STUDENT TESTED, FACULTY APPROVED

THE CB SOLUTION

Every 4LTR Press solution includes:

Heading Numbers Connect Print & eBook

Visually Engaging Textbook

Online Study Tools

Tear-out Review Cards

Interactive eBook

STUDENT RESOURCES:

- Interactive eBook
- Active Listening Guides
- Flashcards
- Media Quizzing
- NEW Trackable Activities
- KnowNOW! Blog
- Career Transitions
- Games: Crossword Puzzles and Beat the Clock
- PowerPoint® Slides
- Videos
- Review Cards

INSTRUCTOR RESOURCES:

- All Student Resources
- Engagement Tracker
- First Day of Class Instructions
- Instructor's Manual
- Test Bank
- PowerPoint® Slides
- Instructor Prep Cards

Students sign in at **www.cengagebrain.com**

Instructors sign in at **www.cengage.com/login**

"I liked the interactive quizzes and power points that outlined the freshened up my studying."

— **Stephanie Wakeley**, Student, *North Central Michigan College*

D1307614

JULY 20

Engagement Tracker launches, giving faculty a window into student usage of digital tools.

1 out of every 3 (1,400) schools has adopted a 4LTR Press solution.

4LTR Press adds eBooks in response to a 10% uptick in digital learning preferences.

750,000 students are IN.

AUGUST 2010

NOVEMBER 2010

Third party research confirms that 4LTR Press digital solutions improve retention and outcomes.

CourseMate
Students access the 4LTR Press website at 4x's the industry average.

IN 2011

60 unique solutions across multiple course areas validates the 4LTR Press concept.

IN 2011

2,000

APRIL 2011

1 out of every 2 (2,000) schools has a 4LTR Press adoption.

AUGUST 2011

Over 1 million students are IN.

We're always evolving. Join the 4LTR Press In-Crowd on Facebook at www.facebook.com/4ltrpress

2013 AND BEYOND

CB, 6th Edition
Barry J. Babin, Louisiana Tech University
Eric G. Harris, Pittsburg State University

Vice President, General Manager, Social Science & Qualitative Business: Erin Joyner

Vice President, General Manager, 4LTR Press: Neil Marquardt

Product Director, 4LTR Press: Steve Joos

Product Director: Mike Schenk

Sr. Product Managers: Jason Fremder, Mike Roche

Content Developer: Julie Klooster

Sr. Product Assistant: Megan Fischer

Sr. Brand Manager: Robin LeFevre

Sr. Content Project Manager: Martha Conway

Sr. Media Developer: John Rich

Sr. Content Digitization Project Manager: Allison Marion

Manufacturing Planner: Ron Montgomery

Production Service: MPS Limited

Sr. Art Director: Stacy Jenkins Shirley

Internal Designer: Ke Design

Cover Designer: Joe Devine/Red Hangar Design

Cover Image: © altrendo images/Getty Images

Rights Acquisitions Specialist, Text and Image: Deanna Ettinger

Inside Front Cover Images: woman with magazine © iStockphoto.com/sdominick; money © iStockphoto.com/alexsl; college hangout © iStockphoto.com/A-Digit

Back Cover Image: © iStockphoto.com/ René Mansi

Title Page Images: laptop © iStockphoto.com/ CostinT; A+ © iStockphoto.com/ photovideostock; crowd © iStockphoto.com/ Leontura

© 2015, 2014 Cengage Learning

ALL RIGHTS RESERVED. No part of this work covered by the copyright herein may be reproduced, transmitted, stored, or used in any form or by any means graphic, electronic, or mechanical, including but not limited to photo-copying, recording, scanning, digitizing, taping, Web distribution, information networks, or information storage and retrieval systems, except as permitted under Section 107 or 108 of the 1976 United States Copyright Act, without the prior written permission of the publisher.

For product information and technology assistance, contact us at
Cengage Learning Customer & Sales Support, 1-800-354-9706

For permission to use material from this text or product,
submit all requests online at **www.cengage.com/permissions**
Further permissions questions can be emailed to
permissionrequest@cengage.com

Library of Congress Control Number: 2013941868

Student Edition ISBN 13: 978-1-285-18948-2
Student Edition ISBN 10: 1-285-18948-5

Student Edition with CourseMate ISBN 13: 978-1-285-18947-5
Student Edition with CourseMate ISBN 10: 1-285-18947-7

Cengage Learning
200 First Stamford Place, 4th Floor
Stamford, CT 06902
USA

Cengage Learning is a leading provider of customized learning solutions with office locations around the globe, including Singapore, the United Kingdom, Australia, Mexico, Brazil, and Japan. Locate your local office at: **www.cengage.com/global**

Cengage Learning products are represented in Canada by Nelson Education, Ltd.

To learn more about Cengage Learning Solutions, visit **www.cengage.com**

Purchase any of our products at your local college store or at our preferred online store **www.cengagebrain.com**

Printed in the United States of America
1 2 3 4 5 6 7 18 17 16 15 14

BRIEF CONTENTS

introduction

Reggie Casagrande/Workbook Stock/Getty Images

internal influences

external influences

Fuse/Jupiter Images

situations and decision making

consumption and beyond

Pixland/Jupiter Images

CONTENTS

introduction

PART **1**

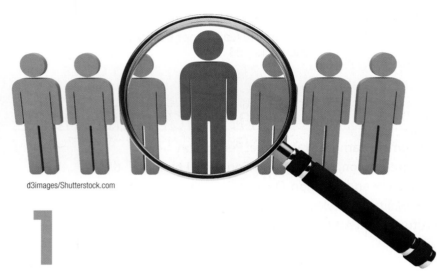

d3images/Shutterstock.com

1

What Is CB and Why Should I Care? 3

Jeff Greenberg/Alamy

2

Value and the Consumer Behavior Value Framework   23

PART **2** *internal influences*

3

Consumer Learning Starts Here: Perception   47

Stockbyte/Jupiter Images

4

Comprehension, Memory, and Cognitive Learning   65

5

Motivation and Emotion: Driving Consumer Behavior   85

CJG-Technology/Alamy

© iStockphoto.com/berekin

6

Personality, Lifestyles, and the Self-Concept 103

7

Attitudes and Attitude Change 121

© kurhan/Shutterstock.com

external influences

PART 3

© Monkey Business Images/Shutterstock.com

8

Group and Interpersonal Influence 147

9

Consumer Culture 169

LHB Photo/Alamy

10

Microcultures 191

PART **4**

*situations and
decision making*

11

Consumers
in Situations 217

12

Decision Making I: Need Recognition and Search   239

© Dmitry Kalinovsky/Shutterstock.com

13

Decision Making II: Alternative Evaluation and Choice   255

PART **5**

consumption and beyond

© Monkey Business Images/Shutterstock.com

16

Consumer and Marketing Misbehavior   307

For my family and my mentors, especially Bill and Joe.
—Barry Babin

For my family, for their wonderful support over the years.
—Eric Harris

PART **1**
CB

© Reggie Casagrande/Workbook Stock/Getty Images

The marketer who
understands consumers will be able to design products that provide more value, and through this process, enhance the well-being of both the company and its customers.

WHAT DO YOU THINK?
In any business, the customer is truly the most important person.

STRONGLY DISAGREE   STRONGLY AGREE

VISIT COURSEMATE AT WWW.CENGAGEBRAIN.COM

What Is CB and Why Should I Care?

1

After studying this chapter, the student should be able to:

1-1 Understand the meaning of *consumption* and *consumer behavior.*

1-2 Describe how competitive marketing environments lead to better outcomes for consumers.

1-3 Explain the role of consumer behavior in business and society.

1-4 Be familiar with basic approaches to studying consumer behavior.

1-5 Appreciate how dynamic the field of consumer behavior continues to be.

Students rarely feel like an expert when they walk into a new college class. However, this course is an exception, because everyone reading this book has years of experience spending! As we will see, spending means that something is being used, perhaps time or perhaps money, and when things are used toward a value-producing activity, consumption takes place. In fact, we act as consumers every day and every waking hour. The reader begins the book with a degree of expertise that makes the subject come alive with relevance.

Just think about how many of a person's daily activities are really consumer activities. We wake, we drink, we eat, we clean, we dress, we ride, we shop, we play, we read, we choose, we talk, we surf, we tweet, and on and on. Practically everything we do involves consumer behavior (CB) in some way. Take a look at Twitter or Facebook and it becomes obvious that many of the tweets and posts on walls are talking about things to buy, places to go, and things to do. Websites like Pinterest mimic real discussions, where one consumer tells others about the things that bring value to their lives. Certainly, these activities help consumers make decisions.

Consumer decisions are sometimes simple, involving few resources, and other times complex, involving large amounts of resources. When consumers make decisions, they set in place a chain of reactions that changes their lives, the lives of those around them, and the lives of people they don't even know. How can even simple decisions be so important to society? The answer to this question is one of the key points of this chapter and of this text. A consumer makes a decision with the intention of improving his or her life—that is, doing something of value. But the value creation doesn't stop here.

As long as consumers continue satisfying needs by shopping and buying, opportunity exists for business.

The process of making a purchase starts a chain reaction of value-creating actions. The economic bust of 2008 and the continued sluggish economy in the United States originated with a drop in housing sales that continued into 2012.[1] When consumers stop buying houses, many industries are affected. Fewer house sales mean fewer appliance and furniture purchases. When fewer appliances and furniture are sold, demand for shipping drops. Fewer new homes sold means less demand for home designers and architects. Eventually, many industries suffer significantly, people lose jobs, and this in turn affects others as their ability to spend gets curtailed.

On the other hand, what happens when people buy things? Lots of consumers have purchased a tablet computer in the last few years and they seem to be satisfied. Both iPad and Kindle owners report about 85% satisfaction. The more videos a consumer views, the higher the reported satisfaction.[2] What happens when a consumer buys an electronic device like an Apple® iPad®? The store must restock its inventory. The manufacturer must produce more product. To do this, the manufacturer purchases raw materials, parts, and services from suppliers. Raw materials and finished products need to be shipped by companies like UPS or FedEx. But that isn't all. Now the iPad owner may well want or need a new service plan to enhance functionality, and now he or she is a potential consumer for some of the more than 250,000 apps made for the device. One can clearly see the iPad customer gets value from the purchase, but the consumption also enhances the life of many other consumers touched by the chain reaction.

Although some may call a course like this one "buyer behavior," consuming involves more than just *buying*. Certainly, businesses are interested in getting someone to buy something. But the fact is that consumption goes on long after purchase and this consumption story ultimately determines how much value results.

As you can see, our behavior as consumers is critically important not just to ourselves, but to many other people. This is why so many people, not just marketing people, are interested in learning about CB. True, the marketer who understands consumers will be able to design products with greater value potential, and thus a greater chance of enhancing the well-being of stakeholders including the company and customers. Policy makers also show interest in CB because the knowledge allows them to make more effective public policy decisions. Last but not least, consumers who understand consumer behavior can make better decisions concerning how they allocate scarce resources—that is, they become better consumers. Thus, an understanding of consumer behavior can mean better business for companies, better public policy for governments, and a better life for individuals and households.

1-1 Consumption and Consumer Behavior

One can look at CB from two unique perspectives. This is because consumer behavior refers to both

1. Human thought and action involved in consumption, and

2. A field of study (human inquiry) that is developing an accumulated body of knowledge.

If we think of the consumer above considering the purchase of a tablet computer, CB can be thought of as the actions, reactions, and consequences that take place as the consumer goes through a decision-making process, reaches a decision, and then puts a product to use. Alternatively, we consider the body of knowledge

Kim White/Bloomberg /Getty Images

Tablets create customers for apps. Consumers drive the economy.

that researchers accumulate as they attempt to explain these actions, reactions, and consequences as the field of study known as consumer behavior. Thus, rather than choosing between the two alternative approaches, we believe the best appreciation of CB requires consideration of both perspectives.

1-1a Consumer Behavior as Human Behavior

Consumer behavior is the set of value-seeking activities that take place as people go about addressing and attempting to address real needs. In other words, when a consumer is motivated by a need, a process kicks in as the consumer sets out to find desirable ways to fill this need. The process involves multiple psychological events, including thinking, feeling and behaving, and the entire process culminates in value. Hopefully, the process creates sufficient value to address the need that began the process.

The Basic CB Process

Exhibit 1.1 illustrates the basic consumption process. We discuss each step in detail in later chapters. However, thinking of the consumer from the introduction, we illustrate the process briefly here in the context of a new tablet computer purchase. At some point, the consumer realizes a need for better access and a better interface to outside media through the Internet, including social media, YouTube, Netflix, and email. This realization may be motivated primarily by a desire to do better on the job and to have better access to friends and family. A **want** is a specific desire that spells out a way a consumer can go about addressing a recognized need. A consumer feels a need to stay in touch, belong, and socialize, and this need enhances desire or want for media access devices.

After weighing some options, the consumer decides to visit an Apple store. After looking at several alternative devices, and talking it over with the salesperson, the consumer chooses the latest iPad. Next, the consumer participates in an exchange in which he or she gives up economic resources in return for receiving the product. An **exchange** is the acting out of a decision to give something up in return for something of greater value. Here, the consumer decides the tablet computer will be worth at least the price of the product plus a 4G service plan that will enhance his ability to use the device.

The consumer then uses the product and experiences all the associated benefits and costs. **Costs** are the negative results of consumption. The costs involve more than just the price of the product. Consumers spend time both shopping for and learning how to use a device. Physical effort also is needed if consumers visit retail stores during the process. The time, money, and effort spent acquiring a tablet computer cannot be allocated toward other activities or processes, resulting in high opportunity costs for the consumer. **Benefits** are positive results of consumption. The benefits are multifaceted, ranging from potentially better job performance, easier Facebook access, and a bigger screen for playing Tiny Zoo.

Over time, the consumer evaluates the costs and benefits and reacts to the purchase in some way. These reactions involve thoughts and feelings. The thoughts may involve reactions to features such as the ease of use. The feelings may sometimes include frustration if the features do not work correctly or conveniently. Ultimately, the process results in a perception of value. We will discuss value in more detail in Chapter 2.

Consumption

Another way to look at the basic consumer behavior process is to consider the steps that occur when consumption takes place. Obviously, a consumer consumes!

> **consumer behavior** set of value-seeking activities that take place as people go about addressing their real needs
>
> **want** a specific desire representing a way a consumer may go about addressing a recognized need
>
> **exchange** acting out of the decision to give something up in return for something of greater value
>
> **costs** negative results of consumption
>
> **benefits** positive results of consumption

EXHIBIT 1.1 The Basic Consumption Process

Need → Want → Exchange → Costs and Benefits → Reaction → Value

© Cengage Learning

iStockphoto.com/Squaredpixels

consumption process by which goods, services, or ideas are used and transformed into value

consumer behavior as a field of study study of consumers as they go about the consumption process; the science of studying how consumers seek value in an effort to address real needs

economics study of production and consumption

Interestingly, very few consumer behavior books define consumption itself. **Consumption** represents the process by which goods, services, or ideas are used and transformed into value. Thus, the actions involved in acquiring and using a mobile communications device like an iPad create value for a consumer. Consumption is a value-producing process in which the marketer and the consumer interact to produce value. When the consumer fails to realize value from the process, something has broken down in the process; perhaps a bad performance from the marketer or perhaps a bad decision by the customer. Thinking about the result of all of these interactions considered together, one easily sees that consumption outcomes affect consumer well-being by affecting quality of life.

1-1b Consumer Behavior as a Field of Study

Consumer behavior as a field of study represents the study of consumers as they go through the consumption process. In this sense, consumer behavior is the science of studying how consumers seek value in an effort to address real needs. This book represents a collection of knowledge resulting as consumer behavior researchers go about studying consumers.

Consumer behavior, as a field of study, is a very young field. The first books that discuss consumer behavior or buyer behavior date from the 1960s.[3] Thus, compared with older disciplines, researchers have had less time to develop the body of knowledge. Therefore, each decade the accumulated body of knowledge grows significantly. Clearly, however, much uncertainty remains, and the body of theory that is accepted by researchers and practitioners is relatively small. This is one reason consumer behavior is so exciting to study. CB researchers continue to expand the knowledge base at a fast pace.

Like other disciplines, the CB field has family roots in other disciplines. Exhibit 1.2 displays the relationship between CB and other disciplines. Research in various disciplines produced relevant knowledge for marketers seeking to understand consumers. The genesis of the CB field lies in business and the growing body of academic research produced by business schools in the late 20th century.[4] The exhibit displays the overlapping nature of CB and marketing. The other fields provide a sample of some of the many fields that sometimes contribute to and to which CB sometimes contributes. A few of these disciplines share a special bond with CB, as we discuss below. CB shares particularly strong interdisciplinary connections with economics, psychology (particularly social psychology), marketing, and anthropology.[5]

⌐ Understanding consumer behavior means better business for companies, better public policy for governments, and a better life for individuals and households. ⌐

Economics and Consumer Behavior

Economics is often defined as the study of production and consumption. A free enterprise system allows individuals to participate freely in the market.[6] Accordingly, it is easy to see that marketing has its origins in economics, particularly with respect to the production and distribution of goods. As the definition implies, economics also involves consumption. Therefore, consumer behavior and economics also have much in common. However, the economist's focus on consumer behavior is generally a broad or macro perspective. For example, economics studies often involve things like commodity consumption of nations over time. This may even involve tracking changes in consumption with

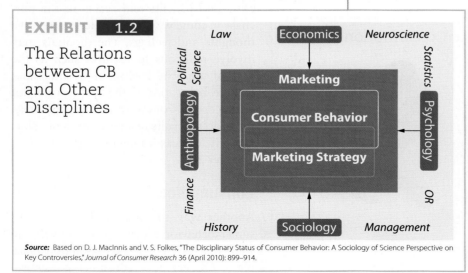

EXHIBIT 1.2

The Relations between CB and Other Disciplines

Source: Based on D. J. MacInnis and V. S. Folkes, "The Disciplinary Status of Consumer Behavior: A Sociology of Science Perspective on Key Controversies," *Journal of Consumer Research* 36 (April 2010): 899–914.

different price levels, enabling price elasticity to be determined. The economist finds data for a study like this in historical sales records. This type of study does not require interviews with individual consumers that may ask for explanations of the behaviors summarized in historical data.

To illustrate a macro perspective, we note that researchers and marketing managers are very interested in emerging markets like China and India. Although these places may seem like very distant lands with little relevance to most business students, nothing could be further from the truth. Economists track all sorts of consumer-related phenomena. In fact, *The Economist* journal tracks the Big Mac Index.[7] The Big Mac Index shows the relative price of hamburgers country by country. The idea was to show relative purchasing power, but economists now realize the Big Mac Index actually predicts currency fluctuations with some accuracy. The prices represent aggregate prices paid by thousands of anonymous consumers within each country.

In contrast, consumer behavior researchers generally study consumer behavior at a more micro level, often focusing on individual consumer behavior. Food and drink consumption studies often require personal interviews or experimentation with individuals. For example, consumer researchers examined the extent to which exposure to advertisements promoting drink specials influences college student drinking. The research drew conclusions from individual student responses to such ads. Results suggest that students had a more positive attitude toward the bar running the specials and intended to buy more because of the specials when exposed to the ad.[8]

Psychology and Social Psychology

Psychology is the study of human reactions to their environment.[9] Psychologists seek to explain the thoughts, feelings, and behaviors that represent human reaction. Psychology itself can be divided into several subdisciplines. Social psychology and cognitive psychology, in particular, are highly relevant to consumer behavior.[10] **Social psychology** focuses on the thoughts, feelings, and behaviors that people have as they interact with other people (group behavior). Consumer behavior most often takes place in some type of social setting; thus, social psychology and consumer behavior overlap significantly. **Cognitive psychology** deals with the intricacies of mental reactions involved in information processing. Every time a consumer evaluates a product, sees an advertisement, or reacts to product consumption, information is processed. Thus, cognitive psychology is also very relevant to consumer behavior.

Marketing

One doesn't have to look very hard to find different definitions of marketing. Many older definitions focus heavily on physical products and profitability. Even though products and profits are very important aspects of marketing, these definitions are relatively narrow.[11] **Marketing** involves the multitude of value-producing seller activities that facilitate *exchanges* between buyers and sellers. These activities include the production, promotion, pricing, distribution, and retailing of goods, services, ideas, and experiences that provide value for consumers and other stakeholders.

CB and marketing are very closely related. Exchange is intimately involved in marketing and as can be seen

psychology study of human reactions to their environment

social psychology study that focuses on the thoughts, feelings, and behaviors that people have as they interact with other people

cognitive psychology study of the intricacies of mental reactions involved in information processing

marketing multitude of activities that facilitate *exchanges* between buyers and sellers, including production, pricing, promotion, distribution, and retailing, which are all focused on providing value for consumers and other stakeholders

Jeff Greenberg/Alamy

Marketing activities are aimed at creating value.

sociology the study of groups of people within a society, with relevance for consumer behavior because a great deal of consumption takes place within group settings or is affected by group behavior

anthropology study in which researchers interpret relationships between consumers and the things they purchase, the products they own, and the activities in which they participate

neuroscience the study of the central nervous system including the brain

from Exhibit 1.1, exchange is central to consumer behavior too. In fact, in some ways, consumer behavior involves "inverse" marketing as consumers operate at the other end of the exchange. Marketing actions are targeted at and affect consumers while consumer actions affect marketers. A marketer without customers won't be a marketer very long! In fact, without consumers, marketing is unnecessary.

Some researchers view the CB discipline as separate and distinct from marketing.[12] Others view CB as a subdiscipline within marketing.[13] The details of the argument are beyond the scope of this text; however, the very fact that such an argument exists illustrates the close bond between the two. Marketing and CB share considerable relevance and both are essential inputs to organizational success.

Consumer Behavior and Other Disciplines

Commerce increased tremendously with the industrial revolution and the coinciding political changes that fostered economic freedom in many countries. Businesses looked to the new field of marketing for practical advice initially about distribution and later about pricing, packaging, advertising, and communication. Thus, although marketing may have originally shared more in common with economics, the turn toward consumer research brought numerous psychologists into the field. Many of these psychologists became the first consumer researchers.

CB research and marketing research overlap with each other more than they do with any other discipline, as illustrated by the overlapping shapes in Exhibit 1.2. Beyond this, CB research shares much in common with psychological research, particularly in terms of shared research approaches and shared theories. Consumer research is based largely on psychology, and to some extent psychology draws from consumer behavior research.

Other disciplines share things in common with consumer behavior. **Sociology** focuses on the study of groups of people within a society. This has relevance for consumer behavior because consumption often takes place within group settings or is in one way or another affected by group behavior.

Anthropology has contributed to consumer behavior research by allowing researchers to interpret the relationships between consumers and the things they purchase, the products they own, and the activities in which they participate. Disciplines such as geography and the medical sciences overlap with consumer behavior in that they draw from some of the same theories and/or research approaches. **Neuroscience**, the study of the central nervous system including the brain, and CB share interest in how the consumer's brain functions during the consumption process. The number of neuroscience applications in CB is growing at a rapid rate.

1-2 The Ways in Which Consumers Are Treated

Is the customer always "king"? Look at this list of familiar service environments:

- A typical Department of Motor Vehicle (DMV) office
- The registrar's office at a state university
- A bank lobby
- A university health clinic
- Cable communication services
- A hair salon
- A New York City fine dining establishment
- A Miami Beach resort

Think about the following questions. Does a consumer receive the same degree of service at each of these places? What is the waiting environment like at each

Competitive pressures motivate marketers to provide good service.

Plush Studios/Jupiter Images

Compared to a restaurant, what motivation does the DMV have to provide a high-value waiting experience?

of these places? Is there a clean, comfortable waiting area with pleasant music? How dedicated are the employees to delivering a high-quality service experience? How likely are employees to view the customer as a nuisance? If you don't see the point of these questions yet, contrast the waiting area at a driver's license bureau with the elaborate lobby where you wait for check-in service (probably not very long) at a Miami Beach resort.

Some organizations can survive while treating customers little better than dirt, and others need to pamper customers just to have a chance of surviving. Consider these two questions in order to understand how important serving customers well should be to any given organization:

1. How competitive is the marketing environment?
2. How dependent is the marketer on repeat business?

1-2a Competition and Consumer Orientation

Where do consumers go if they don't like the service at the DMV? If the choice comes down to visiting the bureau or not driving, nearly all consumers will put up with the less-than-immaculate surroundings, long waits, and poor service that all too typically go along with getting a driver's license. Put yourself into the shoes of the service providers at the bureau. Is there any concern about doing something that would make a customer want to return to do business again? Is there any real incentive to provide a pleasant and valuable experience?

Few Competitive Pressures?

In essence, the DMV typifies a service organization that operates in a market with practically no competitive pressure and a captive audience. In a government service like this, the answers to the two questions above are (1) not at all competitive and (2) not at all dependent on keeping customers. No matter how poor the service is, they know consumers will return to do more business when the term on their license expires or they need to register a vehicle. The incentive for better customer service remains relatively small.

Unlike a restaurant, DMV management may not be compelled to adjust workloads to demand. DMV *customers* can face long lines (sometimes over 100 people in some areas) and wait times counted in hours, not minutes. As state budgets have become increasingly tight with the bad economy, wait times have increased and DMV offices have cut hours—some even operating only four days a week.[14] In Denver, Colorado, the 43 DMV employees (down from 57 in 2009) processed just over 350,000 registration renewals last year (up slightly since 2009). However, the city touts improved customer service with wait times averaging *just under one hour!*[15] Imagine a bank touting wait times of just one hour! A few states have turned to technology and private outsourcing to improve service. Drivers can renew licenses online in some states or go to a company authorized to provide licensing services. The private companies generally provide consumers with better service, and the DMV ends up with better and more accurate information about drivers.[16] Why does the private company improve service? They are the marketer and the city, county, or state is the customer. The company depends on repeat business in the form of a renewed contract.

Many Competitive Pressures?

Now consider the customer dining in New York City. A consumer has over 6,000 full-service restaurants from which to choose—nearly all of them striving to build a loyal clientele. The diner doesn't have to put up with poor treatment. The consumer can simply go next door. While the consumer without a reservation may wait for a table at the establishments with a loyal clientele, many provide a comfortable lounge area where he or she can enjoy a drink, some music, and conversation while waiting. Here the consumer deals with firms operating in a highly competitive market dependent on repeat business. Thus, firms are oriented toward value creation and thus consumers typically receive better treatment.

**consumer (customer)
orientation** way of doing
business in which the actions
and decision making of the
institution prioritize consumer
value and satisfaction above all
other concerns

market orientation
organizational culture that
embodies the importance of
creating value for customers
among all employees

stakeholder marketing
an orientation in which firms
recognize that more than just
the buyer and seller are involved
in the marketing process and a
host of primary and secondary
entities affect and are affected
by the value creation process

The realization that competition in the marketplace is important to protecting consumers is recognized by government. In the United States, many federal laws regulate the market to ensure business competition. The Robinson-Patman Act, the Sherman Act, and the Clayton Act are examples of such legislation. Practices such as price fixing, secret rebates, and customer coercion are restricted by these acts.

Firm Orientations and Consumers

Competition eventually drives companies toward a high degree of consumer orientation. **Consumer (customer) orientation** is a way of doing business in which the actions and decision making of the institution prioritize consumer value and satisfaction above all other concerns. A consumer orientation is a key component of a firm with a market-oriented culture. **Market orientation** is an organizational culture that embodies the importance of creating value for customers among all employees. In addition to understanding customers, a market orientation stresses the need to monitor and understand competitor actions in the marketplace and the need to communicate information about customers and competitors throughout the organization.[17] Profitable firms are usually market oriented, with a few exceptions that will be discussed later.[18]

A market orientation represents a less narrow focus than a strategic orientation that focuses more solely on production. However, an even broader orientation comes when firms adapt **stakeholder marketing**. Under this orientation, firms recognize that more than just the buyer and seller are involved in the marketing process.[19] In fact, primary stakeholders include customers, employees, owners (or shareholders), suppliers, and regulating agencies; secondary stakeholders include the mass media and trade organizations. Stakeholder marketing orientation recognizes that all stakeholders are involved in and/or are affected by the firm's marketing in some way. This means that even secondary stakeholders can alter the value equation and thus marketing strategies should consider all such effects.

1-2b Relationship Marketing and Consumer Behavior

Let's go back to the list of service environments. Certainly, banks and restaurants are generally in very intense competition with rival businesses. Competitive pressures challenge businesses to get customers to repeatedly purchase the goods or services they offer. Even in a city with a population as great as New York, without repeat business, each restaurant would have fewer than ten customers per night. In addition, repeat customers are considered less costly to serve.[20] For instance, while a lot of advertising may be needed for every new customer to learn about a restaurant, old customers already know the place.

Thus, **relationship marketing** means the firm's marketing activities aim to increase repeat business as a route to strong firm performance. Relationship marketing recognizes that customer desires are recurring and that a single purchase act may be only one touchpoint in an ongoing series of interactions with a customer. **Touchpoints** are direct contacts between the firm and a customer. Increasingly, multiple channels or ways of making this contact exist, including phone, email, text messaging, online social networking, and face-to-face contact.[21] Every touchpoint, no matter the channel, should be considered as an opportunity to create value for the customer. Like any type of relationship, a customer-marketer relationship will continue only as long as both parties see the partnership as valuable.

Marketers are increasingly realizing the value of relationship marketing. Wait staff sometimes provide

This consumer is encountering a touchpoint with her stylist. Are there other touchpoints taking place at the same time?

© iStockphoto.com/Izabela Habur

business cards to customers. These customers can use the card to ask for this waiter again on the next visit or to recommend the restaurant and server to a friend. Notice that with relationship marketing, the firm and its employees are very motivated to provide an outstanding overall experience. In sum, both a competitive marketplace and a relationship marketing orientation create exchange environments where firms truly treat customers as "king."

1-3 The CB Field's Role in Business, Society, and for Consumers

As mentioned earlier, multiple reasons for studying consumer behavior exist. Each perspective provides unique and interesting opportunities for study. CB is important in at least three ways:

1. CB provides an input to business/marketing strategy.
2. CB provides a force that shapes society.
3. CB provides an input to making responsible decisions as a consumer.

1-3a Consumer Behavior and Marketing Strategy

What companies do you think of as successful? The ultimate hallmark of success for a business is long-term survival. One hundred years is a blink of an eye in the course of history. But how many companies survive at least 100 years? Exhibit 1.3 lists some famous international companies, their core business, and their age.

None of these companies are 100 years old! Even though we may think about them as lasting forever, chances are some of these giants will not be around 100 years from now. So, surviving is not a trivial goal, and the companies that do survive long term do so by obtaining resources from consumers in return for the value they create. This is a basic tenet of **resource-advantage theory**, a prominent theory that explains why companies succeed or fail.[22] Companies succeed by acquiring more resources from consumers and in turn using those resources to gain advantages in physical and intellectual capital. Consumer research is needed to understand what makes a consumer give up scarce resources. Ultimately, consumers give up resources in the pursuit of value.

In contrast to the companies listed in Exhibit 1.3, consider the Curtis Mathes Corporation. Curtis Mathes produced and sold high quality televisions from 1957 until the 1990s. For much of that time, the Texas-based firm was the leading U.S. name in high-quality televisions. Yet factors in the external environment made it difficult for them to maintain sales relative to increasingly higher-quality imported electronics from companies like Sony and Samsung. Consumers were much more likely to purchase competitor products whose quality was acceptable and whose prices were lower.

relationship marketing activities based on the belief that the firm's performance is enhanced through repeat business

touchpoints direct contacts between the firm and a customer

resource-advantage theory theory that explains why companies succeed or fail; the firm goes about obtaining resources from consumers in return for the value the resources create

EXHIBIT 1.3 How Old Are These Companies?

Company	Core Business	Birthdate	Place of Birth
Home Depot	Retail and Contractor Building Supply	1976	Georgia
FedEx	Express Package Shipping (originally founded as Federal Express in 1973)	2000	Tennessee
Facebook	Online Social Networking	2004	Massachusetts
Tesco	Food Retailing	1919	London, England
McDonald's	Fast Food	1956	Illinois
Samsung	Electronic Equipment	1969	Seoul, South Korea
Toyota	Motor Vehicles	1937	Nagoya, Japan
Microsoft	Computer Software (originally operating systems)	1975	New Mexico

© Cengage Learning

attribute a product feature that delivers a desired consumer benefit

product potentially valuable bundle of benefits

Eventually, the resource drain caused Curtis Mathes to file for bankruptcy; the company exists only as a shell of what it once was, with no production capacity.

What Do People Buy?

When a consumer buys something, he or she gives up resources in the form of time, money, and energy in return for whatever is being sold. Consider a customer who purchases a Kindle. What does he or she really get? Well, the tangibles include mostly plastic and integrated circuitry. These are the parts that make up the product. No reasonable consumer would trade any significant sum of money for plastic and circuitry. A consumer isn't really buying the physical parts of a product. However, the plastic enables the product to be small and light and the integrated circuitry enables this small, light product to function as an electronic reader. Once again, we can ask, is this really what the consumer wants? The fact is, these **attributes** enable the consumer to enjoy the benefits of information availability in a very convenient package. Outcomes like these are valuable and what the customer is ultimately buying.

Marketing firms often implement poor strategies when they don't understand what a product truly is, because they don't understand exactly what they are selling. A **product** is a potentially valuable bundle of benefits. Theodore Levitt, one of the most famous marketing researchers, understood this. He emphasized the importance of the value a customer receives from a product, rather than the product itself.

One consumer researcher studied why people bought milk shakes. In contrast to expectation, the largest share of milk shakes purchased in the study was bought before noon, many before 10 AM, and many were consumed in a car.[23] After studying many milk shake drinkers, one theme emerged. A milk shake is a good solution for consumers with long commutes. They satisfy one's hunger, they are neat, they can be consumed while using one hand, and they take about 20 minutes to finish—the better portion of the commute. The value provided by the milk shake is partly dealing with hunger but also partly dealing with boredom. Thus, the researcher suggested making shakes even thicker so they took even longer to finish as a way of improving the product.

What Are You Fishing For?

Somebody standing on the bank of a lake fishing is pretty certain to want to catch fish. But what about fishing in Fishville?

Zynga is a company whose online revenue has taken off ever since they began to better understand why some people fish—at least virtually fish. After seeing how eager some consumers were to spend virtual currencies for virtual enhancements to their virtual Farmville farms or virtual Fishville fishing, they decided to experiment with selling virtual tractors and virtual fish in exchange for real money. Five dollars for a not-real chicken for a not-real farm in Farmville, $6 for a not-real prize fish in Fishville, $3 for a not-real skyscraper in one's not-real city in Cityville—pretty soon it adds up. Zynga's revenues skyrocketed to over $600 million from less than $1 million in 2008 and perhaps the virtual product market represents an answer to Zynga's revenue problems. Zynga marketing also recognizes that like real products, differentiation is important. Consumer research led them

to offer virtual tractors with a holiday theme, which sell for more than the same not-real but themeless tractor.

These consumers find value in the virtual products—obviously. But what are they buying?

Sources: N. Wingfield, "Virtual Products, Real Profits," *The Wall Street Journal,* December 9, 2011, A1–A11. D. MacMillan and B. Stone, "Feeling Listless Down on the Virtual Farm," *Bloomberg BusinessWeek* (November 23, 2011): 43–4.

Ultimately, companies need to understand why people buy their products to recognize what business they are in. This is also how they identify their competitors. Let's look at the companies that produced buggies (horse-drawn carriages from 100 years ago) and slide rules (rulers used to do calculations). They did not go out of business because their products were flawed. The companies that did well producing those products went out of business because they failed to innovate and because they didn't understand that they were actually competing with Ford automobiles and Texas Instruments calculators, respectively. Products like VHS players, CD players, and tape recorders are all fast on the road to obsolescence as the technologies that provide the benefits of musical or video entertainment change. Thus, in this sense, technologies don't provide value directly; the activities and benefits associated with the technologies do.

Ways of Doing Business

Each company adopts a way of doing business that is epitomized in their corporate culture. Corporate cultures fall roughly into one of several categories representing different ways of doing business. Exhibit 1.4 summarizes different ways of doing business. Each way of marketing coincides with a varying degree of consumer orientation, which as we indicated earlier is a basic component of a market or stakeholder orientation. The ways of doing business often guide a firm's marketing practices.

In **undifferentiated marketing**, the same basic product is offered to all customers. Mass merchandisers typify undifferentiated marketers in that they rely on selling a high volume to be successful. As such, they focus on serving very large segments in which consumers do not have specific desires (are not picky). Undifferentiated marketers generally adopt a **production orientation**, wherein innovation is geared primarily toward making the production process as efficient and economical as possible. In other words, the emphasis is on serving customers while incurring minimum costs. Walmart typifies this approach with their Supercenters and their state-of-the-art distribution network, which ships massive quantities of products to stores around the world at the lowest possible cost. The need for consumer orientation and consumer research is minimal because all consumers are treated the same.

Differentiated marketers serve multiple market segments, each with a unique product offering. A market orientation usually serves a differentiated marketer well. The emphasis here is on matching a product with a segment.

Many people are aware that Lexus and Scion are both Toyota brands. However, other companies in other

undifferentiated marketing plan wherein the same basic product is offered to all customers

production orientation approach where innovation is geared primarily toward making the production process as efficient and economic as possible

differentiated marketers firms that serve multiple market segments each with a unique product offering

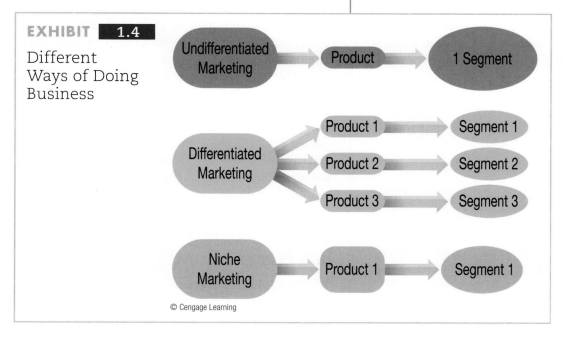

EXHIBIT 1.4

Different Ways of Doing Business

© Cengage Learning

one-to-one marketing
plan wherein a different product is offered for each individual customer so that each customer is treated as a segment of one

niche marketing plan wherein a firm specializes in serving one market segment with particularly unique demand characteristics

industries also create different brands to appeal to different market segments. In much the same way, Prada represents a prestige name in designer accessories (shoes, handbags, etc.), which appeals to the luxury segment. Prada also operates the Miu Miu brand. Prada aims Miu Miu to appeal to women who are design and fashion conscious, but who may be slightly more price sensitive than the Prada shopper. Prada also offers footwear under the Church's brand (English-style shoes for men), and the Car Shoe brand, the ultimate driver's shoe (for the male driver).

Marketers can take differentiated marketing to the extreme with a practice known as **one-to-one marketing**. Here, the company offers a unique product to each individual customer and thereby treats each customer as a segment of one. Computer-aided information processing, design, and production have helped make this a reality on a large scale. Many casinos, for example, develop promotional packages for individual customers based on information collected and stored about that customer's preferences.

Firms that specialize in serving one market segment with particularly unique demand characteristics practice **niche marketing**. Niche marketers may be consumer oriented. However, some niche marketers are product oriented and produce a product that has unique appeal within a segment. Many companies serve the golf market one way or another, and some of them are huge differentiated marketers like Titleist or Callaway, offering many products aimed at multiple markets. However, the Bobby Grace company specializes in one product: the putter. They only make putters and have a very small product offering of accessories beyond that. Their putters are marketed as highly advanced technologically because all of the company's attention is dedicated to this one club, the putter.

1-3b Consumer Behavior and Society

The things that people buy and consume end up determining the type of society in which we live. Things like customs, manners, and rituals all involve consumption—value-producing activities. Certainly, not every society around the world is the same. Just think about the ways we eat and the types of food consumed around the world. Additionally, when governments create laws that govern the way we buy and consume products, consumer behavior is involved. Thus, consumer behavior creates the society in which we live and serves as an important source of input to public policy in a free society.

For example, how does U.S. society treat smoking today? Cigarette advertisements made up a large chunk of all TV advertising before a federal ban took effect on January 2, 1971. Interestingly, popular culture used to glamorize smoking as a valued behavior. In the theater, James Bond smoked, and his image was certainly not harmed by the behavior. On the stage, famous performers like Sammy Davis Jr. and Frank Sinatra often smoked during their acts. At home, practically every room in the house included at least one ashtray. No Smoking sections did not exist, and on airlines, flight attendants (then stewardesses) walked the aisles of the plane offering passengers "coffee, tea, or cigarettes."

My, how things have changed! Smoking has become nearly taboo in the United States. Smoking inside any public building is practically impossible either due to laws restricting smoking or rules created by building owners prohibiting smoking. No Smoking sections in restaurants are now also seen in many parts of Europe and in most cosmopolitan cities around the world. Increasingly, consumers look upon smoking as a non-value-producing activity. Furthermore, politicians realize political advantage in creating more restrictions as consumer opinion continues to turn against the behavior. Policy makers should make such decisions with a thorough understanding of the CB issues involved.

Another current public policy issue concerns the use of mobile phones. Consider how much consumers' widespread adoption of the mobile phone has changed, and continues to change, society. In China alone, consumers account for over 1 billion—that's 1,000 million—mobile phones! Consumers in Africa are adopting mobile phones at an even faster rate, so that today over 70% of all consumers in the world have a mobile phone. This means a total of over 6 billion mobile phones![24] That's not bad for a product that did not exist as we know it 25 years ago. Certainly, the smartphone has been a discontinuous innovation and has altered our behaviors and communications in many significant ways.

1-3c Consumer Behavior and Personal Growth

We face many important decisions as consumers. Among these are choices that will affect our professional careers, our quality of life, and the very fiber of

Hold the Phone! Consumers and Their Phones

Even though "car phones" have provided value to consumers for many years, the mobile phone that we know today really traces back to the Motorola "Brick" of the 1980s. We can safely say that practically all readers of this book own a mobile phone of some type. In fact, the most popular smartphones provide high-speed Internet access, serve as an MP3 player, function as a camera (still or video), and can run many cool apps that do countless things including track the World Cup, the stock market, or commercial airline flight status in real time, or play Angry Birds.

In the United States, 60% of children 8 to 12 years old have their own cell phone, and over one-third of teens say they couldn't live without their phone. One in three teens sends more than 100 text messages per day! A recent study in the United Kingdom suggested that 80% of children have a mobile phone, including over one million kids under the age of ten. As a result, the British government is encouraging public schools to create rules governing mobile phone usage in school.

Restrictions on the use of mobile phones in cars are also being enacted or considered in the interest of public safety. However, will we see greater restrictions such as No Phone sections in restaurants? Some restaurants have already adopted the policy. Consider the following list. In your opinion, do any of these behaviors violate acceptable mobile phone etiquette?

1. Having a mobile phone conversation at the dinner table
2. Texting, browsing, or playing games under the table in class
3. Using profanity on the phone when others can overhear the conversation
4. Using the phone in a movie theater
5. Having a phone conversation in a public bathroom toilet stall

© iStockphoto.com/Neustockimages

6. Speaking so loudly that your phone conversation is easily heard by others ten feet or more away from you
7. Browsing, texting, or using Facebook while involved in a conversation with someone else
8. Using a loud and annoying ring tone
9. Paying more attention to the smartphone than to the road when driving
10. The Baldwin—refusing to power the phone or tablet down on an airplane

The majority of Americans consider mobile phone users to be rude. This is interesting considering that almost all Americans are mobile phone users! Should public restrictions on mobile phone usage be created that govern when, where, and how a phone can be used? Studies of consumer behavior help provide input into public policy decisions on issues like these.

Sources: Joanna L. Krotz, "Cell Phone Etiquette: Dos and Don'ts," Microsoft Business, 2010, http://www.microsoft.com/smallbusiness/resources/ArticleReader/website/default.aspx?Print=1&ArticleId=Cellphoneetiquettedosanddonts, accessed April 3, 2012. Amanda Lenhart, "Teens, Cell Phones and Texting," Pew Research Center Publications, April 20, 2010, http://pewresearch.org/pubs/1572/teens-cell-phones-text-messages, accessed April 3, 2012. "Most Kids 8-12 Now Have Cell Phones: Should Yours?" *Consumer Reports*, 2012, http://news.consumerreports.org/electronics/2012/07/most-kids-8-to-12-now-have-cell-phones-should-yours.html, accessed February 2, 2013.

our families. By this point in your life, you have already experienced many of these decisions. Some decisions are good; some are not. All consumers make dumb decisions occasionally. For instance, modern consumers often carry incredibly high debt relative to our ancestors. Total American consumer debt exceeds $2 trillion. Of that, about $16,000 per family represents credit card debt alone.[25] College students are prime targets for

interpretive research
approach that seeks to explain the inner meanings and motivations associated with specific consumption experiences

qualitative research tools means for gathering data in a relatively unstructured way, including case analysis, clinical interviews, and focus group interviews

researcher dependent subjective data which requires a researcher to interpret the meaning

credit cards, and as can be seen on many college campuses, students are quite willing to apply for cards in exchange for something as mundane as a new t-shirt. Many consumers continue to have negative net worth years into their professional life because of the debt accumulated in early adulthood.

On top of this, the United States faces a national debt crisis, as does much of Europe. Total U.S. government debt has skyrocketed to over $16.5 trillion.[26] Each U.S. taxpayer would have to fork over more than $148,000 to pay that off today. This amount has doubled since 2006. Surely, U.S. consumers and most Western nations' governments know how to spend! Eventually, though, debt can be problematic and drastic changes are needed to the national budgets.

For individuals, decisions that lead to high levels of debt do not seem to be wise, as bankruptcy, financial stress, and lower self-esteem often result. Although often overlooked, decisions about household budget allocation are very relevant aspects of CB. However, budget decisions are not the only way one can choose unwisely when acting as a consumer.

Thus, when consumers learn CB, they should be able to apply that knowledge by making better consumer decisions. Several topics can be particularly helpful in enlightening consumers, including:

1. Consequences associated with poor budget allocation

2. The role of emotions in consumer decision making

3. Avenues for seeking redress for unsatisfactory purchases

4. Social influences on decision making, including peer pressure

5. The effect of the environment on consumer behavior

1-4 Different Approaches to Studying Consumer Behavior

Consumer researchers have many tools and approaches with which to study CB, and researchers don't always agree on which approach is best. In reality, the consumer researcher should realize that no single best way of studying CB exists. Rather, different types of research settings may call for different approaches and the use of different tools. Thus, we provide a brief overview of two basic approaches for studying CB. The purpose is to provide the reader with an idea of how the knowledge found in this book was obtained. For a more detailed view of the different research approaches, the reader is referred elsewhere.[27]

1-4a Interpretive Research

One consumer's music is just noise to another consumer. What creates value in the musical experience? What does music mean and how much does the meaning shape the value of an experience? These are questions that evoke very abstract comments and thoughts from consumers. They are questions that lend themselves well to interpretive research especially when environmental factors like culture shape behaviors.[28] **Interpretive research** seeks to explain the inner meanings and motivations associated with specific consumption experiences. Consumer researchers interpret these meanings through the words that consumers use to describe events or through observation of social interactions. With this approach, researchers interpret meaning rather than analyze data.

Interpretive research generally falls into the broader category of qualitative research.

Qualitative research tools include things such as case analyses, clinical interviews, focus group interviews, and other means by which data are gathered in a relatively unstructured way. In other words, consumer respondents are usually free to respond in their own words or simply through their own behavior. Data of this type requires that the researcher interpret its meaning.

Such results are considered **researcher dependent** because the interpretation is a matter of opinion until corroborated by other findings.

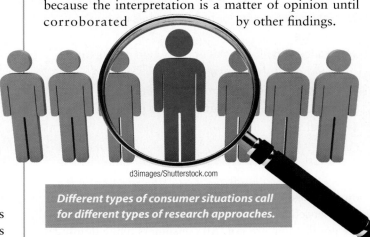

d3images/Shutterstock.com

Different types of consumer situations call for different types of research approaches.

The roots of interpretive consumer research go back over 50 years to the earliest days of consumer research. The focus was on identifying the motivations that lie behind all manner of consumer behavior including mundane things such as coffee drinking or taking an aspirin, to more elaborate issues such as what "drives" one to buy a Ford versus a Chevy.[29] The motivational research era in consumer research, which lasted through the early 1960s, generally proved disappointing in providing satisfying explanations for consumer behavior on a large scale. Unfortunately, many interpretive research tools were scarcely applied for years afterwards. However, these approaches have made a recent comeback and are now commonly applied to many aspects of the field.

Interpretive researchers adopt one of several orientations. Two common interpretative orientations are phenomenology and ethnography. **Phenomenology** represents the study of consumption as a "lived experience."

The phenomenological researcher relies on casual interviews with consumers from whom the researcher has won confidence and trust. This may be supplemented with various other ways that the consumer can tell a story.

Ethnography has roots in anthropology and often involves analyzing the artifacts associated with consumption. An ethnographer may decide to go through trash or ask to see the inside of a consumer's refrigerator in an effort to learn about the consumer. These approaches represent viable options for consumer researchers. More recently, ethnographic CB research takes a twist brought on by the prominence of social networking in everyday

phenomenology qualitative approach to studying consumers that relies on interpretation of the lived experience associated with some aspect of consumption

ethnography qualitative approach to studying consumers that relies on interpretation of artifacts to draw conclusions about consumption

Facing Myopia

Success sometimes leads to complacency and a lack of thought about what changes are needed to perpetuate that success long term. Facebook is the second most visited website on the Internet, meaning the brand does not lack familiarity or traffic. However, because Facebook was created based on an old-fashioned media model in which advertisers are the paying customers, allowing end-users to access content free or nearly free, revenue problems continue to plague the company. Additionally, Facebook has been relatively late to adapt its technology to the many consumers who have changed their preference to mobile access to web platforms, games, and social networking. As a result, consumers now have a plethora of social networking options, many better suited for mobile devices from the start. Twitter is well-known but other more innovative apps like Snapchat and Foursquare, as well as competition from Google + and others leaves analysts wondering about Facebook's long-term viability. Facebook shows that mere consumer familiarity is insufficient for success. Facebook must determine just how it

© iStockphoto.com/Ismail Akin Bostanci

provides value to a set of customer groups that actually might be willing to pay for that value in return. Consumer research may help Facebook understand more precisely what "service" they offer.

Sources: "Facebook Woes Show Investors Wary of Freebies," *Washington Post*, August 22, 2012, D1. E. M. Rusli, "Even Facebook Must Change," *The Wall Street Journal*, January 29, 2013, B1.

netnography a branch of ethnography that studies the behavior of online cultures and communities

quantitative research approach that addresses questions about consumer behavior using numerical measurement and analysis tools

life. **Netnography** applies ethnographic tools to study the behavior of online cultures and communities.[30] While the field is new, researchers believe results will help explore the interplay between brands, products, and belonging based on the virtual relationships played out on Facebook and other social networking sites.

1-4b Quantitative Consumer Research

Which consumer group is most likely to listen to rap music? Statistical models can be applied to retail sales data to identify clusters of consumers who are more likely to be in the market for specific types of products. Sometimes, the results are so spot-on they become controversial. For instance, researhers working for Target stores used patterns of purchases to cluster consumers into groups. One such pattern allowed Target to predict which customers are highly likely to be pregnant.[31] Using this data, the consumers who fall into those groups coincidentally (or not) begin receiving promotions from the store for baby strollers, diapers, and other maternity-related items. One teen's father went to a Target store to complain when his teenage daughter began receiving the maternity-related promotions only to have to apologize when the daughter broke the news to her dad. The fact that individual customer purchases can be recorded and stored by loyalty or credit card numbers makes this type of quantitative modeling possible.

Rather than tracking consumer purchases, a researcher might ask consumers questions about behaviors using a quantitative scaling technique. Survey approaches of this type are used to study all aspects of CB, including the phenomena of video/music piracy.[32] This issue involves the relationship between ethics and consumer behavior. The researcher can design a questionnaire and ask consumers to respond to questions using ten-point rating scales. The questions seek answers to things like the risk of being prosecuted, the extent to which music stars are idolized by the consumer, and the perceived social acceptability of music pirating. Responses can be used to explain how likely a consumer is to illegally pirate music. The researcher may find that one segment of music consumers is more likely to pirate than another segment.

These studies typify quantitative research. **Quantitative research** addresses questions about consumer behavior using numerical measurement and analysis tools. The measurement is usually structured, meaning that the consumer will simply choose a response from among alternatives supplied by the researcher. In other words, structured questionnaires typically involve multiple-choice questions. Alternatively, quantitative research might analyze sales data tracked via the Internet or with point-of-sale scanners.

Unlike qualitative research, the data are not researcher dependent. This is because the numbers are the same no matter who the researcher may be. Typically, quantitative research better enables researchers to test hypotheses as compared to interpretive research. Similarly, quantitative research is more likely to stand on its own and does not require deep interpretation. For example, if consumers have an average attitude score of 50 for brand A and 75 for brand B, we can objectively say that consumers tend to prefer brand B. Exhibit 1.5 summarizes some key differences between quantitative and qualitative research.

1-5 Consumer Behavior Is Dynamic

All one has to do is examine the differences in standards of living between today's American consumers and those living in the years 1875, 1925, 1985, and 2005 to gain an appreciation of how CB has changed over time. As an overall statement, we can say that consumers are never completely satisfied. Actually, this is a good thing, because as companies strive to meet consumer demands, increasingly innovative products are offered, and companies grow in response to increased sales. As a result, they hire more people and raise income levels throughout the economy.

The way marketers respond to consumers is changing dramatically. Marketers have historically used advances in technology to provide consumers with greater opportunities to communicate with companies. Today, billions of consumers around the world have 24-hour, seven-day-a-week access to markets via the Internet. Consumers do not need to wait to go to a retail store to purchase music. They can download their favorite new tunes, movies, and apps while walking down the street. Here are some of the trends beyond changes in technology that are shaping the value received by consumers today.

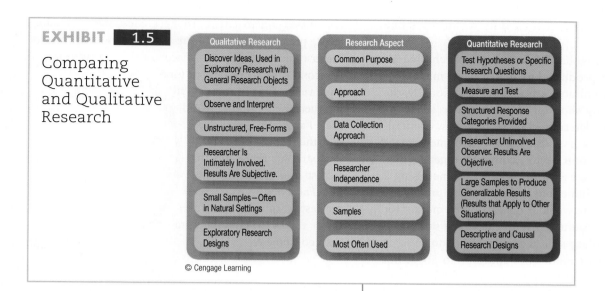

EXHIBIT 1.5

Comparing Quantitative and Qualitative Research

Qualitative Research	Research Aspect	Quantitative Research
Discover Ideas, Used in Exploratory Research with General Research Objects	Common Purpose	Test Hypotheses or Specific Research Questions
Observe and Interpret	Approach	Measure and Test
Unstructured, Free-Forms	Data Collection Approach	Structured Response Categories Provided
Researcher Is Intimately Involved. Results Are Subjective.	Researcher Independence	Researcher Uninvolved Observer. Results Are Objective.
Small Samples—Often in Natural Settings	Samples	Large Samples to Produce Generalizable Results (Results that Apply to Other Situations)
Exploratory Research Designs	Most Often Used	Descriptive and Causal Research Designs

© Cengage Learning

1-5a Internationalization

When Starbucks opened its first store in 1971, the thought may not have occurred that the concept could spread to other parts of the state of Washington or even other parts of the United States. In 1996, Starbucks opened its first store outside the United States in Tokyo, Japan. Today, consumers around the world can order up a latte at one of about 17,000 Starbucks locations in over 55 countries.[33] Whether one is on business in Guadalajara, Mexico; Seoul, South Korea; London, England; Shanghai, China; Nantes, France; or Ruston, Louisiana, he or she can relax at a Starbucks. Almost anywhere the modern consumer travels, he or she can find a familiar place to eat or drink. An Outback Steakhouse, a Pizza Hut, or a McDonald's never seems far away!

Although these chains can be found worldwide, consumers are not alike everywhere these firms operate. An Outback Steakhouse in Seoul will offer *kimchi* (fermented cabbage) on the menu, something neither American nor Australian. Companies must therefore deal with geographical distances as well as cultural distances. The international focus of today's modern company places a greater demand on CB research. Every culture's people will interpret products and behaviors differently. The meanings these consumers perceive will determine the success or failure of the product being offered.

1-5b Technological Changes

It is no secret that we are living in an age of ever-increasing technological advances. These advances seem to be coming at a faster pace all the time. Upon reflection, we may realize that technology has influenced business practices since the advent of industry. Certainly, many retailers felt threatened by mail order technology that was practiced through the Sears Roebuck catalog and the telephone. In 1895, the Sears catalog contained 532 pages of products that enabled rural consumers to obtain things that would have been otherwise difficult to get.[34] Why would people go to a store when they could simply telephone and have products delivered to their door?

In the mid-20th century, television revolutionized consumer behavior. Not only did TV change advertising forever, but true home shopping became a possibility. Now, the consumer could actually see a product in use on television and then make a purchase either by picking up the phone or punching buttons on a cable device (such as the remote control

Joachim Wendler/Shutterstock.com

What do the Sears Catalog from 1895 and an online shopping cart have in common?

for the cable receiver console). Why would someone go to a store?

A consumer now has 24/7 access to purchasing almost any type of product. The Internet has made geographical distance almost a nonissue. Additionally, the consumer can truly shop on his or her own schedule, not on a schedule determined by store hours. Communication technology has also advanced tremendously. Mobile communication devices continue to get smaller, and now one can access stores via the Internet using a Motorola RAZR phone that is thinner than practically any wallet. The entire world is now truly the market for consumers in free countries. With this being said, total U.S. Internet retailing still accounts for about 5% of all retailing. Internet retail sales continue to grow, but using projections from the last quarter of 2012, these sales account for about $216 billion of the $4.4 trillion in 2012 U.S. sales.[35]

What types and amounts of value do consumers seek when shopping online? When a consumer needs an airline ticket, he or she is seeking a solution to a real problem. Buying an airline ticket isn't generally a fun thing to do. Thus, the consumer is primarily seeking "utilitarian" value. Although technology continues to change, the basic consumer desire for value hasn't changed. In fact, the dot-com failures of the late 1990s illustrated that companies that do not enhance the value consumers receive from the current ways of doing things fail. Today, retailers look at web technologies more as complementing traditional retailing than competing with the bricks-and-mortar option. A pure play (Internet only) retailer has a difficult time competing with a shopping adventure to Harrods of London because of the gratification offered by the experience itself.

Shopping online can be a valuable experience, but are virtual shopping and "real" shopping gratifying in the same way?

Changing Communications

As technology has changed, so have the ways that people communicate with each other. Once upon a time, consumers' favorite form of communication was face-to-face. Today, many consumers now rank the telephone as a preferred communication method. However, the preference for voice communication over SMS messages (text messaging) varies. In fact, depending on one's age, both of those may take a back seat to social networking communications. Middle-aged consumers use email for the majority of their communications, as email has replaced a large portion of phone calls. Consumers in their late 20s to 30s prefer

text messaging to email. Younger consumers, including teens, prefer to communicate via Facebook or Twitter rather than email.[36] In fact, Facebook is second only to Google in total page views. One in three of all Internet users in the world use Facebook each day, and the 18- to 24-year-old demographic represents the largest user group for sites like Facebook.[37] Marketers are fast learning how to use these tools to communicate with consumers.

> ⌐ Younger consumers, including teens, prefer communicating via Facebook or Twitter rather than email. ⌐

1-5c Changing Demographics

In most of the Western world, notable demographic trends have shaped consumer behavior patterns greatly over the past quarter century or so. First, households increasingly include two primary income providers. In contrast to the stereotypical working dad and stay-at-home mom, families today often include two parents with a career orientation. Second, family size is decreasing throughout the United States and Europe. In Europe, families are averaging less than one child per family. As a result, the relative importance of countries as consumer markets are changing. Marketers around the world find it hard to ignore the nearly 2 billion consumers in China or the 1 billion in India. We'll discuss demographic trends more in a later chapter.

1-5d Changing Economy

Recent years have seen a downturn in the economy in much of the developed world. With the current high unemployment rate in the U.S., consumers have less money to spend. In 2012, the U.S. unemployment rate was approximately 9% and underemployment was estimated at 20%. In contrast, U.S. unemployment was under 5% as recently as early 2008.[38] Moreover, economic, political, and social turmoil around the world contributes to a picture that leaves many consumers uneasy. As a result, consumer spending has changed in several ways. Consumers are more cautious about spending money and react more favorably to price-cutting policies. Private label brands (such as retail store brands like Walmart's Sam's Choice) become more attractive alternatives as a way of saving money.

Further, consumers perceive themselves as having less discretionary income; one consequence of this is a decrease in charitable giving.[39] If the bad economy continues, consumers will likely continue to be cautious about spending.

Study Tools

Located at the back of the textbook

☐ Rip out Chapter in Review Card

Located at www.cengagebrain.com

☐ Review Key Terms Flashcards (print or online)

☐ Download audio summaries to review on the go

☐ Complete practice quizzes to prepare for tests

☐ Play "Beat the Clock" to master concepts

☐ Watch video on Travelocity for a real company example

WHAT DO YOU THINK?
WHAT OTHERS HAVE THOUGHT

50 45 40 35 30 25 20 15 10 5 0

① Strongly disagree
② Disagree
③ Somewhat disagree
④ Neither agree nor disagree
⑤ Somewhat agree
⑥ Agree
⑦ Strongly agree

In any business, the customer is truly the most important person.

Most respondents agreed with this statement. Nearly 70% of all respondents chose agree or strongly agree. Interestingly, just over 10% of respondents chose strongly disagree. Might a student's major influence his/her response?

Noel Hendrickson/Digital Vision/Jupiter Images

Consumers are sometimes

willing to sacrifice quality and even satisfaction, but consumers never willingly sacrifice value.

WHAT DO YOU THINK?

I get a lot out of shopping even when I don't buy anything.

STRONGLY DISAGREE STRONGLY AGREE

VISIT COURSEMATE AT WWW.CENGAGEBRAIN.COM

Value and the Consumer Behavior Value Framework

2

Raindrops on roses ... warm woolen mittens ... brown paper packages tied up in strings ... these are a few of my favorite things.

Maybe you've heard this famous Rodgers & Hammerstein song from the classic movie, *The Sound of Music*.[1] What are a few of your favorite things? Think about getting a room full of people together that don't know one another. Perhaps they'd have little to talk about but if each person wears a tag listing two favorites, like favorite food and favorite drink, or favorite musician and book author, then conversation likely will fill the room. Seafood gumbo and a village rosé champagne! What are a few of your favorite things?

CB researchers would love to hear these conversations. But they wouldn't be satisfied in only hearing favorites. They would want to know *why* these were a few of your favorite things. One who sets out to study consumers' favorites will quickly spot the fact that favorites relate to identifiable characteristics. This becomes obvious when you ask people of different ages what their favorite branded products are. Exhibit 2.1 shows most preferred brands by age for young U.S. consumers.[2] Clearly, even consumers only a few years apart in age have varied preferences.

Why do preferences change? This is a complicated question and one that becomes only more complicated when other factors are considered besides obvious characteristics like demographics. What about psychological factors, cultural factors, and environmental characteristics? All of these can change a consumer's favorites. This book sheds light on why the things that provide so much value to certain consumers in certain situations don't really do anything for other consumers or even the same consumer in a different situation. This chapter introduces the Consumer Value Framework and some of the core concepts that tie all of CB together and make it actionable in marketing.

After studying this chapter, the student should be able to:

2-1 Describe the consumer value framework, including its basic components.

2-2 Define consumer value and compare and contrast two key types of value.

2-3 Apply the concepts of marketing strategy and marketing tactics to describe the way firms go about creating value for consumers.

2-4 Explain the way market characteristics like market segmentation and product differentiation affect marketing strategy.

2-5 Analyze consumer markets using elementary perceptual maps.

2-6 Justify consumers' lifetime value as an effective focus for long-term business success.

Source: "My Favorite Things" by Richard Rodgers and Oscar Hammerstein II. Copyright © 1959 by Richard Rodgers and Oscar Hammerstein II. Copyright Renewed. International Copyright Secured. All Rights Reserved. Used by Permission of Williamson Music, A Division of The Rodgers & Hammerstein Organization, An Imagem Company.

Consumer Value Framework (CVF) consumer behavior theory that illustrates factors that shape consumption-related behaviors and ultimately determine the value associated with consumption

Customer Relationship Management (CRM) systematic information management system that collects, maintains, and reports detailed information about customers to enable a more customer-oriented managerial approach

EXHIBIT 2.1 — Young Consumers' Favorites

	Tweens (8–12)	Teens (13–17)	Young Adults (18–24)	Overall
First	Nintendo	Reese's PB Cup	Google	M&Ms
Second	Doritos	iPod/iPhone/iPad	Facebook	Google
Third	Oreos	Google	iPod/iPhone/iPad	Reese's PB Cup
Fourth	M&Ms	M&Ms	Gatorade	Oreos
Fifth	Disney Channel	Oreos	Target	iPod/iPhone/iPad

Source: http://www.harrisinteractive.com/Insights/YouthEquiTrendRankings.aspx, accessed April 4, 2012.

2-1 The Consumer Value Framework and Its Components

Consumer behavior is multifaceted. Not only does the study of consumer behavior involve multiple disciplines, but anyone who has ever made a major purchase like a house, an automobile, or an apartment knows that many factors can affect both the purchase decision and the way one feels after the purchase. This book covers many of these factors.

2-1a The Consumer Value Framework

Given the potential complexity involved in explaining consumption, a framework for studying consumer behavior is useful. Exhibit 2.2 displays the framework used in this book. The **Consumer Value Framework (CVF)** represents consumer behavior theory illustrating factors that shape consumption-related behaviors and ultimately determine the value associated with consumption. The different components shown with different colors roughly correspond to the different parts of this book. However, the student of consumer behavior must recognize and accept the fact that each aspect of the CVF is related in some way to other components of the model. The arrows connecting the different components typify these connections.

2-1b Value and the CVF Components

Value is at the heart of experiencing and understanding consumer behavior. Thus, we will never get too far from value in any chapter of this book. We'll expand more on value later in this chapter and throughout the book. In the rest of this section, we present the basic components of the CVF that either contribute to or are outcomes of value.

Relationship Quality

Over the past two decades or so, **Customer Relationship Management (CRM)** has become a popular catchphrase,

EXHIBIT 2.2 — Consumer Value Framework (CVF)

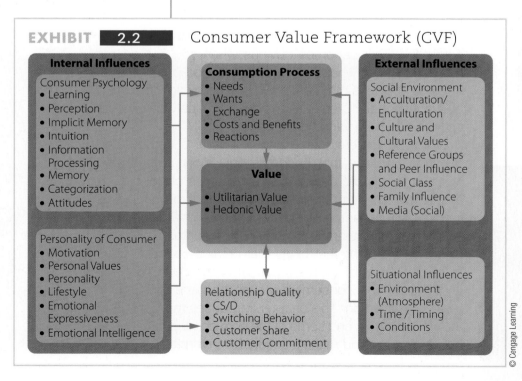

© Cengage Learning

not just in marketing but in all of business. A basic CRM premise is that customers form relationships with companies as opposed to companies conducting individual transactions with customers. A CRM system tracks detailed information about customers so marketers can make more customer-oriented decisions that, hopefully, lead to longer-lasting relationships.

A CRM orientation means each customer represents a potential stream of resources rather than just a single sale. **Relationship quality** reflects the connectedness between a consumer and a retailer, brand, or service provider.[3] In practice, a strong, or high-quality, relationship is typified by a consumer who buys the same brand each time a need for that product arises. Businesses see loyal customers as being more profitable than customers who are prone to switch providers each time they make a purchase.

When a consumer realizes high value from an exchange with a company, relationship quality improves. Over time, a consumer who experiences high value with one company may well become a loyal, committed customer. CVS, a large U.S.-based drugstore chain, successfully implemented a customer loyalty program founded on increased knowledge of the customer.[4] ExtraCare, as the program is known, offers more than just prescription drugs. ExtraCare extends service to a wide assortment of health management services and uses the resulting interactions with customers as a way of gathering additional information about consumers. Along the way, CVS realized that time-starved female consumers made up a large bulk of its business. Armed with information about this segment, CVS designs services aimed at creating value by making health-related services, including getting prescriptions filled, easier to accomplish. Now, rather than advertising heavily to attract new customers, CVS relies more on the same customers to seek health-related services from CVS time and time again. International companies like Dell and Home Depot have also found success in developing high relationship quality.[5]

relationship quality
degree of connectedness between a consumer and a retailer, brand, or service provider

A Consumer's Squeeze

What can a ketchup brand do to add value to its stakeholders? After three years of study, Heinz CB researchers realized these facts:

- Most fast-food consumers use more than one ketchup packet.
- Consumers spend about $2 of every $3 at fast-food restaurants at the drive-through.
- Consumers struggle to use ketchup packages while driving.
- Some consumers dip fries into the package instead of pouring the ketchup out.

The answer was the Dip and Squeeze ketchup packet that holds three times the ketchup as the old packets and makes dipping fries or squeezing the ketchup onto something very easy. Heinz went through all of this knowing full well that virtually all fast-food restaurants give the packets away. Moreover, Heinz planned on charging the restaurants a higher price for this product compared to the old packets. The gamble here is that the fast-food restaurants will invest in enhancing the customer experience with the hopes that customers will come back more often. If this all works, Heinz will have added value to the restaurants' customers and the restaurants themselves and Heinz's other stakeholders. It's really a squeeze play.

Alpha /Landov

Sources: S. Nassauer, "Old Ketchup Packet Heads for Trash," *The Wall Street Journal*, September 19, 2011, B1–B2. "For Heinz, Old Is New," *Brand Packaging* 15 (May 2011): 46.

internal influences things that go on inside of the mind and heart of the consumer

cognition thinking or mental processes that go on as we process and store things that can become knowledge

affect feelings associated with objects or experienced during events

individual differences characteristic traits of individuals, including personality and lifestyle

external influences social and cultural aspects of life as a consumer

Consumption Process

Consumers must decide to do something before they can receive value. This process involves deciding what is needed, what options for exchange are available, and the inevitable reaction to consumption. The consumption process can involve a great deal of decision making and thus represents a consumer decision-making process. Many factors influence this process, and these factors can be divided into different categories, such as internal and external influences.

Internal Influences: The Psychology and Personality of the Consumer

The Psychology of the Consumer. Most consumers can think of a place they try hard to avoid solely because of the irritating music played there. Consumers fear that an irritating song might "get stuck in my head." Is getting a song stuck in someone's head a good idea if you want to sell something? Will consumers remain loyal to a popular brand's product designs when they become increasingly complex with features that only a small portion of consumers can use? Or will they look for a simpler choice? Should marketers sell a product for $99.99 instead of $100? All these questions involve the psychology of the consumer. In other words, these things are **internal influences**, things that go on inside of the consumer or that can be thought of as part of the consumer.

The psychology of the consumer involves both cognitive and affective processes. The term **cognition** refers to the thinking or mental processes that go on as we process and store things that can become knowledge. A child hears parents talk about smoking as a *nasty* thing to do. Smoking becomes associated with nastiness, and the child may develop a dislike of smoking. **Affect** refers to the feelings that are experienced during consumption activities or associated with specific objects. If the child continues to receive negative information about smoking, the belief about its being nasty may result in feelings of disgust.

Many people think of these types of things when they think of CB. Certainly, our perceptions help shape the desirability of products, which can influence decision processes and the value perceived from consuming something. Recall that value is a subjective assessment. Therefore, value is very much a matter of perception.

The Personality of the Consumer. Every consumer has certain characteristics and traits that help define him or her as an individual. We refer to these traits generally as **individual differences**. Individual differences, which include personality and lifestyle, help determine consumer behavior. For example, a consumer with a lifestyle oriented toward spending time outdoors may be more likely to desire a convertible automobile than someone who is happier indoors.

Companies have spent vast amounts of money and time trying to harness individual differences in a way that allows consumer choice to be predicted. They do so because individual differences like these include basic motivations, which trigger consumer desires. Also, individual differences shape the value experienced by consumers and the reaction consumers have to consumption.

External Influences

Why do some consumers like foods like sashimi or habanero peppers while others wouldn't consider eating these things but instead prefer eating a hot dog? Why do consumers in different parts of the world have such different tastes for food? In Korea, a typical breakfast often includes a fish soup of some type, at times made with fish heads. In Australia, one might smear a bit of vegemite (yeast extract made into something resembling peanut butter in texture but not taste) onto toast in the morning. In the United States, a bowl of frosted flakes with cold milk poured over the top is a common way to start the day. Each of these dishes is disgusting as a breakfast food to someone somewhere in the world and just fine to consumers in a different place. Even a simple thing like breakfast can cause quite different reactions in different consumers.

These types of events typify external influences on consumers. **External influences** include the social and cultural aspects of life as a consumer. They directly impact the value of activities, although the influence comes from sources outside of the consumer. Thus, they are critical to a thorough understanding of consumer behavior.

Social Environment. Consumers learn a culture, including important things like rules about what types of food are appropriate for breakfast and how to greet people. In addition, any time a consumer chooses to do something to, at least in part, please or appeal to

External influences like culture shape the value of different behaviors including greetings.

another consumer, he or she has been influenced by the **social environment**. The social environment includes the people and groups who help shape a consumer's everyday experiences. Group influence is one mechanism through which social influences work. A child's tastes for breakfast foods are shaped very much by what he or she learns from parents and an innate desire to conform to their wishes.

Situational Influences.

External influences also include situational influences. **Situational influences** are unique to a time or place that can affect consumer decision making and the value received from consumption. Situational influences include the effect that the physical environment has on consumer behavior. For example, the presence of music in an environment may shape consumer behavior and even change buying patterns. Similarly, music can affect one's feelings when waiting for service. If so, a market for music that creates positive effects on consumers exists. Other characteristics, such as the economic condition at a given time, also affect the value of things.

social environment
elements that specifically deal with the way other people influence consumer decision making and value

situational influences
things unique to a time or place that can affect consumer decision making and the value received from consumption

Fill'er Up!

Although the examples in this book often illustrate businesses selling to individual consumers or households, most principles discussed in this book also apply when businesses sell to other businesses, institutions, or government agencies. Simply put, businesses are consumers too, and at times their purchase decisions are fairly complex and involve very large amounts of resources. A weak economy affects practically all businesses. In these times, businesses, like individual households, become more cautious in their spending.

Among those affected are organizations that rely on corporate sponsorships. Organizations such as NASCAR, the LPGA (Ladies Professional Golf Association), the X Games, and numerous charities hosting community events rely on convincing corporations that a value proposition involving large donations in return for prominent name billing during an event is a good buy. Not only do NASCAR events like the Daytona 500 need sponsors like Budweiser, but individual drivers need sponsors to financially support their teams. Recently, major sponsors like UPS, Home Depot, and Aflac all have reduced their sponsorship involvement with NASCAR. In a tough economy, the sponsorship opportunities don't seem to offer the same value they did in previous years

because the chance of seeing a tangible return seems less likely. Attendance is down at NASCAR events, meaning the sponsor brands get less exposure through their sponsorships. Analysts attribute the reduced attendance primarily to the economic downturn, which has hit the typical NASCAR fan hard, but they also believe the efforts by NASCAR to increase safety have made the races less exciting.

The sponsored events that seem to suffer less in the bad times are those associated with nonprofits. Brand managers become hesitant to sever ties with such brands for emotional reasons and as a way of avoiding any bad publicity that might result. But no organization can hide from external influences.

Sources: V. Bauerlein, "Nascar's Leaky Fuel Tank," *The Wall Street Journal*, November 13, 2012, http://online.wsj.com/article/SB10001424127887324894104578115210175340142 .html#printMode?KEYWORDS=cars; K. Badenhausen, "Matt Kenseth Wins Daytona 500, but Loses with Sponsors," *Forbes*, February 28, 2012, http://www.forbes.com/sites/kurtbadenhausen/2012/02/28 /matt-kenseth-wins-daytona-500-but-loses-with-sponsors/.

value a personal assessment of the net worth obtained from an activity

Much of the remainder of the book will be organized around the Customer Value Framework. The CVF should be a valuable study aid, particularly given that the different theoretical areas of CB are so closely related to each other. Additionally, the CVF is a good analysis tool for solving consumer behavior business problems. Lastly, the CVF is a valuable tool for businesses that are trying to understand the way consumers respond to their product offerings. Thus, the CVF is useful in developing and implementing marketing strategy.

© iStockphoto.com/Godfried Edelman

2-2 Value and Its Two Basic Types

The heart of the Consumer Value Framework, and *the* core concept of CB, is value. **Value** is a personal assessment of the *net worth* a consumer obtains from an activity. From a marketing perspective, the relevant value is that received from activities involving interactions between consumers and the firm or its products. Value is what consumers ultimately pursue, because valuable actions address motivations that manifest themselves in needs and desires. In this sense, value captures how much gratification a consumer receives from consumption.

Most consumers would not list a convenience store as their favorite place to shop. Consumers see the selection as small, the prices high, and the service minimal. Yet consumers return time and time again because, as their name implies, convenience is the key to value in this setting. Consumers in fact will repeat behavior for which they have previously experienced low satisfaction. Walmart stores do not have a relatively high consumer satisfaction index, yet many customers repeatedly visit Walmart. Walmart delivers value, as we will see in a later chapter. In contrast to these examples, contriving a situation where consumers are not seeking value is virtually impossible. In fact, everything we do in life is done in the pursuit of value.

2-2a The Value Equation

Exhibit 2.3 reflects some components of value and how a consumer might put these together to determine the overall worth of something—or its value! Worth to a consumer is actually a function of much more than price. Value can be modeled by playing the "what you get" from dealing with a company against the "what you have to give" to get the product. The "what you get" includes all sorts of benefits or positive consequences of consumption. The "what you give" includes sacrifices or the negative consequences of consumption. For instance, opportunity costs play a role because if a student goes to the movies on a weeknight, he or she may be giving up the opportunity to attend a class. Nearly all components in the value equation come into play when a consumer makes a big purchase like a new home, chooses a college to attend, or uses a dating site.

Later in the book a chapter is devoted to further describing value and other related concepts, including expectations, satisfaction, and quality. However, because value is an essential part of consumer behavior, a basic overview is provided in this chapter.

Value can be understood better by looking at its types. While theoretically one could probably break

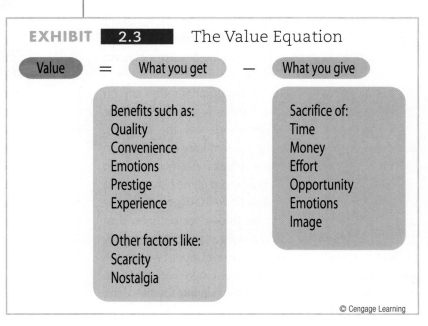

EXHIBIT 2.3 The Value Equation

Value = What you get − What you give

Benefits such as:
Quality
Convenience
Emotions
Prestige
Experience

Other factors like:
Scarcity
Nostalgia

Sacrifice of:
Time
Money
Effort
Opportunity
Emotions
Image

© Cengage Learning

Going to the movies? What are the gets and gives that determine value from the movie experience?

© iStockphoto.com/Blend_Images

down value into many very specific types, a very useful value typology can be developed using only two types. Thus, we distinguish utilitarian value from hedonic value.

2-2b Utilitarian Value

Activities and objects that lead to high utilitarian value do so because they help the consumer accomplish some task. **Utilitarian value** is derived from a product that helps the consumer solve problems and accomplish tasks that are a part of being a consumer. A rational explanation can usually be given by the purchaser when utilitarian value is involved. For instance, when a consumer calls a plumber, he or she undoubtedly has a problem like a stopped-up toilet. Plumbing services are purchased because they accomplish something. In this case, they accomplish the end of getting a toilet working, which is a gratifying end. In this sense, utilitarian value can be thought of as something worthwhile as a means to an end.[6] Value is provided because the object or activity allows something else good to happen or be accomplished.

2-2c Hedonic Value

The second type of value is referred to in CB as hedonic value. **Hedonic value** is the immediate gratification that comes from experiencing some activity. Seldom does one go to a horror film or play an online game on Facebook in an effort to get a job done. With hedonic value, the value is provided entirely by the actual experience and emotions associated with consumption, not because some other end is or will be accomplished.

Conceptually, hedonic value differs from utilitarian value in several ways. First, hedonic value is an end in and of itself rather than a means to an end. Second, hedonic value is very emotional and subjective in nature. Third, when a consumer does something to obtain hedonic value, the action can sometimes be very difficult to explain objectively.

Rather than being viewed as opposites, the two types of value are not mutually exclusive. In other words, the same act of consumption can provide both utilitarian value and hedonic value. Dining in a place like the Hard Rock Café is an event. One doesn't have to go to Hard Rock to eat, but dining there is a lot of fun—an experience! However, the Hard Rock consumer also accomplishes the task of having something to eat—getting nourished. In fact, the very best consumer experiences are those that provide both high utilitarian value and high hedonic value.

If one takes a look at the most popular movies of all time based on box office ticket sales, you might be surprised to see that most of the top hits are family films like the G-rated *Transformers: Dark of the Moon* or the PG-rated *Harry Potter and the Deathly Hollows: Part 2*. Parents can take the kids to the movie and accomplish the job of keeping the kids happy while at the same time enjoying the movie themselves. In this way, movies like these provide high value and the value translates into business success for the studios.

Exhibit 2.4 illustrates the value possibilities associated with consumption. A marketer that provides low

utilitarian value value derived from a product that helps the consumer with some task

hedonic value value derived from the immediate gratification that comes from some activity

---

EXHIBIT 2.4 Consumption Activities Can Fall into Any of These Categories

		Utilitarian Value	
		Low	**High**
Hedonic Value	**Low**	Bad Positioning – slow "fast" food in an unpleasant environment	Okay Positioning – fast, "fast" food
	High	Okay Positioning – restaurant with nice atmosphere but poor service	Superior Positioning – restaurant with great atmosphere, great food, and great service

© Cengage Learning

strategy a planned way of doing something to accomplish some goal

marketing strategy way a company goes about creating value for customers

marketing myopia a common condition in which a company views itself in a product business rather than in a value- or benefits-producing business. In this way, it is short-sighted.

levels of both values is not likely to survive very long. Generally, a consumer goes to a fast-food restaurant to accomplish the task of getting something to eat, and doing this as quickly as possible. Food quality may take a back seat to convenience. When the fast-food experience becomes slow, the consumer receives little value of either type.

In contrast, restaurants can survive by specializing in providing one type of value or the other, as would be the case in a place with a great atmosphere but perhaps less than the best food or service quality. As mentioned earlier, the best experience comes when a place can put everything together—high-quality food and impeccable service all packed in a memorable place with a great atmosphere. These are the types of experiences a consumer is most likely to want to repeat.

2-3 Marketing Strategy and Consumer Value

One way that a company can enhance the chance of long-run survival is to have an effective marketing strategy. To an army general, a strategy provides a way of winning a military conflict. Generally, a **strategy** is a planned way of doing something to accomplish some goal.

2-3a Marketing Strategy

If strategy is a way of doing something, given the purpose of business, a **marketing strategy** is the way a company goes about creating value for customers. The strategy also should provide an effective way of dealing with both competition and eventual technological obsolescence, by making sure that value is delivered in a way that is not easily duplicated by other companies and not defined only in terms of the tangible product offered.

A complete understanding of the value consumers seek is needed to effectively develop and implement a strategy. AT&T may compete directly with Verizon, but AT&T also competes with companies like Skype, which provides local, long-distance, and even international calling via the Internet, all for prices much lower than traditional telephone services. The consumer who uses Internet calling services like Skype no longer needs a telephone to receive the benefits of talking to friends and family who are far away. With these services, consumers can talk to each other anywhere in the world for free as long as they have an Internet connection. If AT&T laid out a marketing strategy that depended on people *buying and owning phones*, technological obsolescence would represent a real threat. A better strategic orientation would focus on providing value by *enabling and facilitating communication*. Rather than fight the new technology, Verizon facilitates the use of Skype calls through the use of select mobile phones. All companies in competitive industries need to focus on the core benefits they provide. For AT&T and Verizon, benefits are derived from electronic communication, but is electronic communication really their business? When firms fail to realize how their products provide value, they run the risk of developing **marketing myopia**, defined as a condition in which a company views itself competing in a product business rather than in a value- or benefits-producing business.[7] Thus, when technology makes the product obsolete, the myopic business goes out of business. In contrast, the company that focuses on value creation builds solutions around consumer needs and wants, not the physical product.

> The best experience comes when a place can put everything together—high-quality food and impeccable service all packed in a memorable place with a great atmosphere.

Technology changes. Consumers do not need phones but they do need to communicate. Why didn't "phone" companies lead the way in this type of communication?

AP Photo/Paul Sakuma

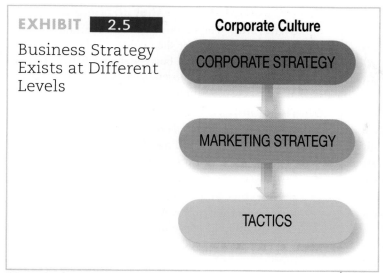

EXHIBIT 2.5

Business Strategy Exists at Different Levels

Corporate Culture

CORPORATE STRATEGY

MARKETING STRATEGY

TACTICS

© Cengage Learning

corporate strategy way a firm is defined, and its general goals

marketing tactics ways marketing management is implemented; involves price, promotion, product, and distribution decisions

Strategies exist at several different levels. Exhibit 2.5 demonstrates this point. Basically, **corporate strategy** deals with how the firm will be defined and sets general goals. This strategy is usually associated with a specific corporate culture, which provides an operating orientation for the company. Marketing strategy then follows. Different business units within the firm may have different marketing strategies. In describing how value is created, the strategies tell why customers will choose to buy things from the company.

Strategies must eventually be implemented. Implementation deals with operational management. In marketing, this level includes activities known as tactics. **Marketing tactics**, which involve price, promotion, product, and distribution decisions, are ways marketing management is implemented. Together, marketing strategy and marketing tactics should maximize the total value received by its customers.

2-3b Total Value Concept

Products are multifaceted and can provide value in many ways. Consider the market for athletic shoes. By all appearances, athletic shoes from different brands appear very similar. A running shoe from Nike appears made from much the same materials and in much the same manner as a running shoe from Adidas or New Balance. Take a look at the prices and one finds that they have shoes at the same price points too. However, the market share for the competing brands is nowhere near the same.

Exhibit 2.6 displays the approximate relative market share for the top athletic shoe companies.[8] If all the products are much the same and sell for about the same prices, then they should have comparable market share. Yet that's not nearly the case. Nike dominates with nearly half the total market. Reebok has less than half the share of Nike, and Puma and New Balance lag far behind. Nike is more than a rubber sole with leather and nylon uppers and laces. The swoosh matters! A couple of interesting facts that may be more than coincidental:

⌐ The company that focuses on value creation builds solutions around consumer needs and wants, not the physical product. ⌐

- Nike's advertising budget is twice the size of its nearest competitor.

- Among consumers who run more than ten miles per week, New Balance has a share comparable to Nike.

Do these facts shed some light on the way these brands' shoes provide value to the consumer? Probably so. Is the Nike image, fueled by massive amounts of advertising, as important to the serious runner as it is to the mass market?

Other products require installation or other types of service before one can enjoy any benefits. Best Buy is

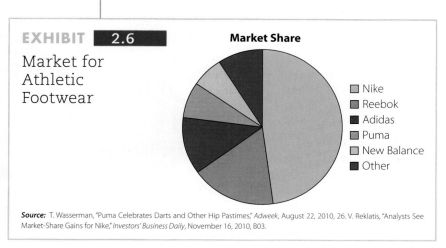

EXHIBIT 2.6

Market for Athletic Footwear

Market Share

- Nike
- Reebok
- Adidas
- Puma
- New Balance
- Other

Source: T. Wasserman, "Puma Celebrates Darts and Other Hip Pastimes," *Adweek*, August 22, 2010, 26. V. Reklatis, "Analysts See Market-Share Gains for Nike," *Investors' Business Daily*, November 16, 2010, B03.

augmented product
actual physical product purchased plus any services such as installation and warranties necessary to use the product and obtain its benefits

total value concept
business practice wherein companies operate with the understanding that products provide value in multiple ways

currently undergoing a change that will position it as more of a services company. While we associate Best Buy with electronic products like computers, the repositioning hopefully will reduce the revenue generated by selling goods and increase the revenue from services that enhance the consumption of electronics. The term **augmented product** means the original product plus the extra things needed to increase the value from consumption.

Thus, every product's value is made up of the basic benefits, plus the augmented product, plus the "feel" benefits. A company must try to understand all the ways a product offers value to its customers. The **total value concept** is practiced when companies operate with the understanding that products provide value in multiple ways. Many products and brands, for instance, provide some benefits that produce utilitarian value and some that provide hedonic value. This value, in turn, helps provide a brand with meaning in the consumer psyche.

2-3c The Total Value Concept Illustrated

Let's consider a consumer who purchases a 2014 Ferrari 458 Italia. Does the consumer buy the car for its 570 horsepower V-8 engine, carbon-filament doors, bright red color, or dual-clutch 7-speed gear box? No, the consumer buys the car because of the total value offered. How does the Ferrari Italia offer value?[9] The answer may not be the same for all consumers, but here are some likely reasons:

1. **Transportation.** In other words, the Ferrari solves the job of getting a consumer from point A to point B. This is one way the Ferrari provides value—utilitarian value in this case.

2. **The Ferrari service plan.** A Ferrari needs TLC. Ferrari offers a three-year warranty, which means for at least three years, the problem of repairing the Ferrari is solved—utilitarian value is added.

3. **The feelings associated with driving the car.** The car is very, very fast and handles well. At a top speed of just over 200 mph, the car will exceed the speed limit, but we know Ferrari owners always obey the speed limit—right?! The excitement that is the Ferrari driving experience provides hedonic value.

4. **The positive feelings that go along with ownership.** The Ferrari owner will certainly take pride in the car. He or she may also believe that social status comes from being seen as a Ferrari owner. He or she can also impress friends with a drive on the Pacific Coast Highway.

5. **The feelings of status and pride that come with ownership.** A Ferrari jacket and cap help make the statement, "I'm a Ferrari owner." The realization of ownership provides a hedonic value.

6. **The negative feelings that go along with ownership.** Hopefully, our Ferrari owner is independently wealthy. At a price tag of about US$250,000, the car loan could be the size of a modest mortgage—not including insurance. If the Ferrari is a financial strain, then worry will result when the owner thinks about the car. In addition, the Ferrari needs servicing every 12,000 miles, servicing that can be quite expensive. Friends may have also suggested that Ferraris are unreliable. All of these feelings may detract from the hedonic value offered by the car.

> Many products and brands, for instance, provide some benefits that produce utilitarian value and some that provide hedonic value.

Altogether, most readers would certainly like to drive the Ferrari but probably not care to pay the high price. Thus, the Ferrari does not offer enough benefits for us to make the necessary sacrifice. A Honda Fit may do the trick, although the hedonic to utilitarian value ratio may not be the same as with a Ferrari.

Automobile marketers sometimes miss the total value equation for their product. In 2005, General Motors began to offer consumers a "total value promise."[10] They hoped this would convey the value of extended warranties, more standard equipment, and lower sticker

AP Photos/Imaginechina

How does the Ferrari provide value? If you understand this, you understand the total value concept.

prices. Was GM missing something if they believed total value is confined to these tangible aspects?

In the 1990s, eBay turned consumers on to the online auction. However, eBay users have increasingly turned toward the use of the buy-it-now price option. Perhaps the traditional online auction just isn't fun anymore. More recently, new online auction sites such as Quibids.com are reinvigorating enthusiasm for online auctions. These auctions work differently than the eBay auction. Unlike eBay's free bids, the Quibids customer must use bids he or she previously purchased for under a dollar each to participate in an auction. Thus, one pays to play. Also, unlike eBay, every time a consumer bids, the price of the product increases by only a penny. The bidding moves at fast pace because if no consumer bids within a few seconds, the last consumer making a bid "wins." Thus, consumers truly can obtain products like laptop computers for a few dollars or less. In this way, Quibids offers utilitarian value through the acquisition of sought-after goods, but it also offers hedonic value potential in that the auction process is exciting to many consumers. Innovation is necessary to provide consumers with high value.

When a firm practices the total value concept, a full understanding of how value can be created from a product is necessary. In the future, Ferrari might consider rolling routine service into the warranty plan as a way of enhancing value—particularly given the reliability of competitors. Total value is also affected by the technologies and infrastructures that exist. For instance, is Ferrari researching a way to provide value if gasoline-powered engines or high-speed highways become obsolete? What value would a Ferrari offer if you couldn't drive it?[11]

2-3d Value Is Co-Created

Alone, a marketer can only propose a way of creating value to consumers. In other words, the marketer cannot create value alone.[12] Rather, the consumer adds resources in the form of knowledge and skills to do his or her own part in the consumption process. Value is not created by the marketer's offering but rather consumption involves **value co-creation**. The marketer serves its customer by making potentially beneficial outcomes of consumption available, but the customer plays a role in whether or not the offering's attributes actually do prove beneficial, and therefore valuable. The consumer and marketer, as a true service provider, are active in turning the offer into value. For example, a 24-hour fitness center serves customers by making workout facilities available

any time of day. However, the consumer can only realize value from the offer by paying for this service and applying diligence, skill, and effort to a workout regime. In many instances, a bad consumption experience is not entirely the fault of the business. The consumer plays a role in the value equation as well.

value co-creation the realization that a consumer is necessary and must play a part in order to produce value

marketing mix combination of product, pricing, promotion, and distribution strategies used to implement a marketing strategy

target market identified segment or segments of a market that a company serves

market segmentation separation of a market into groups based on the different demand curves associated with each group

2-4 Market Characteristics: Market Segments and Product Differentiation

Marketing management involves managing the marketing mix and deciding to whom the effort will be directed. The **marketing mix** is simply the combination of product, pricing, promotion, and distribution strategies used to position some product offering or brand in the marketplace. The marketing mix represents the way a marketing strategy is implemented within a given market or exchange environment. Marketers often use the term **target market** to signify which market segment a company will serve with a specific marketing mix. Thus, target marketing requires that managers identify and understand market segments. But what exactly is market segmentation?

2-4a Market Segmentation

Market segmentation is the separation of a market into groups based on the different demand curves associated with each group. Market segmentation is a marketplace condition; numerous segments exist in some markets, but very few segments may exist in others. We can think of the total quantity of a product sold as a simple mathematical function (f) like this:[13]

$$Q = f(p, w, x, \ldots z)$$

where Q = total quantity sold, p = price, and w, x, and z are other characteristics of the particular product. The function means that as price and the other characteristics are varied, the quantity demanded changes.

elasticity reflects how sensitive a consumer is to changes in some product characteristic

For example, as the price of tablet computers decreases, the quantity sold increases; in other words, there is a negative relationship between price and quantity sold. Negative relationships occur when as one variable increases the other decreases. This type of relationship represents the typical price–quantity relationship commonly depicted in basic economics courses. As the length of the warranty increases (w in this case), more tablets are sold. Thus, if we limit the demand equation to two characteristics (price p and warranty w in this case), the equation representing demand for tablets overall might be:

$$Q = -3p + 2w$$

The numbers, or coefficients, preceding p and w, respectively, for each group represent the sensitivity of each segment to each characteristic. The greater the magnitude (absolute value) of the number, the more sensitive that group is to a change in that characteristic. In economics, **elasticity** is a term used to represent market sensitivity to changes in price or other characteristics.[14] This equation suggests that consumers are more sensitive to price than warranty as indicated by the respective coefficients, -3 for price and $+2$ for warranty in this case.

However, this overall demand "curve" may not accurately reflect any particular consumer. Instead, the market may really consist of two groups of consumers that produce this particular demand curve when aggregated. In other words, the two groups may be of equal size and be represented by equations that look something like this:

$$q_1 = -1p + 3w$$
$$q_2 = -5p + 1w$$

In this case, q_1 and q_2 represent the quantity that would be sold in groups one and two, respectively. Group one is more sensitive to the warranty ($|3| > |1|$), and group two is more sensitive to price ($|-5| > |-1|$). If we put all the segments together, we get total demand once again:

$$Q = q_1 + q_2$$

Thus, a market for any product is really the sum of the demand existing in individual groups or segments of consumers. The fast-food market may consist of many segments including a group most interested in low price, a group most interested in food quality, a group most interested in convenience, and perhaps a group that is not extremely sensitive to any of these characteristics. In this sense, market segmentation is not really a marketing tactic because the segments are created by consumers through their unique preferences. Market segmentation is critically important to effective marketing, though, and the marketing researcher's job becomes identifying segments and describing the segments' members based on characteristics such as age, income, geography, and lifestyle.

Exhibit 2.7 depicts the market segmentation process. For simplicity, we consider the quantity sold as a function of only price. The frame on the left depicts overall quantity demanded. Typically, as price goes up (moves right on the x-axis), the quantity sold goes down, meaning price is negatively related to quantity. The frame on the right breaks this market into three segments:

1. The orange line depicts a segment that is highly sensitive to price. Changes in price correspond to relatively large changes in sales. In this particular case, price increases reduce the quantity demanded.

2. The green line represents a segment also sensitive to price so that higher prices are demanded less, but this segment is not nearly as sensitive as the first segment. Changes in price are not associated with as large of a change in quantity sold.

3. The violet line turns out to be perhaps most interesting. Here, when price goes up, the quantity sold actually goes up, too. Thus, the group is sensitive to price but actually buys more at a higher price than at a lower price.

Actually, although a positive relationship between price and quantity may seem unusual, *backward sloping*

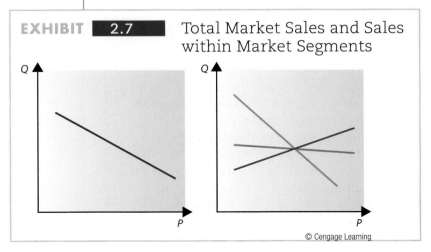

EXHIBIT 2.7 Total Market Sales and Sales within Market Segments

© Cengage Learning

demand, a term used in economics to refer to this situation, is hardly rare. When one considers product category demand, a market segment for many products will feature a positive price–quantity demanded relationship. For instance, how much perfume with a brand name of Très Cher could be sold in a gallon container for $2? Probably not very much! However, Chanel No. 5 is highly demanded at about $325 an ounce!

Earlier, we discussed the athletic shoe market in the context of the total value concept, and how higher-priced brands were the best sellers. If we think of a change in price as the difference in price between the bargain brands and Nike, most consumers seem to prefer higher-priced shoes. At the very least, athletic shoe consumers appear insensitive to price. Although this may seem inconsistent with "rational" economics, consumer behavior theory offers an explanation. Name-brand products like Nike are indeed worth more, meaning they are more valuable, than bargain-brand shoes. The added value comes not just from the tangible characteristics of the shoes but also from the feelings that come along with knowledge of the brand. This is a very important point to understand. Ultimately, consumer segments exist because different consumers do not value different alternatives the same way.[15]

TAKE SPORT. ADD MUSIC.

SOFIA BOUTELLA "MASSIVE FREESTYLE MOVES"
REMIXED BY THE NIKE STUDIO 77 SLASH MIXX CD:
SHOX RHYTHMIC VERSION.

NIKE
www.nikewomen.com

Nike's long-term market dominance illustrates that their value proposition goes beyond footwear.

The Advertising Archives

Market segments are associated with unique value equations just as they are associated with unique demand equations. Thus, if each segment is offered a product that closely matches its particular sensitivities, all segments can receive high value. This brings us to product differentiation.

2-4b Product Differentiation

Product differentiation is a marketplace condition in which consumers do not view all competing products as identical to one another. We refer to commodities very often as products that are indistinguishable across brands and/or manufacturers—that is, no matter who produced them or where they were produced. Regular gasoline approaches a commodity status, but even here, a few consumers will regard certain brands as unique. In contrast, consumers do not all consider Internet retailers the same way. Some purchasers consider a third-party seller like eBay inconvenient and only visit if there is something there that they cannot find easily elsewhere. Conversely, other consumers view the eBay shopping and buying process as intrinsically entertaining and a source of high hedonic value. In this case, market segments can be identified based on the way different consumers view Internet shopping and their differing sensitivities to characteristics of Internet transactions. Fortunately, these segments often align with consumer characteristics like age or generation that enable marketers to reach, communicate with, and serve the segments more efficiently.[16]

2-5 Analyzing Markets with Perceptual Maps

Product differentiation becomes the basis for **product positioning**. Positioning refers to the way a product is perceived by a consumer and can be represented by the number and types of characteristics that consumers perceive. A standard marketing tool is a perceptual map.

> **product differentiation** marketplace condition in which consumers do not view all competing products as identical to one another
>
> **product positioning** way a product is perceived by a consumer

⌐ Cheaper products don't always outsell their higher-priced alternatives. ⌐

perceptual map tool used to depict graphically the positioning of competing products

blue ocean strategy positioning a firm far away from competitors' positions so that it creates an industry of its own and, at least for a time, isolates itself from competitors

ideal points combination of product characteristics that provide the most value to an individual consumer or market segment

2-5a Perceptual Maps

A **perceptual map** is used to depict graphically the positioning of competing products. When marketing analysts examine perceptual maps, they can identify competitors, identify opportunities for doing more business, and diagnose potential problems in the marketing mix. For instance, the analyst may realize that by changing the amount of some product characteristic, they can move closer to some segment's ideal point, and thus increase the competitiveness of the product. Alternatively, a new business may choose to position a product in a way that leaves it facing little direct competition. This can be done by "locating" the product as far away from other brands as possible.

Cirque de Soleil followed a marketing strategy that positioned its offering far away from other circuses by eliminating tents and circus animals (moving into arenas and auditoriums), raising prices (a ticket far above the normal circus ticket), reducing the number of acts, and creating themes for acrobatic shows. In doing so, they created what marketing analysts refer to as a blue ocean.[17] A **blue ocean strategy** seeks to position a firm so far away from competitors that, when successful, the firm creates an industry of its own and, at least for a time, isolates itself from competitors.

2-5b Illustrating a Perceptual Map

Exhibit 2.8 illustrates a perceptual map. Perceptual mapping is used throughout this book as a way to link differences in consumer behavior to changes in marketing strategy or tactics. In this case, the perceptual map depicts consumer beliefs about tourist attractions in New Orleans, Louisiana. Each attraction is listed in a small rectangle.

The researcher identified and collected consumer perceptions of the ten tourist destinations and of the **ideal points**, meaning the combination of tourist destination characteristics providing the most value among the five most prominent consumer segments: Adventure Seekers, Culture Explorers, Relaxers, Knowledge Seekers, and Thrill Seekers.[18] Colored ovals indicate these segments centered on each segment's ideal point. The *x*- and *y*-axes of this plane each represent an important dimension that consumers use to separate competitors on a specific characteristic. Here, the *x*-axis identifies product offerings based on how relaxing to invigorating consumers view each. The *y*-axis separates product offerings based on how relatively modern versus authentic consumers view each. The perceptual map allows several key observations.

1. The competition among attractions viewed as highly authentic and relaxing is intense. Consumers regard the Mississippi River Cruises, a visit to the Jazz Heritage Museum, a Cemetery Visit, and the Audubon Zoo as possessing these characteristics as shown in quadrant IV of the perceptual map. The World War II Museum also competes with these attractions, viewed as a moderately authentic, moderately invigorating attraction.

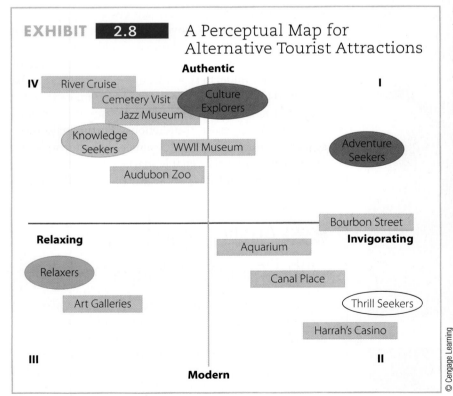

EXHIBIT 2.8 A Perceptual Map for Alternative Tourist Attractions

Michael Bush /UPI/Landov

© Cengage Learning

2. Two segments, Culture Explorers and Knowledge Seekers, possess ideal points near the five segments mentioned above.

3. Harrah's Casino offers an option for the thrill-seeking market with its position as highly exciting, highly modern.

4. The city's numerous art galleries offer the Relaxer segment an attractive option.

5. The Adventure Seeker segment appears underserved, with no option prominent in quadrant I.

The marketing analyst draws several conclusions based on these observations:

1. The highest demand positioning is in quadrant IV (highly authentic, relaxing). The city's overall image as rich in heritage and relatively laid-back—"The Big Easy" being one of the many nicknames—helps attract consumers looking for these types of experiences. An entrepreneur wishing to open another major tourist attraction positioned in this way may see the large number of potential customers desiring this positioning as an opportunity. However, the downside to this positioning is the large amount of entrenched competition. In general, competing directly with large entrenched competitors usually requires a large amount of resources.

2. An opportunity may exist in quadrant I. Here, major competition for the adventure-seeking market appears absent. The advantage of positioning a new business away from the competitors is that it takes fewer resources to get started because the major competitors are not likely to see the new offering as

a threat. Here, the opportunity for rustic, overnight stays in the swamplands that surround New Orleans may provide an attractive offering for this segment. The success of such an offering depends on a steady stream of Adventure Seekers coming to New Orleans.

Perceptual maps are widely used to plot the way consumers view competitors in an industry. As illustrated in the example, they are very useful for spotting opportunities in the marketplace, allowing a business to better understand exactly who they compete with, identifying what-if situations by examining what would happen if they changed an offering by raising or lowering characteristics. Very commonly, brands analyze themselves on a perceptual map with price and quality as the dimensions. If a firm lowers price or raises quality, their competition may well change. Perceptual mapping is used in practically every competitive industry, including in the nonprofit sector.[19] The simple two-dimensional graphics give the user an easy way to analyze a market.

> ⌐ Businesses are constantly using consumer behavior to make better strategic and operational decisions. ⌐

2-5c Using Consumer Behavior Theory in Marketing Strategy

Businesses are constantly using consumer behavior to make better strategic and operational marketing decisions. We will focus considerably on using consumer

Assume Crash Position?

It may be hard to remember now, but BlackBerry was among many consumers' most favorite things until 2010. In about two years time, the BlackBerry smartphone market share dropped from nearly 50% to about 10% in 2012. Where did they go wrong? Unlike an Apple product, BlackBerry smartphones were described as useful, efficient, and simple. They were great to get things done and became particularly dominant in the business market where companies issue phones to employees. In the late 2000s, BlackBerry altered its image by promoting features in their smartphones such as video displays and gaming abilities. With this positioning, they moved closer toward the Apple iPhone and gave up their positioning

Mark Blinch/Reuters /Landov

as the premier utilitarian value phone in the marketplace. Consumer analysts see BlackBerry's strategic move toward the hedonic value positioning as a mistake and a reason for their poor performance. In early 2013, BlackBerry launched the BB10 Smartphone and operating system. With performance specs that match the iPhone 5, BlackBerry hopes to deliver utilitarian value to recapture lost business and hedonic value to appeal to consumers.

Sources: C. Cummins, "BlackBerry Maker's Issue: Gadgets for Work or Play?" *The Wall Street Journal*, September 30, 2011, A1–12. B. S. Bullick, "It Will Take More Than Marketing to Get BlackBerry Back into the Race," *Advertising Age* 83 (February 27, 2012): 18. R. Winkler, "BlackBerry Release Is No Perfect 10," *The Wall Street Journal* (January 31, 2013), C10.

Customer Lifetime Value (CLV) approximate worth of a customer to a company in economic terms; overall profitability of an individual consumer

behavior in business decision making throughout this book. Students, and practicing managers for that matter, sometimes struggle with the application aspect of CB. In other words, how do we translate knowledge of the CVF into more effective analysis and decision making? Checklists can be a useful aid to decision making as a way to develop more creative, thoughtful, and logically sound marketing strategy and tactics. Exhibit 2.9 displays a checklist inspired by the CVF framework—the CB idea checklist.

2-6 Value Today and Tomorrow— Customer Lifetime Value

We defined marketing earlier as value-producing activities that facilitate exchange. In other words, marketing makes exchange more likely. Exchange is far from a one-way street. Consumers enter an exchange seeking value and so do marketers! The value the company receives from exchange may be slightly easier to explain than is the value that a consumer receives. Obviously, when a consumer spends money for a product, the company receives economic resources in the form of revenue, the company then uses these to pay employees, cover costs, and help the firm grow. The company may also receive additional benefits if the consumer becomes a loyal customer who is an advocate for the firm's products.

Thus, not every customer is equally valuable to a firm. Firms increasingly want to know the customer lifetime value associated with a customer or customer segment.[20] **Customer Lifetime Value (CLV)** represents the approximate worth of a customer to a company in economic terms. Put another way, CLV is the overall, long-term profitability of an individual consumer. Although there is no generally accepted formula for the CLV, the basic idea is simple and can be represented as follows:

$$CLV = npv \text{ (sales} - \text{costs)} + npv \text{ (equity)}$$

The customer lifetime value then is equal to the net present value (npv) of the stream of profits over a customer's lifetime, plus the worth attributed to the equity a good customer can bring in the form of positive referrals and word of mouth. Consider a consumer shopping twice weekly at IKEA (see www.ikea.com). On average, this IKEA customer spends $200 per week, or $10,400 per year. If we assume a 5% operating margin, this customer yields IKEA a *net* $520 per year. Even if

EXHIBIT 2.9

The CB Idea Checklist

Question	Idea
What specific consumer needs and desires are involved? • Is a specific product(s) involved in this situation? • Can something else provide the same value or address the same need or desire?	
How is the product positioned (types and amounts of value intended)? • How is our position superior to competitors? • How can we move closer to desirable ideal points? • How is our position inferior to competitors? • How can we isolate ourselves from competition?	
How does the consumer actually receive value from this company? • In the current situation, Has value been diminished? Can value be enhanced? • Can the product be modified to enhance value? • Can the company introduce a new product to enhance value? • Can the company add services to improve value for consumers? • Can communication be improved? • Is a competitor in a better position to provide superior value? • If so, how?	
Where is this product consumed? • Can value be enhanced by changing the consumption setting?	

Who...
• Is buying the product?
  1. Individual consumers
  2. Groups of consumers (families)
  3. Business consumers
• Is not buying the product?	

Why should a consumer... • Buy this product? • Avoid this product?	
When do consumers... • Find the product most valuable? • Find the product least valuable?	
What are the key CVF elements involved in understanding the consumption process in this case?	
Is additional consumer research needed? • Will the information be worth what it would cost to obtain it? • What type of research would be required?	

© Cengage Learning

any potential positive word-of-mouth is not considered, the consumer is worth about $9,000 to IKEA today, assuming a 30-year life span and a 4% annual interest rate.

Interestingly, until recently IKEA did not record customer-level data. Thus, out of over 500 terabytes of data, they had no data on CLV.[21] In contrast, other firms, from convenience stores to Harrah's Casinos, have elaborate systems for tracking individual customer behavior and targeting these consumers with individualized promotions and products. This allows them to practice one-to-one marketing in a real sense and to identify segments of consumers containing a high proportion of very valuable customers. For instance, one retailer found that high CLV customers tend to have the following characteristics:[22]

- Female
- 30–50 years of age
- Married
- $90,000 income
- Loyalty card holder

In contrast, the low CLV customers tended to have quite different characteristics:

- Male
- 24–44 years of age
- Single
- Less than $70,000 income
- Single channel shopper (meaning only Internet or only stores)

Thus, marketers can maximize the value they receive from exchange by concentrating their marketing efforts on consumers with high CLVs. Recently, bargain-conscious consumers have latched on to online closeout retailers like Rue La La. When a consumer names Rue La La as a favorite thing, that consumer is worth a lot to the retailer.

Study Tools

Located at the back of the textbook

☐ Rip out Chapter in Review Card

Located at www.cengagebrain.com

☐ Review Key Terms Flashcards (print or online)

☐ Download audio summaries to review on the go

☐ Complete practice quizzes to prepare for tests

☐ Play "Beat the Clock" to master concepts

☐ Watch video on Evo for a real company example

WHAT DO YOU THINK?
WHAT OTHERS HAVE THOUGHT

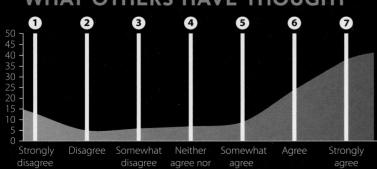

1 2 3 4 5 6 7

50 45 40 35 30 25 20 15 10 5 0

Strongly disagree | Disagree | Somewhat disagree | Neither agree nor disagree | Somewhat agree | Agree | Strongly agree

I get a lot out of shopping even when I don't buy anything.

Respondents tend to agree—but not strongly. More respondents chose the agree response than any other and half of respondents chose some type of agreement (5-7). Almost no respondents chose the neutral response (4), suggesting that consumers do have an opinion on this topic!

PART 1
[CASES]

CASE 1-1

IDEO: Consumer-Focused Innovation

Written by Professor Vicky Szerko, Dominican College

A great example of how companies make use of consumer behavior data is the enormously innovative and influential product design firm, IDEO (www.ideo.com). It has developed products for many of the world's most successful and exciting companies, from technology leader Apple to the venerable consumer packaged goods giant, Procter & Gamble.

While the name IDEO obviously draws from the word *idea*, it is Thomas A. Edison's famous observation regarding genius as being "1% inspiration and 99% perspiration" that actually guides the firm's product development process. Preceding every "flash of genius" is a painstaking and disciplined approach that focuses intently on the consumer experience.

Whenever IDEO is asked by a client to design a new product, it turns to a highly effective form of idea generation called the "deep dive."[1] The "deep dive" consists of a total immersion in the customer experience, requiring IDEO's team of developers and designers to place themselves in the actual situation for which the product is ultimately intended.

For example, a commission to design a better wheelchair would mean living as a disabled person to learn what it's like to be dependent on a wheelchair for tasks most of us take for granted. Besides the physical aspects of navigating the wheelchair, developers have to ask themselves: How does being in a wheelchair make you feel? Does the wheelchair provide a sense of empowerment or frustration? What things about the wheelchair are positive or negative? Once the team has been able to experience the wheelchair from a disabled person's perspective, it can much better address the features and benefits that will be most valuable to the user.

Research tells us that people relate to products from multiple perspectives. Why does someone prefer Brand X to Brand Y—although they both do, essentially, the same thing? It may be because Brand X enhances the person's status (as in a designer

bag), or reassures him that he is receiving high quality (as in an expensive appliance). Simply put, people prefer products that don't just do the job (utilitarian value) but also affect the way they feel (hedonic value). Well-designed wheelchairs must not only get people around, but make them feel good about using them, too.

To illustrate how IDEO takes both utilitarian and hedonic considerations in designing products, consider a recent commission: the re-design of the classroom desk. IDEO was asked by Steelcase, a global company in the office furniture industry, to help them break into the education market. Could IDEO transform the traditional tablet-arm desk?

IDEO's team began by using the desks and observing them in the classroom setting. They saw that the desks were uncomfortable for larger individuals (Americans have been increasing in weight), that the word "tablet" now meant not just spiral notebooks but increasingly referred to digital devices, and that moving and rearranging the desks in the classroom was noisy, cumbersome, and annoying. Also, with many more individuals going to school and class sizes getting larger, the traditional desks produced a sense of overcrowding, an unpleasant feeling for most individuals.

IDEO created a series of prototypes based on their developers' experience in the classroom. They then invited students and faculty to test each prototype in the classroom and provide direct feedback. As feedback was received and considered in light of the desk's role in the classroom experience, the tablet-arm desk was completely redesigned. It was dubbed the Node chair.

"The details betray a remarkable thoughtfulness," wrote Cliff Kuang in *Fast Company*. "The seat is a generously sized bucket, so that students can shift around and adapt their posture to whatever's going on: the seat also swivels, so that students can, for example, swing around to look at other students making class presentations; and a rolling base allows the chairs to move quickly between lecture-based seating and group activities. In group activities, the proportions are such that the chairs and integrated desktops combine into something like a conference table."[2] Clearly, the whole experience of sitting in a classroom had been substantially improved.

In a recent TED Talk, IDEO's founder and president David Kelley discussed how "human-centered design," or looking at things from the user's point of view, can solve what may seem to be insurmountable problems. He used Pittsburgh Children's Hospital's experience with CT scanning of children to illustrate his point.

The problem had to do with the CT scanners themselves. Although the scanners were remarkably accurate and scientifically advanced, they produced a traumatic experience in young children; as many as 80% of children had to be sedated before the scans could take place.

While the scanners delivered a high degree of utility from a medical standpoint, they were woefully lacking in providing a good, or even acceptable, experience for young patients. Doug Dietz, principal designer for GE Global Design, which had developed and produced the scanners, set out to see what could be done to improve the children's experience.

"We did simple things that got overlooked. I mean, some of the most effective insights came from kneeling down and looking at a room from the height of a child," recalled Dietz.[3] The huge machines in the impersonal, utilitarian rooms frightened the children. Dietz's solution was to divert the children's attention from the machine itself by placing it in the context of an exciting fantasy adventure.

The newly redesigned rooms were dubbed the GE Adventure Series™. The rooms and scanners were specially outfitted to resemble a child's fantasy adventure—a pirate ship, a jungle, an underwater journey. Sights, sounds, and even smells (such as the piña colada scent in the pirate ship adventure) engaged the child's attention and turned the scanner into an integral part of the fantasy experience.

The impact of the redesign was dramatic: the number of children having to be sedated dropped from 80% to just around 10%. What better testament to the importance of the hedonic, or experiential, dimension in product design? Before the redesign the scanners were just highly sophisticated medical devices; afterward, they provided a delightful experience to children and even simplified the job experience of the medical technicians involved.

Moral of the story? The best products not only get the job done, but make doing the job a pleasure!

Questions

1. Where does IDEO get inspiration for its product designs?

2. What kind of value do you think successful products deliver to consumers?

3. Why do you think having a product that simply works doesn't always translate to consumer acceptance?

4. What is the relative importance of the utilitarian versus the hedonic value of products, as suggested by the work of IDEO?

5. Do you agree with Edison's observation that "genius is 1% inspiration and 99% perspiration"? Explain your answer.

CASE 1-2

Born or Reinvented in the "Foreign" Land? Examining Brands and Their Country of Origin

Written by Aditi Grover, Plymouth State University

Consumers make choices while considering the expected value they would derive from products and services. Companies likewise seek to enhance the value of their product offering while considering a variety of factors that might guide consumer decision making.

Among the various factors known to play a role in consumer decision making, country of origin—where a certain product or brand was manufactured—is seen to play an important role at least under some circumstances. Research has shown consumers might choose brands manufactured in their own country over the same brands manufactured elsewhere. This preference towards products manufactured within one's own country, called *consumer ethnocentrism*, may be strong enough to persist regardless of price and quality.[1] Furthermore, this phenomenon has been observed not only within the United States but across the globe—in Africa, France, and China, among other regions. Diverse factors may drive people's consumer ethnocentrism. For example, in 2011 the ABC *World News with Diane Sawyer* series "Made in America" tried to promote products made 100% within the United States. According to ABC News, "Economists say that if every one of us spent an extra $3.33 on U.S.-made goods every year, it would create nearly 10,000 new jobs in this country."[2] Note, however, the preference towards products from one's home country does *not* automatically mean animosity towards products from other countries.

Even though data suggests that some consumers might show a preference—overt or covert—towards products manufactured in their country of origin, the question arises whether consumers possess the accurate knowledge of where a product or brand is manufactured, or where the brand originated. For example, consider the famous chocolate hazelnut spread Nutella: did the brand originate in the United States? No, the Nutella spread was born in the 1940s in northwest Italy. How about L'Oreal? How many of us know that BlackBerry is a Canadian company? These examples demonstrate that even though individuals might prefer brands manufactured in their country of birth, consumers might not possess the knowledge to identify a brand's country of origin accurately. Researchers have defined consumers' ability to correctly identify the countries of origin of well-known brands as Brand Origin Knowledge, or BoK.[3]

Table 1 lists selected brands from "2011 Ranking of Top 100 Brands," developed by Interbrand—the world's leading brand consultancy—alongside the brand's country of origin. Examine the table to test your BoK (or lack thereof). Visit Interbrand's website for a complete list of the top 100 brands (www.interbrand.com/).

As consumer behavior students, it would be helpful to further understand how BoK might vary from consumer to consumer, especially if such information makes a difference in consumers' decision making: Would BoK be higher for people who are more educated (versus less educated)? Could BoK vary depending on the demographic factors such as age and gender? Could the extent to which a consumer has traveled across the globe or been exposed to diverse brands be yet another factor? Consider Ms. Sandler, a citizen of the United States and a top executive at SAP, the German firm. She drives a Ferrari and shops only at Cartier for her jewelry and Armani for her clothing, while carrying her cash in her favorite Louis Vuitton bag. She likes to party with friends while sharing a drink of Corona before a

Table 1: Test Your BoK

2011 Rank	Brand	Country	Sector
11	Toyota	Japan	Automotive
12	Mercedes	Germany	Automotive
18	Louis Vuitton	France	Luxury
21	H&M	Sweden	Apparel
24	SAP	Germany	Business Services
30	Nescafé	Switzerland	Beverages
31	IKEA	Sweden	Home Furnishings
38	Gucci	Italy	Luxury
41	Philips	Netherlands	Electronics
48	Nintendo	Japan	Electronics
52	Danone	France	Fast-Moving Consumer Goods
55	Nestlé	Switzerland	Fast-Moving Consumer Goods
70	Cartier	France	Luxury
73	Tiffany & Co.	United States	Luxury
86	Corona	Mexico	Alcohol
93	Armani	Italy	Luxury
95	Burberry	United Kingdom	Luxury
99	Ferrari	Italy	Automotive

Source: 2011 Ranking of the Top 100 Brands (http://www.interbrand.com/en/best-global-brands /best-global-brands-2008/best-global-brands-2011.aspx, accessed April 21, 2012).

final drink of Nestlé's instant coffee. Would such a consumer be more likely to have higher or lower BoK?

While the level of knowledge about the origin of a brand might be attributed to several factors, an important one could be the length of time a "foreign" brand has existed within the United States. This might significantly alter the extent to which it is considered foreign. For example, if we trace the history of Adidas, the German sporting goods company founded in 1948, we learn that the company has had an interesting story as it traversed from Germany into other countries of the world. Even though companies such as Adidas can successfully and seamlessly surpass the preference of products manufactured in one's own country (also known as the country-of-origin effect), it might not always be the case.

Characteristics of certain products might be so inextricably mapped onto a consumer's country that it might be hard to ignore the brand's country of origin while making a consumption decision. For example, consider wine: do people generally prefer to buy wine from France or from the United States? France's history of wine-making is at least as old as the Roman Empire, and France has almost always held the title of the world's largest producer of wine. In a related vein, the United States is known for its edge in Internet services and electronics, for it gave rise to global powerhouses such as Google, Apple, and Amazon. Within the realm of brand and its country of origin, when consumers demonstrate preference for products that map onto the competitiveness of the country in which they originate, it may be referred to as "product ethnicity." Therefore, when product ethnicity is taken into account, consumers might choose to ignore their ethnocentric values while making consumption decisions.

Furthermore, it will be important to see how one brand might be showcased differently in various countries of the brand's presence. For example, a KFC that one sees in the United States has a much different menu offering than does a KFC in China. As another example, consider Wrigley's, the chewing gum. Examining how this brand might be marketed differently in the United States versus in Europe would highlight how the same brand might employ different marketing strategies. Companies analyze varied dimensions (such as culture and corporate regulations) of a country before launching a product in foreign locations. However, the core fundamental lesson of consumer behavior remains consistent around the globe: to be successful, companies need to ensure that the product offering meshes well with consumers' needs and with what they value.

Questions

1. Examine further the "2011 Ranking of Top 100 Brands." Classify these brands while considering the product category or sector and the country of origin. Can you detect a pattern? For example, do you see that strong players in the automotive sector emerge largely in Western Europe?

2. List all the brands that you have in your home. Then research to find the country of origin of all the brands on your list. What do you find? How can marketing professionals make use of the information that you have analyzed?

3. Use the "2011 Ranking of Top 100 Brands" table to test the level of BoK of at least five people (excluding yourself). Examine and write a short reflection on how the extent of their knowledge varies with their lifestyles.

4. Your textbook refers to the concept of perceptual maps. Construct a perceptual map using the following two dimensions: (i) product ethnicity (low vs. high), and (ii) level of BoK (low vs. high). Choose at least ten brands or product categories to represent on the map. You may use the list of brands/categories available at the Interbrand website to populate a list for the map. Use the information from question 3 to identify the average level of knowledge of product ethnicity and extent of BoK.

5. Using the information in question 3, how do you think a company can enhance its understanding of market segmentation so as to efficiently target a marketing message to its potential and existing consumers?

CASE 1-3

DemandTec®: Using Collaborative Analytics in a Fragmented Latin American Market

Written by Kristine Pray, Muskingum University

In February 2012, headlines across America alerted consumers that mass-market retailer Target had discovered a way to predict the gestational state of their female shoppers, even before family members were aware of the pregnancy.[1] With this predictive ability, Target would be able to capitalize on the life-altering events of their customers. Imagine anticipating the changing needs of individual consumers with such accuracy that developing the associated marketing mix brings implementing the marketing concept to a whole other level. Sending targeted promotions to highly segmented markets while the rest of the competition remains unaware offers a strategic advantage to marketers competing in the 21st century.

The accuracy of these predictions is based on models that identify changes in the behavior of consumers. In the case of Target, changes in the purchase behavior of female shoppers, such as increased spending on supplements important to neonatal development, as well as unscented soaps and lotions, were a strong indication of pregnancy.[2] This is, of course, an oversimplification. Aggregating vast amounts of consumer behavior data and creating predictive models to strategically target individual consumers is only made possible by the use of very powerful software, software which has been developed to further the emergent practice known as collaborative analytics.

Although collaborative analytics and cloud-based software company DemandTec made the news recently when it was acquired by IBM for $440 million, it is not likely that anyone outside of the industry is familiar with the San Mateo, California-based company.[3] In the field of collaborative analytics, however, DemandTec is well established, with a client list of over 500 retailers and consumer products companies, including ConAgra Foods, General Mills, Home Depot, PETCO, Sara Lee, Walmart, and, of course, Target.[4] With increased global competition and price-conscious consumers, companies know how important it is to properly segment the market and create the right marketing mix for each of those consumer segments. DemandTec provides companies with the tools they need to optimize those decisions.

American companies, however, are not the only ones faced with increased global competition. Emerging markets in the so-called BRIC countries (Brazil, Russia, India, and China) are increasingly appealing to multinational companies. Domestic as well as foreign corporations can also benefit from the services of companies like DemandTec.

In Sao Paulo, Brazil, the largest market in Latin America, Companhia Brasileira de Distribuicao Grupo Pao de Acucar (GPA), referred to as the "Walmart of Latin America," is striving to hold on to the majority share of the grocery market.[5] French-owned supermarket giant Carrefour maintains a close second place, followed by global retail behemoth Walmart, which plans to invest heavily in the region to edge out the competition for market leader.[6] If that does not make circumstances difficult enough for GPA, the Brazilian market itself is very fragmented. With heterogeneous consumer segments coming from diverse socioeconomic backgrounds and different geographic areas, determining the appropriate marketing strategy becomes even more complex. Enter DemandTec.[7]

Using "everyday price optimization software-as-a-service" from DemandTec, GPA can optimize their pricing strategy at the local level.[8] GPA segments their market using geographic segmentation variables (region); demographic segmentation variables (income and social class); psychographic segmentation variables (lifestyle); and behavioristic segmentation variables (price sensitivity), resulting in twelve distinct target segments.[9] In addition to managing all of the consumer segmentation information, GPA must also integrate stock-keeping unit (SKU) information. Usually in the form of a machine-readable bar code, SKU numbers are assigned to individual items in inventory to help monitor inventory, sales, pricing, transactions, and consumer spending patterns.[10] With 99 variants for each SKU across each of GPA's regions, the amount of data to be processed would be overwhelming without the use of DemandTec's price optimization software.[11]

DemandTec's powerful modeling software collectively analyzes regional competitor prices and then aggregates consumer demand for items, vendor costs, customer characteristics, and consumer segments to arrive at optimal prices for all products across all SKU variants.[12] Collaborative analytics not only helps GPA to optimize prices but also helps them to optimize the price perception of items which have the most elastic demand, in other words, products for which consumers exhibit the most price sensitivity.[13]

The idea of using "loss leaders" as a form of sales promotion is not new to the grocery industry. Consumers tend to be more sensitive to the prices of certain items like bread or milk, so retailers offer these products at a price at or below cost to draw consumers into the store, with the hopes that the consumers will purchase additional, more profitable items. Without the proper intelligence, this promotional strategy can backfire, as consumer price perception of other items in the store discourages value-conscious consumers from buying those items with higher margins, cutting into the profitability of retailers. Collaborative analytics allows marketing managers to process volumes of data to make optimal decisions.

In an era of social media and mobile technology, today's consumers have access to an infinite amount of marketing information in real time. Armed with smart phones and unlimited apps, they can locate product, promotion, and pricing information by typing in a product name or scanning a bar code as they stand in the aisle of their local retailers. In order to meet the needs of these technology-savvy and price-conscious consumers, marketers must arm themselves with the next generation of marketing tools, collaborative analytics.

Questions

1. Predictive models used by Target identified changes in the purchase behavior of female shoppers that indicated they might be pregnant, including increased spending on supplements important to neonatal development as well as unscented soaps and lotions. What other changes in purchase behavior might indicate that a female shopper is expecting?

2. How does the use of collaborative analytics provide value to the consumer and help to facilitate exchanges between buyers and sellers?

3. Based on collaborative analytics, Target created targeted sales promotions for newly expectant mothers, such as mailing coupons to them for purchasing diapers or baby bottles. GPA, in Brazil, uses collaborative analytics to optimize prices for their various customer segments. These are only two of the four marketing mix variables. Can you think of other ways that companies might use collaborative analytics to fine-tune the other marketing mix variables?

4. GPA uses collaborative analytics to look at the shopping behavior of their customers. The next time you purchase food items (groceries), make a list of every item you purchased. Try to organize the items in a meaningful way. Imagine that a researcher was using ethnographic methods to analyze your grocery list. What insights might they have about you based on your purchases?

5. Choose a local retailer that is not part of a national or regional chain. Assume they have decided to expand their efforts internationally and have therefore enlisted the help of DemandTec. How will the use of collaborative analytics help them to better understand consumers in this new market?

CASE 1-4

Sears: A Dying Company?

Written by Dr. Venessa Funches, Auburn University Montgomery

Ashley is on her way to her local mall. She pulls up to the mall and finds a great parking spot close to the Sears entrance. She walks briskly through tools, lawn and garden, as well as kids apparel, noticing nothing. In fact, no one seems to notice her either. She is not approached or greeted by any salespeople. What a relief! The store seems empty. Ashley is a little concerned. She came to hang out with friends but this seems pretty dead. Just as she rounds the corner through the women's department, a shirt catches her attention. But as she glances at the price tag, she decides she can get it cheaper elsewhere. Just then her cell phone rings. It's her friend; everyone is waiting for her at Aeropostale near the food court. She picks up the pace as she rushes through men's apparel, jewelry, and finally bedding. She is relieved as she catches a glimpse of her friends through the crowd in the interior of the mall. She is looking forward to a good time shopping with her friends. As she nears the food court, she is distracted by all the cool outfits displayed in the windows of stores like American Eagle, Abercrombie & Fitch, and Buckle.

Ashley represents many of today's shoppers, who hurry on about their business—shunning department stores like Sears and its competitors. The entire department store category has been experiencing decline in recent years.

Sears has a rich history spanning over 100 years. In the past, Sears was a retail force to be reckoned with. According to the Sears Archives website (www.searsarchives.com), from the 1950s to the 1980s Sears was the largest U.S. retailer. The Sears catalog could be found in virtually every home in America.

Sears has been serving the American consumer since the turn of the century. The firm began in 1886 as a watch company, founded by Richard W. Sears. At that time most Americans lived as farmers in rural areas with limited access to the products they needed. As a result, the local general store served as the farmers' primary retail establishment. Due to the limited availability of products, price gouging was rampant. Richard W. Sears and Alvah Roebuck teamed up to form their own mail order company. They began by selling only jewelry and watches but quickly added other products in order to meet the need in the marketplace. The catalog business flourished and grew quickly.

It was not until the 1920s that the firm's management saw the need to alter their business model. The country was changing and many people were now moving to city centers. As a result, new chain retailers were gaining popularity. Sears joined the fray by opening their own retail locations and expanding vigorously. Sears experienced great success and kept on expanding well into the 1970s. In 1973, Sears built a new headquarters located in Chicago called Sears Tower. At that time it was the tallest building in the world. By the 1980s Sears was not only expanding but also diversifying into different businesses like Allstate car insurance, Dean Witter financial services, and Discover credit cards.

Today, Sears offers a broad array of products and services. Its offerings include appliances, consumer electronics, tools, sporting goods, outdoor living, lawn and garden equipment, certain automotive services and products, home fashion products, as well as apparel, footwear, jewelry and accessories for the whole family. Sears offers proprietary brands like Kenmore, Craftsman, DieHard, Lands' End, Covington, Apostrophe, and Canyon River Blues. These brands are important to the company because they signify quality and drive consumer traffic. Despite the strong brands, many consumers find Sears' selection bland, unattractive, or too costly. Instead they opt for specialty stores like Home Depot, Best Buy, or discounters like Target or Walmart.

The tide has shifted and Sears is struggling. Over the past two decades, Sears has ended its catalog services and closed numerous store locations.[1] In addition, the company has gone through multiple restructurings and divestitures of Dean Witter and Allstate in an effort to refocus and strengthen the business.

In 2005, Kmart bought Sears. The newly formed company became the nation's third largest retailer behind Walmart and Home Depot. The hope was that the combined firm would allow for greater cost savings and result in lower prices to consumers. Many questioned the deal and a lot of the proposed benefits never fully materialized.

More recently, Sears asked the Kardashian sisters, Kim, Kourtney, and Khloé, to develop their own product line. Sears management hoped to use the Kardashians' success and popularity to create excitement, especially among younger consumers. The advertising campaign has tried to capitalize on the sexy Kardashian image. The ad campaign has showcased Kim, Kourtney, and Khloé in seductive lingerie and topless in a denim jean ad. The product line, which includes denim jeans, dresses, shoes, jewelry, handbags, intimates, belts, and sunglasses, has thus far been disappointing and unsuccessful. Despite management's efforts, sales continue to plummet.

Sears has failed to make a profit for ten years. The causes of Sears' problems are multifaceted. Sears' business model has failed to keep step with changing consumer tastes. Many of its locations are out of date and need remodeling. Competitors have outspent Sears in terms of modernizing their locations by a wide margin. Second, many of its stores are located in malls that are decreasing in popularity and expensive to rent. Third, today's consumer has a vast number of shopping options. Many consumers are opting for convenient one-stop shopping at open-air shopping centers rather than enclosed malls, or avoiding them altogether for discount retailers. Finally, Sears' traditional mid-range pricing strategy has left them stranded, unable to compete with the low prices of discount stores or the broad selections of specialty stores.

Sears is down but not out of the game. The remaining stores and brands are still valuable assets. The company's management has a daunting task ahead. Can Sears refocus and find a new way to deliver value to its customers?

Questions

1. Describe how some of the trends mentioned in the textbook are affecting Sears.

2. Describe the external and situational influences that steer shoppers like Ashley away from Sears.

3. Compare and contrast the total value concept for Sears and your favorite retailer.

4. What types of utilitarian and hedonic value does Sears presently provide to its customers?

5. Can Sears be revived? If so what should their new value equation be? If not, explain.

gezzeg/Shutterstock.com

The communication

of value relies on consumer perception and learning.

WHAT DO YOU THINK?

My perceptions of advertisements are usually accurate.

STRONGLY DISAGREE   STRONGLY AGREE

VISIT COURSEMATE AT WWW.CENGAGEBRAIN.COM

Consumer Learning Starts Here: Perception

3

Marketing strategy represents the way a firm goes about creating a unique and valuable bundle of benefits for the consumer and focuses on value creation. Unfortunately, many firms become myopic and never fully understand the value they help create, and this can lead to major problems. For example, the firm Webvan started amid the dot-com boom in the late 1990s. Webvan.com delivered groceries directly to consumers, seemingly a great way to create value for consumers. Webvan attracted tremendous interest among investors but failed in 2001 after a few years in operation. Ultimately, consumers never perceived the value Webvan offered by this service. If consumers don't think that a product will deliver enough value or don't understand a product in the intended way, they won't buy it! Today, hypermarket retailers like Carrefour, Auchan, and LeClerc use the "drive" concept to provide nonstore shopping opportunities. Consumers place an online order and drive to a special pickup station at the store where their purchases are delivered to their car—not their home–in less than five minutes. Many consumers in Europe see the drive concept as more convenient than in-home delivery.

After studying this chapter, the student should be able to:

3-1 Define learning and perception and how the two are connected.

3-2 List and define phases of the consumer perception process.

3-3 Apply the concept of the just noticeable difference.

3-4 Contrast the concepts of implicit and explicit memory.

3-5 Know ways to help get a consumer's attention.

3-6 Understand key differences between intentional and unintentional learning.

3-1 Defining Learning and Perception

Marketers cannot help create value for consumers unless they can effectively communicate the value proposition to consumers in a way that they perceive and learn about the potential benefits. **Learning** refers to a change in behavior resulting from the interaction between a person and a stimulus. **Perception** refers to a consumer's awareness and interpretation of reality. Accordingly, perception serves as a foundation

learning change in behavior resulting from some interaction between a person and a stimulus

perception consumer's awareness and interpretation of reality

exposure process of bringing some stimulus within proximity of a consumer so that the consumer can sense it with one of the five human senses

sensation consumer's immediate response to a stimulus

attention purposeful allocation of information-processing capacity toward developing an understanding of some stimulus

upon which consumer learning takes place. Stated simply, value involves learning, and consumer perception plays a key role in learning because consumers change behavior based on what they perceive. Sometimes, consumers set out to *intentionally* learn marketing-related information. Other times, consumers learn *unintentionally* (or incidentally) by simply being exposed to stimuli and by forming some kind of response to it. Both types of learning rely, to greater or lesser degrees, on perceptual processes.

This chapter focuses on issues relating to the learning process as it applies to consumers. Specifically, the chapter details the earliest phases of perception along with a number of issues related to unintentional learning. The chapter closes with a discussion of *conditioning*, which represents a well-known approach to unintentional learning. Intentional learning and the associated cognitive processes are discussed in a later chapter.

3-1a Consumer Perception

What's more important, perception or reality? This probably seems like a typical academic question, but the issue is very important to consumer researchers. Consumer researchers expend a great deal of effort trying to

understand consumer perception, because the way a consumer perceives something greatly influences learning.

Perception and reality are distinct concepts because the perceptions that consumers develop do not always match the real world. For example, when someone sings in the shower, he or she does not really perceive the actual quality of the music. Our perceptual system protects the singer from that but not somebody else who happens to hear the typical consumer singing to him- or herself. Perception simply doesn't always match reality. Perception can also be ambiguous. Exhibit 3.1 illustrates this point.

We treat perception as a consumer's awareness and interpretation of reality. Perception represents a *subjective* reality, whereas what actually exists in the environment determines objective reality. For example, at a restaurant, the objective reality is that a certain amount of food is served on a plate. A chef can weigh the food so that he knows the actual amount. However, equally hungry consumers may disagree that it is enough. How can this be? The answer to this question illustrates the concept of subjective reality. In this case, subjective and objective reality may differ because the size of the plate affects the quantity of food a consumer perceives.

Exhibit 3.2 illustrates this effect by showing the same amount of food on three different plates. Placing food on a smaller plate can actually increase the chance that diners feel as though they are full, not because they have actually had more food, but because they perceive that they are getting more![1] The same amount of food on a larger plate tends to leave a diner wanting more.

3-1b Exposure, Attention, and Comprehension

During the perceptual process, consumers are *exposed* to stimuli, devote *attention* to stimuli, and attempt to *comprehend* stimuli. **Exposure** refers to the process of bringing some stimulus within the proximity of a consumer so that it can be sensed by one of the five human senses (sight, smell, taste, touch, or sound). The term **sensation** describes a consumer's immediate response to this information.

ExxonMobil uses billboards and other media to send messages about the number of jobs the company creates in the United States, as well as other social responsibility messages, including promoting the Mickelson ExxonMobil Teachers Academy, which provides math camps for teachers of third through fifth graders to spread best practices in teaching math and science.[2] Marketers can expose consumers to messages like this, but that does not guarantee that the consumer will pay attention. **Attention** is the purposeful allocation

---

EXHIBIT **3.1** What Is the Reality in the Image Below?

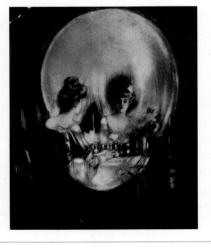

Rykoff Collection/Corbis

EXHIBIT **3.2** Objective and Subjective Reality Don't Always Match

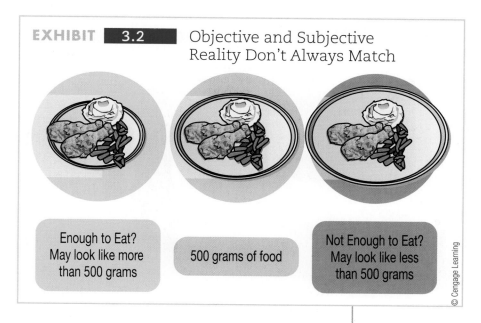

Enough to Eat?
May look like more
than 500 grams

500 grams of food

Not Enough to Eat?
May look like less
than 500 grams

© Cengage Learning

of information-processing capacity toward developing an understanding of some stimulus. Many times, consumers simply cannot pay attention to all the stimuli to which they are exposed. As such, consumers are selective in the information to which they pay attention. Quite simply, there is just too much stimulation in the environment for consumers to pay attention to everything!

Comprehension occurs when consumers attempt to derive meaning from information they receive. Of course, marketers hope that consumers comprehend and interpret information in the intended way, but this is not always the case. As a simple example, a receptionist tells patients there will be a *short* wait. Will all patients think the wait is short? For example, two

When consumers go by a billboard, they are provided with an opportunity to pay attention to the message.

© iStockphoto.com/Paolo Scarlata

consumers that wait 20 minutes may perceive the wait differently. What is short to one may not be so short to another. A professional taking an hour away from her busy day may react differently than a retired person without a hectic daily schedule. Patients' previous experiences will also affect what length of time they associate with *short*. Furthermore, can something be done to change perceptions of the wait time? The receptionist might update the patient every few minutes, explaining what is going on and why the wait is continuing. Alternatively, there could be pleasant music played in the waiting room. In either case, the patient may comprehend a shorter wait than if simply left quietly alone. However, the same patient may also react more negatively to the wait than if left quietly alone.[3]

3-2 Consumer Perception Process

If a friend were to ask, "Do I look good in this outfit?" you would immediately draw upon your perceptions to determine how to respond to the question. (Whether or not you voice your true opinion is an entirely different subject!) As we have stated, in its most basic form, perception describes how consumers become aware of and interpret the environment. Accordingly, we can view consumer perception as including three phases. These phases, *sensing, organizing,* and *reacting,* are shown in Exhibit 3.3.

Notice that the phases of perception overlap with the concepts of exposure, attention, and comprehension. That is, we sense the many stimuli to which we are exposed, we organize the stimuli as we attend and comprehend them, then we react to various stimuli by developing responses.

3-2a Sensing

Consumers sense stimuli to which they are exposed. Sensing is an *immediate* response to stimuli that have come into contact with one of the consumer's five

cognitive organization
process by which the human brain assembles sensory evidence into something recognizable

senses (sight, smell, touch, taste, or sound). Thus, when a consumer enters a store, browses on eBay, reads a Tweet, tastes food, encounters an advertisement, or tries on some clothes, the perceptual process goes into action. However, sensing alone does not allow a consumer to make *sense* out of something. This leads to the second stage of the perceptual process.

3-2b Organizing

Several upscale cosmopolitan restaurants offer dining in complete darkness. Diners don't choose from a menu but eat whatever the chef prepares. The idea is to highlight one's sense of taste. Imagine trying to tell exactly what you are eating. Actually, not just your taste would be involved because food odors activate one's sense of smell. One also feels texture of food and perhaps even hears a crunch. Our brains constantly organize senses in this fashion—not just in the dark!

When we speak of **cognitive organization**, we refer to the process by which the human brain assembles the sensory evidence into something recognizable.

EXHIBIT 3.3 Sensing, Organizing, and Reacting

SENSING → ORGANIZING → REACTING

What will everyone else think?

Does this fit?

© Cengage Learning

© iStockphoto.com/Lise Gagne

This is an important part of perception. Exhibit 3.4 may help you visualize this process. The organization that takes place in your brain is analogous to someone performing a sorting task—such as sorting mail. When an object is first handled, the sorter hasn't a clue what slot the object belongs in. However, information allows the sorter to place the object into progressively more specific categories.

When someone tries to decide if an outfit looks right, the perceptual process goes to work. Consider the clothing pictured in Exhibit 3.3. Is this outfit appropriate for Emilia, a professional consultant? At first, we perceive that the outfit is obviously a woman's dress. However, does the outfit represent proper business

Sensing is Believing!

Sensing is necessary for learning. Sensing feeds both intentional and unintentional learning. Even when we aren't trying to study something, our senses affect our thoughts and reactions.

How do consumers determine if something is luxurious? What we see matters. Consumers judge a product pictured with background vertical images (like high-rise buildings) as more luxurious and more expensive than that same product pictured with background horizontal images.

Imagine yourself in a store standing about 10 feet from a display of a sweater and wondering how comfortable it might be. Research suggests that your feet help answer this

question—yes, your feet! Research shows that if a consumer is standing on a soft carpet, instead of on a hard tile floor, he or she will see the sweater as more comfortable. Turns out that feet have feelings too.

Ariwasabi/Shutterstock.com

Sources: T. J. L. van Rompay, P. W. de Vries, F. Bontekoe, and K. Tanja-Dijkstra, "Embodied Product Perception: Effects of Verticality Cues in Advertising and Packaging Design on Consumer Impressions and Price Expectations," *Psychology & Marketing* 29 (December 2012): 919–928. J. Meyers-Levy, R. Zhu, and L. Jiang, "Context Effects from Bodily Sensations: Examining Bodily Sensations Induced by Flooring and the Moderating Role of Product Viewing Distance," *Journal of Consumer Research* 37 (June 2010): 1–14.

attire? If Emilia's brain organizes the outfit into this category, then she becomes likely to buy it and wear it to work as a consultant. Her clients may perceive the outfit differently and react differently. Again, we see the subjectivity of perception.

Consumers develop an interpretation during this stage of the perceptual process and begin to *comprehend* what the stimulus is. This interpretation provides an initial cognitive and affective meaning. The term *cognitive* refers to a mental or thinking process. A reader of this book almost instantly converts a word into meaning as long as the word on the page matches a known English-language word. Sometimes marketers need to know how consumers will react to unknown words when creating the name for a new product or new company. In fact, the actual sound of a name (that is otherwise nonsense) can evoke different meanings and feelings. Consider the following two sounds (say them each aloud):

Sepfut

Sepsop

Which would make a better name for a new ice cream brand? Actually, when consumers sampled the same new ice cream described with one of these two names, Sepsop was preferred. The researchers theorized that consumers evaluate sounds with a repetitive pattern (like sep-sop) more favorably, and prefer things associated with it, than sounds with no repetition.[4] Consumers' moods can even be affected by sending sounds that produce a favorable evaluation.[5]

Consumers cannot organize everything they sense so easily. When a consumer encounters a stimulus that is difficult to categorize, the brain instinctively continues processing as a way of reconciling inconsistencies. When even this extra effort leaves a consumer uncertain, he or she will generally avoid the stimulus.

In general, depending on the extent to which a stimulus can be categorized, three possible reactions may occur.

assimilation state that results when a stimulus has characteristics such that consumers readily recognize it as belonging to some specific category

accommodation state that results when a stimulus shares some but not all of the characteristics that would lead it to fit neatly in an existing category, and consumers must process exceptions to rules about the category

> When a consumer encounters a stimulus that is difficult to categorize ... he or she will generally avoid the stimulus.

1. **Assimilation. Assimilation** occurs when a stimulus has characteristics such that individuals readily recognize it as an example of a specific category. A light brown, slightly sticky, sweet, round food with a hole in the middle is easily recognized as a doughnut in nearly every part of the world.

2. **Accommodation. Accommodation** occurs when a stimulus shares some, but not all, of the characteristics that allow it to fit neatly in an existing category. At this point, the consumer will begin processing, which allows exceptions to rules about the category. For example, in New Orleans, tourists may encounter a *beignet*, which is a French doughnut. Because the beignet does not have a hole, the tourist's perceptual process may have to make an exception to the rule that all doughnuts have holes. Curiously, research indicates that novel stimuli that are mildly incongruent with expectations are actually preferred.[6] Thus, new products that consumers can categorize through accommodation may produce favorable reactions.

EXHIBIT 3.4

A Visual Image of the Organization Process

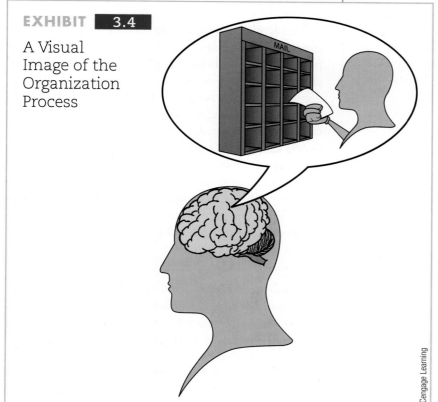

© Cengage Learning

contrast state that results when a stimulus does not share enough in common with existing categories to allow categorization

anthropomorphism giving humanlike characteristics to inanimate objects

selective exposure process of screening out certain stimuli and purposely exposing oneself to other stimuli

selective attention process of paying attention to only certain stimuli

selective distortion process by which consumers interpret information in ways that are biased by their previously held beliefs

3. **Contrast.** Contrast occurs when a stimulus does not share enough in common with existing categories to allow categorization. For example, consumers in Kyrgyzstan routinely enjoy fermented mountain mare's milk, known as *koumiss*. The only similarity to the milk that most western consumers know is the color. When a westerner tastes the milk, particularly if the taster doesn't know what is being consumed, contrast is a nearly certain outcome. People tend to not like things that are so completely unknown. Therefore, contrast is usually associated with negative feelings.

3-2c Reacting

The perceptual process ends with a reaction. If an object is successfully recognized, chances are some nearly automatic reaction takes place. For example, when a driver notices that the car in front of him has its brake lights on, the learned response is to apply brakes as well. Here, the reaction occurs as a response or behavior. Note that reactions can include both physical and mental responses to the stimuli encountered.

Applications to Consumer Behavior

The perceptual process has many implications for consumer behavior. For example, consumers have a need for safety, but just what is it that leads consumers to think some service environment is safe?[7] Subtle cues work to facilitate the perceptual process. Imagine a consumer looking to buy gasoline, milk, and bread late one evening. A convenience store without bright lights, with obscured windows that are difficult to see through, and no sign of a security guard, is not likely to be assimilated as a safe place to stop.

Even subtle cues influence perception. Take a look at an advertisement for a watch. Chances are, time stands still in watch advertisements. The watch almost certainly had a time of about 10 past 10. Why? A watch with that time appears to be smiling at the consumer,

and this subtle difference can cause a watch to be preferred over a frowning watch that says 20 past 8.[8] The term **anthropomorphism** refers to a design that gives humanlike characteristics to inanimate objects.

3-2d Selective Perception

Consumers encounter thousands of stimuli each day. If all stimuli were consciously processed, they would truly be overloaded. Rather than processing all stimuli, consumers practice selective perception. *Selective perception* includes selective exposure, selective attention, and selective distortion. That is, consumers are selective in what they expose themselves to, what they attend to, and what (and how) they comprehend. **Selective exposure** involves screening out most stimuli and exposing oneself to only a small portion of stimuli. **Selective attention** involves paying attention to only certain stimuli.

Consider a tourist walking through downtown Tokyo, Japan. How can he or she possibly pay attention to all of this information? Marketers use the term *clutter* to describe the idea that the environment often bombards consumers with too much information in their daily lives. Consumers can't possibly pay attention to all of this. Instead, they will choose something that stands out, or is personally relevant, and devote attention to that object.

Selective distortion is a process by which consumers interpret information in ways that are biased by their previously held beliefs. This process can be the result of either a conscious or unconscious effort. For example, consumers with strong beliefs about a brand tend to comprehend messages about the brand either positively or negatively, depending on their preexisting attitudes. Sports fans provide good examples of selective distortion. Fans from one team may be enraged when a "bad call" goes against his or her team. Fans for the other team are unlikely to comprehend the controversial play in the same way. Both fans observe the same thing but comprehend and react differently.

Exposure

Exposure occurs when some stimulus is brought within the proximity of a consumer so that it can be sensed. Obviously, marketers who want to inform consumers about their products must first expose them to information. As such, exposure represents a first and necessary step to learning. In fact, exposure is a vital component of both intentional and unintentional learning.

With selective distortion, different consumers can see the same thing but react very differently.

3-2e Subliminal Processing

Subliminal processing refers to the way in which the human brain senses low-strength stimuli, that is, stimuli that occur below the level of conscious awareness. Such stimuli have a strength that is lower than the **absolute threshold** of perception, the minimum strength needed for a consumer to perceive a stimulus. This type of "learning" is unintentional, because the stimuli fall below the absolute threshold. To illustrate effects below the absolute threshold, consider what often happens when a mosquito lands on one's arm. Chances are the mosquito is so small that you will not be consciously aware of the sensation without seeing it. Likewise, sounds often occur that are below the threshold. Images also can be displayed for such a short period of time, or at such a low level of intensity, that the brain cannot organize the image and develop a meaning.

Subliminal persuasion is behavior change induced or brought about based on subliminally processing a message. Popular conceptions about subliminal persuasion have fueled interest in it for many years. For instance, many people believe that:

- Marketers can somehow induce consumers to purchase brands by using subliminal advertising.
- Marketers can subliminally alter products or packages to make them more appealing to consumers.
- Sexual imagery can be hidden in a product itself, the product packaging, or in product advertising.
- People's sense of well-being can be enhanced by listening to subliminally embedded tapes of nature sounds and/or music.[9]

The belief is that communication can influence consumers through mere exposure to subliminal stimuli. The most famous example of subliminal persuasion involves a researcher for an ad firm who claimed that he had embedded subliminal frames within the movie *Picnic* in a New Jersey movie theater several years ago. Exhibit 3.5 illustrates the way this process reportedly took place. Very brief embeds of the phrases "Drink Coke" and "Eat Popcorn" were supposedly placed in the movie. The researcher claimed that popcorn sales rose nearly 60% as a result and that Coke sales rose nearly 20%. This experiment is often called the "Vicary experiment."

This type of "learning" is unintentional, because the stimuli fall below the absolute threshold.

This story grew in such popularity that researchers attempted to replicate the study. Interestingly, these scientific replications failed to produce any increase

subliminal processing way that the human brain deals with very low-strength stimuli, so low that one cannot notice anything

absolute threshold minimum strength of a stimulus that can be perceived

subliminal persuasion behavior change induced by subliminal processing

---

EXHIBIT 3.5 The Vicary Subliminal Persuasion "Study"

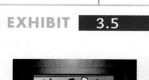

The motion picture *Picnic* is run with a standard projector.

EAT POPCORN!!
A frame is replaced displaying a subliminal message for 1/2000 second.

The movie *Picnic* continues while the audience flocks to concession stand.

in desire for Coke or popcorn. Consumer researchers also conducted experiments testing the effectiveness of sexual embeds involving airbrushed genitalia, the word *sex*, or provocative nudity in advertisements. Results of these experiments generally indicate that these practices do little to nothing that would directly make a consumer more likely to buy the advertised product.[10]

As a general statement, the research examining subliminal processing suggests that subliminal persuasion is ineffective as a marketing tool.[11] This is not to dismiss subliminal processing as having no impact whatsoever on what consumers might learn or how they might behave. But any effects are small in power and far from straightforward.[12]

Despite evidence to the contrary, many consumers are willing to believe that subliminal persuasion is a powerful influential tool.[13] Estimates suggest that over 60% of Americans believe that advertisers can exert subliminal influences strong enough to cause unwanted purchase behavior.[14] Over the years, books have fueled the controversy by promoting the idea that advertisers know about, and use, certain "hidden persuaders" to

create an irresistible urge to buy.[15] Consumers are often willing to attribute their own behavior to some kind of "uncontrollable influence," especially when the consumption involves products like cigarettes or alcoholic beverages.[16] Consumers' willingness to believe that subliminal persuasion tricks them into buying these products may simply be an attempt to downplay their own role in decision making.

The truth is that the Vicary experiment was a *hoax*. Vicary himself never conducted the experiment. Rather, he fabricated the story in an effort to create positive publicity for the advertising firm.[17] Marketers sometimes make light of subliminal persuasion by presenting images in advertisements that they know consumers will see!

3-3 Applying the JND Concept

We have discussed the concept of the absolute threshold as representing a level over which the strength of a stimulus must be greater to

Uncanny!

Earlier, we defined cognitive contrast and described it as usually having a negative reaction. Just what type of negative reaction can result from contrast? Well, one term that may fit is "the creeps!" The uneasy feeling results when a consumer encounters discordant elements that make things difficult to reconcile. Still don't have the creeps? Consider these facts:

- Do you have coulrophobia? If clowns freak you out, make you feel weird, or scare you, then you have coulrophobia. Don't worry, it's not really dangerous, and it's a very common phobia. The reaction is in part due to the way humans categorize humanlike figures and images. As nonhuman things become too humanlike, people can no longer fit the characteristics into known or liked categories, and negative reactions can occur. The advances in animation technology allow cartoon characters to look very real—perhaps too real! A cartoon character is supposed to be a cartoon character, not a human! Consumers reacted with less than a warm reaction to Disney's *Mars Needs Moms*, and coulrophobia most likely played a key role.

- The "uncanny valley theory" tries to explain the negative affect that consumers experience from images with too much human likeness—like images commonly encountered in online games. Researchers demonstrate how uncanny effects become particularly pronounced when images blend features from different categories. Imagine your reaction to a dog with a human face. The researchers explain the reaction as a contrast experience that results as humans sense the blending of incompatible categories.

The creeps are real and driven by perceptions.

Sources: R. Nakashima, "Too Real Means Too Creepy in New Disney Animation," *USA Today*, April 4, 2011, http://www.usatoday.com/tech/news/2011-04-04-creepy-animation_N.htm. T. J. Burleigh, J. R. Schoenherr, and G. L. Lacroix, "Does the Uncanny Valley Exist? An Empirical Test of the Relationship between Eeriness and the Human Likeness of Digitally Created Faces," *Computers in Human Behavior* 29 (2013): 759–771.

activate the perceptual process. A closely related concept deals with changes in the *strength* of stimuli. The **JND** (just noticeable difference) represents how much stronger one stimulus has to be relative to another so that someone can notice that the two are not the same.

The JND concept may be best explained in terms of a physical example. How do people pick out one sound over another? For example, for consumers to be able to physically discern two sounds that originate from the same source, the two sounds must be separated by at least 0.3 second. Separating the sounds by only 0.1 second is likely to produce the perception of one sound. Separating them by 0.3 second or more likely produces the perception of two different sounds.[18]

In general, the ability to detect differences between two levels of a stimulus is affected by the original intensity of the stimulus. This is known as **Weber's Law**. The law states that as the intensity of the initial stimulus increases, a consumer's ability to detect differences between two levels of the stimulus decreases.[19] For example, if the decibel level at a rock concert decreases from 120 to 115 dB, the change likely won't be noticeable. Marketers need to understand that change made a little at a time may be unnoticed by a consumer; change a lot at once and it will be noticed. The JND has numerous implications for marketers who attempt to provide value for consumers, including:

- **Pricing.** Consumers do not perceive very small differences in price as truly different.[20] A price of $29.49 is generally not perceived as being different from a price of $29.99. Thus, marketers may consider increasing prices in small increments to avoid a negative backlash from consumers. Conversely, a price reduction needs to be large enough so that consumers truly perceive the new price as representing significant savings.[21]

- **Quantity.** Small differences in quantity are often not perceived as being different. For instance, if a pack of computer paper changes from 485 sheets to 495 sheets, most consumers won't notice.

- **Quality.** Small improvements in quality may not have any impact on consumers. Thus, if Internet speed changes by a fraction of a second, most consumers will not notice.

- **Add-on Purchases.** A small additional purchase tacked onto a large purchase may not create the perception of increased spending. For instance, a consumer buying a $365 overcoat may be receptive to the suggestion of adding a plaid scarf priced at $45 to the order. The total for the coat is not perceived as being really different than the total for the coat and scarf together.

In general, these examples highlight an important idea: When marketers make a "positive" change they should make sure the difference is large enough to be perceived by consumers. Conversely, when they make a "negative" change, they should think about implementing the change in small increments so that each difference is not distinguished from what existed previously. However, marketers should make sure that changes are not perceived as being deceptive. Deliberately deceptive actions are unethical.

JND just noticeable difference; condition in which one stimulus is sufficiently stronger than another so that someone can actually notice that the two are not the same

Weber's law law that states that a consumer's ability to detect differences between two levels of a stimulus decreases as the intensity of the initial stimulus increases

Small differences between alternatives may not be noticed as different.

Morgan Lane Photography/Shutterstock.com

JMD just meaningful difference; smallest amount of change in a stimulus that would influence consumer consumption and choice

explicit memory memory that develops when a person is exposed to, attends, and tries to remember information

implicit memory memory for things that a person did not try to remember

preattentive effects learning that occurs without attention

mere exposure effect effect that leads consumers to prefer a stimulus to which they've previously been exposed

3-3a Just Meaningful Difference

A topic closely related to the JND is the **JMD** (just meaningful difference). The JMD represents the smallest amount of change in a stimulus that would influence consumer consumption and choice. For instance, how much of a change in price is really needed to *influence* consumer behavior and learning? A consumer can surely "notice" an advertisement stating a price drop of a Rolex from $19,999 to $19,499. Clearly, this is a $500 difference. However, is this price drop really meaningful? Retailers generally follow a rule that states that effective price drops need to be at least 20%.[22]

3-4 Implicit and Explicit Memory

Normally, we associate learning with educational experiences. When we think about learning, we think of people studying and paying close attention, like when you read this book! The knowledge one obtains from this type of experience is stored in **explicit memory**, that is, memory for information one is exposed to, attends to, and applies effort to remember. However, this is not the only kind of memory we develop. **Implicit memory** represents stored information concerning stimuli one is exposed to but does not pay attention to. Implicit memory creates **preattentive effects**, learning that is developed in the absence of attention. The following example illustrates the contrast between implicit and explicit memory.

How effective are banner ads like the ones you see on practically every web page? If a consumer clicks a banner ad to an advertiser's site, that consumer may absorb the resulting advertisement content and develop some explicit memory of the information. However, click-through rates on banner ads are extraordinarily low and continue to decline. Consumers click through fewer than 1 in 100 banners ads to which they are exposed. Do web advertisers waste their resources on the

Nearly every commercial web page presents an opportunity for consumers to learn through explicit and implicit memory.

other 99 plus consumers? Perhaps not. It turns out that consumers' implicit memory system addresses these ads. Even when consumers pay no attention to a banner ad on a crowded computer screen, implicit memory for the brand develops. This implicit memory creates more favorable attitudes towards the brand that increase the likelihood that the consumer would consider buying something associated with the brand.[23] Interestingly, unlike explicit memory, implicit memory becomes stronger the more distracted one is from attending to the stimulus.

3-4a Mere Exposure Effect

The **mere exposure effect** represents another way that consumers can learn unintentionally.[24] The mere exposure effect is the idea that consumers will prefer stimuli they have been previously exposed to over stimuli they

EXHIBIT 3.6	The Mere Exposure Effect Illustrated
August 30	**December 1**
Billécourt	Bernardus
Satturi	Orvôl
Yonsusan	Billécourt
Reinsstressa	Keilenspat
Mersoleil	Monopole
Les Crayers	Jimané
Jeroboams	Apostager

© Cengage Learning

have not seen before. This effect occurs even when there is no recall of the previous stimulus!

Exhibit 3.6 illustrates a classical approach to studying the mere exposure effect. Experiments in mere exposure effect expose subjects to something they do not know. In this case, a group of consumers were shown a list of words that were potential names for a new dining establishment. Some of the words even contain letters that do not exist in the English alphabet.

On August 30, the beginning of the semester, student subjects were exposed to the list of words on the left. Then, on December 1, at the end of the semester, the researcher exposed the same subjects to the list on the right. If you look closely, you'll notice that one word is on both the August 30 and December 1 lists. That word was rated more favorably than the other potential names.

The results of this type of experiment generally show that the "familiar" words will be preferred even though subjects cannot recall ever having seen them before. Consumers not only develop preferences for words, but they learn them as well. In fact, the learning process facilitates positive feelings that become associated with the stimuli. The mere exposure effect therefore has applications in both consumer learning and attitude formation.

The mere exposure effect is very resilient. The effect is true for practically any type of content. If the brand names are replaced with faces, names, Chinese characters, Norwegian words, brand logos, or musical samples, the mere exposure effect still holds.[25] Theoretically, an explanation for the increased preference involves familiarity. Even though consumers can't "remember" seeing the stimuli, some degree of familiarity is created by the mere exposure.

Familiarity

All things equal, consumers prefer the familiar to the unfamiliar. Once exposed to an object, a consumer exhibits a preference for the familiar object over something unfamiliar. An interesting application involves political campaigns. Modern technology allows advertisers to morph one individual's characteristics onto a photograph of another. For instance, a photograph of a political candidate can be modified so that subtle physical characteristics of a particular voter are morphed onto the candidate's appearance. In such a case, the particular voter will express a greater liking of the candidate, even if the changes are too subtle to be noticed.[26] The rationale is that the addition of characteristics, even below the JND, increases the perceived familiarity between the voter and the candidate. Familiarity plays a big role in understanding the way preattentive processes can improve attitudes, and the mere exposure effect highlights this.

Exposed!

Carmen Jaspersen/dpa/Landov

Michael Bublé sings standards, and he's become one of the most popular male vocalists of the modern era by doing so. He has had some tough acts to follow, because some other artist has usually made the song famous in days gone by. Bublé hit the charts with "Crazy Little Thing Called Love" in the mid-2000s, and some people may have heard it for the first time then. However, the rock group Queen made the song popular in the early 1980s. With "Save the Last Dance for Me" Bublé reintroduced a new generation to the song that the Drifters first made popular in the 1960s! "I've Got You Under My Skin" is one of Frank Sinatra's signature songs recently rerecorded by Bublé.

The rerecording of standards inevitably leads to arguments between consumers about which version is better. If you are going to record a Sinatra song you had better be good! But CB research offers some insight into this question. It turns out that consumers show a pronounced tendency to prefer product variations that they are exposed to first. Thus, a consumer who was a teen in the 1980s may well insist that Bublé's version of "Crazy Little Thing Called Love" isn't nearly as good as Queen's recording. In contrast, someone whose first exposure to the song is by Bublé may well argue the reverse.

Sources: M. Pandelaere, K. Millet, and B. V. Bergh, "Madonna or Don McLean? The Effect of Order of Exposure on Liking," *Journal of Consumer Psychology* 20 (October 2010): 442–51.

mere association effect
the transfer of meaning between objects that are similar only by accidental association

product placements
products that have been placed conspicuously in movies or television shows

Several relevant points can be made about the mere exposure effect.

- The mere exposure effect is created in the absence of attention. For this reason, the effect is considered preattentive.

- Preferences associated with the mere exposure effect are easy to elicit. Thus, marketers can use this effect to improve attitudes marginally.

- The mere exposure effect has the greatest effect on novel (previously unfamiliar) objects.

- The size of the effect (increased liking) is not very strong relative to an effect created by a strong cohesive argument. For example, a Notre Dame football fan might develop a preference for a face to which he's repeatedly been exposed, but if he finds that the face belongs to an Alabama fan, the preference will likely go away based on the strong information!

- The mere exposure effect works best when the consumer has a low involvement in processing the object, and indeed when a consumer is distracted from processing the focal stimulus. For example, if a small brand logo is displayed on a magazine page across from an involving story, a greater increase in liking would be found than if the consumer were less distracted from the stimulus.

Note on Subliminal and Mere Exposure Effects

Before moving on, we should distinguish the mere exposure effect from subliminal effects. A subliminal message is one presented below the threshold of perception. In other words, if you are aware of the stimulus or message, then the process is not subliminal. With the mere exposure effect, the stimulus is evident and people could pay attention to it if they wanted to. No attempt is made to keep people from seeing them, as the stimuli are presented with strength above the threshold of perception.

Mere Association

Sometimes, consumers' judgments are influenced by mechanisms that have little to do with reasoning. One effect closely related to mere exposure is the **mere association effect**. This effect occurs when meaning transfers between two unrelated stimuli

that a consumer gets exposed to simultaneously. The mere exposure effect deals specifically with transfers between objects that are dissimilar other than an accidental proximity. An example makes this clearer. A study dealing with the topic demonstrated how a consumer simultaneously exposed to the concept "Mayo Clinic," a famous hospital, and mayonnaise ends up transferring meaning.[27] The exposure to the name "Mayo" activates concepts about hospitals and because the phonics are the same, the same concepts become more active for mayo. In this case, consumers' attitudes toward mayonnaise became less positive when exposed to the Mayo Clinic. For brand managers, the mere exposure effect means care should be taken to avoid any potentially negative but unintended associations. For instance, if Ford announces a safety recall on Ford Fusion models, the mere association by name with Gillette Fusion razors may inadvertently cause consumers to reduce their beliefs about the razor providing a safe shave.

Product Placements

An interesting application of implicit memory and mere exposure involves brand placements in video games. Video games, quite simply, can be very captivating! The person playing a game will likely not be paying attention to things like embedded brand logos. In a manner similar to the way banner ads are processed, implicit memory is created when the logos are executed within a game and an attitude towards the brand develops.[28] As with other preattentive effects, the effect is stronger as the game is more involving.

Product placements represent another way that promotions can impart implicit memory among consumers. Product placements involve branded products placed conspicuously in movies or television shows. These placements can result in implicit memory formation. For instance, researchers in the United Kingdom once demonstrated implicit memory learning by exposing children to the movie *Home Alone*. Half of the children saw the movie with a scene in which the actors consumed unbranded drinks. The other half saw the identical scene but with the drinks changed to Pepsi cans. After the movie, the children were given their choice of soft drink. Those who saw the unbranded drink scene chose Coke and Pepsi in similar proportion to the U.K. market share. However, those who saw the "branded" scene chose Pepsi over Coke by a wide margin.[29]

3-4b Attention

From the discussion above, it's clear that attention plays a key role in distinguishing implicit and explicit memory. Attention is the purposeful allocation of cognitive capacity toward understanding some stimulus. Intentional learning depends on attentive consumers. However, we don't pay attention only to things we wish to. **Involuntary attention** is attention that is beyond the conscious control of the consumer and that occurs as the result of exposure to surprising or novel stimuli. For example, if you were to cut your finger, you would automatically direct attention to the injury due to its pain. When attention is devoted to a stimulus in this way, an orientation reflex occurs. An **orientation reflex** is a natural response to a threat from the environment. In this way, the orientation reflex represents a protective behavior. When consumers pay attention to something, is it more often voluntary or involuntary?

3-5 Enhancing Consumers' Attention

Consumers face a difficult challenge in penetrating the clutter to pay attention to an intended message. What's more, consumers today are continually responding to electronic communication devices, creating an entire other layer of clutter. Getting a consumer's attention, voluntarily or involuntarily, has never been more difficult, but that is the job of effective marketing communication.

3-5a Factors that Get Attention

These factors can help create attention:

- **Intensity of Stimuli.** All things equal, a consumer is more likely to pay attention to stronger stimuli than to weaker stimuli. For example, vivid colors can be used to capture a consumer's attention. Loud sounds capture more attention than quieter sounds and can create an orientation reflex. A television commercial with a louder volume than the rest of the programming tends to get consumers' attention.

- **Contrast.** Contrasting stimuli are extremely effective in getting attention. Contrast occurs in several ways. In days past, a color photo in a newspaper was extremely effective in getting attention. However, today's newspapers are often filled with color, so a color advertisement is less prominent. A black-and-white image in a magazine filled with color, however, can stand out. A period of silence in an otherwise noisy environment can attract attention.[30] Like loud television commercials, silent commercials also usually work in gaining consumer attention. Nonconformity can also create attention because of the contrast with social norms.[31] Marketers often show consumers who stand out from the crowd as a means of capturing attention for an ad.

- **Movement.** With electronic billboards or electronic retail shelf tags, marketers attempt to capture consumer attention by the principle of movement. Items in movement simply gain attention. Flashing lights and "pointing" signage are particularly effective tools for gaining consumer attention.

- **Surprising Stimuli.** Unexpected stimuli gain consumers' attention. Occasionally, retailers replace mannequins with human models. This surprise usually attracts attention.

- **Size of Stimuli.** All else equal, larger items garner more attention than smaller ones. Marketers therefore often attempt to have brands appear large in advertisements. This is a reason advertising copy usually features large headlines.

- **Involvement.** **Involvement** refers to the personal relevance a consumer feels towards a particular

involuntary attention attention that is beyond the conscious control of a consumer

orientation reflex natural reflex that occurs as a response to something threatening

involvement the personal relevance toward, or interest in, a particular product

Kin Cheung/Reuters /Landov

Surprising stimuli can get attention.

unintentional learning
learning that occurs when behavior is modified through a consumer-stimulus interaction without any effortful allocation of cognitive processing capacity toward that stimulus

intentional learning process by which consumers set out to specifically learn information devoted to a certain subject

behaviorist approach to learning theory of learning that focuses on changes in behavior due to association without great concern for the cognitive mechanics of the learning process

information processing (or cognitive) perspective learning perspective that focuses on the cognitive processes associated with comprehension and how these precipitate behavioral changes

product. In general, the more personally relevant (and thus more involving) an object, the greater the chance that the object will be attended to. We discuss involvement in more detail in the cognitive learning chapter.

Gaining consumer attention is an important task for any marketer. Of course, paying attention can be beneficial for consumers as well. Consumers should devote cognitive capacity to comprehend choices that offer the most value for them.

3-5b Comprehension

As stated previously, consumers organize and understand information through comprehension. Comprehension is the interpretation or understanding that a consumer develops about an attended stimulus. As such, comprehension is an especially important topic for marketers because this stage determines the effectiveness of marketing communication. During comprehension, a host of biases can enter into the perceptual process. Furthermore, personal factors such as intelligence and motivation affect comprehension. We'll concentrate more closely on comprehension in the next chapter.

3-6 The Difference between Intentional and Unintentional Learning

Before moving on to cognitive learning and information processing, let's detail the distinction between the two types of consumer learning—intentional and unintentional learning. Both types of learning concern what cognitive psychologists refer to as perceptual processes; however, with **unintentional learning**, consumers simply sense and react (or respond) to the environment. Here, consumers "learn" without trying to learn. They do not attempt to comprehend the information presented. They are exposed to stimuli and respond in some way. With **intentional learning**, consumers set out to specifically learn information devoted to a certain subject. To better explain intentional and unintentional learning, we examine two major theories in the psychology of learning.

3-6a Behaviorism and Cognitive Learning Theories

Recall that perception and learning are closely related topics. As the preeminent behavioral psychologist B. F. Skinner once wrote: "In order to respond effectively to the world around us, we must see, hear, smell, taste and feel it."[32]

Psychologists generally follow one of two basic theories of learning. One theory focuses on changes in behavior occurring as conditioned responses to stimuli, without concern for the cognitive mechanics of the process. The other theory focuses on how changes in thought and knowledge precipitate behavioral changes. Those in the first camp follow a **behaviorist approach to learning** (also referred to as the behavioral learning perspective). This approach suggests that because the brain is a "black box," the focus of inquiry should be on the behavior itself. In fact, Skinner argued that no description of what happens inside the human body can adequately explain human behavior.[33] Thus, the brain is a black box, and we can't look inside.

From the behaviorist perspective, consumers are exposed to stimuli and directly respond in some way. Thus, the argument is that the marketing focus should be on *stimulus and response*. Behaviorists do not deny the existence of mental processes; rather, they consider these processes to be behaviors themselves. For example, thinking is an activity in the same way that walking is; psychological processes are viewed as actions.[34] Note that the term *conditioning* is used in behavioral learning, as behavior becomes conditioned in some way by the external environment.

The second theory of learning involves an **information processing (or cognitive) perspective**. With this approach, the focus is on the cognitive processes

⌐During comprehension, a host of biases can enter into the perceptual process.⌐

associated with comprehension, including that leading to consumer learning. The information processing perspective considers the mind as acting much like a computer. Bits of knowledge are processed electronically to form meaning.

Traditionally, the behavioral learning and cognitive perspectives have competed against one another for theoretical dominance. However, we avoid such debate, because on closer inspection the two theories really share much in common. At the very least, both perspectives focus on changes in behavior as people interact with their environment. We adopt an orientation more directly applicable to consumer learning by separating learning mechanisms into the intentional and unintentional groups that we have presented. The next section discusses unintentional learning and how consumers respond to stimuli they are exposed to.

3-6b Unintentional Learning

Unintentional learning occurs when behavior is modified through a consumer-stimulus interaction without a cognitive effort to understand a stimulus. With this type of learning, consumers respond to stimuli to which they are exposed without thinking about the information. The focus is on *reacting*, not cognitive processing.

Unintentional learning can be approached from the behavioral learning perspective. Two major approaches found in behavioral learning theory are *classical conditioning* and *instrumental conditioning*.

Classical Conditioning

Classical conditioning refers to a change in behavior that occurs simply through associating some stimulus with another stimulus that naturally causes a reaction. The most famous classical conditioning experiment was performed by the behavioral psychologist Ivan Pavlov. Pavlov conducted experiments using dogs, meat powder (an **unconditioned stimulus** that naturally led to a salivation response), and a bell (a **conditioned stimulus** that did not lead to the response before it was paired with the powder).[35] The experiment reveals that the bell eventually evokes the same behavior that the meat powder naturally caused.

In the experiment, Pavlov began ringing the bell every time meat powder was provided to the dogs. Thus, the bell became associated with the meat powder. Eventually, Pavlov rang the bell without providing the meat powder. As predicted, the bell proved enough to increase the amount of saliva the dogs produced. Originally, the dogs would salivate from being exposed to the unconditioned stimulus. The salivation was called an **unconditioned response**, which occurred naturally as a result of exposure to the unconditioned stimulus (the meat powder). The dogs eventually would respond in the same way to the exposure to the bell. This response became known as a **conditioned response**. The response became conditioned by the consistent pairing of the unconditioned and conditioned stimuli. Dogs do not cognitively process in the way we usually think that humans do. So the dogs learned this response without trying to do so.

To be effective, the conditioned stimulus is presented before the unconditioned stimuli, and the pairing of the two should be done consistently (and with repetition). The advertisement at the right illustrates a popular use of unintentional learning through classical conditioning—the use of sexual, or intimate, imagery.

Instrumental Conditioning

Much of what we know about instrumental (or operant) conditioning comes from the work of Skinner. With **instrumental conditioning**, behavior is conditioned

classical conditioning change in behavior that occurs simply through associating some stimulus with another stimulus that naturally causes some reaction; a type of unintentional learning

unconditioned stimulus stimulus with which a behavioral response is already associated

conditioned stimulus object or event that does not cause the desired response naturally but that can be conditioned to do so by pairing with an unconditioned stimulus

unconditioned response response that occurs naturally as a result of exposure to an unconditioned stimulus

conditioned response response that results from exposure to a conditioned stimulus that was originally associated with the unconditioned stimulus

instrumental conditioning type of learning in which a behavioral response can be conditioned through reinforcement—either punishment or rewards associated with undesirable or desirable behavior

RIA Novosti/Alamy

Pavlov got dogs like this one to learn how to produce saliva when they heard a bell ringing.

positive reinforcers
reinforcers that take the form of a reward

discriminative stimuli
stimuli that differentiate one choice from another through the presence of a reinforcer

shaping process through which a desired behavior is altered over time, in small increments

punishers stimuli that decrease the likelihood that a behavior will persist

negative reinforcement
removal of harmful stimuli as a way of encouraging behavior

extinction process through which behaviors cease due to lack of reinforcement

through reinforcement. Reinforcers are stimuli that strengthen a desired response. The focus is on behavior and behavioral change—not on mental processes that lead to learning. With instrumental conditioning, the likelihood that a behavior will increase is influenced by the reinforcers (consequences) of the behavior. The reinforcers are presented after the initial behavior occurs.

As an example of instrumental conditioning, consider childhood development. When a parent is "potty training" a child, he or she is more concerned with getting the desired result than with teaching the child the benefits of using a toilet over a diaper. All parents know that it is very difficult to rationalize with young children. Therefore, attempting to get them to think about the various reasons to become trained is almost useless. The focus is on changing the behavior through reinforcement. When a child performs the desired behavior, he or she receives rewards in the form of hugs, kisses, toys, etc. These rewards reinforce the desired behavior.

Positive reinforcers come in many forms in the consumer environment, and often take the form of some type of reward. The effects can be seen in marketing efforts that encourage repeat purchase behavior. For example, many casinos have players' cards that accumulate points the more a customer plays. The casino keeps track of these points. As the points accumulate, various offers are provided to the consumer, including free hotel rooms, meals, and other things that could otherwise be expensive. In this case, the points are used to elicit a desired response—repeat purchase behavior.

Discriminative Stimuli, Reinforcement, and Shaping. Discriminative stimuli are stimuli that are differentiated from other stimuli because they signal the presence of a reinforcer. These stimuli essentially signal that a type of reward will occur if a behavior is performed. Advertisements that feature special promotions represent marketing examples of discriminative stimuli. Here the ad informs consumers that they will receive some type of reward (for example, 10% off a purchase) if they perform the desirable behavior (for example,

shop at a store). The stimulus serves as a signal presented before the behavior occurs, and the behavior must occur in order for the reinforcement to be delivered. Brand names can be discriminative stimuli because they signal potential customer satisfaction and value. For example, consumers realize that by using FedEx, they can receive overnight delivery with outstanding quality. The reinforcer occurs after the behavior has been performed. Again we see the importance of exposure to the discriminative stimuli, further highlighting the relationship between perception and behavioral learning.

Shaping Behavior

Shaping is a process through which the desired behavior is altered over time, in small increments. Here, the focus is on rewarding small behaviors that lead to the big behavior ultimately desired. For example, universities invite prospective employers to participate in "career day" events. The employers hope that students who come by their booth will pick up some free promotional goods and have a good time interacting with company representatives. The small rewards along the way help shape the desired behavior—which is getting the students interested in a career.

Not all reinforcement is positive. **Punishers** represent stimuli that decrease the likelihood that a behavior will occur again. When children misbehave, they get punished. The hope is that the behavior will not occur again. In the same way, when consumers make poor decisions and purchase products that deliver less value than expected, they are punished. Chances are they won't buy those same products again! **Negative reinforcement**, on the other hand, refers to the *removal* of bad stimuli as a way of encouraging behavior.

Punishers and negative reinforcers are commonly confused. The concepts are not the same. A punisher is the presence of bad stimuli after an undesirable behavior has occurred, whereas a negative reinforcer represents the removal of undesirable events. Companies frequently use negative reinforcement techniques. For example, advertisements that focus on the bad outcomes associated with *not* using a company's products utilize this technique. The message is essentially "If only you had tried us, this bad thing wouldn't have happened!"

Behaviors often cease when reinforcers are no longer present. This represents the concept of **extinction**. For example, consumers may become accustomed to receiving free tea and cookies at a local nail salon every time they get their nails done. If the salon decides to stop offering the free food and drink, the consumers may take their business elsewhere.

Final Thought on Behavioral Conditioning

Conditioning represents a type of learning because it focuses on behavioral change that occurs through a consumer's interaction with the environment. For behaviorists, perception itself is an activity, not a mental process. Through the behavioral approach, consumers are exposed to stimuli and react in some way. Consumer learning through behavioral conditioning occurs without a conscious attempt to learn anything new.

Study Tools

Located at the back of the textbook

❏ Rip out Chapter in Review Card

Located at www.cengagebrain.com

❏ Review Key Terms Flashcards (print or online)

❏ Download audio summaries to review on the go

❏ Complete practice quizzes to prepare for tests

❏ Play "Beat the Clock" to master concepts

❏ Watch video on Culvers for a real company example

WHAT DO YOU THINK?
WHAT OTHERS HAVE THOUGHT

①	②	③	④	⑤	⑥	⑦
Strongly disagree	Disagree	Somewhat disagree	Neither agree nor disagree	Somewhat agree	Agree	Strongly agree

My perceptions of advertisements are usually accurate.

Readers tend to agree with this statement, but the level of agreement falls short of strong agreement. Sixty-five percent of respondents either somewhat agree or agree. Only 8% strongly agree. Overall, the results suggest that readers have some confidence that they accurately perceive advertising messages. Do you?

Andy Kropa/Redux

Consumers can't
realize value without an ability to assign meaning to the things consumed.

WHAT DO YOU THINK?
I can usually remember more from a 30-second television commercial than I can from a 30-minute lecture.

STRONGLY DISAGREE   STRONGLY AGREE

VISIT COURSEMATE AT WWW.CENGAGEBRAIN.COM

Comprehension, Memory, and Cognitive Learning

4

In the previous chapter, we defined consumer learning as a change in behavior resulting from some interaction between a consumer and a stimulus. We learned about a behaviorist approach to learning, which focuses on behaviors rather than inner mental processes, and we introduced human perception as the basis for cognitive learning. Cognitive learning focuses on mental processes occurring as consumers comprehend, elaborate, and act upon information. The cognitive perspective views learning as an active mental process in which a consumer processes information, forms associations between concepts, and gains knowledge.

Exhibit 4.1 shows the basic components of information processing. We have already discussed several of the concepts presented, including exposure, attention, and comprehension. In the current chapter, we look more closely at comprehension and other issues related to cognitive learning, including memory and elaboration.

Any student knows how difficult intentional learning can be even when a GPA provides a strong motivation. Consumers often lack a strong motivation to learn and thus, despite a near constant bombardment of marketing communications via radio, television, social networking sites, printed media, signage, flyers, and more, marketers face a difficult task in creating the learning that they intend to create. Even if one can get over the difficulty in gaining attention, there is no guarantee that any message will be meaningfully encoded and comprehended as intended.

After studying this chapter, the student should be able to:

4-1 Identify factors that influence consumer comprehension.

4-2 Explain how knowledge, meaning, and value are inseparable, using the multiple stores memory theory.

4-3 Understand how the mental associations that consumers develop are a key to learning.

4-4 Use the concept of associative networks to map relevant consumer knowledge.

4-5 Apply the cognitive schema concept in understanding how consumers react to products, brands, and marketing agents.

4-1 What Influences Comprehension?

Consumers can't realize value without an ability to assign meaning to the things consumed. **Comprehension** refers to the interpretation or understanding a consumer develops about some attended stimulus based on the way meaning is assigned. What happens when a consumer sees a "some assembly required" sticker

comprehension the way people cognitively assign meaning to (i.e., understand) things they encounter

signal theory explains ways in which communications convey meaning beyond the explicit or obvious interpretation

on a product? Of course, this means that the consumer will likely have to master a set of detailed instructions before consumption can begin. An easy-to-comprehend set of instructions would certainly contribute to the total value equation for the product. However, we all know how frustrating these instructions can be! In this and many other ways, marketers must teach us things so that we realize the most value from consumption.

Other products contain warning labels that signal specific associated risks. Consider a typical cigarette package. Consumers don't always comprehend messages as intended. A consumer might even see a cigarette warning label as authoritarian and end up mocking the ad, with the end result being that the ad makes smoking more appealing by reinforcing "rebellion" as a benefit. Other times, consumers may actually overestimate the dangers associated with smoking when they read a warning of "rare" side effects.[1] Research suggests that traditional cigarette warning labels actually have only a small effect on consumer behavior.[2] As a result, policy makers now seek the use of images to hopefully convey meaning more strongly. An interesting experiment demonstrated that adult consumers are willing to pay less for a pack of cigarettes with a photographic warning than they would for a pack with a conventional written label.[3] The legality of graphical warnings is currently being debated in court.

The following three factors summarize some key points about comprehension:

1. Internal factors within the consumer powerfully influence the comprehension process. Recall from a previous chapter that factors influencing consumer

In this case, do consumers learn more from pictures or words?

behavior often interact with each other. Numerous components in the Consumer Value Framework alter comprehension.

2. Comprehension includes both *cognitive* and *affective* elements. That is, the process of comprehension involves both thoughts and feelings. As such, comprehension applies not only to consumer learning but also to consumers' attitudes. A number of topics in this chapter apply equally to consumer attitude formation and persuasion (a later chapter is devoted to these topics).

3. Every message sends signals. **Signal theory** tells us that communications provide information in ways beyond the explicit or obvious content. A retailer promises to match competitors' prices (a price-matching guarantee) as a signal to consumers that prices are indeed low.[4] Consumers don't always comprehend messages or get the desired signal, and to this extent, consumer comprehension is not always "correct." After all, perception is subjective reality, which may or may not equal objective reality! Quite simply, consumers sometimes just don't get *it*; however, they act on what they do get.

4-1a Factors Affecting Consumer Comprehension

Meaning and value are inseparable, and consumers must comprehend marketing messages in order to learn the intended value of a product. As marketers attempt to communicate value, many factors

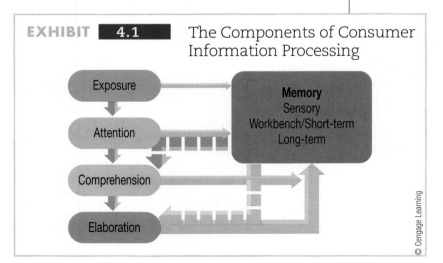

EXHIBIT 4.1 The Components of Consumer Information Processing

EXHIBIT **4.2**

Comprehension Depends on Multiple Factors

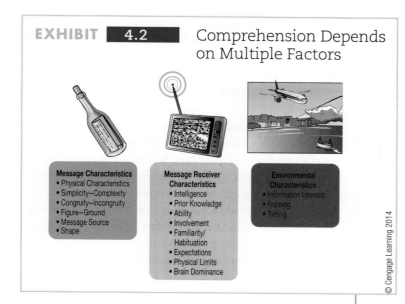

Message Characteristics	Message Receiver Characteristics	Environmental Characteristics
• Physical Characteristics	• Intelligence	• Information Intensity
• Simplicity–Complexity	• Prior Knowledge	• Framing
• Congruity–Incongruity	• Ability	• Timing
• Figure–Ground	• Involvement	
• Message Source	• Familiarity/ Habituation	
• Shape	• Expectations	
	• Physical Limits	
	• Brain Dominance	

© Cengage Learning 2014

influence what a consumer comprehends in a given situation. While consumer researchers still have a great deal to learn about the factors that influence comprehension, Exhibit 4.2 lists things we do know regarding these factors. These factors can be divided into three categories:

- Characteristics of the message
- Characteristics of the message receiver
- Characteristics of the environment (information processing situation)

4-1b Characteristics of the Message

Marketers believe that they can affect consumer learning by carefully planning the execution of marketing communications. If you flip through any popular magazine, you will see advertisements with many different execution styles. Here are a few tools marketers use to potentially influence comprehension and control what consumers learn.

Physical Characteristics

The **physical characteristics** of a message refer to the elements of a message that one senses directly. These parts come together to execute a communication of some type. While these elements affect comprehension, you may note that some of these characteristics also affect the likelihood that consumers pay attention. Here are just a few physical characteristics that can contribute to effective communication.

Intensity. Generally speaking, the greater the movement, the larger the picture, or the louder the sound, the more likely a consumer is to attend and comprehend something from a message. Signage with large numerals communi-

cates the notion of low prices to consumers.

Color. Color affects the likelihood of gaining a consumer's attention, but it can also have an impact on comprehension. Gold signals quality. Similarly, blue is associated with higher quality and higher price expectations. Warm colors like red and orange get attention, but they also lower quality perceptions relative to cool colors. Green signals environmental friendliness today. The mere presence of a green package increases "green" beliefs, although the actual question of what is environmentally friendly is a much more complicated question.[5]

Font. Consumers derive meaning from both the actual text of a message and the visual presentation of the message. Font styles send meaningful signals. The same brand or store name presented in a block font such as Courier

> **physical characteristics**
> tangible elements or the parts of a message that can be sensed

> ⌐ Consumers sometimes just don't get it; however, they act on what they do get. ⌐

If green means good, then this brand is in good shape!

AP Photo/Jim Mone

golden section the preferred ratio of objects, equal to 1.62 to 1.00

may take on a different meaning if presented in a script font. For instance, research suggests that different fonts signal masculinity, femininity, activity, elegance, softness, or tradition, just to name a few. Consider the two examples below:

ACME BRICK COMPANY
ACME BRICK COMPANY

Which sends the better message for a brick company? One can easily see that the signal the font sends should be consistent with the type of service offered.[6]

Numbers. In the 1980s, many discos around the world independently adopted the same name. They were called, in one way or another, 2001! In the 20th century, something with a year indicating the 21st century seemed futuristic. Now, we would have to try a name like 3003 to create the same effect.

Many brand managers rely on alphanumeric names, combining letters and numbers, when creating names for new products, brands, or models. Examples of alphanumeric names include 7-Up, A-1, and Rue 21. Technologically meaningful brands often employ such names. Blackberry recently shifted from a reliance on model names like Pearl, Storm, and Curve to names like BB Z10. Real terms like pearl, storm, and curve evoke specific meanings. In contrast, combinations of numbers and letters have little specific meaning. This gives marketers a better opportunity to shape the intended meaning of brands and products. Alphanumeric names also tend to convey meanings through an association with incremental improvement and advanced technology.

Spacing. All types of communicators, from salespeople to advertisers to teachers, repeat messages as a way of increasing comprehension. If a communicator is going to repeat a message multiple times, is it better to repeat it in sequence or to break up the repetition? Actually, consumers display greater recall of an intended message when information is presented in intervals rather than in sequence.[7] For instance, in media advertising, three 30-second ads spread over three hours achieve better consumer recall of information than a single 90-second advertisement.

Shape. Product designers influence the comprehension of products through many factors but perhaps the shape that they choose is the most basic. Consumers prefer objects that are consistent with the **golden section**. The golden section refers to a ratio of dimensions of about 1.62. Thus, objects that fit into a rectangle of 1.62 × 1.00 (inches, meters, feet, . . .) will be preferred.

Simplicity–Complexity

Generally speaking, the simpler the message, the more likely a consumer develops meaningful comprehension, which, of course, relies on a consumer's ability to process information. For example, research by the U.S.

Are You Lucky?

What do people comprehend when they see the inside of your home for the first time? Chances are, your environment changes the way people comprehend you. Well, imagine how important this comprehension is for retail stores. The store atmosphere sends the strongest signal telling the consumer just what the retail brand means. Lucky Brand applied exhaustive consumer research into designing their store interiors. Lucky Brand management felt this was necessary because consumers were beginning to see the Lucky brand as old, cluttered, and not modern. The fix was to redesign the stores by changing the color scheme from brown to white, changing the merchandising to organize by outfits not by clothing type, eliminating inventory from upper shelves, using those only to display merchandise, and creating more open space, particularly around the dressing rooms. The result is that Lucky customers now view the brand as friendly, cheery, and a place that feels like home. Hopefully, this comprehension is common to all its key market segments.

Source: Christina Binkley, "The Shopping Science Behind Lucky's Revamp," *The Wall Street Journal,* January 19, 2012, D8; S. J. Kim, "Lucky Brands Revamp: Success of Retail Is in the Details," Smartplanet, 2012, http://www .smartplanet.com/blog/design-architecture/lucky-brands-revamp-success-of-retail-is-in-the-details/3642, accessed February 10, 2013.

Food and Drug Administration (FDA) has helped them identify the simplest way to communicate important consumer information. Summary terms like *fat-free* and *low-fat* have replaced more complicated terms that were once linked to specific product attributes.[8] The FDA believes the new terminology allows consumers to better comprehend the desired messages.

Message Congruity

Message congruity represents the extent to which a message is internally consistent and fits surrounding information. To illustrate, consider the question: "Does a consumer more effectively comprehend information when exposed to three different ads about hair care products in a row, or when exposed to one hair care product ad preceded by a detergent ad and followed by an automobile ad?"

The conventional wisdom is that congruent content would lead to improved comprehension. However, this may not always be the case. Think about a typical television advertisement that contains background music. The ad designer can choose music that is either highly consistent or inconsistent with message content. Consider an advertisement encouraging vacations to China. Chinese music could be included in an effort to be consistent with the message content, whereas some type of Western music could be used in an "inconsistent" way. In a situation such as this, consumers may actually comprehend more from the message with inconsistent background music.[9] The reason is that the incongruity motivates deeper processing than when everything in a message is highly congruent. The result is improved comprehension. However, the research also suggests that ads with incongruent music are not liked as much as an ad with congruent music. Thus, if the primary goal is to create a favorable attitude rather than increased comprehension, then marketers should minimize incongruity.

The incongruity of a message with surrounding messages works in much the same way.[10] In fact, consumers will comprehend and remember more from an ad that is presented with incongruent material surrounding it. Consider a brand like L'Oreal Preference hair care products. The consumer will comprehend and remember more when presented with only one hair care message in any three-message sequence (see Exhibit 4.3). In this case, frame B offers better comprehension for the L'Oreal Preference brand.

Figure and Ground

Every message is presented within a background, but sometimes the background becomes the message. A photographer usually concentrates on capturing a focal image in a photo frame. The focal image, or the object intended to capture a person's attention, is much the same as a **figure** in a message. In a message, everything besides the figure should be less important and simply represent the **ground** (or background) relative to the central message. The contrast between the two represents the psychological **figure-ground distinction**.

Look at the simple message in Exhibit 4.4. What would a consumer comprehend? Well, most consumers would easily see the English word *here*. However, look more closely and concentrate on the *T*-shaped image at the left. Most consumers place that in the background. However, if that becomes the figure, then the message may easily become "there" and not "here."

Message Source

The source of a message also can influence comprehension. Message sources include a famous celebrity in an advertisement, a salesperson in a sales context, a family member giving advice,

message congruity extent to which a message is internally consistent and fits surrounding information

figure object that is intended to capture a person's attention, the focal part of any message

ground background in a message

figure–ground distinction notion that each message can be separated into the focal point (figure) and the background (ground)

EXHIBIT 4.3 Congruent or Incongruent Message Sequences?

Congruent Messages

Head and Shoulders Shampoo   L'Oréal Preference   PM Kids Shampoo

Consumer comprehends less about L'Oréal

Incongruent Messages

The Sak   L'Oréal Preference   Lipton Tea & Honey

Consumer comprehends more about L'Oréal

(top images and bottom center) The Advertising Archives; (bottom left) AP Photo/PRNewsFoto/The Sak (bottom right) AP Photo/PRNewsFoto/Lipton

© Cengage Learning

expertise amount of knowledge that a source is perceived to have about a subject

trustworthiness how honest and unbiased the source is perceived to be

credibility extent to which a source is considered to be both an expert in a given area and trustworthy

counterarguments thoughts that contradict a message

support arguments thoughts that further support a message

a Facebook friend, or even a computer-animated avatar. A source influences comprehension to varying degrees based upon characteristics like the following:[11]

1. Likeability
2. Attractiveness
3. Expertise
4. Trustworthiness

A likeable source can change the interpretation of a stimulus. For years, consumers have enjoyed the M&M's characters as the most liked spokes-characters for any product—even before the Super Bowl strip act. However, younger generations also express liking for the Aflac Duck and the Geico Gecko.[12] Most people would find it difficult to argue with Geico's claim, "15 minutes could save you 15% or more on car insurance." Conversely, if one of the less well-liked Geico Cavemen claimed the same, a consumer might be compelled to disagree. Consumers react much the same way to a source perceived as attractive. The Geico Cavemen lose out here too, but Maxwell the Piggy, who really does go "wee, wee, wee," is yet another Geico hit. As a sign of Geico's advertising effectiveness, 98% of consumers correctly associate the ads with the brand.

Expertise refers to the amount of knowledge that a source is perceived to have about a subject. **Trustworthiness** refers to how honest and unbiased a source is perceived to be. Consumers associate expertise and trustworthiness with **credibility**. Like likeability, credible sources tend to lower the chances that consumers will develop **counterarguments** toward a message.

Counterarguments are thoughts that contradict a message. **Support arguments** are thoughts that further support a message. Brand managers should especially rely on a likable, attractive, and credible source. At times, brands will even use celebrity spokespeople to communicate key facts with media. Supermodel Bar Refaeli posts news about her enthusiasm for guns on her Twitter site. Her likability and expertise with guns will likely generate numerous counter and support arguments among fans.

In summary, we can say that desirable source characteristics can help to convey the desired message through cognitive processes. However, sources can influence consumers in other more subtle ways. In a later chapter, we focus on how sources influence persuasion.

4-1c Message Receiver Characteristics

Intelligence/Ability

As a general statement, intelligent, well-educated consumers are more likely to accurately comprehend a message than are less intelligent or less educated consumers. With this being said, we offer two caveats. First, a great deal of knowledge is specific to particular product categories. Therefore, a consumer who does not have a high IQ may be able to comprehend certain product information more readily than another consumer with a high IQ. Second, even a highly intelligent consumer would understand a simpler message better than a more complex message. Marketers should communicate information pertaining to product warnings, usage instructions, or assembly directions in a way that those with relatively low intelligence can understand.[13]

Prior Knowledge

The human brain matches incoming information with preexisting knowledge. This preexisting or prior knowledge provides resources or a way through which other stimuli can be comprehended. Even consumers of very high intelligence may lack prior knowledge to comprehend certain consumer messages. This is why parents sometimes need their children to operate the television remote control. Even young kids have more knowledge of handheld electronic devices than many adults—particularly college professors. Consumers display a preference for things that are consistent with their prior knowledge.

Consider the role that superstition can play in comprehending value propositions. Lucky in Love? Ritz Carlton, and Walmart each offered promotions encouraging consumers to get married on 7/7/07. Consumers could get a seven-night honeymoon stay at the Ritz for $77,777.[14] The same promotion offered on a

---

EXHIBIT **4.4**   The Figure and Ground Distinction

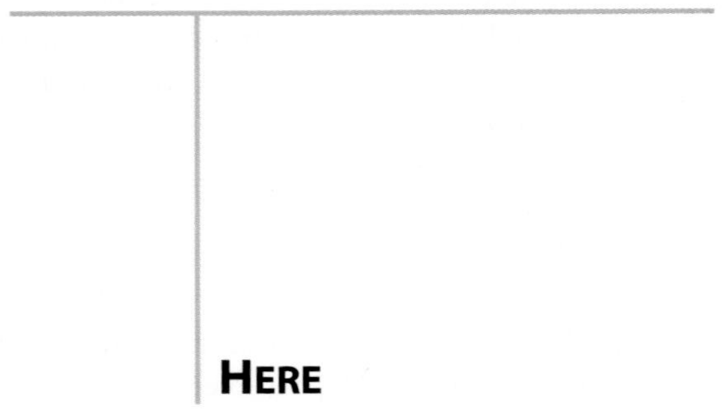

HERE

© Cengage Learning

Brands that Stay in Shape

Comprehension depends on message, consumer, and environment characteristics. Which of the three logos at right do you like the best? Psychology theory allows us to predict and explain why one of the three logos may be interpreted more favorably. The middle logo is quickly eliminated because it does not follow golden section principles. Designs with 1.62 width/length ratios are preferred over other types of shapes. Next, a majority of consumers would prefer the third image to the first. Why? People interpret boxed designs with sharp edges or corners intuitively as potential threats to safety based on the association with things like a rose thorn, a shark's tooth or barbed wire.

Curved edges are preferred. In some periods, such as the 1970s, boxy designs for appliances, autos and furniture became the rule. Some argue that a principle known as *zeitgeist*, taken from the German language and meaning the spirit of a time, can influence the comprehension of a message and the way a consumer receives that message. Consumer input may help design engineers understand such principles. What do you think of the zeitgeist today and how it influences preferred designs?

Sources: C. C. Carbon, "The Cycle of Preference: Long-Term Dynamics of Aesthetic Appreciation," *Acta Psychologica* 134 (2010): 233–44. J. Lander, "Seize the Zeitgeist: How Timing Impacts Success," *Inventor Digest* 26 (March 1, 2010): 40. Lan Luo, "Product Line Design for Consumer Durables: An Integrated Marketing and Engineering Approach," *Journal of Marketing Research* 48 (February 2011): 128–39.

Friday the 13th in 2013 would not likely be so successful. Going beyond lucky and unlucky numbers, consumers in some cultures associate certain colors with good or bad fortune and some associate certain foods with good fortune. Even marketers who are not superstitious would be wise to acknowledge the meanings that such beliefs, examples of prior knowledge, can convey to products.

Involvement

Consumers are not equally involved with every message sent their way. As discussed in Chapter 3, highly involved consumers tend to pay more attention to messages. They also exert more effort in comprehending messages.[15] As a result, these consumers show better recall than consumers with lower levels of involvement.[16] Consider the consumer who views a website describing a new product. The highly involved consumer will click through more hyperlinks, explore more pages, and comprehend more information than a less involved consumer.

Returning to the FDA labeling/instructions issue, marketers face the challenge of designing messages that either highly involved or uninvolved consumers will comprehend. In 1990, the U.S. Congress passed the Nutrition Labeling and Education Act (NLEA) to ensure that consumers would understand product warnings and nutrition labels regardless of their level of involvement. As a result of this act, marketers began to use simpler summary information on their labels. However, evidence suggests that even though this type of information is preferred, highly involved consumers still comprehend more from the labels than consumers with lower levels of involvement.[17]

Familiarity/Habituation

Consumers tend to like the familiar. However, in terms of comprehension, familiarity can *lower* a consumer's motivation to process a message. While some degree of familiarity may improve consumer attitude, high levels of familiarity may actually change or reduce comprehension.[18] Few humorous ads are as enjoyable after ten exposures as they were on the first viewing, so a consumer may tune the message out.

Courtesy of Geico

The Gecko has proved an effective source for Geico; will Maxwell the Piggy?

habituation process by which continuous exposure to a stimulus affects the comprehension of, and response to, the stimulus

adaptation level level of a stimulus to which a consumer has become accustomed

dostats Russian word that can be roughly translated as "acquiring things with great difficulty"

expectations beliefs about what will happen in some future situation

brain dominance refers to the phenomenon of *hemispheric lateralization*. Some people tend to be either right-brain or left-brain dominant

Habituation is the process by which continuous exposure to a stimulus affects the comprehension of and response to some stimulus. Consider the following psychological experiment. Subjects in one treatment group immerse their arms in extremely cold water (2°C) for 60 seconds. Obviously, this is an unpleasant task. Another group of subjects is asked to do the very same thing, except after the first immersion, they are asked to immediately immerse their arms into slightly less frigid (6°C) water for 30 additional seconds. At the end of the procedure, both groups rated the task hedonically. Surprisingly, the group that immersed their arms for 90 seconds rated the task more favorably than did the group that immersed their arms for only 60 seconds.

Habituation theory explains this result. The first 60 seconds of exposure to the extremely cold water habituated the subjects and created an **adaptation level**. As a result, when the second group was exposed to water that was still unpleasant, but slightly warmer than the first, a more favorable evaluation was obtained because the entire experience was framed by the relatively more valuable (less painful) last 30 seconds.

On a global level, consider that consumers in the United States, Canada, Australia, and throughout Western Europe expect fairly pleasant shopping experiences in which many goods and services are readily available in a comfortable setting. This hardly compares with many parts of the developing world, where shopping as we know it hardly exists. A decade after the breakup of the Soviet Union, consumer researchers measured the hedonic and utilitarian shopping value Russian consumers experienced trying to obtain everyday goods and services.[19] The capitalist reforms had been slow to spread throughout Russia and these consumers still faced shops with empty shelves and long lines to buy things like boots or jackets. A Russian word to describe this experience is **dostats**, which roughly means "acquiring things with great difficulty." The surprising result of the research was that the Russian consumers reported similar amounts of shopping value compared to American shoppers. What is the explanation for this outcome? Even though shopping in Russia was certainly worse than shopping in America, shopping was still framed by their life experiences beyond the familiar reality of *dostats*. These life experiences provided a frame of reference in which shopping was *less* unpleasant than were many other routine activities. Over time and improvements to the marketing infrastructure, the mere availability of product selection may cause a different hedonic response.

Expectations

Expectations are beliefs about what will happen in a future situation. They play an important role in many consumer behavior settings and can impact comprehension. We discuss expectations in more detail later when satisfaction becomes the focus. For now, note that what consumers expect to experience has an impact on their comprehension of the environment.

To illustrate, consider how packaging influences consumers' comprehension of products. Beverage marketers have realized for decades that packaging plays a major role in how beverages are perceived. In fact, studies indicate that consumers cannot even identify their "favorite" brand of beer without the label.[20] Removing the label affects consumers' expectations, which affects their comprehension by blocking brand-specific thoughts.

Physical Limits

A consumer's physical limitations can also influence comprehension. For example, we all have limits in our ability to hear, see, smell, taste, and think. Obviously, someone who can't hear an audio message can't comprehend information in it. Also, consumers who are color blind will have difficulty comprehending information related to color. For instance, if a caution or warning label is colored red to signal risk, a color-blind consumer will not likely comprehend this aspect of the message.[21]

Brain Dominance

Brain dominance refers to the phenomenon of *hemispheric lateralization*. Some people tend to be either right-brain or left-brain dominant. This, of course, does not mean that some consumers use *only* the left or right parts of their brains! Right-brain-dominant consumers tend to be visual processors (tend to favor images for communication), whereas left-brain-dominant consumers tend to deal better with verbal processing (words).

Hemispheric lateralization influences metaphor comprehension. Advertisements use metaphors regularly; despite the slogan "you're in good hands with Allstate,"

Making writing fashionable again. **⌀PILOT**

Jacksonville Fashion Week 2012 | P I L O T P E N . U S

Courtesy of Pilot Pen USA and Bright Red/TBWA

Metaphoric messages like this one for Pilot Pens presented at Jacksonville Fashion Week are particularly effective among right brain-dominant consumers.

one isn't really in someone's hands. A **metaphor** communicates a message figuratively rather than literally. Metaphors can increase one's ability to remember an ad message, and they particularly affect consumers when the metaphor is processed in the right brain hemisphere.[22] Thus, consumers who are right-brain dominant may respond particularly well to metaphors. Metaphors are not limited to words, as images often depict animate objects as products and vice versa.

4-1d Environmental Characteristics

Information Intensity

Information intensity refers to the amount of information available for a consumer to process within a given environment. When consumers are overloaded, the overload not only affects their attention but also their comprehension and eventual reaction. For example, evidence suggests that the amount of information presented to consumers participating in online auctions affects their bidding behavior, with highly intense information environments being associated with lower price sensitivity.[23]

Framing

Framing is a phenomenon in which the meaning of something is influenced (perceived differently) by the information environment. Thus, the same event can produce multiple meanings depending on how the information is presented. Framing and the consumer adaptation level (habituation) often work together to affect comprehension. Would you like an ice cream sundae? Most consumers probably would. However, if a consumer has just finished two ice cream sundaes that situational component will probably frame the third so that it doesn't seem so tasty.

Prospect theory hypothesizes that the way in which information is *framed* differentially affect risk assessments and associated consumer decisions. For example, in one store shoppers may see signage saying "save 50%!" In the next store, the consumers see signs saying "you pay half price!" Are they saying the same thing? Which creates a more positive message?

To illustrate prospect theory, consider what you have likely heard about risks associated with prolonged exposure to the sun. The following are two methods of presenting information about those risks:[24]

- Failing to use sunscreen leaves one vulnerable to skin cancer.
- Using sunscreen helps avoid skin cancer.

The first statement frames the behavior negatively. Don't use the product and *get skin cancer*! The second statement frames the behavior positively. Use this product and *stay healthy*!

Priming refers to a cognitive process in which active concepts frame thoughts and therefore affect both value and meaning. Negatively framed information primes losses, which consumers wish to avoid, and encourages consumers to be more willing to take a chance on a product and in this case spend some money on the sunscreen. Also, negatively framed information generally has a greater impact on consumers, and so the perceived value of the sunscreen in the above example may be increased by framing the information negatively.

metaphor in a consumer context, an ad claim that is not literally true but figuratively communicates a message

information intensity amount of information available for a consumer to process within a given environment

framing is a phenomenon in which the meaning of something is influenced (perceived differently) by the information environment

prospect theory theory that suggests that a decision, or argument, can be framed in different ways and that the framing affects risk assessments consumers make

priming cognitive process in which context or environment activates concepts and frames thoughts and therefore affects both value and meaning

memory psychological process by which knowledge is recorded

multiple store theory of memory theory that explains memory as utilizing three different storage areas within the human brain: sensory, workbench, and long-term

sensory memory area in memory where a consumer stores things exposed to one of the five senses

The greater impact of negative information is a key aspect of prospect theory. Exhibit 4.5 illustrates this aspect of framing. Most consumers faced with the first choice set in the exhibit will choose option 2. Notice that the frame is negative.[25] In the second choice set, consumers tend to choose option 1. In the second set, the frame is positive (priming gains—saving money instead of losing money). This happens even though the expected value ($E(v)$) for each choice is the same ($200). Presenting a negative frame primes thoughts that lead to a consumer being more willing to take risks. In terms of prospect theory, we say that losses weigh more heavily than gains. Losing $200 is certainly a loss and hurts hedonic value more than winning $200 helps create hedonic value.[26] As such, consumers more willingly take on a risk when faced with the first choice.

Priming occurs in many subtle ways beyond positive and negative frames. Brand names and logos can serve as primes, for instance. One experiment suggests that the presence of an Apple logo in an environment primes greater creativity among problem solvers compared to an environment that does not expose subjects to the logo.[27] A shopping environment can prime bargain expectations. For instance, a consumer may think $200 is a good price for a watch in a counter filled with watches selling for $1,000 or more. Conversely, the same watch at $200 may not seem like a good deal when it is the most expensive watch in the case.[28]

Timing

Timing also affects comprehension. For our purposes, timing refers to both the *amount of time* a consumer has to process a message and the *point in time* at which the consumer receives the message. For example, consumers who have only a couple of seconds to process a message, such as when driving by a billboard advertisement, cannot possibly comprehend a message in as much depth as a consumer who is not facing a timing issue.

The time of day can also affect the meaning and value of a product. For many consumers, coffee is a morning beverage. Consumers comprehend an advertisement for a brand of coffee quite differently based on the time of day. Most consumers will respond to a coffee advertisement in the morning far more enthusiastically than the same ad shown before bedtime, because of habituation effects associating hot coffee with morning consumption. The way time or age influences the interpretation of things is sometimes called zeitgeist.

As you can see, many factors influence how we comprehend marketing messages. Now we turn our focus to the other major concept in cognitive learning: memory.

4-2 Multiple Store Theory of Acquiring, Storing, and Using Knowledge

Memory is the psychological process by which knowledge is recorded. As shown in Exhibit 4.1, all of the elements of the information processing model are related to memory. In our chapter on perception, we discussed the topics of implicit and explicit memory. Here, we discuss memory from the cognitive learning perspective—the multiple store theory of memory.

4-2a Multiple Store Theory of Memory

The **multiple store theory of memory** views the memory process as utilizing three different storage areas within the human brain. The three areas are sensory memory, workbench (or short-term) memory, and long-term memory. Exhibit 4.6 illustrates this approach.

Sensory Memory

Sensory memory is the area in memory where we store what we encounter with our five human senses. When we hear something, sensory memory is responsible for storing the sounds. The consumer walking through an airport terminal encounters many sounds, smells, and sights.

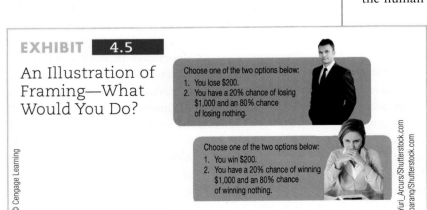

EXHIBIT 4.5

An Illustration of Framing—What Would You Do?

Choose one of the two options below:
1. You lose $200.
2. You have a 20% chance of losing $1,000 and an 80% chance of losing nothing.

Choose one of the two options below:
1. You win $200.
2. You have a 20% chance of winning $1,000 and an 80% chance of winning nothing.

© Cengage Learning

Yuri_Arcurs/Shutterstock.com
barang/Shutterstock.com

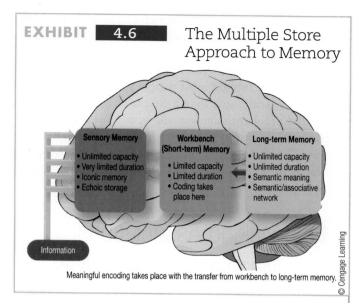

EXHIBIT 4.6 The Multiple Store Approach to Memory

Sensory Memory
- Unlimited capacity
- Very limited duration
- Iconic memory
- Echoic storage

Workbench (Short-term) Memory
- Limited capacity
- Limited duration
- Coding takes place here

Long-term Memory
- Unlimited capacity
- Unlimited duration
- Semantic meaning
- Semantic/associative network

Information

Meaningful encoding takes place with the transfer from workbench to long-term memory.

© Cengage Learning

Sensory memory picks these things out and stores them even though the consumer has not yet allocated attention to any of these sensations. Thus, this portion of memory is considered to be preattentive.

Sensory memory is truly remarkable. For one thing, it has unlimited capacity. Sensory memory stores everything one is exposed to, taking an exact record of what is encountered. Our sensory memory uses multiple distinctive mechanisms. **Iconic storage** is the storage of visual information as an exact representation of the scene. **Echoic storage** is the storage of auditory information as an exact representation of the sound. All sights, sounds, smells, tactile sensations, and tastes are recorded as exact replicas in the mind of the consumer.

If this is the case, then why can we recall only a fraction of what we encounter? Another remarkable aspect of sensory memory concerns duration. Sensory memory is very perishable and lasts only a very short time. In most cases, sensory memory begins to fade immediately after the sensation is recorded and lasts less than a second. Thus, the strength of sensory memory is capacity, but the weakness is duration.

Sensory memory can easily be illustrated. Take a quick look at an object and then close your eyes. What happens in the fractions of a second immediately after you shut your eyes? In most instances, your brain will hold the image immediately after you close your eyes—that is, you will be able to see the image mentally. However, very quickly things will start to fall out of the mental picture until eventually only the most central features can be pictured. If you are familiar with a strobe light, you may have noticed that when the light

speeds up, images look continuous. This is because sensory memory is able to "hold" the image through the dark portion of the strobe—that is, until the next image is physically sensed.

Sensory memory effects are essential for cognitive learning. However, sensory memory alone creates little opportunity for intentional learning because of the short duration. The last images held in sensory memory get transferred to the next storage mechanism where a sensory input like the touch of a package helps create meaning.[29] The term **haptic perception** refers specifically to interpretations created by the way some object feels. Footjoy recently marketed one of its gloves packaged in a black felt container. Inevitably, consumers who picked the package up believed the glove was more expensive than consumers who did not touch the package. Many put the package down immediately without even checking the price. The feel of the package translated into an image evoking an expensive product. Sensory memory works in conjunction with other memory functions in this way.

Workbench Memory

Workbench memory is the storage area in the memory system where information is stored and encoded for placement in long-term memory and, eventually, retrieved for future use. As we will see, workbench memory works very closely with long-term memory. **Encoding** is the process by which information is transferred from workbench memory to long-term memory for permanent storage. **Retrieval** is the process by which information is transferred back into workbench memory for additional processing when needed.

To illustrate workbench memory, imagine a consumer who is walking the aisles of Central Market. The consumer places several items into the cart, including some Camembert, Morbier, Speculoos and multiple household items including paper towels, storage bags, bleach, and toilet tissue. How much do you think all of this is going

iconic storage storage of visual information in sensory memory and the idea that things are stored with a one-to-one representation with reality

echoic storage storage of auditory information in sensory memory

haptic perception interpretations created by the way some object feels

workbench memory storage area in the memory system where information is stored while it is being processed and encoded for later recall

encoding process by which information is transferred from workbench memory to long-term memory for permanent storage

retrieval process by which information is transferred back into workbench memory for additional processing when needed

repetition simple mechanism in which a thought is kept alive in short-term memory by mentally repeating the thought

dual coding coding that occurs when two different sensory traces are available to remember something

meaningful encoding coding that occurs when information from long-term memory is placed on the workbench and attached to the information on the workbench in a way that the information can be recalled and used later

chunking process of grouping stimuli by meaning so that multiple stimuli can become one memory unit

to cost the consumer? If he doesn't physically write down each item's cost, can we expect that he will be able to know what the total bill will be? To some extent, his accuracy will depend on his ability to hold prices in memory long enough to be able to compute a total upon checkout.

Let's consider a single item. He picks up the bleach, checks the price, and puts the item in the cart. The price quickly enters his sensory memory and then moves on to his workbench memory because he is trying to pay attention to the price. The relevancy of duration, capacity, and involvement quickly come into play.

- **Duration.** The term *short-term* is often used when describing workbench memory because this memory storage area, like sensory memory, has limited duration. The duration is not nearly as limited as sensory memory, but stimuli that enter short-term memory may stay there approximately 30 seconds or so without some intervention. Therefore, our consumer can hardly be expected to remember the prices for all items in his cart by the time he reaches the checkout counter.

- **Capacity.** Unlike sensory memory, workbench memory has limited capacity. Generally, the capacity limit for workbench memory is between three and seven units of information. This fact is sometimes known as Miller's Law. Think of a physical workbench. If the bench is almost full, we cannot expect to put additional items on it. Some items must be removed first. Thus, we cannot expect our consumer to remember all the prices, especially if he is buying several products. In fact, working memory is even taxed further if the prices contain more syllables. A price of $13.47 is harder to remember than $12.10 because it contains more sounds, and more syllables contributes to a meaning of more expensive.[30]

- **Involvement.** The capacity of workbench memory expands and contracts based on the level of a consumer's involvement. The more involved a consumer is with a message, the greater will be the capacity of his workbench memory. When involvement is very low, workbench memory capacity contracts to a minimum.

To test your own workbench memory, try to do the following: Without looking back, name all the items purchased by our Central Market customer. How many can you remember? Don't feel bad if you can't remember them all. In fact, most people would not be able to correctly recall more than a couple of items. Many may recall that toilet tissue was one item. Unless a consumer has some knowledge of French cheeses, though, he or she is unlikely to recall Camembert and/or Morbier. We recall things better when we can make meaningful associations.

4-3 Making Associations with Meaning as a Key Way to Learn

So, what kind of work goes on in workbench memory? The task of a consumer may be to recall things, both over a short time period and over a long time period. The consumer should not only recall prices while in the store, but during the days and even weeks following the shopping trip.[31] When we use the expression "remember something," we often are referring to the fact that we can recall some information or make it active in our minds intentionally. Four mental processes help consumers remember things:

1. **Repetition** is a process in which a thought is held in short-term memory by mentally repeating the thought.

2. **Dual Coding** is a process in which two different sensory "traces" are available to remember something. As we shall see, a *trace* is a mental path by which some thought becomes active.

3. **Meaningful Encoding** is a process that occurs when preexisting knowledge is used to assist in storing new information.

4. **Chunking** is a process of grouping stimuli by meaning so that multiple stimuli can become a single memory unit.

Meaningful encoding and chunking rely heavily on making associations between new information and meaning that is stored in long-term memory.

Repetition. Repetition is a commonly employed way of trying to remember something. Picture someone trying to remember the license plate number:

TT 867-53-09

One way to remember this number is by thinking it repeatedly. This process is known as *rehearsal*. However, one major problem with this approach is **cognitive interference**. Cognitive interference simply means that other things are vying for processing capacity when a consumer rehearses information. To illustrate, try to count backwards from 1,000 by 3. This seems like an easy task. But if you try to do this while someone is calling out random numbers at the same time, the task becomes much more difficult. All things equal, repetition is the weakest form of learning.

Dual Coding. Dual coding can be more effective than repetition. To illustrate dual-coding effects, consider Exhibit 4.7. This exhibit illustrates the way a scent can improve recall.[32] Researchers tested the extent to which product feature recall might be enhanced by dual encoding using scents. Consumers in the experiment showed greater recall for product features, even for a product as innocuous as a pencil, when the product was infused with a scent. In a similar way, associating products with music helps consumers remember information. Why is this? A consumer is able to retrieve the information in two ways—by the content of the message and by the sound of the music.

Cows or chickens, Chick-fil-A is easy to remember.

© iStockphoto.com/ivanastar

Some foods can be difficult to spell; does pepperoni have two R's? But generations of Americans have no problem spelling another type of Italian sausage in part due to an Oscar Mayer jingle that finishes like this:

"… cuz Oscar Mayer has a way with B – O – L – O – G – N – A!"

Images also can assist with dual coding.[33] Chick-fil-A employs a logo that turns the C into a chicken. Thus, consumers can easily remember Chick-fil-A and the types of products it sells.

Meaningful Encoding. Meaningful encoding involves the association of active information in short-term memory with other information recalled from long-term memory. By this process, new information is coded with meaning.

To illustrate meaningful encoding, let's return to the license plate example. Consumers often find it difficult to associate anything meaningful with a number. However, a fan of 1980s pop rock would recognize the sequence of digits as the title of a famous hit by the rock artist Tommy Tutone. (The letters *TT* on the plate support this.) A consumer who can retrieve the memory of this song and attach it to the license plate can remember the plate's number much more easily. In a way, this example involves both dual and meaningful encoding, because the music (also stored in memory) serves as a memory aid itself. For a consumer who knows 1980s music, the numbers *867-5309* can only mean Tommy Tutone. (If you know the song, it's probably going to be stuck in your head now.)

Chunking. Chunking is the process of grouping stimuli by *meaning* so that multiple stimuli can become one memory unit. Remember that the capacity of workbench memory is rarely more than seven chunks of information. A **chunk** is a single memory unit. Here's a simple experiment that helps demonstrate what is meant by a chunk of memory. Show someone the following list of numbers for only a few seconds:

1 4 9 2 1 7 7 6 1 9 4 5

After taking the list away, engage them in conversation for a couple of minutes. Then, ask the person to recall

cognitive interference notion that everything else that the consumer is exposed to while trying to remember something is also vying for processing capacity and thus interfering with memory and comprehension

chunk single memory unit

⌐ When we … remember something, we are referring to the fact that we can make it active in our minds intentionally. ⌐

response generation reconstruction of memory traces into a formed recollection of information

long-term memory repository for all information that a person has encountered

semantic coding type of coding wherein stimuli are converted to meaning that can be expressed verbally

memory trace mental path by which some thought becomes active

spreading activation way cognitive activation spreads from one concept (or node) to another

the list. Why is this task so difficult? When someone treats each numeral as a distinct chunk of information, his or her memory capacity is exceeded. After all, 12 numerals, or chunks, are included in the list.

Now look at the list in this way:

1 4 9 2 1 7 7 6 1 9 4 5

If the person did well in American history class, the task should be considerably easier. A history student should recognize that these are all important dates in U.S. history. The set of 12 numbers can now be stored and recalled as only three pieces of information instead of 12!

Retrieval and Workbench Memory. As we have discussed, a task of workbench memory is the retrieval of information from long-term memory. When a consumer retrieves information from long-term memory, it is processed once again in workbench memory. As a part of this process, long-term memory is scanned for relevant information. Through a process of **response generation**, consumers reconstruct memory traces into a formed recollection of the information they are trying to remember.

Marketers can help this process by ensuring that information placed in marketing messages is also placed on in-store promotions, and perhaps product packaging.

One way of doing this is by using *integrated marketing communications* to ensure that a unified promotional message is sent across all consumer contacts.

Clearly, meaning and knowledge are the keys to effective coding and cognitive learning. To illustrate, consider the following list of words:

- Weep Sheep Deep Keep Peep

Suppose a subject is asked to look at this list and the next day asked if the word *sleep* was on the list. Would there be many false recalls (indicating the word was on the list when it was not, or vice versa)?

Now consider another list:

- Night Rest Awake Tired Dream

Would this list produce fewer false memories? The answer is yes. The key is that the second list enables more meaningful encoding and thus better memory.[34]

Long-Term Memory

A consumer's long-term memory plays a very important role in learning. **Long-term memory** is a repository for all information that a person has encountered. This portion of memory has unlimited capacity and unlimited duration. Barring some physical incapacity, long-term memory represents permanent information storage. Information stored in long-term memory is coded with **semantic coding**, which means the stimuli are converted to meaning that can be expressed verbally.

Why can't consumers always recall information when needed if storage is permanent? The problem is not a storage issue as much as it is a retrieval issue. To illustrate, consider that even things consumers process at very low levels leave some memory trace. A **memory trace** is the mental path by which some thought becomes active. For example, in the United States, childhood Easter memories generally include rabbits, eggs, and candy. Memory traces from *Easter* for many consumers also spread to specific brands like Russell Stover and Cadbury (chocolates) and of course, no Easter memory is complete without Peeps.

Psychologically, a memory trace shows how cognitive activation spreads from one concept to another. This process is known as **spreading activation**. Marketers want their brand names to cause cognitive activation to spread to favorable, rather than unfavorable, thoughts. For example, consider the following brands:

- Tabasco
- KFC

Tabasco is most often associated with "hot." Generally, hot things are good. Hot music is good, hot fashions are

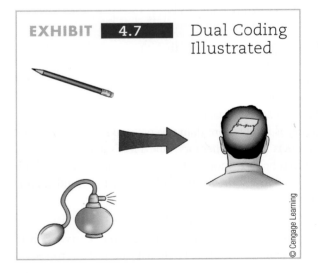

EXHIBIT 4.7 Dual Coding Illustrated

© Cengage Learning

good, and hot food is good. Therefore, consumers are willing to purchase Tabasco brand clothing (ties, shirts, etc.). From the concept of KFC, activation still spreads quickly to fried chicken and perhaps the notion of unhealthy food. KFC introduced grilled chicken and at many outlets emphasized the fact by proclaiming it was Kentucky Grilled Chicken—not KFC.

Mental Tagging. Let's look again at Exhibit 4.1. In psychological terms, a **tag** is a small piece of coded information that helps that particular piece of knowledge get retrieved. The tags function much like the bar-coded information on checked luggage. When everything works right, the information on the tag allows the luggage to be located. However, we all realize that not everything always goes right and luggage sometimes ends up in the wrong place. Similarly, if consumers do not tag information in a meaningful way, the encoding process results in errors.

As adults, most people have recalled some innocuous childhood memory for seemingly no apparent reason. These types of memories illustrate how long-term memory is permanent and how events that were poorly tagged during encoding can emerge at practically any time. Stimuli that consumers pay attention to but do not really comprehend or elaborate upon tend to be poorly tagged.

Rumination. **Rumination** refers to unintentional but recurrent memory of long-ago events that are not triggered by anything in the environment.[35] These thoughts frequently include consumption-related activities. Brand meaning can be clouded by bad feelings that accompany rumination. Not all rumination is bad, however, and nostalgic rumination may include positive associations with brands. **Nostalgia**, a mental yearning to relive the past, produces emotions of longing. Often nostalgic memories are tagged with product and brand associations. For example, Cracker Barrel stores are filled with products like Mallo Cups, Moon Pies, and Pixie Sticks, which seem to assimilate well with memories of childhood and childhood vacations.

Elaboration

The multiple stores theory of memory is an active process of association. **Elaboration** refers to the extent to which a person continues processing a message even after she develops an initial understanding in the comprehension stage.[36] With elaboration, increased information is retrieved from long-term memory and attached to the new information and understanding. This means more and richer tags and a better chance of recall. In particular, **personal elaboration**, in which people imagine themselves associating with a stimulus being processed, provides the deepest comprehension and greatest chance of accurate recall.

In Exhibit 4.1, notice the information processing steps linked to memory get more pronounced from exposure through elaboration. The darker and more pronounced lines linking comprehension and elaboration to memory represent the strength with which incoming information is tagged. Remember, our brains tag information so that we can understand it. Consumers who reach the elaboration stage are most likely to meaningfully encode information so that intentional retrieval is possible later. In a marketing context, therefore, appeals to a consumer to associate aspects of their own lives are likely to lead to deeper comprehension and better recall.[37] When an advertisement says, "Have you ever been in this situation?" or, "Imagine yourself on a deserted island," these primes can trigger personal elaboration in a consumer, resulting in better recall. For anyone trying to gain knowledge on purpose, personal elaboration provides the strongest link to meaningfully encoding information so that it can be useful in decision making.

4-4 Associative Networks and Consumer Knowledge

4-4a Associative Networks

Knowledge in long-term memory is stored in an associative network. An **associative network**, sometimes referred to as a semantic network, is a network of mental pathways linking knowledge within memory. These networks are similar to family trees, as they represent known linkages between objects.

Exhibit 4.8 illustrates the concept by showing a portion of a consumer's associative network that shows spreading activation from the Southwest Airlines

tag small piece of coded information that helps with the retrieval of knowledge

rumination unintentional but recurrent memory of long-ago events that are spontaneously (not evoked by the environment) triggered

nostalgia a yearning to relive the past that can produce lingering emotions

elaboration extent to which a consumer continues processing a message even after an initial understanding is achieved

personal elaboration process by which people imagine themselves somehow associating with a stimulus that is being processed

associative network network of mental pathways linking knowledge within memory; sometimes referred to as a semantic network

declarative knowledge cognitive components that represent facts

nodes concepts found in an associative network

paths representations of the association between nodes in an associative network

schema cognitive representation of a phenomenon that provides meaning to that entity

brand.[38] This illustrates the knowledge that can help identify the Southwest Airlines experience within a consumer's long-term memory. The network illustration also shows where cognitive activation flows after the Southwest Airlines concept becomes active.

4-4b Declarative Knowledge

Declarative knowledge is a term used in psychology to refer to cognitive components that represent facts. Declarative knowledge is represented in an associative network when two nodes are linked by a path. **Nodes** simply represent concepts in the network, while **paths** show the association between nodes in the network. Consumers' declarative knowledge may not always be correct, but consumers do act upon the beliefs this knowledge represents. The following are examples of declarative knowledge based on the associative network in Exhibit 4.8:

> *Southwest Airlines has cheap fares. . . . Southwest is orange and orange things are cheap. . . . Southwest Airlines has friendly attendants who use corny humor. . . . Southwest Airlines means waiting in A,B,C boarding lines. . . . Southwest Airlines is in Texas, and they have plenty of cattle in Texas, where they wait in line and stink. . . .*

In everyday experiences, a consumer compares all of these bits of knowledge with reality. Every time a consumer encounters a supportive instance of declarative knowledge, that knowledge becomes stronger. Consider: "A Southwest plane is blue and orange." Not all of their planes are blue and orange, but when some consumers think of their planes, they picture them as blue and orange. Every time a consumer actually sees a blue and orange Southwest plane, this belief becomes stronger even further building the strength of the Southwest-blue-orange association. If a consumer sees a white Southwest plane, the rule may diminish in strength. In this way, the associations represent rules that determine consumer reactions (SW airplanes are orange). When an intermediary node like peanuts comes between the brand and another concept, like "stinks," the indirect association still affects the brand's meaning.

Amazingly, every concept within a consumer's associative network is linked to every other concept. Consider the following request:

> List at least 10 snack foods in 60 seconds or less.

A typical consumer would list things like potato chips, an energy bar, a Twinkie, and a candy bar. Few would argue that these are indeed snack foods. All are linked to the snack concept and distinct from other food categories—like dinner entrees. A glass of milk may also be a snack, but the association between milk and snack food must first pass through several nodes. By that time, the association is weak. Selling milk as a snack, therefore, would be difficult. However, if a dairy packages milk in a small container reminiscent of a snack food's plastic wrapper, the likelihood that consumers would view milk as a snack will increase, and the rule that milk can be a snack would subsequently increase in strength.

4-5 Product and Brand Schemas

A consumer's knowledge for a brand or product is contained in a **schema**. A schema is a type of associative network that works as a cognitive representation of a phenomenon that provides meaning to that entity. Exhibit 4.8 illustrates a brand schema for Southwest Airlines while Exhibit 4.9 illustrates a product schema for snack food. A brand schema is the smaller part within one's total associative network responsible for defining a particular marketing entity. Similarly, product schemas function in much the same way. Each time a consumer encounters something that could be a snack food, the mind quickly compares all the associations in the schema to see if indeed the thought is correct. Several types of *schemata* (plural for schema) exist.

EXHIBIT 4.8

The Schema and Associative Network for Southwest Airlines

© Cengage Learning

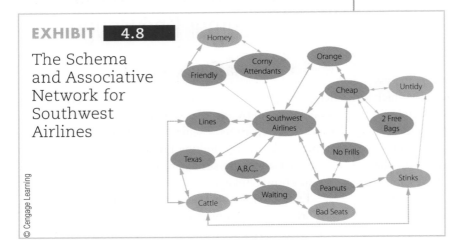

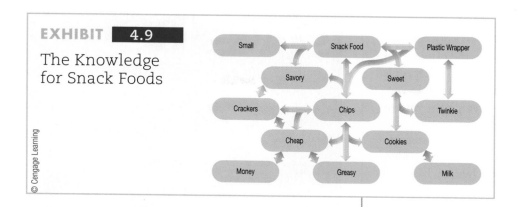

EXHIBIT 4.9

The Knowledge for Snack Foods

© Cengage Learning

exemplar concept within a schema that is the single best representative of some category; schema for something that really exists

prototype schema that is the best representative of some category but that is not represented by an existing entity; conglomeration of the most associated characteristics of a category

script schema representing an event

4-5a Exemplars

An **exemplar** is a concept within a schema that is the single best representative of some category. Exemplars can be different for different people. In a snack food schema, potato chips may be the exemplar. Beyoncé may be the category exemplar for a female pop singer. Disney World may be the exemplar for a vacation destination. Other examples in a category are compared to the exemplar. When a consumer encounters a carrot, the association with chips as the exemplar of a snack food may not be close. But if the retailer offers small bite-sized carrots wrapped enclosed in a small plastic bag, they may be associated with a bag of chips and fit into the snack food category. Exhibit 4.10 illustrates other possible category exemplars.

4-5b Prototypes

Some categories are not well represented by an exemplar. For instance, a "pharmaceutical sales rep" category likely does not evoke a specific person who best represents that category. However, an image is associated in one's mind with the category. The image contains the characteristics most associated with a pharma rep. Several characteristics may come to mind

and they are active in your own mind at this moment. This type of schema is known as a **prototype**. Whether represented by a prototype or an exemplar, consumers compare new and unknown examples to the standard by comparing features with those found in the schema. If interviewing for a pharma rep job, one probably wants to evoke assimilation with that category.

4-5c Reaction to New Products/Brands

When consumers encounter new products or brands, they react to them by comparing them to the existing schema. Sometimes, new products fail because they are too different or just way ahead of their time. Tablet computer–type devices first appeared in the 1990s but didn't catch on. New offerings often involve cobranding: multiple brands partnering together to develop and market an offering. Consumers are more receptive to cobranding efforts among brands with shared associations. Disney and Crocs offer cobranded footwear ideal for strolling the huge theme parks. TGI Friday's restaurants team with Jack Daniels for a host of branded menu items. In contrast, cobranding efforts between L'Oréal (makeup) and Nestlé (food) don't present as much overlap in meaning or opportunity.

4-5d Script

A **script** is a schema representing an event. Consumers derive expectations for service encounters from these scripts. For instance, when a consumer dines in a fine Italian restaurant, the script probably contains things such as valet parking, a greeting by a maitre d' in a nice suit, a table covered with a tablecloth, perhaps music by Dean Martin, etc. Since the script is positive (Italian fine dining is a good experience), restaurant managers try to not vary too much from expectations or risk confusing, and even frustrating, consumers.

EXHIBIT 4.10 Category Exemplars

Product Category	Exemplar
Fast Food	McDonald's
Motorcycle	Harley-Davidson
Dollar Store	Dollar General Store
Supercenter	Walmart
Cartoon Character	Bugs Bunny
Golf Ball	Titleist Pro V1
Social Network	Facebook

© Cengage Learning

episodic memory memory for past events in one's life

social schema cognitive representation that gives a specific type of person meaning

social stereotype another word for social schema

Similarly, salespeople employ scripts in performing their jobs. For instance, salespeople making charitable appeals employ various scripts to employ the best sequence of steps to gain compliance from a consumer.[39] Health care providers may develop unique scripts to use with children, based on the belief that children are less knowledgeable and more anxious than adult patients.

4-5e Episodic Memory

Closely related to the concept of a script is **episodic memory.** Episodic memory refers to the memory for past events, or episodes, in one's life. A consumer may have fond memories of childhood holiday celebrations. Another consumer may remember graduating from college or getting a first job. Both of these are episodes and they involve products and brands. Brands associated with positive events stored in episodic memory receive something of a halo, and tend to be preferred by consumers.[40] Episodic memories and scripts both can include knowledge necessary for consumers to use products. Younger consumers' memories likely are much better developed than older consumers when it comes to ways to use social networks like Facebook and Twitter to find and post important marketing information.

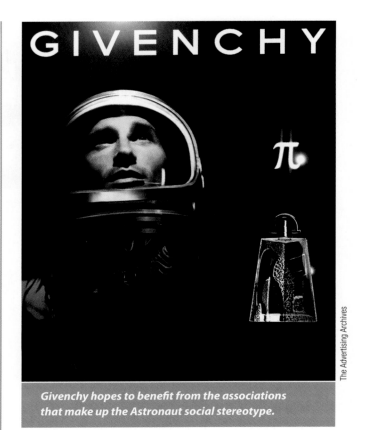

Givenchy hopes to benefit from the associations that make up the Astronaut social stereotype.

The Advertising Archives

4-5f Social Schemata

A **social schema** is the cognitive representation that gives a specific type of person meaning. Another word for social schema is **social stereotype.** The stereotype captures

Bike, Trike, or Hike?

What is an Elio? When a company enters into a product market for the first time, the hope is that the new offering has characteristics that allow it to fit into the product schema. That isn't always the case. Elio Inc. is a U.S. start-up venture that intends to appeal to consumers' thriftiness and/or concern for the environment.

An Elio has one door, three wheels (not counting a steering wheel), place for two passengers (one behind the other), optional leather seats and air conditioning, and gets up to 84 miles per gallon. The company plans to price the vehicle from about $7,000. But what is this vehicle? Is it a bike, motorcycle, trike, Spyder, Cushman, or

car? Will the driver need a helmet? The answers to these questions are ultimately up to the consumers more than the marketers. Similarly, as more intellectual products become digitized, their success also depends on consumer categorization processes.

Courtesy of Elio Motors

Sources: N. Bunkley, "Pony Up $1,000. Get an Elio T-shirt, . . . and Maybe a Discounted 3-wheeled Car" Autonews.com, January 24, 2013, http://www.autonews.com/article/20130124/BLOG06/130129939/pony-up-1-000-get-an-elio-t-shirt-maybe-a-discounted-3-wheeled#axzz2KWI6VYF3, accessed February 10, 2013. S. Chen and N. Granitz, "Adoption, Rejection or Convergence: Consumer Attitudes toward Book Digitization," *Journal of Business Research* 65 (2012): 1219–25.

the role expectations of a person of a specific type. For instance, consumers generally like when a service provider matches an existing stereotype. Consumers are comforted by a surgeon that looks like a surgeon and acts like a surgeon. But consumer behavior may be altered when a service provider does not fit a social schema. A waitress that does not match the stereotype, in this case by being over- or underweight, may cause consumers to eat more or less than they might otherwise![41]

Consumers also realize that, as consumers, they belong to certain categories of person types. This phenomenon falls under the general heading of *social identity*. Many consumers will try to match the characteristics associated with a stereotype. For instance, male consumers often exhibit characteristics that confirm their fit with the male stereotype. Male consumers' reactions to feminine-based advertising may be less positive when viewed in the presence of another male consumer. This may be the result of trying to protect their male identity.[42] A male consumer may sometimes seek out products that allow him to fit better into this category.

A social schema can be based on practically any characteristic that can describe a person, including occupation, age, sex, ethnicity, religion, and even product ownership. What type of person is a typical Taco Bell customer? What does a Taco Bell customer do? When do they patronize Taco Bell? Taco Bell's 2013 Super Bowl commercial played on stereotypes by depicting senior citizens performing behaviors more consistent with typical Taco Bell customers. Even children associate certain stereotypes, like a "cool kid," with specific types of brands and products (e.g., A&F clothing).[43]

Also, attempts to demarket a product can be implemented by stigmatizing consumption with a negative stereotype. Perhaps no better example exists than the stigmatization of smoking. A "smoker," as opposed to a nonsmoker, is more likely to be attributed with the following characteristics: *energetic, interesting, disgusting, offending,* and *unkempt.* Additionally, a person described as a smoker is liked less than a similar person described as a nonsmoker, and interestingly, even smokers are more likely to describe a fellow smoker as disgusting and offensive.[44] Thus, the stereotype seems pervasive. Obviously, a product associated with increasing the belief that a consumer is disgusting and offensive is more difficult to sell. To the extent that anti-smoking public policy messages have tried to stigmatize smokers, the messages have been effective.

Study Tools

Located at the back of the textbook

❑ Rip out Chapter in Review Card

Located at www.cengagebrain.com

❑ Review Key Terms Flashcards (print or online)

❑ Download audio summaries to review on the go

❑ Complete practice quizzes to prepare for tests

❑ Play "Beat the Clock" to master concepts

❑ Watch video on Cold Stone Creamery for a real company example

study tools

WHAT DO YOU THINK?
WHAT OTHERS HAVE THOUGHT

| | 1 | 2 | 3 | 4 | 5 | 6 | 7 |

Strongly disagree · Disagree · Somewhat disagree · Neither agree nor disagree · Somewhat agree · Agree · Strongly agree

I can usually remember more from a 30-second television commercial than I can from a 30-minute lecture.

Results from this question may be somewhat depressing for instructors. Sixty-two percent of respondents expressed at least some agreement with this statement and only 14 percent disagree or strongly disagree. Can professors teach in 30-second jingles?

Juice Images/Cultura/Jupiter Images

Basic needs are

addressed with utilitarian value, and as needs become more elaborate, hedonic value is often needed to satiate the need state.

WHAT DO YOU THINK?

I do not allow emotions to control my behavior.

STRONGLY DISAGREE   STRONGLY AGREE

VISIT COURSEMATE AT WWW.CENGAGEBRAIN.COM

Motivation and Emotion: Driving Consumer Behavior

5

How many times do people ask, "Why did I do that?" Sometimes the reason is simple. A consumer might ask, "Why did I eat two whole Snickers bars?" The reason may be as simple as "I was hungry." Many consumers may also relate to another familiar question, "Why did I drink so much?" People usually ask this question the morning after a long night out. The reason here may not be as simple or obvious as "I was hungry" or "I was thirsty." But ultimately, excessive drinking, like all acts, does indeed have an explanation. Often times, the explanations for CB like this involve motivation and emotion.

5-1 What Drives Human Behavior?

The basic consumption process (recall from Chapter 1) is a central component of the CVF and includes consumer needs as the first component. Consumer needs start the process because they kick-start or *motivate* subsequent thoughts, feelings, and behavior. Simply put, **motivations** are the inner reasons or driving forces behind human actions that drive consumers to address real needs. As the CVF indicates, motivations do not completely determine behavior. Other sources, including situational factors like the physical environment, influence behavior. However, motivations do much to provide the intended reason for a consumer's actions.

5-1a Homeostasis

Human motivations are oriented around two key groups of behavior. The first is behavior aimed at maintaining one in a current acceptable state. **Homeostasis** refers to the fact that the body naturally reacts in a way so as to maintain a constant, normal bloodstream. Shivering motivates consumers to wear coats to keep their blood from becoming too cold. When one's blood sugar falls below an acceptable state, the physiological reaction is hunger. Hunger then

After studying this chapter, the student should be able to:

5-1 Understand what initiates human behavior.

5-2 Classify basic consumer motivations.

5-3 Describe consumer emotions and demonstrate how they help shape value.

5-4 Apply different approaches to measuring consumer emotions.

5-5 Understand how different consumers express emotions in different ways.

5-6 Define and apply the concepts of schema-based affect and emotional contagion.

motivations inner reasons or driving forces behind human actions that drive consumers to address real needs

homeostasis state of equilibrium wherein the body naturally reacts in a way so as to maintain a constant, normal bloodstream

self-improvement motivation motivations aimed at changing the current state to a level that is more ideal, not at simply maintaining the current state

regulatory focus theory puts forward the notion that consumers orient their behavior either through a prevention or promotion focus

Maslow's hierarchy of needs a theory of human motivation which describes consumers as addressing a finite set of prioritized needs

motivates a consumer to eat something and restore the body to an acceptable state. In this way, a consumer comes to want a Snickers or something else to eat as a way of restoring a normal state. Thus, consumers act to maintain things the way they are and their wants are a function of the need driven by homeostasis.

5-1b Self-Improvement

The second group of behavior results from **self-improvement motivation**. These behaviors are aimed at changing one's current state to a level that is more ideal—not simply maintaining the current state of existence. Consider why one exercises. Beyond some level, consumers exercise not to maintain themselves but to improve their health and well-being. In much the same way, when a consumer upgrades from a Touchup handbag to a Prada handbag, she is not acting out a decision to maintain herself, but she sees Prada as a way of improving her status in life. Self-improvement leads consumers to perform acts that cause emotions that help create hedonic value.

5-1c Regulatory Focus

Consumer researchers try to capture the manner through which motivation orients consumers through various theories about how we try to control our behaviors. **Regulatory focus theory**, following closely from the contrast between homeostasis and self-improvement, puts forward the notion that consumers orient their behavior either through a prevention focus or a promotion focus. A prevention focus orients consumers toward avoiding negative consequences, while a promotion focus orients consumers toward the pursuit of their aspirations or ideals.[1] The prevention terminology captures the motivation to maintain homeostasis and the promotion focus shares similarity with self-improvement goals. Consider the following two toothpaste brands:

1. White-Bright: White-Bright gives you an appealing white smile!

2. Drill-Not: Drill-Not is the leader in preventing tooth decay.

White-Bright appeals more to a promotion focus and achieving the ideal of a sexy, white smile. Drill-Not

Purestock/Jupiter Images

Regulatory focus theory explains that even simple acts like this are driven either by a prevention (maintenace) or promotion (self-improvement) orientation.

appeals more to a prevention focus and trying to avoid the pain, discomfort, and inconvenience of tooth decay and related diseases.

Basic motivations are relatively simple to understand. As with many psychological concepts, researchers classify motives in several ways. We turn now to two related classification schemes—one a classic, general motivational classification and another aimed more specifically at CB and value creation.

5-2 General Hierarchy of Motivation

Perhaps the most popular theory of human motivation in consumer and organizational behavior is **Maslow's hierarchy of needs**. This theory describes consumers as addressing a finite set of prioritized needs. The following list displays the set of needs, starting with the most basic.

- **Physiological.** Basic survival (food, drink, shelter, etc.)
- **Safety and security.** The need to be secure and protected
- **Belongingness and love.** The need to feel like a member of a family or community
- **Esteem.** The need to be recognized as a person of worth
- **Self-actualization.** The need for personal fulfillment

According to Maslow's theory, consumers first seek value by satisfying the most basic needs. Thus, a starving consumer will risk safety to get something to eat. A consumer whose survival is in doubt would find little value in things that might provide esteem or self-actualization. In contrast, when successful businesspeople retire, they may indeed find the most value in things that do not bring esteem, love, or safety, but instead provide self-fulfillment. Several financial firms run advertisements showing retirees leaving high-paying careers to travel to far-off places or go off and work in a mission. This appeal typifies how CB can provide value by addressing the self-actualization need.

Further, consider how Maslow's hierarchy may operate differently around the world. In war-torn areas of the world, consumers may indeed risk their lives to buy basic necessities. Clearly, this type of shopping is providing only utilitarian value. In the United States, consumers may find esteem through performing well on the job and owning a large house. In Japan, however, space is so scarce that very few people own large homes. Therefore, esteem may manifest itself more in owning a nice car or in one's manner of dress.

Similarly, the things that address self-actualization needs are likely to vary in different places around the world. Motivations can determine the type and amounts of value consumers seek. Generally, the most basic needs are addressed with utilitarian value, and as needs become more elaborate, hedonic value is often needed to satiate the need state. Exhibit 5.1 illustrates the hierarchical aspect of needs and includes an example of a consumer behavior that goes with each need.

5-2a Simpler Classification of Consumer Motivations

The preceding discussion suggests an even simpler classification of consumer motivations. Not surprisingly, the types of motivations match up with the types of needs. A simple but very useful way to understand CB is to classify motives based on whether a consumption act can best address a particular need by realizing utilitarian or hedonic value.[2]

Utilitarian Motivation

Utilitarian motivation is a drive to acquire products that consumers can use to accomplish things. Utilitarian motivation bears much in common with the idea of maintaining behavior. When the consumer runs out of toothpaste, there will be a strong motivation to do something about this problem and acquire more toothpaste. He or she may want to buy some Crest toothpaste. In the sense that utilitarian motivation helps a consumer maintain his or her state, these motivations work much like homeostasis.

Hedonic Motivation

Hedonic motivation involves a drive to experience something personally gratifying. These behaviors are usually emotionally satisfying. Interestingly, although sales via the Internet continue to grow, they account for no more than 5% of all retailing. Perhaps part of the reason is that the process itself is not very rewarding. For people who really love to shop, the Internet may not provide the multisensory experience that a rich shopping environment can deliver. For these consumers, the Internet may be fine for acquiring things but disappointing as a rewarding shopping experience. Exhibit 5.2 illustrates some typical behaviors that are motivated by utilitarian or hedonic shopping motives.

5-2b Consumer Involvement

CB researchers use the word involvement a great deal. In most families, everyone knows which family member to go to with questions about how to work some electronic appliance or get some app to work on a media device. Much to the other family members' amazement, that individual just seems to stroke a few keys and voilà, the task is accomplished. What makes this person so different?

Involvement is synonymous with motivation in the sense that a highly involved consumer is strongly motivated to expend effort and resources in consuming that particular thing.[3] **Consumer involvement** represents the

utilitarian motivation drive to acquire products that can be used to accomplish something

hedonic motivation drive to experience something emotionally gratifying

consumer involvement degree of personal relevance a consumer finds in pursuing value from a particular category of consumption

EXHIBIT 5.1

An Illustration of Consumer Motivations According to Maslow's Hierarchy

© Cengage Learning 2015

Self-actualization — Pursuing a degree during retirement

Esteem — Posting achievements in online gaming

Belongingness and love — Fitting in with college group

Safety and Security — Gated apartment complex

Physiological Needs — Dining on ramen noodles in the dorm

Hedonic Value

Utilitarian Value

moderating variable
variable that changes the nature of the relationship between two other variables

product involvement the personal relevance of a particular product category

product enthusiasts consumers with very high involvement in some product category

---

EXHIBIT 5.2 Utilitarian and Hedonic Motivations Lead to Consumer Behaviors

Utilitarian Motivations Lead to	Hedonic Motivations Lead to
Joining LinkedIn to network professionally	Joining Facebook to have fun spreading "news"
Visiting the health clinic because of a high fever	Going to a health club to have fun playing racquetball with friends
Choosing to shop with retailers that are seen as useful and easy to use	Choosing to shop with retailers that are seen as fun and exciting
Using air freshener to cover up a strange smell in the apartment	Using air freshener because one really enjoys the smell
Going gift shopping out of a sense of obligation to give a gift	Giving a gift to enjoy the giving process and the joy the recipient experiences when opening the gift

© Cengage Learning 2015

degree of personal relevance a consumer finds in pursuing value from a given category of consumption. Thus, when a consumer is highly involved, there is a greater chance that relatively high value can be achieved, as long as things go as expected. The consumer above captures more value from electronic media devices than does a less involved consumer.

Consumer Involvement as a Moderator

Consumer researchers often consider involvement a key moderating variable. A **moderating variable** is one that changes the nature of a relationship between two other variables. For example, consider the relationship between the number of alternative brands of a product, perhaps running shoes, and the amount of time and effort a consumer spends choosing a pair of shoes. Logically, one might expect that the larger the selection, the greater the time needed to make a decision. However, would this be the case for all consumers?

Highly involved consumers are likely to take more time because they recognize a greater number of attractive alternatives. She is willing (motivated) to spend time evaluating multiple pairs of shoes, trying them on, and comparing their attributes. Value is closely tied to making the right choice. On the other hand, a consumer who lacks motivation to study shoes is quickly overwhelmed by a large selection and falls back to some simple choice decision like "pick the cutest." A consumer needs some degree of involvement to have an ability to evaluate multiple brands effectively. A consumer with low involvement will not spend more time just because there are more types of shoes. A consumer

with high involvement, though, is likely to spend more time making a decision, since there are more alternatives from which to choose.

Different Types of Involvement

Involvement can mean different things to different people. However, one way to bring different perspectives together is to realize that there are different types of involvement. In each case, high involvement still means high personal relevance and the importance of receiving high value. Here are some key types of consumer involvement:

- **Product involvement** means that some product category has personal relevance. **Product enthusiasts** are consumers with very high involvement in some category. A relatively large segment of product enthusiasts find fashion highly relevant. These consumers find great value in learning about fashions, shopping for fashions, and wearing fashionable clothes and accessories. For every consumer. some product categories are much more involving than others. Exhibit 5.3 contrasts products that are generally associated with low and high consumer product involvement.

Igor Grochev/Shutterstock.com

EXHIBIT 5.3 Typical High and Low Product Involvement

High Product Involvement	Low Product Involvement
Handbags	Detergents
Computers	Band-Aids
Vacations	Toothpaste
High heels	Bananas

© Cengage Learning 2015

- **Shopping involvement** represents the personal relevance of shopping activities. This relevance enhances personal shopping value. From a utilitarian value perspective, highly involved shoppers are more likely to process information about deals and are more likely to react to price reductions and limited offers that create better deals.[4]

- **Situational involvement** represents the temporary involvement associated with some imminent purchase situation. Situational involvement often comes about when consumers are shopping for something that they have little interest in but that comes with a relatively high price. Things like household and kitchen appliances often qualify as evoking situation involvement. For instance, few consumers are highly involved with air conditioners. However, when a consumer is about to purchase a water heater, he may temporarily learn a lot about water heaters to avoid paying too much or choosing an inappropriate unit.

- **Enduring involvement** is not temporary but rather represents a continuing interest in some product or activity. The consumer is always searching for opportunities to consume the product or participate in the activity. Enduring involvement is associated with hedonic value, because learning about, shopping for, or consuming a product for which a consumer has high enduring involvement is personally gratifying. Consumers with high enduring involvement typically find hedonic value in learning more about that particular product or activity.

- **Emotional involvement** represents how emotional a consumer gets during some specific consumption activity. Emotional involvement shares much in common with enduring involvement because the things that consumers care most about will eventually create highly emotional responses. Sports fans typify consumers with high emotional involvement, and as we know, sports fans can be rowdy and do wild and crazy things.

Enduring involvement is emotional. Consumers often show passion for activities in which they are enduringly involved.

Sean Nel/Shutterstock.com

shopping involvement personal relevance of shopping activities

situational involvement temporary interest in some imminent purchase situation

enduring involvement ongoing interest in some product or opportunity

emotional involvement type of deep personal interest that evokes strongly felt feelings simply from the thoughts or behavior associated with some object or activity

emotion a specific psychobiological reaction to a human appraisal

psychobiological a response involving both psychological and physical human responses

5-3 Consumer Emotions and Value

5-3a Emotion

What is *emotion*? Emotion is a difficult term to define. In fact, some refer to emotion as a "fuzzy" concept, believing that no exact definition exists. According to this view, the best that one can do is list examples of emotions. Love, for example, is a primary example of an emotion, and all readers can relate to the experience of love. Yet, how is *love* defined?

Ask someone to put love into words and people will usually provide examples or types of love such as romantic love, brotherly love, maternal love, or love for one's school. Although quite different from love, anger is also a typical emotion and shares something in common with love. Both love and anger are controlling emotions, in that they tend to shape one's behavior strongly.

While emotions seem a bit "fuzzy," we can offer a straightforward definition. **Emotions** are specific psychobiological reactions to appraisals. Thus, when a consumer receives bad service in a restaurant, she appraises the situation and then reacts emotionally. When a consumer is contemplating vacation, he appraises different sites and thinks about the total vacation experience.[5] A consumer reacts differently to Maui, Hawaii, than Branson, Missouri. Emotions are considered **psychobiological** because they involve both psychological processing and physical responses.[6] Indeed,

visceral responses certain feeling states that are tied to physical reactions/behavior in a very direct way

cognitive appraisal theory school of thought proposing that specific types of appraisal thoughts can be linked to specific types of emotions

anticipation appraisals appraisals focusing on the future and can elicit anticipatory emotions like hopefulness or anxiety

emotions create **visceral responses**, meaning that certain feeling states are tied to behavior in a very direct way. Exhibit 5.4 lists some typical visceral responses to emotions.

Emotions are extremely important to CB and marketing because consumers react most immediately to their feelings. Notice that the word *motivation* and the word *emotion* both contain "motion" as a root. The fact that emotions are hard-wired to behavior has been explained as follows:

> *"[Emotions are] fuels for drives, for all motion, every performance, and any behavioral act."*[7]

Behaviors are closely tied to emotion, creating close links between emotions, CB, and value. Thus, marketing success is determined by emotions, because actions bring value to a consumer to the extent that desirable emotional states can be created.[8] One of the secrets to Starbucks's success is an environment that creates relaxing feelings. These emotions end up contributing to the overall value of the Starbucks experience. Price discounts also create emotions that drive consumer behavior. A $200 discount on a $20,000 necklace may not create a lot of emotion, but a $200 discount on a $500 suit creates emotion that can cause consumers to drive out of their way to buy the product.[9]

db2stock/Purestock/Jupiterimages

Emotions create visceral responses— such as a smile.

5-3b Cognitive Appraisal Theory

What gives rise to consumer emotions? Psychologists have debated the different sources of emotions for decades, but **cognitive appraisal theory** represents an increasingly popular school of thought. Cognitive appraisal theory describes how specific types of thoughts can serve as a basis for specific emotions. When a consumer makes an appraisal, he or she is assessing some past, present, or future situation. Four types of cognitive appraisals are especially relevant for consumer behavior.[10]

> Marketers would like to create appraisals leading to consumer emotions that evoke approach behaviors.

1. **Anticipation appraisal.** Focuses on the future and can elicit anticipatory emotions like hopefulness or anxiety

EXHIBIT 5.4 Visceral Responses to Emotions by Consumers

Type of Appraisal/Situation	Emotion	Behavioral Reaction
Anticipation appraisal—Consumer waits while doctor examines X-rays	Worry	Grim face with turned-down eyebrows and cheeks. Hands likely near face. Consumer would rather avoid situation.
Outcome appraisal—Consumer wins a contest	Joy	Genuine smile including turned-up cheeks and eyebrows and open hands. The consumer approaches the situation.
Equity appraisal—Consumer sees one customer receive faster and better service than he or she receives	Anger	Turned-down cheeks and eyebrows with clenched fists and hunched back. The consumer seeks to approach an agent of the company.
Agency appraisal—Consumer sees a waiter sneeze near a food preparation area	Disgust	Pinched-in facial expression and turned head. The body naturally withdraws from (avoids) the situation.
Outcome appraisal—Consumer shows up at an important party inappropriately dressed	Embarrassment	Face blushes (turns red and feels hot), head cowers, and a strong desire to flee is experienced.

© Cengage Learning

2. **Agency appraisal.** Reviews responsibility for events and can evoke consequential emotions like gratefulness, frustration, guilt, or sadness

3. **Equity appraisal.** Considers how fair some event is and can evoke emotions like warmth or anger

4. **Outcomes appraisal.** Considers how something turned out relative to one's goals and can evoke emotions like joyfulness, satisfaction, sadness, or pride

Exhibit 5.4 illustrates each of these appraisal types. A basic behavioral response is to either approach or avoid. Marketers generally benefit from approach responses; thus, they would like to create appraisals leading to emotions evoking approach behaviors, and avoid appraisals and emotions evoking avoidance.

Appraisals are often complicated enough to involve more than one type of appraisal and sometimes conflicting behavioral responses. Anticipatory appraisals can involve suspenseful emotions such as hope. A consumer may appraise an ad for a charitable cause in a manner that evokes hope and she may become more willing to consider donation to that cause. However, the same ad could cause a consumer to feel guilty if he makes an agency appraisal and ends up feeling a sense of responsibility for the problem that the charity addresses. Guilt may be less effective than hope in gaining compliance to an appeal.[11] Consumers also make equity appraisals such as the perception of very unfair treatment. They end up feeling angry and may cope with the anger by seeking revenge.[12] Health services often create situations involving both anticipation and outcome appraisals. A consumer visiting the dentist may be worried about having cavities but feel joyful when the dentist provides a clean bill of health. Cognitive appraisal theory emphasizes the fact that emotions result from appraisals.

5-3c Emotion Terminology

Mood

Moods can be distinguished from the broader concept of emotion based on specificity and time. Consumer **mood** represents a transient (temporary and changing) and general feeling state often characterized with simple descriptors such as a "good mood," "bad mood," or even a "funky mood." Moods are generally considered less intense than many other emotional experiences; nevertheless, moods can influence CB. Consumers in good moods tend to make decisions faster and to outspend their bad-mood counterparts. In addition, consumer mood affects satisfaction, with a bad mood being particularly detrimental to consumer satisfaction.[13] In this sense, marketers do not

have complete control of the satisfaction they deliver.

Employees' moods can also affect consumption outcomes as they interact with consumer mood. A salesperson in a bad mood can negatively affect a consumer's overall attitude and willingness to buy. Perhaps curiously, consumers who enter a situation in a bad mood react better to service providers who are also in a bad mood than they do to service providers in a good mood. Consumers seem to be most receptive to an employee with a matching mood rather than to an employee who always has a positive mood.[14]

A consumer's mood can serve as a type of frame that can transfer into product value judgments. For example, when consumers are evaluating alternative vacation sites, they tend to rate sites more favorably when they evaluate them in a good mood as opposed to when they are in a bad mood.[15] Consumers make **mood-congruent judgments**, an evaluation in which they judge the value of a target in a mood-consistent way. As a result, marketers should prefer consumers to buy and consume their products when they are in a good mood. Many cues can make a consumer's mood more positive, including music, smells, and even exposure to lucky numbers![16] Conversely, things that lower one's mood make consumers less likely to trust market information.[17] Environmental cues that can affect mood then do much to influence the value consumers get from shopping and service experiences, as we will see later.

Sometimes, a consumer intentionally goes about some action as a way of altering mood. Consumers may purchase a gift for themselves, for instance, as a way of improving their mood. In much the same way, research shows that consumers who are in bad moods can be more likely to be generous to others. The rationale is based on the hedonic value produced when one is generous.[18]

Affect

Affect is another term used to represent the feelings a consumer experiences during the consumption process. At times, affect is used as a general term encompassing both emotion and mood. However, in CB,

agency appraisals reviews responsibility for events and can evoke consequential emotions like gratefulness, frustration, guilt, or sadness

equity appraisal considers how fair some event is and can evoke emotions like warmth or anger

outcomes appraisal considers how something turned out relative to one's goals and can evoke emotions like joyfulness, satisfaction, sadness, or pride

mood transient and general affective state

mood-congruent judgments evaluations in which the value of a target is influenced in a consistent way by one's mood

consumer affect feelings a consumer has about a particular product or activity

autonomic measures means of recording responses based on either automatic visceral reactions or neurological brain activity

© Cengage Learning

EXHIBIT 5.5

The Interplay between Emotion, Mood, and Affect

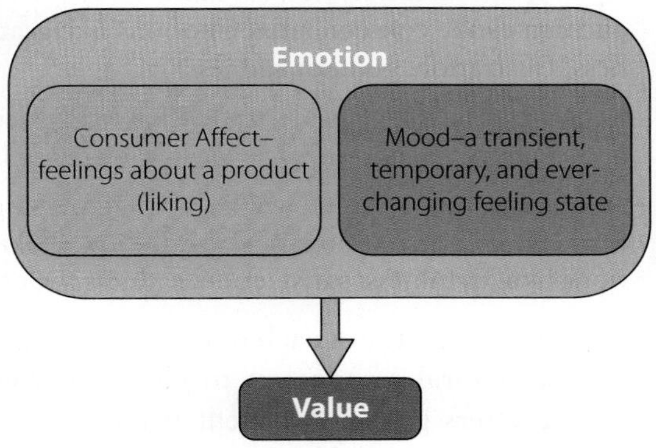

consumer affect is more often used to represent the feelings a consumer has about a particular product or activity.[19] Thus, when a consumer likes Dairy Queen (DQ) more than KFC, she is expressing her affect toward the DQ brand. Exhibit 5.5 illustrates the interplay between emotion, consumer mood, and consumer affect.

5-4 Measuring Emotion

Marketing and consumer researchers place a great deal of emphasis on properly measuring consumer emotion, because emotions play such a key role in shaping value. However, there is no consensus on the best way to measure consumer emotions. Two issues that regularly arise are whether consumers have introspection (can express verbally) connected to their emotions, and how to best categorize these emotions if they can be communicated.

5-4a Autonomic Measures

Perhaps autonomic measures offer the greatest validity in representing consumer emotions. **Autonomic measures** are means for automatically recording visceral reactions or neurological brain activity. Autonomic emotion measures monitor things like facial reactions, physiological responses such as sweating in a GSR (galvanic skin response) or lie detector test, heart rate, and activity in areas of the brain responsible for certain specific emotions, which can be documented via brain imaging.[20]

While these measurement approaches have the advantage of assessing emotional activity without requiring a volitional response from the consumer, they have the drawback of being intrusive. The researcher must attach some type of device to the consumer. Imagine a consumer wearing a net stocking cap attached to a computer by wires, in a lab, while a researcher tells him to watch some ads and act naturally, as if in his own living room. This would be very difficult to do. So the disadvantage of this approach is the obtrusiveness created by the measuring device. Interestingly, however, research suggests that these autonomic responses generally correspond fairly well to introspective self-reports of emotional experience.[21]

5-4b Self-Report Measures

Self-report measures are less obtrusive than biological measures, because they don't involve physical contraptions like imaging machines or lie detectors. Self-report affect measures require consumers to recall their affect state from a recent experience, or to state the affect they are feeling at a given point in time. These survey approaches usually involve a questionnaire; the process is not perfect, but generally results are valid enough to be useful to consumer and marketing researchers. Exhibit 5.6 illustrates a web-based survey approach for assessing emotion using slider scales. The respondent moves the slider from 0 to 100 until the scale indicates how much they feel a certain emotion. Many different options exist for applying self-report measures, with each option usually based on a somewhat different perspective of emotion theory.

PANAS

One of the most commonly applied ways to assess one's emotional state is by using the PANAS. PANAS stands for positive-affect-negative-affect scale and allows respondents to self-report the extent to which they feel one of 20 emotional adjectives.

Researchers generally apply the PANAS to capture the relative amount of positive and negative emotion experienced by a consumer at a given point in time. However, this raises several questions about the nature of emotion, including whether or not positive and negative emotions can coexist.

Every PANAS item represents either a good or a bad feeling. Thus, one might wonder why "inspired" and "upset" would both need to be measured. If a new product inspired a consumer, it would seem that the

PAD pleasure–arousal–dominance; a self-report measure that asks respondents to rate feelings using semantic differential items

bipolar situation wherein if one feels joy he or she cannot also experience sadness

EXHIBIT 5.6 A Slider Scale to Measure Consumption Emotion

Thank you for your recent visit to our service center. Please use the slider scales below to rate the extent to which you felt each emotion listed during service experience.

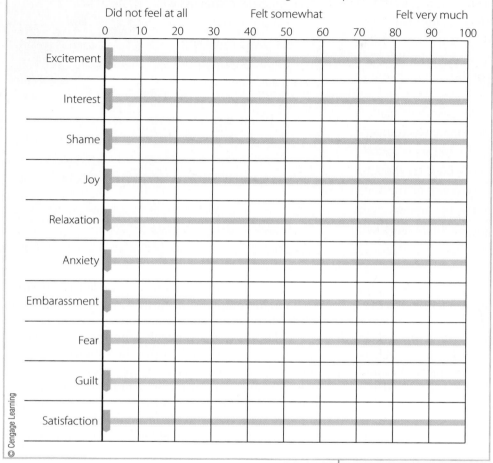

The first situation is quite simple. In situations like these, positive and negative emotions tend to be opposites. If people have bad feelings during the experience, they are unlikely to have any good feelings. The second situation is more complex and extends over a longer period. In situations such as these, bad and good feelings do not cancel each other out completely, and people can indeed experience some levels of both.

Thus, when consumer researchers are studying highly complex situations, a scale like the PANAS allows them to capture both positive and negative dimensions of emotional experience. The possibility exists that each dimension might explain somewhat unique experiences. For example, positive affect is highly related to increased spending, but

consumer could not be upset at the same time. If feeling good excludes feeling bad, then wouldn't a researcher need only measure positive terms or negative terms to account for a consumer's feelings?

This might be an interesting academic question, but the issue also has practical implications if consumers react differently to equal amounts of positive and negative emotions. Does a mad consumer or a glad consumer react more strongly? Considerable attention in psychology and marketing research addresses this question, and the evidence isn't crystal clear. The best we can say in addressing whether feeling bad is more influential than feeling good is "sometimes." Take a look at the following situations:

- A consumer rating the feelings experienced when a pop-up box shows up on an online Facebook game
- A consumer rating the feelings experienced when planning a wedding.

negative emotion is not. The more good feelings a consumer has, the more she buys. A consumer experiencing negative emotions may still complete the shopping task, but she may also be more likely to look for another place to shop next time.

> The things that tap our deepest emotions have the ability to evoke the greatest value.

PAD

PAD is an acronym that stands for pleasure–arousal–dominance. This scale asks consumers to rate their feelings using a number of semantic differential (bipolar opposites) items that capture emotions in these three dimensions. The theory behind PAD, unlike PANAS, is that pleasure—the evaluative dimension of emotion—is **bipolar**, meaning that if one feels joyful, one cannot also

Feeling Guilty?

How do you feel when you see an advertisement aimed at encouraging you to donate to some program to prevent animal cruelty? Usually, these ads include disturbing images of distressed animals. Do the ads that encourage donations to prevent starvation among developing-world children, with their images of distressed children, evoke the same feelings?

Ads like this evoke negative emotions like guilt, shame, or disgust. The negative emotions are sometimes counteracted by empathetic feelings that encourage approach behaviors like giving. This is really a tricky business though, because negative reactions create avoidance as the consumer feels distressed by having to see the images. Here are a few things that research suggests about the situation:

1. Consumers who feel personally distressed will give as much as those who are truly feeling sympathy if they cannot escape viewing the ads.
2. Consumers feel more empathy and give more when an ad provides a victim's personal identity.
3. Although some consumers are more prone to feel empathy, they don't always respond better to an individual appeal because they feel empathetic to many appeals.

Sources: G. A. Verhaert and D. Van den Poel, "Empathy as Added Value in Predicting Donation Behavior," *Journal of Business Research* 64 (2011): 1288–95. E. G. Danit and L. Levontin, "Giving from a Distance: Putting the Charitable Organization at the Center of the Donation Appeal," *Journal of Consumer Psychology*, April 2013, http://dx.doi.org/10.1016/j.jcps.2012.09.002.

experience sadness.[22] Arousal, which is the degree to which one feels energized, excited, or interested, is also seen as bipolar, in that a consumer is either aroused or bored. Likewise, dominance, the degree that one feels in control of a situation, is also bipolar. Thus, researchers have combined the PAD and PANAS approaches and applied adjectives taken from the PAD scale and put them in a format similar to that in Exhibit 5.6, rather than a semantic differential.

Many researchers use the PAD or a modified PAD approach to study retail atmospherics across many environments, including museums and parks and even advertising contexts.[23] Because the scale captures arousal separately, the approach is advantageous when the degree of activation or excitement is of particular interest. For example, when consumers go to a movie, they may feel pleased but not excited. Similarly, the PAD approach allows a separate accounting for feelings of dominance, sometimes known as control. When consumers feel lower control, situational influences play a greater role in shaping their behavior.

5-5 Differences in Emotional Behavior

Not all consumers react emotionally or show their emotions to the same extent or in the same way.[24] Two consumers, for instance, may receive the same poor service from a crowded retail store. One might complain furiously to store management, while the other simply walks away to find a more quiet shopping environment. Emotions, as discussed earlier, are deeply tied to personal motivations and traits. Thus, personality characteristics can affect the way consumers respond or demonstrate their emotions. For instance, neuroticism, an important personality trait, is positively related with the amount of negative affect a consumer reports in various service settings.[25]

Fortunately, consumers know how they feel, so measuring emotion is possible.

5-5a Emotional Involvement

Motivation and involvement are closely related, as we discussed earlier in the chapter. The things that tap our deepest emotions have the ability to evoke the greatest value. This brings us to emotional involvement, meaning the type of deep personal interest that evokes strongly felt feelings associated with some object or activity. Emotional involvement drives one to consume generally through relatively strong hedonic motivations. Often, emotional involvement can make a consumer appear irrational. Consider the amount of money and time a college alumnus and football fan will spend following his team. Some spend hundreds of thousands of dollars on motor homes used only on football weekends for tailgating. The consumer is deeply and emotionally involved with the team and in many ways becomes one with the team.

Other consumers may experience deeply held feelings over certain fashion products, jewelry, music, travel, food, and wine or even over online gaming. A consumer experiencing a fantastic dinner with a fantastic bottle of wine is achieving a maximum value experience through a combination of high emotional involvement and products that served as expected or better than expected.[26]

Emotional involvement increases when the consumer receives something extra with products purchased. For instance, if someone buys a nice leather backpack, the company might consider adding a premium, which may include a phone holster, calculator, or gift certificate to a local pub. In this way, the consumer may develop an emotional attachment or become emotionally involved with the product and with the brand.[27]

Perhaps there is no better example of how different consumers react emotionally than the responses different consumers get when involved with a motion picture. Some consumers have difficulty getting through any heart-touching scene without tears coming to their eyes—which generally means they like the movie. Other consumers see the same scene and are bored. They would rather be watching a classic slapstick movie like *Caddyshack* or *Dumb and Dumber*, which may bring them to tears through laughter.

Flow

All consumers can probably relate to the experience of enjoying a good book or movie so much that one loses awareness of time passing. When this occurs, a consumer has achieved a state of **flow**, meaning extremely high emotional involvement in which a consumer is engrossed in an activity.

A great deal of the work on flow deals with computer-related activities. For instance, consumers can become so involved in video games or online social networking that they have little physical awareness of their surroundings.[28] When a parent calls a child for dinner and the child seems to be ignoring her, the child may be so caught up in gaming that there is no conscious awareness of being called. In the extreme, consumers can become addicted to playing video games or surfing the Internet.[29] Similarly, more and more consumers face Facebook addiction. Consumers can become addicted when their level of obsession with an activity becomes too high. Here are a few signs that might indicate Facebook addiction:[30]

flow extremely high emotional involvement in which a consumer is engrossed in an activity.

> Highly involved consumers sometimes obtain a flow experience.

- Spending more than one hour a day dedicated to Facebook
- Ignoring work to stay on Facebook
- Keeping Facebook page constantly minimized on computer and mobile device
- Feeling a constant urge to refresh the Facebook page
- Feeling more attached to the Facebook world than the real world
- Replacing sleep with time on Facebook
- Becoming nervous or depressed when facing an extended period away from Facebook (more than a day)
- Getting irritated when someone or something interrupts your use of Facebook
- Checking Facebook while driving or walking across a street

CJG-Technology/Alamy

The state of flow is value enhancing, but can it facilitate addiction—such as Facebook addiction?

emotional expressiveness extent to which a consumer shows outward behavioral signs and otherwise reacts obviously to emotional experiences

emotional intelligence awareness of the emotions experienced in a given situation and the ability to control reactions to these emotions

Addictions like this are driven in part by a desire to achieve the state of flow where one escapes the real world and realizes high hedonic value.[31]

Highly involved shoppers sometimes achieve a flow experience. When this occurs, the consumer is more likely to spend time browsing, spend more money, make repeat purchases, and be more prone to impulse purchasing.[32] Online consumers can pursue a flow state while shopping; however, interruptions in Internet service, poor navigational clues, or slow page load times can inhibit the flow experience and lower both utilitarian and hedonic shopping value.[33] If the consumer achieves hedonic value, positive outcomes can result for both the consumer and the marketer. However, the consumer must be able to maintain control of the situation to avoid compulsive or addictive behaviors.

5-5b Emotional Expressiveness

Not all consumers express their emotions as obviously as others do. **Emotional expressiveness** represents the extent to which a consumer shows outward behavioral signs and otherwise reacts obviously to emotional experiences. The consumer with relatively high emotional expressiveness is likely to react in some way to outcomes that are unexpected. A bad poker player, for example, is unable to hide emotions from other players, so his reaction displays high emotional expressiveness.

Many who study emotions ask whether women are more emotional than men. Researchers do not provide a clear answer to this question. For instance, psychologists interested in studying the human experience of, and reaction to, disgust have conducted experiments in which subjects are exposed to films depicting either an actual amputation or a man being swarmed by cockroaches.[34] Male and female subjects report on average the same level of disgust while viewing the films. However, female respondents are more likely than males to react to the disgusting experience by leaving the room before the film is finished. Studies show similar emotional expression by females for other emotions beside disgust, both positive and negative.[35] Research suggests that when male and female consumers react with similar emotions, women express the emotions more noticeably.[36] Because of this, to the extent that a marketer can judge a consumer's emotional reaction, female consumers may prove more valuable in signaling poor or outstanding service than would male consumers.

5-5c Emotional Intelligence

Emotions can be useful in determining the most appropriate reaction to events. **Emotional intelligence** is a term used to capture one's awareness of the emotions experienced in a situation, and an ability to control reactions to these emotions. This includes awareness of the emotions experienced by the individual as well as an awareness and sympathy for the emotions experienced by others. Emotional intelligence (EI) is a multifaceted concept; Exhibit 5.7 illustrates EI components. High EI consumers are able to use awareness of emotions in decision making and are better able to manage their own emotions and exhibit self-control.[37]

In a marketing context, salespeople with high emotional intelligence are more effective in closing sales with consumers than are salespeople with low emotional intelligence.[38] Sales companies are increasingly realizing the benefits of employees with high EI. Similarly, high EI service employees in hospitality and healthcare industries tend to create more valuable experiences for customers. EI training is becoming commonplace as marketers attempt to get consumers to buy more and to be more satisfied with the things they buy.[39]

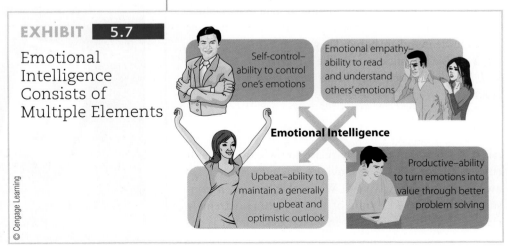

EXHIBIT 5.7

Emotional Intelligence Consists of Multiple Elements

© Cengage Learning

Self-control—ability to control one's emotions

Emotional empathy—ability to read and understand others' emotions

Emotional Intelligence

Upbeat—ability to maintain a generally upbeat and optimistic outlook

Productive—ability to turn emotions into value through better problem solving

Humorous ads like this one can create schema-based affect which helps shape a brand's meaning.

AP Photo/Skechers USA

5-5d What's Funny

Laughter is almost always a positive experience and can add a lot of value to one's life. Marketers often try to evoke laughter as a way of getting attention or creating positive affect that may become associated with a brand. What makes something funny? Generally, funny things cause some surprise or at least present some mental incongruity that one tries to resolve. Advertising appeals can be funny based on a comedic appeal, best represented by slapstick humor, such as Volkswagen's 2013 Super Bowl ad depicting a staid male office worker speaking happily to coworkers in a thick Jamaican accent, requiring little thought to evoke laughter. In contrast, clever appeals require consumers to think. A recent Sony Bravia ad consisted of thousands of bouncing tennis balls and people reaching to catch them, only to find they are really not there—tagline, Wimbledon on 3-D, as you've never seen it before! Comedic ads often push the boundaries of good taste, and consumers do not always "get" clever ads. Each appeal engages consumers differently. Comedic ads work best for common consumer products, whereas clever ads are usually more appropriate for higher-end, luxury, or high-involvement products. Consumers low in need for cognition are not as likely to respond well to clever ads as are other consumers.

5-6 Emotion, Meaning, and Schema-Based Affect

What is the relation between cognition and emotion? Intuitively, emotion and cognition seem so different that one might easily presume the two are completely independent. However, emotion and cognition are actually quite closely related. One can easily see the close relationship in the role that affect, mood, and emotion can play in signaling and developing meaning. This section focuses on the interplay between emotion and cognitive learning.

5-6a Semantic Wiring

In the previous chapter, we learned that in our memory, a network connects all concepts to other concepts. A concept such as a "toaster" is closely linked with a concept like "breakfast" but very remotely linked with another concept like "zoo." A consumer's ability to remember things about brands and products can be explained using theory developed around the principles of *semantic or associative* networks. Remember, all concepts are linked to all other concepts but some are linked strongly and others very weakly. It's difficult to put weak concepts together.

Although the term *semantic* refers to cognitive thought processes, the active processing and storage of knowledge depends on emotions in several ways. The general expression **"emotional effect on memory"** refers to relatively superior recall for information presented with mild affective content compared to similar information presented in an affectively neutral way.[40]

The implications for marketing are fairly direct. Marketing communications that present product information in a way that evokes mild levels of emotions will tend to be more effective in producing recall than communications that are affectively neutral.[41] Caution is needed in executing such communications because intense emotions are more complicated to deal with and can sometimes even distract consumers from the task of actually processing information. But Exhibit 5.8 illustrates the way that emotion shapes the meaning of a brand.

5-6b Mood-Congruent Recall

Many consumers can remember their first day of school, first airplane trip, or first visit to a theme park. In each case, products and brands are associated with the experience. Likewise, in each case, each event is associated with a fairly specific mood. For many consumers, apprehension fills the first day of school, the first airplane ride may be a blend of fear and excitement, and a visit to a theme park is associated with joy.

Autobiographical memories are memories of previous meaningful events in one's life. Consumers are more likely to recall autobiographical memories characterized by specific moods when the same mood occurs

emotional effect on memory relatively superior recall for information presented with mild affective content compared to similar information presented in an affectively neutral way

autobiographical memories cognitive representation of meaningful events in one's life

mood-congruent recall
consumers will remember information better when the mood they are currently in matches the mood they were in when originally exposed to the information

schema-based affect
emotions that become stored as part of the meaning for a category (a schema)

aesthetic labor effort put forth by employees in carefully managing their appearance as a requisite for performing their job well

again in the future.[42] Simply put, moods tend to match memories.

Mood-congruent recall means that to the extent that a consumer's mood can be controlled, their memories and evaluations can be influenced. Music is one tool useful in inducing moods. When music sets a mood, consumers will recall products associated with that mood more readily. In addition, consumers in good moods tend to evaluate products positively compared to consumers in bad moods, and vice versa.[43]

5-6c Nostalgia

Nostalgia affects consumers in a manner similar to that of mood-congruent recall and autobiographical memory. Recall that we introduced nostalgia in an earlier chapter as a yearning for the past motivated by the belief that previous times were somehow more pleasant. Nostalgia can motivate product purchases as consumers attempt to relive the pleasant feelings of the past. Music, toys, magazines, and movies are products that consumers report commonly buying in association with feelings of nostalgia.[44] The large number of advertisements that include popular "oldies" songs illustrate attempts at evoking nostalgic feelings. Further, consumers become more willing to make purchases when a nostalgic ad evokes or recaptures a childhood mood.

5-6d Schema-Based Affect

As we know from consumer information processing theory, knowledge of familiar things becomes organized in a cognitive unit of meaning known as a *schema*. A schema contains the knowledge of a brand, a product, or any concept. However, a schema is not a purely cognitive entity. Schemata are developed and reinforced through actual experience.

© Cengage Learning

EXHIBIT 5.8 Illustration of Emotion Aiding Learning

TOMS

AP Photos/PRNewsFoto/TOMS Shoes

For instance, we come to perceive what a car salesperson truly is based on our total experience with that category. Experience involves more than cognition. When we encounter a car salesperson or hear stories that involve car salespeople, we also experience some type of affect or emotion. These emotions become part of the meaning for a category in the form of **schema-based affect**.

Schema-based affect helps provide meaning and thus is another example of how affect and cognition are wired together. However, a consumer can actually experience schema-based affect once a schema becomes active. For example, a consumer who fears going to a dentist can actually experience true nervousness and apprehension simply by thinking about a visit to the dentist. This makes the dentist visit script active. Social schemata, or stereotypes, are characterized by specific schema-based affect. A politician schema usually evokes suspicion or skepticism. A seasoned airline pilot may create a sense of calm. Exhibit 5.9 displays examples of schema-based affect that can influence consumers' reactions to consumption experiences.

Aesthetic Labor

Aesthetic labor deals specifically with employees who most carefully manage their own personal appearance as a requisite to performing their job well, and fitting what managers see as the stereotype for their particular company's service. Many service employees perform aesthetic labor, including cosmetic representatives and fashion models for companies like L'Oréal and Victoria's Secret, and flight attendants and table servers for such companies like Korean Air and Hooters. The belief is that a specific appearance generates the appropriate emotional reaction in the consumer. These emotions promote behavior that can ultimately create value and potentially lead to loyalty.

Golden Pixels LLC/Shutterstock.com

EXHIBIT 5.9   Examples of Schema-Based Affect

Schema	Affect	Typical Consumer Reaction
Apple	Confidence, pride	Apple consumers feel a sense of superiority that comes along with the products.
Individual countries (United Kingdom, France, United States, Japan, Israel, China)	Consumers may have slightly different affect associated with each country	Consumers are less favorable toward products manufactured in countries for which that consumer's schema evokes negative affect.
Dentist	Anxiety	Consumers avoid scheduling an appointment and cringe in anticipation.
Puppies	Tenderness, warmth	Products depicted with puppies benefit from the warm feelings.
Champagne	Anticipation, excitement	The product is associated with parties, celebrations, rituals, and joyful good times.
Stereotypes	Each stereotype evokes slightly different affect	The affect associated with the stereotype can cause consumers to be more or less willing to approach and may alter information processing.

© Cengage Learning 2015

5-6e Self-Conscious Emotions

Getting laughed at can be painful. Marketers sometimes execute communications designed to take advantage of consumers' natural tendency to avoid ridicule. Apple advertising often tries to evoke humor at the expense of PC users. Other brands emphasize how embarrassed one should feel for having less than pearly-white teeth, body odor (BO), bad hair, ED, a bad figure, and on and on. These appeals work because they cause consumers

Feels Like Work!

By now, it's clear to see that emotions play a huge role in shaping the value of consumer experiences. Emotion isn't all fun, though—particularly not for employees who deal with consumers. Service management is a lot about managing emotion. Consider the health care provider dealing with a seriously injured or ill consumer. The ability to manage the patient's emotion is critical to a successful service encounter. In a different way, imagine the role that retail employees play in dealing with consumers concerned about their appearance and overall self-image, or Disney cast members who try to make sure customers experience Disney magic. Often, service providers in jobs like these perform work that falls into the category of emotional labor. They literally labor to not only sympathize with consumer emotions but to try to effect changes in their emotions. Emotional

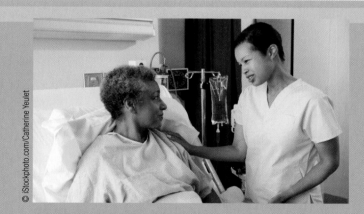

© iStockphoto.com/Catherine Yeulet

labor can indeed be very stressful and take a long-term toll on an employee's well-being. Effective management of emotion in consumption environments involves concepts like emotional intelligence and aesthetic labor, all discussed in this chapter.

Sources: For more on emotional labor, see K. H. Chu, M. A. Baker, and S. K. Murrmann, "When We Are Onstage, We Smile: The Effects of Emotional Labor on Employee Work Outcomes," *International Journal of Hospitality Management* 31 (2012): 906–15.

self-conscious emotions specific emotions that result from some evaluation or reflection of one's own behavior, including pride, shame, guilt, and embarrassment

emotional contagion extent to which an emotional display by one person influences the emotional state of a bystander

emotional labor effort put forth by service workers who have to overtly manage their own emotional displays as part of the requirements of the job

to appraise themselves in some way and play on any resulting negative self-conscious emotions.[45] Self-conscious emotions result from some evaluation or reflection of one's own behavior—which can include both actions and failures to act. **Self-conscious emotions** include pride, embarrassment, guilt, regret, shame, and hope. Consumers experiencing negative self-conscious emotions can perceive not only the need to rectify some problem, but also the need to restore their self-esteem.

The feeling of guilt can play a role in CB in many ways. Consumers may feel guilty for the way they treat a service provider. For instance, a consumer using the same hair stylists for several years may feel guilty for saving a few dollars and going to a different person to get a haircut. Consumers sometimes feel self-conscious when they see consumers who are not as wealthy and lack buying power. In all these instances, a consumer may perform some counterbalancing behavior such as recommending the old service provider to others or making a charitable contribution.

5-6f Emotional Contagion

Are emotions contagious? This is the idea behind **emotional contagion**, which represents the extent to which an emotional display by one person influences the emotional state of a bystander. Consumers who perceive other consumers or employees surrounding them as either happy or sad may experience a corresponding change in actual happiness or sadness themselves. Emotional contagion means marketing managers who have a mantra of "service with a smile" may have a good reason to do so. When service providers maintain an expression signaling positive affect (service with a smile), consumers report higher incidences of positive affect themselves.[46]

Emotional Labor

Emotional contagion relates closely to another topic, emotional labor. **Emotional labor** is performed by service workers who must overtly manage their own emotional displays as part of the requirements of the job. As an example, when airline flight attendants themselves feel angry, the requirements of their job ask them to hide their true feelings and express more positive emotions. Practically all service employees must perform some emotional labor, including professional service providers such as physicians. The long-term impact of emotional labor on psychological well-being may not be positive unless the employees learn how to cope with the emotional conflict.

Can Money Buy Love?

Good feelings create hedonic value. Keep that in mind, especially when considering the role of price. Prices evoke emotions. To understand the way consumers respond to various value propositions, the CB student must consider emotions. Consider two customers shopping for business clothes. One buys suit A for $300 and suit B for $200. A second consumer buys the same two suits but the price for suit A is $400 and suit B is half price with the purchase of suit A. Both pay $500 and get the same two suits—even deal, right?? Well, it turns out that the second consumer extracts more value out of the deal because of the hedonic response to the promotion. The increased happiness at the half-price suit more than compensates

for paying a higher price for suit A. Compulsive buyers also respond to price promotions emotionally but, despite some issues in controlling the amount of purchase, they turn out to be very price aware and price conscious. So, if you need some price advice, ask a compulsive consumer.

Sources: S. Yoon and P. T. Vargas, "Feeling Happier When Paying More: Dysfunctional Counterfactual Thinking in Consumer Affect," *Psychology & Marketing* 27 (December 2010): 1075–1100. M. Kukar-Kinney, N. M. Ridgway, and K. B. Monroe, "The Role of Price in the Behavior and Purchase Decisions of Compulsive Buyers," *Journal of Retailing* 88 (2012): 63–71.

© iStockphoto.com/Neustockimages

Flight attendants practice emotional labor with the hope that good feelings will be contagious.

that they have seen others handling. However, in an interesting twist, research shows that through a type of emotional contagion process, a product's value can actually increase after a consumer sees the product handled by an attractive member of the opposite sex.[47] Instead of avoiding that product, the consumer will actually seek it out.

product contamination
refers to the diminished positive feelings someone has about a product because another consumer has handled the product

Product Contamination

Picture this. A consumer sees a price reduction on a shirt he has wanted for a long time. He buys it, but when he gets home and begins to put it on, he realizes it no longer has the pins and cardboard backing that should come with a new shirt. "Has somebody already purchased this and returned it?" he asks himself. All of a sudden, the value in wearing the new shirt is diminished because the idea that someone else may have worn the shirt creates uneasiness. **Product contamination** refers to the fact that consumers feel uneasy about buying things that others have previously touched. Supermarket consumers can be seen searching the back of the shelf for an untouched package or avoiding produce

Study Tools

Located at the back of the textbook

☐ Rip out Chapter in Review Card

Located at www.cengagebrain.com

☐ Review Key Terms Flashcards (print or online)

☐ Download audio summaries to review on the go

☐ Complete practice quizzes to prepare for tests

☐ Play "Beat the Clock" to master concepts

☐ Watch video on Jordan's Furniture for a real company example

WHAT DO YOU THINK?
WHAT OTHERS HAVE THOUGHT

	①	②	③	④	⑤	⑥	⑦
Strongly disagree	Disagree	Somewhat disagree	Neither agree nor disagree	Somewhat agree	Agree	Strongly agree

(y-axis: 0, 5, 10, 15, 20, 25, 30, 35)

I do not allow emotions to control my behavior.

Only 41% of respondents express some level of disagreement, 52% express some level of agreement, and 7% neither agree nor disagree. Are some consumers able to feel emotions but not react to them? Well, some consumers think so.

Galyna Andrushko/Shutterstock.com

Individual difference

variables help explain why some consumers focus more highly on value than do others.

WHAT DO YOU THINK?

My personality can easily be seen in the products that I buy.

STRONGLY DISAGREE   STRONGLY AGREE

VISIT COURSEMATE AT WWW.CENGAGEBRAIN.COM

Personality, Lifestyles, and the Self-Concept

This chapter focuses on consumer personality, lifestyles, and the self-concept. These concepts are often included when referring to **individual difference variables**, which are descriptions of how individual consumers differ according to specific traits or patterns of behavior.[1] Personality, lifestyles, and the self-concept all have several applications to both consumer research and marketing practice. Marketing managers are especially interested in identifying consumer characteristics that are associated with the likelihood of purchasing products. Concepts like personality, lifestyle, and self-concept help to describe these likelihoods. Demographics are also important, and we include this issue in our discussion. These concepts have been studied for many years and there are several ways to approach each subject area.

6-1 Personality and Consumer Behavior

Personality has been studied for many years, and the term has been defined in a number of different ways. We define **personality** as the totality of thoughts, emotions, intentions, tendencies, and behaviors that a person exhibits consistently as he or she adapts to the environment.[2] This definition highlights the *cognitive* (thoughts), *affective* (emotions), *motivational* (intentions), and *behavioral* (behaviors) aspects that are central to the study of personality. Personality is but one characteristic that helps explain why a particular behavior, for example listening to the band Kings of Leon, provides great value to one consumer but none to another.

Personality exhibits a number of distinct qualities, including:

1. *Personality is unique to an individual.* Personality helps distinguish consumers based on the specific characteristics each exhibits. Consumers differ in personalities, although some characteristics, or traits, may be shared across individuals.

After studying this chapter, the student should be able to:

6-1 Define personality and know how various approaches to studying personality can be applied to consumer behavior.

6-2 Discuss major traits that have been examined in consumer research.

6-3 Understand why lifestyles, psychographics, and demographics are important to the study of consumer behavior.

6-4 Comprehend the role of the self-concept in consumer behavior.

6-5 Understand the concept of self-congruency and how it applies to consumer behavior issues.

---

individual difference variables descriptions of how individual consumers differ according to specific trait patterns of behavior

personality totality of thoughts, emotions, intentions, tendencies, and behaviors that a person exhibits consistently as he or she adapts to the environment

aggregation approach
approach to studying personality in which behavior is assessed at a number of points in time

psychoanalytic approach to personality
approach to personality research, advocated by Sigmund Freud, that suggests personality results from a struggle between inner motives and societal pressures to follow rules and expectations

id the personality component in psychoanalytic theory that focuses on pleasure-seeking motives and immediate gratification

pleasure principle
principle found in psychoanalytic theory that describes the factor that motivates pleasure-seeking behavior within the id

superego component in psychoanalytic theory that works against the id by motivating behavior that matches the expectations and norms of society

ego component in psychoanalytic theory that attempts to balance the struggle between the superego and the id

reality principle the principle in psychoanalytic theory under which the ego attempts to satisfy the id within societal constraints

2. *Personality can be conceptualized as a combination of specific traits or characteristics.* Like all consumers, your overall personality is really a combination of many stable characteristics, or traits. In fact, for many psychologists, personality psychology deals exclusively with the study of human traits.[3]

3. *Personality traits are relatively stable and interact with situations to influence behavior.* Personality traits are expected to remain consistent across situations. However, consumer researchers realize the importance of situational influencers, and the combined influence of situations and traits greatly influences specific behaviors (this is referred to as an *interaction* between the person and the situation).[4] To illustrate, imagine how an unstable person might act when she has to wait a long time at a restaurant.

4. *Specific behaviors can vary across time.* Simply knowing a consumer possesses a specific trait does not allow us to predict a particular behavior. For example, knowing that a consumer is "materialistic" does not allow us to predict the exact type of product the person may buy. For this reason, personality researchers often advocate an **aggregation approach** in which behaviors and tendencies are measured over time.

As we have mentioned, marketing managers are particularly interested in how consumers differ according to their personalities. Consistent patterns of thoughts, emotions, intentions, and behaviors can signal the need for individualized marketing campaigns, and today's marketers are becoming quite adept at individualizing messages. To understand how personalities differ across consumers, it is important to begin with a description of the various approaches to studying the concept. Here we focus on two popular approaches: the psychoanalytic approach and the trait approach.

6-1a Psychoanalytic Approach to Personality

According to the famous psychologist Sigmund Freud, human behavior is influenced by an inner struggle between various systems within the personality system.[5] His approach, commonly referred to as the **psychoanalytic approach to personality**, is applicable to both motivation and personality inquiry. Freud's approach highlights the importance of unconscious mental processes in influencing behavior.

For Freud, the human personality consists of three important components: the *id*, the *superego*, and the *ego*. The **id** focuses on pleasure-seeking and immediate gratification. It operates on a **pleasure principle** that motivates a person to focus on maximizing pleasure and minimizing pain. One's id, therefore, focuses on hedonic value. Indeed, a key concept in the id is the *libido*. The libido represents a drive for sexual pleasure, although some researchers view it in slightly different ways. The **superego** works against the id by motivating behavior that matches societal norms and expectations, much like the consumer's conscience. The **ego** focuses on resolving the conflicts between the id and the superego. The ego works largely in accordance with the **reality principle**. Under this principle, the ego seeks to satisfy the id within the constraints of society. As such, the ego attempts to balance the desires of the id with the constraints of, and expectations found in, the superego.

> Freud's approach highlights the importance of unconscious mental processes in influencing behavior.

Luis Andrade/Shutterstock.com

Psychoanalytic Approach and Motivation Research

In the early days of consumer research, researchers applied psychoanalytic tools to try to identify explanations for behavior. This was known as the **motivational research era**. Consumer researchers in this era utilized tools such as *depth interviews* and *focus groups* to improve their understanding of inner motives and needs.[6] Here, researchers used depth interviews to explore deep-seated motivations by asking consumers a series of probing questions.

Suppose a researcher is studying a consumer who enjoys Live Action Role Play (LARP). The researcher might ask the following probing questions:

- "How do you feel when you are LARPing?"
- "What does it mean to you to feel this way?"
- "What kinds of things do you think about when you participate in a LARP?"
- "What would you do if you could no longer do any LARPing?

A LARP fan might reveal that role playing is a way to escape and that escape is necessary to combat the stresses of everyday life. Participating in experiences that offer fantasy and escape, like LARP, provides consumers with hedonic value. From this example we can see how motivational research can uncover a number of consumer behaviors related to fantasy and escape.

In general, the motivational research era proved disappointing because it did not spawn any compelling, practical consumer behavior theories or guidelines for marketing actions. Nonetheless, Freud clearly influenced the study of personality and consumer behavior, and researchers remain interested in deep-seated motivations.[7] In fact, the saying "Sex sells!" may be tied to the Freudian and motivational approaches.

The Advertising Archives

Does this ad appeal to some deeply held motivation?

6-1b Trait Approach to Personality

While the psychoanalytic approach helped set the groundwork for much of consumer personality research, the **trait approach to personality** has received significant attention over the past few decades and many consumer researchers focus on this approach today. A **trait** is defined as a distinguishable characteristic that describes one's tendency to act in a relatively consistent manner.

Not surprisingly, there are multiple approaches available for consumer researchers. Here, we discuss the differences between nomothetic and idiographic approaches, and between single-versus multi-trait approaches.

Nomothetic versus Idiographic Approaches

The nomothetic perspective and the idiographic perspective can be distinguished as follows.[8] The **nomothetic perspective** is a "variable-centered" approach that focuses on particular variables, or traits, that exist across a number of consumers. The goal of this perspective is to find common personality traits that can be studied across people.

An example helps to explain the nomothetic approach. Consider college student Nick. Nick's friends notice that he is very competitive in all that he does. He hates losing, pays attention to how he compares to others, and is vocal about his abilities. Of course, many other people can be described in this way. Here, the focus is on the competitiveness trait, and it is used to describe the characteristics of a number of consumers. Competitive

motivational research era era in consumer research that focused heavily on psychoanalytic approaches

trait approach to personality approaches in personality research that focus on specific consumer traits as motivators of various consumer behaviors

trait distinguishable characteristic that describes one's tendency to act in a relatively consistent manner

nomothetic perspective variable-centered approach to personality that focuses on particular traits that exist across a number of people

idiographic perspective
approach to personality that focuses on understanding the complexity of each individual consumer

single-trait approach
approach in trait research wherein the focus is on one particular trait

multiple-trait approach
approach in trait research wherein the focus remains on combinations of traits

consumers would represent a market segment for marketers selling products that are promoted largely on image.

The **idiographic perspective** focuses on the total person and the uniqueness of his psychological makeup. Attention is not placed on individual traits or how they can be studied across multiple consumers. Rather, the focus is on understanding the complexity of each individual consumer. Some researchers today focus on what is referred to as consumer introspections and how they explain behavior. *Consumer Introspection Theory* views the consumer herself as the research instrument and examines how her introspections can explain things like product involvement and choice.[9] Introspections can reveal much about the inner motivations and psychology of consumers. Although this approach has been around for several years, it has recently gained significant research attention.

The trait approach takes a nomothetic approach to personality. That is, the trait approach assumes that the human personality can be described as a combination of traits that can be studied across consumers. From this perspective, individuals can be described by using various trait descriptors.

Single-Trait and Multiple-Trait Approaches

We can further distinguish between single-trait and multi-trait approaches to consumer research. With the **single-trait approach**, the focus of the researcher is on one particular trait. Here, researchers can learn more about the trait and how it affects behavior. For example, a researcher may want to investigate how a consumer's tendency to be productive affects his leisure activities, such as what he does on a family vacation.[10]

With the **multiple-trait approach**, combinations of traits are examined and the total effect of the collection of traits is considered. Here, the researcher is interested in trait scores on numerous traits as potential predictors of consumer behavior. The prediction of individual behavior tends to be stronger with the multiple-trait approach.[11] However, both the single- and multiple-trait approaches have been used extensively in consumer research.

6-2 Major Traits Examined in Consumer Research

To say that there are many traits that can be studied would be a serious understatement! To illustrate, researchers Gordon Allport and Henry Odbert identified nearly 18,000 names for human characteristics found in Webster's Dictionary. And that was in 1936![12] Many trait names are simple descriptions that are used in everyday life. For example, we commonly use terms like "talkative" or "social" to describe people. Other trait names are very specific and originate in the psychology literature.

6-2a Many Traits Examined in CB

When there are thousands of ways to describe people it obviously becomes difficult to know exactly what trait should be examined. Although numerous traits have received research attention, we will discuss only a handful of important traits found in consumer research. We emphasize that the traits here represent only a very small sampling of the many traits that could be included. We discuss value consciousness, materialism, innovativeness, complaint proneness, competitiveness, and self-monitoring.

Value Consciousness

As we have stated throughout this text, value is at the heart of consumer behavior. Although all consumers

Personality can be studied in many ways

© iStockphoto.com/franckreporter

ultimately seek value, some consumers are more highly focused on value than are others. As such, value consciousness is often studied as a trait. **Value consciousness** represents the tendency for consumers to focus on maximizing what is received from a transaction as compared to what is given.

Research reveals that value consciousness is an important concept in consumer behavior. For example, value consciousness underlies tendencies to perform behaviors like redeeming coupons.[13] Value-conscious consumers can be expected to pay close attention to the resources that they devote to transactions and to the benefits that they receive. In today's turbulent economy, value consciousness is an important trait to study.

Materialism

Materialism refers to the extent to which material goods are important in a consumer's life. Most Western cultures are generally thought of as being relatively materialistic. However, within each culture, the degree to which each individual is materialistic varies. Studying this trait has been very popular among consumer researchers, and numerous studies have examined the impact of materialism on various consumer behaviors.

Materialism is seen as consisting of three separate dimensions:[14]

- *Possessiveness.* A tendency to retain control and ownership over possessions
- *Nongenerosity.* An unwillingness to share with others
- *Envy.* Resentment that arises as a result of another's belongings and a desire to acquire similar possessions

Highly materialistic consumers tend to be possessive, nongenerous, and envious of other's possessions. These consumers view possessions as a means of achieving happiness and they may hold onto possessions as long as possible.[15] Research even indicates that materialistic people establish strong bonds with products in order to ease fears regarding their own mortality![16] Products can be a real source of comfort for materialistic consumers.

Interestingly, consumers today commonly bring many of their favorite material possessions into the workplace. Personal possessions in the workplace can produce calm feelings and stabilize an employee's sense of self.[17] In this way,

© iStockphoto.com/berekin

material possessions play an important part in self-expression. That is, material possessions help consumers express who they think they are, and even who they would like to be.[18]

Materialism tends to differ among generations, with lower materialism scores typically found among older consumers.[19] Indeed, younger consumers have long been thought of as relatively materialistic. A change in the prevalence of materialism does appear to be occurring, however. Although the U.S. culture is widely viewed as materialistic, research suggests that consumers are beginning to "downshift." Downshifting refers to a conscious decision to reduce one's material consumption. This may be a positive development as high levels of materialism can adversely affect debt levels and personal relationships.[20] The "great recession" also contributed to a growth in consumer *frugality*, or the extent to which consumers exhibit restraint when purchasing and using material goods.[21]

Innovativeness

Consumer **innovativeness** refers to the degree to which a consumer is open to new ideas and quick to adopt, buying new products, services, or experiences soon after they are introduced. Innovative consumers are also generally dynamic and curious, and they are often young, educated, and relatively affluent.[22] Obviously, consumer innovativeness is an important trait for marketers to consider when introducing new products.

Although researchers do not necessarily agree on the extent to which innovativeness is exhibited across product categories, a consumer with a strong degree of innovativeness may be expected to be innovative in a number of situations. For example, innovativeness has been shown to relate to a number of behaviors, including new product adoption, novelty seeking,

value consciousness the extent to which consumers tend to maximize what they receive from a transaction as compared to what they give

materialism extent to which material goods have importance in a consumer's life

innovativeness degree to which an individual is open to new ideas and tends to be relatively early in adopting new products, services, or experiences

need for cognition refers to the degree to which consumers enjoy engaging in effortful cognitive information processing

competitiveness enduring tendency to strive to be better than others

information seeking, and online shopping.[23]

Need for Cognition

Need for cognition refers to the degree to which consumers tend to engage in effortful cognitive information processing.[24] Consumers who have a high degree of this trait tend to think carefully about products, problems, and even marketing messages. For example, research has shown that consumers with a high need for cognition tend to be influenced heavily by the quality of the arguments in an advertisement. Conversely, consumers with low need for cognition tend to be influenced by things like an endorser's attractiveness and cues that are not central to a message.[25]

Research also indicates that the effect of humorous advertising is impacted by need for cognition. Humorous ads tend to lead to more positive consumer attitudes and purchase intentions for consumers who have a low degree of need for cognition. Studies also indicate that the need for cognition trait influences consumers' reactions to ads with sexual content. For example, consumers with a low degree of need for cognition have exhibited more positive attitudes and purchase intentions toward brands that are advertised using sexual imagery than consumers with a high degree of need for cognition.[26]

Competitiveness

The **competitiveness** trait may be defined as an enduring tendency to strive to be better than others. The predominance of competitiveness in consumer society is easy to see, and the use of competitive themes in marketing messages is widespread.

A competitive person is generally easy to identify; research reveals that the trait often emerges in the following ways:[27]

- When a consumer is directly competing with others. Competitive cheer competitions like

---

A Sisyphean Effort

Are you a maximizer or a satisficer? What does this even mean?

Maximizers consistently focus on making the best product choices possible. Satisficers simply try to make decisions that are good enough.

Maximizing tendencies impact how consumers think and how they integrate information that is learned from previous experience. And while we might expect that maximizers would focus heavily on information learned from previous product experiences, researchers Francois Carrillat, Daniel Ladik, and Renaud Legoux find that they don't rely on past experiences like satisficers do. Rather, maximizers continue to consider previous alternatives even if those options were less than satisfying, thereby minimizing the value of the previously learned information. The researchers label this phenomenon the "Sisyphus" effect, named for the Greek god who was condemned for all eternity to continually roll a boulder up a hill. Each time the boulder would reach the top, it would roll back down and Sisyphus would have to start over again. Much like the Greek god, maximizers "start over" each time they have to make a decision.

While scholars might not agree on whether maximizing is truly a personality trait, it does represent a tendency to act in a consistent manner. If you are a maximizer, that boulder will probably start to get very heavy!

Sources: F. Carrillat, D. Ladik, and R. Legoux, "When the Decision Ball Keeps Rolling: An Investigation of the Sisyphus Effect Among Maximizing Consumers," *Marketing Letters* 22, no. 3 (2011): 283–96; T. G. Chowdhury, S. Ratneshwar, and P. Mohanty, "The Time Harried Shopper: Exploring the Differences Between Maximizers and Satisficers," *Marketing Letters* 20, no. 2 (2009): 155–67; B. Schwartz, A. Ward, J. Monterosso, S. Lyubomirsky, K. White, and D.R. Lehman, "Maximizing versus Satisficing: Happiness is a Matter of Choice," *Journal of Personality and Social Psychology* 83, no. 5 (2002): 1178–97; H. A. Simon, *Models of Man, Social and Rational: Mathematical Essays on Rational Human Behavior*, New York: Wiley, 1957.

America's Best, Jamfest, and Cheersport are growing in popularity.

- When a consumer enjoys winning vicariously through the efforts of others (as when we enjoy seeing our team win). Sports fans often *bask in reflected glory* (BIRG) when their team wins. This means that they will wear team apparel and display team merchandise when their team is successful (As researchers point out, you hardly ever hear them say things like "They're number one!"[28]). Interestingly, fans may also CORF. That is, they *cut off reflected failure* by hiding their association with losing teams.

- When a consumer attempts to display superiority over others by openly flaunting exclusive products, especially publicly visible products. The term *conspicuous consumption* describes a tendency of the wealthy to flaunt their material possessions as a way of displaying their social class. Products ranging from automobiles to jewelry help to signal a consumer's status and can be used to convey images of consumer "superiority."

Self-Monitoring

Self-monitoring represents the tendency for consumers to observe and control behavior in ways that agree with social cues and influence.[29] High self-monitors care deeply about what others think and say about their behaviors and they care much about how they present themselves in social situations. Low self-monitors are not sensitive to the opinions of others. Evidence reveals that high self-monitors are influenced by advertising messages that provide information about how products will affect their image. Low self-monitors tend to care more about the functionality of products and tend to think more positively about generic versus brand-name products.[30]

Other Traits Found in Consumer Research

It should be emphasized that the preceding traits represent only a small fraction of the many traits that have been investigated in consumer research. Exhibit 6.1 highlights other traits that are often studied. There are many, many more!

The Five-Factor Model Approach

One of the most popular multiple-trait approaches found in both personality psychology and consumer research is the **five-factor model** (FFM) approach.[31] Numerous studies have examined the influence of the traits in the FFM on a wide range of behaviors, both inside and outside the field of consumer research. The FFM proposes that five dominant traits are found in the human personality, including:

1. Extroversion
2. Agreeableness
3. Openness to Experience (also referred to as *creativity*)
4. Stability (or Instability; sometimes referred to clinically as *neuroticism*)
5. Conscientiousness

Extroverted consumers are outgoing and talkative with others. Agreeable consumers are kindhearted to others and sympathetic. Creative consumers are imaginative and enjoy new ideas. Stable consumers tend to be able to control their emotions and avoid mood swings. Conscientious consumers are careful, orderly, and precise. These traits are presented in Exhibit 6.2.

As we have stated, the FFM approach is a multiple-trait approach, meaning that a consumer's personality is conceptualized as a *combination* of these traits and that each consumer will vary on the respective traits. For example, Joey might possess relatively strong degrees of extroversion, agreeableness, and openness, but he

self-monitoring tendency for consumers to observe and control behavior in ways that agree with social cues and influence.

five-factor model multiple-trait perspective that proposes that the human personality consists of five traits: agreeableness, extroversion, openness to experience (or creativity), conscientiousness, and neuroticism (or stability)

EXHIBIT 6.1

Examples of Other Traits in Consumer Research

© Cengage Learning

Frugality	The tendency of a consumer to exhibit restraint when facing purchases and using resources.
Trait Superstition	A tendency to follow superstitions and superstitious beliefs.
Trait Impulsivity	A tendency to buy products and engage in experiences on impulse.
Bargaining Proneness	The tendency for a consumer to engage in bargaining behaviors when making purchases.
Trait Vanity	The tendency for consumers to take excessive pride in themselves, including their appearance and accomplishments.

hierarchical approaches to personality approaches to personality inquiry that assume that personality traits exist at varying levels of abstraction

may not be very stable or conscientious. By examining consumers across the five dimensions of the FFM, we gain an expanded view of how multiple traits influence specific consumer behaviors.

The FFM approach is indeed popular with consumer researchers, and the traits found in the FFM have been shown to impact consumer behaviors such as complaining, bargaining, banking, compulsive shopping, mass media consumption, and commitment to buying environmentally friendly products.

Even though the FFM has proved useful for presenting an integrative approach to personality, the model is not universally accepted by all researchers. In fact, there have been some lively debates regarding its usefulness.

Hierarchical Approaches to Personality Traits

If you are beginning to think that there are so many different approaches to trait psychology theory that it is hard to keep them all straight, you are not alone! Organizing all of these traits is one of the goals of what are known as **hierarchical approaches to personality.**

Hierarchical approaches begin with the assumption that personality traits exist at varying levels of abstraction. That is, some traits are specific (bargaining proneness), and others are more broad (extroversion). Specific traits refer to tendencies to behave in very well-defined situations. For example, a bargaining-prone consumer will bargain when shopping for products. Here, the situation is very specific. Broad traits refer to tendencies to behave across many different situations. For example, an extroverted consumer may be very outgoing when with friends, when in a restaurant, or when discussing a group project with classmates. As a general statement, specific traits tend to be better predictors of individual behaviors than broad traits. A number of researchers have argued for the existence of these hierarchies, with

EXHIBIT 6.2 Five-Factor Model

Personality Trait	Description
Extroversion	Talkative, outgoing
Agreeableness	Kindhearted, sympathetic
Openness to Experience	Creative, open to new ideas, imaginative
Stability	Even-keeled, avoids mood swings
Conscientiousness	Precise, efficient, organized

Source: Based on R. R. McCrae and P. T. Costa, *Personality in Adulthood: A Five-Factor Theory Perspective,* 2nd ed. (New York: Guilford, 2005).

many suggesting that abstract traits influence more specific traits in a hierarchical fashion.[32]

Final Thoughts on the Trait Approach

The trait approach in consumer research is very popular today in large part due to its ability to objectively assign a personality trait score, from a survey for example, to a consumer. In this way, the approach has an advantage over the psychoanalytic approach in which personality dimensions are assigned based on the psychologist's subjective interpretation. We should emphasize, however, that the trait approach is not without criticism. Exhibit 6.3 reveals a number of criticisms that have been leveled against trait research.[33]

Personology

We discussed previously that personality and motivation are closely related topics. A relatively new approach to researching consumers, which combines personality theory and motivation, is the "personology" approach. This approach allows consumer researchers to better understand the uniqueness of the individual consumer by combining information on traits, goals, and even consumer life stories.[34]

As you can see, many ways to view the human personality exist, and several different approaches to exploring the influence of personality on consumer behavior

EXHIBIT 6.3 Criticisms of the Trait Approach

- Personality traits have not traditionally been shown to be strong predictors of consumer behavior relative to other explanatory variables.
- So many personality traits exist that researchers often select traits for study without any logical theoretical basis.
- Personality traits are sometimes hard to measure, and researchers often use measures with questionable validity.
- Personality inventories used to measure traits are often meant for use on specific populations, but they are frequently applied to practically any consumer group.
- Researchers often measure and use traits in ways not originally intended.
- Consumer traits generally do not predict specific brand selections.

© Cengage Learning

brand personality collection of human characteristics that can be associated with a brand

brand personality appeal a product's ability to appeal to consumers based on the human characteristics associated with it

EXHIBIT 6.4 Brand Personality Dimensions

Personality Trait	Description	Example
Competence	Responsible, reliable, dependable	Maytag—"Depend on Us"
Excitement	Daring, spirited	Monster Energy —"Unleash the Beast"
Ruggedness	Tough, strong	Ford Trucks—"Built Ford Tough"
Sincerity	Honest, genuine	Wrangler Jeans— "Genuine. Wrangler"
Sophistication	Glamorous, charming	Cartier jewelry— "Brilliance, Elegance, Exuberance"

Source: Based on Jennifer Aaker, "Dimensions of Brand Personality," *Journal of Marketing Research* (August 1997): 347–56.

have been used. Personality inquiry, while controversial and not without limitations, continues to be a fruitful avenue of research for consumer researchers.

6-2b Brand Personality

Do brands have personalities? This question may sound a bit strange at first, but upon reflection, consumers do describe brands with human-like qualities. How would you describe the personality of CNN news? How is Spencer's different from JCP?

Marketing managers and consumer researchers alike are very interested in the "personalities" of products. **Brand personality** refers to human characteristics that can be associated with a brand.[35] Brand personalities can be described across five dimensions including competence, excitement, ruggedness, sincerity, and sophistication. These dimensions are described in Exhibit 6.4.

Brand personalities represent opportunities for companies to differentiate their products. Accordingly, a brand's personality may be viewed as a part of its overall image.[36] Brand personalities also provide marketers with opportunities to build strong brand relationships with consumers, especially when they have an understanding of their customer's personality.[37] A well-known Old Spice campaign says "Smell Like a Man, Man," signifying how the products relate to this overall image. Hallmark cards may be seen as sincere and trustworthy. Guess is considered to be sophisticated clothing and Mercedes-Benz is a sophisticated automobile. Recent research indicates that the brand personality concept applies to sports teams as well.[37a]

Formation of Brand Personality

Many factors contribute to the development of a brand's personality.[38] You can infer certain qualities from a product's category. For example, if you hear the name *Sampson, Whitten, and Taylor* and find out that it is a law firm, you may develop an idea that the firm is serious, professional, and competent. In order for the perceived personality to match the intended personality that is promoted, managers should be sure to present a strong concept, differentiate the product well, create credible messages about the brand, involve the consumer to a high degree, and generate a positive attitude toward the brand.[38a]

Brand Personality Appeal

The brand personality concept has proven to be valuable for both consumer researchers and marketers alike. However, current research reveals that understanding a brand's personality is not enough. Rather, the appeal of the brand's personality should be considered. **Brand personality appeal** refers to a brand's ability to appeal to consumers based on the human characteristics

The Advertising Archives

A brand's personality is an important part of its image

Fashionistas

Are you a person who lives and breathes fashion? Do you follow the latest trends in the fashion industry and see fashion as a form of art? Do you pay close attention to your body image and consider your body to be a canvas for fashion expression? If so, you might be what some would call a *fashionista*.

© iStockphoto.com/Izabela Habur

Fashionistas are very fashionable by definition. They pay close attention to fashion knowledge and sensibility and tend to present themselves with confidence. Curiously, they don't necessarily flaunt fashion; rather, they embrace it and see it as an important part of who they are.

Fashionistas have become quite popular in consumer culture. There are blogs and websites devoted to them, there are advertisements that target them, and there is even a line of Barbie® dolls known as the Fashionistas. While consumers have followed fashion trends for generations, fashionistas take it to a whole new level. Fashion designers are keenly aware of the fashionistas because they can be influential in persuading other consumers regarding fashion decisions. Accordingly, they have become an important part of many companies' marketing strategies. Identifying and communicating with fashionistas can be an effective marketing strategy.

Sources: Krystine Sykes, "The Definition of a True Fashionista," October 27, 2008, http://voices.yahoo.com/the-definition-true-fashionista-2065453.html, accessed April 10, 2012. "What Is a Fashionista?" n.d., http://www.wisegeek.com/what-is-a-fashionista.htm, accessed April 11, 2012. Marlene Montanez, "What the Heck Is a Fashionista?" n.d., http://stylesizzle.com/fashion/define-fashionista, accessed April 11, 2012.

associated with it.[39] A brand's personality should be perceived as having strong degrees of *favorability*, *originality*, and *clarity*. When consumers view a brand's personality in these terms, they are more likely to purchase the brand in question.

Personality and Brand Relationships

The brand personality concept is especially important when one considers that consumers, to a certain extent, have relationships with brands, and that personality traits are important in the formation and maintenance of these relationships.[40] To illustrate, Coca-Cola's sincere and traditional personality enables the Coca-Cola Company to easily remind consumers that the brand has always been and will always be a part of their lives. In fact, "Always Coca-Cola" is one of Coke's best-known advertising campaigns. A clearly defined brand personality and a strong brand personality appeal help with consumer-brand relationship formation.

The concept of consumer–brand relationships has received considerable research attention, and several factors help indicate the level of relationship between a consumer and a brand. Consumer researcher Susan Fournier proposes that the overall quality of such relationships can be explained by:

- **Love and Passion.** A consumer may have such strong feelings about a brand that they actually describe it with the term *love*. A consumer may say, "I love my Chi flat iron" or "I love 'Very Sexy' cologne." Service employees play a part in the formation of brand love.[40a]

- **Self-Connection.** Brands may help to express some central component of a consumer's identity. Research indicates that the correct match between consumer and brand personality leads to higher overall satisfaction.[41]

- **Commitment.** In a strong consumer–brand relationship, consumers are very committed to their brands and feel very loyal to them. Miss Me clothing owners are well-known for their commitment to the brand.

- **Interdependence.** Consumer–brand relationships may be marked by interdependence between the product and consumer. This can be described in terms of the frequency of use, the diversity of brand-related situations, and the intensity of usage. Consumers are often reminded that "Like a good neighbor, State Farm is there."

- **Intimacy.** Strong relationships between consumers and brands can be described as intimate. Deep-seated needs and desires of consumers can be tied directly to specific brands. For example, a need for intimacy and passion can be directly tied to a specific brand of perfume or Victoria's Secret apparel.

- **Brand Partner Quality.** In general, brands that are perceived to be of high quality contribute to the formation of consumer–brand relationships. In this sense, consumers develop feelings of trust regarding specific brands, and these feelings of trust foster consumer–brand relationships. Brand personality traits also affect relationship quality when service problems occur, with sincere brands suffering more than exciting brands.[42]

6-3 Consumer Lifestyles, Psychographics, and Demographics

Consumer lifestyles, psychographics, and demographics are all important variables that highlight differences between consumers. Many consumer research companies focus nearly exclusively on these variables because they give very good information regarding consumer behavior. Each of the concepts is discussed below.

6-3a Lifestyles

The term *lifestyle* is used commonly in everyday life. For example, we often speak of healthy lifestyles, unhealthy lifestyles, alternative lifestyles, and even dangerous lifestyles. The word has also been used in many ways in consumer research. Stated simply, **lifestyles** refer to the ways consumers live and spend their time and money.

Personality and lifestyles are closely related topics. In fact, lifestyles may be referred to as context-specific personality traits. This has implications for how the concepts are measured. That is, instead of asking a consumer if she is an "outdoor type," a lifestyle approach will ask the consumer about the amount of time she spends outdoors and what she does when she is outdoors. Importantly, lifestyles aren't completely determined by personality. Instead, they emerge from the influence of culture, groups, and individual processes, including personality.[43] Not surprisingly, consumer lifestyles vary considerably across cultures.

Lifestyles have proved extremely valuable to marketers and others interested in predicting behavior. Purchase patterns are often influenced by consumer lifestyles, and numerous lifestyle categories can be identified. It shouldn't be surprising, therefore, that marketers

often target consumers based on lifestyles. For example, "Beats by Dr. Dre" has been aimed at active, young consumers, and "Body by Vi" appeals to the health-conscious market. Because lifestyle can be directly tied to product purchase and consumption, consumer lifestyles are considered an important manifestation of social stratification.[44] In other words, they are very useful in identifying viable market segments. Appealing to a consumer's lifestyle is so important that it's not uncommon to see advertisements focusing as much on lifestyle as on the actual product or service itself.

> Consumer lifestyles, psychographics, and demographics are all important variables that highlight differences between consumers.

6-3b Psychographics

The term **psychographics** refers to the way consumer lifestyles are measured. Psychographic techniques use quantitative methods that can be used in developing lifestyle profiles. Psychographic research has been used to investigate lifestyles for many years, and advances in technology have helped psychographics become very popular with consumer researchers. Psychographic analysis involves surveying consumers using **AIO statements**, which are used to gain an understanding of consumers' activities, interests, and opinions. These measurements can be narrowly defined (as relating to a specific product or category) or broadly defined (as pertaining to activities that the consumer enjoys).

Consumer segments very often contain consumers with similar lifestyles. Although the categorization of segments is rarely based on consumer behavior theory, the process can be very helpful in identifying marketing opportunities. As an example, one effort to identify segments in the European tourism industry resulted in the following lifestyle segment profiles:[45]

- **Home Loving.** Fundamentally focused on the family, this segment values product quality. These consumers enjoy cultural activities such as visiting art exhibits and monuments. The home-loving group takes the greatest number of long, family-oriented travel vacations.

- **Idealistic.** These responsible consumers believe that the road to success is based on bettering the world. They enjoy classical music and theater and travel

lifestyles distinctive modes of living, including how people spend their time and money

psychographics quantitative investigation of consumer lifestyles

AIO statements activity, interest, and opinion statements that are used in lifestyle studies

VALS popular psychographic method in consumer research that divides consumers into groups based on resources and consumer behavior motivations

geodemographic techniques techniques that combine data on consumer expenditures and socioeconomic variables with geographic information in order to identify commonalities in consumption patterns of households in various regions

PRIZM popular geodemographic technique that stands for Potential Ratings Index by ZIP Market

to destinations that include rural locations and country villages.

- **Autonomous.** These independent-thinking consumers strive to be upwardly mobile. They enjoy the nightlife and read few newspapers. This segment enjoys weekend travel.

- **Hedonistic.** The hedonistic segment values human relationships and work. They are interested in new product offerings and enjoy listening to music. These consumers enjoy visiting large cities.

- **Conservative.** Like the home-loving segment, this segment focuses largely on the family. These consumers tend to view success simply in terms of their work careers. This group dislikes nightlife and modern music and instead focuses on issues related to religion, law, and order.

Psychographic profiles of various other consumer groups have resulted in lifestyle segments such as: Harley-Davidson owners (including "cocky misfits" and "classy capitalists"), wine drinkers (including "conservatives," "experimenters," and "image oriented"), Porsche owners (including "top guns," "elitists," and "fantasists"), and health, wellness, and sustainability focused consumers (including "lifestyle of health and sustainability").[46] There are numerous ways in which to segment consumers based on lifestyles.

Lifestyles explain how people spend their time

Specificity of Lifestyle Segments

The lifestyle approaches that we have discussed here can be categorized in terms of specificity—either narrowly defined or more broadly defined. Generally, lifestyles are indeed quite specific. The magazine industry is particularly efficient at identifying consumer lifestyles and developing products around lifestyle segments. For example, consumers who skateboard can read magazines such as *Thrasher*, while those who play paintball can read *PaintballX3*.

VALS

When using lifestyle segmentation, a marketer can either identify his or her own segments or use established methods that are already available. One popular method in consumer research is the VALS™ approach.[47] Developed and marketed by Strategic Business Insights, VALS is a very successful segmentation approach that has been adopted by several companies. **VALS** stands for "Values and Lifestyles." VALS classifies consumers into eight distinct segments based on resources available to the consumer (including financial, educational, and intellectual resources), as well as three primary motivations (ideals motivation, achievement motivation, and self-expression motivation). The VALS segments are presented in Exhibit 6.5.

PRIZM

Another popular tool for lifestyle analysis is a geodemographic procedure known as PRIZM®.[48] **Geodemographic techniques** combine data on consumer expenditures and socioeconomic variables with geographic information in order to identify commonalities in consumption patterns of households in various regions. **PRIZM** is a popular lifestyle analysis technique that was developed by Nielsen Claritas. PRIZM, which stands for Potential Ratings Index by ZIP Market, is based on the premise that people with similar backgrounds and means tend to live close to one another and emulate each other's behaviors and lifestyles.

PRIZM combines demographic and behavioral information in a manner that enables marketers to better understand and target their customers. The technique uses 66 different segments as descriptors of individual households, which are ranked according to socioeconomic variables. Segments found using the PRIZM technique include "Movers and Shakers," "Money and Brains," "Red, White and Blues," and "Back Country Folks." There are other geodemographic techniques available as well, including ESRI's GIS and Mapping Software.

EXHIBIT 6.5 VALS Segments

- **Innovators.** Innovators are successful, sophisticated people who have high self-esteem. They are motivated by achievement, ideals, and self-expression. Image is important to these consumers.

- **Thinkers.** Thinkers are ideal motivated. They are mature, reflective people who value order and knowledge. They have relatively high income and are conservative, practical consumers.

- **Achievers.** Achievers have an achievement motivation and are politically conservative. Their lives largely center around church, family, and career. Image is important to this group, and they prefer to purchase prestige products.

- **Experiencers.** Experiencers are self-expressive consumers who tend to be young, impulsive, and enthusiastic. These consumers value novelty and excitement.

- **Believers.** In some ways, believers are like thinkers. They are ideal motivated and conservative. They follow routines, and their lives largely center around home, family, and church. They do not have the amount of resources that thinkers have, however.

- **Strivers.** Strivers are achievement motivated, but they do not have the amount of resources that are available to achievers. For strivers, shopping is a way to demonstrate to others their ability to buy.

- **Makers.** Makers are like experiencers in that they are motivated by self-expression. They have fewer resources than experiencers. They tend to express themselves through their activities such as raising children, fixing cars, and building houses.

- **Survivors.** Survivors are very low on resources and are constricted by this lack of resources. They tend to be elderly consumers who are concerned with health issues and who believe that the world is changing too quickly. They are not active in the marketplace, as their primary concerns center around safety, family, and security.

© Cengage Learning

6-3c Demographics

Demographics refer to observable, statistical aspects of populations including such factors as age, gender, or income. Notice that this is very different from either lifestyles or psychographics. The study of demographics is known as *demography*. Demographic variables include age, ethnicity, family size, occupation, and sometimes income.

Age. Age is important not only because of its descriptive nature, but also because consumers who experience significant life events at approximately the same age are influenced greatly by the events. This is the "cohort effect." Groups such as "Generation Y" or "Millennials" (born between 1981 and 1995), "Generation X" (born between 1965 and 1980), "Baby Boomers" (born between 1946 and 1964), and "The Greatest Generation" (born prior to 1946) are identifiable segments. Baby Boomers receive a lot of attention because of the group's size and spending power. Younger consumers like Gen Z'ers also receive attention.

demographics observable, statistical aspects of populations such as age, gender, or income

Ethnicity. Diversity is growing in the United States. Minority groups (such as Hispanics, African-Americans, and Asian-Americans) are expected to grow considerably in the years to come. In fact, projections reveal that by 2050, the "minority" segment will exceed more than half of the total population!

Income. Income is another important variable. Although it is often discussed in terms of socioeconomic variables, we include it here because it is often present in several popular demographic publications such as the U.S. Census. Income obviously affects consumer behavior in numerous ways. Engel's Law states that as income increases, a smaller percentage of expenditure is devoted to food, and the percentage devoted to consumption rises slower than the rise in income.

Demographics can be used in conjunction with psychographic analysis. In fact, demographics can be used to help locate and understand lifestyle segments. Failing to consider psychographic measures leads to the trap of assuming that all consumers of a certain demographic have the exact same tastes. An example is found in the concept of "psychological age." A person's actual age and his or her psychological age can be very different. As some have said, "today's sixty is yesterday's forty."

Ixpert/Shutterstock.com

Demographics help to describe consumer groups.

self-concept totality of thoughts and feelings that an individual has about himself or herself

symbolic interactionism perspective that proposes that consumers live in a symbolic environment and interpret the myriad of symbols around them, and that members of a society agree on the meanings of symbols

semiotics study of symbols and their meanings

6-4 The Role of Self-Concept in Consumer Behavior

The self-concept is another important topic in consumer behavior. The term **self-concept** refers to the totality of thoughts and feelings that an individual has about him- or herself. Self-concept can also be thought of as the way a person defines or gives meaning to his or her own identity, as in a type of self-schema.

Consumers are motivated to act in accordance with their self-concepts. As such, consumers often use products as ways of revealing their self-concepts to others. According to a **symbolic interactionism** perspective, consumers agree on the shared meaning of products and symbols.[49] These symbols can become part of the self-concept if the consumer identifies with them strongly.

An important field of study that relates to the symbolic interactionism approach is semiotics. **Semiotics** refers to the study of symbols and their meanings. As we have stated, consumers use products as symbols to convey their self-concepts to others. In this sense, products are an essential part of self-expression.[50] Popular websites like MySpace, Facebook, and Twitter give consumers easy ways of expressing themselves.[51]

Let's first explore various dimensions of the "self" before examining how a consumer's self-concept influences various behaviors. First, we note that a consumer will have a number of "concepts" about himself that may emerge over time and surface in different social situations.[52] A few of the different "self-concepts" that may emerge include the actual self, the ideal self, the social self, the ideal social self, the possible self, and the extended self.[53]

The *actual self* refers to how consumers currently perceives themselves (that is, who I am). The *ideal self* refers to how consumers would like to perceive themselves (that is, who I would like to be in the future). The *social self* refers to the beliefs that consumers have about how they are seen by others. The social self is also called the

The Cyber Self

It will probably come as no surprise that estimates indicate that nearly three-quarters of online teens and young adults use social networking sites, with millions of young consumers updating their profiles several times per day. Popular websites such as Facebook, MySpace, and Twitter allow users to post various aspects of their lives and present themselves in almost limitless ways. Some young consumers even lie about their age in order to post.

Consumers who pay close attention to their online social self are motivated by a need to socialize, a disposition to trust others, and a high degree of self-efficacy. Unfortunately, many website users don't care about the image they portray and feel that almost any detail of their lives is fair game. Many young consumers seem to think that posting explicit information related to sexual behavior, drugs, or violence is not a problem. Of course, the downside is when too much information is given out and bad things happen. This is becoming all too common. From employers reviewing online profiles to websites

like "pleaserobme.com," highlighting the dangers of revealing when consumers are, and are not, at home, the implications of

social networking are far-reaching. This brings a new perspective to the ideal social self! Although the Internet allows consumers to post all kinds of material about themselves, common sense should still apply.

Sources: Based on Tao Sun and Guohua Wu, "Traits, Predictors, and Consequences of Facebook Self-Presentation," *Social Science Computer Review*, December 7, 2011, http://ssc.sagepub.com/content/early/2011/10/18/0894439311425978, accessed April 11, 2012. Amanda Lenhart, Kristen Purcell, Aaron Smith, and Kathryn Zickuh, "Social Media and Young Adults," Pew Internet & American Life Project, February 3, 2010, http://pewinternet.org/Reports/2010/Social-Media-and-Young-Adults.aspx, accessed May 25, 2010. Matt Richtel and Miguel Helft, "Facebook Users Who Are Under Age Raise Concerns," *New York Times*, March 12, 2011, http://www.nytimes.com/2011/03/12/technology/internet/12underage.html?_r=1&pagewanted=all, accessed April 7, 2011.

"looking-glass" self because it denotes the image that a consumer has when she looks into the mirror and imagines how others see her. The *ideal social self* represents the image that a consumer would like others to have about her. The *possible self*, much like the ideal self, presents an image of what the consumer could become, whereas the *extended self* represents the various possessions that a consumer owns that help him form perceptions about himself.

The relationship between consumer self-concept and product consumption is a two-way street. That is, consumers express their self-concepts by purchasing and displaying various products, while products help to define how they see themselves.[54] Note that the relationship between the self-concept and consumption is not limited to adult consumers only, as consumer–brand connections have been shown to form as early as childhood![55]

6-4a Self-Concept and Body Presentation

The issue of self-concept in consumer behavior has several practical implications. For example, the cosmetics and weight-loss industries are well-known for offering products that purportedly help improve one's self-image. The term **self-esteem** refers to the positivity of an individual's self-concept. The effect of advertising on consumers' self-esteem is an important consumer research topic and one that has often been overlooked.[56]

self-esteem positivity of the self-concept that one holds

body esteem positivity with which people hold their body image

The fashion industry is often criticized for promoting overly thin models and body types. Research confirms that consumers compare their bodies with those of models in advertisements, and that these comparisons can have harmful effects. This is particularly the case for young females.[57] **Body esteem** refers to the positivity with which people hold their body image.[58] Low body esteem can result in a number of negative behaviors and attitudes.

In response to growing public concern regarding this issue, the Council of Fashion Designers of America (CFDA) updated guidelines to encourage healthy eating habits and to discourage the use of overly thin models in advertisements. "The fashion business should be sensitive to the fact that we do have a responsibility in affecting young girls and their self-image," CFDA president Diane von Furstenberg commented.[59] The problem is not solely for women, however, as evidence suggests that male consumers are also affected by unrealistic body imagery in advertising.[60] Although the industry has received much negative publicity, not all model effects are negative. Consumers can feel better about themselves when they find similarities between their bodies and those of models.[61]

Unilever Corp. addressed the issue of unrealistic body types with their Real Beauty campaign for the brand Dove. The campaign seeks to provide more realistic views of beauty and to improve the self-esteem of both women and young girls.

Cosmetic Surgery and Body Modification

Because of the many ways consumers compare themselves to others, it is easy to understand why many medical procedures that promise to improve consumers' perceptions of their bodies are now available. According to the American Society for Aesthetic Plastic surgery, approximately 9 million cosmetic and nonsurgical procedures are performed in the U.S. annually. It seems that even in times of economic uncertainty, people are still willing to pay for cosmetic surgery. In fact, American consumers spent nearly $10 billion on cosmetic procedures in 2011. Liposuction was the most popular cosmetic surgical

Henglein and Steets/Jupiter Images

Unrealistic body images affect consumers' self-esteem.

self-congruency theory
theory that proposes that much of consumer behavior can be explained by the congruence of a consumer's self-concept with the image of typical users of a focal product

procedure, followed by breast augmentation, abdominoplasty, eyelid surgery, and breast lift. Women had 91% of the procedures while men had 9%. The top procedures for women were breast augmentation, liposuction, abdominoplasty, eyelid surgery, and breast lift. The most popular for men were liposuction, rhinoplasty, eyelid surgery, breast reduction, and facelift. Most procedures were found among consumers aged 35–50.[62]

Body Piercings and Tattoos

Body piercings and other forms of body decorations, such as tattoos, represent other methods of promoting one's self-concept. Estimates vary widely, with one recent study revealing that as many as 51% of teenagers and young adults have some form of body piercing. The same estimates reveal that up to 14% of the general population has body piercings. Interestingly, piercings tend to be more popular with female consumers than with male consumers.[63] The growth in body art suggests that new attitudes about the body's role in self-presentation are emerging.[64]

While body piercings are popular forms of self-expression and are frequently used as innocent methods of self-expression, research also indicates that the use of piercings can sometimes be associated with increased levels of drug and alcohol use, unprotected sexual activity, trait anxiety, and depression.[65] Consumers also form impressions of employees who have tattoos and piercings, and these perceptions may impact how they view organizations with such employees.[66] For consumers, body piercings and tattoos have become more popular than ever.

6-5 Self-Congruency Theory and Consumer Behavior

Reference group members share symbolic meanings. This is an assumption of **self-congruency theory**, which proposes that behavior can be explained by the congruence (match) between a consumer's self-concept and the image of typical users of a focal product.[67] For example, one study found that store loyalty is influenced by the congruency between self-image and store image.[68] Another study found that passengers on a cruise ship rated their experience based on the congruence between their self-image and their images of other passengers.[68a]

6-5a Segmentation and Self-Congruency

Marketers can use congruency theory by segmenting markets into groups of consumers who perceive high self-concept congruence with product-user image. Imagine a consumer who sees himself as being a stylish person. If he believes that people who drive Corvettes are stylish, then he will be motivated to drive a Corvette. In this way, brands become vehicles for self-expression.

As discussed earlier, there are several types of self-concepts, and different products may relate to each concept. That is, one product may relate quite well to the actual self-concept, but not as strongly to the ideal self-concept. One study found that the purchase of privately consumable items (such as frozen dinners or suntan lotion) is heavily influenced by the actual self-concept, while the purchase of publicly visible products (like clothing) is more strongly related to the ideal self-concept.[69]

A popular advertising campaign for Ford trucks illustrates the role of self-congruency theory in marketing. The successful ad campaign, which centers on the "Built Ford Tough" theme, sends the message that if you are a hardworking man you need a hardworking truck like Ford. Rolex watches are well-known for being watches for people who have arrived or who soon will be "arriving."

Consumer Identity and Product Ownership

Beyond consumer–product congruity, some consumers view brands much more intensely. Given the many

Brands are vehicles for self-expression

Valentin Flauraud/Bloomberg/Getty Images

ways in which consumers use and display brands, some researchers suggest that brands are used to express and validate *consumer identity*.[70] For these consumers, the task of self-expression through product ownership is one of identity maintenance and communication. This is found when consumers have very strong ties to brands and feel as if they are one with the brand. The classic "I'm a Pepper" advertising slogan for Dr. Pepper is a good example. The campaign, which has spanned generations, boasts of the strong role that the soft-drink brand plays in consumer identity.

Organizational Identification

Consumers also form close associations with companies and organizations. When consumers feel very close to organizations, *organizational identification* is said to be present.[71] For consumers, the organization becomes a vehicle for self-expression, and for organizations, consumer loyalty and commitment become quite strong. Identifying with an organization also helps consumers to forge stronger social identities.[71a] Consumer and organizational identification illustrate the important role that products and organizations can play in the expression of the self.

Final Thought on Personality, Lifestyles, and the Self-Concept

Personality, lifestyles, and the self-concept are all important topics in the study of consumer behavior. Consumers differ across each of these concepts, and these differences help signal the need for targeted marketing communications. As technological advancements continue to develop, it can be expected that consumer researchers and marketing managers alike will continue to be interested in these topics.

Study Tools

Located at back of the textbook

❑ Rip out Chapter in Review Card

Located at www.cengagebrain.com

❑ Review Key Terms Flashcards (print or online)

❑ Download audio summaries to review on the go

❑ Complete practice quizzes to prepare for tests

❑ Play "Beat the Clock" to master concepts

❑ Watch video on Wheelworks for a real company example

study tools

WHAT DO YOU THINK?
WHAT OTHERS HAVE THOUGHT

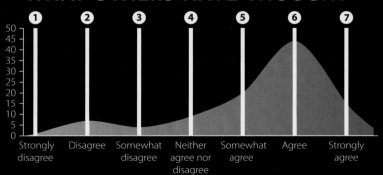

| 1 Strongly disagree | 2 Disagree | 3 Somewhat disagree | 4 Neither agree nor disagree | 5 Somewhat agree | 6 Agree | 7 Strongly agree |

My personality can easily be seen in the products that I buy.

The vast majority of students, 79%, at least somewhat agree with this statement, with 44% indicating "agree." Our personalities and the products that we buy usually are closely related. This is a central theme in self-congruency theory.

© Jenkedco/Shutterstock.com

Attitudes
play a critical role in consumer behavior.

WHAT DO YOU THINK?

It's pretty hard to change my attitude about products that I dislike.

STRONGLY DISAGREE   STRONGLY AGREE

VISIT COURSEMATE AT WWW.CENGAGEBRAIN.COM

Attitudes and Attitude Change

It's no secret that millions of consumers love their iPhones. The wildly successful phone has become a mainstay of everyday life for consumers around the world. Taylor recently bought an Apple iPhone 5s. She's been a fan of iPhones for years and the iPhone 5s was the next logical purchase. As it turns out, she really likes it a lot and she thinks it is well worth the price that she paid. She's quick to talk about the phone with others and she follows an "iPhone Fans" page on Facebook.

Getting consumers to feel strongly about a product is something that marketers constantly try to achieve. When consumers have positive attitudes toward products they often promote them to others. This is a win-win situation for both the customer and the company. Conversely, negative attitudes can have a profound impact as well. Some people become so upset with a company and its products that they boycott everything the company sells—and tell others that they should do the same.

Understanding the factors that influence consumer attitudes is very important for marketers. This may seem obvious for companies, but consumer attitudes are important in nontraditional settings as well. For example, politicians want to know how voters *feel* about candidates. City managers want to know if citizens *believe* that a new construction project is a good idea. Musicians want to know if consumers *intend* to buy their new album. Consumer attitudes are important in each of these examples.

After studying this chapter, the student should be able to:

7-1 Define attitudes and describe attitude components.

7-2 Describe the functions of attitudes.

7-3 Understand how the hierarchy of effects concept applies to attitude theory.

7-4 Comprehend the major consumer attitude models.

7-5 Describe attitude change theories and their role in persuasion.

7-6 Understand how message and source effects influence persuasion.

7-1 Attitudes and Attitude Components

The term *attitude* has been used in many ways. **Attitudes** are relatively enduring overall evaluations of objects, products, services, issues, or people.[1] Attitudes play a critical role in consumer behavior. They are particularly important because they motivate people to behave in relatively consistent ways. Because they are so important, it shouldn't be surprising that the attitude concept is one

attitudes relatively enduring overall evaluations of objects, products, services, issues, or people

ABC approach to attitudes approach that suggests that attitudes encompass one's affect, behavior, and cognitions (or beliefs) toward an object

functional theory of attitudes theory of attitudes that suggests that attitudes perform four basic functions

utilitarian function of attitudes function of attitudes in which consumers use attitudes as ways to maximize rewards and minimize punishment

of the most researched topics in the entire field of consumer research. In fact, attitude is one of the most popular concepts in all of the social sciences.

Attitudes and value are closely related. Recall from our opening example that Taylor really likes her iPhone 5s and the value it provides. In general, consumers have positive attitudes toward products that deliver value. Likewise, when products deliver poor value, consumer attitudes are usually negative. In order to appreciate how attitudes influence consumer behavior, we need to distinguish between the components of attitudes and the functions that attitudes perform.

7-1a Components of Attitude

According to the **ABC approach to attitudes**, attitudes possess three components: *a*ffect, *b*ehavior, and *c*ognitions. *Affect* refers to feelings about an object and *cognitions*, as used here, refers to beliefs that the consumer has about the object. *Behavior* refers to the overt behavior that consumers exhibit as well as their intentions to behave. To understand these components, consider the following statements:

- "I really like the iPhone 5s."
- "I always buy Apple products."
- "My iPhone 5s keeps me connected."

These statements reflect the three components of a consumer's attitude found in the ABC approach. "I really like the iPhone 5s" is a statement of affect because it describes the feelings, or affection, a consumer has about the product. "I always buy Apple products" refers to one's behavior regarding Apple products. "My iPhone 5s keeps me connected" is a cognitive statement that expresses the owner's belief about the usefulness of the phone.

7-2 Functions of Attitudes

Knowing that attitudes represent relatively enduring evaluations of products, and that attitudes can be broken into three components, is valuable. But what's the big deal about attitudes? What do they do for the consumer? Understanding the answer to these questions gives marketers an opportunity to develop better promotional messages.

According to the **functional theory of attitudes**, attitudes perform four functions.[2] The four functions are the *utilitarian* function, the *knowledge* function, the *value-expressive* function, and the *ego-defensive* function. These functions are summarized in Exhibit 7.1.

7-2a Utilitarian Function

The **utilitarian function of attitudes** is based on the concept of reward and punishment. This means that consumers learn to use attitudes as ways to maximize

EXHIBIT 7.1 Functions of Consumer Attitudes

Attitude Function	Description	Example
Utilitarian	Attitudes are used as a method to obtain rewards and to minimize punishment.	High school boys wear cool brands so they fit in.
Knowledge	The knowledge function of attitudes allows consumers to simplify their decision-making processes.	A student avoids a party because he knows there will be a lot of drinking and he doesn't like to get drunk.
Value-expressive	This function of attitudes enables consumers to express their core values, self-concept, and beliefs to others.	A consumer supports Greenpeace because he places much value on environmentalism.
Ego-defensive	The ego-defensive function of attitudes works as a defense mechanism for consumers to avoid facts or to defend themselves from their own low self-concept.	Smokers discount information that suggests that smoking is bad for their health.

© Cengage Learning

© iStockphoto.com/Thepalmer

rewards and minimize punishment. Buying and liking a product because it delivers a specific benefit is one example of the utilitarian function of attitudes. The consumer is rewarded through a desired product benefit. For example, many high school boys pay a lot of attention to the brands of clothing they wear. By wearing the right clothes, they are able to feel as though they fit in with the expectations of others. Consumers can reap social rewards through expressing attitudes, and they often express their attitudes as an attempt to develop or maintain relationships. A study of college sports fans presents an example. In the study, football fans revealed that one of the many reasons they wear their team's apparel is to fit in and make connections with new friends.[3]

7-2b Knowledge Function

The **knowledge function of attitudes** allows consumers to simplify decision-making processes. For example, consumers may not like credit card offers because they want to stay out of debt. The decision to shred the offers would then be easy. Attitudes perform the important function of helping consumers avoid undesirable situations and approach more desirable situations. They also help consumers select objects that they do like. Brand loyalty is important here. It is usually much easier to buy a product that you know you like than it is to try a new one. Attitude components become stored in the associated network in consumers' long-term memory and become linked together to form rules that guide behavior. Here, we can see again that attitudes are linked to comprehension and knowledge.

7-2c Value-Expressive Function

The **value-expressive function of attitudes** is found in a number of consumer settings. This function enables consumers to express their core values, self-concept, and beliefs to others. Accordingly, this function of attitude provides a positive expression of the type of person a consumer perceives herself to be and the values that she holds. For example, consumers who believe in the protection of the environment might support a group like Greenpeace. Consumers also express core values by displaying products such as bumper stickers, posters, or t-shirts. It is easy to learn about consumers' values by looking at the bumper stickers they place on their cars, the posters that place in their apartments, and the types of t-shirts they wear.

7-2d Ego-Defensive Function

The **ego-defensive function of attitudes** works as a defense mechanism for consumers. There are a couple of ways in which this function works. First, the ego-defensive function enables consumers to protect themselves from information that may be threatening. For example, people who like to smoke may discount evidence that smoking is bad for their health. In this case, the attitude works as a defense mechanism that protects the individual from the reality that smoking isn't healthy.

Another example of the ego-defensive function is when consumers develop positive attitudes toward products that enhance their self-image. Many college-aged male students wear athletic apparel to enhance their image of being in shape and active. This function also works as a protection mechanism. For some consumers this behavior compensates for a general feeling of being out-of-shape, thereby protecting the ego and self-image.

7-3 Hierarchy of Effects

Research indicates that the three components of attitudes may be formed in a sequential pattern. This process is known as the **hierarchy of effects**.[4] According to this approach, affect, behavior, and cognitions (beliefs) form by following one of four hierarchies:

Wearing the right clothes is a way to enhance your self-image.

knowledge function of attitudes function of attitudes whereby attitudes allow consumers to simplify decision-making processes

value-expressive function of attitudes function of attitudes whereby attitudes allow consumers to express their core values, self-concept, and beliefs to others

ego-defensive function of attitudes function of attitudes whereby attitudes work as a defense mechanism for consumers

hierarchy of effects attitude approach that suggests that affect, behavior, and cognitions form in a sequential order

Adrian Sherratt/Alamy

1. High-involvement (or "standard learning") hierarchy
2. Low-involvement hierarchy
3. Experiential hierarchy
4. Behavioral influence hierarchy

These hierarchies are discussed in the next section and presented in Exhibit 7.2.

7-3a High-Involvement Hierarchy

The high-involvement, or standard learning, hierarchy of effects occurs when a consumer faces a high-involvement decision or addresses a significant problem. High-involvement decisions are important to a consumer and often contain significant risk. In this hierarchy, beliefs about products are formed first. The consumer carefully considers various product features and develops beliefs and thoughts about each feature. Next, feelings, or evaluations, about the product are formed. The consumer may begin to think the product is good and will suit his needs based on the beliefs that have been formed. Finally, after beliefs and feelings are formed, the consumer decides to act in some way toward the product. Here, a purchase decision is made. The consumer decides to either buy the product or not.

Imagine the process that Andre went through when he bought a new television. He knew that it would be a significant purchase, and he was careful about his selection. He first considered the various attributes of each TV and began to develop favorable

EXHIBIT 7.2 Hierarchy of Effects

Purchase Context	Hierarchy of Effects
High involvement	Cognition—affect—behavior
Low involvement	Cognition—behavior—affect
Experiential	Affect—behavior—cognition
Behavioral Influence	Behavior—cognition—affect

© Cengage Learning

evaluations toward a few of the brands. Realizing that he felt best about the Samsung, he decided that this would be the one to buy.

7-3b Low-Involvement Hierarchy

The standard learning approach was once considered the best approach to explain consumer attitude formation. Marketers began to realize, however, that many consumer purchases and problems are not very risky or even significant. In fact, many purchases are routine and boring.[5]

When low-involvement purchases are made, consumers often have some basic beliefs about products without necessarily having strong feelings toward them. Devon, a self-proclaimed hardcore gamer, may not consider the feelings he has about a mundane product like printer paper. In fact, he probably doesn't think much about printer paper at all. He may just think, "Staples is a popular brand, so I'll buy it." Only after he buys and

I Like This Store!

Retail managers are well aware of the powerful effects that music has on consumer behavior. In general, consumers tend to walk faster through a store when fast music is played, and they tend to slow down (and buy more!) when slower music is played. Music can even impact consumers' perceptions of wait time.

What is equally important for managers, however, is that the wrong choice of music may actually drive customers away. Of course, different segments of consumers like different types of music, and consumers can become quickly turned off if the wrong kind of music is played.

In fact, companies like DMX Music and Muzak know that the tendency to leave a store if unappealing music is played cuts across demographic segments. Quite simply, no one likes to be bombarded with bad music! The right choice of background music can be a critical factor in retail success. Managers should pay close attention. Background music is very, very important!

© LOU DEMATTEIS/Reuters/Landow

Sources: DMX, http://www.dmx.com/services/music/why-dmx-music, accessed April 18, 2012; Muzak, www.muzak.com, accessed April 18, 2012; Becky Ebenkamp, "Songs in the Key of Flee," *Brandweek*, February 16, 2004, 17.

uses the product will he develop any type of feeling, or evaluation, of the paper. In reality, the feelings may be very mild. At first, he thinks "Staples is popular" (belief) and he decides to buy it (behavior). Only later does he say "I like it" (affect). Of course, he'd think very carefully about videogame equipment and probably follow the standard learning hierarchy. It is easy to see that the purchase of an expensive gaming system is much more involving for Devon than a $3 ream of paper.

7-3c Experiential Hierarchy

Many purchases are based on feelings, and consumers often purchase products or try experiences simply because they "feel good" or "feel right." For example, when a student decides to visit a new dance club, she makes the decision simply because it sounds like a fun thing to do.

Impulse purchases can be explained from the experiential perspective. These purchases are often motivated by feelings. Impulse purchasing means that a consumer buys a product spontaneously and with little concern for consequences. Dessert items are often purchased on impulse. When the waiter brings the tray by, the chocoholic feels strongly about one of the desserts and simply buys it on impulse. Here, he feels strongly and acts on those feelings. A great deal of research focuses on the experiential hierarchy.[6]

7-3d Behavioral Influence Hierarchy

The behavioral influence hierarchy suggests that some behaviors occur without either beliefs or affect being strongly formed beforehand. Strong environmental pressures lead to behaviors without belief or affect formation. An example of this may be found when a consumer eats at a restaurant playing soft, slow music. Restaurant managers know that one way to get people to relax and order more drinks is to play soft, soothing music. Retail store managers know that by placing a product display in appropriate locations, consumers can be propelled to buy a product seemingly with very little or no thought at all. As such, behavior is influenced by environmental cues. This means that there are times when behaviors may be performed in the absence of strong beliefs or feelings.

7-4 Consumer Attitude Models

As you can see, understanding consumer attitudes is very important for understanding consumer behavior. This leads to the question of how to measure attitudes. In this section, we review a major approach

to measuring attitudes which was developed by Martin Fishbein and Icek Ajzen, the attitude-toward-the-object model.[7] This model is known as a **multiattribute attitude model** because it combines information about a number of beliefs and evaluations pertaining to an object's attributes.

multiattribute attitude model a model that combines a number of pieces of information about belief and evaluations of attributes of an object

attitude-toward-the-object (ATO) model attitude model that considers three key elements, including beliefs consumers have about salient attributes, the strength of the belief that an object possesses the attribute, and evaluation of the particular attribute

7-4a Attitude-Toward-the-Object Model

The **attitude-toward-the-object (ATO) model** (sometimes simply referred to as the *Fishbein model*) proposes that three key elements must be assessed to understand and predict a consumer's attitude. The first element consists of the *salient beliefs* that a person has about the attributes of an object. The second element is the *strength of the belief* that a certain object under consideration does indeed have the attribute. The third element is an *evaluation of the attribute* in question. These elements are combined to form the overall attitude toward the object (referred to as A_o, or attitude toward the object). The formula for predicting attitudes with this approach is

$$A_o = \sum_{I=1}^{N} (b_i)(e_i)$$

where A_o = attitude toward the object in question (or A_{brand}), b_i = strength of belief that the object possesses attribute i, e_i = evaluation of the attractiveness or goodness of attribute i, and N = number of attributes and beliefs.

The formula states that belief (b) and evaluative ratings (e) for product attributes are combined (multiplied) and the resulting product terms are added together to give a numerical expression of a consumer's attitude toward a product. This model can be used both for predicting a consumer's attitude and for understanding how beliefs, strength of beliefs, and evaluations influence attitude formation.

Using the ATO Approach

To understand this model, first consider how the various elements are measured. To begin, note that belief ratings (b) can be measured on a 10-point scale such as:

How likely is it that the Sony television will give you a clear picture?

1   2   3   4   5   6   7   8   9   10
Extremely unlikely   *Extremely likely*

The evaluative (*e*) rating can then be measured on a −3 to +3 scale such as:

How bad/good is it that a television has a clear picture?

−3   −2   −1   0   +1   +2   +3
Very bad   *Very good*

The consumer would rate the Sony television and any other brand being considered on each relevant attribute. They would also consider their evaluations of the attributes, and ultimately combine the information.

An example may help to clarify the use of this formula. Think of the situation that Jamal faces selecting a new apartment. Jamal recently graduated from college and received a job offer in a large city. He is now considering three different apartment complexes that currently have vacancies. How could we predict his attitude toward each one? This information is presented in Exhibit 7.3.

Jamal is evaluating the following three complexes: *City Pointe*, *Crown View*, and *Kings Landing*. He first thinks of the attributes, or features, that come to mind when he thinks of apartment complexes. He decides that the following attributes are relevant: location, high rent/fees, security, fitness center, and pet friendliness. It is important to emphasize that the attributes need to really be relevant to the product under consideration.

After identifying the relevant attributes, Jamal thinks of how likely it is that each apartment will perform well on the various attributes, or how likely it is that the complexes have these attributes. Jamal would be answering questions such as:

How likely is it that City Pointe is pet-friendly?

1   2   3   4   5   6   7   8   9   10
Extremely unlikely   *Extremely likely*

Jamal rates each apartment across all relevant attributes. His belief (*b*) ratings for the apartments are shown in Exhibit 7.3. From his belief ratings, we can see that he thinks that Kings Landing is most pet-friendly. This complex allows dogs of any size. City Pointe allows dogs under fifty pounds with a large damage deposit, and Crown View does not allow any pet over twenty pounds.

Next, Jamal considers how he *feels* about the relevant attributes, or how good (or bad) the attributes are. An example from the model would be:

How good/bad is it that an apartment complex is pet-friendly?

−3   −2   −1   0   +1   +2   +3
Very bad   *Very good*

Jamal has a number of pet allergies and would prefer to stay away from complexes that he considers to be overly pet-friendly (*e* = −3). Unfortunately, all three complexes that have vacancies allow pets. Most complexes require some fee for pets and they also limit the size of pets that are allowed. He evaluates the other attributes as well. He highly values a location that is close

EXHIBIT 7.3 Attitude-Toward-the-Object Model Applied to Apartment Complexes

Attribute	e	City Pointe		Crown View		Kings Landing	
		b	(b)(e)	b	(b)(e)	b	(b)(e)
Location	3	7	21	9	27	6	18
High rent/fees	−2	8	−16	9	−18	7	−14
Security	3	7	21	8	24	6	18
Fitness center	1	5	5	7	7	10	10
Pet friendliness	−3	5	−15	2	−6	9	−27
A_o			16		34		5

Note: *e* = evaluative ratings. These ratings are generally scaled from −3 to +3, with −3 being very negative and +3 being very positive. *b* = strength of belief that the object possesses the attribute in question. Beliefs are generally scaled from 1 to 10, with 1 meaning "highly unlikely" and 10 meaning "highly likely." (*b*)(*e*) is the product term that is derived by multiplying the evaluative ratings (*e*) by belief strength (*b*). A_o is the overall attitude toward the object. This is determined by adding the (*b*)(*e*) product terms for each object.

© Cengage Learning

Attitudes play an important role in searching for an apartment.

to the downtown entertainment district ($e = +3$) and a complex with its own security force ($e = +3$). Jamal knows that the fees and limitations can vary greatly and he really doesn't want to have problems with his allergies. He also values a fitness center but realizes that these centers usually raise the overall costs associated with a lease ($e = +1$). He would naturally like to pay as little as possible in rent. He does believe, however, in the old adage "you get what you pay for," so he thinks that higher rent probably signals higher quality ($e = -2$). As such, he doesn't view higher rent as a completely bad thing. *It is important to emphasize that the evaluation ratings (e) do not vary across the brands under consideration, while the belief ratings do.* That is, consumers know what attributes they like regardless of which product they are considering.

Using this model, Jamal's attitude would be calculated by multiplying each belief rating (b) by the corresponding evaluation (e). For example, the belief rating of 7 for City Pointe (security) would be multiplied by the evaluation of 3 to arrive at 21. Similarly, the belief rating of 2 for Crown View (pet friendliness) would be multiplied by the evaluation of -3 to arrive at -6. This is performed for all belief ratings and evaluations. Finally, the product terms are added together to arrive at a predicted attitude score. From Exhibit 7.3, we see that his most positive attitude is toward Crown View ($A_o = 34$), followed by City Pointe ($A_o = 16$), and finally Kings Landing ($A_o = 5$).

What was it that led to the higher attitude toward Crown View versus the other complexes? An examination of Exhibit 7.3 reveals that Crown View was rated higher than the other two complexes on the two highly valued attributes, location and security. Kings Landing has an excellent fitness center, but it is also the most pet-friendly of the three complexes, with practically no limitations on pets. He also views City Pointe as relatively pet-friendly. Notice that Crown View was considered to be the most expensive complex ($b = 9$), but this is still the complex to which Jamal holds the most positive attitude. How could this be? The higher ratings on other attributes compensated for the belief that Crown View would be the most expensive complex. Accordingly, the ATO approach is known as a **compensatory model**. With compensatory models, attitudes are formed holistically across a number of attributes, with poor ratings on one attribute being compensated for by higher ratings on another attribute.

Implications of the ATO Approach

Information obtained from this model has important marketing implications. First, we note that attitude research is most often performed on entire market segments rather than on individuals. Marketing researchers would generally want to understand how an entire segment of consumers feel about apartment complexes. Information would be gathered from a sample of several consumers in the segment.

An equally important issue for managers would be learning if consumers believe that products offer relevant attributes. Does the target segment know that Crown View offers excellent security? Do they know that Kings Landing offers a high-quality fitness center? If targeted segments do not know these things, then they could be emphasized in advertising campaigns. This would particularly be the case if the attribute was highly valued by the consumers. Therefore, both belief (b) and evaluative (e) ratings have important implications.

As a general statement, it would be easier for managers to convince a targeted segment that they do offer a specific

> **compensatory model**
> attitudinal model wherein low ratings for one attribute are compensated for by higher ratings on another

> The attitude-toward-the-object model has value from both an academic and a practical viewpoint.

attitude–behavior consistency extent to which a strong relationship exists between attitudes and actual behavior

behavioral intentions model model developed to improve on the ATO model, focusing on behavioral intentions, subjective norms, and attitude toward a particular behavior

feature (like an excellent fitness center) than it would be to attempt to change how consumers evaluate the attribute (in other words, how people feel about fitness centers). This is why marketers need to perform extensive research up front to gain clear understandings of attributes that are highly valued, and then develop their products and services around these features.

A couple of questions commonly arise regarding this approach. "Do consumers really form attitudes in this way?" Most consumer researchers would respond "Yes." Think of a person considering the purchase of a new cell phone. Chances are that they will first think of the features that are relevant. Next, they will rate each brand on how well it performs on those features. They will also consider how they feel about each of the features. Finally, they will combine their beliefs with the evaluations and make a decision. Granted, *they probably won't write down the formula when they evaluate different cell phones,* but consumers think about relevant features of products, how much they value the features, and how each product rates on the features.

The next question that is commonly asked is, "Do consumer researchers really do this?" Again, the answer is yes. Researchers are very interested in how attitudes are formed, and the approach presented here can easily be performed through consumer surveys. The resultant information can have a significant impact on marketing strategy. As the apartment example reveals, this type of research can affect both product development and promotional strategy. For example, a manager could decide that he or she should improve features that are desired by the targeted segment. Or the manager could focus on improving customer awareness that a complex actually does have the features that the targeted consumers want. The manager could also do both of these things.

Overall, the attitude-toward-the-object model has value from both an academic and a practical viewpoint. We do note, however, that one difficulty with the model is that the weights that are associated with the various attributes do not necessarily remain constant over time, and the list of relevant attributes may indeed change. For this reason, managers should try to stay current on these issues.

Do Attitudes Always Predict Behavior?

Marketing managers and researchers alike realize that just because a consumer has a positive attitude toward a product, this doesn't mean that he will always purchase the product. In fact, there would be little need for sales promotion if this were the case. **Attitude–behavior consistency** refers to the extent to which a strong relationship exists between attitudes and actual behavior. A number of situations may keep consumers from selecting products they hold positive attitudes toward.[8] In general, attitudes are stronger predictors of behavior when the decision to be made is classified as high involvement, when situational factors do not impede the product selection (for example, the product is out of stock or the consumer doesn't have enough money), and when the attitude is held quite strongly. Because attitudes don't always predict behavior, other approaches, including the behavioral intentions model, have been developed to improve upon the ATO approach.

7-4b Behavioral Intentions Model

The **behavioral intentions model**, sometimes referred to as the *theory of reasoned action*, has been offered as an improvement over the attitude-toward-the-object model. This model differs from the attitude-toward-the-object model in a number of important ways.[9] First, rather than focusing explicitly on attitudes, the model focuses on intentions to act in some way. Second, the model adds a component that assesses the consumer's perceptions of what other people think they should do. This is referred to as the *subjective norm*. Finally, the model explicitly focuses on the consumer's attitude toward the behavior of buying rather than the attitude toward the object.

The formula for the behavioral intentions model is as follows:[10]

$$B \approx BI = w_1(A_{\text{behavior}}) + w_2(SN)$$

where B = behavior, BI = behavioral intention, A_{behavior} = attitude toward performing the behavior (or A_{act}), SN = subjective norm, and w_1, w_2 = empirical weights.

This model states that a consumer's behavior is influenced by the intention to perform that behavior (BI), and that this intention is determined by the attitude toward performing the behavior (A_{behavior}) and *subjective norms* (SN).

From our apartment complex example, the A_{behavior} component includes the belief that the behavior will lead to a consequence (for example, "If I rent from Crown View, I'll be safe") and an evaluation of the consequence (for example: "Being safe is a good thing"). The *SN* component includes a consumer's belief that a reference group thinks that he or she should (or should not) perform the behavior (for example, Jamal's friends think he should choose Kings Landing because of its excellent fitness center) and the extent to which the consumer wants to comply with the suggestions of others (for example, will Jamal follow his friends' recommendations?).

The aspects of the behavioral intentions model are presented in Exhibit 7.4.

The behavioral intentions model was introduced as an improvement to the ATO model. Again, two major differences are found in the attitude toward the behavior and subjective norm components. For marketers, a clear understanding of the perceived consequences of product selection is crucial. Researchers must determine the consequences that are highly valued by their targeted consumer segments. Consumers don't always select products for the most predictable reason. Renters don't always choose an apartment based on rent or location. They may rent based largely on pet policies.

Marketing managers should also pay close attention to the subjective norm component of the model. Word-of-mouth communications are becoming critical for marketers. What do referent others think that the consumer should do? To what extent are they motivated to comply with the input of these people? The answers to these questions are quite valuable.

Factors That Weaken Attitude–Behavior Relationship

Although consumer attitude models are very popular in consumer research, researchers note that a number of factors can detract from the accuracy of this approach. For example, as the length of time between attitude measurement and overt behavior grows, the predictive ability of attitudinal models weakens. The specificity with which attitudes are measured also has an impact on accuracy. For example, measuring the intentions of buying a new Sony television would be more appropriate for Sony managers than would measuring one's intentions to buy any new television in the next month.

Strong environmental pressures can also keep consumers from performing intended behaviors. For example, when consumers feel rushed, decisions are often made in haste. Finally, attitude–behavior models tend to not perform very well in impulse-buying situations. As discussed earlier, these behaviors are quite common in a number of consumer contexts.

Alternative Approaches to Attitude

One small variation of this theory is the **theory of planned action**, which expands upon the behavioral intentions model by including a *perceived control* component. This component assesses the difficulty involved in performing the behavior and the extent to which the consumers perceive that they are in control of the product selection.[11] Products can be difficult to purchase, especially if they are in short supply.

Expanding the Attitude Object

The definition of attitudes presented earlier states that attitudes are relatively enduring evaluations of objects, products, services, issues, or people. For this reason, consumer researchers often study attitudes toward several different entities, not just brands or products.

One area that has received considerable consumer research attention is *attitude toward the advertisement*. Research has shown that there is generally a positive relationship between a consumer's attitude toward an advertisement and her attitude toward a particular product.[12]

> **theory of planned action** attitudinal measurement approach that expands upon the behavioral intentions model by including a perceived control component

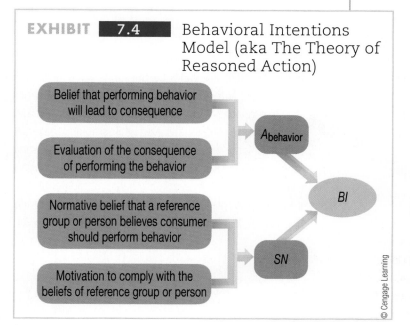

EXHIBIT 7.4 Behavioral Intentions Model (aka The Theory of Reasoned Action)

Belief that performing behavior will lead to consequence

Evaluation of the consequence of performing the behavior

A_behavior

Normative belief that a reference group or person believes consumer should perform behavior

Motivation to comply with the beliefs of reference group or person

SN

BI

© Cengage Learning

attitude tracking effort of a marketer or researcher to track changes in consumer attitudes over time

persuasion attempt to change attitudes

We note, however, that several factors have been shown to affect this relationship, including the overall liking of the television program in which the ad is embedded, the vividness of the imagery in the ad, the ad context, and the mood of the consumer.[13]

A growing area of research interest has also focused on attitude toward the company. What consumers know or believe about a company (sometimes referred to as *corporate associations*) can influence the attitude they have toward its products.[14] The study of consumer beliefs toward companies is therefore gaining considerable attention from consumer researchers. Of particular importance for many consumers is the question of how responsible companies are with their business practices. In general, consumers who feel positively about a company's business practices are likely to react more favorably toward the brands that the company markets.[15]

Attitude Tracking

Assessing one's attitude toward a specific product, brand, purchase act, advertisement, or company at only one specific point in time can also limit the accuracy of attitudinal models. Researchers therefore track how attitudes change over time. Because attitudes toward a brand can be influenced by several things, including attitude toward advertisements and companies, it is especially important to study changes in consumer attitudes. **Attitude tracking** refers to the extent to which a company actively monitors its customers' attitudes over time. What is important to understand is that even though attitudes are relatively enduring evaluations of objects, products, services, issues, or people, these attitudes should be monitored over time to gauge changes that may occur.

7-5 Attitude Change Theories and Persuasion

An important issue in the study of consumer behavior is how attitudes are changed. Marketers frequently want to change consumer attitudes about their products, and they focus their efforts on developing persuasive messages. Advertising obviously plays a major role in this effort. The term **persuasion** refers to specific attempts to change attitudes. Usually, the hope is that by changing beliefs or feelings, marketers can also change behavior.

There are many different persuasive techniques, and the following discussion presents the theoretical mechanisms through which persuasion may occur. These include the ATO approach, the behavioral influence approach, the schema-based affect approach,

Make the Switch

We have email and e-commerce, so why not e-cigarettes? Given the well-documented health risks that come from smoking traditional cigarettes, it was just a matter of time before marketers would deliver a seemingly safer alternative.

Electronic cigarettes (e-cigarettes) turn nicotine into a vapor that is inhaled by the smoker, thereby giving a smoke-free alternative in a healthier device. The beauty of the product for smokers is that the sensation of smoking remains while the urge for nicotine is satisfied. Because the product doesn't burn tobacco, it is marketed as being a healthier alternative to regular cigarettes. Many smokers have changed their attitudes about the relatively new product and a number of major tobacco companies have slowly ventured into the market.

However, there are currently questions about just how healthy these products really are. Some evidence suggests that smokers still inhale dangerous materials like carcinogens even while smoking the e-cigarette. This has led to a number of lawmakers introducing regulations to an industry that is otherwise largely unregulated. Time will tell if e-cigarettes eventually beat out traditional cigarettes in the marketplace. For now, however, many consumers are changing their attitudes and behaviors towards "smoking."

janceluch/Shutterstock.com

Sources: Josh Sanburn, "Can Electronic Cigarettes Challenge Big Tobacco?, *Time,* January 8, 2013, http://business.time.com/2013/01/08/can-electronic-cigarettes-challenge-big-tobacco/, accessed February 4, 2013; Mike Esterl, "E-Cigarettes Draw Fire from Legislatures," *The Wall Street Journal,* March 12, 2012, http://online.wsj.com/article/SB10001424052970203833004577249223276225382.html, accessed February 4, 2013; U.S. Food and Drug Administration, "FDA and Public Health Experts Warn About Electronic Cigarettes," July 22, 2009, http://www.fda.gov/NewsEvents/Newsroom/PressAnnouncements/ucm173222.htm, accessed February 4, 2013.

the elaboration likelihood model, the balance theory approach, and the social judgment theory approach.

7-5a Attitude-Toward-the-Object Approach

According to the ATO model, both beliefs about product attributes and evaluations of those attributes play important roles in attitude formation. By focusing on these components, the ATO approach presents marketers with a number of alternatives for changing consumer attitudes. To change attitudes according to this approach, marketers can attempt to change beliefs, create new beliefs about product features, or change evaluations of product attributes.

Changing Beliefs

As discussed in our apartment complex example, marketers may attempt to change consumers' beliefs. If consumers do not believe that Crown Pointe offers an excellent fitness center, then managers could focus on improving its facilities. Or let's assume that the complex already does have an excellent center, but consumers simply don't realize that they do. In this case, managers would need to focus more on this attribute in advertisements. With each effort, the focus is on improving the belief rating for an attribute that is evaluated positively (here, fitness center).

Another approach would be to focus on decreasing the strength of belief regarding a negatively evaluated attribute. For example, since pet friendliness is evaluated negatively in this case (−3), managers might decide to promote the idea that the walls of the apartments are quite thick and pet allergies shouldn't be a problem in their apartments. Here, the focus is on decreasing the belief rating of a negatively evaluated attribute. As we have discussed throughout this text, communicating value is an important marketing task.

Adding Beliefs about New Attributes

Another strategy for changing attitudes under the ATO approach is adding a salient attribute to the product or service. Like the changing beliefs approach, this may require a physical change to the product itself. For example, an apartment complex might add basic DirecTV service to all units. Here, a new attribute that is likely to be evaluated positively by consumers is added. When a valued attribute that was not previously considered is added, the overall attitude toward the complex may be improved.

At other times, the new beliefs may not be tied to an actual new attribute. Rather, they may simply

À votre santé! The belief that wine is healthy can lead people to like it even more.

emphasize something that consumers had previously not considered. To illustrate, consider what has happened with the marketing of red wine. In the 1980s, Robert Mondavi Winery added labeling to its wines that referred to the health benefits of drinking wine. Initially, the FDA stopped this practice, based on the notion that the label was misleading and detrimental to consumers. However, after years of research, the health-giving properties of wine are widely accepted. Red wine is associated with a reduced risk of heart disease and cancer, and this information has now been widely promoted. Thus, although the health-related benefits of red wine are nothing new, only in the last few years has the belief become prominently known and accepted. By adding a new belief, wine marketers have increased the market share of wine relative to beer and spirits. Recently, the advantages of apple cider vinegar have been promoted. Several health experts suggest consuming the vinegar daily as it reportedly leads to many health advantages. The vinegar purportedly helps the body break down fats, decrease bad cholesterol, and improve blood pressure.[16]

> Changing evaluations of an attribute is usually more difficult than changing the strength of a belief regarding an attribute.

Changing Evaluations

As noted earlier, marketers may also attempt to change the evaluation of an attribute. Here, the marketer would try to convince consumers that an attribute is not as positive (or negative) as they may think. For example, an apartment complex may attempt to persuade consumers that a downtown location is not necessarily a good

elaboration likelihood model attitudinal change model that shows attitudes are changed based on differing levels of consumer involvement through either central or peripheral processing

thing and that living in the suburbs is better. As discussed previously, changing evaluations of an attribute is usually more difficult than changing the strength of a belief regarding that attribute. Quite simply, consumers know what they like, and they make selections accordingly.

7-5b Behavioral Influence Approach

Another strategy commonly applied by marketers follows the Behavioral Influence hierarchy. You may remember that this hierarchy proposes that behavior precedes cognition and affect. Marketers may use this approach in many ways. Changing a retail store's design or atmospherics can have a direct influence on behavior. In fact, an entire industry called scent marketing (using scents to influence behavior) is emerging.

You may remember from our discussion on conditioning in an earlier chapter that behavioral conditioning can be very effective. Consumers respond to marketing stimuli in certain ways, and behaviors frequently result without either beliefs or affect changing first.

7-5c Changing Schema-Based Affect

We introduced the notion of schema-based affect in a previous chapter. From an attitude perspective, schema-based affect refers to the idea that schemas contain affective and emotional meanings. If the affect found in a schema can be changed, then the attitude toward a brand or product will change as well.

To illustrate, consider what happened when Domino's Pizza first entered Japan. Initially, the company had to deal with commonly held beliefs that tomatoes were unhealthy and that delivery food was not clean. Rather than trying to change these beliefs directly, Domino's created funny delivery carts and advertisements that attempted to attach positive feelings to the product schema and their brand. Thus, a positive attitude was shaped by this feeling found within the schema. This attitude-change technique can be effective if performed properly.

7-5d The Elaboration Likelihood Model

Another popular approach for conceptualizing attitude change is found in the **elaboration likelihood model**.[17] The elaboration likelihood model (ELM) illustrates

Don't Cross the Line

The recent MTV campaign entitled "A Thin Line" highlights how companies can partner with each other in order to stop harmful consumer behavior like cyberbullying.

Recent studies have revealed that cyberbullying and digital abuse are particularly harmful acts that are often aimed at teenagers. According to the A Thin Line website, 29% of young people have had rumors spread about them online or via text. MTV took the lead on the campaign and partnered with organizations such as the Anti-Defamation League, ConnectSafely.org, Facebook, DoSomething.org, iKeepSafe, and Family Violence Prevention Fund. The campaign, which is a multi-year effort, aims to stop the spread of actions like cyberbullying, digital date abuse, and "sexting." Distinguishing between digital use and digital abuse is a key part of the campaign. The campaign reminds consumers not to cross the line between the two areas.

© NLshop /Shutterstock.com

Efforts like A Thin Line focus on changing beliefs, affect, and behaviors. Beliefs about what is appropriate regarding online behaviors can be changed, feelings about digital abuse can be altered, and harmful behaviors can be stopped as well. Thanks to MTV and its partners, the Internet can be a safer place for all.

Sources: Based on online content, including Richard Webster, "MTV: New PSAs, New Original Movie on Cyberbullying, and More," Examiner.com, March 13, 2011, http://www.examiner.com /domestic-crimes-in-national/mtv-new-psas-new-original-movie-on-cyberbullying-and-more, accessed April 12, 2011; "Get the Facts," A Thin Line, http://www.athinline.org/facts, accessed April 18, 2012; "MTV Launches 'A Thin Line' to Stop Digital Abuse," MTV.com, http://www.mtv.com/news /articles/1627487/mtv-launches-thin-line-stop-digital-abuse.jhtml; Colleen Moody, "Protect Yourself from Digital Abuse," Seventeen.com, December 9, 2009, http://www.seventeen.com/cosmogirl /mtv-digital-abuse-campaign, accessed April 12, 2011.

how attitudes are changed based on differing levels of consumer involvement. Numerous research studies have examined the usefulness of the ELM in explaining the attitude change process. This model is shown in Exhibit 7.5.

According to the ELM, a consumer begins to process a message as soon as it is received. Depending on the level of involvement and a consumer's ability and motivation to process a message, the persuasion process then follows one of two routes: a *central route* or a *peripheral route*.[18]

The Central Route

If consumers find that the incoming message is particularly relevant to their situation (and thus highly involved), they will likely expend considerable effort in comprehending the message. In this case, high-involvement processing occurs, and the **central route to persuasion** is activated. Here, the consumer develops a number of thoughts (or cognitive responses) regarding the incoming message that may either support or contradict the information. Contradicting thoughts are known as counterarguments. Thoughts that support the main argument presented are known as support arguments.

In the central route, the consumer relies on **central cues**. Central cues refer specifically to information found in the message that pertains directly to the product, its attributes, its advantages, or the consequences of its use.

To illustrate this process, consider an experienced photographer who sees an advertisement for Sony cameras. Because he knows a lot about cameras and is highly interested in them, he will likely think carefully about the message he sees and the arguments presented as to why Sony cameras are the best cameras on the market. The arguments presented in the ad are critical. The photographer will consider the arguments and compare them to his current beliefs. He may even form counterarguments against the ad. For example, he may think "Canons are better." Or, he may think "Sony cameras really are better than Canons after all." (It is important to note that responses can be either negative or positive.)

If the consumer's beliefs are changed as a result of message exposure, attitude and behavior change will follow. Because the consumer is highly involved, and because he has made an effort to carefully attend to the message, it is likely that the attitude change will be relatively enduring. This is an important aspect of the central route to persuasion: *Attitude change tends to be relatively enduring when it occurs in the central route.*

The Peripheral Route

If consumers are not involved with a message or lack either the motivation or ability to process information, the **peripheral route to persuasion** will be followed. In this route, consumers are unlikely to develop cognitive responses to the message (either supporting arguments or counterarguments), and are more likely to pay attention to things like the attractiveness of the person delivering the message, the number of arguments presented, the expertise of the spokesperson, and the imagery or music presented along with the message. These elements of the message (that is, nonproduct-related information) are referred to as **peripheral cues**.

Many products, ranging from beer to cologne to clothing, use peripheral cues in their advertisements. If the consumer is influenced more by peripheral cues than central cues, any resulting belief or attitude change will likely be only temporary. That is, because the consumer is not highly engaged in the process, it is unlikely that attitude change will be enduring.

central route to persuasion path to persuasion found in ELM where the consumer has high involvement, motivation, and/or ability to process a message

central cues information presented in a message about the product itself, its attributes, or the consequences of its use

peripheral route to persuasion path to persuasion found in ELM where the consumer has low involvement, motivation, and/or ability to process a message

peripheral cues non-product-related information presented in a message

EXHIBIT 7.5 The Elaboration Likelihood Model

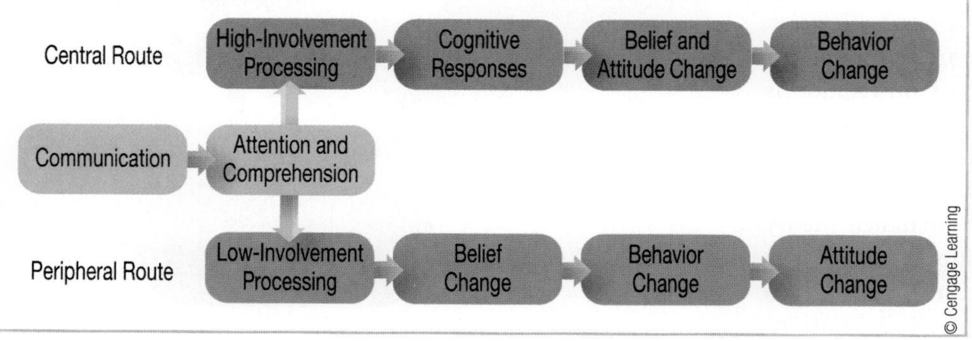

Central Route: High-Involvement Processing → Cognitive Responses → Belief and Attitude Change → Behavior Change

Communication → Attention and Comprehension

Peripheral Route: Low-Involvement Processing → Belief Change → Behavior Change → Attitude Change

© Cengage Learning

balance theory theory that states that consumers are motivated to maintain perceived consistency in the relations found in a system

consistency principle principle that states that human beings prefer consistency among their beliefs, attitudes, and behaviors

Low-Involvement Processing in the Consumer Environment

It is important to note that the vast majority of advertisements to which consumers are exposed are processed with low-involvement processing. Consumers are simply not motivated to carefully attend to the thousands of ads that they are exposed to each day! Therefore, advertisers tend to rely heavily on the use of peripheral cues—attractive models, enticing imagery, upbeat music—when developing advertisements.

7-5e Balance Theory

Another way to conceptualize attitude change processes is through balance theory. The **balance theory** approach was introduced by social psychologist Fritz Heider.[19] The basic premise of balance theory is that consumers are motivated to maintain perceived consistency in the relations found in mental systems. Accordingly, this approach is based on the **consistency principle**. This principle states that human beings prefer consistency among their beliefs, attitudes, and behaviors.

Balance theory focuses on the associations, or relations, that are perceived between a person (or observer), another person, and an attitudinal object. The relations between these elements may be perceived as being either positive or negative. An example is shown in Exhibit 7.6.

Note that the system (composed of observer, person, and object) is referred to as a *triad* because it consists of a set of three elements. The relations between the elements are referred to either as sentiment relations or as unit relations. *Sentiment relations* are the relations between the observer (consumer) and the other elements in the system. In Exhibit 7.6, the observer-person relation and the observer-object relation are referred to as sentiment relations. The object-person relation is referred to as a *unit relation*. Unit relations are based on the idea that two elements are in some way connected to one another.

Again, the basic premise of balance theory is that consumers are motivated to maintain perceived consistency in the relations found in the triad. Importantly, the perceived relations

An attractive model represents a peripheral cue.

between the cognitive elements in the balance theory system may be changed when inconsistency occurs.

To illustrate, look carefully at Exhibit 7.6. Assume that Isaiah, a quarterback on the local college team, is a fan of Peyton Manning. Here, there would be a positive (+) sentiment connection between Isaiah and Peyton. Isaiah notices that Peyton endorses Papa John's pizza. He sees advertisements for Papa John's during many NFL

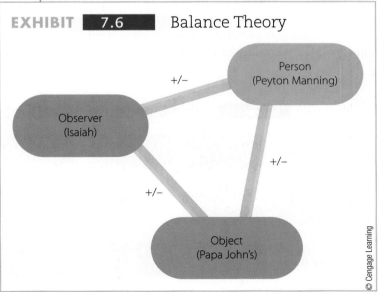

EXHIBIT 7.6 Balance Theory

Person (Peyton Manning)

Observer (Isaiah)

Object (Papa John's)

+/−

+/−

+/−

games on television. He's never felt strongly about Papa John's, but he really likes Peyton. Isaiah would perceive a positive unit relation (+) between Peyton and Papa John's. That is, Isaiah assumes the star endorses the product because he really likes it. How would Isaiah feel about the product? Well, in order to maintain balance in this triad, he would develop positive feelings toward Papa John's, resulting in a positive sentiment connection between himself and the brand.

This example illustrates a key premise of balance theory: *Consistency in the triad is maintained when the multiplication of the signs in the sentiment and unit relations results in a positive value.* When the resulting value is negative, consumers are motivated to change the signs (feelings) associated with one of the relations.

Suppose Isaiah didn't like Peyton Manning. That is, suppose there is a negative (−) sentiment relation between Isaiah and the star. Because he perceives a positive unit relation between Peyton and Papa John's he will be motivated to form a negative sentiment relation between himself and the brand (note that $[-] \times [+] \times [-] = +$). According to the theory, weak perceived relations are generally changed, while stronger relations remain unchanged. Here, Isaiah would be turned off by the advertisement and would develop a negative sentiment relation between himself and the brand. We note that while balance theory is often used to explain endorser effectiveness, the theory has also been applied in several other contexts, including product placements in television shows, goal-oriented behavior, consumer-brand relationships, and sports fan/team identification.[21]

It should also be noted that marketers who rely on this approach should be careful to monitor any changes that occur in how a target market perceives an endorser. As we have seen, public attitudes toward celebrities can change nearly overnight. In this case, the sentiment connection between the endorser and the consumer can become negative, leading to trouble for the brand advertised!

7-5f Social Judgment Theory

Social judgment theory is yet another theory for explaining attitude change.[22] This theory proposes that consumers compare incoming information to their existing attitudes about a particular object or issue. The initial attitude acts as a frame of reference, or standard, against which the incoming message is compared. Around these initial reference points are *latitudes of acceptance* and *latitudes of rejection*. For a message to fall within

the latitude of acceptance, the information presented must be perceived as being close to the original attitude position. A message that is perceived as being far away from, or opposed to, the original attitude position will fall within the latitude of rejection. These aspects of the theory are presented in Exhibit 7.7.

According to the theory, when an incoming message falls within the latitude of acceptance, *assimilation* occurs. This means that the message is viewed as being congruent with the initial attitudinal position, and the message is received favorably. In fact, the message may be viewed as being even more congruent with the initial attitudinal position than it really is. As a result, the consumer is likely to agree with the content of a message falling within the latitude of acceptance, and the attitude would change in the direction of the message.

If the message is perceived as falling in the latitude of rejection, an opposite effect occurs. In fact, the message will be viewed as being even more opposed to the original attitude than it really is, and the message will be rejected. In this way, a *contrast effect* is said to occur.

The implication for marketers is that messages should be constructed so that they fall within the latitude of acceptance of the targeted consumer. An important finding in this line of research is that when the original attitude is held with much conviction (either positive or negative), the latitude of acceptance is quite small and the latitude of rejection is large. On the contrary, when the original attitude is weak

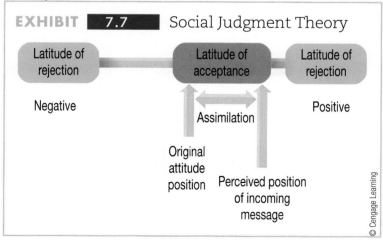

social judgment theory theory that proposes that consumers compare incoming information to their existing attitudes about a particular object or issue and that attitude change depends upon how consistent the information is with the initial attitude

EXHIBIT 7.7 Social Judgment Theory

© Cengage Learning

message effects how the appeal of a message and its construction affect persuasiveness

source effects characteristics of a source that influence the persuasiveness of a message

(either positive or negative), the latitude of acceptance is large and the latitude of rejection is small. This finding helps to explain why it is difficult to change a person's attitude when his or her attitude is very strong. Anyone who has tried to change a friend's mind will understand!

7-6 Message and Source Effects and Persuasion

An important part of understanding persuasion is comprehending how communication occurs. As we have discussed, consumers are exposed to thousands of messages every day and attention spans are decreasing. In response, some marketers are making their messages very brief. In fact, some radio ads are now only two seconds long![22a] Communicating in such a short time span is obviously difficult. Regardless of attention spans, both the message being sent and the source of the message affect persuasion.

The term **message effects** is used to describe how the appeal of a message and its construction affect persuasion. **Source effects** refer to the characteristics of the person or character delivering a message that influence persuasion. To understand how message and source effects work, we must begin by introducing a simple communication model. A basic communication model is shown in Exhibit 7.8.

According to this model, a source encodes a message and delivers the message through some medium. The medium could be personal (for example, when one consumer talks to another, or when a salesperson speaks with a customer) or impersonal (for example, when a company places an ad on television, on radio, or on a web page). The receiver (consumer) decodes the message and responds to it in some way. Feedback consists of the responses that the receiver sends back to the source. For example, a consumer might voice an objection to a sales pitch or decide to call a toll-free number to receive additional product information.

The *noise* concept is very important to this model. Noise represents all the stimuli in the environment that disrupt the communication process. In today's environment, noise comes in many different forms. For example, the popularity of online pop-up blockers is evidence of the number of distractions found on the web. From a traditional advertising perspective, the basic communication model is referred to as a "one-to-many" approach, because it illustrates how a marketer may attempt to communicate with numerous consumers.[23]

7-6a Interactive Communications

The one-to-many communications model works well when examining personal communications or traditional advertising media such as television, newspapers, or radio. However, interactive communications have radically changed the communication paradigm. In fact, recent estimates reveal that over 34% of the world's population now uses the Internet (over 2.4 billion consumers) and literally trillions of text messages are sent every year.[24] Due to the rapid adoption of the Internet and cell phones, we must consider its effect on the communication process.

Importantly, information flow is no longer considered a "one-way street," in which consumers passively receive messages from marketers. Rather, communication is seen as an interactive process that enables a flow of information among consumers and/or firms in what might be referred to as a many-to-many approach.[25] Senders can place content (web pages, blogs, interactive TV ads) into a medium and communicate directly with receivers through social networking sites, or text messages. This dramatically changes the communication model, with a newer conceptualization being presented in Exhibit 7.9. Research confirms that social media significantly influence consumer loyalty and WOM today.[25a]

As we have discussed, both the message itself and the person delivering the message have an impact on the overall effectiveness of an advertisement. For this reason, marketers

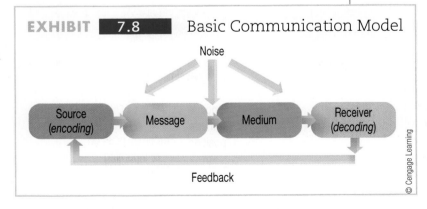

EXHIBIT 7.8 Basic Communication Model

Noise

Source (encoding) → Message → Medium → Receiver (decoding)

Feedback

© Cengage Learning

EXHIBIT 7.9

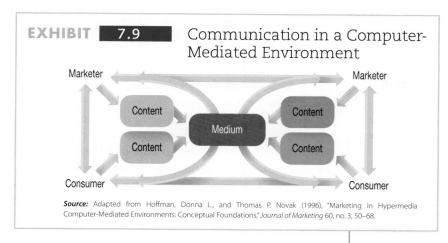

Communication in a Computer-Mediated Environment

Marketer

Marketer

Content

Content

Medium

Content

Content

Consumer

Consumer

Source: Adapted from Hoffman, Donna L., and Thomas P. Novak (1996), "Marketing in Hypermedia Computer-Mediated Environments: Conceptual Foundations," *Journal of Marketing* 60, no. 3, 50–68.

must consider both elements when developing communication strategies. This section discusses a number of findings regarding message and source effects. As you may remember, some of these topics were first introduced in our chapter on comprehension.

7-6b Message Appeal

There are several ways to conceptualize how a message may impact the persuasiveness of an advertisement. Here, we focus on the appeal (or general content) of an advertisement. A number of appeals are used by advertisers, including sex appeals, humor appeals, and fear appeals.

Sex Appeals

A popular saying in marketing is that "sex sells!" Using sexual imagery in advertisements certainly is popular in many parts of the world. In fact, European media usually contain stronger and more explicit sexual appeals than do American media. As we discussed in another chapter, the rationale for this approach is found within the psychoanalytic approach, and these appeals are often used as peripheral cues in the Elaboration Likelihood Model.

Interestingly, consumers often find sexually appealing ads to be persuasive, even when they consider them to be exploitative or offensive![26] However, consumers' reactions to the strategy depend on a number of factors. Moderate levels of nudity appear to be most preferred, as highly explicit content tends to direct attention away from the product.

Gender plays a role in advertising effectiveness regarding nudity. For example, one study found that women react negatively to the use of female nudity in advertising, but that men respond favorably toward the practice.[27] Conversely, a later study revealed men react

negatively toward the use of male nudity in ads, and that women responded favorably. The type of product being advertised also plays an important role. That is, the use of nudity is most effective for products that have some level of intimate appeal.[28]

Finally, research also reveals that including a romantic theme (rather than focusing on the explicit pleasure of sex) may have positive benefits for marketers. This is good news for fragrance marketers, who often focus their ads on romantic situations and settings.[29]

Humor Appeals

Marketers also frequently use humorous ads. In today's age of intense advertising clutter, ads that are humorous can be effective. One recent study confirmed that humorous ads can attract attention, create a positive mood, and enhance both attitude toward a brand and purchase intentions. However, humor appeals can also decrease the credibility of a message source.[30] Research also suggests that the use of humor should relate to the product being advertised.[31]

The overall effectiveness of a humorous ad depends, in part, on the characteristics of both the individual

Humorous ads can attract attention and create a positive mood.

consumer and the advertisement. As discussed in another chapter, research indicates that humor is more effective when a consumer's need for cognition is low rather than high,[32] and also when a consumer has a high need for humor.[33] Furthermore, the initial attitude that a consumer has regarding the product plays an important role, as humorous ads appear to be most effective when the consumer's attitudes are initially positive rather than negative.[34]

The amount of humor to place in an advertisement is another issue. High levels of humor can cause consumers to fail to pay attention to the product being advertised, and high levels can also limit information processing.[35] Obviously, marketers don't want to spend millions of dollars on ad campaigns simply for entertainment purposes.

Fear Appeals

In addition to using sexual and humor appeals, advertisers also frequently attempt to evoke some level of fear in their target audiences as a means of changing attitudes and behaviors. These ads often rely on the relationship between a threat (an undesirable consequence of behavior) and fear (an emotional response).[36] The product being advertised is often promoted as a type of a solution that will remove the threat.

For example, an insurance company might try to evoke fear in consumers by suggesting that their loved ones may fall into financial hardship if the consumer doesn't carry enough life insurance. Public service announcements may attempt to evoke fear in consumers by highlighting the tragic consequences of unsafe sexual practices (for example, HIV). Security monitoring services may use fear appeals to draw attention to the frightening consequences of home invasions.

Numerous research studies have addressed the effectiveness of fear appeals in marketing. As a general statement, research suggests that the use of fear appeals can be effective. However, the level of fear that results is very important. Overly high levels of fear may lead consumers to focus on the threat so much that they lose focus on the proposed solution.[37] Paradoxically, if fear arousal is not strong enough consumers may either discount the message or develop more positive attitudes towards the behavior that is being discouraged.[38] Also, different consumers are likely to react in different ways to the exact same fear appeal, complicating the issue further.[39] As a result, it is very difficult to predict how an individual consumer will react to any fear appeal. The context in which fear appeals are placed can also influence their effectiveness. For example, attitudes toward a fear-inducing ad have been found to be less positive when the ad is embedded in a sad television program than when the ad is placed in a happy (comedic) program.[40]

As an overall statement, fear appeals appear to be effective when they (1) introduce the severity of a threat, (2) present the probability of occurrence, (3) explain the effectiveness of a coping strategy, and (4) show how easy it is to implement the desired response.[41]

Although the use of fear appeals is popular among advertisers, it is important to note that there is an ethical question regarding their use. Critics often argue that the use of fear appeals in advertising is essentially a means of unfair manipulation.[42]

Violence Appeals

One trend that has been growing over the last few decades is the use of violent scenes in advertisements. There is much variety in violent themes, from the seemingly innocent to the downright shocking. The effects on viewers often go beyond marketing-related reactions. For example, children who view violent ads are more likely to develop aggressive thoughts, which can eventually lead to aggressive behavior.[43] Evidence has also shown that women are less receptive to violence in advertisements regardless of the level of severity of the violence, and that younger consumers are generally more receptive to violence in advertising.[44] It is interesting to note that many violent ads also use elements of humor, seemingly in an attempt to lessen the degree to which the ad is disturbing. In fact, many popular commercials have a combination of violence and humor, and a recent study found that the most popular Super Bowl ads include both humor and violence.[45] This area is likely to continue to gain research attention in CB.

7-6c Message Construction

The way that the message is constructed also impacts its persuasiveness. Advertisers must consider a number of issues when constructing a message. Here, we present a number of questions that marketers must answer.

- *Should an ad present a conclusion or should the consumer be allowed to reach his own conclusion?*

    Advertisements that allow consumers to arrive at their own conclusions tend to be more persuasive when the audience has a high level of involvement with the product. Conversely, when the audience is not engaged with the message, it is generally better to draw the conclusion for consumers.[46]

- *Should comparative ads that directly compare one brand against another be developed?*

Advertisers generally have three alternatives when developing an ad. First, they can promote their brands without mentioning competing brands. Second, advertisers can promote their brands and compare them generically to "the competition." Third, they can actively compare their products against specific competitors by explicitly naming the competing brands in the advertisement.

Directly comparing one brand against specific competitors can be effective—especially when the brand being promoted is not already the market leader.[47] Promoting a brand as being "superior to all competition" can also be very persuasive when a firm hopes to court users away from all competing brands.[48]

- *Where should important information be placed?*

The placement of information in a specific message at the beginning, middle, or end of the message impacts the recall of the information. This is a basic tenet of what is known as the **serial position effect**.[49] When material presented early in a message is most influential, a **primacy effect** is said to occur. When material presented later in the message has the most impact, a **recency effect** is said to occur.[50]

Research suggests that primacy effects are likely to occur when the audience is highly engaged (highly involved) and when verbal (versus pictorial) content is present.[51] If marketers are attempting to reach a highly involved audience, important information should be placed early in the message. Marketers can also attempt to gain the consumer's attention as early as possible and encourage careful processing of information by using statements such as "an important message" or "listen carefully." For audiences with lower levels of involvement, important information can be placed late in the message. These effects also occur in series of messages, and can impact the recall of commercials placed in any particular block of commercials. For example, research has revealed that primacy effects prevail for the recall of Super Bowl commercials. That is, commercials placed at the beginning of a block resulted in higher levels of consumer recall.[52]

- *Should the message be straightforward and simple, or complex?*

Advertisers must consider both message and source effects. In general, complex ads take more effort on the part of the consumer and require deep information processing. Overly complex messages can cause frustration within consumers and lead to unfavorable reactions. As presented earlier in the section on the ELM, the number of arguments presented in an ad is considered a peripheral cue. Highly involved consumers are more motivated to attend to a larger number of arguments than are less motivated consumers.

7-6d Source Effects

Another important issue in the study of persuasion is how the source of a message (a spokesperson or model, for example) influences consumers' attitudes. Source effects include issues such as credibility, attractiveness, likeability, and meaningfulness. You may notice that some of these effects were presented as peripheral cues in the ELM.

Source Credibility

Source credibility plays an important role in advertising effectiveness. In general, credible sources tend to be more persuasive than less credible sources. This effect tends to be highest when consumers lack the ability or motivation to expend effort attending to the details of an ad (low involvement).[53] However, credible sources also influence highly involved consumers, especially if their credentials are clearly communicated early in a message.[54] The credibility of sources also impacts the certainty with which consumer attitudes are held, with lower levels of credibility leading to higher levels of certainty.[55]

As we discussed in our comprehension chapter, credibility consists of two elements: expertise and trustworthiness. *Expertise* refers to the amount of

serial position effect occurs when the placement of information in a message impacts recall of the information

primacy effect occurs when the information placed early in a message has the most impact

recency effect occurs when the information placed late in a message has the most impact

Source credibility is important in advertising.

© iStockphoto.com/GYI NSEA

matchup hypothesis
hypothesis that states that a source feature is most effective when it is matched with relevant products

knowledge that a spokesperson is perceived to have about the product or issue in question. You may remember from our presentation on the ELM that source expertise represents a peripheral cue in advertising. Expertise can be an important quality for a spokesperson to possess. In fact, a major review of source effects has revealed that source expertise has the biggest influence of all source effects on consumer responses to advertisements.[56]

Trustworthiness refers to a perception of the extent to which a spokesperson is presenting a message that he or she truly believes, with no reason to present false information. Interestingly, expertise and trustworthiness can independently influence persuasion. That is, trustworthy sources can be persuasive even if they're not experts, and expert sources can be persuasive even if they're perceived as being untrustworthy.[57]

Finally, we note that source credibility, although generally conceptualized as pertaining to a spokesperson or model, also applies to the sponsoring company. In fact, research reveals that the credibility of both the spokesperson and the company influences the effectiveness of an advertisement, with the credibility of the spokesperson having a stronger influence than the credibility of the company.[58]

Source Attractiveness

Source attractiveness is another quality that has received a great deal of attention. Attractive models are often thought to possess desirable qualities and personalities. They also tend to be more persuasive than unattractive spokespeople.[59] However, the type of product plays an important role in the process. Much like the research regarding the use of sex appeals, research into attractiveness reveals that attractive models are more effective when promoting products that have an intimate appeal, whereas unattractive models are more effective when promoting products that have no intimate appeal.[60] This is particularly the case when consumers have the ability and motivation to process the message being presented and elaboration likelihood is high.[61]

Source Likeability

Source likeability also affects a spokesperson's effectiveness. Likeable sources tend to be persuasive. Of course, individuals differ in terms of which celebrities they like and dislike, and marketers are very interested in finding the best possible spokesperson for a given market segment. The advertising industry relies heavily on a Q-score rating provided by Marketing Evaluations, Inc. as an indication of the overall appeal of celebrities.[62] Interestingly, it has been found that source likeability affects persuasion more for consumers with low need for cognition than for those with a high degree of this trait. This again highlights the importance of individual difference variables in persuasion.[63]

Source Meaningfulness

Celebrities have images and cultural meanings that resonate with consumers. For example, a famous athlete like Dwayne Wade embodies the image of hard work and success. Pairing Dwayne with athletic apparel or footwear simply makes sense. You should recall that research on the use of sexual imagery and source attractiveness suggests that these characteristics should be matched with the type of product being advertised. This is true for source meaningfulness as well. That is, the dominant characteristics of a source should match the characteristics of the product. This is a key concept that is found in the **matchup hypothesis**, which states that a source feature is most effective when it is matched with relevant products.[64] As such, we should expect NBA star Dwayne Wade to be an effective spokesperson for footwear and less effective when promoting a product that has no athletic qualities at all.

As you can see, marketers face a number of decisions when constructing campaigns that are aimed at changing consumer attitudes.

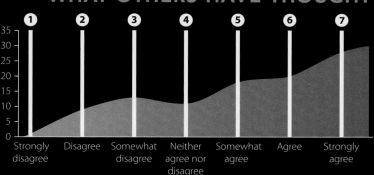

WHAT DO YOU THINK?
WHAT OTHERS HAVE THOUGHT

❶	❷	❸	❹	❺	❻	❼

35
30
25
20
15
10
5
0

Strongly disagree | Disagree | Somewhat disagree | Neither agree nor disagree | Somewhat agree | Agree | Strongly agree

It's pretty hard to change my attitude about products that I dislike.

Responses to this question have varied greatly and there are many reasons for these findings. Attitude change is affected by the theories that have been discussed in this chapter. One common finding, however, is that the stronger the attitude, the harder it is to change the attitude. We all know what we like and it's hard to change how we feel!

Study Tools

Located at back of the textbook

❑ Rip out Chapter in Review Card

Located at www.cengagebrain.com

❑ Review Key Terms Flashcards (print or online)

❑ Download audio summaries to review on the go

❑ Complete practice quizzes to prepare for tests

❑ Play "Beat the Clock" and "Quizbowl" to master concepts

❑ Watch video on Southwest Airlines for a real company example

study tools

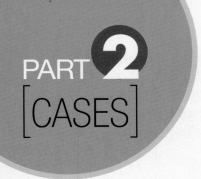

CASE 2-1

CLIMBING TO THE TOP!

*Written by Dr. David Matthews, SUNY Adirondack; students
Sandra Dickinson and Christina Green, SUNY Adirondack*

Where can one go and relax while having a thrill-seeking adventure? Ever heard of vertical yoga? Would you, could you, imagine being 30 feet off the ground in a tranquil state of mind, knowing you have just reached a new high? Tom Rosecrans began an adventure of a lifetime when he bought out two partners of Rock Sport Indoor Rock Climbing (www.rocksportny.com). A small-scale facility with varying degrees of difficulty ranging from beginner to advanced bouldering, the setting may be small in square footage but it sure fills the desires of experienced climbers. Never having owned his own business, this high school teacher powdered his hands and held on tight taking his venture to new levels ten years later. With over 36 years of rock climbing experience, Tom has experienced destinations on a global scale, including two expeditions to the Himalayas.

Running a business of passion could be overwhelming, so Tom kept things relatively manageable, never really trying to outdo or grow the business beyond modest proportions, satisfied to own a part-time "hobby" business. However, the situation has changed and Tom has decided now is the time for adjustment, and with good reason. A few months ago a newer, bigger, brassier indoor rock climbing gym opened just 20 minutes away and is drawing excitement from Rock Sport's current customer base as well as the public. With few choices and immediate need, Tom must determine through market research what is best for Rock Sport, especially increasing his target market, client base, and innovative new programs.

Outdoor rock climbing, or mountaineering, began in Europe in the early 1800s, though the first mountaineering club wasn't started until 1857. Rock climbing for recreation came much later in the 20th century, when styles, grading, and equipment were all brought together and turned the adventure into a sport.[1] In the 1980s alternatives were made for busy climbers; indoor facilities that took less time to manage were designed to have different degrees of difficulty and to allow realistic experiences for the sport enthusiast.[2]

Climbing is both challenging and rewarding, physically and psychologically. Designed to promote problem solving, teamwork, and self-confidence, other benefits are purely physical. For example, major progress can be made in improving one's cardiovascular health, muscle tone, and weight loss. But one of the great benefits of rock climbing is the thrill and joy it brings, as well as a pure sense of achievement. Children love the challenge in a risky environment, while parents enjoy the safety features in today's indoor gyms. Having fun with family, friends, or finally reaching one's personal "trail" goal is satisfying. A simple focus group conducted at the gym even revealed customers speaking of "peak performances and experiences," conditions indicative of the intrinsically satisfying "flow" state of motivation.

However, there are some negative perceptions in society today regarding rock climbing, many stemming from cautious Baby Boomers. Survey research revealed the following possible obstacles: fear of falling, fear of heights, low self-image while climbing (embarrassment), and even the fear of failure. All were cited as reasons why the sport has declined in adult participation over the years. On top of this, cost and time limitations were also mentioned by survey respondents. Tom's biggest challenge is drawing in new people or markets to try rock climbing. He is convinced the sport can be viewed as another "soft recreation" alternative similar to kayaking and bicycling. In fact, he has made it a personal mission to try and get more Baby Boomers like himself to try the sport. The children's market is not the problem. Hundreds of Generation Y parents are bringing their kids to the facility for birthday parties and non-competitive meets. In addition, students from the local community college are also regular customers who share their experiences on social media like Facebook. No, the younger demographic segments are not the issue. As such, Tom is now challenged to try and change this negative attitude among the Generation X and Baby Boomer market segments.

Other indoor gyms have reacted to grow their business and made the needed changes in facility offerings and programs. In the past, strong athletic men were the avid climbers; today the average climber is in his or her mid-20s, with the number of children right behind and growing rapidly.[3] There are stories of toddlers climbing indoor rock walls in just diapers, and even five- and six-year-olds on open mountain ranges climbing better than most adults, which shows how they will become the new generation of the sport. Women have slowly gained interest in the sport mainly due to themed nights and special events. Many believe that rock climbing is for the 130-pound, athletic, outgoing type and miss that rock climbing can fit anyone who is willing to try. There has even been a national marketing campaign introduced to stress the safety of climbing.

Currently, most of Rock Sport's customers are the children of Generation Xers in the athletic programs and some college students. Tom would like to encourage Baby Boomers and parents of the children that use his facility to give indoor climbing a try. Convincing the older generations of the health benefits and the fun and exciting adventures is tricky in today's society. Their opinion of adventurers is young and fit, not parents and grandparents. Changing the views of these age groups is challenging and can cost quite a bit of money and time if not done correctly.

Soon Tom will pass the business off to his daughter, but not without leaving her a strategy that ensures sustainable growth forward. Ideas include moving into a larger facility, revamping the website, increasing social media use, and creating strategic alliances with lifestyle, service firms like yoga, and Pilates training. Creating large competitive events that showcase the facility and spread awareness are other possible ideas. As such, Tom is challenged by what the future holds and eager to turn ideas into action plans.

Questions

1. What types of programs or tactics would you suggest the owner institute to break the fear of Baby Boomers and change their attitude towards rock climbing?

2. What do you think motivates one to rock climb or try this sport? Is the value provided utilitarian or hedonic? If you never tried rock climbing, would you now consider it? If so, what would be your motivation?

3. Explain how the intrinsic motivation state of flow might occur in rock climbing.

4. Using the multiple trait approach to consumer behavior, analyze which specific consumer traits would explain one's motivation to rock climb. For example, the Five Factor Model of personality traits is one framework that can be used.

5. Using the ABC approach to attitudes, explain why a Baby Boomer might feel that rock climbing is a "young person's sport." Then, create a program for Rock Sport that attempts to change this negative attitude and invites Baby Boomers to try indoor rock climbing.

CASE 2-2

Plasma vs. LCD TVs – Much Ado About Nothing?

Written by Rob Rouwenhorst, Ph.D., University of Iowa

There are numerous factors consumers need to consider as they upgrade their televisions to newer high-definition (HD) sets. Bulky cathode ray tubes, weighing sometimes hundreds of pounds, are dead and rear-projection TVs are dying, leaving three distinct types of HDTVs: plasma, liquid crystal displays (LCD) backlit with cold cathode fluorescent lights (CCFL), and LCDs backlit with light-emitting diodes (LED). As technology is constantly evolving and improving, audio-video enthusiasts debate which technology is best and provides the most value. Can consumers really tell the difference, and what are ways marketers can influence viewers' perceptions of HDTVs?

When HDTVs first came on the scene, the only real choice was plasma. The phosphors that make a plasma television's image light up themselves and do not require backlighting. Because they do not require backlighting, plasma provides dark blacks and great picture quality. On the down side, they literally can be hot to the touch and are power-hungry. In general, they will consume two to three times the power consumed by a LCD TV.[1]

Gradually, thinner, energy-efficient LCDs lit with CCFL backlighting became less expensive and began gaining ground on plasma TVs. The liquid crystal screen does not light up itself, so a backlight is required. CCFL were in many of the first LCDs produced and are still used in more inexpensive sets available today. CCFLs are similar to the fluorescent lights you may use in an overhead fixture. Because of the need for a backlight, CCFL LCDs were worse in picture quality compared to plasma TVs.

Today, LED-backlit LCDs are increasingly popular. With their ability to backlight portions of the screen that you want lit up (e.g., a character talking), and stay off in other parts that should remain black (e.g., a night sky or black bars), LED technology promises the best of both worlds: picture quality to match plasma sets, with the energy efficiency and thinness of LCDs.

To further complicate television buying, a TV's resolution has become another statistic. Terms such as 720i, 720p, 1080i, and 1080p are used to describe the HD signal being shown. The number represents the number of lines being displayed from the top to the bottom of the screen. To put this in perspective, older standard-definition televisions and DVDs had only 480 lines. While more lines leads to a better image, it is difficult to tell the difference between 720 and 1080 lines on a small screen (those less than 32 inches).

There was a large debate about whether the average consumer could notice the difference several years ago, when sets that topped out at 720p cost less than 1080p sets. However, the debate has been ruled largely academic, as most large (40 inches and more) HDTVs nowadays are capable of displaying a 1080p signal. However, smaller screens (those less than 32 inches) come in both 720 and 1080 flavors.

HD signals are denoted with an *i* for interlaced and a *p* for progressive. Interlaced signals mean the screen is divided into even and odd lines that are alternately refreshed or redrawn, meaning there is a slight delay between odd and even line refreshes, which can cause some jaggedness. This occurs because half of the lines are keeping up with a moving image while the other half are waiting to be refreshed. Progressive signals mean that every line on the screen is redrawn or refreshed. The distinction is nuanced, but progressive signals look better. However, the progressive signals also come with the drawback of having to carry more information, so many cable and satellite providers only provide interlaced signals to decrease their bandwidth costs.

Refresh rates get a lot of talk in the marketing of TV sets. Saying that more frames shown per second leads to a smoother look sounds great, but in practice there is not much of a difference. Television can be thought of as 30 pictures shown each second. Those pictures or *frames* are interlaced to 60 frames per second to match the 60Hz refresh rate of the majority of LCD TVs you can buy today. Movies are shot at 24 frames per second, and to make the footage look as close to the film as possible, Blu-ray players display 24 frames per second. When HDTVs were in their infancy, they would suffer from blurriness during very fast movement (e.g., sports). But technology has progressed such that motion blur has mostly been eliminated. So if you are considering an LCD with 120HZ or 240Hz or a plasma with 600Hz, know that the various technologies that increase refresh rate on HDTVs do not actually add any detail to the video and are another way to market TVs that will not be that discernable from one another.

Finally, there is the consideration of size and price. Do not assume that bigger is always better. Much like with a computer monitor, if you sit too close to the TV, images will become jagged and pixelated. For instance, do not get a 60" TV if you will be sitting within six feet of the screen.[2]

All of us have walked down the TV aisle of a large discount or electronics store and seen the wall of televisions. While comparing two TVs may seem easy as they are next to one another, you must consider the motivations of the store. There are a myriad of settings that can be adjusted on each TV. For instance, the brightness can be controlled to make one television brighter than the other. Is the store displaying the ideal, calibrated settings? Or are they displaying the settings out of the box? Are they making one TV that has a higher margin for the retailer look especially good?

In conclusion, do not buy on price alone. Most plasma and LCD TVs have an expected life of 100,000 hours. Picking the right technology and screen is critical to the HDTV experience. Relying on the opinion of experts and others may help consumers make the best choice, because in the hands of a well-trained employee, the worst television can be made to look the best and vice versa.

Questions

1. In what ways are TV manufacturers practicing the total value concept? What features are consumers coming to expect in a modern TV?

2. Say you manage the electronics department at your local Best Buy. Would you tweak the TV settings so each TV displays an ideal picture or would you leave them as they are out of the box? How would your decision influence returns and customer satisfaction?

3. Apple has made a case for the "retina" display on the latest iPhone and iPad, saying the pixels are so small the human eye cannot detect them. This gets away from official statistics like 2048-by-1536 screen resolution. In what ways is this positive or negative for consumers?

4. Say you are the product manager for a line of plasma televisions. What features would you emphasize the most with customers? Why?

5. Given what you now know about HDTVs, in what ways does marketing influence consumers' perceptions of products such as TVs?

CASE 2-3

Virtually Free!

Written by Barry J. Babin, Louisiana Tech University

An old marketing adage puts forward the importance of creating customers. In times gone by, companies like Kodak were heralded for using inexpensive cameras like the Kodak 110 to create customers for film and film services. Kodak's success lay in film, not in cameras.

Perhaps the connection between Kodak and video games isn't so obvious, but success in gaming is all about creating customers. Before the widespread adoption of online gaming, companies like Nintendo used game consoles as loss leaders to create customers for games. The online gaming companies don't even have to manufacture or sell consoles as loss leaders.

Zynga is one of the major players in online gaming. While Zynga's original marketing strategy was to provide games free to users and generate revenue from advertisers, they've morphed into a revenue model strongly driven by Facebook users. Zynga games like Castleville, Cityville, Farmville, Fishville, and Zynga Poker have become a social networking phenomenon in recent years. Zynga and other online gamers now use the "freemium" as the primary tool to create customers. The term *freemium* refers to the free games that companies offer to consumers as a tool to sell virtual products that help freemium customers succeed in their game play. Zynga grew on this business model to revenues topping $600 million in 2010 (from $1 million in 2008).[1] Zynga went public with an intial stock offering in late 2011. Initially shares sold for $10 and showed a decline to about $5 by the middle of 2012.[2]

Zynga's hope is to create more *whales*, a term referring to heavy consumers of virtual products. However, Zynga faces a lot more competition today than it did in 2011, as consumers find many more options for online games.[3] Take for example TinyCo, makers of Tiny Zoo, available as an app in iTunes or for Android systems through Google. After playing Tiny Zoo for only 60 seconds, new users receive a message saying "looks like you need more Coins to buy a Chickity Puff." The idea behind the game is to amass a prized collection of virtual (not real) animals to display in the virtual (not real) zoo. Perhaps with more than a touch of irony, one of the prized animals is known as the Cash Cow! In case you haven't guessed by now, TinyCo sells Tiny Zoo virtual coins for real money. One market segment for virtual products is children. One eight-year-old spent two months' allowance ($50) when Tiny Zoo released a new batch of animals. These kids are not playing the games on computers but on their parents' smartphones and tablets—or on their own tablets and iPods. Many parents willingly allow their kids to use payment apps to buy virtual products as a sort of babysitting device. After all, parents have always given in to kids in toy stores. Trouble is, unlike a real toy store, the app store is open 24-7 and the kid is in the store any time the smartphone is in their hands.[4] Industry analysts expect the mobile gaming business to grow fivefold to nearly $20 billion per year by 2015.[5]

The growth may seem like good news for Zynga, but many questions linger. Among these questions are the following:

- Zynga games are predominantly played on PCs through Facebook. Consumer trends seem to be moving toward gaming on mobile devices. Zynga would be a latecomer to this market. Will consumers continue to play games like Farmville on Facebook or will consumers substitute gaming on mobile devices at the expense of Zynga?

- Zynga is closely tied to Facebook. Is this risky?

- Apple's new operating system will facilitate social networking simultaneously with the use of many online games. Will this make Zynga's typical distribution outdated?

- Can Zynga continue to develop new and creative freemiums given the large number of app designers entering the gaming market?

With these issues in mind, Zynga may need to rethink their marketing strategy. Consumer behavior knowledge may be useful to them in better understanding their customers.

Questions

1. Consumers, whether adults are children, have to learn how to play online games like Tiny Zoo or Castleville. In this part of the book, learning is described as being either intentional or unintentional. Explain your opinion on whether these games are learned more by intentional or unintentional learning mechanisms.

2. Brand loyalty is an important marketing concept. Define the concept of schema. How important is the brand schema in consumer decisions to play these games? Do you think consumers think of the company (Zynga), the game (Cityville), or the host (Facebook) when playing the games?

3. All consumer behavior is motivated by something. What motivations underlie online gaming and purchasing of online games? In the case of parents paying for virtual goods used by their kids, what value is involved in the consumption?

4. Do consumer attitudes play a role in online gaming?

Fuse/Jupiterimages

PART **3**
CB

Networking has
taken on a new meaning in the digital age.

WHAT DO YOU THINK?
The groups I belong to have a great impact on how I see myself.

STRONGLY DISAGREE   STRONGLY AGREE

VISIT COURSEMATE AT WWW.CENGAGEBRAIN.COM

Group and Interpersonal Influence

One common motivation that people share is the need to belong. Belonging to groups is an important part of human life, because humans are social creatures who desire contact and affiliation with others. Consumers often belong to, or desire to join, a number of formal or informal groups. These groups can exert significant influence on consumer behavior. Consumers are also influenced by other individual consumers. This is especially true through social media. The popular website Pinterest allows individual consumers to influence others regarding things like crafts, recipes, and clothing. In this chapter, we discuss a number of issues relating to the concept of group and interpersonal influence and how these concepts apply to value. We begin by discussing the various types of reference groups that influence CB.

8-1 Reference Groups

A **reference group** is a group of individuals who have significant relevance for a consumer and who have an impact on the consumer's evaluations, aspirations, and behavior.[1] This influence affects the ways that consumers seek and receive value from consumption. Most people don't realize all the ways that reference groups influence their behavior. However, we can start to understand this better when we think of all the groups that we belong to. Consumers become members of many groups that either meet physically or, thanks to the Internet, meet in cyberspace. How many Facebook groups do you "like"? How many people or companies do you follow on Twitter? Have you discovered any new music from Myspace or learned about a new hobby on Pinterest? Have your friends sent you a Snapchat photo? All of these examples illustrate how social media shape group and individual behavior. To begin a discussion of these issues, we must first define what we mean by group influence.

After studying this chapter, the student should be able to:

8-1 Understand the different types of reference groups that influence consumers and how reference groups influence value perceptions.

8-2 Describe the various types of social power that reference groups exert on members.

8-3 Comprehend the difference between informational, utilitarian, and value-expressive reference group influence.

8-4 Understand social media's role in consumer behavior.

8-5 Understand the importance of word-of-mouth in influencing consumer behavior.

8-6 Comprehend the role of household influence in consumer behavior.

reference group
individuals who have significant relevance for a consumer and who have an impact on the consumer's evaluations, aspirations, and behavior

group influence ways in which group members influence attitudes, behaviors, and opinions of others within the group

primary group group that includes members who have frequent, direct contact with one another

secondary group group to which a consumer belongs whose contact is less frequent than that found in a primary group

brand community group of consumers who develop relationships based on shared interests or product usage

8-1a Group Influence

Group influence refers to ways in which group members influence attitudes, opinions, and behaviors of others within the group. Groups are an important part of social life, and they profoundly affect consumer behavior by changing the perceived value of products. In fact, gaining acceptance into a group provides value for consumers directly by satisfying their needs for belonging. Consider the following aspects of group life:

- Group members share common goals and interests.
- Group members communicate with and influence one another.
- Group members share a set of expectations, rules, and roles.
- Group members view themselves as members of a common social unit.[2]

These qualities of group membership are important. A college international club shares a common set of expectations that ultimately influences members' decisions about things such as activities, attire, and social involvement. A Girl Scouts troop organizes fundraisers to help finance their activities. A divorce support group meets regularly to discuss the difficulties associated with adjusting to a single lifestyle. A Facebook group shares common interests in products and services. When you join (or like) a Facebook group or page, you share some common interest in the relevant subject.

Group influence does not just affect buying behavior. Consumer attitudes, opinions, and value perceptions also are heavily influenced by groups, even if a specific purchase does not directly result. This is particularly the case with social networking website groups. Some groups, whether online or otherwise, have more influence on consumers than do others.

Primary/Secondary Groups

A **primary group** is a group that includes members who have frequent, direct contact with one another. Primary reference groups generally have the most influence on their members, and *social ties* for these groups are very strong. A social tie is a measure of the strength of connection between group members. An example of a primary reference group is the family unit. Family members generally have much influence on one another, and many times it directly affects behavior in the marketplace. For example, studies reveal that parental influence on children's shopping and saving behavior can be quite strong.[3] Parents who openly discuss financial matters, such as developing savings accounts, can greatly influence these behaviors.

In a **secondary group**, interaction within the group is much less frequent than in a primary group. Professional organizations and social clubs are examples of secondary groups. Usually, the influence of these groups on members is not as strong as the influence of primary groups on their members. Furthermore, social ties are not as strong in secondary groups as they are in primary groups.

One special type of secondary group is a **brand community**. Brand communities are groups of consumers who develop relationships based on shared interests or product usage.[4] A popular example of a brand community is the KISS Army. The KISS Army is a group of fans of the legendary rock group who form close bonds with each other and who regularly attend band conventions that may be referred to as *brandfests*.

In general, personal connections originating in brand communities lead to positive outcomes for consumers and companies. Consumers learn more about the products they enjoy, and they develop bonds with other users. Companies reap the rewards of positive

Becoming a Girl Scout provides many opportunities for girls.

ZUMA Wire Service/Alamy

consumer commitment, which they can build by sponsoring events.[4a] The commitment members share helps them form tight bonds.[5]

Formal/Informal Groups

A **formal group** is a group in which a consumer formally becomes a member. For example, a consumer becomes a formal member of a church congregation. Formal groups generally have a set of stated rules, accepted values, and codes of conduct that members are expected to adhere to.

An **informal group** is a group that has no membership or application requirements, and codes of conduct may be nonexistent. Examples of informal groups include groups that meet regularly to exercise, have coffee, or go to sporting events. Although informal group influence may not be as strong as formal group influence, these groups can have an impact on consumer behavior.

Aspirational/Dissociative Groups

An **aspirational group** is a group in which a consumer desires to become a member. Aspirational group membership often appeals to the consumer's *ideal* self. The ideal self is an important part of the consumer's self-concept, and consumers often visualize themselves as belonging to certain groups. For example, a business student may desire to become a member of a professional business association once he earns his degree. Consumers frequently emulate the members of aspirational groups and perform behaviors that they believe will lead to formal acceptance into the group. Getting the first job would be the first step for joining a business organization.

A **dissociative group** is a group to which a consumer does not want to belong. For example, a Republican might want to avoid being perceived as belonging to a Democratic group (and vice versa). Recent college graduates may want to disassociate themselves from groups from their past as they take the next step into adulthood.

8-1b Conformity

An important topic in the study of reference group influence is conformity. **Conformity** occurs when an individual yields to the attitudes and behaviors of other consumers. Conformity is similar in some ways to the concept of persuasion. The key difference between persuasion and conformity is that with conformity, the other party does not necessarily defend its position. That is, a group may give no reason for why it expects its group members to act or think a certain way. Persuasion, on the other hand, relies on one party defending its position in an attempt to change behavior.[6]

Peer Pressure

Peer pressure and conformity are also closely related topics. **Peer pressure**, the pressure an individual feels to behave in accordance with group expectations, can greatly influence behavior. In fact, peer pressure is often the strongest type of influence a consumer experiences in daily life.

Consumers of all ages feel peer pressure. In fact, very young children often desire to wear the types of clothing and brands that will allow them to feel accepted. One study found that children as young as ten prefer to wear brand-name footwear (e.g., Nike) so that they will fit in with their peers.[7]

Peer pressure and conformity share some similarities. Both are based on behaviors that are in line with what others expect. With peer pressure, there is usually some type of sanction that is threatened if the consumer does not go along with the group. With conformity, behavioral choices are generally more strongly based on internal desires to belong, even when the threat of sanction is not present.

Negative Peer Pressure

Peer pressure to wear a certain brand of clothing is not necessarily a bad thing. Unfortunately, negative consumer behaviors are often heavily influenced by peer pressure. Consumers sometimes succumb to group pressures that subtly or not so subtly encourage counterproductive or unethical—perhaps illegal—behaviors.

Experts frequently cite peer pressure as particularly persuasive among young consumers. The media direct

formal group group in which a consumer formally becomes a member

informal group group that has no membership or application requirements and that may have no code of conduct

aspirational group group in which a consumer desires to become a member

dissociative group group to which a consumer does not want to belong

conformity result of group influence in which an individual yields to the attitudes and behaviors of others

peer pressure extent to which group members feel pressure to behave in accordance with group expectations

> Consumers frequently emulate the members of aspirational groups.

social power ability of an individual or a group to alter the actions of others

a lot of attention to peer pressure and illegal alcohol or tobacco consumption. Binge drinking among underage consumers is a serious societal problem that can have disastrous, and sometimes fatal, effects. Peer pressure often plays a large role in this behavior. Even virtual group pressure, such as exerted through social networking sites, is sometimes blamed for encouraging underage smoking.[8] Although this form of peer pressure is negative, marketers can harness the power of peer pressure in positive ways. For example, advertisements that encourage young consumers to abstain from negative behaviors (like underage drinking) can be effective when peer group members deliver the message.[9] And consumers who stick together can change together, as illustrated by a Facebook group that encourages friending among those who want to stop smoking.

Adolescents are particularly susceptible to peer pressure and are often compelled to rebel against their families in favor of behaviors that win acceptance from their peers. Teens commonly go against family expectations and parental rules. At this stage in social development, friends begin to take on additional importance and exert greater influence in teens' lives. This can be considered a natural part of a child's development; nevertheless, negative influences, including conflict within the family, can result.

Adults also feel and yield to peer pressure, and sometimes the pressure is directed toward negative behaviors. In fact, one study of adult consumers reveals that respondents reported a greater likelihood to buy an illicit product (counterfeit or stolen merchandise) if their friends did the same.[10] As with influence on children, this form of peer pressure is negative and can affect consumers, marketers, and society as a whole.

8-2 Social Power

Another important topic in the study of reference groups and group influence is social power. **Social power** refers to the ability of an individual or a group to alter the actions of others.[11] Consumers often believe that others hold a great deal of power over their own behavior. As a result, social power can greatly influence the types of products that consumers buy, the attitudes they hold, and the activities in which they participate.

8-2a Types of Social Power

Social power can be classified into five categories.[12] These categories include *referent power*, *legitimate power*, *expert power*, *reward power*, and *coercive power*. These forms of power can be exerted both by referent groups and by other individuals. These power bases are presented in Exhibit 8.1 and then discussed in more detail.

Referent Power

Consumers often imitate the behaviors and attitudes of groups as a means of identifying with the group. For example, a new resident of a city might desire to join the local Rotary Club, or perhaps a country club. In these cases, it is likely that the behaviors of other group members will be imitated. Belonging to such groups often allows consumers to feel as though they are fitting in.

Legitimate Power

In many situations, social arrangements dictate that differing levels of power are dependent upon one's position in a group. Legitimate power is used to describe this type of power, and it is associated with authority. For example, bosses have legitimate power and authority over their employee, including the authority to fire their employees. Notice that employees are usually very limited in any power that they can exert over a boss.

Expert Power

An important motivation in CB is the motivation to understand the environment. Expert power refers to the

Social power can be very strong, as in the case of peer pressure.

© iStockphoto.com/Maria Pavlova

ability of a group or individual to influence a consumer due to the group's or individual's knowledge of, or experience with, a specific subject matter. For example, consumers often find advice on health issues by consulting groups such as the American Heart Association or American Diabetes Association. Medical patients also often consult various online discussion groups for information. By consulting these groups for advice and direction relating to specific medical issues, consumers can alter their behaviors based on the perceived expertise of the source of information.

Reward Power

Groups frequently have the power to reward members for compliance with expectations. For example, at season's end, sports teams often distribute "most valuable player" awards based on performance. The desirability of the rewards is very important. If the reward isn't valued by the group members, then the motivation to perform the desired behavior is not overly strong.

Coercive Power

Groups may also exert coercive power over their members. When consumers fail to give in to group expectations or rules, disapproval can be harsh and may even result in loss of membership. For example, college athletes can be kicked off sports teams for using illegal substances like steroids. As mentioned earlier, groups may sanction members based on their legitimate power to do so, or they may revoke the membership of group members who do not comply with group rules.

How does social power originate? Social power depends upon a member's agreement to, or acceptance of, the fact that the power bases do indeed exist. That is, members must (a) *be aware that the power base exists* and (b) *desire to maintain or establish membership in the group* in order for the power base to be effective.

informational influence
ways in which a consumer uses the behaviors and attitudes of reference groups as information for making his or her own decisions

8-3 Reference Group Influence

The study of reference groups requires an understanding of group influence processes. Reference group influence generally falls into one of three categories: *informational influence*, *utilitarian influence*, and *value-expressive influence*. These categories of influence are discussed next.[13]

8-3a Informational Influence

The **informational influence** of groups refers to the ways in which consumers use the behaviors and attitudes of reference groups as information for making their own decisions. Reference groups often provide members with product- or issue-related information, and consumers often consider group-related information when purchasing products or services. Consumers desire to make informed decisions, and reference groups are often perceived as being effective sources of information.[14] Groups can be very influential in this way. Informational influence can be a result of explicit searching behavior. For example, when

EXHIBIT 8.1 — Types of Social Power

Type of Power	Description	Example
Referent Power	A consumer admires the qualities of a group and emulates their behavior.	A student joins Enactus and emulates that group's behaviors.
Legitimate Power	Specific agreements are made regarding membership and the punishment for non-conformity is understood.	A neighborhood association has the power to annually increase membership fees.
Expert Power	Groups possess knowledge that members, prospective members, or other consumers seek.	Consumers seek out medical information from groups such as the American Dental Association.
Reward Power	Groups have the power to reward members for various behaviors.	Weight loss clubs give out prizes for weight loss goals.
Coercive Power	Groups have the power to sanction group members for breaking rules or failing to follow expectations.	A member of a professional association is excused for breaking a code of conduct.

© Cengage Learning 2015

utilitarian influence ways in which a consumer conforms to group expectations in order to receive a reward or avoid punishment

value-expressive influence ways in which a consumer internalizes a group's values or the extent to which consumers join groups in order to express their own closely held values and beliefs

a consumer is seeking a doctor, friends may influence the choice by saying, "This doctor is very good."

Informational influence is also present even when the consumer is *not* explicitly searching for product-related information, but rather observing others' behaviors. For example, a consumer may simply see another person drinking a new soft drink and decide to try one.[15]

Informational influence helps to explain why word-of-mouth communication is so persuasive. Consumers share all kinds of information about products, services, and experiences, and this information can have a significant impact on consumer behavior. Internet discussion groups, in particular, have rapidly become important sources of information for group members.

The informational influence of a group is particularly strong if the group is seen as being credible. Credibility is often associated with expertise. Professional groups are often perceived as being very credible, and for this reason, they can exert significant informational influence even if a consumer is not a member of the group. For example, a consumer may be persuaded by a message that proclaims that "four of five dentists recommend brand X."

This same information obtained from the American Dental Association can affect a dentist's decisions as well, as informational influence is directly related to expert power.

8-3b Utilitarian Influence

The **utilitarian influence** occurs when consumers conform to group expectations to receive a reward or avoid punishment (this is sometimes referred to as "normative" influence). This is similar in many ways to the utilitarian function of attitudes. Compliance with group expectations often leads to valued rewards.

As discussed earlier, young consumers often think they need to buy the correct brand of shoes or clothing to fit in. By wearing apparel approved by the reference group, a child feels accepted (the reward). If the wrong clothing is selected, the child may feel shunned by the group (a punishment). When the group is perceived as being able to give rewards and punishment based on compliance, then this influence is quite strong.

Utilitarian influence of groups is not limited to any age group or demographic profile. Adult consumers often perceive a great deal of utilitarian influence from reference groups. Driving the right car, living in the right neighborhood, and belonging to the right clubs can make adults feel accepted. Here, we can see that utilitarian influence is related to reward power.

8-3c Value-Expressive Influence

Consumers often desire to seek membership in groups that hold values that are similar to their own. They also choose to adopt the values that are held by the desirable group. The **value-expressive influence** of groups refers to the ways in which consumers internalize a group's values or the extent to which consumers join groups to express their own closely held values and beliefs. This influence is related to referent power. Occupy Wall Street became a popular movement in 2011, which essentially became a vehicle for many consumers to express their displeasure with economic policies in the United States. This group took on many different forms throughout the United States that year.

Consumers may also use group membership as a way to project their own self-image. Importantly, the self-image of the individual is influenced by the group, and group membership helps the individual project the desired image. For example, a consumer may choose to join Mothers Against Drunk Driving because she feels strongly

© iStockphoto.com/Neustockimages

Student Groups Bring Value

You might have heard it by now. Getting involved is an important part of student life. Numerous student organizations and groups exist across college campuses, and these groups bring value to students in many ways.

Both utilitarian and hedonic value apply to student groups. Most employers look for graduates who have gone beyond the classroom and worked on personal development through membership in organizations. Employers also like to see that students can handle more responsibilities than simply going to class and studying. They especially like to see leadership activities in student groups. Increasing the chances of getting a job is a utilitarian benefit for students. However, it's also fun to belong to groups. Many groups present opportunities to enjoy experiences that wouldn't otherwise be available. For example, groups allow students to participate in special events, projects, and sometimes travel opportunities.

These experiences not only provide learning experiences, they also provide hedonic value.

Most career counselors stress the importance of networking, building relationships, and being involved. Student groups are great for this. It's a safe bet that your university has several student groups. Being a part of these groups allows students to become well-rounded and connected, and to have fun in the process.

Sources: C. Adler, "College Students: Why You Should Join a Student Organization," Myfootpath.com, January 6, 2012, http://myfootpath.com/mypathfinder/college-students-join-student-organization/, accessed February 11, 2013; A. Martini, "Student Organizations: Benefitting the Present and Your Future," Fastweb.com, November 17, 2011, http://www.fastweb.com/student-life/articles/3344-student-organizations-benefitting-the-present-and-your-future, accessed February 11, 2013; E. Driskoll, "What Employers Want from College Grads," Fox Business, June 4, 2012, http://www.foxbusiness.com/personal-finance/2012/06/04/what-are-employers-want-from-college-grads/, accessed February 13, 2013.

about the drunk driving issue. Once she has joined, she can project the values of the group as well. This is also similar to the value expressive function of attitudes.

8-3d Value and Reference Groups

External influences have a direct impact on the value of many activities. Reference groups and value are related in various ways.

From a utilitarian value perspective, joining a campus organization like Students in Free Enterprise, can be quite a valuable experience. The benefits associated with membership (networking, work experience, accomplishment) may be greater than the work that is put into the organization (work performed to complete a project, hours devoted to planning and meetings). In this way, utilitarian value is derived from belonging to the group, and membership becomes a means to a valued end state. Group membership also involves hedonic value perceptions. Value can be derived from simply enjoying group meetings and activities. Here, value is an end in itself. Members of the KISS Army receive both utilitarian and hedonic value from membership. They are able to enjoy interacting with other fans while also

obtaining special deals on concert tickets and other memorabilia from the band.

Reference group influences affect value perceptions in other ways. Because consumers learn about products and services from referent others, the information that is obtained from groups directly affects consumer expectations about product benefits such as quality and convenience. If you hear from your friends that a product is good, you'll probably believe it! These expectations, in turn, affect value perceptions and satisfaction.

8-3e Reference Group Influence on Product Selection

A number of things affect how much influence reference groups have on product selection. First, the situation in which the product is consumed must be considered. "Public" products (for example, a watch) are easily seen by others. "Private" products (for example, socks) usually are not. Second, the extent to which the product is considered to be a necessity or a luxury affects the level of reference group influence.[16] We really do need some products (for example, a bed).

social media media through which communication occurs

social networks consumers connecting with one another based on common interests, associations, or goals

social networking website website that facilitates online social networking

Others aren't really necessary (for example, an espresso maker). Third, reference group influence differs depending on whether a type of product or a particular brand is being selected. Obviously, a watch is a product. Rolex is a very expensive brand of watch. These elements are presented in Exhibit 8.2. Keep in mind that the meaning of necessity and luxury varies by consumer.

For necessities, reference group influence is weak for product selection (boxes #1 and #3). Reference groups rarely influence the decision to buy shoes, in general. With public necessities, however, the influence of reference groups on brand selection is strong (for example, "You should get some Sperry's"; box #1). For luxuries, reference group influence is strong for *product* selection (boxes #2 and #4). However, group influence on *brand* selection is only strong for public luxuries (for example, "You need to join *our* country club!") A careful look at the exhibit reveals that group influence on brand selection is strong for all publicly viewed products. This highlights the importance that brands play in the everyday life of consumers.

8-4 Social Media's Role in Group and Interpersonal Influence

To say that social media and the Internet are radically changing consumer behavior and group influence would be an understatement. Social media and social networking now play big roles in CB. As discussed previously, consumers get both hedonic and utilitarian value from interacting through social networking websites. Because some of these sites revolve specifically around causes, interests, and activities, they also directly impact behavior in different ways. Few groups ever meet physically, making most of them informal and secondary for group members. However, their importance shouldn't be overlooked. Even when the physical proximity of other people is close, many consumers choose to connect through social media rather than face to face. One study found that 20% of adults in the United States use digital tools to "talk" with neighbors![17]

8-4a Social Media and Consumer Behavior

It is important to distinguish among several concepts that pertain to online behavior. **Social media** refers to media through which communication occurs. As used most often today, the term is nearly synonymous with the Internet. **Social networks** are networks of consumers that are formed based on common interest, associations, or goals. In sociology, a social network is viewed as a group of individuals who share information and experiences. **Social networking websites** (sometimes referred to as "online social network sites") are websites that facilitate online social networking. Networking has taken on a new meaning in the digital age.

Interestingly, social networking has quickly become primarily a mobile activity, as friends stay in virtual touch with others through iPads, BlackBerry smartphones, cell phones, or other devices. Recent statistics reveal that the majority of social media usage now originates from mobile devices rather than from desktop computers.[18] This finding also highlights the important role that smartphone apps play in CB today.

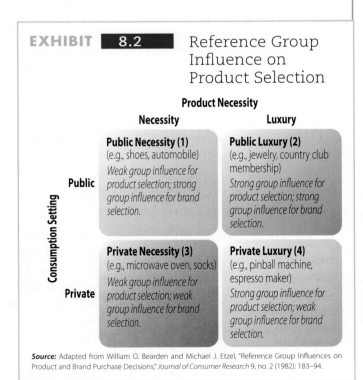

EXHIBIT 8.2 Reference Group Influence on Product Selection

Product Necessity

		Necessity	Luxury
Consumption Setting	**Public**	**Public Necessity (1)** (e.g., shoes, automobile) *Weak group influence for product selection; strong group influence for brand selection.*	**Public Luxury (2)** (e.g., jewelry, country club membership) *Strong group influence for product selection; strong group influence for brand selection.*
	Private	**Private Necessity (3)** (e.g., microwave oven, socks) *Weak group influence for product selection; weak group influence for brand selection.*	**Private Luxury (4)** (e.g., pinball machine, espresso maker) *Strong group influence for product selection; weak group influence for brand selection.*

Source: Adapted from William O. Bearden and Michael J. Etzel, "Reference Group Influences on Product and Brand Purchase Decisions," *Journal of Consumer Research* 9, no. 2 (1982): 183–94.

Popularity of Social Networking Websites

Two websites in particular highlight the role that the Internet plays in daily life: Facebook and Twitter. As of mid-2012, Facebook was the most popular website in the world, surpassing Google in popularity.[19] Although statistics change daily, Facebook reported more than 1.15 billion active monthly users as of June 2013. To put that in perspective, if Facebook were a country, it'd be the third largest country in the world! The worldwide dominance of Facebook is reflected in the fact that the site is available in more than 70 languages.[20] The majority of users check Facebook frequently throughout the day and post daily as well. There's no question that Facebook has become *the* major player in online social networking. Facebook applies well to our discussion of groups because of all of the groups that consumers can join or "like."

Twitter also continues to grow in popularity. Twitter's own statistics reveal that there were more than 200 million active users as of mid-2013 and 400 million tweets per day.[21] Twitter appears to be more popular with men than with women, especially compared to Facebook and Myspace. In today's information age, Twitter has become an important part of information flow, with many news stories breaking on Twitter before they are covered on network news stations. Myspace continues to be popular, although it currently lags well behind Facebook and Twitter in web traffic. According to recent rankings, Twitter was the tenth most popular site in the world, while Myspace ranked 221st worldwide.[22]

It is important to emphasize that the motivation to join social networking groups goes beyond a simple need to communicate. For many consumers, it's about connection. In this way, social networking helps to fulfill the need to belong. Of course, there are countless other websites that are popular, with each one attempting to satisfy a unique niche. For example, sites like YouTube and Flikr allow users to share online video and photo content. Sharing photo content has become a very big business, as evidenced by the fact that Facebook acquired Instagram for approximately $1 billion in early 2012 and by the popularity of Snapchat.[23] Other sites such as LinkedIn, Classmates, Tagged, Meetup, Friendster, Ning, Bebo, and Ourtime continue to grow in popularity.

Value and Social Media

Recall from an earlier discussion that consumers derive both utilitarian and hedonic value from group membership. This pertains to social media as well. To illustrate, consider the website SocialVibe. This site allows users to connect with brands and share content with others to benefit a cause of their choice. By using SocialVibe, consumers can positively impact charities of their choice by completing various branded activities.[24]

Another example of value from social media sites can be found at Stylehive. Stylehive is a social shopping community where people share fashion ideas and products. The site allows consumers to organize their shopping activities, learn about other consumers with similar fashion styles, and connect with popular fashion retailers. Users are also able to learn about special deals (a utilitarian benefit) and enjoy connections with other consumers (a hedonic benefit). Foursquare, a popular social networking application website that centers around geolocation and mobile technologies, not only allows users to inform friends of their location, but also allows users to earn rewards, to leave tips about particular destinations, and to collect coupons for various retailers.[25] Game apps like Words with Friends, Ruzzle, and What's the Word also allow consumers to enjoy playing games with one another.

Pinterest has also become very popular. The site, which allows users to organize and share their interests with others, draws millions of unique visitors each month. The site is most popular with women, who regularly post images of their favorite fashions, foods, and other interests.[26] By "pinning" on categorized boards, consumers can follow others with similar interests. They can even "re-pin" content onto their own boards. This way content can be spread quickly from consumer to consumer.

Social networking websites like Pinterest are very influential.

© iStockphoto.com/Rossella De Berti

social buying consumer buying behavior that takes place on social networking sites

social couponing type of buying where consumers receive a coupon, or deal, by joining a special social networking website

susceptibility to interpersonal influence individual difference variable that assesses a consumer's need to enhance the image others hold of him or her by acquiring and using products, conforming to the expectations of others, and learning about products by observing others

attention to social comparison information (ATSCI) individual difference variable that assesses the extent to which consumers are concerned about how other people react to their behavior

separated self-schema self-conceptualization of the extent to which a consumer perceives himself or herself as distinct and separate from others

connected self-schema self-conceptualization of the extent to which a consumer perceives himself or herself as being an integral part of a group

Social Buying and Couponing

Social buying refers to consumer buying behavior that takes place on social networking sites. Social couponing is a closely related topic. **Social couponing** refers to a type of buying where consumers receive a coupon, or deal, by joining a special social networking website. In some cases, the coupons become valid after a certain number of consumers choose to take advantage of the offer.

There are a number of popular social buying and social couponing websites. One of the most popular is Groupon. Groupon allows members to take advantage of several deals daily when enough consumers join in for a specified deal. One of the advantages to consumers and businesses alike is that consumers are often persuaded to try new things that they might not have otherwise tried. Similar sites like Livingsocial, Yipit, and Scoutmob have also gained in popularity.

Social media sites like the ones discussed in this section have dramatically influenced consumer behavior. Consumers receive both utilitarian and hedonic value from these sites and there is little reason to believe that the popularity of the sites will wane in the foreseeable future.

8-4b Individual Differences in Susceptibility to Group Influence

Although group influence plays an important role in influencing consumer behavior, not all consumers conform to group expectations equally. Individual difference variables play an important role in the extent to which consumers conform to the expectations of others. They also influence how one behaves in the presence of others. Three important variables are susceptibility to interpersonal influence, attention to social comparison information, and separateness-connectedness.

Susceptibility to Interpersonal Influence

One individual difference variable, **susceptibility to interpersonal influence**, assesses an individual's need to enhance the image others hold of him or her by acquiring and using products, conforming to the expectations of others, and learning about products by observing others.[27]

Studies reveal that consumers who are particularly susceptible to interpersonal influence are more likely to value conspicuous items (that is, highly valued items like luxury automobiles or jewelry).[28] In the value equation (value = what you get − what you give), the benefits of quality and image would be weighted heavily in their perception of value.

Seeking approval of others through product ownership is very important to these consumers. Consumers who score high on the susceptibility to interpersonal influence scale are also more likely to desire avoiding negative impressions in public settings.[29] For example, wearing "uncool" clothes in a shopping mall would be much more distressing to a consumer who is highly susceptible to interpersonal influence than to other consumers.

Attention to Social Comparison Information

Another individual difference variable that affects consumer behavior related to group influence is **attention to social comparison information (ATSCI)**. Consumers who score high on this measure are concerned about how other people react to their behavior.[30] The trait is closely related to susceptibility to interpersonal influence. Sample items from this scale are presented in Exhibit 8.3.

The ATSCI trait often emerges when a consumer is shopping, as consumers with a strong degree of the trait tend to modify their purchasing behaviors when they are shopping with others. For example, a consumer who has a strong degree of ATSCI might buy an imported beer when he is shopping with others but a less expensive beer when he is shopping alone. Paying attention to what others think is likely to lead consumers to conform to others' expectations, and studies have shown that consumers with a strong degree of ATSCI are more likely to conform to the expectations of others.[31]

Separateness-Connectedness

Consumers differ in their feelings of "connectedness" to other consumers. A consumer with a **separated self-schema** perceives himself as distinct and separate from others, while a consumer with a **connected self-schema** sees herself as an integral part of a group.[32] Marketers are well aware of the differences in how people view their relationships with groups, and marketing

EXHIBIT 8.3

Sample Items from Attention to Social Comparison Information Scale

It's important to me to fit into the group I'm with.
At parties I usually try to behave in a manner that makes me fit in.
I tend to pay attention to what others are wearing.
I actively avoid wearing clothes that are not in style.
My behavior often depends on how I feel others wish me to behave.

Source: Adapted from William O. Bearden and Randall L. Rose, "Attention to Social Comparison Information: An Individual Difference Factor Affecting Consumer Conformity," *Journal of Consumer Research* 16 (March 1990): 461–71.

word-of-mouth (WOM) information about products, services, and experiences that is transmitted from consumer to consumer

messages are often based on "connected" or "separated" themes. One study found that consumers who feel connected respond more favorably to advertisements that promote group belonging and cohesion.[33] Another study found that consumers with a high need for connection respond quite favorably to salespeople with whom they share some degree of similarity.[34]

Culture plays an important role in how separated or connected consumers feel. For example, consumers in Eastern cultures tend to feel more connected to others, while consumers in Western cultures tend to feel more separate and distinct. Advertising themes in a collectivist culture (a culture that focuses heavily on the interdependence of citizens) therefore often promote connected themes, while advertisements in the United States tend to emphasize separate themes.[35]

Apps help consumers connect with friends and have fun!

© iStockphoto.com/mbbirdy

Social Presence and Embarrassment

The influence of other people on consumer behavior is strongest when consumers know they are being observed. In some cases, the presence of others in a specific situation (referred to as *social presence*) can make one feel uncomfortable.[36] This is especially the case when consumers are consuming or buying personal products. Consumers can even feel embarrassed by the presence of others when purchasing these items. One study revealed that college students were particularly embarrassed with the purchase of condoms when other consumers were present.[37] This influence was affected, however, by the amount of experience the students had with buying condoms. Consumers who were familiar with the act of buying the product did not feel significantly high levels of embarrassment if others were present during the purchase. Many consumers are uncomfortable working out in a gym for fear of how they appear to others!

Social presence can also have positive effects. One recent study concluded that the presence of others in a service setting can make a customer feel more satisfied with a positive experience than they would be if they were alone when the positive experience occurred. Importantly, the same study concluded that consumers can be even more dissatisfied with a bad experience when other consumers are present.[38] It seems that social presence intensifies feelings of satisfaction and dissatisfaction.

8-5 Word-of-Mouth and Consumer Behavior

Another important concept in the study of interpersonal influence is word-of-mouth behavior. **Word-of-mouth (WOM)** is information about products, services, and experiences that is transmitted from consumer to consumer. WOM includes all kinds of information that can be spread about various consumer behaviors. Although word-of-mouth processes have been important in marketing for years, they've taken on even more importance in the digital age.

Two types of WOM influences can be distinguished: *organic* and *amplified*. The distinction between the concepts is highlighted by the Word of Mouth Marketing Association (WOMMA). According to WOMMA, organic WOM occurs naturally when consumers truly enjoy a product or service and they want to share their experiences with others. Amplified WOM occurs when marketers attempt to accelerate WOM in existing customer circles, or when they develop entirely new forums for WOM, like blogs or web pages.[39]

Consumers are heavily influenced by WOM, and its power is impressive. Consumers tell each other about products, services, and experiences all day long. If a movie is really good, moviegoers tell others. It's no wonder that word-of-mouth influences the vast majority of consumer product sales! WOM is influential because in general consumers tend to believe other consumers more than they believe advertisements and explicit marketing messages from companies.

8-5a Positive and Negative WOM

The more satisfied consumers are with a company or product, the more likely they are to spread positive WOM. If consumers believe strongly in a company and its products, they are more likely to talk to others about it.[40] Terms such as *brand advocate* or *brand ambassador* describe consumers who believe strongly in a brand and tell others about it. Consumers are also more likely to spread WOM when a product is particularly relevant to their own self-concept and when they are highly involved with the product category.[41] For example, a drummer is more likely to spread WOM about musical products than a consumer who doesn't play any instruments.

Marketers realize that negative WOM can be extremely damaging. The reason why negative WOM is so damaging to a company is that this form of WOM is especially influential. In general, negative word-of-mouth is more influential than positive word-of-mouth.[42] Hearing that the food at a restaurant is terrible is much more influential than hearing that it is good! Consumers also tend to tell more people about unsatisfactory experiences than pleasing ones.

Value and Word-of-Mouth

As noted earlier, group influence processes are closely related to consumer perceptions of value. Similarly, WOM is affected in large part by the perceived value that consumers receive from products and services.

One study, performed in a South Korean service setting, found that both utilitarian and hedonic value positively influence WOM intentions.[43] Customers who believed the restaurant allowed them to efficiently address their hunger received utilitarian value, and those who enjoyed the experience beyond addressing hunger received hedonic value. When this value was perceived as being particularly high, consumers were motivated to encourage their families and friends to go to that restaurant as well. The more value that consumers receive, the more likely they are to tell others about their experiences with products and services!

> Eighty percent of Internet users have sought online advice for health issues.

Word-of-Mouth in the Digital Age

As we have mentioned, the digital world has drastically affected the effectiveness of consumer word-of-mouth. Consumers seek out other online users for advice on all kinds of issues, ranging from what types of products to buy, to input into health, personal, and financial decisions. In fact, recent estimates reveal that 80% of Internet users have sought online advice for health issues.[44] Consumers also regularly spread WOM through text messaging. Consider that one in three teens sends more than 100 texts per day, and it's easy to see how this can impact WOM.[45] And that's just teens!

Many websites encourage the spread of information from consumer to consumer. Some sites are even dedicated specifically to WOM, like BzzAgent, Yelp, and Digg.[46] BzzAgent only allows consumers to spread WOM and also to share web content. By becoming a "bzzagent" consumers are able to participate in a popular online WOM network. Yelp.com allows consumers to learn about places to eat, shop, and relax based on the opinions of knowledgeable locals. Digg also focuses on sharing web content. Using this site, users submit content for others to see and then other users vote on what they like best. The content comes in many forms, including other web pages, images, or videos. If the content gets enough votes, it is placed on the front page for millions of visitors to see. It also allows users to comment and share discussions about the content.

Many companies actively encourage WOM by including discussion boards on their own websites. This also allows companies to assist in the development and maintenance of brand communities. They may also hire their customers to blog about their products. Although marketers can encourage the spread of positive WOM, they must also be mindful of the spread of negative WOM in the online world. Because negative WOM is so influential, it is important for companies to monitor the content that is posted on various websites. It is becoming quite common to see what can be called *anti-brand communities*, or communities in which members spread negative information about companies and products to other users. Marketers should pay close attention to these communities.

Measuring Online WOM

Given the importance of online WOM and how it influences CB, it is important for consumer researchers and marketers alike to be able to gather valid information on WOM statistics. Many services measure web traffic, such as the Google Doubleclick Adplanner site, Quantcast, Alexa, and Comscore. Some web traffic services allow users to focus on specific topics or trends, as would be the case with WOM. For example, the site Trendrr monitors the popularity of trends across social networks, blogs, and video views. Some services, such as Tweetreach, Trendistic, and Whatthetrend focus specifically on Twitter tweets and trends. Popular trends generally include tweets about products, movies, celebrities, and news events. Google Trends monitors the popularity of search terms on its search engine, and Bing offers a similar listing. All of these services can be quite valuable for understanding popular online topics, trends, and WOM.

buzz marketing marketing efforts that focus on generating excitement among consumers and that are spread from consumer to consumer

guerrilla marketing marketing of a product using unconventional means

8-5b Buzz Marketing

One marketing tactic that continues to evolve is called **buzz marketing**. Buzz marketing includes marketing efforts that focus on generating excitement (or buzz) that is spread among market segments. Quite often, this type of marketing utilizes some form of WOM, as is found with the BzzAgent website. Successful buzz marketing can be a powerful tool for marketers, as information about products and services can spread quickly. Buzz marketing is one form of what is called **guerrilla marketing**, or the marketing of a product using unconventional means.

Maybe Talk Isn't Cheap

Marketers are excited about the many opportunities that are available in cyberspace. One valuable opportunity can be found in blogging (a term formed from the words "web logging"). Blogging allows consumers to voice their opinions on a number of different topics, products, and services. Blogging has become so popular that the practice is now a part of the marketing mix for many companies!

A number of websites now allow companies to hire bloggers to write blogs about their products and services. Sites such as PayPerPost, Buy Blog Reviews, and blogsvertise have grown in popularity. Although the requirements for each site vary, the basic idea is that bloggers are given the opportunity to blog about products or companies for pay. Advertisers tell bloggers what products or services they want included in the blog, and the blogger agrees to write about it. The arrangement can be a win-win situation for both the blogger and advertiser. Of course, this practice may be considered to be unethical by some. Nevertheless, this form of Internet promotion is rapidly becoming an important component of buzz marketing, and given the popularity of the blog, it is likely that this practice will continue to grow in popularity.

© iStockphoto.com/Andresr

Sources: "How It Works," PayPerPost.com, https://payperpost.com/bloggers/blogger-how-it-works/ (accessed April 14, 2012); www.buyblogreviews.com (accessed April 14, 2012).; M. Schwartz, "Can Paid Blog Reviews Pay Off?" *B to B* 92, no. 2 (2007), 1–3; M. Frazier, "Want to Build Up Blog Buzz? Starting Writing Checks for $8," *Advertising Age* 77, no. 44 (2006): 3–4.

viral marketing marketing method that uses online technologies to facilitate WOM by having consumers spread messages through their online conversations

stealth marketing guerrilla marketing tactic in which consumers do not realize that they are being targeted for a marketing message

Although marketers have attempted to create a buzz about their products for years, buzz marketing is currently becoming popular in large part as a response to mass media fragmentation and advertising clutter. The techniques can be quite clever. For example, automobile companies can give customers automobiles to simply ride around and be seen in. This was a tactic the Ford Motor Company utilized when it gave a handful of consumers Ford Fiesta automobiles to drive around while performing activities assigned by the company. By having consumers see the new automobile in use and receive WOM from others, Ford was able to take advantage of the power of buzz marketing.[47]

The spreading of WOM online through social networking sites can be considered another form of buzz marketing. In fact, buzz marketing uses social media tools and websites regularly. As we have discussed, companies sometimes hire consumers to spread such messages. One buzz marketing tactic that relates directly to WOM is termed viral marketing. **Viral marketing** uses online technologies to facilitate WOM by having consumers spread marketing messages through their online connections. A great example of viral marketing was when Columbia Records and Legacy Recordings developed a viral campaign to promote a Bob Dylan greatest hits collection. Consumers were able to make personalized notes superimposed over the famous rock video for the song "Subterranean Homesick Blues" and to send the video to friends. Hundreds of thousands of consumers joined in on the fun, making the campaign a success. Companies sometimes attach their own viral messages to messages that are sent by consumers. For example, HTC and Sprint use viral marketing by including the message "Sent from my HTC on the Now Network from Sprint!" on text messages sent from the popular phone.

Although buzz marketing may be facilitated through online message boards and networking sites, this type of marketing is not limited to online content. The term *buzz marketing* is used much more broadly than that, with messages being delivered in many different ways to create buzz.

8-5c Stealth Marketing

Another more controversial form of marketing that uses WOM is stealth marketing. **Stealth marketing** is a guerrilla marketing tactic that is similar to buzz marketing, but a key difference is that with stealth marketing consumers are completely unaware that they are being marketed to (hence the term *stealth*). As an example of stealth marketing, imagine a camera marketer who has employees pose as tourists. These "tourists" then ask others to take their pictures with a new camera. Of course, the picture takers don't realize that the tourists are employed by the company and that they are being targeted by a marketing message.[48] A movie entitled *The Joneses,* starring Demi Moore, presents an entertaining, albeit exaggerated example of stealth marketing. Some consider *product placements* in television shows and movies to be a type of stealth marketing, because consumers generally don't realize that companies pay for these placements. Soap operas, such as *Days of Our Lives*, have recently turned to product placements as a marketing tool.[49] Research suggests that female consumers have more positive attitudes toward product placements than do male consumers.[50] Product placements were once considered to be unique but in today's environment they are becoming commonplace. Marketers often use the terms *branded content* or *advertainment* when using these strategies.

The use of stealth marketing techniques, though growing, is considered questionable by many marketing professional organizations, and WOMMA is opposed to the stealth tactics. In fact, WOMMA has developed several categories of what it considers "unethical"

Columbia/The Kobal Collections/Hanover, Suzanne/Picture Desk

Product placements in movies have become quite common.

marketing practices, including the following types of marketing techniques:[51]

- **Stealth marketing.** Deceiving consumers about the involvement of marketers in a communication
- **Shilling.** Compensating consumers to talk about or promote products without disclosing that they are working for the company
- **Infiltrating.** Using fake identities in online discussions to promote a product

8-5d Opinion Leaders

Buzz marketing techniques are especially effective when opinion leaders are used. **Opinion leaders** are consumers who have great influence on the behavior of others relating to product adoption and purchase. Opinion leaders are knowledgeable about specific products or services and have a high level of involvement with those products. Characteristics of opinion leaders depend largely on the type of product under consideration, but in general, opinion leaders are socially active and self-confident.

With online social networking and media sites, it's easy to find a few key posters that other users tend to listen to. With Twitter, you can even track the number of followers for each user. Recently, the Ford Motor Company included influential women bloggers in their "What Women Want" campaign. Popular bloggers were invited to test new Ford products and interact with company executives. Inviting the bloggers was a good way of ensuring some online buzz.[52] As with the Ford Fiesta example, it appears the company is becoming quite adept with buzz marketing campaigns.

Market Mavens and Surrogate Consumers

Opinion leaders are not the only influential consumers that have been identified. Market mavens and surrogate consumers also exert much influence on others. A **market maven** is a consumer who spreads information about all types of products and services that are available in the marketplace. The key difference between an opinion leader and a market maven is that the market maven's influence is not category specific. That is, market mavens spread information about numerous products and services.

Consumers can also be heavily influenced by what are termed surrogate consumers. A **surrogate consumer** is a consumer who is hired by another to provide input into a purchase decision. Interior decorators, travel consultants, and stockbrokers can all be considered surrogate consumers. Surrogate consumers can be very influential, and marketers should carefully consider the level of influence of these individuals.[53] Because of their extensive product expertise, surrogate consumers can often help others derive the maximum amount of value out of their transactions by maximizing the benefits associated with product purchase.

8-5e Diffusion Processes

One area of interest in the study of group processes is the diffusion process. The **diffusion process** refers to the way in which new products are adopted and spread throughout a marketplace. Researchers have learned that different groups of consumers tend to adopt new products at different rates. One group may adopt a new product (for example, a hybrid automobile) very early in the product's life cycle, while another group may be very slow to adopt the product, if it adopts the product at all. A product life cycle is a description of the life of a product from the time it is introduced to the time it dies off.

In all, five categories of consumers have been identified. They include innovators, early adopters, early majority, late majority, and laggards. These groups are presented in Exhibit 8.4.[54]

What makes group influence relevant to the diffusion process is that each group learns about new products not only from seeing marketing messages, but also from talking with other consumers and observing their behavior. Group influence processes therefore apply to these categories.

Innovators and early adopter consumers tend to be influential when discussing products and services with members of other groups. As such, they tend to be opinion leaders for specific product categories. Innovators are often risk takers and financially well-off. Early adopter consumers are generally young and well educated. Members of other groups, including late majority consumers and laggards, tend to be more

opinion leader consumer who has a great deal of influence on the behavior of others relating to product adoption and purchase

market maven consumer who spreads information about all types of products and services that are available in the marketplace

surrogate consumer consumer who is hired by another to provide input into a purchase decision

diffusion process way in which new products are adopted and spread throughout a marketplace

household decision making process by which decisions are made in household units

family household at least two people who are related by blood or marriage who occupy a housing unit

nuclear family a mother, a father, and a set of siblings

extended family three or more generations of family members

EXHIBIT 8.4

Adopter Categories

Consumer Innovators	Early Adopters	Early Majority	Late Majority	Laggards
2.5%	13.5%	34%	34%	16%

Adapted from Rogers, Everett M. *Diffusion of Innovation*, 4th ed., New York: The Free Press, 1995.

cautious about buying new products and wait significantly longer to buy the latest innovations. These consumers also tend to be somewhat older, with lower levels of education and spending power.

8-6 Household Decision Making and Consumer Behavior

As we discussed previously, the family unit is an important primary reference group for consumers. Family members typically have a great deal of influence over one another's attitudes, thoughts, and behaviors. Consider the many ways that the family has an impact on consumer behavior. **Household decision making** is the process by which household units choose between alternative courses of action. One interesting finding relates to what has been termed the *consumer doppelganger effect*.[55] Research reveals that mothers often mimic their daughters' identities through clothing and fashion choice. Some might realize that this is similar to mothers living vicariously through their children, but it more strongly emphasizes the fact that parents can be influenced by their children just as easily as children can be influenced by their parents. To begin our discussion of household decision making, we first discuss the various conceptualizations of the term *household*.

8-6a Traditional Family Structure

The ways in which society views the family unit have changed dramatically in recent decades. Traditionally, the **family household** has been viewed as at least two people who are related by blood or marriage and who occupy a housing unit. In fact, this is how the U.S. Census Bureau defines a family unit. Other traditional family definitions include the *nuclear* family and the *extended* family.

The **nuclear family** consists of a mother, a father, and a set of siblings. The **extended family** consists of three or more generations of family members, including grandparents, parents, children, and grandchildren. In individualistic cultures like the United States, emphasis is placed on the nuclear family. However, in collectivist cultures, more focus is placed on the extended family, and it is not uncommon to see households that are comprised of extended family members living together.

Family members greatly influence one another.

Monkey Business Images/Shutterstock.com

With this being said, the growth in multigenerational households in the United States (an individualistic culture) has been significant in recent years, with a 2011 study revealing the greatest growth coming in the economically turbulent years of 2007–9.[56]

Emerging Trends in Family Structure

As mentioned previously, the traditional views of the family have changed over time. Today, many nontraditional household arrangements exist throughout the United States. Societal trends toward people of opposite sex sharing living quarters (termed POSSLQ or cohabitation) and homosexual households have altered the way in which family households are conceptualized. In fact, 33% of households are defined as nonfamily households (that is, consumers sharing the same living quarters who are not related by blood or marriage).[57] Nonfamily households grew twice as fast as traditional households from 2000–2010.[57a]

Divorce rates tend to be quite high in the United States. It is widely quoted that nearly 50% of all marriages in the United States end in divorce, but the exact number is really unknown. Regardless, even higher rates are seen in second and third marriages, as estimates reveal that 67% of second marriages and 74% of third marriages end this way.[58] Divorces have clearly altered the composition of the American family, and they have led to *blended families*. Blended families consist of previously married spouses and their children. On the bright side, estimates reveal that divorce rates are currently at their lowest point in over 30 years, at approximately 3.6 per 1,000 people. However, some researchers suggest that this is simply because many consumers cannot afford to divorce in the shaky economy. In fact, it has been estimated that as the unemployment rates rises 1%, the divorce rate drops 1%.[59] A sluggish economy may also explain relatively low birth rates. The most current census data reveal that the birth rate of 63.2 births per thousand is the lowest since 1920.[60]

Many people simply decide to never marry. And many other people delay marriage. In the United States, the median age of first marriages for men is 28.7 and 26.5 for women. This has been an increase since the 1960s, when the median ages were in the early 20s.[61] Also, more American women are living without a husband than with one.[62] As a result of this trend and the high divorce rate, single-parent households have increased. Approximately 28% of U.S. children lived with only one parent in the year 2012,[63] and approximately 40% of births are to unmarried women.[64] Of course, not all women have children. In fact, a 2010 report revealed that nearly one in five American women ends her childbearing years without having borne a child.[65] Yet another trend is that single men are adopting children at a record rate.[66]

Finally, the meaning of the term *nonfamily* is open to debate and interpretation. For many, the term itself is plagued by personal beliefs and biases and it has evolved based on societal changes. One topic of current interest is same-sex marriages. Same-sex marriages are becoming increasingly common. Marketers increasingly target same-sex couples in many of their advertisements.

Despite widespread attention to nontraditional households, census data reveal that the largest portion of American consumers still live in something resembling a "traditional" household, consisting of a married couple who either have yet to have children, have children living under the same roof, or have already raised children who no longer live at home. Also, the data reveal that the majority of American children reside in a traditional household, as is shown in Exhibit 8.5. The prevalence of products such as SUVs and minivans as well as family-oriented movies such as *Cars* and *Dolphin Tale*, and the profitability of retailers such as Walmart and Target, owe at least a portion of their success to the large number of traditional family units.

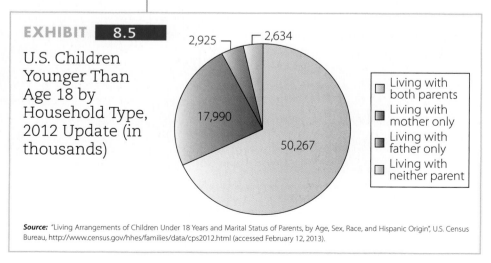

EXHIBIT 8.5

U.S. Children Younger Than Age 18 by Household Type, 2012 Update (in thousands)

2,925 — 2,634

17,990

50,267

- Living with both parents
- Living with mother only
- Living with father only
- Living with neither parent

Source: "Living Arrangements of Children Under 18 Years and Marital Status of Parents, by Age, Sex, Race, and Hispanic Origin", U.S. Census Bureau, http://www.census.gov/hhes/families/data/cps2012.html (accessed February 12, 2013).

household life cycle (HLC) segmentation technique that acknowledges that changes in family composition and income alter household demand for products and services

boomerang kids young adults, between the ages of 18 and 34, who move back home with their parents after they graduate from college

8-6b Household Life Cycle

An important concept in the study of the family unit is the **household life cycle (HLC)**. The HLC represents a segmentation technique that acknowledges that changes in family composition and income alter household demand for products and services.

The traditional HLC segments families into a number of groups based on the number of adults present and the age of the head of household. This conceptualization is presented in Exhibit 8.6. Based on this conceptualization, a number of segments are present, including consumers who never marry (Bachelor 1, 2, and 3); two-adult, childless households (Young Couple, Childless Couple, and Older Couple); two adults with children (Full Nest 1, 2, and 3 and Delayed Full Nest); and one adult with children (Single Parent 1, 2, and 3).

The categorization of the household is important for consumer researchers.[67] Product expenditures vary greatly by stage in the HLC, and at each stage, consumers often try to obtain the most value that they can from their purchases. For example, Full Nest 1 consumers often face costly expenses related to raising young children, including the cost of baby clothes, furniture, and day care. These young consumers often have to search for new living accommodations in the form of larger apartments or a starter home when children are born. Single parents face the same challenges as two-adult families, but they must face these challenges alone. A great strain is therefore placed on the income of single parents. Older, childless couples have more disposable income to spend on their own needs. They are much more likely to enjoy luxuries such as vacation homes, financial investments, and upscale automobiles. Couples older than 64 often enjoy their retirement years, or choose to remain employed beyond retirement age.

The categories and assumptions in the HLC are representative of general patterns of spending behavior. Not every consumer will fall neatly into one specific category. Rather, the categories help to explain the living situations and expenditures of many consumers. Obviously, consumers face their own situations.

Boomerang Kids and the Sandwich Generation

Two important groups that are of interest to researchers are boomerang kids and members of the sandwich generation. **Boomerang kids** are young adults, aged 18 to 34, who graduate from college and move back home with their parents. Quite often, the motivation is to reduce debt that has accumulated in the college

---

EXHIBIT 8.6 Traditional Household Life Cycle Categories

	Under 35 Years	35–64 Years	Older than 64 Years
One-adult household	Bachelor 1	Bachelor 2	Bachelor 3
Two-adult household	Young Couple	Childless Couple	Older Couple
Two adults + children	Full Nest 1 (children < 6 years old)	Delayed Full Nest (children < 6 years old)	
	Full Nest 2 (children > 6 years old)	Full Nest 3 (children > 6 years old)	
One adult + children	Single Parent 1 (children < 6 years old)	Single Parent 3	
	Single Parent 2 (children > 6 years old)		

Source: Adapted from M. C. Gilly and B. M. Enis, "Recycling the Family Lifecycle: A Proposal for Redefinition," in *Advances in Consumer Research*, Vol. 9, ed. Andrew A. Mitchell, 271–76 (Ann Arbor, MI: Association for Consumer Research, 1982).

years. Some have suggested the term *adultolescence* to describe this stage. The trend is growing, and a 2010 report estimated that nearly 53% of college graduates planned to move back home with their parents.[68]

The economy plays a big role in influencing boomerang kids. A 2011 study revealed that nearly 30% of adults aged 25–34 lived with their parents due to the shaky economy.[69] A more recent survey found that 78% of consumers in this segment stated they couldn't afford to live on their own.[69a] This trend challenges the traditional HLC, and it impacts how middle-aged consumers spend their money. A humorous view of adult children at home can be found in the movie *Failure to Launch*, starring Matthew McConaughey. The issue, however, is not a laughing matter. In fact, it has been estimated that boomerang kids cost their parents $5,000 per year in disposable income.[70]

Financial and emotional strains on middle-aged consumers also come from belonging to the sandwich generation. The **sandwich generation** consists of those consumers who must take care of both their own children and their aging parents. An estimated 20 million consumers in the United States are members of the sandwich generation.[71] This number is expected to increase dramatically over the next decade, as millions of Baby Boomers enter their retirement years. Taking care of both children and parents obviously affects the behavior of these consumers, as income is devoted to the needs of others. In fact, the average cost of caring for others aged 50-plus is nearly $6,000 per year. For consumers who must care for others long distance, the cost is nearly $9,000 per year.[72] Caregivers also lose much time at work and they lose income and benefits as a result. These losses can be substantial and average over $300,000 over the lifetime of the caregiver. Businesses also lose money due to the lost productivity, in the amount of as much as $34 billion per year due to sandwich generation employees missing work.[73]

8-6c Household Purchase Roles

Each member of a household plays a specific role in product purchase. Five important roles in the household purchase process can be identified:

- *Influencer.* The person in the household who recognizes a need and provides information about a potential purchase to others

- *Gatekeeper.* The person who controls information flow into the household (for example, a mother who blocks unwanted email solicitations from her child's email account)

- *User.* The actual user of the product under consideration

- *Decision maker.* The person who makes the final decision regarding product purchase or nonpurchase

- *Purchaser.* The person who actually buys the product under consideration

Each role is important in product consideration and selection. The final purchase of the product is largely influenced by beliefs regarding the role of each person in the household.

Gender Roles and Household Decision Making

Like many of the concepts pertaining to household composition, societal views on gender roles and family decision making have evolved over time. Traditionally, men were viewed as having the primary responsibility of providing for the family, while women were expected to meet everyday family needs and take care of the home.[74] However, changes in the education of women and the acceleration in the number of double-income families have challenged these conceptualizations.

An important concept in gender roles and family decision making is **sex role orientation (SRO)**. A family's SRO influences the ways in which household decisions are reached. Families that have a traditional SRO believe that it is the responsibility of the male head of household to make large purchase decisions, while families with a "modern" SRO believe in a more democratic approach.[75] Given the evolving nature of the typical household in the United States, it is not surprising that SROs are changing. In particular, the role of women in household decision making is more prevalent than in previous years. Indeed, studies have revealed that women are playing a bigger role in decision making in all household decision areas. This, in part, reflects the fact that the percentage of women with higher education and income levels than their spouses has grown significantly over the last few decades.[76]

sandwich generation consumers who must take care of both their own children and their aging parents

sex role orientation (SRO) family's set of beliefs regarding the ways in which household decisions are reached

consumer socialization the process through which young consumers develop attitudes and learn skills that help them function in the marketplace

Kid Power

The role of children in household decision making is also evolving.[77] Although children were once thought to have little impact on purchasing decisions beyond what toy to buy, marketers are realizing that children are playing a large role in influencing many household purchases. One study found that 36% of parents with children between the ages of 6 and 11 reported that kids significantly influence their purchases. Even in times of economic instability, parents still try to spend on their kids, even if it means cutting back on other things.

The power of the children's market has grown. Consumers between the ages of 8 and 12 spend $30 billion per year of their own money and influence another $700 billion per year in total household spending. Furthermore, the teen segment frequently sees its disposable income grow at a rate that is unlike that found in any other segment. For example, the typical American 12-year-old has $1,500 per year to spend.

However, this number leaps to $4,500 per year by the time the child reaches age 17. Much of this income is earned income, even if it is simply a weekly allowance. Older children earn much of their income from jobs outside of the house.

An important issue in the development of the child consumer is known as consumer socialization.[78] **Consumer socialization** is defined as the process through which young consumers develop attitudes and learn skills that help them function in the marketplace.[78] Sometimes these skills are learned at a surprisingly young age, and children have largely begun to seek products that were once considered "too old" for their age segment. This has led to the development of a common marketing acronym, KGOY (Kids Growing Older, Younger).

Although many consider the issue of kid power and marketing to children controversial, it is clear that children do exert a significant influence on household decision making, and it is likely that this trend will continue.

Pets Are Family Too!

It will probably come as no surprise that pets are considered to be family members for millions of consumers worldwide. Dogs, cats, fish, birds, and reptiles are all popular pets for millions of consumers. Taking care of these pets can be costly, and the industry continues to grow. In the United States alone, consumers spend an estimated $53 billion on pet care annually, and the total is expected to increase. To put this into perspective, this is more than consumers spend on personal entertainment like watching movies, playing video games, or listening to music.

While most of the spending is attributed to food and basic medical care, one growing segment in the industry is pet services. Pet services include things like walking, boarding, and even doggie daycare! Another booming segment is pet insurance. In fact, it is becoming popular for insurance policies to include coverage for pets. It seems that there is no limit to what some people will do for their pets. For most consumers, the money is well spent, considering the loyalty, comfort, and friendship that come from our furry friends.

Liliya Kulianionak/Shutterstock.com

Soures: "Industry Statistics & Trends," American Pet Products Association, http:www.americanpetproducts. org/press_industrytrends.asp (accessed April 13, 2012); Amy Silverstein, "Americans Spent Record Amount of Money Grooming Their Pets Last Year," Globalpost.com, March 3, 2012, http://www.globalpost .com/dispatches/globalpost-blogs/weird-wide-web/americans-spent-record-amount-money -grooming-their-pets (accessed April 13, 2012); "The Pet Economy: More than Movies, Music & Video Games Combined," Globalanimal.org, http://www.globalanimal.org/2010/10/20/the-pet-economy -more-than-movies-music-video-games-combined/20226/ (accessed April 12, 2012); C. Taylor, "The U.S. Pet Economy Didn't Go to the Dogs", Reuters, http://www.reuters.com/article/2013/02/08 /us-economy-spending-pets-idUSBRE9170ZP20130208 (accessed February 11, 2013).

WHAT DO YOU THINK?
WHAT OTHERS HAVE THOUGHT

① ② ③ ④ ⑤ ⑥ ⑦

40
35
30
25
20
15
10
5
0

Strongly disagree | Disagree | Somewhat disagree | Neither agree nor disagree | Somewhat agree | Agree | Strongly agree

The groups I belong to have a great impact on how I see myself.

It seems that most students agree with this statement. Our data reveals that approximately 60% of students at least somewhat agree with this. Groups do impact all of us in many ways, and they even impact how we see ourselves!

Study Tools

Located at back of the textbook

☐ Rip out Chapter in Review Card

Located at www.cengagebrain.com

☐ Review Key Terms Flashcards (print or online)

☐ Download audio summaries to review on the go

☐ Complete practice quizzes to prepare for tests

☐ Play "Beat the Clock" to master concepts

☐ Watch video on Teenage Research Unlimited for a real company example

study tools

© iStockphoto.com/Clerkenwell_Images

In all cases

what a person consumes helps determine how accepted one is by other consumers in society.

WHAT DO YOU THINK?

A man should always pay for his date's dinner.

STRONGLY DISAGREE   STRONGLY AGREE

VISIT COURSEMATE AT WWW.CENGAGEBRAIN.COM

Consumer Culture

9

9-1 Culture and Meaning Are Inseparable

Do love and marriage go together? One thing that might be even more certain is the fact that marriage and consumption go together! No matter where one gets married, the wedding typically involves an elaborate celebration. Estimates suggest that an average U.S. wedding costs over $28,000.[1] The high cost of getting hitched is not confined to the United States— Chinese weddings cost an average 200,000 Yuan![2] If you do the currency conversion you'll find that's a little bit more than the typical U.S. wedding. Spending money on weddings seems to be a universal phenomenon.

The way consumers find mates, however, is not so universal. In Western cultures, romantic marriage rules so much that other concepts come across as strange, unusual, or even illegal. Consumers in other cultures often do not have so much say in exactly whom they marry. However, although this seems strange for most readers of this book, consumers from those cultures accept and even find comfort in the notion of an arranged marriage. Arab and Eastern consumers often end up getting married based on arrangements between families. This eliminates the need for dating rituals, anxiety, and stress over popping the question—the couples never face this climactic moment. Polygamy is even an accepted form of marriage in some cultures, although it's illegal in many Western cultures. Also, while spending on wedding ceremonies is a constant, the customs associated with weddings and even marriages are very much determined by culture.

9-1a What Is Culture?

Consumers make very simple decisions involving things like coffee drinking and very important and meaningful decisions involving things like getting married. In all cases, what a person consumes helps determine how accepted one is by other consumers in society. Likewise, the consumption act itself generally

After studying this chapter, the student should be able to:

9-1 Understand how culture provides the true meaning of objects and activities.

9-2 Use the key dimensions of core societal values to apply the concept of cultural distance.

9-3 Define acculturation and enculturation.

9-4 List fundamental elements of verbal and nonverbal communication.

9-5 Discuss current emerging consumer markets and scan for opportunities.

consumer culture
commonly held societal beliefs that define what is socially gratifying

has no absolute meaning, only meaning relative to the environment in which the act takes place. Culture, therefore, embodies meaning.

Consumer culture represents the commonly held societal beliefs that define what is socially gratifying within a specific society. Culture shapes value by framing everyday life in terms of these commonly held beliefs. The fact that the average price for a cup of coffee in the United States has risen in the last quarter century indicates that American beliefs about the coffee-drinking experience have certainly changed and define a more valuable experience than in decades past. In contrast, although the average wedding still represents a large sum of money, the average spending on weddings in the U.S.A. actually has dropped since 2008. Is this due to the economy or to changing values? The answer is uncertain at this point but culture ultimately determines what consumption behaviors are acceptable.

At what age is it okay to have a cup of coffee, drink a glass of wine with the family, or go to the mall without an adult chaperone? Like other activities, the appropriateness of these activities varies. Exhibit 9.1

EXHIBIT 9.1	Culture, Meaning, and Value	
Behavior	**Typical Meaning in United States**	**Alternate Meaning**
Consumer age 14–18 consuming beer or wine in a restaurant	Unacceptable or even illegal in most areas.	Wine is part of a nice family meal in other areas, including much of Western Europe.
People gathering to eat barbecue pork ribs	This menu is part of a pleasant social event.	Pork is not an acceptable food item among Jews and Muslims.
Supervisors and employees socializing together	Supervisors and coworkers can be friendly with each other.	Employees and supervisors should keep their distance away from work. An employee who acts too casually with a "senior" could incur a sanction.
Kissing	Purely a family or romantic activity.	In many nations, kissing is common when making a new acquaintance or greeting a friend.

© Cengage Learning

lists some consumption behaviors that vary in meaning, value, and acceptability from culture to culture.

9-1b Culture, Meaning, and Value

The focus of this chapter is on culture. This focus acknowledges that the marketplace today truly is global. Modern technology has greatly reduced the geographic barriers that prevented consumers from doing business with marketers in other parts of the world. Without culture, consumers would have little guidance as to the appropriate actions in many common consumer situations. Thus, culture performs important functions for consumers. These functions shape the value of consumer activities and include:

Time to Go McGlobal

© ERIC PIERMONT/AFP/GettyImages

McDonald's can be found around the world, but don't expect to find typical McDonald's offerings across the globe. The French really find eating good bread gratifying. The average French consumer eats about 121 pounds of bread every year, much of it in the form of a baguette (the typical, long but slim, crusty French bread). McDonald's appeals to this culturally rewarding habit through the 2012 introduction of the "McBaguette." Blending traditional burger concepts with the traditional French tastes, this small square baguette holds a ground beef patty made from famous French Charolais beef. The experiment by McDo, as the French call it, is not unique, as Starbucks and Dunkin Donuts are both entering the Indian market. Although Indians aren't known for coffee drinking, both chains hope that blending brand and cultural concepts will prove to be a recipe for success.

Sources: M. Issard, "To Tailor Burgers for France, McDonald's Enlists Baguette," *The Wall Street Journal,* February 24, 2012, B4. R. Ahmed, "Dunkin Donuts and Starbucks to Duke It Out in India," *The Wall Street Journal,* February 22, 2012, B8.

1. **Giving meaning to objects.** Consider how much culture defines the meaning of furniture, religious objects, and everyday items like food and drink. For instance, Dunkin Donuts sells more cups of coffee in the United States than even Starbucks, but in India, consumers already like the donuts but are slower to catch on to coffee as a morning beverage.[3]

2. **Giving meaning to activities.** Consider, for example, the role of things as simple as recreational activities and even washing (hygiene). A daily shower is not a universally accepted norm.

3. **Facilitating communication.** The shared meaning of things facilitates communication. When strangers meet, culture indicates whether a handshake, hug, or kiss is most appropriate. Things as simple as making eye contact can take on dramatically different meanings from one culture to another.

9-1c Cultural Norms

Culture, meaning, and value are very closely intertwined. For this reason, culture determines things that are socially rewarding (valuable) or socially unrewarding (not valuable). A consumer who acts inconsistently with cultural expectations risks getting the cold shoulder or worse from others. The term **cultural norm** refers to a rule that specifies the appropriate behavior in a given situation within a specific culture. Most, but not all, cultural norms are unwritten and simply understood by members of a cultural group.

In many countries, consumers do not routinely drink out of a bottle or can. It's considered impolite. Rather, particularly when one is at the table, a server always provides a glass and the cultural expectation means a consumer should pour their drink into the glass before drinking. Koreans hold this custom very strongly, many European cultures also practice this custom but perhaps not as strongly, whereas in most North American cultures, drinking from a bottle is routine even in public places like bars and restaurants. Thus, in places like Korea and Europe, by pouring the drink into a glass before drinking, the consumer has performed a socially rewarding (valuable) act consistent with the norms of that society.

9-1d Cultural Sanctions

So, what happens to a consumer who performs an act inconsistent with cultural norms? Unfortunately, the consumer is likely to experience a cultural sanction. A **cultural sanction** refers to the penalties associated with performing a nongratifying or culturally inconsistent behavior. Cultural sanctions often are relatively innocuous. For instance, if one were to drink a soda from a bottle in Korea, he would be likely to get only a curious look or suffer some innocent teasing from members of the group. In other instances however, a consumer performing a culturally inconsistent act may be shunned or suffer banishment from a group.

Many societies still have strong cultural norms about marrying outside of one's social class, religion, or ethnic group. Violation of this norm can result in isolation from family or worse. Physically or socially harming a family member for fraternizing beyond one's cultural group represents a fairly strong cultural sanction.

Popular Culture

Popular culture captures cultural trends and shapes norms and sanctions within society. A few decades ago, U.S. college students routinely smoked cigarettes in college classroom buildings, filling the hallways with clouds of smoke. This is not only against university and local regulations in most places, but other students would likely find the

cultural norm rule that specifies the appropriate consumer behavior in a given situation within a specific culture

cultural sanction penalty associated with performing a nongratifying or culturally inconsistent behavior

Pop star icons like this may establish cultural norms among pop culture members.

© s_bukley/Shutterstock.com

role expectations the specific expectations that are associated with each type of person within a culture or society

behavior offensive today. Pop icons such as Miley Cyrus or Justin Bieber help determine acceptable style for many groups of admirers who desire to fit in with today's popular culture. For example, before Miley Cyrus's 20th birthday, she generated quite a bit of controversy by taking part in public displays of nudity and sensual behavior aimed at members of both sexes, as well as flaunting her use of marijuana.[4] Do such behaviors challenge cultural norms?

Role Expectations

Every consumer plays various roles within society. Culture expects people to play these roles in a culturally rewarding fashion. In other words, when a consumer interacts with another person, any characteristic upon which that person can be categorized activates certain behavioral expectations. Recall that in a previous chapter we described how social schemata (stereotypes) help consumers organize knowledge about people. **Role expectations** are the specific expectations that are associated with each type of person. One's sex, one's occupation, one's social class, one's age: all are relevant bases for forming societal role expectations. Role expectations become a primary basis for cultural norms and sanctions. They define not only the way one should act to play the role but also the types of products that are appropriate for a person within a role. When a consumer travels to a foreign country, she may well find that expectations for a given role are different from those at home. As a result, the consumption activities associated with roles can also vary from culture to culture.

In most parts of the United States, for example, a typical service employee in a restaurant, department store, or even a hotel plays their societal role well by speaking English only. However, in much of Scandinavia, for instance Norway, consumers expect that a service employee can respond in at least two languages, if not more. A service employee in Norway would generally be somewhat surprised even to be asked if he can speak English, because it is very much expected of them within their role. Exhibit 9.2 provides some other examples of cultural role expectations. In the next chapter, we focus more specifically on societal roles tied to demographic characteristics.

9-2 Using Core Societal Values

9-2a Where Does Culture Come From?

Consumer researchers commonly use culture to explain and predict consumer behavior.[5] Estimates suggest that out of all academic explanations of consumer behavior, more than 10% of all explanations include culture as a key factor.[6] Cultural beliefs define what religion is acceptable, what types of art and recreation are preferred, what manners are considered polite, the roles for different types of individuals including expectations for men and women in a society, and much more. Distinguishing the unique effects of culture over these more specific things is extremely difficult since as part of culture these things tend to function together. But as a whole there is little doubt that culture causes differences in the value consumers perceive from different products and experiences.[7]

How do people in one nation end up with a culture distinct from that of people in another? In other words, what causes culture? The answer to this question involves two important components.

EXHIBIT 9.2 Societal Role Expectations Vary

Role	Role Expectations within USA	Role Expectations outside of USA
Hotel Clerk	Speak English	Europe: Speak multiple languages and adjust language to customer
Retail Employee	Treat customers promptly, courteously, and as a priority	Russia: Customers not treated quite so promptly or courteously—the worker is prioritized over the customer
Table Server	Serves customers promptly, brings check when service is done, expects a tip of 15% or more	Europe: Serves customers professionally, brings check only when customer asks for it, does not expect a tip
Motorcyle Driver	Dress down and generally follow the same driving rules as automobile drivers	Italy: Dressed up (often going to the office) and generally ignore the rules for automobiles—particularly traffic lanes

© Cengage Learning 2015

Religious traditions shape consumption experiences.

© m.bonotto/Shutterstock.com

ecological factors physical characteristics that describe the physical environment and habitat of a particular place

tradition customs and accepted ways of everyday behavior in a given culture

household, and the key decision maker is the oldest male living in the house. Thus, consumer advertising may need to differ based on the traditional family decision-making style associated with a culture. While tradition can be thought of as influencing culture, one can safely say that, in the long run, culture also defines tradition.

Exhibit 9.3 illustrates how tradition and ecology come together to influence culture, with each culture being described by different amounts of core societal values (discussed later in this chapter), and these values driving differences in consumer behaviors and the value derived from them.

> ⌈ While tradition can be thought of as influencing culture, one can safely say that, in the long run, culture also defines tradition. ⌋

Over time, traditions become embedded in culture and become relatively stable. However, while stable, they do slowly change, as illustrated by the changes in places where people could traditionally smoke without fear of sanctions. In this sense, not only are the choices and behaviors of consumers influenced by culture, but in the long run subtle changes in these choices and behaviors also influence culture.

First, ecological factors cause differences in culture because they change the relative value of objects. **Ecological factors** are the physical characteristics that describe the physical environment and habitat of a particular place. Thus, for example, consumers from groups that have traditionally lived in desert areas place a great value on water relative to consumers from areas filled with freshwater lakes. As a result, consumers from this area may have different habits when it comes to hygiene, including the frequency and duration of baths or showers. This can affect sales of beauty products, soaps, and toilet water and also things like hotel room and building design.

Second, over time tradition develops among groups of peoples, and these traditions carry forward to structure society. **Tradition** in this sense refers to the customs and accepted ways of structuring society. Traditions include things like the family and political structures of a society. In the United States, Australia, Canada, and much of Europe, families traditionally consist of two generations (parents and children) living in a household, where a husband and wife share decision making. In other cultures, India for instance, more than two generations (grandparents, parents, and children) may share a

9-2b Dimensions of Cultural Values

Although conflicting views exist on what exactly are the best dimensions to describe differences in cultural values, the most widely applied dimensions are those developed by Geert Hofstede.[8] This theory of value-based

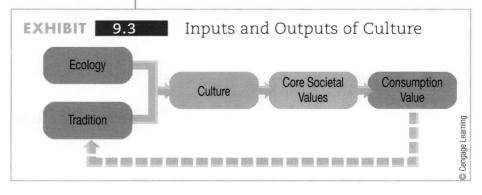

EXHIBIT 9.3 Inputs and Outputs of Culture

Ecology / Tradition → Culture → Core Societal Values → Consumption Value

© Cengage Learning

core societal values (CSV) commonly agreed-upon consensus about the most preferable ways of living within a society, also known as cultural values

individualism extent to which people are expected to take care of themselves and their immediate families

collectivism extent to which an individual's life is intertwined with a large cohesive group

masculinity role distinction within a group that values assertiveness and control; CSV opposite of femininity

femininity sex role distinction within a group that emphasizes the prioritization of relational variables such as caring, conciliation, and community; CSV opposite of masculinity

power distance extent to which authority and privileges are divided among different groups within society and the extent to which these facts of life are accepted by the people within the society

differences in cultures is based on five key dimensions, with each dimension representing a core societal value. **Core societal values (CSV)**, or cultural values, represent a commonly agreed-upon consensus about the most preferable ways of living within a society. Even though not all members of a culture may share precisely the same values to the same degree, a specific cultural group will tend to have common worldviews along these dimensions. Exhibit 9.3 illustrates how core societal values serve as the mechanism by which culture affects value. Cultural values can be classified using multiple dimensions. In some cases, the dimensions overlap with each other or are related to one another.

Individualism

The first CSV dimension contrasts cultures based on relative amounts of individualism and collectivism.[9] **Individualism** as a CSV means the extent to which people expect each other to take responsibility for themselves and their immediate family. Highly individualistic societies place high value on self-reliance, individual initiative, and personal achievement. In contrast, nations with low individualism are seen as high in **collectivism**, which refers to the extent to which an individual's life is intertwined with a large cohesive group. Highly collectivistic societies tend to live in extended families, take their identity from the groups to which they belong, and be very loyal to these groups.

Clearly, this dimension has important implications for the way consumers make decisions and the way that consumers extract value from consumption (see the CVF in Chapter 2 for an illustration). In the U.S.A., marketers often communicate the value of various products by illustrating the extent to which they help one achieve personal freedom. American consumers often see important purchases as an extension of

themselves. Advertisements for jeans, shoes, and even laptop computers commonly use adjectives such as *rugged, tough,* and *dependable*.[10] In contrast, an advertisement for a collective culture may rely more on adjectives such as *honest* or *friendly*.

Generally, Western societies tend to be more individualistic, whereas Eastern nations tend to be more collectivistic. Collectivist societies tend to be more compliant with requests from group members. American consumers, for instance, once they have made a choice, are more likely to repeat that choice a second time because its value is enhanced by virtue of having been personally selected originally. In contrast, consumers from Korea are more susceptible to making a choice that someone in their group has chosen previously, because the cohesiveness of the group adds value more than the confirmation of individual merit.[11] This generality is just that—a generality! There are exceptions to this rule. Later, we'll discuss specific scores on all dimensions across many countries.

Masculinity

The **masculinity** CSV dimension captures distinctions existing in societies based on mannerisms typically associated with Western male traits such as valuing assertiveness and control over traditional feminine traits such as caring, conciliation, and community. **Femininity** represents the opposite of masculinity, but in this case, the term does not refer to a political or social movement or even to the prominence that women have within a society. In fact, women's traits tend to vary less from nation to nation than do those of men, so this dimension is most clearly obvious within a masculine culture. In other words, in a culture with low masculinity, men also tend to share some *feminine* traits.[12]

Advertisements for tablet computers in a highly masculine nation such as Japan may emphasize product benefits such as one's ability to get ahead. So a newer, faster computer with more features can help one assert himself in the workplace or at school. In contrast, in a more feminine country such as Brazil, an advertisement for the same tablet might emphasize the benefit of being able to stay in touch with family and friends through ready access to social networks via various apps.

Power Distance

Power distance is the extent to which people accept as fact the principle of the division of authority and privilege among different groups within society. Social

How might differing cultural values create different meanings for this product?

YURIKO NAKAO/Reuters /Landov

class distinctions become a very real issue among consumers in high-power-distance nations. These distinctions go beyond just social class and affect relationships between supervisory and subordinate employees and even between students and teachers.

Low-power-distance nations tend to be more egalitarian. As a result, people refer commonly to each other by first names even when a discussion involves people from different social classes and often even between employees and supervisors. In high-power-distance nations, those with less status must show deference to those with greater status; therefore, the lower-status person would not likely call a person of higher status by first name.

In many Asian nations, where power distance is relatively high compared to that in the United States, people often use the terms *senior* and *junior* to capture status distinctions. A student might be junior to a faculty supervisor or even to another student who preceded her through a program of study. When one is unclear about whether or not she is junior or senior to another, she might well ask the other consumer, "How old are you?" Age would be a tiebreaker, with older people having more status than younger people. Senior and junior status can affect simple things such as seating arrangements and whether or not one gets served first or last. Juniors may need to be careful in what they buy and do so as not to seem superior in any substantive way to a senior. A consumer violating a custom and acting more "senior" than appropriate may well

face cultural sanctions for the behavior.

In high-power-distance nations, certain consumer behaviors are designated exclusively to individuals by class or status. For example, in high-power-distance nations people view activities like tennis as only for those with very high status. Additionally, authority appeals in marketing are more effective when power distance is high.[13]

uncertainty avoidance
extent to which a culture is uncomfortable with things that are ambiguous or unknown

> The task becomes making the unfamiliar seem familiar in appealing to consumers who are high in uncertainty avoidance.

Uncertainty Avoidance

Uncertainty avoidance is just what the term implies. A culture high in uncertainty avoidance is uncomfortable with things that are ambiguous or unknown. Consumers high in uncertainty avoidance prefer the known, avoid taking risks, and like life to be structured and routine. Uncertainty avoidance has important implications for consumer behavior, because marketing success and improved quality of life often depend on obtaining value from something innovative and therefore somewhat unfamiliar. The task becomes making the unfamiliar seem familiar in appealing to consumers who are high in uncertainty avoidance.

Nations that are high in uncertainty avoidance will be slower to adopt product innovations. Additionally, nations that are relatively high in uncertainty avoidance, such as France, will react differently to basic CB generalizations. For instance, one such generalization is that scarcity affects the perceived value of products. A scarce product is worth more, and consumers are more likely to purchase a product perceived to be scarce. However, the extent to which scarcity drives actual purchase intentions is more pronounced among cultures high in uncertainty avoidance.[14] In other words, consumers in high-uncertainty-avoidance cultures are quicker to buy something because of perceived scarcity possibly because of doubt over when the product might be available again.

Differing CSV values also define basic consumer principles such as the price–quality relationship. For instance, the price–quality relationship is not as strong among cultures with high uncertainty avoidance. These consumers are more skeptical and likely to discern individual features of products separately. Such is the case with Chinese consumers, who are more likely to perceive a price–risk relationship than a price–quality relationship.

long-term orientation
values consistent with Confucian philosophy and a prioritization of future rewards over short-term benefits

guanxi (pronounced "gawn-zeye") Chinese term for a way of doing business in which parties must first invest time and resources in getting to know one another and becoming comfortable with one another before consummating any important deal

renquing the idea that favors given to another are reciprocal and must be returned

In other words, a higher price means higher risk in conditions of uncertainty.[15] Superstitions and myths also play a bigger role among cultures high in uncertainty avoidance.[16] Consumers in these cultures may even use astrological charts to help plan visits to casinos. Thus, the casinos in these cultures can somewhat predict peak periods of traffic based on these types of beliefs. Recent research also suggests that low uncertainty avoidance leads to a higher degree of implicit trust as the exchange partners' ethics guide marketing transactions. This means that fewer issues need to be governed by explicit rules.[17]

Consumers from high-uncertainty-avoidance cultures also demand greater amounts of product information and explanation. Bosch Industries, based in Germany, designs different packages for products sold in Europe and products sold in the United States. A packet containing appliance replacement parts, for instance, can be a simple cellophane wrapper in the United States. In Germany, Bosch may use a box because consumers can easily read more information than from a wrapper. The Bosch website includes different presentations by country, with the German site going into elaborate explanations. German consumers, like other consumers high in uncertainty avoidance, find more value from the detailed product presentations.

Long-Term Orientation

The final CSV dimension is long-term orientation. **Long-term orientation** reflects values consistent with Confucian philosophy and a prioritization of future rewards over short-term benefits. As such, high long-term orientation means that a consumer values thriftiness and perseverance as well as the maintenance of long-term relationships.[18] Relationships need time to develop and are intended to last for a lifetime. As a result, negotiations between suppliers and buyers are more likely to consider long-term effects to both parties in high-long-term-orientation cultures such as Japan.[19] At the other end of the spectrum, a short-term orientation is associated more with immediate payoffs and face saving.[20]

anekoho/Shutterstock.com

Guanxi (pronounced "gawn-zeye") is the Chinese term for a way of doing business in which parties must first invest time and resources in getting to know one another and becoming comfortable with one another before consummating any important deal. Guanxi is a common mode of operation among cultures with high long-term orientation—as with many nations in the Far East.[21] Western consumers depend on credit cards for everyday purchases and even in many cases as instant financing for luxury items. Thus, American consumers often have multiple credit cards, each from a different bank or credit company. As the Chinese economy develops, the principles of guanxi and long-term orientation present barriers for credit card companies.[22] In a country where smartphones cost about two months' salary, global marketers that present consumer credit to Chinese consumers in a palatable way are likely to perform well.

Renquing is another phenomenon associated with long-term orientation. **Renquing** is the idea that when someone does a good deed for you, you are expected to return that good deed. The reciprocation need not be immediate, however. In fact, the expectation of reciprocation at some point in the future fosters long-term relationships, since individuals are forever trying to balance the renquing score with each other.[23] Thus, a consumer and personal service provider may end up in a long-term relationship facilitated in part by renquing.

9-2c The CSV Scoreboard

A CSV scoreboard can be put together using historical CSV dimension scores found in many resources, including the Hofstede website **www.geert-hofstede.com**. How does your country stack up on the CSV scoreboard? The CSV scores for a given country can be essential information for marketers wishing to appeal to consumers in another country. The more similar the CSV scores, the more likely consumers find value in the same or similar products and experiences.

EXHIBIT 9.4 CSV Scoreboard for the United States, Australia, United Kingdom, Brazil, Russia, India, Pakistan, and China

	Power Distance	Individualism	Masculinity	Uncertainty Avoidance	Long-Term Orientation
United States	40	91	62	46	29
Australia	36	90	61	51	31
United Kingdom	35	89	66	35	25
Brazil	69	38	49	76	65
Russia	93	39	36	95	55[a]
India	77	48	56	40	61
Pakistan	55	14	50	70	0
China*	80	20	66	30	118

*No LTO score available for Russia. The mean LTO is inserted as an estimate.

© Cengage Learning

BRIC acronym that refers to the collective economies of Brazil, Russia, India, and China

BRIC

Exhibit 9.4 shows a CSV scoreboard for a few select nations. Brazil, Russia, India, and China represent typical emerging economies. The acronym **BRIC** refers to the collective economies of these nations. These nations are key targets for foreign investment, and the ripple effect is that consumers in these nations are becoming wealthier and better targets for all manner of goods and services. Doing business in these nations is hardly the same, though, as their CSV scores show. Thus, in this truly global marketplace, serving consumers in emerging markets can be an important route to business success. Some are now considering where the next emerging nations will be.[24]

CSV Leaders

Among all nations with CSV scores, Austria has the lowest power-distance scores and Malaysia has the highest. The United States has relatively low power distance, with only 15 nations reporting lower scores. For individualism, Guatemala reports the lowest score, and the United States has the highest. Sweden reports the lowest masculinity score, and Japan the highest, with the exception of the Slovak nations. The United States is neither clearly masculine nor clearly feminine. Singapore reports the lowest uncertainty avoidance score and Greece the highest. The United States is relatively low on uncertainty avoidance, with only 12 nations reporting a lower score. Long-term orientation scores are available for only a few nations. But, among those with scores, Pakistan has the lowest (meaning that it is the most short-term oriented), and China has the highest.

9-2d Cultural Distance

More and more businesses are considering reaching out to markets outside of their own country. Certainly, the Internet has helped reduce the market separations caused by geographic distance. However, consider businesses like Subway, IKEA, Sephora, and Zara. Each already operates many stores in many countries. How should a company decide where it should expand internationally? In other words, where will it be successful?

Two approaches to this important question can be taken. First, perhaps the most intuitive response is to look to neighboring countries with which the home country shares a border. Certainly, many U.S. businesses exist in Canada and vice versa. This approach is based on geographic distance. Countries are attractive because they are nearby and can be easily reached both in terms of marketing communications and physical distribution.

How should a company decide where it should expand internationally?

© iStockphoto.com/winhorse

cultural distance representation of how disparate one nation is from another in terms of their CSV

CANZUS acronym that refers to the close similarity in values between Canada, Australia, New Zealand, and the United States

socialization learning through observation of and the active processing of information about lived, everyday experience

The second approach looks more at how similar a target nation's consumers are to the home consumers. This approach is based more on **cultural distance (CD)**, which represents how disparate one nation is from another in terms of their CSVs. Thus, with this approach, consumers can be compared by using scores available in a CSV scoreboard. For example, Exhibit 9.5 shows the difference scores for all nations depicted in the CSV scoreboard compared to those of the U.S.A. These are obtained simply by subtracting the score for each nation on each dimension from the corresponding score for U.S. consumers.

Notice the small scores on each dimension for the differences between Australia, the United Kingdom, and the United States compared to the other nations. A simple distance formula can summarize the cultural differences between nations. One might consider simply adding up the difference scores; however, the negative and positive scores could cancel each other out, making two nations that are really quite different appear similar. Thus, one way to correct this problem is by using the squared differences, much as would be the case in computing statistical variation. For example, the following formula is used to compute the total cultural distances from the United States for each nation shown in Exhibit 9.5:

$$CD = \sqrt{\sum_{i=1}^{5}(TCSV_i - BCSV_i)^2}$$

where CD = cultural distance, TCSV = target country value score on dimension i, and BCSV = baseline country value score on dimension i.

Thus, for example, the CD for Australia from the United States is 6.9:

$$CD = \sqrt{\begin{matrix}(36-40)^2 + (90-91)^2 + (61-62)^2 + \\ (51-46)^2 + (31-29)^2\end{matrix}} = \sqrt{47} = 6.9$$

Among all comparisons, few would show as little difference as this. Compare these with the CD scores for the BRIC countries. The CD score between any two countries is easily computed for all nations for which CSV scores are available.

Countries with relatively low CD scores are more similar, and thus they tend to value the same types of consumption experiences. In fact, the term **CANZUS** is sometimes used to refer to the close similarity in values between Canada, Australia, New Zealand, and the United States.[25] Additionally, the U could also represent the United Kingdom because the nations are nearly identical from a CD perspective. Not surprisingly, common consumer products, retailers, and restaurant chains that are successful in one of these countries tend to be successful in the others as well.

International expansion decisions should consider CD as well as geography.

9-3 How Is Culture Learned?

Culture is a learned process. Consumers learn culture through one of the two socialization processes discussed in this section. **Socialization** involves learning through observation and the active

---

EXHIBIT 9.5 CSV Difference Scores Relative to American Consumers

	Power Distance	Individualism	Masculinity	Uncertainty Avoidance	Long-Term Orientation	Total Distance Score
Australia	−4	−1	−1	5	2	6.9
United Kingdom	−5	−2	4	−11	−4	13.5
Brazil	29	−53	−13	30	36	77.6
Russia	53	−52	−26	49	26	96.3
India	37	−43	−6	−6	32	65.7
Pakistan	15	−77	−12	24	−29	87.8
China	40	−71	4	−6	89	121.8

© Cengage Learning

processing of information about lived, everyday experience. The process takes place in a sequence something like this:

Social interaction $\mapsto$ modeling $\mapsto$ reinforcement

As consumers interact they begin to model (meaning enact) behaviors learned or seen. Reinforcement occurs through the process of rewarding reactions or sanctions. Additionally, learning results in CSVs that are relatively enduring. Societal values are not easily changed, and the clash between peoples with differing CSVs has been around since the beginning of time.

9-3a Enculturation

The most basic way by which consumers learn a culture is through an enculturation process. **Enculturation** represents the way people learn their native culture. In other words, enculturation represents the way in which consumers learn and develop shared understandings of things with their families.

Why do some consumers like wasabi or hot peppers? The answer is enculturation. Consumers are not born liking very pungent food. But, early in life, children observe the diets of their parents and relatives and come to mimic those behaviors. When they do, they receive overt social rewards, thereby reinforcing their dietary choice. In Kyrgyzstan, children grow up drinking fermented mare's milk. Although koumiss, or fermented mare's milk, has what can kindly be called a "peculiar" flavor by most standards, the fact that one grows up drinking this creates the acquired taste that makes it palatable or even tasty. The entire idea of habituation, discussed in an earlier chapter, provides a mechanism that helps make this type of enculturation possible.

Tatiana Morozova/Shutterstock.com

9-3b Acculturation

Acculturation is the process by which consumers come to learn a culture other than their natural, native culture—that is, the culture to which one may adapt when exposed to a new set of CSVs. Acculturation is a learning process. When a consumer becomes acculturated, chances are that old beliefs have been replaced by new beliefs. Therefore, children generally become acculturated more quickly than adults because the old rules are not as old and are thereby less resistant to change.[26] Retail managers at Sainsbury's supermarket in the U.K. are aiming more lines of food products specifically at children. As a marketing tool, this may attract more shoppers, but as an image tool, the move positions Sainsbury as a more healthy alternative for children.[27]

However, not all consumers who are introduced into a new culture acculturate. Several factors can inhibit acculturation. For example, strong **ethnic identification**, the degree to which consumers feel a sense of belonging to the culture of their ethnic origins, can make consumers feel close-minded about adopting products from a different culture. When ethnic identification is strong, consumers in a new land may even avoid learning the language of the new land. For instance, pockets of Chinese immigrants in Canada with strong ethnic identification choose to live the majority of their lives interacting only with other Chinese immigrants, purchasing Chinese products nearly exclusively, and paying attention only to Chinese language media.[28]

Consumer ethnocentrism is a belief among consumers that their ethnic group is superior to others and that the products that come from their native land are superior to other products. Consumers who are highly ethnocentric believe that it is only right to support workers in their native country by buying products from that country. Ethnocentrism is highly related to the concept of uncertainty avoidance. When ethnocentrism is very high, consumers who are in a foreign land may create their own communities within a larger enclave and display little interaction with the outside world.

Exhibit 9.6 illustrates factors that either inhibit or encourage consumer acculturation. Simply put, male consumers who have high ethnic identification, high ethnocentrism, and are relatively old are the worst targets for adopting products of a different or new culture. Interestingly, from an international marketing perspective, CSV profiles characterized by high uncertainty avoidance and strong masculinity are likely not good targets for imported goods relative to other countries. The inhibitions that consumers have about "foreign" products distract from the value the

enculturation way people learn their native culture

acculturation process by which consumers come to learn a culture other than their natural, native culture

ethnic identification degree to which consumers feel a sense of belonging to the culture of their ethnic origins

consumer ethnocentrism belief among consumers that their ethnic group is superior to others and that the products that come from their native land are superior to other products

quartet of institutions
four groups responsible for communicating the CSVs through both formal and informal processes from one generation to another: family, school, church, and media

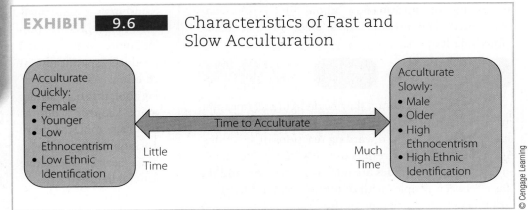

EXHIBIT 9.6 Characteristics of Fast and Slow Acculturation

Acculturate Quickly:
• Female
• Younger
• Low Ethnocentrism
• Low Ethnic Identification

Little Time

Time to Acculturate

Much Time

Acculturate Slowly:
• Male
• Older
• High Ethnocentrism
• High Ethnic Identification

© Cengage Learning

products offer, because their very meaning is inconsistent with the consumer's current belief structure.

9-3c Quartet of Institutions

So consumers *get* culture through either enculturation or acculturation. Each of these is a learning process. Consumers learn primarily through the influence of cultural institutions. Previously, consumer behavior theory suggested that a triad of institutions accounted for much of the cultural learning process. However, more recently a fourth institution has been recognized. Thus, we now recognize a **quartet of institutions** that are responsible for communicating the CSVs through both formal and informal processes from one generation to another. The four institutions comprising the quartet are (see Exhibit 9.7):

1. **Family**
2. **School**
3. **Church**
4. **Media**

Family, school, and church have long been recognized as primary agents for acculturation and enculturation. Each of these is recognized as a vehicle for teaching values to children; therefore, they are agents of enculturation. Consumers become socialized by the behaviors that are affiliated with specific institutions.

Many consumers, particularly young consumers, spend a lot of time interacting with media ranging from radio to Facebook. Here, they observe behavior (sometimes acted out in fiction), receive information about celebrities and pop culture, and exchange ideas, likes, and thoughts with both real and virtual acquaintances. Media offers a channel through which consumers learn. The relative influence pushed through the media raises concerns about public policy potentially restricting media access. Many governments actively limit the amount of "American" media allowed in the country in the belief that this will protect their culture from becoming overly Americanized or Westernized. An influx of nonnative media can indeed influence the rate of acculturation.[29] Children may be particularly susceptible to media influence. Children who watch more television have a more distorted view of reality and generally presume that

EXHIBIT 9.7 The Quartet of Institutions Shape a Consumer's Culture

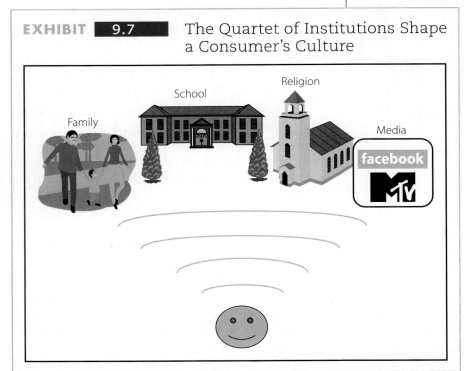

Family   School   Religion   Media

facebook   MTV

© Cengage Learning

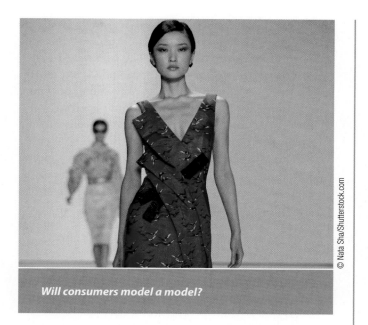
Will consumers model a model?

the typical family owns more luxury items and is better off materialistically than families in that particular culture really are. Children who watch more television become more materialistic than children who view less television.[30] Teens and young adults, particularly immigrants, who are more involved with media such as MTV may end up with different ideas about what makes up appropriate dating behavior based on idealized portrayals of attraction often depicted in media.[31] Therefore, many families try to actively limit the amount of Internet media and television exposure to their children.[32]

Culture and Policy-Related Consumer Communication

Differences in CSVs may have public policy implications as well. A study of teen consumers in countries such as Italy, Austria, Slovenia, Uzbekistan, Russia, and the United States, among others, found that antismoking ads were not equally effective. The results suggest that antismoking ads targeted toward countries high in individualism should emphasize the ill effects of smoking to one's self. In contrast, in countries with high collectivism, antismoking ads that emphasize the negative effects of smoking on other consumers are more effective.[33]

Studies measuring CSV among consumers still show distinctions consistent with the profiles discussed earlier. Thus, beyond the teen years particularly, differences in

tastes, political views, and preferences are expected to remain somewhat distinct from culture to culture.

modeling process of imitating others' behavior; a form of observational learning

Modeling

Modeling is an important way in which consumers are socialized into a specific culture either through acculturation or enculturation. A famous cliché says that imitation is the sincerest form of flattery. Well, **modeling** is precisely a process of imitating others' behavior.

Young children, for instance, observe their parents and model their behavior—at least until adolescence. As children become older, they may choose to model the behavior of older peers more than they model that of their parents. Adolescent children's attitudes toward smoking as well as their actual smoking behavior are largely influenced by the activities of peer referents.[34] In other words, adolescents will tend to model the behavior of those they aspire to become. In fact, the noun *model* captures this concept's essence. When it comes to fashion, designers hope that consumers will want to model their fashion models by selecting the clothes these models wear on the runway. Exhibit 9.8 displays ways institutions facilitate modeling.

Shaping

Shaping is a socialization process by which consumers' behaviors slowly adapt to a culture through a series of rewards and sanctions. Think about how one might modify his or her behavior to win acceptance from a group. A student might decide to wear different clothes to school as a way of trying to fit in. The way that other

EXHIBIT 9.8 Modeling and the Quartet

Institution	Behavior	Description
School	Meals	Younger students observe senior students' behaviors and learn when it is appropriate to use the dining hall versus other options on or off campus.
Family	Timeliness	Children observe parents to see if they are on time to events.
Church	Prayer	People observe others in the church to learn the appropriate way to behave when in a church.
Media	Language	Consumers learn slang by repeating terms learned through television, movies, music, and Internet media.

© Cengage Learning 2015

verbal communication
transfer of information through either the literal spoken or written word

dialects variations of a common language

students react to the new attire can serve to shape the student's future behavior.

The CSV profile of a culture can influence the effectiveness of cultural shaping. For instance, more individualistic cultures are less susceptible to these types of normative influences.[35] Not all cultures reward complaining in the same way.[36] In collectivistic cultures, complaining can be a sign of disrespect and may be looked at as inappropriate for minor inconveniences. American consumers who complain about their hotel room being slightly too warm are not likely to risk sanction. However, in a more collectivistic culture, hotel staff may look down upon someone complaining about a room that is slightly warm. Therefore, the extra added value that comes from group acceptance is greater among cultures where collectivism is stronger than individualism.

9-4 Fundamental Elements of Communication

9-4a Verbal Communication

Obviously, language can sometimes be a problem. If you have ever needed directions to some location in a place where you don't know the language, you can

appreciate this. However, sometimes even when the correct language is used communication can still be awkward or difficult. The term *Chinglish* is used to refer to the awkward use of English traditionally common in China.[37] "Execution in progress" may sound alarming but it's Chinglish for "caution, work in progress."

In this section, **verbal communication** refers to the transfer of information through the literal spoken or written word. Consumers will have difficulty finding value in things they cannot understand. Marketers have long wrestled with the problem of translating advertisements, research instruments, product labels, and promotional materials into foreign languages for foreign markets. This problem is only made more widespread in today's truly international marketplace.

Verbal communication can even be difficult within a single language. Almost every language is spoken slightly differently from place to place—or with several unique **dialects**. English in the United States isn't exactly the same as English in England, which is not the same as English in Australia, which is not the same as English in Ireland or other places where English is spoken. In the same way, Chinese is not always Chinese and Spanish not always Spanish. Thus, translation alone is insufficient to guarantee effective communication. Exhibit 9.9 provides some examples of difficulties in communicating even simple ideas through the spoken or written word.

Translation Equivalence

Bilingual speakers often may think of more than one way to try to express the meaning of something from

Horse of a Different Color

Socialization processes teach us many things, including what makes appropriate food. Recently, horse meat traces appeared in ground meat across Europe, including in Burger King burgers and IKEA's famous "Swedish Meatballs." Plants that processed the ground beef in both cases also processed horse meat destined for other uses. As a result, traces of horse ended up in meat labeled ground beef.

Although the news had little effect on Burger King, IKEA took swift action to remove the product from their stores in many countries. IKEA products, particularly in Scandinavia, are regarded as good value, trustworthy, and wholesome. Thus, despite the fact that horse is not

that unusual a food in many parts of Europe, IKEA chose not to risk cultural sanctions from consumers in non-horse-eating cultures.

© Ilona Baha/Shutterstock.com

Sources: A. Molin and J. D. Stoll, "IKEA's Iconic Meatball Drawn Into Horse-Meat Scandal," *The Wall Street Journal*, February 26, 2013, B1. AP (2013), "Horsemeat Found in IKEA's Swedish Meatballs," *Fox News*, http://www.foxnews.com/health/2013/02/25/horse-meat-found-in-IKEA-swedish-meatballs/, accessed March 14, 2013.

one language in another. In some cases, words exist in one language that have no precise equivalent in another. In other instances, even when the same word may exist, people in other cultures do not use the word the same way. Thus, interpretation errors and blunders occur unless one takes great care.

Translational equivalence exists when two phrases share the same precise meaning in two different cultures. Translation–back translation is a way to try to produce translational equivalence. With this process, one bilingual speaker takes the original phrase and translates it from the original language into the new language. Then, a second, independent bilingual speaker translates the phrase from the new language back into the original language. Assuming the retranslated phrase matches the first, translational equivalence exists. If not, either the phrase needs to be dropped or more work, possibly involving even other speakers fluent in both languages, is needed to determine if a common meaning can be found by changing the words in one or both languages.

Metric Equivalence

Once a common meaning is established, things could still go wrong when consumer researchers compare consumer reactions from one country with those from another. Researchers who apply typical survey techniques such as Likert scales or semantic differentials may wish to compare scores from one culture with those from another. This is valid only if the two culture–language combinations use numbers in a somewhat similar fashion. For example, if a Chinese consumer rated a woman who was 5 feet 3 inches tall for height, she might be rated tall. However, if a Norwegian rated the same woman, she would be rated as quite short.

Metric equivalence refers to the state in which consumers are shown to use numbers to represent quantities the same way across cultures. Metric equivalence is necessary to draw basic comparisons about consumers from different countries concerning important consumer relationships. Comparing average scores for consumer attitudes from one culture to the next requires another form of equivalence known as *scalar equivalence*. The procedures for performing tests of metric equivalence are beyond the scope of this text, but students of consumer behavior and international marketing should be aware of these approaches, because comparing quantities across cultures can be tricky.[38]

> **translational equivalence** two phrases share the same precise meaning in two different cultures
>
> **metric equivalence** statistical tests used to validate the way people use numbers to represent quantities across cultures

---

EXHIBIT 9.9 Example Problems with Verbal Communication

Communication	Situation	Intended Communication	Problem
"Yo vi la Papa!"	Spanish-language slogan on t-shirts prior to Pope's visit to Mexico	"I saw the Pope!"	"La Papa" is "the potato." El (or al) Papa is the Pope. So, the t-shirts said "I saw the potato."
"Boy, am I stuffed!"	English-language restaurant slogan spoken by middle-aged man.	"Boy, am I full!" (meaning had a lot to eat)	Slogan works fine in the United States; however, in Australia, "stuffed" means pregnant. So, slogan depicts middle-aged, slightly overweight man saying "Boy, am I pregnant!"
"Strawberry Crap Dessert"	English placed on pre-prepared, refrigerated pancakes by Japanese firm intending product for Chinese market.	"Strawberry crêpe"	English can convey a quality image to products in much of Asia even if most consumers can't read the words. Here, the phonics are probably just a little off.
"Bite the waxed tadpole"	Chinese label for Coca-Cola	"Coca-Cola"	Coke tried to find the best phonetic way to produce something sounding like "Coca-Cola." In some Chinese dialects, but not all, strange interpretations like this resulted.
"miststueck!"	Clairol's name for a new hair care product introduced in Germany	Literally a Mist Stick that helped to tame unmanageable hair.	The English *mist stick* phonetically sounds like "miststueck," which is at best an impolite term to use for a women's product!

© Cengage Learning

Globish simplified form of English that reduces the vocabulary to around 1500 words and eliminates grammatical complications

nonverbal communication information passed through some nonverbal act

Globish

Through history, different languages have emerged as the international language of business communication. At one time, French was that language, but today most would consider English the language of international business. Certainly English is most common on the Internet and is the international language of marketing. About 1 out of 5 people in the BRIC study English—more than the number of students in the United States. English has become the language of marketing. But English grammar can be difficult as illustrated by Chinglish—and some linguists believe a new form of English with simpler rules is developing. **Globish** reduces the English vocabulary to around 1500 words and gets rid of nasty complications like contractions and silent letters.[39] Grammatically incorrect but easily recognized, Globish slogans and advertising are spreading through developing countries.

9-4b Nonverbal Communication

A conductor at a train station in Germany is approached by an American tourist who wants to know how many stops it will be until he reaches his destination. The train is noisy and filled with people so the conductor holds up his pointer finger in response. When the train stops, the tourist quickly exits. However, he'll soon realize he is not in the right location. Why? In Germany, one would be indicated by holding up the thumb.

Nonverbal communication refers to information passed through some nonverbal act—in other words, communication not involving the literal spoken or written word. This example illustrates intentional nonverbal communication; however, much communication through this means is unintentional or automatic. Many nonverbal communication cues are culturally laden so that the meaning depends on culture.

Exhibit 9.10 depicts several aspects of nonverbal communication and the way they come together to create effective communication. High-context cultures emphasize communication through nonverbal elements. In contrast, low-context cultures, such as Denmark, emphasize the spoken word and what you say is truly what you mean. The elements of nonverbal communication are touched on briefly in the following sections.

Time

In America, the expression "time is money" is often used. Americans typically place a high value on time and timeliness. The high value placed on timeliness may be due to the importance of individualism and achievement as core values. When an American consumer plans a dinner meeting for 7:00 P.M., he or she expects everyone to be present at 7:00 P.M.

Honey, I Brought the Kids!

Marriage can have a big impact on a consumer's life, but that change may pale in comparison to the change that comes when children are introduced into the equation. Both marriage and children can impact one's social life and particularly the types of places someone frequents to have dinner or just relax. In some cultures, for instance, the idea of bringing the kids along is taboo. In others, the idea of young children in an adult environment is taboo. In France, for example, children may be welcome at a brasserie but not so much at a Michelin-rated restaurant. Thus, dinner out means the added expense and complication of arranging someone to take care of the children. One French couple became so frustrated that they went to a nice restaurant and asked for a seat near the window. Why? Well, they left their young son outside the window where they could watch him while they had a nice dinner. This may seem awkward but in a culture such as this, the awkward looks one might get by bringing in a young child also would be clearly uncomfortable. Perhaps this may seem strange, but interesting: A couple may routinely bring their pet dog into the same restaurant and not even get an odd glance.

© iStockphoto.com/Figure8Photos/Mark Rose

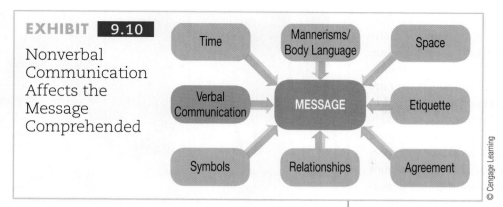

EXHIBIT 9.10

Nonverbal Communication Affects the Message Comprehended

Time → MESSAGE
Mannerisms/Body Language → MESSAGE
Space → MESSAGE
Verbal Communication → MESSAGE
Etiquette → MESSAGE
Symbols → MESSAGE
Relationships → MESSAGE
Agreement → MESSAGE

© Cengage Learning

body language nonverbal communication cues signaled by somatic responses

Consumers from some other cultures do not value timeliness in the same way. For example, in Spain, where individualism is much lower than the United States, a formal dinner scheduled for 9:00 P.M. is early by Spanish standards and will probably not begin at 9:00 P.M. The exact starting time is uncertain, but dinner will almost certainly not be served until sometime much later than 9:00 P.M.

Asian cultures also show much more patience consistent with high long-term orientation. Thus, while CANZUS and many Western European salespeople will want to close a sale on the first meeting, such an approach with Asian buyers will not come across well. Asian exchange partners need time to get to know one another and are not anxious to either close a sale or be closed until guanxi is established.

Mannerisms/Body Language

Body language refers to the nonverbal communication cues signaled by somatic (uncontrollable biological) responses. Consumers may use certain mannerisms when discussing issues with other consumers or salespeople. These cues can be more telling than the words that are spoken. The mannerisms that reveal meaning include the following characteristics:

- Facial expressions
- Posture
- Arm/leg position
- Skin conditions
- Voice

Sometimes, we feel compelled to look happy just to be polite. This requires a fake smile. While most people can easily make their mouths produce a grin, smiling eyebrows, slightly dilated pupils, and a tilted head (back) also occur with true happiness. Similarly, the posture of a truly happy person generally indicates

a willingness to approach the object of the emotion.

Service providers sometimes receive training aimed at making them better able to guess which consumers will complain out of anger long before any negative words are voiced.[40] Thus, if a customer's reaction signals anger, intervention may actually turn the experience into something positive through proactive measures to remedy the situation causing the anger. In Japan and similar cultures, managing the appearance of one's emotions becomes very important because one needs to avoid doing something that may shame another. If a Japanese consumer gives a gift to another person, the reaction in written and verbal communication means a great deal to the gift giver.

In addition, in today's virtual marketplace, nonverbal communication extends to virtual employees. Marketers study the mannerisms of avatars to investigate the messages they send. In other words, does an avatar seem agreeable, or disagreeable, or welcoming, or even trustful? Currently, the effects of avatars alone are small; however, the combination of verbal communication along with an avatar may contribute to higher trust and to increased hedonic value from the shopping experience.[41] Real or virtual, body language can affect the value of an interaction.

Space

In places like the United States and Australia, there is a lot of space! Relative to many parts of the world, like Japan or Western Europe, the United States and Australia are relatively sparsely populated. Thus, space varies in importance. The typical consumer in Seoul lives in a large high-rise building in a small flat identical to that of many neighbors living in the same building. For many Americans or Australians, the fact that so many people would be packed into a tight space may make them uncomfortable. For citizens of Seoul, being very close to other people is a fact of life.

The value that consumers place on space affects communication styles, too. Generally, CANZUS consumers, for instance, do not like to be too close to each other. When having a conversation, they remain at "arm's

etiquette customary mannerisms consumers use in common social situations

length." However, Italian, Armenian, or many Arabian consumers are comfortable communicating when they are so close to each other that they are physically touching. The CANZUS consumer engaged in a conversation with an Armenian, for instance, will likely instinctively try to obtain some space in the conversation by leaning backward at the waist as if an escape were possible! The differing approaches to space have implications for sales approaches, the way other consumers are depicted in advertising, and the design of retail environments.

Etiquette/Manners

When Americans greet each other, the typical response, particularly if a man is involved, is a handshake. Different handshakes may communicate different impressions. However, Asian consumers would expect a bow as a greeting and show of respect, while many Europeans may plant a kiss or two on the cheek. Greeting a business client with a kiss on the cheek would be a definite no-no in the United States; however, in France, a couple of kisses to the cheek could be an appropriate greeting.

Different cultures have different etiquettes for handling various social situations. **Etiquette** represents the customary mannerisms consumers use in common social situations. Dining etiquette varies considerably from one culture to another. In the United States, a consumer cuts food with the right hand, places the knife down, then

Politeness is gratifying—but what is polite, like appropriate table manners, varies with culture.

places a fork in the right hand to place food into his or her mouth. In Europe, however, good manners dictate that the knife stays in the right hand and the fork in the other. One cuts with the one hand and uses the left to efficiently scoop food into one's mouth. In any event, violating etiquette can lead to a cultural sanction.

Service providers need to be sensitive to the various differences in etiquette. For example, although no formal airline passenger etiquette exists, there is an informal code, and passengers who break these unwritten rules can actually decrease the satisfaction of other passengers. This situation is exaggerated by airlines carrying multinational groups of passengers. These passengers have different rules about space, privacy, dress, and hygiene.

"I Do? Or, I Do Not?"

Think about how different wedding rituals may be from culture to culture. Now consider all the material about cultural values, norms, sanctions, and verbal and nonverbal communications. Think about all the ways a stranger invited to a wedding in a different culture could end up in awkward situations. Here are a few issues that might arise:

- What time does a guest arrive to the wedding? Is it okay to arrive late? Can one leave early?
- If the wedding includes a wedding ceremony, does the guest participate fully (as with a non-Catholic participating in Holy Communion)?
- Is it okay to have an alcoholic beverage?
- Is it okay to dance?

- What is the proper way to greet the bride and groom?

  Burke/Triolo Productions/Botanica/Getty Images
- If others begin pinning money on the bride and groom, does the guest do so too?
- Does the guest bring a gift and if so, what types of gifts are inappropriate?
- Should the guest try to "catch the bouquet," if there is one?
- Does the guest have to try the food and drink?
- How should one dress? Should the guest try to dress as well as or better than members of the family?

Passengers with body odor or who dress inappropriately (for example, men in tank tops are generally considered inappropriate for such close company in Western cultures) can ruin the experience for other consumers. When consumers are unaware or lack concern for the proper etiquette in a given situation, the result can be awkward and diminish the value of the experience.

Relationships

How do consumers respond to attempts by marketers to build a personal relationship? Earlier, we discussed the Asian principle of guanxi and the different ways that a relationship may develop under this principle as opposed to conventional Western principles. However, differing CSVs have other implications for consumer–brand or consumer–service provider relationships.

For example, with high collectivism, the idea of a relationship is no longer personal. Consumers from collectivist nations define relationships in terms of the ties between a brand or service provider and a family or relevant group of consumers. Therefore, marketing appeals aimed at building personal relationships should emphasize the collective preference of this group rather than the individual.[42]

Agreement

How is agreement indicated and what does it mean? An Asian consumer who responds to a sales appeal with yes is not indicating agreement. Instead, this "yes" is more a way of indicating that she understands what is being said. Further, many Asian cultures will avoid strong affirmative or negative responses and instead use expressions like "that is possible" or "that may be difficult" to indicate agreement or lack of agreement.

Additionally, the extent to which a contract is seen as binding varies from place to place. Traditionally, South Koreans have not been accustomed to signing contracts. The fact that one would be asked to sign such an agreement was seen as a bit of an insult. Thus, Western firms may have to adjust their practices to indicate formal agreements when doing business in these cultures.

Symbols

The chapter began by emphasizing the link between culture and meaning. Because different cultures have different value profiles, objects and activities take on different symbolic or semiotic meaning. Perhaps nowhere is this more obvious than in the arena of religious objects. A large wooden cross is a device used to execute people in some cultures, but to Christians, a cross is an important symbol signifying everlasting life.

The symbolic meaning of objects also affects gift giving from culture to culture. In some Western cultures, particularly among the French cultures of Quebec and south Louisiana, a knife is seen as an inappropriate gift because of the risk that a knife symbolizes cutting a relationship. In China, clocks and watches are inappropriate as gift items because they symbolize the finite nature of life—time is running out. Also in Japan, the term *omiyage* refers to the custom of bringing gifts to friends from foreign trips. In particular, an omiyage gift of a famous brand can help symbolize freedom for the typical female office worker.[43] Marketers need to take care not to unintentionally promote offensive items based on cultural symbolism.

> When consumers are unaware or lack concern for the proper etiquette in a given situation, the result can be awkward and diminish the value of the experience.

9-5 Emerging Cultures

Marketing efforts are largely directed at consumers from developed nations. However, less-developed nations can offer attractive markets and many may represent emerging economies. Even low-income consumers in third-world nations can represent attractive markets to serve, particularly if low-priced, basic products can be offered. Market segments in developing nations offer tremendous opportunities, but communicating and delivering value in these segments means that the nuances of culture must be known and understood.

Exhibit 9.11 displays the most attractive national consumer markets. Countries like the United States, United Kingdom, and Germany have long been recognized as important consumer markets; however, many nations on this list are emerging in the sense that they would not have been considered leading consumer markets a decade or two ago. Sociopolitical changes have allowed these markets to emerge.

9-5a BRIC Markets

As discussed previously, the acronym BRIC stands for Brazil, Russia, India, and China. These four nations are often singled out as having economies that are growing very rapidly. In each market, large middle classes are emerging as consumers who formerly would have had

purchasing power parity (PPP) total size of the consumer market in each country in terms of total buying power

Chindia combined market and business potential of China and India

glocalization idea that marketing strategy may be global but the implementation of that strategy at the marketing tactics level should be local

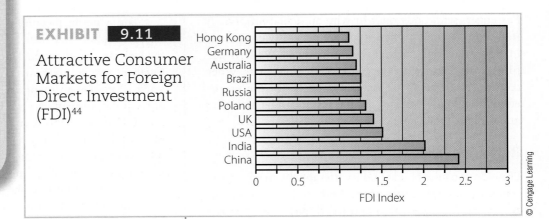

EXHIBIT 9.11

Attractive Consumer Markets for Foreign Direct Investment (FDI)[44]

© Cengage Learning

little opportunity for a good job have benefited from corporate capital investment. As a result, consumers in these nations have rising standards of living and have become attractive markets for many goods and services.

Exhibit 9.12 tracks the **purchasing power parity (PPP)** of the 10 most attractive consumer markets. The PPP gives an idea of the total size of the consumer market in each country in terms of total buying power. By 2020, China is expected to match or exceed the total purchasing power of the United States.

9-5b Chindia

The term **Chindia** refers to the combined market and business potential of China and India. The consumer demographics of India today compare favorably to those of the United States in 1970. Just over one billion consumers live in India. Today, the largest group of consumers is between 12 and 20 years old. This cohort group is similar to the baby-boomer generation in the United States, which was responsible for tremendous economic growth domestically and abroad.

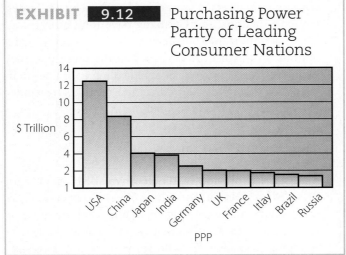

EXHIBIT 9.12 Purchasing Power Parity of Leading Consumer Nations

© Cengage Learning

Over 190 million households call India home. In 2005, 140 million of those households were considered aspiring consumers with household incomes equal to about $2,500 per year. Today, the Indian middle class has grown to just over 100 million households. As Indian incomes rise, the market potential of India expands as well.

The market potential for India and China is made clear in the fact that population is assessed in billions rather than millions. More and more Chindian consumers are stepping up to some luxuries that would have been out of their reach previously. Starbucks is growing in both countries, and the cosmetics market in China is about $25 billion annually.[44a] The Chinese cosmetics consumer remains price conscious though, and much of the growth in the industry is through discount e-tailing.

9-5c Glocalization

How should a company from another country appeal to these emerging but foreign consumer markets? Certainly, these countries offer a significantly different CSV profile than those in the United States. The term *glocalization* represents one alternative that allows flexibility in responding to the unique value profiles of consumers. **Glocalization** represents the idea that the marketing strategy may be global but the implementation of that strategy at the marketing tactics level should be local.

Reef Brazil beachwear executes a global branding strategy that appeals to the youth market by portraying a cool, carefree image.[45] This corporate strategy may be set by executives in Brazil. However, rather than dictating how this plan would be implemented, Reef could practice glocalization by letting managers and consultants in the foreign markets decide how this strategy should be carried out in their own particular markets.[46] In this way, local consumers can comprehend the global theme and share the same meaning for the brand.

What's Next?

During the days of the cold war, consumer markets like those in Russia and China were hardly seen as attractive to marketers in North America and Europe. However, times have changed. The advancement of free market economies has led to increased standards of living in many corners of the globe.

However, the fact is that half the world's consumer population remains illiterate and struggles to maintain anything more than a meager way of life. As the emerging economies advance today, so will the cost of doing business in those countries. Companies will search for cheaper places to do business, and through this process new emerging economies will develop. Much of Africa, for example, remains without the type of industrial or technological development necessary to create good jobs and the incomes that lead to a higher standard of living. Africa has a total population of nearly 800 million people. Even though parts of South Africa and northern Africa are developed, much of the rest remains destitute. Perhaps this area too will be a new emerging market for later in this century.

Like other places, though, the cultural barriers presented there are more than trivial. The cultural barriers go beyond dealing with consumers, but they also are ingrained in the sociopolitical environment. Therefore, changes in the government institutions will probably be needed before many companies will feel comfortable doing business there.[47]

Study Tools

Located at the back of the textbook

☐ Rip out Chapter in Review Card

Located at www.cengagebrain.com

☐ Review Key Terms Flashcards (print or online)

☐ Download audio summaries to review on the go

☐ Complete practice quizzes to prepare for tests

☐ Play "Beat the Clock" to master concepts

☐ Watch video on Lonely Planet for a real company example

WHAT DO YOU THINK?
WHAT OTHERS HAVE THOUGHT

① ② ③ ④ ⑤ ⑥ ⑦

35
30
25
20
15
10
5
0

Strongly disagree | Disagree | Somewhat disagree | Neither agree nor disagree | Somewhat agree | Agree | Strongly agree

A man should always pay for his date's dinner.

Opinions are almost evenly split on this question but most interestingly, almost nobody is neutral! Approximately 40% of respondents express some level of disagreement, leaving nearly 60% expressing some agreement. The neutral response accounts for practically no respondents!

Hill Street Studios/Blend Images/Jupiter Images

Consumers often
choose membership in microcultures in an effort to stand out or define themselves from the crowd.

WHAT DO YOU THINK?

The microcultures I belong to greatly influence the value I receive from products.

STRONGLY DISAGREE   STRONGLY AGREE

① ② ③ ④ ⑤ ⑥ ⑦

VISIT COURSEMATE AT WWW.CENGAGEBRAIN.COM

Microcultures

10

10-1 Microculture and Consumer Behavior

The climate is remarkable in many ways. On a June day, Kevin drives westward through northern California, and in just a few minutes time the temperature indicator on the car has fluctuated from 92 to 58 degrees. The sky has gone from absolutely clear to partly cloudy to a foggy mist. East of a ridge it is hot and dry, west of a ridge, cool and damp. Drive into a valley, and it is something in between. Meteorologists explain that regional climates contain many microclimates within them. Many Americans envy Californians because of the good weather associated with California. But truly, California's weather presents many different climates. The microclimates that exist throughout central and northern California are responsible for high-quality grapes that are used to make many outstanding wines.

In a similar way, we can think of a given culture containing multiple smaller and more specific microcultures. A **microculture** is indeed a culture, only smaller. We define a microculture as a group of people who share similar values and tastes that are subsumed within a larger culture. The smaller group can be quite distinct from the larger group or overall culture. The term *subculture* is often used to capture much the same idea as microculture. However, the term *microculture* is used here to portray the idea that the group is smaller but in no way less significant in terms of the potential influence on consumer behavior. You may notice that the microculture concept is similar in some ways to the group influence topic. Microcultures, however, are generally based on specific variables that we detail in this chapter. How many microcultures do you belong to? Let's take a look.

10-1a Culture Is Hierarchical

Culture is a universal phenomenon. It is everywhere and ultimately explains the habits and idiosyncrasies of all groups of consumers. In fact, each consumer belongs to many cultural groups—or more

After studying this chapter, the student should be able to:

10-1 Apply the concept of microculture as it influences consumer behavior.

10-2 Know the major U.S. microcultural groups.

10-3 Realize that microculture is not a uniquely American phenomenon.

10-4 Perform a demographic analysis.

10-5 Identify major cultural and demographic trends.

microculture a group of people who share similar values and tastes that are subsumed within a larger culture

role conflict a situation involving conflicting expectations based on cultural role expectations

precisely, they move in and out of microcultures. For instance, a college student from Texas who is attending a state university in that state is likely part of American culture, Texas culture, an ethnically defined culture such as Hispanic culture, university culture, and possibly Greek culture, should he or she belong to a fraternity or sorority. In this way, culture is hierarchical. A consumer belongs to one large, overall culture and then to many smaller cultural groups—microcultures—existing and interlinking within the overall culture. Exhibit 10.1 illustrates a cultural hierarchy.

Each microculture brings with it role expectations for its members. The role provides a signal as to the behaviors that one should perform to truly belong to the group; or, in other words, what it takes to be an authentic member of the group.[1] Obviously, some of the roles are inconsistent with each group and the consumer makes a choice to behave in ways more consistent with one group than with another. When a consumer faces a situation involving conflicting expectations based on cultural expectations, he is experiencing **role conflict**. For instance, when students attend a career fair for the first time they may experience some conflict over how to dress. Sorority sisters may see a certain outfit as business attire, but the career-oriented woman representing a company at the event may see it as too sexy and inappropriate for the office.

The fact that the college student mentioned earlier is a Texan clearly typifies culture. Texas has a unique and identifiable culture, and this point is illustrated by the fact that by now, the reader has an image of a Texan in mind. In other words, consumers have generally consistent associations with the "Texan" social schema. A college student who wears boots, jeans, and a Stetson in Massachusetts may stand out in the crowd, but this manner of dress may help a Texan fit in. This particular consumer likely also identifies with a specific age-based or generational culture, and makes consumer choices that either reinforce this social identity or send the signal that he does not wish to be part

EXHIBIT 10.1 The Hierarchical Nature of Culture and Microculture

- National Culture
  - Regional Culture
    - State Culture
      - Urban Culture
    - Neighborhood Culture
  - Ethnic Culture
  - Social Culture
    - University Culture
      - Class Culture (Undergrad/Grad)
      - Greek Culture
    - Sex-Role Culture
    - Age and Generational Cultures
    - Consumer Culture
      - Brand Cultures
      - Virtual Cultures

© Cengage Learning

of this group. Think about how these decisions explain simple things like music preferences. Polka music may be traditional in Austria, but an Austrian university student is not likely to find being a huge polka fan very gratifying among his peers. Similarly, an authentic goth may well have to hide a liking of a country music song or two.

> ⌐ Each microculture brings with it role expectations for its members. ⌐

Texas culture is part of American culture.

© iStockphoto.com/Mlenny Photography

10-1b Microcultural Roles and Value

Microculture membership changes the value of things. American consumers, for instance, generally find watching soccer dull, and thus consider it to be a low-value activity. In contrast, soccer is the number one spectator sport all around Europe and in other parts of the world. Cultural groups even arise within sports fans, and an extreme soccer fan may even become a *soccer hooligan* who participates in extreme and sometimes violent behaviors as a way of creating a personally meaningful soccer experience. Anthropologists have studied this cultural phenomenon by immersing themselves within the hooligan group. Some hooligans are professional people who find involvement in soccer to be a way to escape other realities, and thus they find hedonic value in hooligan activities. However, when soccer hooligans took up Burberry caps as preferred headwear, then young, male British business professionals abandoned the caps so as not to have a preference overlapping that could identify them as hooligans. We again see how culture is hierarchical in this example. Indeed, consumers often choose membership in microcultures in an effort to stand out or define themselves from the crowd. This phenomenon is known as **divergence**.[2]

10-2 Major U.S. Microcultures

Marketers can divide the U.S. population into consumer groups along a number of dimensions relative to market segmentation. These groupings are particularly effective when microcultures are involved, because the consumers within these groups likely have very similar preferences. There are many types of microcultures in the United States. These include regional, sex role, age-based, generational, religious, ethnic, income/social class, and street microcultures.

10-2a Regional Microculture

We don't think about it much today, but the U.S. Declaration of Independence declares each of the original 13 colonies "free and independent states." In much of early U.S. history, the country's name was plural. "These United States are free and independent" was a commonly used phrase, as opposed to "The United States is free and independent."[3] Using the plural form more clearly reflects the fact that lifestyles and culture vary as you travel around the United States and North America. Within America, many cultural groups can be identified. In 1981, Joel Garreau published the book *The Nine Nations of North America*.[4] The book identifies nine geographical regions that supposedly share similar value profiles and thus contain consumers with similar preferences. However, they don't neatly fit with conventional regional distinctions. For example, Florida is split, with the northern part belonging to "Dixie" and the southern part belonging to "The Islands." Chicago is part of the "Breadbasket," but Indianapolis is part of Dixie. Exhibit 10.2 illustrates this concept.

divergence situation in which consumers choose membership in microcultures in an effort to stand out or define themselves from the crowd

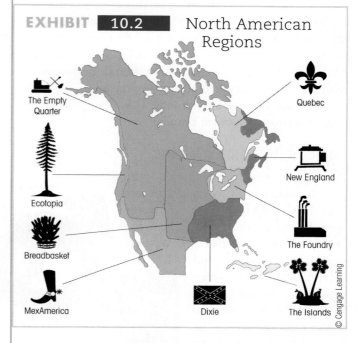

EXHIBIT 10.2 North American Regions

The Empty Quarter · Quebec · Ecotopia · New England · Breadbasket · The Foundry · MexAmerica · Dixie · The Islands

© Cengage Learning

The relative usefulness of the nine nation approach in segmentation is questionable, but it captures the fact that priorities among consumers do vary regionally.[5] Brand and food preferences, choices of favorite beverages, favorite sports, and even the names of things vary by region. For example, a soda is something with ice cream in it in the South, but a soda is another term for a soft drink in much of the Northeast. Debating the best pizza—either Chicago style or New York style—is very likely to get some consumers fighting!

One area in the United States that receives significant attention is the "Borderland" region, a region that was not included in the original Nine Nations approach. The Borderland covers the southwestern U.S. states that share a border with Mexico.[6] A large Hispanic population lives in this region; consumer researchers

sex roles societal
expectations for men and
women among members of a
cultural group

and marketers alike pay close attention to the composition and culture of the region. It is common to experience both Mexican and American culture in the area, and many marketing communications are presented in both English and Spanish. Exhibit 10.3 presents differences and preferences among U.S. consumers by region.

10-2b Sex Roles and Microculture

Sex roles refer to the societal expectations for men and women among members of a cultural group. Sex roles are ubiquitous in society, and inconsistency with them can be a source of sanctions. The differences between societal expectations of men and women vary less in Western cultures than they do in Eastern cultures, in which sex-based divisions in roles remain more obvious.[7] Recent comparisons of brand personality tend to show greater androgyny—meaning neither clearly male nor female—among U.S. perceptions of brands relative to Korean brands.[8]

Societal Role Expectations

Even in Western cultures, certain responsibilities such as child care and household cleaning are unevenly spread among cultures. In Italy, a relatively feminine culture by Western standards, women spend a great deal of time keeping their houses clean. Even an Italian woman who works outside of the home is likely to wash the floors of her home at least

© YAKOBCHUK VASYL/Shutterstock.com

twice a week. Women who do not work outside the home likely wash the floors nearly every day. In addition, they tend to use stronger cleaners than their U.S. counterparts. Clearly, all of this cleaning provides utilitarian value through the result of a clean house, but Italian women also take inner gratification from the activities because they help fulfill their specific societal sex role.[9] In Western culture, men have traditionally picked up the tab during a date, but as cultures become more androgynous, this tradition may be falling by the wayside.

Marketers need to be aware of the relative sex roles within societies. Men and women may share purchasing responsibilities differently from culture to culture. In the United States, the woman in the family remains the primary purchasing agent for most things. Men are generally allowed to make purchase decisions for things such as lawn care equipment and beer. Men also play a much larger role in the purchase of big-ticket items. Women tend to purchase the majority of clothing for males in U.S. households. However, in Italy, men place great pride in their business attire and are more likely to want control of these purchase decisions. Marketers therefore need to do research to help identify these roles, or else run the risk of targeting the wrong family member with marketing communications.

Male and Female Segments

A great deal of marketing communication is directed toward either a male or female market segment. Media are often distinguished easily based on the proportion of male and female customers. ESPN channels, for example, offer an opportunity to

EXHIBIT 10.3 Regional Differences and Preferences among U.S. Consumers

Actual Place	"9 Nation Region" (Garreau)	Geographical Designation	Core Societal Value Priority	Example Preference
Birmingham, AL	Dixie	South	Security and self-respect	Watch Discovery Health Channel
Los Angeles, CA	MexAmerica	West	Warm relationships with others and self-fulfillment	In-home cosmetics
Boston, MA	New England	Northeast	Self-fulfillment, achievement	Viewing foreign movies
Chicago, IL	Breadbasket	Midwest	Security and warm relationships	Chicago pizza

© Cengage Learning 2015

reach out to a predominantly male market. *Cosmopolitan* and *Harper's Bazaar* magazines offer an opportunity to reach a female market. These media clearly contain appeals geared toward the respective sex.

Although role expectations associate certain types of purchases with men or women, marketers sometimes reach out to the opposite sex. Men traditionally are the household buying agent for electronics. However, Best Buy altered its marketing strategy in a special effort to appeal to female shoppers. Consumer research showed that women were not particularly enamored with the big box format, so Best Buy launched Best Buy Mobile. Best Buy Mobile units are relatively small and located in shopping centers and malls.[10] Now, female consumers are exposed to electronic gadgets in an environment more suited to their tastes. Marketers outside the United States are also taking this approach. Vespa, the world's top name in scooters, redesigned their basic model into the "Indian Vespa" by adding a foot-rest extension to the left side because Indian women, who wear relatively close-fitting foot-length garments, only ride in a side-saddle style. The effort to provide cheap transportation to relatively low-income women may pay off in a big way in the long run.

Conversely, online fashion retailers like Gilt Groupe and Rue La La have changed their marketing approach to better appeal to men.[11] Currently, only about one in four adult men regularly purchase clothing products online. These retailers seek to entice more men to their sites by offering more sports-oriented merchandise lines, such as golf apparel. The retailers believe that appealing to men will be successful based on the relatively high amount of disposable income of many middle-aged professional men.

Marketers need to keep in mind that women and men do not make consumer decisions in the same way. Perhaps the biggest difference is in the way men and women process information. Relative to women, men tend to be more heuristic/intuitive in their processing. **Cognitive structuring** is a term that refers to the reliance on schema-based heuristics in making decisions. In contrast, women tend to process information in a more piecemeal fashion.[12] Thus, men are more likely to process information based on the way it is framed and on the categories (schema, stereotypes, scripts) it evokes, rather than on a detailed breakdown of all the information. Interestingly, this doesn't mean that men make poorer choices than women, only that they make them in a different way.

10-2c Age-Based Microculture

The term **age-based microculture** describes the finding that people of the same age end up sharing many of the same values and develop similar consumer preferences. Perhaps no age-based group receives more attention

---

cognitive structuring
term that refers to the reliance on schema-based heuristics in making decisions

age-based microculture
term that describes the finding that people of the same age end up sharing many of the same values and develop similar consumer preferences

---

Changing Class?

Middle-class growth characterizes much of the developing world as typified by China, India, and Brazil. The United States, however, bucks this demographic trend with respect to income groups. In the United States, a shrinking middle class and a growing lower class characterizes recent times. In 2012, 32% of U.S. residents classify themselves as lower class, which is up from 25% in 2008. Less than half consider themselves middle class. Upper-class consumer households were down to 17% from 21% in the same time period.

If household incomes continue to decrease, consumer spending may remain low overall and premium products formerly enjoyed by middle-class consumers, such as frequently dining out, private school education, and new cars, will be in less demand. Further, over half of American consumers are on some kind of government aid, and a record 15% (over 45 million) receive food stamps. As a result, even American companies look increasingly to foreign markets for growth. Ford and GM both look to Brazil's growth in middle-class consumers as a reason to be optimistic about their near-term sales prospects.

© ALLERIM/Shutterstock.com

Sources: C. Morello, "Census: Middle Class Shrinks to an All-Time Low," *The Washington Post*, September 12, 2012, http://www.articles.washingtonpost.com/2012-09-12/35496368_1_income-inequality-median-household-income-middle-class (accessed March 19, 2013); J. Cox, "Report: 15% of Americans on Food Stamps," http://www.nbcnews.com/business/report-15-americans-food-stamps-980690 (accessed March 19, 2013); J. Muller, "Going South," *Forbes*, (October 22, 2012): 46–48.

world teen culture
speculation that teenagers around the world are more similar to each other than to people from other generations in the same culture

cohort a group of people who have lived the same major experiences in their lives

than teens. Nearly 21,000,000 Americans are between 15 and 19 years of age.[13] Teens seem to share many similar behaviors. In fact, some argue that teen behavior is not just similar within a given country, but similar across countries. Part of the similarity in behavior allows teens to fill the role expectations for a teenager in U.S. society.

World Teen Culture?

Consumer media involve more than just television. Radio, print publications, music, and web-based communication all can play a role in shaping culture and, therefore, the things that consumers value.[14] The Internet facilitates communication among consumers around the world, contributing to what some believe is a more universally similar **world teen culture**. Evidence of similar tastes among teenaged consumers around the world is obvious if one takes a look at teen purchase and consumption patterns. Many of these tastes are influenced by the Western media's depiction of celebrities. Thus, fashion and entertainment companies in particular may find segmenting based on age as useful as geography.

Brands listed in Exhibit 10.4 have particular appeal to teens in practically all corners of the world.

EXHIBIT 10.4	Similarities and Differences among Teen Consumers	
Favorite Brands	**Similar Activities**	**Less Similar Choices**
Coca-Cola	Listening to music	Religious ideas/activities
McDonald's	Using mobile phone	Cosmetic brands
Nike	Surfing the Internet	Political ideas
Disney	Video games	Equality of sexes
Cadbury	Smoking	
Apple		

© Cengage Learning

Coca-Cola and McDonald's, for example, are brand names that are listed among teens' favorite brands throughout much of the world.[15] Coca-Cola takes advantage of virtual media to help stay on top. A 2013 Coke Super Bowl ad encouraged fans to go online to vote for their favorite way of ending the commercial. Coke fans voted on which team would win a desert race to the nearest Coca-Cola. Coke invites participation in marketing and engages young consumers worldwide in doing so.

Although teens around the world may find value in many of the same types of music and clothing, research suggests that the cultural values of their home nation remain relatively distinct from nation to nation, particularly concerning personal products.[17] American teen consumers, for instance, still rate freedom as the most important CSV. In contrast, teens from Arab countries list faith as the most important CSV.[18] These differences translate into different consumption habits. For example, even though McDonald's is popular among teens practically everywhere, preferences for fast-food brands still differ between Asians and Americans.[19] Young consumers from different cultures around the world do appear to have similar tastes in apparel.

10-2d Generation Microculture

Age-based groups can be distinguished from generational groups. Consumers grow out of age groups. When a consumer reaches age 20, she is no longer in the teen microculture. However, she still "belongs" to a group with her peers. Notice that people who age in the same generation still belong to the same cohort. A **cohort** is a group of people who have lived the same major experiences in their lives, and the experiences end up shaping their core values. Life experiences have many different effects on a cohort. For instance, while teens tend to share some behaviors in common,

Teens share some preferences across cultures, including pizza!

© iStockphoto.com/Blend_Images

such as experimenting with tobacco, their preference for music tends to be much more of a generational effect. Consumers tend to enjoy music from their own generation and each generation seems to carry its taste for music with it to a large extent. Here, we briefly introduce some of the main generational groups in the United States. It is important to remember that not everyone always agrees on the exact dates of these groups or specific labels that are attached to them.[20]

Greatest Generation

The term "greatest generation" refers to American consumers who were young adults during World War II. These consumers were born prior to 1928. They represent approximately 11,500,000 consumers living today. Their lives and values are shaped very much by World War II and their post-war experiences. These consumers tend to be more thrifty than other consumers and thus are highly price conscious. These consumers have reached their elderly years.

Silent Generation

Silent generation consumers were born between 1928 and 1945. Two major events occurred during this time period. The first major event was the Great Depression, which began in 1929. The second major event was, of course, World War II. These consumers were greatly impacted by these events and, like their predecessors, are known for civic duty, conformity, and responsibility. They tend to be frugal and follow, largely, utilitarian motivations with their purchases. This segment is comprised of approximately 40,000,000 consumers in the United States today.

Baby Boomers

The Baby Boomers were born between 1946 and 1964. Over 60,000,000 Americans are Boomers. Boomers were born during a time in the United States that was marked by optimism and relative economic security. Many of these consumers came of age during the very turbulent 1960s, and they clearly left a mark on popular culture.

Boomers represent a major force in consumer culture and they are a substantial force in the economy. It should not be surprising, therefore, that they receive significant marketing attention. Many Boomers have saved significant sums of money for retirement and plan to enjoy good times well into their elderly years. Boomers, by and large, have a huge amount of spending power relative to other generations. They are characterized by a preference for wine and the finer things.

Generation X

Generation X consumers were born between 1965 and 1980. They represent just over 40,000,000 consumers. Generation X consumers were long thought to be a group that was marked by alienation and cynicism. They have also been referred to as "latchkey" kids to signify the idea that many of these consumers spent a great deal of time alone due to having both parents at work. Many Generation Xers also came from divorced households, which may explain why a good number of these consumers today focus strongly on the family and traditional family values. Although marketers often viewed Generation Xers as slackers, many of these consumers have become successful business people and community leaders. Research also reveals that the majority of these consumers started saving money relatively early in life.[21]

Millennials

Millennials were born between 1981 and 1995. They represent approximately 60,000,000 consumers in the United States. This group was originally referred to as Generation Y. A lot of research attention has been focused on this group not only because of its sheer size, but also because its members are so different from other cohorts.

These consumers tend to wholeheartedly embrace technology as no other generation before them. Many of them were cocooned by protective parents when they were young and tend to view technology as a means to build community and relationships. They also tend to keep close contact with their parents.[22] They tend to be relatively impulsive and optimistic. One of the consumer

Excited about an RV?? Well, Baby Boomers with disposable income find lots of value in the RV!!

Lisa F. Young/Shutterstock.com

behaviors that Millennials enjoy is visiting coffee shops with in-store WiFi. In this way, they stay connected to their friends and to their interests. In fact, they are so technologically savvy that they have been referred to as the first "always connected" generation, meaning that they are constantly in touch with other consumers through various technologies.[23] Of course, the older Millennials did not grow up in the same technological environment as did the younger consumers in this group. This is why only a part of this group, those in their early twenties, are referred to as "digital natives."[24] Regardless, even the older Millennials are more tech-savvy than the general population and they do tend to be always connected.

Millennials would prefer to walk than drive, live in urban settings than in rural settings, and live in smaller, rather than larger, homes. The very way in which they view the concept of "freedom" is also unique. For Millennials, freedom is more closely associated with having access to the Internet and social networking sites than with the automobile. Their parents tended to view the automobile as the key to freedom. Millennials, as a group, do not.

Millennials tend to be optimistic even though older consumers in this group have been greatly impacted by economic challenges. Many of these consumers are underemployed, taking whatever job will help to pay bills, and a number of them have taken unpaid internships simply to gain experience. Economic pressures have led many of them to delay marriage and even to move in with parents for financial reasons. Research also reveals that these pressures lead many Millennials to make poor choices with their finances, such as accumulating debt and saving little.[25]

Generation Z

Much attention has been given to the Millennial group, and rightfully so. However, another group of interest is "Generation Z." This group follows the Millennials and represents young consumers born between 1995 and 2010. The total number of consumers in this group is similar to the Millennials, with approximately 60,000,000 consumers in the United States. Research suggests that they will be the most educated, diverse, and mobile group to date. They will also be the first truly "global" generation, due to racial and cultural diversity, increased population mobility and migration, and comfort with mobile technologies.[26] They also tend to embody the "KGOY" concept (kids growing older, younger) since information is spread so quickly through the group by social media and texting. Given that many of these young consumers grew up with concepts like "tagging" and "liking" Facebook pages, they are also more attuned to concepts like viral marketing and self-endorsements

than is any other group.[27] Consumer researchers will continue to monitor this group as they come of age.

Generational Influence and Marketing

Generations provide a good basis for marketing segments because the consumer's age identifies his or her generation. Not every person that is age 21 right now matches the tastes of all the other Millennial generation consumers, but the largest number of people within a generation are similar to some extent. McDonald's recent strategies illustrate the difference between appealing to an age group versus a cohort group. For decades, practically every McDonald's featured a playground built conspicuously at the front of each restaurant. Not only that, consumers also strongly associated the Happy Meal with McDonald's. Thus, in consumers' long-term memories, McDonald's was strongly defined by the play area, Happy Meals, and children. In the past few years, McDonald's has moved away from that strategy and has even removed the play areas from many of their restaurants. In some cases, they have been replaced with sections called McCafé. The Happy Meal still remains, but the shift in their marketing corresponds to the fact that they are more interested in serving the markets that grew up playing in the playgrounds and eating Happy Meals than they are in directly appealing to children themselves. In a way, McDonald's has shifted from looking at the markets based on their age to one where they are capitalizing on a cohort group. Millennial generation consumers won't be found in the play area any longer, but you can still find them at McDonald's.

Generational effects can also explain why country music has changed so dramatically over the years. Have you ever wondered why today's country music doesn't sound like your grandpa's country? The answer lies largely in the fact that many of today's biggest stars grew up listening to classic or even alternative rock music. As you may have noticed, much of country music has a rock-edge sound to it. In some cases, it's even hard to tell the difference between today's country and rock music. Many of today's younger country music stars were just as likely to listen to rock groups such as Van Halen, Aerosmith, or Guns N' Roses when they were growing up as to traditional country legends like Willie Nelson or Johnny Cash. Comparing today's country music star in his 30s with a country music star of the same age in 1950 clearly illustrates how generations change.

10-2e Religious Microculture

Recall that religion represents one of the key institutions that shape consumer culture. Not surprisingly, then,

The Young and the Tweety

Today's marketer realizes that communicating with all consumers through a single media channel is impossible. Young consumers present a unique problem. To communicate with or understand these consumers, multiple media are needed and communication takes place at a torrid pace. As an example, "digital natives," consumers who are now in their early 20s, switch media an average of 27 times per hour! That's a constant shift from one medium to another. Getting somebody to view an entire 30-second commercial is now a major accomplishment.

Digital natives have little fear about leaving messages on social networking sites, and these messages represent a wealth of information for researchers. However, the data that are collected are not always helpful. Nevertheless, researchers are beginning to understand the advantages of using these data as they attempt to apply sophisticated statistical tools to code dimensions of meaning to statements that reflect consumer opinions about issues.

Twitter feeds provide an intriguing means of gathering data. Imagine trying to predict election outcomes from

© iStockphoto.com/Sadeugra

Twitter feeds. Researchers try to code tweets based on the mention of a candidate by name. The assumption is that a Twitter mention signals who a Twitter user will vote for. In 2008, such attempts proved inaccurate in predicting results in part because tweeters don't represent voters very well. Perhaps these problems would be less significant when trying to predict reactions to new product ideas or advertising campaigns. What do you think?

Sources: J. Maneyso and K. Stuth, "What Qualitative Researchers Can Learn from Facebook," *Marketing Research*, 23 (Summer 2011): 32. M. Griessmair, G. Strunk, and K. J. Aver-Srnka, "Dimensional Mapping: Applying DQR and MDS to Explore Perceptions of Seniors' Role in Advertising," *Psychology & Marketing* 28 (October 2011): 1061–86. A. Branthwaite and S. Patterson, "The Power of Qualitative Research in the Era of Social Media," *Qualitative Market Research: An International Journal* 14 (September 2011), 430–44. B. Steinberg, "Study: Young Consumers Switch Media 27 Times in an Hour," *Advertising Age*, April 9, 2012, http://adage.com/article/news/study-young-consumers-switch-media-27-times-hour/234008/ (accessed June 6, 2012).

religious affiliation provides a basis for microcultures within national or regional cultures. Religion affects all manner of daily life, sometimes even among those who are not devout followers of any religion. For instance, in the United States and throughout the Western world, the weekend occurs on Saturday and Sunday. But in Arab lands and others where Islam is the predominant religion, Friday is the day of prayer, so the weekend occurs on Thursday and Friday. Exhibit 10.5 illustrates the proportion of consumers belonging to the main religions in the United States, other diverse nations, and the world at large.

Perhaps more than in other countries, U.S. Christians represent a large number of different religions. Just over half (51.3%) of Americans report belonging to a Protestant religion, with the remainder of Christians being Catholic (23.9%). One can hardly say that all Protestant denominations are the same, but generally speaking, Protestants are relatively conservative in their approach to life, and emphasize hard work and

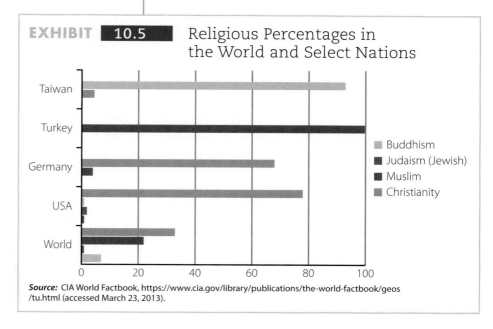

EXHIBIT 10.5 Religious Percentages in the World and Select Nations

Legend:
- Buddhism
- Judaism (Jewish)
- Muslim
- Christianity

(Bar chart showing religious percentages for Taiwan, Turkey, Germany, USA, and World on a scale from 0 to 100)

Source: CIA World Factbook, https://www.cia.gov/library/publications/the-world-factbook/geos/tu.html (accessed March 23, 2013).

stigmatization a situation in which consumers are marked in some way that indicates their place in society

accomplishment as important goals. They also tend to be more comfortable with material acquisitions than are Catholics.[28] Some Protestant denominations are more likely than Catholics to have a moral prohibition against the consumption of beer, wine, and other forms of alcoholic beverages. In the southern United States, where large portions of the population belong to relatively conservative Protestant religions such as Southern Baptist or Pentecostal, many counties are "dry," meaning the purchase and/or possession of alcohol is prohibited by law.

Budget allocations also are associated with religion. Church organizations have not been immune from the recent economic downturn. Many Protestant denominations have tithing requirements that strongly encourage church members to give 10% of their gross income to the church. This is a relatively high proportion compared to other religions, even while the bad economy has hit church finances very hard.[29] The resulting strain comes at a bad time for church groups as they seek to provide assistance for the unemployed. Furthermore, many church groups provide a source of low-price and free products for lower income consumers. Groups such as St. Vincent de Paul operate stores where second-hand items and retailer overstocks are made available at a small fraction of normal retail price or even for free for the more needy consumers. The Jewish Federation also implements *tzedakah*, meaning giving assistance to the poor, which enables the poor to access products they may not otherwise be able to access.

Consumer research examines the extent to which an overt Christian appeal influences Christians.[30] For example, an advertisement containing the ichthys symbol (Christian fish emblem) caused Evangelical Christians to rate the perceived quality of service, and their intention to use that particular service, higher than an ad that was otherwise identical. No such effect was seen among consumers of other religious affiliations. In fact, the authors of that particular research suggest that the symbol may even backfire and have negative effects on non-Evangelicals.

Religion also affects consumers' diets and the clothing they wear. During Lent each year, fast-food restaurants heavily advertise fish offerings as a way of capitalizing on the Catholic tradition of abstaining from meat during Lent, particularly on Fridays. Jewish consumers often follow a *kosher* diet. This places a high standard on cleanliness and purity of foods. Some common

Christian foods like shrimp and bacon are inconsistent with this standard. Kosher restrictions include:

- Food must be prepared with a very high degree of cleanliness. Kosher packing plants are inspected by a rabbi to certify cleanliness.
- Certain meats are prohibited, such as pork and rabbit.
- Dairy products cannot be consumed simultaneously with meat.
- Fish with scales are allowed, but shellfish are not.

In many urban areas around the United States, where relatively large Jewish populations exist, grocers dedicate entire sections of their stores to kosher goods. The Islamic religion also places dietary restrictions on its followers, and it strictly prohibits the consumption of pork. The word *halal* describes the dietary restrictions that prohibit alcohol, pork, and meats that are not slaughtered in the prescribed manner. Restaurateurs who serve these markets need to be well aware of the dietary restrictions and the sensitivity of these cultures to violations of the restrictions.

Additionally, various religions have rules and customs about public displays of the body. Muslim women often sport veils, or even cover their entire face. Although this practice is often stigmatized in the United States, some fashion retailers have offered fashionable veils that may even cross over into the secular market.[31] **Stigmatization** means that the consumers are marked in some way that indicates their place in society. Sometimes the mark is not particularly flattering. A fashionable veil can help overcome negative feelings about this stigmatized product. In 2010, France's legislature voted to make the public wearing of full veils (those covering the face as well as the head) illegal, arguing that the practice was demeaning to women. Other European countries are considering adopting similar legislation.[32] Friction is often inevitable as cultures interact and as consumers choose to follow their religious beliefs rather than laws that they perceive to clash with these beliefs. Consumers of all faiths often make decisions to follow their religious beliefs and customs. Without question, religion plays a major role in both culture and microculture.

⌐ Stigmatization means that the consumers are marked in some way ⌐

10-2f Ethnic Microculture

The United States is sometimes referred to as a melting pot. The analogy tries to make the point that

bicultural used to describe immigrants as they face decisions and form preferences based on their old or new cultures

EXHIBIT 10.6

Ethnic/Racial Groups in the United States Based on U.S. Census Projections (2015)[1]

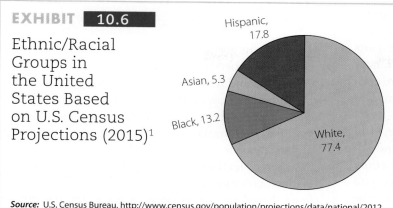

Hispanic, 17.8

Asian, 5.3

Black, 13.2

White, 77.4

Source: U.S. Census Bureau, http://www.census.gov/population/projections/data/national/2012/summarytables.html (accessed March 24, 2013).

[1]The percentages do not add to 100 because the U.S. Census classifies Hispanics by racial color (white or black) and reports the percentage of Hispanic people separately.

America is a land filled with people from a wide range of ethnic backgrounds. According to this view, these people all blend together into a single American culture. This may be an oversimplification, but the fact that the American people are very diverse is undeniable. Most Americans are aware of their heritage beyond the United States and are often proud of it. Thus, even for multi-generational Americans, consumption is affected by heritage. This can be much stronger for families with shorter roots in America, including recent immigrants. Another chapter discussed the acculturation process of consumers arriving in a new land like America. Consumption in the United States, however, remains tied to ethnicity to varying extents. We choose to use the term *culture* with these groups due to the strong ties that consumers often feel to their ethnic roots. Exhibit 10.6 breaks down the major ethnic groups in the United States.

Hispanic Culture

The largest ethnic group (aside from whites) is now Hispanic. Hispanics will account for nearly 18% of the U.S. population by 2015. Nearly 11% of Americans list Spanish as their primary language. Perhaps the most important rule to remember in dealing with any large ethnic market segment is that the group is not homogeneous. Hispanic consumers vary a great deal from one another, based on their own personal preferences, their degree of acculturation, how many generations removed they are from their ancestral country, what the ancestral country is (Mexico, the Dominican Republic, Cuba, etc.), and other demographic characteristics. Thus, we can only talk about general tendencies for this market.

The more generations removed from the ancestral country, the closer a consumer is likely to be to the mainstream culture. Hispanic consumers several generations removed from the ancestral country are likely to communicate in English, while first generation Hispanic immigrants may still communicate primarily in Spanish. However, care needs to be taken when trying to appeal to an ethnic group in their native language. Even if the children of American-born Hispanics (third generation or more) can speak Spanish, they may be somewhat insulted by being presented an ad in Spanish. Also, in all cultures, there is some risk of a backlash from other consumers who may resent an advertisement in something other than their native language. The safest approach is to use Spanish language ads only when dealing with immigrant Hispanic populations or Spanish language media (Spanish language radio, printed media, television). The term **bicultural** is used to describe immigrants as they face decisions and form preferences based on their old or new

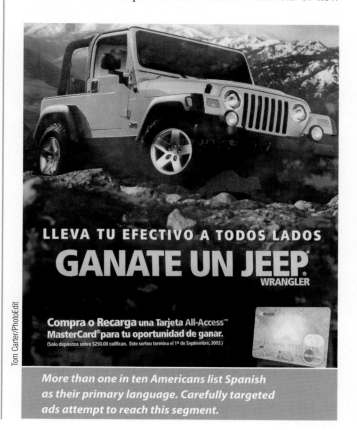

Tom Carter/PhotoEdit

More than one in ten Americans list Spanish as their primary language. Carefully targeted ads attempt to reach this segment.

social class a culturally defined group to which a consumer belongs based on resources like prestige, income, occupation, and education

habitus mental and cognitive structures through which individuals perceive the world based largely on their standing in a social class

cultures. Bicultural consumers begin to express lower ethnocentrism than their counterparts in the native country and thus are more open to products from their new country.[33]

Hispanics tend to place a high value on family-oriented values and social intimacy. Thus, products that appeal to the entire family or that somehow bring the family together tend to provide high value for Hispanic consumers. The Hispanic market cannot be ignored, as it is the fastest growing market segment in the United States.

African-American Culture

The African-American market segment represents about 13% of the total U.S. market. Like the Hispanic culture, the African-American microculture can be broken down into other more specific microcultures. Obviously, this is an important American market segment. Again, factors such as social class may have more influence in a given situation than ethnicity (such as which restaurants to patronize), but many companies, including McDonald's, have successfully capitalized on a special effort to tailor products toward the African-American consumer. One of the most important trends among African-American consumers is their growing affluence. The number of these Americans in professional occupations has multiplied many times over in the past few decades, as has the number of African-American owned businesses. Each of these factors contributes to an even higher buying power for this important segment.

Asian Culture

The Asian segment also is growing rapidly. This segment represents between four and five percent of the U.S. population. Relative to other minority groups, the Asian-American culture is highly educated and highly affluent.[34] Asian-American consumers are very favorable toward luxury brands, tend to own their homes, and retain a preference for Asian foods. Asian-Americans also are concentrated in large numbers in a few areas of the United States. For example, all the major cities of California contain high proportions of Asian-Americans. The fact that they are concentrated in specific locations in the United States facilitates marketers' ability to effectively reach this market.

10-2g Income and Social Class Microculture

Two very important topics in consumer behavior are income and social class. The concepts permeate our everyday life and it seems that consumers are always trying to better themselves by moving up the income and class ladders. To say that income and social class are variables that marketers track closely would be a huge understatement.

Income level and social class are closely related, but distinct, concepts. Income level is truly a demographic issue, based on the amount of monetary resources a person receives. We define **social class** as a culturally defined group to which a consumer belongs based on resources like prestige, income, occupation, and education. Income and occupation are two of the most recognizable determinants of social class.

Tastes and preferences are largely determined by social class, a finding that falls under the sociological concept of habitus. The term **habitus** refers to mental and cognitive structures through which individuals perceive the world based largely on their standing in a social class.[35] Although concrete generalizations regarding the influence of income and social class on purchase behavior are difficult, it can be said that social class tends to be a better predictor of purchases that involve value and lifestyles, as well as symbolic and highly visible products. Income tends to be a better predictor of purchases that require very substantial expenditures.[36]

Social Class in the United States

Six major social classes have been identified in the United States. These include *Upper Class, Lower Upper Class, Upper Middle Class, Lower Middle Class, Upper Lower Class,* and *Lower Lower Class.*[37] Many consumers strive to move up the social ladder throughout their lifetimes, but this is not true of all consumers. Some consumers are simply content with their social standing and do not aspire to move up the social ladder. Some consumers are born into a social class (termed an *ascribed* status) while others work their way into a class (termed an *achieved* status).

Social class is an important concept because a class strongly influences lifestyles, opinions, attitudes, and behaviors. Sayings such as "birds of a feather flock together" and "keeping up with the Joneses" typify the social class conceptualization. That is to say, consumers in a particular class tend to behave similarly in the marketplace. Again, it should be emphasized that this does not mean that *every* consumer in a social class will exhibit the *exact* same behaviors, attitudes, and opinions. However, in general it is a good rule of thumb that they will act similarly.

Two issues regarding social class that have been discussed here illustrate the difficulties with considering class in consumer behavior. The facts that not all consumers strive to move up the social ladder, and that not every consumer in a social class will act similarly, highlight the limitations of using the concept in consumer research. Nevertheless, social class is a very important societal and cultural issue that we observe in everyday life. A simple example of the influence of social class on behavior is the finding that most marriages comprise people from similar classes. In sociology, this is referred to as **homogamy,** or *assortative mating.*[38]

Social Stratification

The concept of social stratification underscores the role of social class in society. **Social stratification** can be defined as the division of society into classes that have unequal access to scarce and valuable resources.[39] Of course, the finer things in life are generally enjoyed by the Upper Class or Lower Upper Class. Luxury items and **status symbols** are enjoyed by these groups, while the bare essentials are relegated to the Lower Lower Class. Many of the Lower Lower Class even find themselves homeless.

The huge disparity between the upper and lower classes can be found in many parts of the United States. As a sad, ironic example, consider the number of homeless people that currently live in the tunnel systems under the city of Las Vegas. Under the very streets where excess is flaunted live some of the poorest and most destitute consumers in the nation.[40] The problems of poverty and homelessness are found worldwide.

Social Class Worldwide

Social classes obviously exist throughout the world. China, with its enormous population, exhibits a range of social classes. Rapid economic development has led to recent gains in the Chinese middle class. Forecasts reveal that as many as 700 million consumers will be in the Chinese middle class by the year 2020. Middle class consumers occupy a variety of positions in the Chinese workplace, from entrepreneurs to managers of high-tech companies.[41] Japan, on the other hand, has witnessed a gradual widening of the gap between the haves and the have-nots, along with a generally shrinking middle class. India, like China, has a large middle class, estimated at approximately 170 million. Many of these consumers are young, with nearly half of India's billion-plus population

less than 25 years old. Estimates reveal that as much as 40% of the population of India will be middle class in the next two decades.[42]

10-2h Street Microculture

Microcultures can grow around any number of phenomena, not just around differences in ethnicity, income/social class, generation, region, or religion. As we have seen, sports can provide a basis for microculture. Music can as well. One way to refer to these microcultures is by using the label *street microcultures.*

The hip-hop microculture illustrates one such group. Obviously, hip-hop culture has influenced consumer tastes outside of its group (consider the pervasiveness of hip-hop apparel). "Gothic" (or "goth") microculture represents another prevalent microculture in the United States. Gothic influence can be very strong, as group members almost universally wear dark, macabre attire. The goth microculture is a great example of how strong microculture influence can be. In fact, some argue that gothic identification is even more important than gender identification.[43] The "emo" subculture has received a lot of media attention in recent years, though its roots are thought to go back at least a few decades. Most consumers can recognize a goth or emo person easily, further evidence of how microcultures permeate our daily lives and are observed by many consumers.

Microcultures can even grow out of gaming experiences, virtual communities, and practically any other consumer activity that brings consumers with something in common together. The more easily microcultures can be reached, either physically or with various media, the better marketers can connect with them through value-added communications and products.

homogamy the finding that most marriages comprise people from similar classes

social stratification the division of society into classes that have unequal access to scarce and valuable resources

status symbols products or objects that are used to signal one's place in society

10-3 Microculture Is Not Uniquely American

From this discussion of microcultures, it is easy to see why this consumer behavior topic is important to researchers and managers alike. Microculture membership affects the value of things. It is important to remember that like other concepts discussed in this text,

demographic analysis
a profile of a consumer group
based on their demographics

microcultures are truly global phenomena and are not confined to any one region or country.

10-3a Microcultures Around the World

We often think of foreign countries with a single stereotype. A Parisian may represent all French people to some consumers. Even a country as diverse as China might be looked at very narrowly, with unfounded stereotypes. Yet other countries also have many bases around which microcultures are formed.

Many of the examples we've discussed transcend any specific country. Germany, Spain, and South Africa, for instance, are all countries where different languages are spoken in different regions of the country. Bavarians, from the German Alps, feel quite distinct from the typical German population. Over 1,800 languages are spoken on the continent of Africa, across 53 countries. Furthermore, immigration is fast spreading through Europe, and the influx of Muslim microcultures in many European countries is adding to the diversity of these nations.

10-3b Street Microcultures Worldwide

Many street microcultures, including music, sports, and fashion, exist around the world as well. Punk,

Some microcultures end up being defined by things that are not related to generational, regional, or social bases.

LHB Photo/Alamy

goth, and emo microcultures are all good examples. Emo, for example, represents a popular microculture in Japan. Japanese "gothic Lolita" is another popular microculture that can best be illustrated by imagining a gothic China doll. Some Japanese girls also follow the "decora" microculture, which is marked by wearing extremely bright clothing and plastic accessories. Given the pervasiveness of microcultures throughout the world, firms' efforts to market products in virtually any part of the world need to take into account not only culture, but also microculture.

10-4 Demographic Analysis

Ultimately, any group or microculture has to be reached before a value proposition can be effectively delivered to them. Demographics is a term that we have used throughout this text, and it is an important concept for marketers and consumer researchers alike. Demographics refer to observable, statistical aspects of populations such as age, gender, or income.

Demographic variables are closely related to microculture. In fact, you may have noticed from previous sections that demographic variables help one to describe microcultures. As an example, we previously discussed the fact that age distinctions can be used to describe generational microcultures. Consider the fact that consumers in the Millennial microculture can be described as currently falling between the ages of 17 and 31. As such, the demographic variable "age" helps us to better understand and describe this microculture. The combination of demographic and microcultural information is therefore very valuable for today's marketers. This information becomes even more valuable when it is combined with geodemographic information, because members of many microcultures often live in close proximity to one another. Geodemographic tools such as PRIZM assist the consumer researcher with these analyses.

A **demographic analysis** develops a profile of a consumer group based on their demographics. As we have discussed, these analyses often include geodemographic approaches, because marketers find it advantageous to know where targeted consumers live. These analyses become important components of a demographic segmentation strategy. If marketers can identify where their targeted consumers live, they can implement marketing campaigns much more efficiently. Newspapers, radio, television, and even Internet communications can then be geared to specific regions.

10-4a U.S. Census Data

One very important source for performing a demographic analysis is the U.S. Census Bureau's website (www.census.gov). Exhibit 10.7 shows the interface from www.census.gov.

The website provides a real-time estimate of the U.S. population. The top category of options provides an entry into the search mechanisms to find details about people and households in the United States. One can find the actual counts from the most recent census, or get estimates and projections of populations up to the current date. Generally, the search engine can be used to find statistics on a region of interest. Exhibit 10.8 shows the demographic profile for the state of Missouri.

This simple profile contains a great deal of useful information. For example, if a company were interested in marketing a product toward Hispanics, Missouri might not be the best target. Less than 4% of the population is Hispanic, which does not compare favorably to the percentage in the nation overall. In contrast, the relative proportion of white Americans versus African-Americans is quite similar to that of the national profile. In other instances, one may wish to obtain these data for a smaller region. The website makes the data available at the county level, and with a bit of additional assistance, the data can be broken down by ZIP code. Also, a marketer may sometimes need a market to be of at least a certain minimum size in order for the market to be considered a viable target. A product might be targeted toward Millennials and may require a market of at least two million consumers to be viable. The target can be compared to the demographic numbers to see if the option should be pursued.

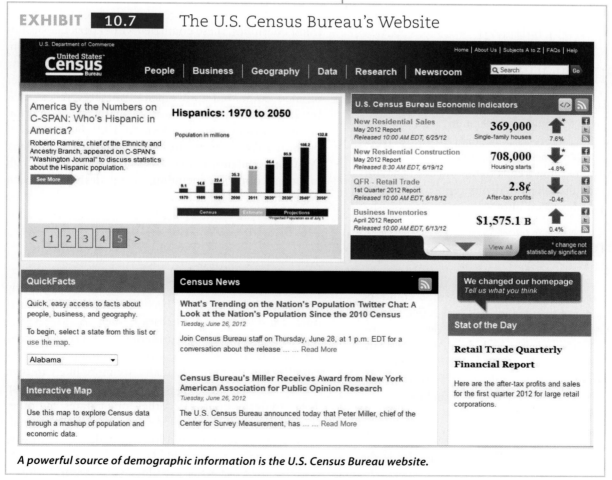

EXHIBIT 10.7 The U.S. Census Bureau's Website

A powerful source of demographic information is the U.S. Census Bureau website.

Source: U.S. Census Bureau, http://www.census.gov/2012, accessed June 18, 2012.

EXHIBIT **10.8** Demographic Profile for the State of Missouri

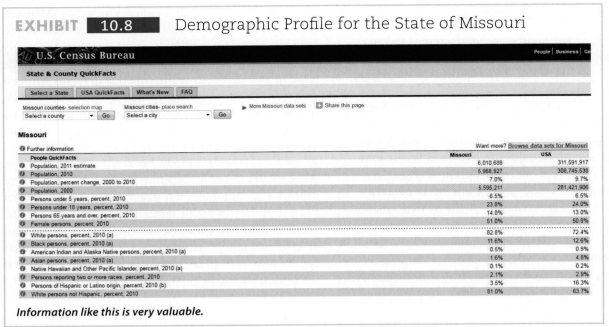

Information like this is very valuable.

Source: http://quickfacts.census.gov/qfd/states/29000.html, accessed March 25, 2013.

10-5 Major Cultural and Demographic Trends

As with other consumer behavior topics, it is not enough to simply understand cultural and demographic factors as they currently exist. These factors evolve over time. For this reason, it is important to identify emerging trends that influence behavior. Cultural, microcultural, and demographic trends are especially important to monitor.

10-5a Trends Affecting Consumer Behavior

While there are a number of trends that could be discussed, four notable trends that are relevant to consumer researchers and managers deserve careful attention. These trends include declining birthrates, increasing consumer affluence, increasing life expectancy, and increasing cultural diversity worldwide. Each of these trends are discussed below.

Declining Birthrates

One of the biggest trends in Western countries is the declining birthrate. In many European countries, the birthrate has dropped to 0.5 per person. That means that each couple is having at most one child. If this trend continues, these countries will experience declining populations. One particularly important trend in China, thought to be the result of the country's "one child" policy, is a relative imbalance in the number of men compared to women. Estimates reveal that by 2020, China could have as many as 30 million more men than women.[44] Exhibit 10.9 displays select birthrates. While birthrates are relatively low in many Western countries, notice that birthrates remain high in other countries, including Bangladesh, India, and Nigeria.

Increasing Consumer Affluence

The combination of working couples and lower birthrates has led to greater levels of consumer affluence, particularly in the United States. As a result, many consumer segments have become targets for products once considered to be luxuries, such as cruises and high-end automobiles. Furthermore, consumers have generally become less price sensitive in many categories. Families eat out more often and are more likely to own the latest electronic devices than consumers of the past. These trends not only affect the United States, but other countries as well. As detailed earlier, the rise in the middle class in both China and India is evidence of growing consumer affluence worldwide.

To say that consumer affluence is a trend is not to imply that poverty is not a major problem worldwide. To the contrary, poverty remains a major problem in

Success at the Bottom

Over 4 billion consumers worldwide live in poverty. That segment isn't expected to shrink anytime soon. However, these consumers are not to be ignored. First, they share the same basic needs as other consumers, and success can be found in the marketplace for products that provide these consumers economical ways to address basic needs for sustenance, safety, and esteem. Entrepreneurs sometimes go into these areas with the idea of providing basic goods and services to this segment, but also realize that without a way for consumers to make a living, poverty will continue.

In many instances, agricultural products still offer entrepreneurial opportunities, particularly as upper-level consumers become more attuned to natural, authentic products and avoid the synthetic. If these consumers can become part of an enterprise that nurtures the natural resources where they live into a product that offers value for other consumers, then they have a chance to earn a living and in turn become consumers for an ever-increasing array of products. For example, in many coffee-producing areas,

entrepreneurs have capitalized on upper-level segments' increasing taste for gourmet coffee by teaching farmers and workers in these areas to nurture the *terroir* (the specific geographical location along with its natural and cultural resources) into a uniquely differentiated product. After all, nobody else has that terroir! Such strategic efforts provide an avenue up from the bottom of the pyramid.

Sources: C. Nakata and M. Viswanathan, "From Impactful Research to Sustainable Innovations for Subsistence Marktplaces," *Journal of Business Research*, in press. Raed Elaydi and Josetta McLaughlin, "Cultivating Terroir in Subsistence Markets: Development of Terroir Strategy through Harmony-with-Community Framework," *Journal of Business Research*, doi.org/10.1016/j.jbusres.2012.02.016.

many nations, as evidenced by the approximately 4 billion "bottom of the pyramid" consumers. Nevertheless, the growth in consumer affluence is a recognizable trend.

Increasing Life Expectancy and the Aging Consumer

The right pane of Exhibit 10.9 displays the life expectancy for citizens of a number of different countries. Life expectancy is increasing in many, but not all, countries. The most obvious increase is found in developed nations. If we consider life expectancy as a proxy for standard of living, we can see that as the birthrate declines, the standard of living increases. Thus, unfortunately, the countries with the highest birthrates in the world are among the poorest. In developed countries, more wealth is spread over fewer consumers.

The growth trends in population, along with birthrate and life expectancy trends, all affect consumer culture in many ways. One major issue in the United States today is the aging Baby Boomer population. This segment of the consumer population is expected to dramatically affect business practices for many years to come. As discussed earlier, this segment attracts much marketing attention due to its large size and overall spending power.

Increasing Cultural Diversity

Many societies worldwide are becoming increasingly culturally diverse. One way in which cultures become more diverse is through immigration and the growth of microcultures. There are numerous trends that could be discussed, and they range from religious to street microcultural diversity. Regarding religious microcultures, one significant trend in European countries is the growth of the Muslim faith. Islam is rapidly growing in popularity in Europe and this religious microculture is influencing consumer behavior throughout the region. In the United States, ethnic microcultures continue to become increasingly diverse due to both legal and illegal immigration. This issue is greatly impacting the Borderland region discussed earlier in this chapter.

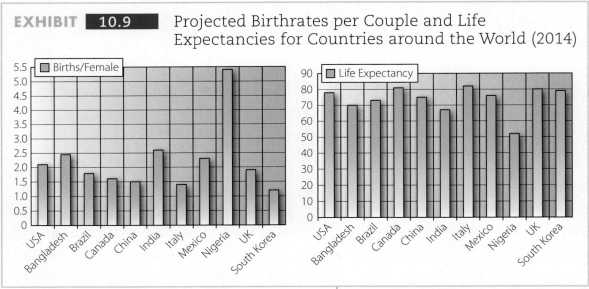

EXHIBIT 10.9 Projected Birthrates per Couple and Life Expectancies for Countries around the World (2014)

Source: U.S. Census Bureau, International Data Base, 2013, accessed March 25, 2013.

The United Kingdom is also experiencing a general increase in immigration, with many immigrants arriving from the European Union. As such, the U.K. is realizing a growth in microcultural diversity, particularly pertaining to ethnic and religious microcultural diversity. The continued expansion of the world teen culture market is expected as many Western brands, such as Coca-Cola, McDonald's, and Starbucks, continue to succeed with foreign expansion. The influence of Western ideals and practice on the world teen culture continues. This is not to say that all young consumers will completely think and act alike. In fact, many Asian teens are carving out new and developing microcultures unlike those found in the United States. Some teens worldwide are breaking away from punk, goth, and emo microcultures to focus on more traditional clean-cut, even conservative styles.[45] As mentioned, there are many ways in which cultural diversity is increasing worldwide.

As we have seen, microcultures influence consumer behavior throughout the world, and for this reason, the study of microculture is very important for consumer researchers and marketers alike.

WHAT DO YOU THINK?
WHAT OTHERS HAVE THOUGHT

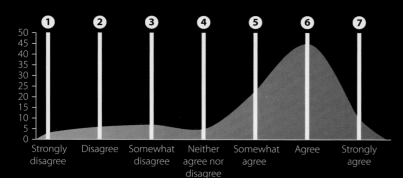

Strongly disagree	Disagree	Somewhat disagree	Neither agree nor disagree	Somewhat agree	Agree	Strongly agree

The microcultures I belong to greatly influence the value I receive from products.

Over 3 out of 4 respondents express some level of agreement! Thus, users recognize that our choices are influenced by others and especially by the cultural groups we belong to, no matter if those cultural groups are large are small.

Study Tools

Located at back of the textbook

❏ Rip out Chapter in Review Card

Located at www.cengagebrain.com

❏ Review Key Terms Flashcards (print or online)

❏ Download audio summaries to review on the go

❏ Complete practice quizzes to prepare for tests

❏ Play "Beat the Clock" to master concepts

❏ Watch video on Vans for a real company example

study tools

CASE 3-1

RateMyProfessors.com: Does This Site Really Help in Choosing Classes?

Written by Robert A. Bergman, College of Business, Lewis University

When registration time comes around, convenient class times and a great schedule are just part of the picture. You also want the best professors who make the class relevant, interesting, informative, and fun. And don't forget . . . easy. As one student remarked, "keep me awake and give me an A."

Tom and Alex are a couple of marketing majors finishing their second year at State University. They're kicking back at the student union on a warm afternoon in late April, schedule books in hand. It's time to register for fall term, and they're discussing a lot more than just day and time of the available classes.

They've already met with their academic advisors and determined the classes they should take in the fall term to stay on schedule and graduate on time. They've chosen six classes to target when it's their turn for online registration. They've also determined a contingency plan in the event the courses they want are full. They've each chosen two alternative courses.

On average, each of these eight courses has a half dozen sections to choose from, and each section seems to have a different professor. It's a confusing quest for the perfect schedule.

As business students, they take a managerial approach to their decision-making process—to maximize their probability of success in taking classes. In their minds, "success" is measured in:

1. convenient schedule

2. easy coursework

3. interesting lectures

The schedule book allows them to evaluate each course by:

a) day-of-week

b) time-of-day

c) professor

While they can make educated decisions about (a) day-of-week, and (b) time-of-day, which happen to be their first evaluative criteria to consider for a *Convenient Schedule*, they are stumped to know an easy and effective way to evaluate *Easy Coursework* and *Interesting Lectures* without further data on the various professors.

Success factors		Evaluative criteria
Convenient Schedule	}	Day-of-week
		Time-of-day
Easy Coursework	}	Professor
Interesting Lectures		

They could create a list of all the professors teaching the classes on their list—over 40 professors. Then they could poll fellow students about their experiences with each professor, document the results, and churn the data to make the most effective decisions in choosing their class schedule for the next term.

Tom and Alex realize they are members of the generational microculture termed Millennial by their *Principles of Marketing* textbook. They are technologically savvy and experts in using the Internet and social media. As they crack open a Red Bull and ponder this revelation, they think out loud: "there must be a website where professors are rated by students." Tom pulls out his smartphone, opens a browser window and types in "rate professors" in the search bar. In a few seconds his eyes widen to see listed a website called "Rate My Professors" at www.ratemyprofessors.com.

	NAME	DEPARTMENT	TOTAL RATINGS	OVERALL QUALITY	EASINESS	HOT?	SHARE
	Bergman, Robert	**Marketing**	28	5.0	3.8		

Source: http://www.ratemyprofessors.com/SelectTeacher.jsp?the_dept=All&sid=515&orderby=TLName&letter=B, accessed April 8, 2012.

Name: Robert Bergman
School: Lewis University
Location: Romeoville, IL
Department: Marketing

no photo

5.0	5.0	5.0	3.8	HOTNESS
OVERALL QUALITY	HELPFULNESS	CLARITY	EASINESS	

ⓘ Submit a Correction

Number of ratings 28

Source: http://www.ratemyprofessors.com/ShowRatings.jsp?tid=517521, accessed April 8, 2012.

Their hearts start to race. Is it an adrenalin rush from finding the kind of site that would solve their dilemma, or the slurry of stimulants in the Red Bull? With a few taps of the screen, they find the "gold" they were digging for—priceless information about their university professors.

On RateMyProfessors.com, Tom and Alex find all the professors from State U listed in alphabetical order, making it easy to locate each professor's rating they need to evaluate.

Both Tom and Alex must take Consumer Behavior in the fall. There are six sections, with four different professors. Registration is just a couple of days away and they need to make the right decision, factoring in the day, time, and quality of the professor.

They find the list of professors at State U rated in the following ways;

• Total ratings (number of ratings students have made)

• Overall quality

• Easiness

• Hot?

Overall quality and easiness have numerical values from 0 to 5, 5 being the highest.

The term "hot?" is noted with the graphic of a red chili pepper to designate if the professor is considered good looking.

Tom and Alex note the numerical values representing *overall quality* and *easiness* of each professor they are researching, and make their decisions based on these numbers alone.

In addition, visitors to the site can click on the name of any professor and see their ratings in more detail. The following categories and their rating are presented:

• Overall quality

• Helpfulness

• Clarity

• Easiness

• Hotness

Below these rating summaries are the individual User Comments and Ratings.

Tom and Alex are used to reading customer reviews of products and services on Amazon, Zappos, and Best Buy websites. They've come to rely on the feedback and opinions of people they perceive to be just like them. While they don't always read the dialogue or text of each customer review, they base a lot of their purchase decisions on the rating, or number of stars the product or service receives in the ratings. They figure the rating tells enough of the story to make an informed decision, and "why waste time reading the entire review."

Tom hypothesizes another thing about the ratings, and muses to Alex, "if girls are rating male professors with a chili pepper to signify they're 'hot', then there might be more girls in the class." Alex punches him in the arm and they continue studying the ratings.

When they finish planning their schedule, Tom and Alex look to have the perfect schedules—classes just three days a week, all taught by professors who have an overall rating of 4-5 stars and an easiness rating of 3.5 or higher. Life is good!

Tom and Alex close their schedule books, put them in their backpacks and head to the cafeteria. Their next mission is evaluating the selection of lunch entries at the university cafeteria, affectionately known as "the slop house." They only wish there was a website called "RateMyCafeteriaFood.com."

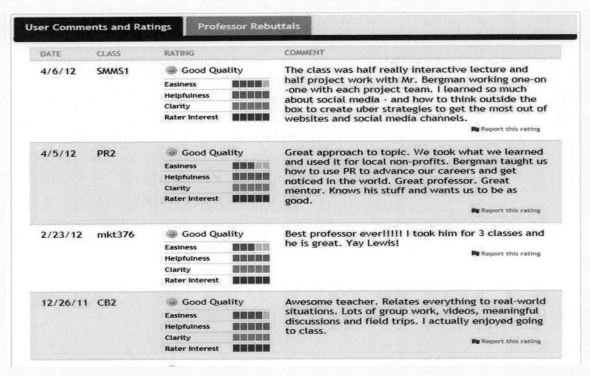

| User Comments and Ratings | Professor Rebuttals |

DATE	CLASS	RATING	COMMENT
4/6/12	SMMS1	Good Quality Easiness Helpfulness Clarity Rater Interest	The class was half really interactive lecture and half project work with Mr. Bergman working one-on-one with each project team. I learned so much about social media - and how to think outside the box to create uber strategies to get the most out of websites and social media channels. *Report this rating*
4/5/12	PR2	Good Quality Easiness Helpfulness Clarity Rater Interest	Great approach to topic. We took what we learned and used it for local non-profits. Bergman taught us how to use PR to advance our careers and get noticed in the world. Great professor. Great mentor. Knows his stuff and wants us to be as good. *Report this rating*
2/23/12	mkt376	Good Quality Easiness Helpfulness Clarity Rater Interest	Best professor ever!!!!! I took him for 3 classes and he is great. Yay Lewis! *Report this rating*
12/26/11	CB2	Good Quality Easiness Helpfulness Clarity Rater Interest	Awesome teacher. Relates everything to real-world situations. Lots of group work, videos, meaningful discussions and field trips. I actually enjoyed going to class. *Report this rating*

Source: http://www.ratemyprofessors.com/ShowRatings.jsp?tid=517521, accessed April 8, 2012.

Questions

1. What assumptions can you make about managerial decision making, as it relates to the Millennial generation, from the case?

2. Did Tom and Alex follow a logical and rational managerial decision-making process in determining their class schedules? Why or why not?

3. Identify the group influence that the information provided on RateMyProfessors.com places on Tom and Alex.

4. Describe the types of interpersonal influence that the information provided on RateMyProfessors.com places on Tom and Alex.

5. What influence do consumer ratings that fall either above or below the norm have on your managerial decision-making process? For example, when a professor (or an Amazon.com product) is rated with 3 stars, what strength do you place on the few individual reviews that rate them with 1 star or 5 stars?

CASE 3-2

Collegiate Sporting Events Attendance: Reaching Students through Social Media

Written by Sarah Fischbach, PhD Candidate, New Mexico State University

Attendance at university sports has a unique position. Sports at the collegiate level either have a strong following where it is nearly impossible to obtain seats to the season games, or a weak following where it is a struggle to bring in fans week after week. The administration for universities with attendance challenges find themselves focusing on all target markets. Campaigns are developed to increase community involvement by bringing in local high school, even elementary school students and families. Potential attendees are offered free products such as shirts, megaphones, and meet and greet with the players. Additionally, theme nights become popular techniques for influencing attendance for the entire population. For example, the college administration may reduce hot dog and drink prices by 25 cents for every free throw made or three-point shot hit by the home team, to the point that the hot dogs and drinks are free to the attendees.

Although promoting to the local community and their families is important, it is not really what students are looking for at a basketball game. Students are looking for a much different environment than are families with children. In a recent survey, students were asked about family and children's attendance at games.[1] Their response was somewhat of a surprise; they didn't understand why people outside the college would want to attend the games. The consensus was that college sports were meant for the students and the students' families, not the rest of the community. Encouraging local participation would only decrease their desire to attend the game.

Whatever marketing approach the university uses to increase attendance, they need to consider the impact on the students. Students seem to be forgotten in the typical sports marketing campaign. During a recent focus group of students and faculty at a university struggling with game attendance, one participant asked what kind of motivation it is for younger kids (high school and even elementary) to come to a game and see all the empty seats. If or when the students begin their tenure at the university, they will follow suit and continue to limit their attendance at games. It's not personal, it's popularity. It doesn't create much fun for potential students when current university students don't attend the games. This is why it is so important to include collegiate sports when developing the culture of the university. It's in their best interest for universities to make attending sporting events an important part of college life and not a burden on the student's time.

So why are students not attending the games? During the same qualitative research, students unanimously stated that the main reason they don't attend is because the team doesn't win.[2] It's hard to sit in the bleachers game after game watching the other team win. There are a hundred other things students could be doing rather than attending a losing basketball game. However, winning or losing doesn't matter as much if the student is having fun and hanging out with friends. Building the sports attendance culture at the university may be just what is needed to improve overall attendance. But where does administration start? The cultural selection process includes finding out how to produce a system with both formal and informal gatekeepers. Informal gatekeepers include friends, spouses, family members, and neighbors, just for a few examples. Formal gatekeepers include radio, TV, and celebrities. College administrators must take these gatekeepers' choices and opinions into consideration and continue to mold the changes students find in mass media. Building the hype

among the students even if the team is failing to meet the league records will create this awareness, at least to attend. But how do universities build this hype? Where else but social media.

Social media is the component of the online world where people interact with one another, often changing roles from reader to author and seeking various benefits from social interaction.[3] Over the last two decades, research from the literacy field has been incorporated into marketing research. The researchers who pursue this avenue discuss how the characteristics of literature or drama have been important factors in consumer development of perspectives regarding ads. Academic researchers, marketing practitioners, and sports marketing professionals agree that you must use social media to gain awareness for younger generations. But merely being on the social media radar is not enough. You have to track your social return on investment. As more companies become players of social media tools, it is important for academic researchers, practitioners, and especially sports marketers to establish relevant ground rules.

Social media can be used to tap into the social media network that students communicate through on a daily basis. Even outside of the student network, individuals of the younger generation are using social media to bring awareness to organizations and companies. Many organizations use social media to create a buzz around a new project or an event. Facebook, LinkedIn, and Twitter have become popular forms of communication for companies worldwide. Mobile communication and mobile marketing have recently become resources for companies looking for a new edge. For example, individuals may communicate through texting and other forms of social media to create a flash mob. A flash mob is when individuals get together to promote a product or organization through spontaneous, choreographed dancing. A recent episode of *Modern Family* featured a flash mob scenario. The type of organization utilizing this new wave of social media marketing is not limited to any specific category. Suave, Oscar Mayer, and Cox Wireless are just a few companies to step into this growing segment.[4]

Mobile marketing including the use of a flash mob is just one example of how organizations can reach out through new innovative ways to communicate with the next technology-friendly generations. Collegiate sports are no different. Connecting with students to conduct a flash mob at a basketball game or football game could increase attendance and create a buzz for students to come and watch. These new forms of communication such as mobile marketing can be incorporated into the university sporting culture. Feeding the me generation frenzy takes new forms of marketing that might not be seen as marketing techniques. This allows the student to become part of the game instead of just a bystander. During a day and age when demands on our time keep increasing, creating the desire for students to attend games can be challenging. Using social media can help.

Questions

1. What factors will likely have the greatest impact on student attendance at a basketball game for your university?

2. Describe culture. How would your university go about creating a unique culture to capture student attendance for your university?

3. What are the benefits and dangers that universities face by including social media in their marketing campaigns?

4. What types of social media campaigns could a sports marketing director implement to gain student awareness? Explain your answer.

5. Not all college sports venues are the same. For example, football is played in a stadium and golf is an event where smaller crowds follow along with the players. What challenges and benefits does this create for a university trying to increase attendance at sporting events?

CASE 3-3

The Millennial Generation

Written by Henry Schrader, Department of Business Administration, Central State University

Julie is the owner and manager of Julie Marchese Photography (www.mar-k-zphotography.photoreflect.com). Her business has grown to more than she can handle alone and she decided to hire another photographer. Julie, being of the late Baby Boomer generation, wanted to hire a photographer from a younger generation to bring a new and different creative viewpoint to her customers. She hired Maggie, a twenty-something photographer who she believed would bring in fresh ideas to her company. What Julie wasn't expecting was having a hard time understanding and working with someone from the Millennial generation. Julie said, "Maggie does a good job taking pictures, but seems to have a problem staying focused on the other responsibilities of the position."

Many employers are now trying to work with and understand the generation that is called by so many names, including the Millennial Generation, Millennium Generation, Millennials, Generation Y, Generation Next, Net Generation, Always Connected Generation, Eighties Babies, or Echo Boomers. This generation is described as "jugglers" who value being both footloose and connected to their peers 24/7.[1] They stay connected via technology such as Facebook, IM, and texting, and are totally comfortable in a thumb culture that communicates online and by cell phone. To an employer these could seem like distracted employees who are more interested in their best friend's dating life than serving their customers. So is this the most misunderstood generation yet or the most distracted? We really can't look at the generation born

between 1981 and 1995 (give or take a few years) as baby-faced teenagers anymore. The bulk of the Millennials have struggled to find their place in the 21st century. They are the most diverse generation ever and have often grown up in nontraditional families.[2] As they age, some of the adult pressure and strain has started eating away at their celebrated optimism and good cheer as it does with every generation. Happiness is higher on their agenda than past generations, but many Millennials remain motivated by material things. They will not forgo their comfort to make a difference.[3]

The Millennial generation has been raised in a culture that places more focus on the self and less on group, society, and community.[4] The aphorisms have shifted to "believe in yourself" and "you're special." The culture emphasizes individualism, and this gets reflected in personality traits and attitudes.[5] In the same way, older generations may view Millennials' willingness to trade high pay for fewer billable hours, flexible schedules, and a better work life as a lack of commitment, discipline, and drive. Is this true? Or are they just more focused on what is really important in life? Perception seems to be a major factor in understanding the younger generations. Julie has found that Maggie's generation is looking for meaningful work and a solid learning curve. They have high expectations of their employers and don't want to do anything they feel is beneath them.

Julie has also found that Maggie works better when they work as a team versus working alone. The Millennial generation has grown up playing on teams with no winners or losers, or even all winners. They have been laden with trophies just for participating.[6] Julie may want to focus more attention on giving Maggie different forms of feedback and guidance. Millennials like to be kept in the loop and seek frequent praise and reassurance. Honesty, humor, and information are important to this generation.[7] Employers may want to be aware that this generation has a tendency to move on to other employers when they feel they are not advancing or achieving in a timely manner. You can expect your Millennial employees to stay with your company three to five years on average.

Maggie has been a large help to Julie when it comes to marketing to her fellow Millennials. Where Julie's generation was easy to reach via television, Maggie's generation has grown up in the media-saturated world of their parents and responds differently to advertisements.[8] They are more likely to respond to advertisements on the Internet, at a snowboarding tournament, or on cable television. The ads may be funny or disarmingly direct. The thing to avoid is assuming that you know this generation better than they know themselves. They are more pragmatic than the Baby Boomers ever were, and they have a BS alarm that goes off quickly. They walk in and usually make up their minds very quickly about whether they want something or don't want it. They know a lot of advertising is based on lies and hype.[9]

So as soon as you have them figured out, it is likely to change tomorrow. Millennials live in a fluid world that requires an unprecedented mutability of mind and action, and flexibility of identity and disposition. Millennials expect to live their lives in constant transition, always upgrading, changing, and leapfrogging to the latest technology. Markets that are wholly dissimilar in almost every other way look strikingly alike when it comes to Millennials.[10]

Julie has seen an increase in sales and new customers, and has learned to work with her Millennial. Just as in times past, passing knowledge from one generation to the next takes place, and learning to work with the individual not the generation turns out to be the most important thing on the road to success. Keeping an open mind, staying flexible, and using nontraditional methods to reach today's consumers including the Millennials has become the next step on the road of marketing.

Questions

1. Can the Millennial generation be considered a microculture?

2. What type of social power, if any, does the Millennial generation hold?

3. How has social media and group influence helped to define the Millennial generation?

4. What generation has been called the boomerang kids? Why?

5. What makes the Millennial generation so much different than generations before?

MGP/Photodisc/Getty Images

PART **4**
CB

CB is dynamic in
many ways, and the way situations alter the
value of things illustrates its dynamism.

WHAT DO YOU THINK?
**I never let anything get in the way of
preparing for my consumer behavior
class.**

STRONGLY DISAGREE   STRONGLY AGREE

VISIT COURSEMATE AT WWW.CENGAGEBRAIN.COM

Consumers in Situations

11

This chapter focuses on a dynamic aspect of value. Value indeed changes not only between consumers, but within consumers. Here, the focus is on ways that a particular situation alters how much value a consumer associates with some particular consumption act. In doing so, we recognize that consumers are always free to change their minds about something, and they very frequently do!

11-1 Value in Situations?

Some consumers like to travel and others find traveling a royal pain. In either case, think about the way traveling alters a consumers' preferences and behaviors. Ordinarily, $25 would seem like a high price to pay for breakfast, but a consumer traveling on business and staying in an urban hotel in a strange city may very well pay $25 or more to avoid hunting down a cheaper breakfast. If the travel is to a country where the consumer is unfamiliar with the language, staying in the hotel where servers are used to English-speaking guests may enhance the value of the breakfast. Think also about whether the traveling consumer will seek out help from a store clerk based on the travel destination. Also, think about how someone traveling for business will make different decisions than someone traveling for leisure. Thus, a great deal of temporary factors shape the value the consumer experiences from even mundane activities. A partial list of considerations that might shape value for traveling consumers includes:

- Is the consumer getting reimbursed (third-party payer)?
- What time of year is it?
- What are the economic conditions like?
- Does the business accept credit cards?
- How much time is the consumer spending in the location?
- What is the exchange rate?
- Is the consumer traveling alone?

11-1a Situations and Value

This chapter focuses on precisely how the value a consumer obtains from a purchase or consumption act varies based on the context in which the act takes place. Situational influences is the term that captures these contextual effects, meaning effects independent of enduring consumer, brand, or product characteristics. As can be seen in the CVF framework, situational influences directly affect both consumer decision making and the eventual value experienced. Situational influences are enduring characteristics of neither a particular consumer nor a product or brand. Indeed, situational influences are ephemeral, meaning they are temporary conditions in a very real sense. Contexts can affect communication, shopping, brand preference, purchase, actual consumption, and the evaluation of that consumption.

The movie theater experience typifies situational influences. If the movie is a matinee, the consumer expects to pay a lower price than he would pay in the evening. Even though the movie hasn't changed, the number of people available to go to the movie has changed from the evening hours. Therefore, the lower demand entices the theater to offer lower prices. Far fewer people work in the evenings, and thus more people are free to take in a movie.

How much is too much for one margarita? Well, a consumer attending an event at the $1 billion Cowboy Stadium in the DFW area must think a margarita, or "Cowboy" Rita as they are called, is worth at least $16. Each time a big game is played there, thousands of "Cowboy" Ritas are sold. Outside the stadium, the consumer could mix a margarita for a couple of dollars. However, they are not allowed to bring those inside, so the convenience factors, along with the souvenir cowboy boot cup, add to its value. Situational influences change the desirability of consuming things and therefore change the value of these things.

Three categories of situational influences can be described based on these influences:

- Time
- Place
- Conditions

Ten bucks for nachos? Only at the ball park!

© iStockphoto.com/nazdravie

Exhibit 11.1 provides a snapshot of examples of these influences and the way they operate. The following sections discuss each of these groups of influence in more detail, with an emphasis on how value changes with each.

⌐Time is a consumer's only real resource, because when we work, we convert time into money.⌐

EXHIBIT 11.1

Categories of Situational Influences

Time – the amount of time available influences how able a consumer is to obtain and process relevant information; time of day, time of year also change the types of things consumers find desirable.

Place – one's enviroment, both geographical location and any interior structure, serve to frame the way products are viewed. Italian food is best in an environment that looks and feels italian. A casino should sound, look, and feel like a casino—not a church!

Conditions – how temporary states such as weather shape the value of products. Consider how the value of a cup of hot tea changes with weather conditions. Crowding also represents a temporary condition.

© Cengage Learning 2014

11-2 Time and Consumer Behavior

Is time a consumer's most valuable resource? Time is truly scarce. In some ways, time is a consumer's only real resource because when we work, we convert time into economic resources. In addition, time is necessary for consumption to occur. Time-related factors also affect a consumer's thoughts, feelings, and behavior, all of which come together to create differing perceptions of value. Time can affect consumption in any of these forms:

- Time pressure
- Time of year
- Time of day

The term **temporal factor** refers to situational characteristics related to time. Thus, each of the time forms listed here represents a different temporal factor.

11-2a Time Pressure

A consumer sits down with five coworkers for lunch. Almost immediately, the waiter comes and asks, "Are you ready to order?" All the others at the table are ready. The consumer experiences a sense of urgency and hastily settles for a hamburger. Would the consumer have made a different choice if she had not felt rushed to make a decision rather than make the others wait?

This situation exemplifies an intense time pressure. **Time pressure** represents an urgency to act based on some real or self-imposed deadline. In the situation above, the consumer imposed a deadline of ordering at the same time as the others at the table. Therefore, she rushed to make a decision without the due deliberation that would likely take place otherwise.

Time pressure affects consumers in several ways. First, when time is scarce, consumers process less information because time is a critical resource necessary for problem solving. Consumers who experience time pressure, for instance, are able to recall less information about product choices than are consumers in the same situation who are not under the situational influence of time pressure.[1] Second, consumers experiencing time pressure are more likely to rely on simple choice heuristics than are those in less-tense situations. Thus, rather than deciding which restaurant option is more nutritious, the consumer simply chooses the fastest option.[2] Often, this means relying on habit (habitual decision making) such as choosing a burger.[3] Third, time pressure can switch a consumer's orientation from hedonic to utilitarian. Consider a highly involved shopper. This consumer would ordinarily enjoy taking time leisurely enjoying the shopping activity. However, time pressure may prevent any enjoyment and shopping just becomes something that needs to be done. Consistent with this line of reasoning, consumers are more likely to shop alone than with others under time pressure.[4]

Consumers who might otherwise consider many attributes in reaching a decision may simply rely on a price–quality heuristic under time pressure.[5] Time pressure shapes the value consumers perceive in products by influencing both quality and price perceptions.[6] Because consumers rely more on price-quality heuristics than they do beliefs about financial sacrifice, brands positioned as relatively high quality may benefit in situations characterized by high time pressure. Consumers may simply choose the well-known and potentially higher-priced brand because they don't have time to weigh different attributes against the price. Conversely, other consumers may simply choose the lowest price alternative and risk disappointment if a brand does not deliver the expected benefits.

11-2b Time of Year

Seasonality refers to regularly occurring conditions that vary with the time of year. The fact is, consumers' value perceptions also vary with the time of the year. Iced tea is worth more to a consumer on a hot, sunny summer afternoon than it might be on a cold, cloudy winter day.

Even though this tendency may seem as obvious as consumers purchasing more coats and sweaters during the winter, seasonality has other effects that are perhaps not so obvious.[7] Consumers tend to shop earlier in the day during winter months, and, overall, they tend to spend more during the summer months.[8] Almost all products are susceptible to some type of seasonal influence. Fashion may lead the way with traditional spring, summer, fall, and winter fashions. However, many food items vary in demand with the season. People consume champagne predominantly during the holidays. The challenge for those who sell seasonal products like champagne is to position the product more as an everyday option.

11-2c Cycles

The increase in coffee consumption in the United States over the last few years has come largely at the expense

temporal factors situational characteristics related to time

time pressure urgency to act based on some real or self-imposed deadline

seasonality regularly occurring conditions that vary with the time of year

circadian cycle rhythm (level of energy) of the human body that varies with the time of day

advertiming ad buys that include a schedule that runs the advertisement primarily at times when customers will be most receptive to the message

of carbonated soft drinks. Tea sales are also increasing in the United States, and although tea has largely been an afternoon and evening beverage in the past, Americans now are turning to tea as a beverage to wake up to. Whether it's beverage consumption, attire, or choice of entertainment, the time of day affects the value of products and activities. Some of this influence is due to scheduled events during the day such as one's working hours. But part is also biological. In fact, our bodies have a rhythm that varies with the time of day, or a **circadian cycle**. One aspect of the circadian cycle deals with our sleeping and waking times. Consumers would prefer to sleep between the hours of midnight and 6 AM and from about 1 to 3 PM Consumers who tend to shop during the "odd hours" will do so with less energy and efficiency, and deprived cognitive capacity.[9] However, they can also do so with less interference from other consumers.

Our circadian cycle is responsible for productivity in many activities. A host of products exist to try to aid consumers through the low-energy periods of the day, but perhaps the best fix is a quick nap! Research shows that diminished capacity will affect consumers who get less than 5 hours of sleep each day.[10] Products like 5-Hour Energy, a vitamin B–based pick-me-up, offer a value proposition built around trying to help consumers get through the sleepy times of day.

Other types of physical cycles also can create situational influences on consumers. Consumer researchers examined women's purchasing patterns over the menstrual cycle. The research demonstrates that women purchase more beauty-related products during the fertile phase and more food-related products during the non-fertile phase.[11] The explanation involves instinctive mechanisms related to the need for a mate, which are heightened cyclically during this time.

11-2d Advertiming

Companies sometimes buy advertising with a schedule that runs the advertisement primarily at times when customers will be most receptive to the message. This practice is known as **advertiming**. Advertisers practice advertiming based on seasonal patterns and even on day-to-day changes in the weather. Advertisers offering insurance-related products or those offering the sale of metals as a safe investment time their advertising to appear during news-related shows, hoping that consumers will be more receptive when fears about instability in the world are heightened.

11-3 Place Shapes Shopping Activities

The economy depends on consumers buying things. Consumers depend on purchases to receive value. Buying is the result of the shopping process. Thus, marketers understand that shopping holds the key to value creation that stimulates economies and ultimately raises standards of living.

Many of the activities involved in the CVF and consumer behavior theory in general take place in the shopping process. What exactly is shopping? Perhaps the following questions can help put shopping in perspective:

- Do consumers have to buy to shop?
- Is a store necessary for shopping?
- What motivates consumer shopping?

Marketers naturally hope that consumers will purchase things while shopping. But not every shopping act culminates in a purchase. Sometimes a consumer goes shopping only to find out that the desired product is out of stock. Rather than buying a less desirable product, the consumer may simply pass or put off product acquisition indefinitely.

More and more, a physical store isn't necessary for shopping to take place. Consumers shop using their computers, tablets, phones, vending machines, or more traditional nonstore alternatives, like catalogs. Sometimes, consumers facing an important decision like a new home or an upcoming vacation are so involved in

© iStockphoto.com/Brandon Alms

The value of products like 5-Hour Energy depends on the circadian cycle.

the buying process that they can't stop thinking about their choices. In this case, they may be shopping simply from the things they hold in memory.

11-3a What Is Shopping?

Shopping can be defined as the set of potentially value-producing consumer activities that directly increase the likelihood that something will be purchased. Thus, when a consumer surfs iTunes looking for a song for his iPod, he is shopping. A consumer searching Pinterest at 3 AM for comments about new dress shoes because she can't sleep is shopping. When a consumer visits the mall as a regular weekend activity, she is shopping. Earlier, we described marketing as business activities that enhance the likelihood of purchase. In this sense, shopping represents the inverse of marketing. Both marketing and shopping make purchase more likely, but one involves activities of marketing people and the other involves activities of shoppers.

11-3b Shopping Activities

Shopping activities take place in specific places, over time, and under specific conditions or contexts. Shopping thus occurs in situations that are not easily controlled by a consumer and often not by the marketer either. The consumer may be either alone or in a crowded place, rushed or relaxed, in a good mood or a bad mood. In other words, shoppers are subject to many situational influences that affect decision making and value. Whether the shoppers are American, European, or Asian, situational variables are at least as important in explaining eventual buying behavior as are personal characteristics or product beliefs.[12] Practically all shopping activities are influenced by contextual sources.

Four different types of shopping activities exist. At least one of these types characterizes any given shopping experience, but sometimes the shopper can combine more than one type into a single shopping trip. The four types of shopping activities are:

1. **Acquisitional shopping.** Activities oriented toward a specific, intended purchase or purchases

2. **Epistemic shopping.** Activities oriented toward acquiring knowledge about products

shopping set of value-producing consumer activities that directly increase the likelihood that something will be purchased

acquisitional shopping activities oriented toward a specific, intended purchase or purchases

epistemic shopping activities oriented toward acquiring knowledge about products

> Both marketing and shopping make purchase more likely, but one involves activities of marketing people and the other involves activities of shoppers.

Shopping Pals?

Is it better to shop with a shopping pal? Maybe, if the consumer has the time. Married consumers report that one of the main reasons for not shopping with a spouse is time pressure. Men in particular see an advantage in shopping together, because of the reduced financial risk that comes from being able to make a joint decision. Thus, if there isn't enough time to shop together, the couple may spend more than they would otherwise, reducing the utilitarian value from the situation. However, consumers also report that shopping with a family member can reduce hedonic value. Specifically, consumers appear to have more pleasure and report greater hedonic value when shopping alone or with a friend as opposed to shopping with a family member. Family members create greater anxiety about purchase decisions and can even increase the sense of time pressure as a consumer worries about the other family member being bored when she is enjoying an extended shopping period. Thus, shopping pals don't always enhance shopping value.

Sources: J. Lim and S. E. Beatty, "Factors Affecting Couples' Decisions to Jointly Shop," *Journal of Business Research* 64, no. 7 (2011): 774–81. A. Borges, J. C. Chebat, and B. J. Babin, "Does a Companion Always Enhance the Shopping Experience?" *Journal of Retailing and Consumer Services* 17 (July 2010): 294–99. D. Grace, "An Examination of Consumer Embarrassment and Repatronage Intentions in the Context of Emotional Service Encounters," *Journal of Retailing and Consumer Services* 16 (January 2009): 1–9.

© shironosov/iStockphoto.com

experiential shopping
recreationally oriented activities designed to provide interest, excitement, relaxation, fun, social interaction, or some other desired feeling

impulsive shopping
spontaneous activities characterized by a diminished regard for consequences, spontaneity, and a desire for immediate self-fulfillment

outshopping shopping in a city or town to which consumers must travel rather than in their own hometowns

EXHIBIT 11.2

Types of Shopping Activities

Type of Shopping Activity	Example	Utilitarian Shopping Value	Hedonic Shopping Value
Acquisitional Shopping	Buying Printer Cartridges	☆ ☆ ☆	
Epistemic Shopping	Studying Vacation Destinations	☆ ☆	★ ★
Experiential Shopping	Shopping with Friends		★ ★ ★
Impulsive Shopping	Buying 4 Pairs of Shoes	☆	★ ★

© Cengage Learning 2015

3. **Experiential shopping.** Recreationally oriented activities designed to provide interest, excitement, relaxation, fun, social interaction, or some other desired feeling

4. **Impulsive shopping.** Spontaneous activities characterized by a diminished regard for consequences, heightened emotional involvement, and a desire for immediate self-fulfillment

Exhibit 11.2 lists each type of shopping activity and depicts the type of shopping value generally associated with each type.

Acquisitional Shopping

A consumer who runs out to the store on her lunch hour to buy laundry detergent so she can wash clothes after work seeks to acquire detergent. Thus, shopping is more like a task, and this particular activity depends on high utilitarian value as an outcome.

Epistemic Shopping

An epistemic orientation motivates the shopper to increase knowledge. Epistemic activities include finding information on some imminent purchase. After the purchase situation is finished, the consumer stops looking for information. Alternatively, epistemic activities also include shopping simply to increase an ever-growing body of knowledge about some product category of interest. In this sense, epistemic activities can be associated with either situational involvement or enduring involvement, respectively. Online shopping provides a convenient forum for epistemic shopping activities that can be directly gratifying and value producing.[13] A consumer reading restaurant reviews while traveling to a city is practicing epistemic shopping. Depending on the situation, the activity could produce utilitarian value (the consumer is taking a client to dinner just after arrival) and/or hedonic value (the consumer is curious about the local restaurants).

Experiential Shopping

Experiential activities include things done just for the experience. Many consumers go shopping on the weekends just to do something. In other words, experiential shopping can be motivated by boredom or loneliness. On the other hand, consumers who are on vacation often take in the local shopping venues. In this way, they experience something new and possibly unique. **Outshopping** is a term used to refer to consumers who are shopping in a city or town they must travel to rather than in their own hometown. Outshopping is often motivated simply by the desire for the experience. The outshopping consumer sees this as a value opportunity and is more likely to make purchases in this less familiar and perhaps more intriguing place.

Outshopping provides value by allowing consumers to experience new or unique things.

Blend Images/John Lund/Marc Romanelli/the Agency Collection/Jupiterimages

People who live alone also go shopping to experience interacting with other people. These consumers desire more of a social experience when shopping, as might be expected. Experiential shoppers also tend to be less averse to crowds and thus can better cope with a crowded shopping environment.[14] Experiential shopping activities demonstrate that a lot of the reason for shopping lies in the experience itself.

Impulsive Shopping

Impulsive behaviors represent a unique group of shopping activities, as we will see in detail later. However, impulsive activities also illustrate how a single shopping trip can result in more than one type of activity. The shopper described above may go to a mall simply to acquire the baby shower gift. However, while there, she may get into the environment of the store and experience strong emotions. A store has shoes at half off! So the consumer buys four pairs of shoes and "saves a lot of money" doing so. In this instance, the consumer may have entered the store with an acquisitional orientation but the environment triggers a reversal which leads to more impulsive activities. A body of theory known as **reversal theory** tries to explain how environmental elements can lead to near 180-degree changes in shopping orientation.

11-3c Shopping Value

All shopping activities are aimed at one key result—value. Consistent with the view of value from a previous chapter, **personal shopping value**, or **PSV**, is the overall subjective worth of a shopping activity considering all associated costs and benefits. Like value overall, PSV can be usefully divided into two types. **Utilitarian shopping value** represents the worth obtained because some shopping task or job is completed successfully. **Hedonic shopping value** represents the worth of an activity because the time spent doing the activity itself is personally gratifying.[15]

Value and Shopping Activities

Thus, the activities shown in Exhibit 11.2 all provide value, but they provide value in different ways to different consumers. The old term *window shopping* illustrates this point. Some consumers *window-shop* to find information so that an upcoming shopping trip might be more successful. In this way, window shopping is epistemic and provides a means to the end of a more successful future shopping task. Consumers may also window-shop simply as a way of passing time in a gratifying way. Thus, window shopping can provide utilitarian and/or hedonic shopping value, respectively. A lot of *window shopping* takes place on the screen of a consumer's smartphone or tablet and serves much the same purposes as actual window shopping.[16]

Situational influences may affect the type of shopping value desired by consumers. Time pressure, for example, may lead consumers to be more concerned with simple product acquisition than they might otherwise be. On the other hand, consumers who are in a bad mood may choose to change it by going shopping. The pleasant emotions can be personally gratifying and can potentially improve a shopper's mood.

Retail Personality

Retailers specializing in things like a wide selection of goods, low prices, guarantees, and knowledgeable employees can provide high proportions of utilitarian shopping value. This type of positioning emphasizes the **functional quality** of a retail store by facilitating the task of shopping. In contrast, retailers specializing in a unique environment, an impressive décor, friendly employees, and pleasant emotions can provide relatively high hedonic shopping value. This type of positioning emphasizes the **affective quality** of a retail store. The affective quality can be managed to create an emotionally rewarding environment capable of producing high hedonic shopping value. Together, the functional and affective qualities come together to shape retail personality. More specifically, **retail personality** is the way a retail store is defined in the mind of a shopper based on the combination of functional and affective qualities.[17]

reversal theory tries to explain how environmental elements can lead to near 180-degree changes in shopping orientation

personal shopping value (PSV) overall subjective worth of a shopping activity considering all associated costs and benefits

utilitarian shopping value worth obtained because some shopping task or job is completed successfully

hedonic shopping value worth of a shopping activity because the time spent doing the activity itself is personally gratifying

functional quality retail positioning that emphasizes tangible things like a wide selection of goods, low prices, guarantees, and knowledgeable employees

affective quality retail positioning that emphasizes a unique environment, exciting décor, friendly employees, and, in general, the feelings experienced in a retail place

retail personality way a retail store is defined in the mind of a shopper based on the combination of functional and affective qualities

impulsive consumption
consumption acts characterized by spontaneity, a diminished regard for consequences, and a need for self-fulfillment

From a strategic perspective, these two retail personality dimensions are extremely useful as perceptual map dimensions (see Exhibit 11.3). Once again, a perceptual map of this type reveals which retail choices consumers view as most similar. As consumers' choices become more similar, they are more likely to compete with each other.

11-4 Impulsive Shopping and Consumption

Impulsive shopping activities take place every day. Some retailers and service providers survive largely as a result of consumers' impulsive activities. For instance, many behaviors associated with indulgence can be driven by impulsive motivations.

EXHIBIT 11.3

A Retail Personality Perceptual Map

© Cengage Learning

So, just what is an impulsive consumption act? **Impulsive consumption** is largely characterized by three components:

1. Impulsive acts are usually spontaneous and involve at least short-term feelings of liberation.

2. Impulsive acts are usually associated with a diminished regard for any costs or consequences (negative aspects) associated with the act.

3. Impulsive acts are usually motivated by a need for immediate self-fulfillment and are thus usually highly involving emotionally and associated with hedonic shopping value.

Will I Respect Myself in the Morning?

Impulsive shopping can contribute to negative self-conscious emotions like guilt and shame. Impulsive acts are characterized by a diminished regard for the consequences; the consequences having been learned from previous impulsive shopping experiences. Thus, consumers sometimes face shopping in a situation created by a previous shopping trip involving impulsive overspending. One way that a consumer may cope with such a situation is by avoiding the next shopping trip, particularly to the scene of the previous crime (where the impulsive spending occurred).

This situation stands in contrast to one created by consecutive shopping trips, the first in which a consumer practiced considerable constraint from spending and the second

© Edyta Pawlowska/Shutterstock.com

shaped by a great opportunity to act impulsively. What happens now? Although the consumer avoided feelings of guilt or shame on the first trip, some consumers reward themselves for the good behavior on the first trip by indulging themselves with an expensive self-reward on the second trip. The self-reward pleases the consumer temporarily but second thoughts that occur later can reintroduce feelings of guilt and shame into the equation. In a way, then, one shopping trip frames the next!

Sources: A. Mukhopadhyay and G. V. Johar, "Indulgence as Self-Reward for Prior Shopping Restraint: A Justification-Based Mechanism," *Journal of Consumer Psychology* 19 (2009): 334–45. S. Yi and H. Baumgartner, "Coping with Guilt and Shame in the Impulse Buying Context," *Journal of Economics Psychology* 32 (2011): 456–67.

Activities characterized by these features are likely to be impulsive. For example, a consumer might have a bad morning at work and decide to cancel a business lunch to take a break shopping for self-gifts or "happies" via the Internet. This activity is likely characterized as impulsive and can be a way to suppress negative emotions and evoke more positive feelings.[18] The behavior can be broken down to demonstrate the impulsiveness involved as follows:

1. The act involves willingly deviating from previous plans and thus shows spontaneity and no doubt feelings of liberation from the negative events of the day.

2. The act shows diminished regard for consequences either for missing the business lunch or for any expense incurred.

3. The act fulfills the need to maintain a positive outlook on the self and thus provides hedonic value.

Internet shopping, although often viewed as utilitarian in nature, can provide hedonic value in this way.[19] Additionally, consumers who feel they have restrained their spending behavior in the past may indulge in impulsive purchases as a reward for past good behavior.[20] Thus, when the economy eventually turns around, consumers may let loose with a lot of impulsive purchases.

11-4a Impulsive versus Unplanned Consumer Behavior

Impulsive purchasing is not synonymous with unplanned purchasing behavior. **Unplanned shopping,** buying, and consuming share some, but not all, characteristics of truly impulsive consumer behavior. Exhibit 11.4 illustrates the relationship between impulsive and unplanned consumer activity. The right side of the exhibit shows that unplanned consumer acts are characterized by:

1. Situational memory
2. Utilitarian orientation
3. Spontaneity

Situational memory characterizes unplanned acts because something in the environment, such as a point-of-purchase display, usually triggers the knowledge in memory that something is needed. A consumer may enter the grocery store without AA batteries on her grocery list. However, the battery display at the checkout provides a convenient reminder that her office inventory of batteries for wireless devices is depleted.

Simply put, utilitarian motivations drive many unplanned purchases. This consumer who purchases AA batteries is probably not very emotionally moved by the purchase. However, the purchase allows her to fulfill a need to maintain items needed to work efficiently.

Unplanned acts are spontaneous and, to some extent, they share this characteristic with impulsivity. They are, by definition, unplanned and therefore done without any significant deliberation or prior decision making. The grocery shopper certainly had not thought about buying AA batteries as she planned the shopping trip.

11-4b Distinguishing Impulsive and Unplanned Consumer Behavior

The line between impulsive and unplanned purchases is not always clear, because some unplanned acts are impulsive and many impulsive acts are unplanned. Las Vegas tourism for years has used a tagline that says:

What Happens in Vegas, Stays in Vegas

While some trips to Vegas may be completely spontaneous, most involve some degree of planning. But

unplanned shopping
shopping activity that shares some, but not all, characteristics of truly impulsive consumer behavior; being characterized by situational memory, a utilitarian orientation, and feelings of spontaneity

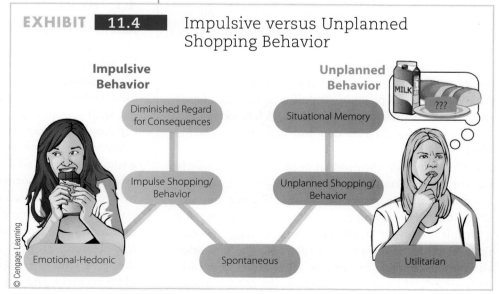

EXHIBIT 11.4 Impulsive versus Unplanned Shopping Behavior

Impulsive Behavior

Unplanned Behavior

Diminished Regard for Consequences

Situational Memory

Impulse Shopping/Behavior

Unplanned Shopping/Behavior

Emotional-Hedonic

Spontaneous

Utilitarian

© Cengage Learning

impulsivity *personality trait that represents how sensitive a consumer is to immediate rewards*

consumer self-regulation *tendency for consumers to inhibit outside, or situational, influences from interfering with shopping intentions*

action-oriented *consumers with a high capacity to self-regulate their behavior*

state-oriented *consumers with a low capacity to self-regulate their behavior*

the tagline emphasizes the impulsive nature of consumer behavior in Las Vegas. Certainly, the campaign illustrates the high hedonic value that can be obtained and encourages consumers not to worry so much about the consequences. So perhaps an impulsive consumption act, like going to Vegas, can even be planned. Simple unplanned purchases may lack the impulsive characteristics captured so well by this campaign.

Simple unplanned purchases usually lack any real emotional involvement or significant amounts of self-gratification. Additionally, unplanned purchases often involve only minimal negative consequences and thus fail to really qualify as having negative consequences. A pack of gum or breath mints is not likely to cause severe financial problems for very many consumers.

11-4c Susceptibility to Situational Effects

Are all consumers susceptible to unplanned and impulsive behavior? The answer is yes, but not all consumers are equally susceptible. Individual difference characteristics can play a role. For example, **impulsivity** is a personality trait that represents how sensitive a consumer is to immediate *rewards*. A consumer shopping for a gift for a friend may see shoes on sale at half off and be compelled to purchase these and obtain the *reward*.[21] Naturally, consumers with high impulsivity are more prone to impulsive acts.[22]

Consumers with attention deficit disorder, for example, typically have high degrees of impulsivity, which makes them more prone to impulsive acts. One consequence is that such consumers are even less likely than others to follow step-by-step instructions for assembling or using a product.[23] Thus, they may fail to get the full value from the product because the assembly is incomplete or wrong.

Situational characteristics also influence impulse shopping.[24] For example, a consumer shopping for a purple dress for a special occasion may encounter a black dress on the 40% off rack. The low-price cue may encourage an impulse purchase in this case. Atmospheric characteristics such as the colors, music,

A great deal of the allure of Las Vegas vacations is the opportunity to participate in a lot of impulsive behavior.

© ittleny/Shutterstock.com

free samples, merchandising, and salespeople also can encourage purchase. Online retailers can facilitate the actual buying process by making the transaction a simple one-step process.[25] Exhibit 11.5 summarizes things that retailers can do to encourage unplanned and impulse purchasing.

11-4d Consumer Self-Regulation

Another key personality trait that affects a consumer's tendency to do things that are unplanned or impulsive is self-regulatory capacity. **Consumer self-regulation** in this sense, refers to a tendency for consumers to inhibit outside, or situational, influences from interfering with shopping intentions. Consumers with a high capacity to self-regulate their behavior are sometimes referred to as **action-oriented**, whereas consumers with a low capacity to self-regulate are referred to as **state-oriented**.[26] Action-oriented consumers are affected less by emotions generated by a retail atmosphere than are state-oriented consumers. Recall the three dimensions of atmospheric emotions discussed in an earlier chapter: pleasure, arousal, and dominance. State-oriented shoppers who are emotionally aroused are far more likely to make additional purchases beyond what was

EXHIBIT 11.5 Retail Approaches at Encouraging Impulse Purchases

Tool	Example
1. Merchandise complementary products together	Peruse social networking entries on the Internet for consumers talking about recent purchases and generate push advertising aimed at complementary products.
2. Encourage "add-on" purchases	Asking consumers to buy socks after they have agreed to buy shoes seems like a small request, and turning the request down risks creating negative feelings. Add-on purchases also serve as a trigger in memory.
3. Create an emotionally charged atmosphere	Creating an upbeat, exciting dining atmosphere encourages customers to linger and order something extra.
4. Make things easy to buy	Storing credit card information using an instant pay app, which makes transactions easy and quick, reduces time for consumers to have second thoughts.
5. Provide a discount	Offering an instant discount at checkout diminishes the perceived consequences associated with a purchase.

© Cengage Learning 2015

planned than are action-oriented shoppers. Likewise, state-oriented shoppers' spending behavior is strongly affected by feelings of dominance in the environment. Further, feelings of dominance among state-oriented shoppers increase hedonic shopping value and decrease utilitarian shopping value. In contrast, action-oriented shoppers' purchasing and shopping value perceptions are unaffected by dominance.

New technologies represent tempting items in a shopping environment. Self-regulation is related to a consumer's desire, and intention, to purchase such new products. A state-oriented consumer who discovers an innovative new technology is more likely to buy the new product than would be an action-oriented consumer in the same situation.[27] Retailers with a high proportion of state-oriented consumers in their target market are more likely to thrive on consumers' impulse purchases.

Exhibit 11.6 lists some questions that help distinguish consumers based on self-regulatory capacity. The exhibit shows a statement and then demonstrates the way a consumer would respond to the situation. Consumers with a high ability to self-regulate their behavior—in other words, the action-oriented consumers—generally form rules that they stick by to limit the extent to which situational influences determine their behavior. For example, if they know they will be tempted to overspend during a shopping trip, they may decide not to take their credit cards with them while shopping. In this way, they can resist the overspending that sometimes accompanies unplanned and impulse purchases.

Considering that consumers are more or less vulnerable to certain marketing approaches to encourage impulsive buying, one might ask, are such actions ethical? Or do such actions simply encourage consumers to

EXHIBIT 11.6 Questions Distinguishing Low from High Self-Regulatory Capacity

Statement	Action-Oriented Consumers' Typical Response	State-Oriented Consumers' Typical Response
If I had to work at home…	I would get started right away	I would often have problems getting started
When I have important things to buy…	I make a shopping plan and stick to it	I don't know how to get started
When I have an important assignment to finish in an afternoon…	I can easily concentrate on the assignment	It often happens that things will distract me
When it is absolutely necessary to do some unpleasant task…	I finish it as soon as possible	It takes a while before I can start on it

© Cengage Learning

atmospherics emotional nature of an environment or the feelings created by the total aura of physical attributes that comprise a physical environment

servicescape physical environment in which consumer services are performed

buy things wastefully? This certainly can be the case, but unplanned purchases are often simply things consumers would indeed intend to buy if they had remembered them before they started shopping. Impulse purchases can also be a relatively harmless way that consumers control their emotions and improve their outlook on life. Impulse purchases do provide value as long as the consequences of the purchases are relatively harmless. In this way, impulse shopping can be therapeutic and emotionally uplifting. This isn't always the case though.

11-4e Impulsive versus Compulsive Behavior

Impulsive and compulsive consumer behavior share many of the same characteristics. Compulsive behavior can be emotionally involving and certainly entails the possibility of negative consequences. Compulsive consumer behavior can be distinguished from impulsive consumer behavior. The three distinguishing characteristics are:

- Compulsive consumer behavior is harmful.
- Compulsive CB seems to be uncontrollable.
- Compulsive CB is driven by chronic depression.

Compulsive consumer behavior is defined and discussed in more detail in a later chapter.

11-5 Places Have Atmospheres

All consumer behavior takes place in some physical space. This statement isn't really profound. Sometimes marketing managers easily forget that the physical environment can play a significant role in shaping buying behavior and the value a consumer receives from shopping or service. Perhaps nowhere is the true impact of place more obvious than in retail and service environments.

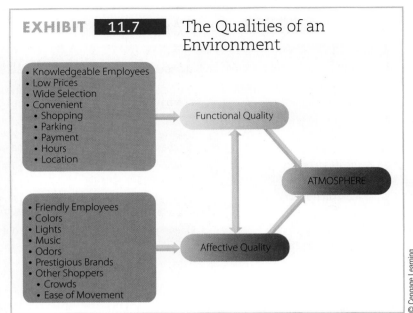

EXHIBIT 11.7 The Qualities of an Environment

- Knowledgeable Employees
- Low Prices
- Wide Selection
- Convenient
  - Shopping
  - Parking
  - Payment
  - Hours
  - Location

→ Functional Quality

- Friendly Employees
- Colors
- Lights
- Music
- Odors
- Prestigious Brands
- Other Shoppers
  - Crowds
  - Ease of Movement

→ Affective Quality

ATMOSPHERE

© Cengage Learning

11-5a Retail and Service Atmospherics

In consumer behavior, **atmospherics** refers to the emotional nature of an environment or, more precisely, to the feelings created by the total aura of physical attributes that comprise the physical environment. A total list of things that make up the atmosphere would be difficult to compile; however, they can be summarized by two dimensions.[28] Exhibit 11.7 provides a summary of the dimensions and what they can create.

The term **servicescape** is sometimes used to refer to the physical environment in which consumer services are performed.[29] Each servicescape has its own unique environment. Others have used terms like *e-scape* to refer to a virtual shopping environment as portrayed by a website or *festivalscape* to refer to the array of environmental characteristics a consumer encounters when attending a festival.[30] Thus, Mardi Gras in New Orleans creates an atmosphere where consumers feel uninhibited and sometimes perform extreme behaviors, including acts of public nudity, that they probably would not even consider doing in another atmosphere. While consumers sometimes do things they may regret later, this feeling is a defining part of the Mardi Gras experience. No matter the "scape," atmosphere works through the same sequence:

Environment ⊢→ Thoughts ⊢→ Feelings ⊢→ Behavior ⊢→ Value

Functional Quality

As mentioned earlier, the functional quality of an environment describes the meaning created by the total result of attributes that facilitate and make efficient the function performed there. In a shopping environment, this includes convenience in all forms: the price levels, the number and helpfulness of employees, and the breadth and depth of merchandise, along with other characteristics that facilitate the shopping task. In a service environment, the amount and expertise of service employees, the convenience of the environment, and the capability of the support staff, among other things, all contribute to the functional quality of the service environment.[31] These are often thought of as core aspects of service, as some are essential for the benefits to be realized by consumers.

Affective Quality

The affective quality represents the emotional meaning of an environment, which results from the sum effect of all ambient attributes that affect the way one feels in that place. A friendly nurse can make a health-care environment less anxious, cool colors can be relaxing, upbeat music can be exciting, and a crowded environment that restricts movement can be distressing. Although many managers focus more on core aspects, these more relational aspects also influence value and satisfaction.

Restaurants, for example, often go out of business despite having excellent food and a good location. A primary reason for their lack of competitiveness is a lack of attention to the environment. As a result, the restaurant lacks style or creates a distressing or boring affective quality. All consumers are susceptible to the effects of affective quality, but female consumers appear much more demanding based on how they react to a place with a negative affective quality.[32]

So, does a retail environment with a distinctly high functional quality necessarily have an uninteresting or poor affective quality? Quite the contrary! If anything, the two dimensions are positively related. An environment with a favorable functional quality tends to be associated with some degree of positive affect. Adolescent girls, for example, find an environment with high levels of functional qualities like accessibility and safety features to also be more pleasing places to shop.[33] Thus, retailers should keep this in mind and realize that even things they build

to create shopper safety can affect both the functional and affective meaning of a particular retailer.

fit how appropriate the elements of a given environment are

congruity how consistent the elements of an environment are with one another

11-5b Atmosphere Elements

The way an atmosphere makes a consumer feel is really determined by the consumer's perception of all the elements in a given environment working together. Therefore, naming all the elements that eventually affect the retail or service atmosphere is impossible. However, a more distinct atmosphere creates a feeling that can ultimately result in a core competitive advantage based on the unique feeling. Two factors help merchandisers and retail designers create just such an atmosphere:[34]

- **Fit** refers to how appropriate the elements of an environment are for a given environment.
- **Congruity** refers to how consistent the elements of an environment are with each other.

Panera Bread is one of the fastest growing food chains in the United States. Panera illustrates that it takes more than good food to deliver a total value experience. A big secret to their success is the relaxing atmosphere. The design concept is visually appealing with interesting shapes and colors. This design is accented by soft jazz music and wonderful aromas of fresh baked bread. Like Starbucks, consumers feel comfortable just being in the Panera Bread atmosphere and many will linger there even after their meal is done. Panera also presents an inviting atmosphere for families—including families with small children. The informality of the design makes everyone feel welcome.

When all of the environment's elements are congruent, a restaurant can add experience to food in delivering hedonic and utilitarian value.

ZUMA Wire Service/Alamy

olfactory refers to humans' physical and psychological processing of smells

foreground music music that becomes the focal point of attention and can have strong effects on a consumer's willingness to approach or avoid an environment

background music music played below the audible threshold that would make it the center of attention

Although a combination of elements come together to create an atmosphere, researchers often study the elements in isolation or in combination with only one or two other elements. The following sections single out a few of the more prominent environmental elements as being particularly effective in controlling an environment's atmosphere.

Odors

Believe it or not, in Manchester, U.K., the industrial revolution museum includes a tribute to sewerage systems with a sewer exhibit. What should a sewer exhibit smell like? Well, the folks at the museum in Manchester have a sewer that smells like a sewer—it certainly wouldn't be authentic with the scent of roses piped in. The fact is, odors are prominent environmental elements that affect both a consumer's cognitive processing and affective reaction.

Olfactory is a term that refers to humans' physical and psychological processing of smells. When shoppers process ambient citrus odors, they tend to feel higher levels of pleasant emotions while shopping and to be more receptive to product information. Citrus odors produce positive responses in practically all consumers. Even more positive reactions can be obtained by matching odors with a target market. For example, women respond more favorably to floral scents while men respond more favorably to food scents like pumpkin pie. No kidding! Perhaps the way to a man's heart, or wallet, really is through his stomach. Panera's bread aromas set the tone for its relaxing atmosphere.

Designers need to keep in mind that a scent, like other elements, works best when it fits with the setting. In an experimental study, wine store consumers paid more attention to label information when an incongruent and slightly less pleasant odor was present and became less risk aversive and more willing to try different wines when more pleasing and consistent odors were present.[35] Odors also seem to have a greater effect when other more intrusive elements like crowding are not too strong.[36]

Music

Fast music means fast dancing. Slow music means slow dancing. Even though consumers don't always dance through the aisles of stores, this image is fairly accurate in describing the way background music affects consumers. Both foreground and background music affect consumers, but they do so in different ways. **Foreground music** is music that becomes the focal point of attention and can have strong effects on a consumer's willingness to approach or avoid an environment. Consumers who dislike rap or country music will likely have a difficult time hanging around a place with loud rap or country music.

From a consumer behavior standpoint, **background music**, which is music played below the audible threshold that would make it the center of attention, is perhaps more interesting than foreground music. Service providers and retailers generally provide some type of background music for customers. Muzak is one of several companies whose business is providing the appropriate background music for a particular service or retail setting. Several effects are attributable to background music:

- The speed of the background music determines the speed at which consumers shop. Slower music means slower shopping. Faster music means faster shopping.
- The tempo of music affects the patience of consumers. Faster music makes consumers less patient.
- The presence of background music enhances service quality perceptions relative to an environment with no background music.
- Pop music used in the background contributes to discount store perceptions.
- Incongruent music lowers consumers' quality perceptions.

These factors are important for retail managers interested in managing quality and value perceptions. However, background music can also affect the bottom line. In restaurants, for instance, consumers who dine with slow background music are more patient and in less of a hurry to leave. As a result, they linger longer and tend to buy more beverages than consumers dining with faster background music. Thus, gross margins can actually be increased by slowing down the background music, particularly in light of the higher margins realized on drink sales relative to food sales.[37]

Color

Color is another tool that marketing managers can use to alter consumer reactions by enhancing visual appeal. Some colors are more liked than other colors, but liking isn't really the key to understanding consumer

Fascinating

Ever just want to get it away from it all? Escaping a mundane or troubling reality can bring value to a consumer. Designers sometimes create spaces with escape in mind. When effective, such an environment creates sensations of escape and even fascination. More and more, consumer and service environments incorporate elements of the outdoors such as plant life, waterfalls, and an abundance of natural light. A large atrium can cost a lot to build and maintain, but the result is that consumers feel attracted to the space. In the extreme, a consumer can become so fascinated with the place that they lose the sense of time passing. Research suggests that consumers often mention elements like these in characterizing "favorite places." In fact, such environments possess restorative properties that can refresh a consumer both cognitively and emotionally.

In service environments or retail shopping venues, escape and fascination provide hedonic value through the emotional sensations they can create. Additionally, the environments restore cognitive functioning and allow consumers to become more effective problem solvers while in this place!

Sources: D. Shows, "Escapist Environments, Restorative Experiences and Consumer Self-Regulation" (PhD dissertation, Louisiana Tech University, 2013). B. Wöran and A. Arnberger, "Exploring Relationships Between Recreation Specialization, Restorative Environments and Mountain Hikers' Flow Experience," *Leisure Sciences* 34 (2012): 95–114.

reactions to color. Blue is perhaps the most universally liked color. Blue presents few cultural taboos. Red, white, and black, however, all present cultural barriers associated with bad omens and death in some cultures. Red is a risky color in Japan, as is white in China and black in Western cultures. Color, like other environmental elements, helps frame the shopping experience. Therefore, choosing the right color depends on how consumers react in terms of both their thoughts and their feelings.

Color, for example, affects both quality and price perceptions. Consumers who perceive a product in a predominantly blue background tend to think the product is of higher quality, and they are willing to pay more for that product.[38] In contrast, warm colors like red and orange tend to promote expectations of poor quality and low price. Exhibit 11.8 illustrates the way these effects can play out in a retail environment. Color changes behavior by framing the way one thinks about a product and also by changing the way one feels. Thus, the perceived value of an object can vary with color.

Exhibit 11.8 clearly illustrates how color can frame consumer information processing. The same product at the identical price, in this case $100, will be viewed as priced more fairly with a blue background than with an orange or red background. Consumers also express more positive feelings when presented with a blue background. Not surprisingly, consumers are also more willing to buy a product presented in a blue background than a red or orange background.

So is blue always a good color? Like many aspects of consumer behavior, the story isn't quite that simple.

EXHIBIT 11.8 The Way Color Works

$100

- High Quality
- Worth $100
- Believe Price Is Fair
- Feel Pleased
- More Willing to Buy

$100

- Low Quality/Discount
- Not Worth $100
- Believe Price Is Not as Fair
- Feel More Distressed
- Less Willing to Buy

© Cengage Learning

crowding density of people and objects within a given space

nonlinear effect a plot of an effect that does not make a straight line

Blue has drawbacks. For instance, blue is a cool color. Thus, blue does not attract attention as effectively as a warm color like red or orange does. Also, like other situational effects due to the environment, color does not work alone. Lighting can have dramatic effects on the environment and even reverse color's effect. For example, the effects above hold for bright lights. Change a store's lighting to soft lights and consumers' opinions regarding the product change considerably. For instance, soft lights and an orange background can eliminate the advantage for blue in that the price fairness perceptions, quality perceptions, affect, and purchase intentions are now equal to or slightly better than the combination of blue and soft lights.[39] Luxury retailers including designers like Burberry and Victoria's Secret pay careful attention to their lighting and colors to create the right mood and get good reactions to their merchandise.

Like other elements too, a marketer must be aware of the image. If the brand is closely associated with a color, then that association may be more important than the effects discussed here. So, if you are in a bad mood, change the color of your space, and things may improve!

Merchandising

Merchandising's point is to provide the customer with the best opportunity to purchase something. This is done by the placement of goods and store fixtures, along with the use of signage. The angles or racks and the visual image of the store provide a way for consumers to view and move through a store. Signs change consumers' perceptions. For example, signs that emphasize price by using large numerals create the perception of a discount store. An up-scale store uses little signage. Increasingly, digital signage is delivered with electronic display boards. These seem to attract the attention of shoppers and can be used toward creating a specific feeling.[40] In some cases, the consumer can even interact with the display board.

Social Settings

An old saying about Bishop Berkeley's forest goes:

If a tree falls in the forest and nobody is there to hear it, does it make any noise?

Well, if a consumer shops on the Champs Elysées in Paris and no other shoppers are present is there an

Jeff Greenberg/age fotostock /SuperStock

Poor merchandising can increase the sense of crowding in a store environment.

atmosphere? People are a huge part of the environment, and if the people are removed the atmosphere changes entirely. Thus, the social environment, referring to the other customers and employees in a service or shopping environment, cannot be ignored when explaining how atmosphere affects CB.

Crowding refers to the density of people and objects within a given space. A space can be crowded without any people. However, *shopper density*, meaning the number of consumers in a given space, can still exert relatively strong influences on consumer behavior. Crowding actually exerts a **nonlinear effect** on consumers, meaning that a plot of the effect by the amount of crowding does not make a straight line.

Exhibit 11.9 illustrates the way crowding works, particularly with respect to shopper density. Generally, consumers are not particularly attracted to an environment with no other consumers. The lack of consumers might signal poor quality or, in other cases, an absence of other consumers is simply awkward. For example, a consumer who enters a restaurant alone, particularly with no other diners, may well feel quite uncomfortable. In contrast, a mild degree of crowding produces the most positive outcomes in terms of shopping affect, purchase behavior, consumer satisfaction, and shopping value; high degrees of crowding lower these outcomes.[41] For instance, crowding affects utilitarian shopping value less

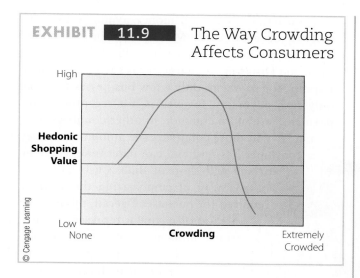

EXHIBIT 11.9 The Way Crowding Affects Consumers

© Cengage Learning

strongly than hedonic shopping value in part because of the negative affect caused by crowding.

Hypermarket chains like Carrefour, Target, and Walmart can unintentionally diminish the hedonic shopping value consumers experience by placing large displays on the sales floor that compound the negative affect occurring during busy shopping times. In contrast, savvy retailers can actually increase sales by decreasing the amount of merchandise on the sales floor and creating a less crowded shopping environment.

Both the number and type of salespeople can also affect shoppers. For example, the presence of more salespeople in a shopping environment can actually increase shopper purchase intentions. However, the type of salespeople can also influence shoppers' purchasing and value perceptions. In particular, salespeople and service providers should have an appropriate appearance for the type of product sold. The salespeople should simply fit the part. At Disney theme parks, employees are referred to as "cast members" in part because their appearance is tightly controlled to fit the particular environment in which they work.

Salespeople and service providers are an important source of information and influence. **Source attractiveness** is defined as the degree to which a source's physical appearance matches a consumer's prototype (expectations) for beauty and elicits a favorable or desirous response. Intuitively, one would think that a more attractive person always is a good idea relative to a relatively less attractive person. This idea is known as the "beauty is good" hypothesis.

However, a consumer who encounters an attractive salesperson may end up making an upward social comparison. **Social comparison** is a naturally occurring

mental personal comparison of the self with a target individual. Simply, it's a self–other comparison that helps give the self relative meaning. An upward comparison means the target is better and a downward comparison means the target is inferior. In the case of attractiveness, an upward comparison (the salesperson perceived as more attractive than the consumer) can cause negative feelings that reduce the likelihood of purchase.[42] The presence of other attractive customers may even cause another consumer to feel embarrassed if the upward comparison is strong. This effect is more likely for same-sex comparisons when the service is unrelated to beauty-related products. Think about how a very attractive appliance salesperson may come across.

Shopping buddies, meaning shopping companions, also cause consumers to react differently than when shopping alone. A shopping companion can be more fun and be a source of objective opinion. In this way, the companion can affect hedonic and utilitarian value. The shopping buddy can help reinforce positive feelings about products and thus encourage purchase. A simple statement like "those jeans look great on you" can tilt the scale toward purchase. Partly as a result, consumers who shop with a companion tend to buy more than those who shop alone. Teens' behavior is particularly affected by mall shopping companions who are members of their peer group. Research shows limits to positive effects of group shopping, however. Consumers who shop with a spouse or other family member report lower hedonic value. The family members interfere or get in the way of what could otherwise be a gratifying time alone or with a friend.[43] The presence of a shopping buddy does change things.

Virtual Shopping Situations

Shopping via the Internet is just about as commonplace as catalog shopping. Many effects seen in real bricks-and-mortar shopping environments exist in the virtual shopping world too. For example, color and sounds can work in much the same way. A website with a blue background enhances quality perceptions just as the background in a real store might. Additionally, images placed in the background of a website can produce active thoughts, particularly when consumer expertise or knowledge is low. A web-based furniture retailer using pictures of

source attractiveness the degree to which a source's physical appearance matches a prototype for beauty and elicits a favorable or desirous response

social comparison a naturally occurring mental personal comparison of the self with a target individual within the environment

antecedent conditions
situational characteristics that a consumer brings to information processing

clouds in the web background, for instance, can produce thoughts of soft and comfortable furniture. Similarly, images related to money can produce thoughts related to discounts.[44] Online retailers, like real retail environments, can enhance the shopping experience by making the site visually appealing.[45] However, care should be taken, as aesthetics often take a backseat to the need for an easy-to-use site that facilitates easy transactions—especially for task-oriented shoppers that frequent the Internet. This is particularly the case for shoppers interacting through a smartphone or tablet computer, due to the smaller screen and limited functionality.

Virtual retail sites now sometimes include avatars or images of real people playing the social role of a helpful salesclerk. Does a virtual salesperson have any effect on shoppers? The answer is yes![46] The advantages to these sites include increased purchase likelihood and utilitarian shopping value as the virtual people are helpful, but the additional social context particularly improves hedonic shopping value. The body of evidence suggests that online shoppers respond better to images of real people than to avatars.

© iStockphoto.com/Baris Simsek

11-6 Antecedent Conditions

The term **antecedent conditions** refers to situational characteristics that a consumer brings to a particular information processing, purchase, or consumption environment. Events occurring prior to this particular point in time have created a situation. Antecedent conditions include things like economic resources, orientation, mood, and other emotional perceptions such as fear. They can shape the value in a situation by framing the events that take place. The following sections elaborate.

11-6a Economic Resources

Buying Power

The economic resources a consumer brings to a particular purchase setting refer to the consumer's buying power. Buying power can be in the form of

cash on hand, credit and money available by draft (check), or debit card. Most places in the United States today accept credit cards such as Visa, Mastercard, and Discover, or charge cards such as American Express, for payment; only a few businesses still take only cash payments. Businesses not accepting "card payment" are more common in other countries. Particularly in those countries, the amount of money a consumer has on hand can determine where he or she will shop or dine. Cash payments have a way of emphasizing the sacrifice required for purchase. Overall, though, the method of payment represents a situational influence on consumers in several ways. Perhaps the most prominent is that consumers are less price sensitive when using plastic compared to when using cash.[47]

However, other issues arise. What if consumers are near their credit limits? This can also change their shopping behavior. Companies may put together special financing packages to deal with consumers whose credit is good enough to receive a major credit card, even though they maintain high debt levels. Many consumers live paycheck to paycheck. If so, buying may increase around the day that consumers are paid. Then, the awareness that they are financially better off because of payday may stimulate increased spending. Check advance services take advantage of payday timing by offering to prepay consumers in return for a portion of the total paycheck. Thus, these consumer services offer utilitarian value to consumers by providing a way for them to receive their pay before the company they work for actually issues a check.

Consumer Budgeting

During the 1990s, consumer debt began increasing to unprecedented levels, and it remains that way today. Much of the consumer debt can be attributed to credit cards. The fact is, credit card companies charge a high interest rate (such as 18% or more), allowing them to take credit risks and still maintain a profitable business. Thus, credit became easy to get, even for some consumers with low incomes and poor credit histories. Today, consumers see credit cards as necessary given that some exchanges, such as on the Internet, are difficult if not impossible without one.

Instant credit enables consumers to avoid delaying gratification. "Why wait when you can buy it today?"

However, when consumers find themselves having difficulty making payments, their spending habits must change or they run the risk of losing their credit and worse. Even the manner with which one uses a credit card can influence spending. The easier it is to use the card, the more consumers spend. Consumers who store their card numbers online or use smartphone apps to make payments are more willing to spend than are consumers who actually have to take their card out and swipe it in a card reader.[48] Consumers concerned about spending habits may find this fact useful as a tip to saving money.

A mortgage crisis in the United States rippled through financial markets around the world during the late 2000s. Many consumers had taken variable rate mortgages that offered very low rates in the first few years of the loan. However, as interest rates rose, these very same consumers sometimes found themselves in a position where their home mortgage was taking 50% or more of their total income. The higher budget allocation to make a house payment lowered their buying power. Many consumers who faced foreclosure learned the hard way about the risks of a variable rate loan.

Most consumers do not prepare a formal budget and instead rely on mental budgeting. **Mental budgeting** is simply a memory accounting for recent spending.[49] One result is that a consumer who has recently splurged on spending in one category will tend to make up for the exuberance through underconsumption in another category. In other words, they buy less than they typically would. Thus, the fact that the consumer has splurged recently in one area creates an antecedent condition that affects spending in another.

Gift (Prepaid) Cards

How do you feel when you get a gift card for a gift? U.S. consumers report purchasing an average of nearly five and one-half gift cards per year, and apparently consumers like getting them.[50] Consider this question:

Would you prefer receiving a gift valued at $45 or a $25 gift card?

Surprisingly, just over half (52%) of consumers surveyed favored the $25 gift card! Retailers see benefits from these purchases as well, based on the way a gift card frames the buying situation. Not only do consumers

with closed-loop gift cards, meaning those redeemable at a specific retailer(s), become likely to shop at that retailer, but typically the consumers spend far more than the value of the gift card. Closed-loop (as opposed to open-loop, which can be spent anywhere) gift cards average $42, but the average amount spent by consumers redeeming these cards tops $200. Gift cards may lower price sensitivity in much the same way as the easy use of a credit card.

However, between six and ten percent of gift cards go unclaimed. Estimates are that in the last five years, over $40 billion of gift cards went unclaimed in the United States. When a card reaches its expiration date without being spent, it legally becomes unclaimed property. Each state regulates what happens to such property. About half of the states provide mechanisms by which they claim the income, and in other cases retailers may eventually convert the liability into income on their financial statements.[51] For some consumers, gift cards offer no great allure and are either forgotten or seen as too much trouble to redeem, illustrating that costs beyond money costs are involved in the total value equation.

mental budgeting
memory accounting for recent spending

> For some consumers, gift cards offer no great allure and are either forgotten or seen as too much trouble to redeem, illustrating that costs beyond money costs are involved in the total value equation.

© iStockphoto.com/Catherine Lane

11-6b Orientation

Consumers enter each exchange environment with a specific orientation. However, some orientations are temporary. Consumers in uncertain economic times may adopt a temporary orientation toward increased price consciousness. Even a consumer with a tendency toward an experiential orientation may temporarily face a strong task orientation. Gift shopping can change a consumer's orientation in this way. With this reversal, things that might otherwise be pleasant distract the consumer. This effect is even true on the Internet, as an aesthetically pleasing website can actually cause lower satisfaction among consumers that are highly task-oriented.[52] Employees who sense the orientation and can adjust their approach will create higher value for the consumer. Gift shopping can dramatically shift a shopper's orientation and change the shopping experience altogether.

11-6c Mood

Mood was defined earlier as a transient affective state. While shopping and consuming can alter a consumer's mood, consumers bring their current moods to the particular consumption situation. Consumers in particularly bad moods may have a tendency to binge-consume. For example, a consumer in a foul mood may down an entire pint of Ben & Jerry's ice cream. If the mood is particularly disagreeable, perhaps a quart is more likely to do the trick. The foul mood enhances the value of the ice cream temporarily because it provides the normal hedonic value from the good taste, but it is also therapeutic and, at least temporarily, helps restores a more favorable affective state.

Mood can also affect shopping. The mood that consumers bring to the shopping environment can exaggerate the actual experience. A consumer in a good mood may find even greater hedonic shopping value in a pleasant shopping experience than he may otherwise find.[53] Mood can also affect spending and consumer satisfaction. Shoppers who go shopping in a bad mood are particularly likely to buy only what they absolutely need and experience lower consumer satisfaction than consumers in good moods.

11-6d Security and Fearfulness

Consumers today live with ever-present reminders of vandalism, crime, and even terrorism. Large parking lots such as commonly found at Walmart stores or conventional shopping centers attract criminals who prey on seemingly defenseless consumers. Stories of abductions, muggings, assaults, carjackings, and other heinous criminal acts taking place understandably create fear among some shoppers, particularly those who view themselves as vulnerable.[54] Shopping malls, markets, airports, and other places where large numbers of consumers gather are consistently mentioned as potential terrorist targets, providing another reason for consumers to feel less secure.

Fearfulness can affect consumers in multiple ways. A consumer who goes shopping in a fearful mood will not go about her shopping in the same way. A fearful consumer will tend to buy less and enjoy the experience less. Alternatively, a consumer may cope with fear of shopping by turning to nonstore outlets such as the Internet as a seemingly safer way of doing business. But, even here, consumers sometimes fear providing private information often needed to complete a transaction. Thus, retailers who pay attention to making their parking and shopping environments more secure can help eliminate the feelings of fear some shoppers may have otherwise. Exhibit 11.10 lists some ways fearfulness may be reduced among consumers.

EXHIBIT 11.10   Enhancing Value by Making Consumers Feel Safer

- Increase number and visibility of security personnel
- Increase number and prominence of security cameras in parking lots
- Have brightly lit parking lots
- Add carry-out service for consumers—particularly for those shopping alone
- Maintain an uncrowded, open entrance
- Clearly mark all exits
- Prevent loitering
- Discourage gangs from visiting the center

© Cengage Learning

WHAT DO YOU THINK?
WHAT OTHERS HAVE THOUGHT

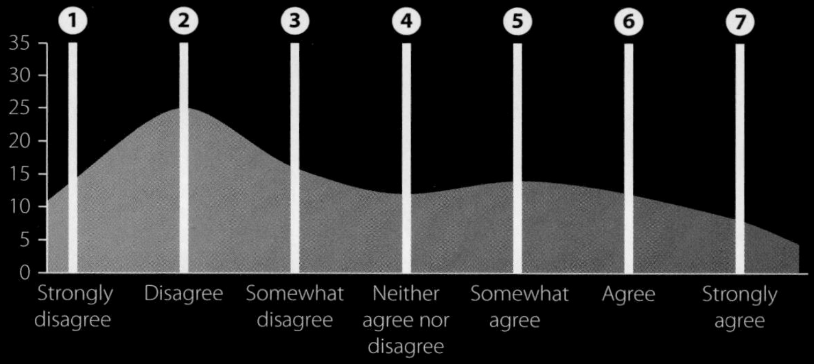

Chart with responses numbered 1–7:

- ① Strongly disagree
- ② Disagree
- ③ Somewhat disagree
- ④ Neither agree nor disagree
- ⑤ Somewhat agree
- ⑥ Agree
- ⑦ Strongly agree

Y-axis: 0, 5, 10, 15, 20, 25, 30, 35

I never let anything get in the way of preparing for my consumer behavior class.

We can see that students responded anonymously! One out of four respondents selected the "disagree" (2) response. Thus, quite a few students seem to recognize that situational influences can get in the way of even their best made plans. Eight percent strongly agree. Are those "A" students?

Study Tools

Located at the back of the textbook

❏ Rip out Chapter in Review Card

Located at www.cengagebrain.com

❏ Review Key Terms Flashcards (print or online)

❏ Download audio summaries to review on the go

❏ Complete practice quizzes to prepare for tests

❏ Play "Beat the Clock" to master concepts

❏ Watch video on Murray's Cheese for a real company example

study tools

© VLADGRIN/Shutterstock.com

Decision making
processes lead to consumer choice.

WHAT DO YOU THINK?
Most of the time I am a rational decision maker.

STRONGLY DISAGREE   **STRONGLY AGREE**

VISIT COURSEMATE AT WWW.CENGAGEBRAIN.COM

Decision Making I: Need Recognition and Search

12-1 Consumer Decision Making

Consumers encounter problem situations each and every day. Most of the time there are so many situations that it's hard to recall them all. You can run out of milk, be low on gasoline, search for a new apartment, take your car to the shop, and look for an outfit for a job interview all in the same day. In each of these situations, needs are recognized. When needs occur, decision making must take place. Where should I buy milk? Who has the cheapest gasoline? Should I buy a suit at Men's Wearhouse or Dillard's?

Some situations require big decisions. For example, when a college graduate needs to find a new apartment, a big decision usually follows. In other situations, the decisions are relatively small. For example, when you blow a lightbulb, you might simply grab any brand you see or perhaps prefer a green brand.

You may recall the basic consumer behavior consumption process that was presented in our opening chapter. This process is shown again in Exhibit 12.1. The process revolves around value-seeking activities that consumers perform as they go about satisfying needs. The consumer first realizes she has a particular need. She then moves through a series of steps that will help her find a desirable way to fill the need. Exchange then takes place, and she ultimately derives value from the process. As with other consumer behavior concepts, we see that value is at the heart of the process.

The decision-making process has been added to the exhibit. As you can see, decision-making processes generally include five activities: (1) need recognition, (2) search for information, (3) evaluation of alternatives, (4) choice, and (5) postchoice evaluation. In the current chapter, we focus on the first two stages of the process: need recognition and information search. The following chapter discusses evaluation of alternatives and choice.

To better visualize this process, consider Exhibit 12.2. Here, James is faced with a need for a new business suit as he begins interviewing for jobs. To learn about his options, he begins to

After studying this chapter, the student should be able to:

12-1 Understand the activities involved in the consumer decision-making process.

12-2 Describe the three major decision-making research perspectives.

12-3 Explain the three major types of decision-making approaches.

12-4 Understand the importance of the consideration set in the decision-making process.

12-5 Understand the factors that influence the type and amount of search performed by consumers.

EXHIBIT 12.1

Basic Consumption Process and Decision Making

Need → Need Recognition

Want → Search for Information

Evaluation of Alternatives

Exchange ← Choice

Costs and Benefits

Reaction → Postchoice Evaluation

Value

© Cengage Learning

pay attention to ads for men's apparel and may begin doing a search on the Internet. He asks friends for their input while scanning QR codes and using visual search apps on his smartphone. After considering all of the information that he has gathered, he evaluates the alternatives that are realistically available. From there, he makes a choice and an exchange occurs. He then considers all the costs and benefits of his purchase and the overall value that he has received.

Note that the activities found in the decision-making process are not referred to as steps. The reason is that consumers do not always proceed through the activities in sequential fashion, nor do they always complete the process. Because consumers face numerous decision-making situations daily, they often decide to simply defer a decision until a later time.

Consumers can also uncover additional problems or unmet needs as they search for information—moving them from information search to need recognition.

12-1a Decision Making and Choice

Decision-making processes lead to consumer choice. The term *choice* is important. *Choice* does not necessarily mean identifying what brand of product to buy. In fact, one of the very first choices that consumers need to make when facing a decision is whether any purchase will be made at all.[1] Consumers commonly either delay the purchase of a product or forgo the purchase altogether.

Decision-making processes don't always involve a tangible product. And consumers make choices about behaviors not relating directly to a purchase. For example, a consumer may be trying to decide if she should volunteer at a community theater. Here, the decision involves whether time should be exchanged in return for greater involvement with the theater. Thus, consumer decision making does not always focus on the purchase of a tangible product, but always involves choices linked to value.

Decision Making and Value

Both utilitarian value and hedonic value are associated with consumer decision making. As we have discussed

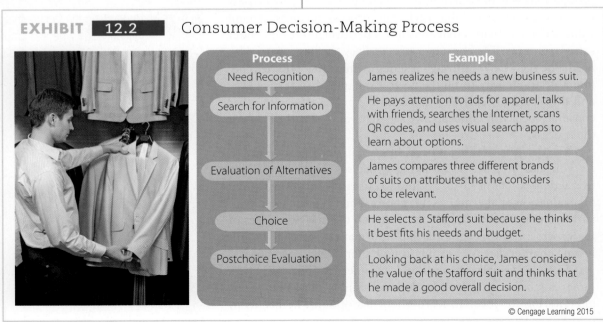

EXHIBIT 12.2 Consumer Decision-Making Process

Process	Example
Need Recognition	James realizes he needs a new business suit.
Search for Information	He pays attention to ads for apparel, talks with friends, searches the Internet, scans QR codes, and uses visual search apps to learn about options.
Evaluation of Alternatives	James compares three different brands of suits on attributes that he considers to be relevant.
Choice	He selects a Stafford suit because he thinks it best fits his needs and budget.
Postchoice Evaluation	Looking back at his choice, James considers the value of the Stafford suit and thinks that he made a good overall decision.

Dmitry Kalinovsky/Shutterstock.com

© Cengage Learning 2015

previously, the car-buying experience involves both value types. First, a car is in itself a means to an end. That is, owning cars enables consumers to transport themselves from place to place. As such, an automobile delivers utilitarian value. Second, much of the car-buying (and car-owning) experience is based on hedonic value. The image associated with a particular model of car and the feelings that go with sporty handling or comfort are hedonic benefits. Many other consumption activities also provide both hedonic value and utilitarian value. For example, a $5,000 Gibson Les Paul guitar may provide the same utilitarian value as a $300 Squire Stratocaster guitar. However, guitarists will recognize that the hedonic value of each would differ based on the feelings involved with consumption.

Value perceptions also influence the activities found in the decision-making process itself. For example, consumers generally continue searching for information about products only as long as the perceived benefits that come from searching exceed the perceived costs associated with the process. In today's smartphone world, it is easier than ever to obtain information very quickly and easily, thereby making it beneficial for consumers to extend the search process. QR codes, visual search, and augmented reality applications have made search much easier.

Decision Making and Motivation

As discussed in the motivation chapter, motivations are the inner reasons or driving forces behind human actions as consumers are driven to address needs. It isn't surprising, therefore, that decision making and motivation are closely related concepts.[2] For example, a student may notice that the ink in his printer is low and perceive a need to fix the problem (a utilitarian motivation). Or the same student may be bored on a Saturday afternoon and decide to go longboarding (a hedonic motivation). The relationship between decision making and motivation is well-known, and almost all consumer decisions revolve around goal pursuit.[3]

Decision Making and Emotion

Consumer decision making is also closely related to emotion. Quite frankly, some decisions can be very emotional and exhausting. Because the decision-making process can be draining, consumers frequently have feelings of frustration, irritation, or even anger as they attempt to satisfy needs. This is especially true when consumers must make difficult decisions, cannot find acceptable solutions to problems, or must make trade-offs by giving up one alternative for another.[4] As a college student, you may soon face the difficult task of deciding which job offer to take. Perhaps there will be a job offer many miles away, or one that is closer to your family. Decisions like these can be quite emotional.

⌈Codes, visual search, and augmented reality apps have made search much easier.⌋

12-2 Decision-Making Perspectives

Consumer researchers view the decision-making process from three perspectives: the rational decision-making perspective, the experiential decision-making perspective, and the behavioral influence decision-making perspective.[5] These perspectives are similar to the attitude hierarchies that we discussed in the attitude chapter.

It is important to remember two important aspects of these perspectives. First, each perspective serves as a theoretical framework from which decision making can be viewed. That is, the perspectives pertain to how consumer researchers view the decision-making process, and they are not consumer decision-making approaches. Second, most consumer decisions can be analyzed from a combination of these perspectives. The perspectives are presented in Exhibit 12.3.

Advances in technology affect information search.

© rangizzz/Shutterstock.com

rational decision-making perspective
assumes consumers diligently gather information about purchases, carefully compare various brands of products on salient attributes, and make informed decisions regarding what brand to buy

experiential decision-making perspective
assumes consumers often make purchases and reach decisions based on the affect, or feeling, attached to the product or behavior under consideration

behavioral influence decision-making perspective assumes many consumer decisions are actually learned responses to environmental influences

12-2a Rational Decision-Making Perspective

In the early days of consumer research, researchers focused on what is referred to as the rational decision-making perspective. This perspective is considered by many to be the traditional approach to studying decision making. The **rational decision-making perspective** assumes that consumers diligently gather information about purchases, carefully compare various brands of products on salient attributes, and make informed decisions regarding what brand to buy. This approach centers on the assumption that human beings are rational creatures who carefully consider their decisions and that they can identify the expected value associated with a purchase. The act of selecting a cell-phone plan often follows a rational process. Consumers compare service, features, and prices carefully when making these purchases. The rational perspective fits well within the concept of utilitarian value.

A problem with this perspective is that we cannot assume that consumers are always rational, nor do they always follow a well-planned decision-making process. In fact, consumers often make purchases and satisfy needs with very little cognitive effort or rationality. We simply don't want to think extensively about every single product choice that we make. Nor could we!

The assumption that consumers are rational is debatable. Of course, what is rational to some may be irrational to others. Paying over $1,000 for enjoying a wine-tasting event may seem irrational to many consumers, but some people do it regularly. Although researchers focused on the rational perspective for several years, the experiential and behavioral influence perspectives have recently gained significant attention.

12-2b Experiential Decision-Making Perspective

The **experiential decision-making perspective** assumes that consumers often make purchases and reach decisions based on the affect, or feeling, attached to the product or behavior under consideration. Recall from the discussion in our attitude chapter that consumers sometimes follow an "affect-behavior-cognition" hierarchy. That is, behaviors are based largely on the sheer enjoyment involved with consumption rather than on extensive cognitive effort.

Experiential decision processes often focus on hedonic value. For example, a consumer may decide to spend time at a day spa as the result of an experiential decision-making process. Here, decisions are based on feeling—not on a drawn-out decision-making process. That is, the value comes from the experience, not from an end result.

12-2c Behavioral Influence Decision-Making Perspective

The **behavioral influence decision-making perspective** assumes that many decisions are learned responses to environmental influences. For example, soft music and dim lighting can have a strong influence on consumer behavior in a restaurant. These influences generally lead consumers to slow down, stay in the restaurant for a longer time, and buy more drinks and dessert. This perspective follows the behavioral learning concept that was discussed in a previous chapter.

EXHIBIT 12.3 Perspectives on Consumer Decision Making

Perspective	Description	Example
Rational Perspective	Consumers are rational and they carefully arrive at decisions.	Valarie considers the various features of a new dishwasher.
Experiential Perspective	Decision making is often influenced by the feelings associated with consumption.	Riley goes longboarding just for the fun of it.
Behavioral Influence Perspective	Decisions are responses to environmental influences.	A product display leads Karissa to buy a snack.

© Cengage Learning

Product displays impact consumer behavior.

The behavioral influence perspective also helps to explain how consumers react to store layout, store design, and POP (point-of-purchase) displays. Traffic flows in a grocery store greatly influence grocery shopping behavior. In fact, consumers often buy products that are placed on display simply because they are on display! Retailers use the "brand-lift index" to measure the incremental sales that occur when a product is on display. Lift indices can be impressive. In fact, one study indicated that POP displays in convenience stores can increase product sales by nearly 10%. This is a sizable amount. Considering that incremental sales opportunities for POP materials in grocery stores can be in the billions of dollars, retailers should pay close attention to the behavioral influence perspective![6]

12-3 Decision-Making Approaches

Consumers reach decisions in a number of different ways. The decision-making approach that is used depends heavily on the amount of involvement a consumer has with a product category or purchase and the amount of perceived risk involved with the decision. Note that involvement can be associated with the product, the purchase situation, or both. In general, as involvement and risk increase, consumers are motivated to move more carefully through the decision-making process.

You may remember from an earlier chapter that consumer involvement represents the degree of personal relevance that a consumer finds in pursuing value from a given act. **Perceived risk** refers to the perception of the negative consequences that are likely to result from a course of action and the uncertainty of which course of action is best to take. Consumers face several types of risk, including:[7]

- **Financial risk.** Risk associated with the cost of the product
- **Social risk.** Risk associated with how other consumers will view the purchase
- **Performance risk.** Risk associated with the likelihood of a product performing as expected
- **Physical risk.** Risk associated with the safety of the product and the likelihood that physical harm will result from its consumption
- **Time risk.** Risk associated with the time required to search for the product and the time necessary for the product to be serviced or maintained

Risk varies across consumers and situations. Signing a year-long apartment lease is a financially risky process for most consumers. For the very wealthy, this may not be the case at all. Some risks are hidden or not completely understood. For example, some evidence suggests that mp3 players can damage hearing, though few consumers think of this.

Decision-making approaches can be classified into three categories: extended decision making, limited decision making, and habitual (or "routine") decision making. Remember, these are approaches that consumers use, and they differ from the researcher perspectives discussed previously. Exhibit 12.4 presents these categories in the form of a continuum based on involvement and risk.

12-3a Extended Decision Making

When consumers engage in **extended decision making**, they tend to search diligently for information that will help them reach a satisfactory decision. This information can come from both internal sources (for

perceived risk perception of the negative consequences that are likely to result from a course of action and the uncertainty of which course of action is best to take

extended decision making consumers move diligently through various problem-solving activities in search of the best information that will help them reach a decision

limited decision making
consumers search very little for information and often reach decisions based largely on prior beliefs about products and their attributes

EXHIBIT 12.4 Decision-Making Approaches

Low Involvement — **High Involvement**

Habitual Decision Making | Limited Decision Making | Extended Decision Making

Low Risk — **High Risk**

© Cengage Learning

example, previous experiences) and external sources (for example, websites such as Shopping.com). Consumers carefully assimilate the information they have gathered and evaluate each alternative based on its potential to satisfy their need. This process is generally rather lengthy. Extended decision making occurs when involvement is high and when there is a significant amount of purchase risk involved with the decision. Expensive products such as houses, automobiles, and televisions are usually purchased only after an extended decision-making process has occurred.

12-3b Limited Decision Making

With **limited decision making**, consumers search very little for information and often reach decisions based on prior beliefs about products and their attributes. There is little comparison between brands. Given the time constraints that consumers often feel, this type of decision making occurs with great frequency.

Limited decision making usually occurs when there are relatively low amounts of purchase risk and product involvement. For example, a consumer may need to buy a new a roll of adhesive tape, and there may be very few attributes that are considered in the process. Perhaps the consumer will want to find a roll that is designed to be "invisible." Any brand that offers this feature would likely be selected.

Safety Risks?

Energy drinks, or "shots," have become popular in consumer culture today. Brands such as Monster, 5-Hour Energy, Red Bull, and Rockstar have gained in popularity due to successful marketing campaigns and rapid consumer adoption.

Safety concerns are also growing. A number of consumer deaths have been alleged to have occurred due to the consumption of energy drinks. And, questions have arisen regarding both caffeine content and the combination of ingredients in the products. Questions have also arisen regarding whether they are safe for consumption by vulnerable populations, such as the very young or sick.

The key issues seem to be what level of caffeine intake is safe, whether consumers understand the amount of caffeine they are consuming, what the effects of the combination of ingredients are, what role the Food and Drug Administration should take in regulating these products, and how the products should be classified. Are they "dietary

supplements"? Or, are they simply "traditional" drinks? The labeling requirements for these categories differ. Another issue is whether the deaths and adverse effects are directly related to the products.

© iStockphoto.com/Skip Odonnell

Answers to these and other questions will go a long way toward determining the future marketing and labeling requirements. Without question, energy drinks are popular even if all the risks associated with their consumption are not completely understood.

Sources: David Kroll, "What You Really Need to Know About the Safety of Five-Hour Energy Drink," *Forbes*, November 16, 2012, http://www.forbes.com/sites/davidkroll/2012/11/16/what-you-really-need-to-know-about-the-safety-of-5-hour-energy-drink/, accessed February 22, 2013; Doug Podolsky, "FDA Looking Into Safety of Energy Drinks," *Consumer Reports*, November 29, 2012, http://news.consumerreports.org/health/2012/11/fda-update-on-energy-drink-probe.html, accessed February 22, 2013; Jayne O'Donnell, "Deaths Linked to Energy Drinks Could Prompt Action," *USA Today*, October 23, 2012, http://www.usatoday.com/story/money/business/2012/10/23/monster-energy-drinks-five-deaths/1652819/, accessed February 22, 2013.

12-3c Habitual Decision Making

With **habitual decision making** (sometimes referred to as "routine" decision making), consumers generally do not seek information at all when a problem is recognized. Choice is often based on habit. Here, consumers generally have a specific brand in mind that will solve the problem, and they believe that the consumption of the product will deliver value. For example, most consumers have a favorite type of soft drink that they habitually buy when they are thirsty.

Two topics are of special importance concerning habitual decision making: *brand loyalty* and *brand inertia*. **Brand loyalty** may be defined as a deeply held commitment to rebuy a product or service regardless of situational influences that could lead to switching behavior.[8] For a consumer to truly be brand loyal, he must have a bond with the product and believe that the consumption activity delivers value. Companies often attempt to reward loyalty with rewards programs as found in frequent flier miles, hotel reward points, and credit card cash-back deals. However, in order for these tactics to be successful, consumers must ultimately value both the product and the incentives offered.[9] This leads to a key difference between loyalty and what is referred to as brand inertia. **Brand inertia** is present when a consumer simply buys a product repeatedly without any real attachment. Loyalty includes an attitudinal component that reflects a true affection for the product.[10] Strictly speaking, a consumer is not considered loyal if she simply buys the same product habitually.

Brand loyalty affects consumption value in a number of ways. First, loyalty enables consumers to reduce searching time drastically by insisting on the brand to which they are loyal. This leads to a benefit of convenience. Second, loyalty creates value for a consumer through the benefits associated with brand image. Ford trucks are well-known for their ruggedness and durability. Ford owners benefit from this image. Finally, loyalty enables consumers to enjoy the benefits that come from long-term relationships with companies. For example, a consumer might enjoy special incentives that are offered to long-time Ford purchasers.

Brand loyalty also has an impact on the value of the brand to the firm. As branding expert David Aaker asserts, consumer brand loyalty influences the value of a product to a firm because (a) it costs much less to retain current customers than to attract new ones, and (b) highly loyal customers generate predictable revenue streams.[11] As can be seen, brand loyalty has benefits for both the consumer and the marketer. Brand loyalty is discussed in more detail in a subsequent chapter.

Final Thought on Decision-Making Approaches

Consumers go through decision-making processes, but these processes do not guarantee maximum value. Consumers often make mistakes or settle for alternatives that they are unsure about. In reality, many purchases are made with little prepurchase decision effort.[12] Most purchases made daily are low-involvement purchases that do not entail significant risk. Also, consumers are not always motivated to make the "best" decision. In many situations, consumers engage in what is called **satisficing**, the practice of using decision-making shortcuts to arrive at satisfactory, rather than optimal, decisions.[13] Other consumers, like "maximizers," work to find the best solution. Research also indicates that consumer decision making may be influenced by heredity.[14] Some consumers may be predisposed genetically to arrive at some

Realimage/Alamy

habitual decision making consumers generally do not seek information at all when a problem is recognized and select a product based on habit

brand loyalty deeply held commitment to rebuy a product or service regardless of situational influences that could lead to switching behavior

brand inertia what occurs when a consumer simply buys a product repeatedly without any real attachment

satisficing practice of using decision-making shortcuts to arrive at satisfactory, rather than optimal, decisions

Reward cards can be a successful method of rewarding loyalty if consumers value both the product and the incentives offered.

actual state consumer's perceived current state

desired state perceived state for which a consumer strives

decisions. One recent study found that some decisions, including compromises, can be influenced by heredity.

12-4 Need Recognition, Internal Search, and the Consideration Set

As we have discussed, the recognition of a need leads the consumer to begin searching for information. Several important issues are relevant here.

12-4a Need Recognition

The decision-making process begins with the recognition of a need. Simply put, a need is recognized when a consumer perceives a difference between an actual state and a desired state. A consumer's **actual state** is his perceived current state, while the **desired state** is the perceived state for which the consumer strives. A consumer recognizes a need when there is a gap between these two. Note that either the actual state or the desired state can change, leading to a perceptual imbalance between the two. When the actual state begins to drop, for example when a consumer runs out of deodorant, a need is recognized. Obviously, needs like this are recognized many times each day. Importantly, however, marketers also focus on what they term *opportunity recognition*. Here, a consumer's actual state doesn't change, but her desired state changes in some significant way.

To illustrate how a desired state can be changed, consider how happy consumers once were with their cell phones—that is, before the iPhone was released. After the iPhone was introduced, the desired state for many consumers changed dramatically. Phones became much more than just phones. Apple then introduced the iPad, and now tablets are overtaking laptops in popularity!

Desired states can be affected by many factors, including reference group information, consumer novelty seeking, and cognitive thought processes.[15] As we discussed in the group influence chapter, reference groups are important sources of information for consumers and the information that is gathered from others directly affects what consumers think they should do and what types of products they think they should

buy. Desired states are also influenced by novelty. Many times consumers desire to try a new product simply because of boredom or because of a motivation to engage in variety seeking. Finally, consumers have the ability to plan their actions by anticipating future needs. For example, college graduates realize after graduation that they face the need for all types of insurance they may not have considered before, including life, health, and homeowner's insurance.

Not all needs are satisfied quickly, nor does the recognition of a need always trigger the other activities found in the decision-making process. Value is again important here. If the end goal is not highly valued, consumers may simply put off a decision. For example, a consumer may realize that the leather cushion on her couch is ripped but this does not necessarily mean that she will begin to search for information on where to buy a new couch. She may simply realize that there is a problem that eventually needs to be fixed. In fact, she may have to be reminded of this need several times before she does anything about it. Or, she may simply

WWW.SWAROVSKI.COM
PHONE: + 44 (0)1737 856 814

SWAROVSKI

Wants and needs are often confused.

decide to do nothing about it at all. From this example, we are again reminded of why we don't refer to the activities found in decision making as steps. That is, the sequential ordering of the activities is not concrete.

We should once again clarify the distinction between a want and a need. Both of these terms have been discussed in a previous chapter. As you may remember, a want is the way in which a consumer goes about addressing a need. It's quite common for marketers to be criticized for attempting to turn wants into needs. For example, a consumer may want to fulfill a need for a watch by purchasing a Michael Kors, even though a much less expensive watch would suffice.

12-4b Search Behavior

When consumers perceive a difference between an actual state (an empty gas tank) and a desired state (a full tank), the decision-making process is triggered.[16] **Consumer search behavior** refers to the behaviors that consumers engage in as they seek information that can be used to satisfy needs. Consumers seek all types of information about potential solutions to needs, including: (1) the number of alternatives available, (2) the price of various alternatives, (3) the relevant attributes that should be considered and their importance, and (4) the performance of each alternative on the attributes.[17] Consumer search behaviors can be categorized in a number of ways, including ongoing search, prepurchase search, internal search, and external search.

consumer search behavior behaviors that consumers engage in as they seek information that can be used to satisfy needs

ongoing search search effort that is not necessarily focused on an upcoming purchase or decision but rather on staying up to date on the topic

prepurchase search search effort aimed at finding information to solve an immediate problem

Ongoing and Prepurchase Search

A consumer performs an **ongoing search** when she seeks information simply because she is interested in a particular topic (such as a product or an organization). Here, the search effort is not necessarily focused on an upcoming purchase or decision; rather, the effort is focused on simply staying up to date on a topic of interest. Consumers who perform ongoing searches are usually highly involved with the product category and seek information simply for enjoyment. They also tend to spend more in the relevant product category than do consumers who do not regularly search for information.[18]

Prepurchase search activities are focused on locating information that will enable the consumer to reach

"Give Me Shelter"

Many problems that consumers face are routine. We run out of milk or gasoline. But sometimes, our problems can be unexpected and very serious. Researchers refer to unforeseen needs as "unanticipated needs."

The last few years have brought about a number of severe weather incidents around the world and tornado outbreaks in the United States have been particularly deadly. The storm shelter industry has been greatly impacted. The monster tornadoes that recently struck Tuscaloosa, Joplin, and Moore, Oklahoma, have greatly increased the demand for shelters in recent years. Shelters of all types, including both underground and above-ground models, are in high demand throughout the U.S. heartland.

Sometimes the perception of a need is greater than the real need. Nevertheless, the demand for shelters is likely to grow as consumers witness the

horrors that tornadoes bring. The need for safety and security is a critical part of Maslow's Hierarchy of Needs and the storm shelter industry works hard to meet this need. Taking shelter from the storm is definitely serious business.

Sources: Sheila Stogsdill, "High Demand for Storm Shelters Mean the Wait Is Long," *Tulsa World*, October 28, 2011, http://www.tulsaworld.com/news/article.aspx?subjectid=11&articleid=20110528_19_A10_CUTLIN111108 (accessed April 25, 2012); Brian Richardson, "Storm Shelters in High Demand Following Joplin Tornado," Ozarksfirst, June 6, 2011, http://ozarksfirst.com/fulltext?nxd_id=467967 (accessed April 25, 2012); Meghan McCormick, "Demand Is Up for Storm Shelters," *The Norman Transcript*, May 10, 2011, http://normantranscript.com/x74960437/Demand-is-up-for-storm-shelters (accessed April 25, 2012).

information overload
situation in which consumers are presented with so much information that they cannot assimilate the variety of information presented

internal search retrieval of knowledge stored in memory about products, services, and experiences

consideration set alternatives that are considered acceptable for further consideration in decision making

universal set total collection of all possible solutions to a consumer problem

awareness set set of alternatives of which a consumer is aware

a decision for a specific problem. These searches are purchase-specific. Prepurchase search can also be exhibited in browsing behavior. When consumers browse, they are simply gathering information that can be used in decisions that involve a longer time frame. Note that browsing and ongoing searches are similar. The difference between ongoing searches and browsing behavior is that an ongoing search is performed when consumers have an enduring interest or involvement with the product, not simply when information is being gathered for a specific purchase.

The concept of information search has changed dramatically in recent years due to the mass adoption of the Internet as well as the proliferation of mobile information technologies like cell phones and personal data assistants. In today's environment, finding information generally isn't a problem. The problem is that there is simply too much information out there! Information overload is an important research topic.[19] **Information overload** refers to the situation in which consumers are presented with so much information that they cannot assimilate it all. The search engine Bing humorously devised an advertising campaign aimed at highlighting the downside of what they term "search overload." The campaign targeted Google as presenting too much information in an unfiltered way.

One way that consumers can try to minimize information overload in the online environment is by joining a specific group for a product or brand on a site like Facebook. By focusing specifically on a group or fan page, consumers are able to look for relevant information in one place and can gain a sense of what other posters they can and cannot trust for information. Information search on social network sites can be either ongoing or prepurchase.

12-4c The Consideration Set

Internal search includes the retrieval of knowledge about products, services, and experiences that is stored in memory. This type of knowledge is related directly

AP Photos/PRNewsFoto/Kraft Foods

Consumers are able to learn about new developments with products by following them online.

to consumers' experiences with products and services. When confronted with a need, consumers begin to scan their memories for available solutions to the problem that can aid in decision making. As such, consumers most often perform internal searches before any other type of search begins.

Marketers find it valuable to understand the **consideration set** of their customers in order to learn about the total number of brands, or alternatives, that are considered in consumer decision making.[20] The conceptualization of a consideration set is presented in Exhibit 12.5.

The total collection of all possible solutions to a recognized need (for example, the total number of brands of deodorant available on the market) is referred to as the **universal set** of alternatives. Although the universal set may be quite large, consumers generally do not realize how many solutions are potentially available when a need arises. In fact, decision making is limited by what is referred to as the awareness set. The **awareness set** includes, quite simply, the set of brands or alternatives of which a consumer is aware. Alternatives that have been previously selected are included in this set and the size of the awareness set increases as external search proceeds.[21]

Within the awareness set, three categories of alternatives are found. The first is the consideration set (or the "evoked set"). The consideration set includes the brands or alternatives that are considered acceptable for further consideration in decision making. There are

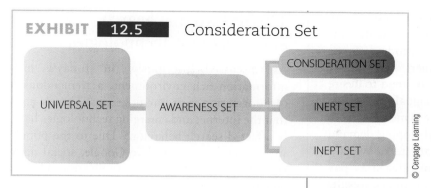

EXHIBIT 12.5 Consideration Set

CONSIDERATION SET

INERT SET

INEPT SET

UNIVERSAL SET

AWARENESS SET

© Cengage Learning

inept set alternatives in the awareness set that are deemed to be unacceptable for further consideration

inert set alternatives in the awareness set about which consumers are indifferent or do not hold strong feelings

external search gathering of information from sources external to the consumer such as friends, family, salespeople, advertising, independent research reports, and the Internet

price information that signals the amount of potential value contained in a product

also alternatives in the awareness set that are deemed to be unacceptable for further consideration. These alternatives comprise the **inept set**. The **inert set** includes those alternatives to which consumers are indifferent, or for which strong feelings are not held.

Exhibit 12.5 demonstrates how the size of both the awareness set and the consideration set is smaller than the universal set—a situation typical for most decisions. Research confirms that consumers generally consider only a small fraction of the actual number of problem solutions that are available.[22] Note that although the consideration set is held internally in a consumer's memory, alternatives that are found in external search can be added to the set as the decision-making process continues. As such, the consideration set plays an important role in advertising effectiveness.[23]

12-5 External Search

Frequently, consumers don't have enough information stored in memory that will enable them to reach a decision. For this reason, external search efforts are often necessary. **External search** includes the gathering of information from sources external to the consumer, including friends, family, salespeople, advertising, independent research reports (such as *Consumer Reports*), the Internet, and smartphone technologies. In selecting the best information source, consumers consider factors such as:

- The ease of obtaining information from the source
- The objectivity of the source
- The trustworthiness of the source
- The speed with which the information can be obtained

In general, consumers find that information from family and friends is dependable but that information from commercial sources (like advertising or salespeople) is less credible for input into decision making.[24]

Personal factors like self-esteem play a role, however. Research indicates that consumers with low self-esteem tend to favor impersonal sources of information such as media advertising and the Internet.[25]

12-5a The Role of Price and Quality in the Search Process

The term *evaluative criteria* is used to refer to the product attributes that consumers consider when reviewing possible solutions to a problem. Many things can become evaluative criteria. However, two evaluative criteria are used across almost all consumer decisions: price and quality. Consumers turn to price and quality very quickly as they consider most products.

Price represents an important type of information that consumers generally seek. But what is a price? A price is really a piece of information. More specifically, price is information signaling how much potential value may be derived from consuming something. In this sense, price is like the physical concept of potential energy.

Generally, we think of a high price as being a bad thing. In other words, a higher price means greater sacrifice to obtain some product. This view of price is referred to as the negative role of price. From this view, needless to say, a lower price is more desirable. Some consumers are very sensitive to the negative role of price. They tend to be very bargain conscious and do things like collect and redeem coupons.

However, a positive role for price also exists. In this sense, price signals how desirable a product is and

⌐A positive role for price exists. In this sense, price signals how desirable a product is.⌐

quality perceived overall goodness or badness of some product

how much prestige may be associated with owning the product. Some consumers are more sensitive to the positive role of price and tend to desire things with high prices as a way of signaling prestige and desirability to others.[26] You may remember from an earlier discussion that a backward sloping demand curve is not necessarily rare. Some marketers have taken this finding to a new level and introduced a "pay what you want" strategy for certain products. Results have revealed that many consumers are quite happy to pay a higher price for products they think are of good quality and also as a means of feeling good about themselves.[27]

Consider a consumer shopping for a new outfit to wear during an evening on the town. She may find a cute outfit at Target, but this outfit may not offer enough value given that it will be worn in a socially sensitive situation. Therefore, she may opt for a higher-priced outfit that may be somewhat similar. The higher price will signal more prestige. Thus, she may feel more comfortable shopping at Chico's or some other more prestigious fashion retailer.

Consumers also commonly search for information about a product's quality. Consumers nearly always consider quality an important evaluative criterion. Although quality can mean many things to many people, from a consumer perspective, **quality** represents the perceived overall goodness or badness of some product. In other words, consumers generally use the word *quality* as a synonym for relative goodness. A high-quality hotel room is a good hotel room; a low-quality hotel room is a bad one.

Quality perceptions take place both before and after purchase. However, consumers do not always seek high quality, because many times consumers do not need the "best" product available. Although Holiday Inn Express may not offer as high quality an experience as does a Hyatt Regency hotel, it does adequately address the need for a place to sleep on a cross-country drive.

Consumers almost always use price and quality when making decisions. Indeed, price and quality perceptions are related, as consumers generally assume that higher prices mean higher quality. This relationship is altered, however, by other variables. For example, when consumers view a purchase as coming in the distant future they tend to view price as a stronger indicator of quality (the positive role of price). When the purchase is imminent, however, they tend to view price as more of a monetary sacrifice (the negative role of price).[28]

12-5b External Search and Emerging Technologies

As discussed previously, in today's fast-paced, information-rich environment, a tremendous amount of information is at our fingertips. There's no denying that the Internet and emerging technologies have quickly affected search behavior.[29] Due to the popularity of various search engines like Google, social networking sites like Facebook, and new applications like QR codes and augmented reality, consumers can find solutions to all sorts of problems at their fingertips.

The Internet has improved search activities in several ways. First, it lower the costs associated with search and can make the process more productive.[30] Second, the search process itself can be enjoyable and deliver hedonic value to the consumer. This is especially the case for younger versus older consumers.[31] Third, consumers have the ability to control information flow much more efficiently than if they are viewing product information on a television commercial. The ability to control information flow increases the value of information and increases the consumers' ability to remember information that is gathered.[32] Of course, consumers may also buy products online. This greatly impacts the ease of consumer online shopping behavior.

Website construction is important. One study found that consumers spend more time searching in three-dimensional interactive web environments than in two-dimensional web spaces. However, the study also revealed that the number of brands examined was actually higher for two-dimensional web pages than for three-dimensional sites.[33] Consumers can become so immersed in virtual worlds that they neglect to consider brand information. Consumers will continue to use the Internet for search activities as computer availability becomes more widespread.

12-5c Consumer Search and Smartphone Applications

Students will quickly recognize that the Internet is not the only place to find information today. Smartphone capabilities have greatly impacted search. Recall that one criterion that consumers consider when searching for information is the ease of obtaining information from the source. Smartphone applications (apps) have made it easier for consumers to search for information from practically any location, and they have played a major role in the advent of mobile commerce. Although new technologies are introduced daily, the following four advancements apply very well to smartphone apps and mobile commerce. These technologies have also contributed to the growing use of the phrase *consumer discovery*, which describes how consumers are constantly discovering new information about products, services, experiences, and locations. [34]

QR Codes. QR codes *(quick response codes)* have dramatically changed information availability. With a QR code reader, consumers can easily gain access to all types of product-related information. Many marketers view QR codes as an essential part of marketing strategy whereby *promotional conversion rates* (that is, the rate at which a promotion is transitioned into a sale) are greatly improved. Essentially, technologies such as these allow consumers to move beyond simple text search in a search engine like Google to a whole new realm of information availability.

Augmented Reality. A number of apps are currently available that bring the physical and virtual worlds together in new and exciting ways. Augmented reality apps do simply that—they *augment* reality with computer simulated information. Apps such as *Blippar*, *Aurasma*, *Wikitude*, and *Layar* create entirely new interactive experiences for the consumer. Other apps, such as *Snapshot Showroom*, allow consumers to visualize how products purchased will look in their homes.

Visual Search. Visual search allows consumers to simply take a photo of an object or scan it into their screen and quickly receive information about it. *Google Goggles* is one product that enables consumers to perform visual search without having to enter text into a search engine. Not only does this make it easier for consumers to gain information, it also makes the process faster.

GPS-Based Technologies. Other search technologies combine elements of GPS capabilities with consumer needs. Apps like *Airyell*, *Around Me*, and *iWant* allow consumers to find information about nearby points of interest like restaurants, gas stations, hospitals, and parks. These apps allow consumers to quickly address specific needs that they have while they are traveling.

It is easy to see how these technologies have affected consumer search processes. In fact, some might argue that the terms *search* and *discovery* don't clearly describe what these technologies enable the consumer to do. Rather, the search and discovery processes really become branded consumer experiences. The experience enables the consumer to learn about the product, interact with it, and begin to forge relationships with it.

12-5d Amount of Search

The amount of search that a consumer performs related to decision making can be measured in a number of ways, including the number of stores visited, the number of websites visited, the number of personal sources (friends, family, salespeople) used, the number of alternatives considered, and the number of advertisements studied.

Many factors influence information search effort, including previous experience with a product, involvement, perceived risk, value of search effort, time availability, attitudes toward shopping, personal factors, and situational influencers. [35]

Product Experience. Prior experience with a product has been shown to influence how much a consumer searches. A number of researchers have examined this issue, sometimes with conflicting results. As a general statement, evidence shows that moderately experienced consumers search for purchase-related information more than do either experienced or inexperienced consumers. This finding is shown in Exhibit 12.6. [36]

One explanation for the finding that moderately experienced consumers search more than other consumers is that individuals with little experience are unable to make fine distinctions between product differences and will likely see product alternatives as being similar. As such, they find little value in extensive information search. Highly experienced consumers can make fine distinctions between products and may know so much about products that they do not need to search at all. Moderately

© iStockphoto.com/Stephen Krow

GPS technologies have greatly impacted CB.

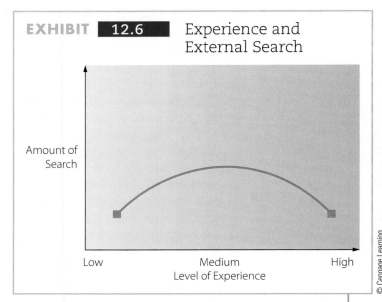

EXHIBIT 12.6 Experience and External Search

Amount of Search

Low | Medium | High
Level of Experience

© Cengage Learning

experienced consumers, on the other hand, perceive some differences among brands and are more likely to value information about these distinctions.[37]

Involvement. As noted earlier, purchase involvement is positively associated with search activities, especially for ongoing searches. Because involvement represents a level of arousal and interest in a product, search tends to increase when a consumer possesses a high level of purchase involvement.[38]

Perceived Risk. As perceived risk increases, search effort increases.[39] As discussed earlier in the chapter, a number of risks can be associated with the consumption act, including financial, social, performance, physical, and time risks. Consumers are usually motivated to reduce these risks as much as possible and will therefore expend considerable time and effort in searching for information.

Value of Search Effort. Value can be obtained from the search process itself. When the benefits received from searching exceed the associated costs, consumers derive value. When searching costs are greater than the benefits of the search process, consumers no longer value the activity and search stops.[40] Costs associated with search can be either monetary (for example, the cost of driving around town looking for a new bedroom dresser) or nonmonetary (for example, psychological or physical exhaustion or stress). Even online searching brings about certain mental costs.[41] As we have discussed, mobile technologies have increased the ease of search activities.

Time Availability. All other things being equal, more time to spend on search usually results in increased search activity.[42] Because time is valued so highly by most consumers, search will decrease when time constraints are present.

Pay to Play

One controversial method for introducing new products to consumers requires marketers to pay retailers what are known as "slotting allowances" or "slotting fees." Slotting allowances are sums of money that are paid by a vendor to a retailer for specific locations or shelf placement in a store. These fees are often required for new products and can play a big role in the success of these products.

One advantage of slotting allowances is that they help to balance the risk of introducing new products between both vendors and retailers. They also signal how valuable a new product is for a vendor. Vendors often have better information about the likely success of a new product than do retailers.

© Elnur/Shutterstock.com

Accordingly, the amount paid by a vendor can be a signal of the attractiveness of the product.

Critics often charge that these allowances represent a type of extortion on the part of retailers. Retailers, on the other hand, recognize the value of prime retail location in supporting product success. While these allowances are generally legal, they can violate anti-trust laws. Regardless of the views of vendors or retailers, consumers are often unaware that slotting fees may have been paid in an effort to introduce new products. New products enter the consumer's consideration set . . . at a cost!

Sources: Adapted from K. Sudhir and V. Rao, "Do Slotting Allowances Enhance Efficiency or Hinder Competition?" *Journal of Marketing Research* 43 (May 2006): 137–55; R. W. Davis, "Slotting Allowances and Antitrust," *Antitrust* 15 (2), Spring, 69–76; "Slotting Allowances—A Good Thing," *Chain Store Age* (May 2005): 43.

252 PART 4: SITUATIONS AND DECISION MAKING

Attitude toward Shopping. Consumers who value shopping and who possess positive attitudes toward shopping generally spend more time searching for product information.[43]

Personal Factors. Search tends to increase as a consumer's level of education and income increases. Search also tends to decrease as consumers become older.[44]

Situational Influencers. Situational factors also influence the amount of search that takes place. Perceived urgency, financial pressure, and mood can all impact search behavior. The purchase occasion can also affect the search. Consumers sometimes have such an urgent need for a product that they will select the first option they come across. When a product is being purchased as a gift, the amount of search will depend on the relationship between the giver and the receiver and on the amount of time before the occasion.

External Search Often Minimized

While many factors influence the amount of search that takes place, consumers tend to search surprisingly little for most products.[45] This is true for both high- and low-involvement products. Consumers may already have a stored rule in memory for low-involvement products and may engage in extensive ongoing search activities and have acceptable alternative solutions in mind for high-involvement categories.[46]

12-5e Search Regret

As we have discussed, emotions and decision making are closely related topics. The search process can lead directly to emotional responses for consumers as well. The term **search regret** refers to the negative emotions that come from failed search processes. Many times, consumers are simply not able to find an acceptable solution to their problems. As a result, the decision-making process stops. In these situations, consumers may feel as if the entire search process was a waste of time, and they will start to feel search regret. Regret is related to the amount of search effort, the emotions felt during the process, and the use of unfamiliar search techniques.[47] Regret is more likely to be experienced when consumers exert much energy, experience more emotion, and utilize unfamiliar techniques during the search process.

Many issues relate to the topics of need recognition and search. Our next chapter discusses evaluation of alternatives and choice.

search regret negative emotions that come from failed search processes

Study Tools

Located at back of the textbook

- ❏ Rip out Chapter in Review card

Located at www.cengagebrain.com

- ❏ Review Key Terms Flashcards (print or online)
- ❏ Download audio summaries to review on the go
- ❏ Complete practice quizzes to prepare for tests
- ❏ Play "Beat the Clock" to master concepts
- ❏ Watch video on Scholfield Honda for a real company example

study tools

WHAT DO YOU THINK?
WHAT OTHERS HAVE THOUGHT

① ② ③ ④ ⑤ ⑥ ⑦

50 45 40 35 30 25 20 15 10 5 0

Strongly disagree | Disagree | Somewhat disagree | Neither agree nor disagree | Somewhat agree | Agree | Strongly agree

Most of the time I am a rational decision maker.

We can see that most students claim to be rational decision makers. A strong majority of students have indicated at least some level of agreement with our survey question. There's a pretty good chance that this doesn't apply to all purchases, however. We can all be a bit irrational some of the time!

Kraig Scarbinsky/Riser/Getty Images

Marketers often
promote both utilitarian and hedonic potential
of a product.

WHAT DO YOU THINK?
**Getting a hair style for under $10 is a
very good thing.**

STRONGLY DISAGREE   STRONGLY AGREE

VISIT COURSEMATE AT WWW.CENGAGEBRAIN.COM

Decision Making II: Alternative Evaluation and Choice

Selecting a new apartment is obviously a big decision. There are many issues to consider. Which location is best? How much is rent? Is the complex safe? Does the apartment allow pets? Making a final decision can be draining. Thankfully, not every decision we face is this difficult.

As you will remember from the first decision-making chapter, the decision-making process includes need recognition, search for information, alternative evaluation, choice, and postchoice evaluation. The decision-making model is shown once again in Exhibit 13.1.

After studying this chapter, the student should be able to:

13-1 Understand the difference between evaluative criteria and determinant criteria.

13-2 Comprehend how value affects the evaluation of alternatives.

13-3 Explain the importance of product categorization in the evaluation of alternatives process.

13-4 Distinguish between compensatory and noncompensatory rules that guide consumer choice.

EXHIBIT 13.1 Consumer Decision-Making Process

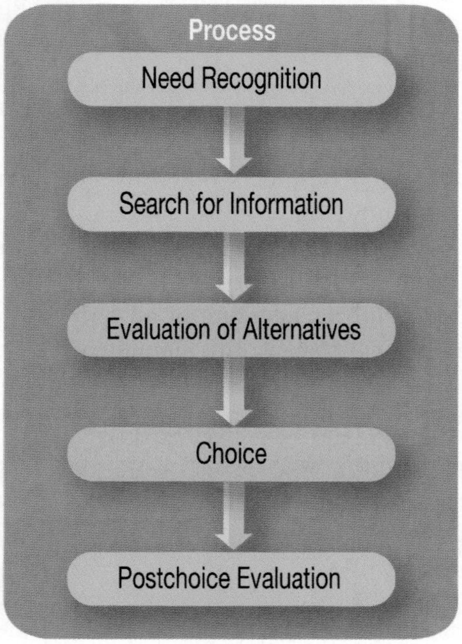

Process
- Need Recognition
- Search for Information
- Evaluation of Alternatives
- Choice
- Postchoice Evaluation

© Cengage Learning

evaluative criteria
attributes that consumers consider when reviewing alternative solutions to a problem

feature performance characteristic of an object

benefit perceived favorable results derived from a particular feature

determinant criteria
criteria that are most carefully considered and directly related to the actual choice that is made

In the current chapter, we focus on evaluation of alternatives and choice.

Benefits play an important role in the value equation. Consumers don't really buy a garage door because of programmable codes. They are seeking security! If there was some other way to deliver this benefit without the feature, consumers would be quick to buy this other solution. You may remember that benefits represent "what you get" in the value equation.

$$\text{Value} = \frac{\text{What you get}}{\text{(Benefits)}} - \frac{\text{What you give}}{\text{(Costs)}}$$

13-1 Evaluation of Alternatives: Criteria

An important part of decision making is evaluating alternative solutions to problems. As we have discussed throughout this text, consumers are bombarded daily by a dizzying array of product varieties, brands, and experiences from which to choose. For example, consumers can select from dozens of varieties of athletic shoes and deodorants. Marketers sometimes refer to this situation as "hyperchoice" because so many alternatives are available. Trying to make sense out of all the alternatives can be very difficult. Fortunately, consumer researchers have learned much about how consumers evaluate alternatives. In some situations, consumers simply look for one or two attributes to consider. In other cases, they consider products across several different attributes. The first thing to understand is how consumers select criteria to differentiate one alternative from another.

13-1a Evaluative Criteria

After a need is recognized and a search process has taken place, consumers begin to examine the criteria that will be used for making a choice. **Evaluative criteria** are the attributes, features, or potential benefits that consumers consider when reviewing possible solutions to a problem. A **feature** is a performance characteristic of an object. Remember from our attitude chapter that features are often referred to as attributes. A **benefit** is a perceived favorable result that is derived from the presence of a particular feature.[1] A solar panel on a set of landscape lights is a feature. The benefit is environmental friendliness. These concepts are illustrated in Exhibit 13.2.

13-1b Determinant Criteria

Not all evaluative criteria are equally important. **Determinant criteria** (sometimes called determinant attributes) are the evaluative criteria that are related to the actual choice that is made.[2]

Sean Gallup/Getty Images News/Getty Images

Television marketers add new features regularly.

Consumers don't always reveal, or may not even know, the criteria that truly are determinant. This is true even when several attributes are considered to be important. For example, airline safety is definitely an important feature of an airline, and consumers would quickly voice this opinion. But because consumers do

EXHIBIT 13.2		Product, Feature, and Benefit
Product	**Feature**	**Benefit**
Landscape Lights	Solar Panel	Environmentally Friendly
Garage Door Opener	Programmable Code	Security
Tablet Case	Detachable Front	Ease of Use

© Cengage Learning

not perceive a difference in safety among major airlines, safety does not actually determine the airline that is eventually selected. For this reason, statistical tools are often needed to establish determinance.

Which criteria are determinant can depend largely on the situation in which a product is consumed. For example, a consumer might consider gas mileage as a determinant criterion when buying a car for himself. However, the safety of a car would likely be a determinant factor if he were buying a car for his daughter. Marketers therefore position products on the determinant criteria that apply to a specific situation.

13-2 Value and Alternative Evaluation

To understand how alternatives are evaluated and how final choices are made, we must again highlight the key role that value plays in decision making. The value that consumers believe they will receive from a product has a direct impact on their evaluation of that product. In fact, the word *evaluate* literally means to set a value or worth to an object. Remember that benefits are at the heart of the value equation, and value is a function of both benefits and costs.

13-2a Hedonic and Utilitarian Value

It should be clear that consumers seek both hedonic and utilitarian value. The criteria that consumers use when evaluating a product can also often be classified as either hedonic or utilitarian.[3] Hedonic criteria include emotional, symbolic, and subjective attributes or benefits that are associated with an alternative. For example, the prestige that one associates with owning a BMW is a hedonic criterion. These criteria are largely experiential. Utilitarian criteria pertain to functional or economic aspects associated with an alternative. For example, safety of a BMW is a utilitarian criterion.

Marketers often promote both utilitarian and hedonic potential of a product. For example, the advertisements presented in Exhibit 13.3 promote utilitarian and hedonic automobile attributes. Consumers often use both categories of criteria when evaluating alternatives and making a final choice.

Rationality, Effort, and Variety

As discussed previously, consumers are not always rational when they are evaluating and choosing from possible solutions to a problem. What's more, consumers often have limited ability to process all the information that's available in the environment. The term **bounded rationality** describes the idea that perfectly rational decisions are not always feasible due to constraints found in information processing.

Even when consumers have the ability to consider all possible solutions to a problem, they do not always do so. Quite simply, sometimes the task just isn't worth it. In fact, consumers often minimize the effort that they put into alternative evaluation and choice. As we discussed in our need recognition and information search chapter, consumers often settle for a

bounded rationality idea that consumers attempt to act rationally within their information-processing constraints

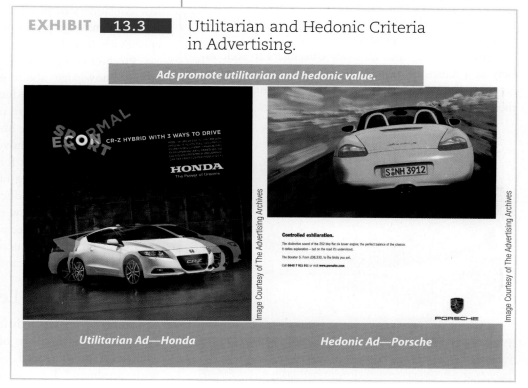

EXHIBIT 13.3 Utilitarian and Hedonic Criteria in Advertising.

Ads promote utilitarian and hedonic value.

Utilitarian Ad—Honda

Hedonic Ad—Porsche

affect-based evaluation evaluative process wherein consumers evaluate products based on the overall feeling that is evoked by the alternative

attribute-based evaluation evaluative process wherein alternatives are evaluated across a set of attributes that are considered relevant to the purchase situation

product categories mental representations of stored knowledge about groups of products

solution that is simply good enough to solve a problem. Realistically, there are just too many choices out there. In fact, even though variety is a good thing, studies indicate that too much variety actually contributes to feelings of discontent and unhappiness![4]

13-2b Affect-Based and Attribute-Based Evaluations

We can distinguish between two major types of evaluation processes: affect-based and attribute-based. With **affect-based evaluation**, consumers evaluate products based on the overall feeling that is evoked by the alternative.[5] A consumer remark like "I'm not even sure why I bought this sweater; I just liked it" reflects an affect-based process. Emotions play a big role in affect-based evaluation, as do mood states.[6]

In general, positive mood states lead to positive evaluations, while negative mood states lead to negative evaluations. Mood is also influential when limited information is found about an alternative.[7] For example, when you are in a good mood, you may evaluate a product positively even if there is not a lot of information given about the product.

Strong feelings also motivate consumers to seek variety as a means of escaping boredom. Beverage marketers like Coca-Cola and Pepsi-Cola frequently update their offerings in order to combat consumer boredom.

Stephen VanHorn/Shutterstock.com

Subway is synonymous with a sub sandwich. However, Subway now focuses on the breakfast market.

Fast food marketers continually add new products and flavors in order to combat boredom. Subway restaurants recently moved into the breakfast market. The move not only fulfills consumers' needs, but it also helps build interest and excitement towards the brand. The fast food industry knows that consumer excitement plays a key role in success.

> Mood is influential when limited information is found about an alternative.

With **attribute-based evaluation**, alternatives are evaluated across a set of attributes that are considered relevant to the purchase situation. As we have noted, the rational decision-making process assumes that consumers carefully integrate information about product attributes and make careful comparisons between products. This process illustrates attribute-based evaluation.

13-3 Product Categorization and Criteria Selection

One of the first things that a consumer does when she receives information from the environment is attempt to make sense of the information by placing it in the context of a familiar category. Existing schemas, as discussed in our comprehension chapter, allow consumers to provide meaning to objects. Within these schemas, both product categories and brand categories are found.

Product categories are mental representations of stored knowledge about groups of products. When considering a new product, consumers rely on the knowledge that they have regarding the relevant product category. Knowledge about the existing category is then transferred to the novel item. For example, when consumers view a tablet for the first time they start to compare it with existing tablets. Even if a product is very different from products that are currently available, consumers still draw on existing category knowledge to guide their expectations and attitudes toward the new product.[8] The successful launch of the iPad in recent years is a good example of this.

13-3a Category Levels

Consumers possess different levels of product categories. The number of levels and details within each level is influenced by familiarity and expertise with products.[9] For example, consumers know the

Tastes Like...Water!

If you had to choose one type of bottled water, what would it be? Drinking water? Spring water? Purified water? Do you even know the difference between these types?

There are some big problems in the bottled water industry. First, some bottled waters are mislabeled or promoted incorrectly. Some purified water is promoted as spring water. Mislabeling and misleading consumers is a serious offense, particularly given that the Food and Drug Administration regulates these products. Second, many consumers either do not know the differences between the types of water or may not even care.

Critics argue that labeling laws should be much more specific so that consumers know what they are getting. In general, drinking water is any type of water, spring water must come from some natural spring source, and purified water may come from any source as long as it has been filtered.

The bottled water industry applies well to categorization and judgment. If you can name some popular bottled water brands, do you know to which categories these brands belong? How do you assess the quality of the water? Which is better, purified water or spring water? For many consumers, bottled water is somewhat of a mystery.

Sources: Kevin McCoy, "Disputes Spring Up Over Bottled Water Sources," *USA Today,* December 13, 2013, http://www.usatoday.com/story/money/business/2012/12/13/bottled-water-sources-disputed/1768417/, accessed March 1, 2013; Nadia Atumugam, "Nestlé Sued AGAIN For Falsely Representing Bottled Tap Water As Naturally Spring-Sourced," *Forbes,* October 19, 2012, http://www.forbes.com/sites/nadiaarumugam/2012/10/19/nestle-sued-again-for-falsely-representing-bottled-tap-water-as-naturally-spring-sourced/, accessed March 1, 2013; Devin Dwyer, "Water Wars: Is Bottled Water Better Than Tap? *ABC News* (*online edition*), July 8, 2009, http://abcnews.go.com/Politics/Health/story?id=8031551&page=1, accessed March 1, 2013.

differences between snacks, breakfast, and dinner. Further distinctions can be made within any of these categories. Within the snack category, distinctions can be made between salty snacks, sweet snacks, fruits, and vegetables. Even finer distinctions can be made at yet a third level. Salty snacks may be broken down into crackers, chips, snack mix, and so on. Therefore, distinctions at basic levels are generally made across product categories (for example, snacks, breakfast foods, dinner foods). Distinctions at subsequent levels increase in specificity, ultimately to the brand and attribute level.[10] Expertise and familiarity play important roles in this process.

Superordinate and Subordinate Categories

The different levels of product categories are referred to as being either superordinate or subordinate.[11] *Superordinate categories* are abstract in nature and represent the highest level of categorization. An example of a superordinate category would be "beverages." *Subordinate categories* are more detailed. Here, the consumer examines the knowledge that

she has stored about various options. For example, a consumer would proceed through the beverage superordinate category to the subordinate categories of "colas," "sports drinks," and "juices." As a hypothetical example, assume that Sharleen visited the websites for sports drinks and found the information listed in Exhibit 13.4.

We should note that evaluations are generally more relevant and meaningful at subordinate levels.[12] For

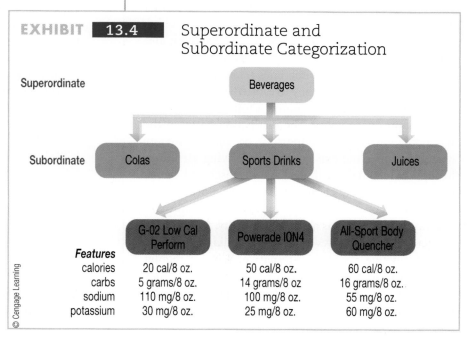

EXHIBIT 13.4 Superordinate and Subordinate Categorization

Features	G-02 Low Cal Perform	Powerade ION4	All-Sport Body Quencher
calories	20 cal/8 oz.	50 cal/8 oz.	60 cal/8 oz.
carbs	5 grams/8 oz.	14 grams/8 oz	16 grams/8 oz.
sodium	110 mg/8 oz.	100 mg/8 oz.	55 mg/8 oz.
potassium	30 mg/8 oz.	25 mg/8 oz.	60 mg/8 oz.

© Cengage Learning

perceptual attributes
attributes that are visually apparent and easily recognizable

underlying attributes
attributes that are not readily apparent and can be learned only through experience or contact with the product

signal attribute that consumers use to infer something about another attribute

example, assume that Sharleen notices specific differences in the brands at the subordinate level. Hypothetically, she may notice that G-02 has fewer calories than the other products. Or she may notice that All-Sport has less sodium than the competitors. Or she may notice that Powerade ION4 has less potassium than the others. This information would then guide her final decision for which sports drink to buy.

Recall from the memory chapter that exemplars are first thought of within any category. An exemplar for sports drinks may be G. New alternatives will be compared to exemplars first and then to other brands that are found in the brand category. For example, when Sharleen sees an advertisement for a new brand of sports drink, she will quickly move through the beverage and sports drinks categories and arrive at G and use G as the first benchmark. Other brand comparisons will then occur.

Perceptual and Underlying Attributes

When evaluating products, consumers also distinguish between perceptual and underlying attributes. **Perceptual attributes** are visually apparent and easily recognizable. Size, shape, color, and price are perceptual attributes. These attributes are sometimes referred to as search qualities because they can easily be evaluated prior to actual purchase.

Underlying attributes are not readily apparent and can only be learned through experience with the product. These attributes are sometimes referred to as experience qualities because they are often perceived only during consumption. An example of an underlying attribute is product quality. The distinction between the two types of attributes is important, because consumers most often infer the existence of underlying attributes through perceptual attributes. As we discussed in the first decision-making chapter, the price of a product often tells the consumer something about its quality. In this way, price is used as a signal of quality. A **signal** is a characteristic that allows a consumer to diagnose something distinctive about an alternative. When a retailer offers a price-matching guarantee, meaning that they will match any competitor's advertised price, they give off a signal that consumers will enjoy low prices when they shop at this particular store.

Signals such as brand name, price, appearance, and retailer reputation often convey information about product quality. This is particularly so in the following situations:

- When the consumer is trying to reduce risk
- When purchase involvement is low
- When the consumer lacks product expertise[13]

Interestingly, young and inexperienced consumers rely more heavily on perceptual attributes than do older consumers.[14]

13-3b Criteria Selection

There are a number of issues that relate to the selection of criteria that consumers use when evaluating products. What determines the type of evaluative criteria that consumers use? Are consumers accurate in their assessment of evaluative criteria? How many criteria are necessary to evaluate alternatives effectively? What if information is missing? How do marketers determine which criteria consumers use? These issues are discussed below.

What Determines the Type of Evaluative Criteria that Consumers Use?

A number of factors influence the type of criteria that consumers use when evaluating alternatives. Situational influences, product knowledge, social influences, expert opinions, online sources, and marketing communications all influence the type of criteria that are used.

1. **Situational Influences.** As discussed in the chapter on consumers in situations, situations play a big role in CB. The type of criteria that are considered depends heavily on situational influences. If a product is being purchased as a gift, the buyer may pay close attention to hedonic attributes such as the image of the product and its reputation. When a girl buys a dress for a high school prom or college formal, attributes like quality and look are important and are weighted heavily in the evaluation process. When purchasing a dress for other occasions, the consumer would likely rely more heavily on other criteria such as price and, perhaps, convenience.

2. **Product Knowledge.** As a consumer's level of knowledge increases, he is able to focus on criteria that are most important in making a selection and to discount irrelevant information.[15] A college basketball player would be able to quickly discern what information about athletic shoes is important.

3. **Expert Opinions.** Because brand experts have well-developed knowledge banks for products and services, they can be used to help others determine what types

of information to pay attention to when evaluating products. For example, a lapidary would be able to guide consumers in the types of evaluative criteria to consider when buying a diamond ring. Market mavens are also trusted sources who can guide consumers in focusing on various product attributes.

4. **Social Influences.** Friends, family members, and reference groups also have an impact on the type of criteria that are used for decision making. This is especially true for socially visible products like automobiles or clothing.[16] Friends and families are considered to be trustworthy sources of information, and guidance that they give as to what type of attributes to consider is usually closely followed.

5. **Online Sources.** Numerous websites can assist consumers with information on product attributes and brand differences. ConsumerReports.com explains what types of criteria to consider when buying products. Popular retail sites like Staples.com also explain what attributes consumers should consider.

6. **Marketing Communications.** Marketers assist consumers in deciding what features to consider when buying a particular product. They generally promote the attributes that their products excel on and attempt to convince consumers that these are the most important. For example, Hallmark Cards tells consumers to choose their cards when they "care enough to send the very best."

judgments mental assessments of the presence of attributes and the consequences associated with those attributes

Are Consumers Accurate in Their Assessment of Evaluative Criteria?

The accuracy of a consumer's evaluation depends heavily on the quality of judgments that they make. **Judgments** are mental assessments of the presence of attributes and the benefits associated with those attributes. Consumer judgments are affected by the amount of knowledge or experience a consumer has with a particular object. During the evaluation process, consumers make judgments about the following:

- **Presence of features.** Does this car stereo store music?
- **Feature levels.** How many songs does it store?
- **Benefits associated with features.** I won't have to carry my mp3 player or CDs with me.
- **Value associated with the benefit.** Both utilitarian and hedonic value are derived.
- **How objects differ from each other.** The other stereos don't offer this attribute.

This Looks Good!

You've heard it many times before: "Eat your fruits and vegetables!" This is an old saying that has withstood the test of time because fruits and vegetables are definitely good for you. Unfortunately, relatively few people consume the recommended servings of these foods.

But, how do you choose the best fruit or vegetable if you don't know about their nutrition content? One way is to look at their color. You may know that green bananas taste tart. But what do colors signal about nutrition? In general, dark-colored fruits and vegetables are full of healthy nutrients. Specific colors matter too. For example, research shows that red fruits and vegetables may help reduce the risk of several cancers, blue fruits may reduce the risk of stroke and heart disease, white vegetables may help lower cholesterol and blood pressure, and orange fruits are a good source of beta carotene, which

has also been linked to decreased risk of cardiovascular disease and certain cancers. The good news is that you may just need to look for brightly colored fruits and vegetables, because these options are usually full of healthy nutrients.

When it comes to fruits and vegetables, what you see (perceptual attribute) tells you something about what you don't see (underlying attribute). So, maybe we should add the saying: "Study your CB!"

Sources: Heike Wersching, "An Apple a Day Keeps Stroke Away?" *Stroke: Journal of the American Heart Association* 42: 3001-3002; Brady Williams, "What Health Benefits Do Colorful Fruits and Vegetables Provide?" Livestrong.com, November 22, 2010, http://www.livestrong.com/article/315111-what-health-benefits-do-colorful-fruits-and-vegetables-provide/, accessed March 1, 2013; D. Heber, "Vegetables, Fruits and Phytoestrogens in the Prevention of Diseases," *Journal of Postgraduate Medicine* 50 no. 2 (2004): 145–49.

attribute correlation
perceived relationship between
product features

There are several issues that affect consumer judgments. We review a few of these issues here.

1. **Just Noticeable Difference.** The ability of consumers to make accurate judgments when evaluating alternatives is influenced by their ability to perceive differences in levels of stimuli between two options. As was discussed in our perception chapter, the just noticeable difference (JND) represents how much stronger one stimulus must be compared to another if someone is to notice that the two are not the same. For example, when judging picture quality on a HDTV, a consumer may not be able to discern the difference between refresh rates of 120 Hz and 240 Hz. In fact, most consumers can't see the difference. If consumers cannot tell the difference, then their judgments about the products may not be accurate.

Sometimes, the same manufacturer offers different brands or models that are very similar to each other. The term *branded variants* is used to describe the practice of offering essentially identical products with different model numbers or names.[17] Even if differences are perceived, the differences might not be very meaningful.

The impact of the JND on consumer judgments applies to how consumers react to counterfeit products. Some counterfeits are so much like the original that consumers simply can't perceive the difference. This is, of course, a bad situation for marketers of the original.

2. **Attribute Correlation.** Consumers often make judgments about features based on their perceived

Personality traits also affect consumer judgments.

Dmitry Kalinovsky/Shutterstock.com

relationship with other features. For example, earlier we stated that price is often used as a signal for quality. Here, consumers rely on **attribute correlation** to describe the perceived relationship between attributes of products.[18] Recall from the discussion of consumer search that price and quality are often assumed to be positively correlated. That is, when a product has a high price, consumers often assume it will be high quality.

Attributes can also be negatively correlated. For example, if a consumer's wait time at a bank is long, he might think that the bank offers poor service. Here, the consumer assumes that as wait time goes up, service quality goes down (hence, a negative correlation). This can be a faulty assumption because a long wait time may simply mean that consumers get individualized attention and really good service. Some things are worth waiting for. In fact, perceived quality, purchase intentions, and customer satisfaction can even be improved by making consumers wait![19]

3. **Quality Perceptions.** Marketers have long realized that consumer perception is critical to marketing success. As we have discussed, perceptions are not always in line with reality. One issue that pertains to consumer judgments is the difference between objective quality and perceived quality. *Objective quality* refers to the actual quality of a product that can be assessed through industry specification or expert rating. For example, a cell phone provider may advertise that its service has been proven to have the fewest dropped calls in the industry. *Perceived quality* is based on consumer perceptions. Even if the cell phone has objectively been shown to have the best coverage in the industry, consumers may still perceive poor quality if the coverage in their immediate area is not good.

Companies spend a great deal of time and money on improving the objective quality of their products. These efforts are limited, however, by consumer perceptions of quality. In fact, a recent study revealed that improvements in objective quality may take as many as six years to be fully recognized by consumers![20] You may remember from our discussion in the comprehension chapter that consumers act on declarative knowledge even if the knowledge is incorrect. The Ford Motor Company has been successful with its "Swap Your Ride" promotion, which allows consumers to directly experience the quality of its products, influencing their perceptions.[21]

4. **Brand Name Associations.** Brand names also have an impact on consumer judgments. Much like price, brand names can be used as signals of quality.

In fact, studies have found that brand names are even stronger signals of quality than is price.[22] For example, Energizer batteries are assumed to last a long time and Gillette razors are believed to be the best a man can get.

Unusual product names also influence consumer judgments. Marketers therefore pay close attention to the names they place on their products. This is true across consumer product industries. Chewing gum brands are known for being very descriptive and sometimes humorous. Names like "Double Bubble," "CinnaBurst," and "Extra" tell consumers what to expect from the products. Research indicates that unexpected and novel names can lead to increased product preference and choice.[23]

5. **Consumer Personality.** Personality traits also affect consumer judgments. Highly impulsive consumers often make poor judgments, while consumers with a high need for cognition can overthink their decisions and sometimes regret the judgments that they've made. High self-monitors can also ruminate on their judgments by focusing too intensely on the consequences associated with various attributes.

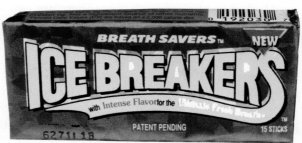
© iStockphoto.com/camilla wisbauer/evemilla

How Many Criteria Are Necessary to Evaluate Alternatives Effectively?

As we have discussed, too many alternatives can be draining for consumers. However, research suggests that consumers can handle a surprisingly high number of comparisons before overload sets in. One study revealed that consumers can evaluate as many as ten product alternatives and fifteen attributes before overload occurs.[24] Even though consumers can handle this much information, they rarely like to do so. And they generally do not consider this many alternatives. In fact, consumers are often able to make good choices when considering only a single attribute.[25]

What if Information Is Missing?

Consumers may have a good understanding of the types of attributes that they would like to use for alternative evaluation, but sometimes attribute information is not available. This actually happens quite frequently in the marketplace. For example, consider the information given in Exhibit 13.5. Here, information is given for two televisions that a consumer collects from print advertisements. Assume that both televisions cost roughly the same amount, say $1,000. As you can see, the information for television A lacks the details for picture quality, while the information given for television B lacks the details regarding the product's warranty. Consumer satisfaction ratings are available for both products.

To help solve this dilemma, consumers tend to weigh the criteria that are common to both alternatives quite heavily in the evaluation. They also tend to discount information that is missing for the option that performs better on the common criteria. For example, satisfaction ratings are given for both sets in this exhibit. Consumers would likely discount the missing warranty information for television B because this alternative performs better on the common criterion of consumer satisfaction ratings.[26]

⌈Conjoint analysis is used to understand attributes that guide preferences.⌋

How Do Marketers Determine Which Criteria Consumers Use?

Marketers can use several techniques to determine the criteria that consumers use when judging products. They can directly ask consumers through surveys. They can also gather information from warranty registrations that ask consumers to indicate the specific criteria that were used in arriving at a purchase decision.

EXHIBIT 13.5 Missing Information

Features	Television A	Television B
Consumer satisfaction ratings	Good	Excellent
Warranty	2 years parts & labor	Not given
Picture quality	Not given	Good

Source: Kivetz, R., and I. Simonson (2000), "The Effects of Incomplete Information on Consumer Choice," *Journal of Marketing Research*, 37 (4), 427–448.

conjoint analysis technique used to develop an understanding of the attributes that guide consumer preferences by having consumers compare product preferences across varying levels of evaluative criteria and expected utility

compensatory rule decision rule that allows consumers to select products that may perform poorly on one criterion by compensating for the poor performance on one attribute by good performance on another

noncompensatory rule decision rule in which strict guidelines are set prior to selection and any option that does not meet the guidelines is eliminated from consideration

Marketers also use techniques such as perceptual mapping and conjoint analysis to assess choice criteria. Perceptual mapping was discussed in a previous chapter. **Conjoint analysis** is used to understand the attributes that guide preferences by having consumers compare products across levels of evaluative criteria and the expected utility associated with the alternatives.[27]

13-4 Consumer Choice: Decision Rules

Once consumers have evaluated alternative solutions to a problem, they begin to make a choice. *Choice* does not mean that a particular alternative will be chosen, as consumers may simply choose to delay a choice until a future date or to forgo a selection indefinitely.

There are two major types of rules that consumers use when selecting products: compensatory rules and noncompensatory rules. **Compensatory rules** allow consumers to select products that may perform poorly on one attribute by compensating for the poor performance by good performance on another attribute. A consumer using a compensatory rule might say something like "It's OK that this car isn't very stylish; it gets good gas mileage. I'll buy it."

Noncompensatory models do not allow for this process to take place. Rather, when **noncompensatory rules** are used, strict guidelines are set prior to selection, and any option that does not meet the specifications is eliminated from consideration. For example, a consumer might say, "I'll only choose a car that gets good gas mileage. I am not budging on that."

13-4a Compensatory Models

The attitude-toward-the-object model (Fishbein model) that was presented in our attitude chapter represents a compensatory approach. The formula $A_o = \Sigma(b_i)(e_i)$ allows for poor scores on one attribute to be compensated for by good scores on another. Our example from that chapter is again shown in Exhibit 13.6. This example revealed that Crown View was the apartment complex to which Jamal held the most positive attitude, even though it scored highest on

Birds of Prey

What do bulls, raptors, bobcats, grizzlies, and timberwolves all have in common? If you're an NBA fan you'll quickly recognize that they're all NBA team names, and even if you're not a fan you'll probably think that all of these creatures can be scary.

As is the case with all brand names, team names are very important. One of the newest teams in the NBA is the Oklahoma City Thunder. If you've been to Oklahoma, you'll know that thunderstorms in that area can mean trouble. So even thunder can be scary.

Now enter the Pelicans! In case you don't know, the New Orleans Hornets recently became the New Orleans Pelicans. While this name has seemed silly to a lot of NBA fans, it actually makes a lot of sense. Louisiana is known as the "Pelican State," and the pelican is considered

a bird of prey. There was also a popular minor league baseball team with this name in New Orleans. The bird has important symbolic qualities as well. It helps to symbolize the resurgence of the state after both the BP oil spill and the devastation that was Hurricane Katrina. When you think about it, a pelican is one tough bird. So don't laugh when you hear "Pelicans." It actually makes a lot of sense.

Tischenko Irina/Shutterstock.com

Sources: Kelly Dwyer, "The New Orleans Pelicans Unveil the Team's New Logo," Yahoo.com, January 24, 2013, http://sports.yahoo.com/blogs/nba-ball-dont-lie/orleans-pelicans-unveil-team-logo-214138275--nba.html, accessed March 1, 2013; Ryan Gerhardt, "The Logic Behind the New Orleans' Pelicans Rebranding," PSFK.com, February 6, 2013, http://www.psfk.com/2013/02/new-orleans-pelicans-nba.html, accessed March 1, 2013; Jeremy Gordon, "The Pelicans Are Happening," *The Wall Street Journal*, January 24, 2013, http://blogs.wsj.com/dailyfix/2013/01/24/new-orleans-hornets-the-pelicans-are-happening/, accessed March 1, 2013.

the attribute that Jamal rated very poorly, high rent/fees. The high ratings on other attributes compensated for his belief that the complex has high fees.

13-4b Noncompensatory Models

Consumer researchers have identified four major categories of noncompensatory decision rules.[28] They include the conjunctive rule, the disjunctive rule, the lexicographic rule, and the elimination-by-aspects (EBA) rule.

1. Following the **conjunctive rule**, the consumer sets a minimum mental cutoff point for various features and rejects any product that fails to meet or exceed this cutoff point across all features.

2. Following the **disjunctive rule**, the consumer sets a minimum mental cutoff for various features. This is similar to the conjunctive rule. However, with the disjunctive rule, the cutoff point is usually high. The product that meets or exceeds this cutoff on any feature is selected.

3. Following the **lexicographic rule**, consumers select the product that they believe performs best on the most important feature.

4. Following the **elimination-by-aspects rule (EBA)**, consumers set minimum cutoff points for the attributes. Beginning with the most important feature, they then eliminate options that don't meet or surpass the cutoff point on this important feature. The consumer then moves on to the next most important feature and repeats the process, doing this until only one option remains and a choice is made.

To illustrate these rules, consider the information that is presented in Exhibit 13.7. Here, the consumer is evaluating different makes and models of cars. She is considering the Chevy Sonic, Ford Fiesta, Honda Fit, and Hyundai Accent.

The process involved with each decision rule would be as follows:

1. **Conjunctive Rule.** Assume that all features must meet or surpass a mental cutoff of 5 in order for the car to be selected. Looking across the various features for the cars, we see that only the Ford Fiesta has performance ratings at or above 5 on all features. Using this rule, the Ford Fiesta would therefore be selected. Its performance ratings are, respectively, 7, 6, 8, 8, 6, 5. Notice that at least one of the performance ratings for the attributes of the other cars falls below the cutoff of 5.

2. **Disjunctive Rule.** Assume that the consumer wants a car that excels at any of the features. Here, she would set a high cutoff of, say, 10. The only car that offers a performance rating of 10 on any attribute is the Hyundai Accent. The "low price" criterion is particularly strong for this car, and the consumer rates this feature as a 10. Using the disjunctive rule, the Hyundai Accent would be selected. She is considering performance ratings, not the importance of the attributes.

conjunctive rule noncompensatory decision rule where the option selected must surpass a minimum cutoff across all relevant attributes

disjunctive rule noncompensatory decision rule where the option selected surpasses a relatively high cutoff point on any attribute

lexicographic rule noncompensatory decision rule where the option selected is thought to perform best on the most important attribute

elimination-by-aspects rule (EBA) noncompensatory decision rule where the consumer begins evaluating options by first looking at the most important attribute and eliminating any option that does not meet a minimum cutoff point for that attribute and where subsequent evaluations proceed in order of importance until only one option remains

EXHIBIT 13.6 Attitude-Toward-the-Object Model Applied to Apartment Complexes

Attribute	e	City Pointe b	City Pointe (b)(e)	Crown View b	Crown View (b)(e)	Kings Landing b	Kings Landing (b)(e)
Location	3	7	21	9	27	6	18
High rent/fees	−2	8	−16	9	−18	7	−14
Security	3	7	21	8	24	6	18
Fitness center	1	5	5	7	7	10	10
Pet friendliness	−3	5	−15	2	−6	9	−27
A_o			16		34		5

Note: e = evaluative ratings. These ratings are generally scaled from −3 to +3, with −3 being very negative and +3 being very positive. b = strength of belief that the object possesses the attribute in question. Beliefs are generally scaled from 1 to 10, with 1 meaning "highly unlikely" and 10 meaning "highly likely." $(b)(e)$ is the product term that is derived by multiplying the evaluative ratings (e) by belief strength (b). A_o is the overall attitude toward the object. This is determined by adding the $(b)(e)$ product terms for each object.

© Cengage Learning

EXHIBIT **13.7**   Noncompensatory Decision Approaches

Attribute	Importance	Chevy Sonic Belief Ratings	Ford Fiesta Belief Ratings	Honda Fit Belief Ratings	Hyundai Accent Belief Ratings
Gas mileage	10	5	7	9	8
Low price	9	8	6	7	10
Styling	8	9	8	4	4
Warranty	5	4	8	9	8
Service	6	5	6	7	3
Handling	7	6	5	3	3

Note: Belief ratings are performance judgments scaled from 1 = very poor to 10 = very good. Importance ratings are scaled so that 10 = most important, 9 = next most important, and so on.
Source: P. Wright, "Consumer Choice Strategies: Simplifying vs. Optimizing," *Journal of Marketing Research* 12, no. 1 (1975): 60–67.

3. **Lexicographic Rule.** Here, the product that is thought to perform best on the most important attribute is selected. In this example, the consumer would select the Honda Fit because it scores highest (9) on the most important attribute, gas mileage.

4. **EBA Rule.** Assuming a minimum cutoff point of 5 once again, the consumer begins with the most important attribute, gas mileage. Any product that does not meet or surpass the cutoff of 5 on this attribute would be eliminated. All options meet or surpass 5 on the gas mileage attribute and no products are eliminated. Next, the consumer looks at the next most important attribute, low price. Again, all options meet the 5 criterion and no options are eliminated.

Choosing a car is a highly involving decision and probably involves both compensatory and noncompensatory rules.

On the next most important attribute, styling, two options are eliminated because they don't reach the 5 cutoff—the Honda Fit and the Hyundai Accent. The consumer continues on with the next most important attribute, handling. Both the Sonic and the Fiesta surpass the 5 cutoff on this attribute. The same is true for the next most important attribute, service. Finally, on the final attribute, warranty, the Sonic is eliminated from consideration because it does not reach the cutoff and the Ford Fiesta is ultimately selected. Notice that the conjunctive and EBA rules can result in the same decision. This will occur if the same cutoff points are used for both rules.

13-4c Use of Decision Rules

Noncompensatory rules are often used in low-involvement situations because these rules allow consumers to simplify their thought processes. However, these rules are also used in high-involvement purchase situations. The decision of what car to buy is certainly a high-involvement decision for most people.

Consumers can combine decision rules in order to arrive at a final solution. For example, a consumer might begin with a conjunctive rule to narrow down the choices and then use a compensatory approach to finalize the decision.

You may be wondering what type of rule consumers use most often. Studies have revealed that the lexicographic rule is very common. This is because consumers usually know what features are most important, and they simply select the product that offers the best performance on that feature.

You may also wonder how often consumers use these rules. Actually, the rules are used quite frequently. We should emphasize, however, that the processes are indeed mental. That is, the comparisons are almost always made mentally, without the strict use of a mathematical formula. Nevertheless, by considering issues such as cutoff points, researchers are able to gain a better understanding of the processes behind consumer choice.

13-4d Retail Outlet Selection

Up to this point, we have emphasized the processes that consumers use when selecting from alternative solutions to a problem. Consumers must also choose where they will buy the product. Sometimes, consumers will decide *where* they will buy before they determine *what* they will buy. One consumer says to another, "I'm going to the store; what do we need?" The other replies, "Where are you going?" Here, the decision of what product to buy hinges on where you are shopping. In fact, one trend that researchers have noticed is that consumers have gradually become less brand-loyal and more store-loyal. This means that consumers tend to have favorite stores that they visit regularly and first consider the products that are carried by those stores. Of course, retail marketers encourage this behavior by offering club memberships and reward points. Marketing managers realize that much of the power in the marketing channel has moved from manufacturer to retailer.

Several factors influence the choice of retail outlet, including objective and subjective criteria such as product variety, store image, location, service, and product quality.[29] Location is particularly important, as is store image. Consumers still prefer to shop in shopping malls, although many cities have successfully implemented "shop downtown" or "Main Street" campaigns. The Internet has also become the channel of choice for many consumers. The actual decision of which website to use is based on several factors, including the availability of product variety and information, customer service, security, and navigational ease.[30] Of course, many large retailers have both physical presence (a bricks-and-mortar store) and an online presence (website). Best Buy is a good example of a store that has successful physical and online presence.

As you can tell, evaluating alternatives and making final purchase decisions are part of an involved process. Our next chapter will consider the processes that occur after a choice has been made.

Study Tools

Located at the back of the textbook

❏ Rip out Chapter in Review Card

Located at www.cengagebrain.com

❏ Review Key Terms Flashcards (print or online)

❏ Download audio summaries to review on the go

❏ Complete practice quizzes to prepare for tests

❏ Play "Beat the Clock" to master concepts

❏ Watch video on Ford for a real company example

study tools

WHAT DO YOU THINK?
WHAT OTHERS HAVE THOUGHT

①	②	③	④	⑤	⑥	⑦
Strongly disagree	Disagree	Somewhat disagree	Neither agree nor disagree	Somewhat agree	Agree	Strongly agree

Getting a hair style for under $10 is a very good thing.

The responses to this question vary widely. Some students think getting a cheap haircut is a good thing while some think it's bad! Personal factors will greatly impact these responses. Students who pay close attention to social comparison information probably care deeply. Others simply don't. Quality and price are related after all!

PART 4 [CASES]

CASE 4-1

Smartphones, Tablets, Laptops, and PCs: What's the World Coming To?

Written by Eric G. Harris, Pittsburg State University

2011 was a very significant year in the computer world. It was during 2011 that smartphones officially outsold personal computers (PCs) for the first time ever. For a society that is always "on the go," the PC and laptop can stay at home. Smartphones and tablets are changing both the consumer and business worlds, and they are greatly impacting the global economy.

The numbers are truly astonishing. In the fourth quarter alone, 158 million smartphones were shipped, as compared to a total of 120 million PCs, tablets, netbooks, and laptops combined![1] The total shipments of smartphones totaled 488 million in 2011, which was an increase of over 60% from 2010.[2] These numbers indicate that smartphones are currently the hot consumer electronic product. Even though smartphones are hot, tablets are gaining ground very quickly. Their sales grew 274% in 2011 (63 million total units shipped for the year).[3] To put these growth rates into perspective, desktops and laptops grew only 2% and 7% respectively, while netbook sales declined 25%. The proliferation of mobile devices, including laptops, is a clear indication that we truly live in a mobile society and that mobile technology is the wave of the future.

So what is driving the demand for these devices? As smartphones and tablets have quickly gained consumer acceptance, the products are approaching the point where they've gained mass-market appeal, analysts say. They are no longer considered a niche market for businesspeople or the affluent. Consumers from all demographic groups seek mobile access to the Internet. And the popularity of social media and smartphone apps continues to grow in popularity for most all consumer groups at the same time that consumers realize that they don't have to be home to enjoy their availability. What this means is that consumers are no longer content with just surfing the web, they now consider mobile technologies as essential parts of their social lives. It seems that maintaining a presence in cyberspace all but requires mobile technologies today. More consumers access social media sites by mobile technologies than through desktop computers.

What consumer need do mobile devices fill? Smartphones and tablets deliver both utilitarian and hedonic value. For many businesspeople, smartphones and tablets have become an essential part of everyday work life. Many business travelers prefer the smaller size of smartphones and tablets to the larger, more bulky, laptops.[4] Business travelers can perform many work-related duties on smartphones, from checking email to checking warehouse inventories. And many nonusers report the intention to adopt them if manufacturers can improve applications, power, and projection availabilities. Cloud technologies also make it more reasonable for the business traveler to access vital company information from the cloud. These are very rational reasons to use smartphones or tablets.

The average consumer also tends to prefer the smartphone and tablet to laptops when they are traveling. And, of course, they're fun to use! Most consumers are familiar with all of the apps that are available. Consumers also enjoy having a music player, camera, Internet connectivity, and games at their fingertips. For many consumers, social media connectivity also provides hedonic value. Many consumers simply enjoy the ability to keep up on sites such as Facebook, Twitter, and MySpace through their smartphones or tablets while they are on the go.

What attributes and benefits do consumers seek with mobile devices? Attributes such as screen size, battery life, and storage capability are important. For some consumers, computing power is a consideration. App availability is also very important for most consumers. Of course, the reputation of the manufacturer and the warranty are important as well. The physical design of the products is also important, as are their accessories such as carrying cases and external keyboards.

So what has happened with the laptop? Laptop sales, as previously mentioned, have grown but they haven't kept up with smartphone or tablet sales growth. That doesn't mean that there aren't hardcore laptop fans out there. In fact, many consumers insist on the laptop. Laptop fans tend to lament the small size of the smartphone and the lack of computing power of the tablet.[5] In response, smartphone marketers have developed a number of projection techniques for screens and keyboards, along with motion technologies such as Microsoft Kinect technologies for smartphones. Tablet manufacturers are researching ways to make their products more powerful. Will tablets overtake the laptop in the business world? At a growth rate of over 200% in the last year, this appears likely. Most consumers prefer to type on a regular keyboard versus a tablet keyboard (even when external keyboards are available for many tablets).[6] But tablets tend to be more portable than are laptops. Also, tablets are less intrusive in business meetings because they fit nicely on a desk without having to extend a viewing screen abruptly. They also tend to have much better battery life as compared to the battery life of the average laptop. Of course, it takes more power to handle the computing strength of the laptop.

For many consumers, the debate is not really about tablets versus laptops, but rather about tablets versus smartphones. It may be that smartphone sales will eventually fall victim to tablets and that it won't be laptops or even PCs that disappear. Some analysts already predict this, suggesting that the most dramatic decrease in sales will soon be found with smartphones. Given that most consumers use smartphones for data capabilities, they really don't have many advantages over tablets other than simply having the telephone feature.[7] The key question appears to be what the optimal size should be. But are tablets better than smartphones simply because of their size? One interesting thing to note is that smartphones are getting bigger while tablets are getting smaller. However, this doesn't address the issue of telephone capability. What if you could speak through a tablet like you can through a smartphone? Many tablets already include technologies such as FaceTime and Skype. As such, telephone capabilities might not be that big of an issue.

There is a possibility that smartphones will begin to decline in 2012 or shortly thereafter. If laptops or PCs do not disappear, then the growth in tablets will most likely come at the expense of smartphones. Will smartphones, which have enjoyed record sales, soon be in decline? The answer to this question is largely based on consumer needs, value, and decision making.

Questions

1. What type of decision-making approach do most consumers use when deciding between smartphones, tablets, laptops, or PCs?

2. What factors influence the amount of search that most consumers will exert when buying a smartphone or a tablet?

3. How does superordinate and subordinate categorization apply to this case from a consumer's perspective?

4. What factors do consumers consider when making judgments about smartphones?

5. What type of decision rule would a consumer most likely use when selecting between smartphone brands? How could they use such a rule?

CASE 4-2

New Balance, Out of Step?

Written by Kristen Regine, Johnson & Wales University

New Balance (NB) is a privately held corporation based out of Brighton, MA, selling men's and women's athletic shoes and apparel for running, hiking, tennis, cross-training, golf, and fitness. The company operates in 120 countries worldwide. There are 157 licensed New Balance stores in North America; 140 are independently owned and operated.[1] This number does not include its three corporate stores located in Dedham, MA. The experience stores are in the Flatiron district in New York and the Pentagon in Washington, DC. The company expects to open another twelve stores over the next year.[2]

Some of their top competitors include Nike, K-Swiss, Saucony, Adidas, and Fila USA. The NB claim is substance over style, unlike their competitors; they do not promote their products with celebrity endorsements. They have developed an "endorsed by no one" philosophy. When compared to their competitors, this might be viewed as a weakness, since brands such as Nike, Adidas, and Reebok have developed well-established brands based on the premise of using celebrities as endorsers to build brand awareness.

Their focus in the marketplace is on technology and innovation, with a wide product portfolio. In 2011, the company's products NBX and WW86 were named as "Best Fitness Buys" by *Health* magazine, and the MR/WR890 and MR/WR1080 shoes were selected as the "Best Neutral Shoe" by *Women's Running* and *Running Network* magazines. In such a competitive market, New Balance expects a 15% growth this year, and for the first time since 2004 expects double-digit growth globally.[3]

New Balance Brand Goals[4]

- Solidify top placement within the athletic shoe market and among the key target market/core consumers with research, development, and strategic tactics that showcase NB as an innovator/cutting-edge brand in the athletic shoe category.

- Reinforce the brand anthem of "Make Excellent Happen" by raising awareness to the fact that NB is invested in the consumer's performance as an athlete, comfort as an athlete, and investment in fashion as a man or woman. The idea is to market to all the needs and wants of the consumer athlete: fashion/form/function/fun.

- Demonstrate a dedication to "American-made"/"made in the USA" products. (This is a critical attribute that NB is proud of and promotes with enthusiasm.)

- Expand upon the brand legacy of being a runners' shoe company and grow into a holistic brand that is a leader in the athletic show category and serves not just the runner, but the athlete.

- Promote a fashion-forward, functional perception among consumers that builds upon the trusted New Balance product legacy.

Judy Piktelis, the general market manager from New Balance, explained that their new experience store opened in the Flatiron district due to its historic roots in New York City to unprecedented numbers. The 4000-square-foot Flatiron store opened in August 2011. Consumers are able to see their shoes completed in an hour. "I think customers expect a lot more in their shopping experience," said Tracy Knauer, New Balance's head of marketing for retail. There's a running track, a shoemaker from Maine in a glass booth assembling shoes, and an over-the-top shopping experience. In New York, a creative tactic was utilized to drive traffic into the store: customization of the 875 shoe.[5] Shoppers were even able to purchase shoes from the glass booth with an "assembled in New York" tote bag. The shoe was a sellout. This is not the first experience store for New Balance. The others are located in Beijing, Hong Kong, and Australia.[6]

However, in New Balance's backyard and home market the company-owned store in Dedham, MA, a suburb located south of Boston,[7] is showing a slowdown in sales. Dedham's demographics are mainly families (56%). Eighty percent of families own their own homes, the median age is 39 years, and the largest age group is 35–44 years old with an average household income of $80,000 per year, which is substantially higher than the national average of $51,914.[8] Legacy Place was a prime target to develop a new retail center in 2009. The open-air shopping center covers 675,000 square feet, featuring over 60 retail shops, restaurants, and entertainment such as a movie theater and bowling alley.[9]

However, the Dedham store in Legacy Place is problematic. There is a lot of competition: City Sports, Urban Outfitters, and Lu Lu Lemon Athletica. One destination in particular was always jam-packed; King's Bowling Alley.[10]

The Dedham New Balance store decided to start with a grassroots marketing program, since discounting was a tactic employed only twice a year for friends and family days. Their grassroots campaign included partnering with King's Bowling Alley. King's offers its patrons a trivia night, karaoke nights, all-you-can-bowl nights for $10, live music, bowling leagues, and industry nights.[11] New Balance posted information in the restrooms and offered employees of King's a discount. Additionally, the marketing program included the formation of a walking club for the outdoor shopping plaza, which was sponsored by Whole Foods.

The one tactic that did require a small budget was to partner with the local Massachusetts Red Cross mobile unit where blood donors would receive a gift from New Balance.[12] Recently, the company struck a deal with the Boston Red Sox to become the official apparel and footwear sponsor of the team.[13] Could the Legacy Place store feature a Boston sports connection to get foot traffic moving their way? Would their grassroots marketing program develop a loyal customer? What type of experience can Legacy Place create for its customers?

Questions

1. Explain the consumer decision-making process when purchasing a new pair of sneakers.

2. What is the consumer's motivation for wanting to have the customized pair of 875 New Balance sneakers? Explain.

3. Should New Balance consider a specialty sneaker for the Boston market? If so, what do you envision?

4. What is the effect of the New Balance brand on the consumers' judgment to buy or not to buy?

5. Discuss the atmospherics of the two shopping areas, Legacy Place in Dedham, MA, and the Flatiron district in New York City.

6. Visit three stores selling sneakers. Describe how the atmospherics differ across the stores. Why do these difference exist?

CASE 4-3

Consumer Confidence: Preparation Pays Off

Written by Mohan Menon, University of South Alabama

It's time to make a decision on a new car. Maya has been preparing for the moment when she would finally buy her own new car for the first time in her life, but she didn't want to break the news to her family until she got closer to her graduation date. She now feels that she has done her homework and is ready to discuss her choices with her family before making the purchase.

It all started about a year ago, when she was in the last year of medical school. Maya had been thinking about her residency in a city hospital, one that is well known for her specialty, neuroradiology. Along with moving away from home and fitting into the hospital culture, Maya would have to buy a car. Until now, she has been driving an older model Prius that was given to her by her dad, who bought it new. She has liked the car, but wants to upgrade to a new car when she starts her residency. She has never had a new car and believes that the transition in her life the following year would warrant one.

She feels confident in her ability to select a suitable new car. Having grown up in a family that subscribed to *Consumer Reports* ever since she can remember, she seems well informed about many products, including automobiles. Her parents were careful shoppers. They taught her and her older brother how to save money, spend less, and not to give in to impulses. Moreover, her dad and brother are knowledgeable about cars. Her brother, who has just started his private practice, would be of tremendous help in the process. With his extensive toy car collection from childhood, he has been a car enthusiast and is highly knowledgeable about automobiles.

However, she wanted to go through with the new car–buying process on her own with minimal help. Maya set aside time to do some serious research on cars she was considering. She had a set of basic criteria, such as miles per gallon (MPG) of 40 or more, interior (leather only), body style (4-door), no built-in GPS-Nav system, iPhone/iPad and bluetooth connectivity, ample trunk space, low maintenance, minimum 4-star safety rating, ABS system, electronic displays on the dashboard, smooth handling and ride, manual transmission, and so on. Since she is likely to move to a northern city, having heated seats would be preferable but not a must. She has also heard of other features such as independent suspension and all-wheel-drive options, but is not quite sure how they would benefit her. At that same time Maya was also sure of features or options she did not care for: acceleration/performance, V-6 engine, off-road ability, extended warranty, towing capacity, sun or moon roof, etc. She knew she would never find her ideal car and would have to compromise on a few items along the way.

Even though price was not likely to be a major factor in her decision, she had an upper limit of $35,000 for her car. But Maya is not very familiar with financing options available to her. Also, leaving the nest for the very first time, she knew she would have to buy her own car insurance. Despite her accident-free record, she was concerned about her premiums. Understanding the options with regard to financing and insurance are two areas she might need help with from her family.

Maya was anxious about starting out on her own in a new city, yet when it came to buying her own car for the very first time, she seemed to feel confident. She also had the luxury of time, since she was not planning to buy the car until after her graduation but before leaving for the residency. She found most of the information in magazines and from various websites. She watched very little TV and thus paid scant attention to the car ads. She was more interested in non-biased sources of car information. Even though she sometimes steered family conversations to include cars, she had not informed them of her intent to buy a new car before her residency begins. She would also bring up the topic subtly with her friends, who had a variety of opinions on various makes and models. She wanted to first gather information from trustworthy sources, mull over it, and possibly narrow down her options before seeking some assistance from her family.

She began with positive impressions of the Prius she had been driving and knew she wanted an environmentally friendly vehicle. Given the number of cars that fit the description, she knew she had a long road ahead. But her informal discussions with family and friends helped.

Maya considers herself to be a very logical person and thus was more interested in the functional aspects of the car. Not that she did not care for the look and feel of the car, but they were secondary in nature. Her color choices were basic: silver or black.

Yet one aspect of research she avoided at this point was visits to the dealerships. Having gone car shopping with her family in the past, she was realistic about her own experience. For instance, she is not comfortable negotiating prices or making instant decisions about certain aspects of the purchase. She planned to take her dad or brother along when visiting dealerships.

After mulling over the information she had gathered, she felt confident about four specific models: Toyota Prius V, Hyundai Sonata Hybrid, Ford Fiesta Hybrid, and Volkswagen TDI Diesel. Brands she rejected for one reason or the other included Chevy Volt, Nissan Leaf, Toyota Camry Hybrid, and Honda Civic Hybrid. Having been involved in her family's car buying decisions in the past, she knew that she had to also order *Consumer Reports'* new car pricing reports before visiting car dealerships. Also, given how selective her dad and brother can be about cars, she wanted to narrow down her choices before seeking specific brand advice from them. She was sure that they would approve of her initial choices.

It's now a few days after the graduation ceremony. Maya and her family were preparing for her move to New York-Presbyterian Hospital for her residency. It's time to finally decide and buy that new car.

Questions

1. Based on the various perspectives of consumer decision making, what type of a shopper is Maya and why?

2. Apply the consumer decision-making process stages to Maya's actions as a consumer, or describe Maya's actions within the framework of the consumer decision-making process.

3. Is Maya utilizing the affect-based or attribute-based evaluation process? Justify your answer.

4. Based on the information provided in the case, what are the determinants of the evaluative criteria that the customer is using? Explain each in detail.

5. In your opinion, which decision rule (compensatory or non-compensatory) is Maya utilizing in her car-buying process?

PART **5**
CB

Pixland/Jupiter Images

Is satisfaction the
key outcome variable for marketers
and consumers?

WHAT DO YOU THINK?
When I'm treated unfairly by a
business, dissatisfaction describes my
feelings well.

STRONGLY DISAGREE   STRONGLY AGREE

VISIT COURSEMATE AT WWW.CENGAGEBRAIN.COM

Consumption to Satisfaction

14

For several reasons, one might think that the CB ends when a consumer is satisfied. However, as the CVF illustrates, a host of other things go on after exchange and consumption, not just satisfaction. This chapter focuses on what happens after consumption takes place. This is a critical stage for marketers, because among those things is the decision of whether or not to do business again with the marketers who helped create the value.

14-1 Consumption, Value, and Satisfaction

Consumption is at the heart of all consumer behavior. Obviously, a consumer *consumes*! In fact, one might say that all human activity focuses on some form of consumption. Even when we work, we consume time so that we can earn money to consume other things! In the consumption process, consumers use the product, service, or experience that has been selected. Ultimately, consumers consume products and receive value in return.

14-1a Consumption Leads to Value

The important role of consumption becomes apparent when one considers that without consumption, there is no value. Consumers derive value from consumption and marketers derive value from continued exchange.[1] Earlier, we defined consumption as the process that converts time, goods, ideas, or services into value. Consumption experiences potentially produce utilitarian and/or hedonic value. The basic consumption process that is at the heart of the CVF is shown again in Exhibit 14.1.

After studying this chapter, the student should be able to:

14-1 Gain an appreciation of the link from consumption to value to satisfaction.

14-2 Discuss the relative importance of satisfaction and value in consumer behavior.

14-3 Know that emotions other than satisfaction can affect postconsumption behavior.

14-4 Use expectancy disconfirmation, equity, and attribution theory approaches to explain consumers' postconsumption reactions.

14-5 Understand problems with commonly applied satisfaction measures.

14-6 Describe some ways that consumers dispose of products.

durable goods goods that are usually consumed over a long period of time

nondurable goods goods that are usually consumed quickly

consumption frequency number of times a product or service is consumed in a given period of time

14-1b Consumption and Product Classification

Many issues go along with the consumption of goods, services, and experiences. Important differences exist for the consumption of durable and nondurable goods. **Durable goods** are goods that are consumed over long periods of time. A dishwasher is a durable good. **Nondurable goods** are consumed quickly. Soft drinks are nondurable goods.

For nondurable goods especially, marketers try to increase consumption frequency as much as possible. **Consumption frequency** refers to the number of times a product or service is consumed in a given time period. Credit card companies have made it easier and easier for consumers to use their cards on routine shopping trips. Not so long ago, consumers viewed credit cards as inappropriate for routine transactions like groceries or fast food. Consumers today, though, routinely use cards for all types of purchases. The card number can even be stored for ready use online via Paypal or Google Checkout.

Marketers also attempt to increase the amount of product consumed per occasion. For example, soft drink marketers gradually increased the average size of soft drinks over time. Many students may be surprised to find out that the traditional Coke bottle was much smaller than today—holding a mere $6\frac{1}{2}$ ounces. Pepsi's selling point was a 10-ounce bottle at the same price. Today consumers often consume 20-ounce or even 1-liter bottles a number of times per day! The soft-drink industry has slowly facilitated an increase in the average soft drink serving size.

Services and experiences are usually classified as nondurable by default. However, some services are more clearly consumed over extended time periods. For example, we consume insurance daily even though consumers may pay premiums only periodically. Experiences

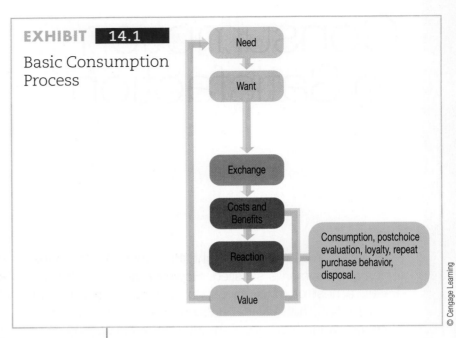

EXHIBIT 14.1

Basic Consumption Process

Need → Want → Exchange → Costs and Benefits → Reaction → Value

Consumption, postchoice evaluation, loyalty, repeat purchase behavior, disposal.

© Cengage Learning

Today, people use credit cards in many ways, making buying all types of things very easy—sometimes too easy?

Diego Cervo/Shutterstock.com

are complete when consumption stops. However, marketers of these products encourage repeat consumption of their products by offering season tickets, club memberships, and special invitations to events. By encouraging increased consumption, these marketers are able to foster customer relationships.

14-1c Situations and Consumer Reactions

As discussed previously, consumption situations and settings have a significant impact on the consumer experience. The temporal factors, antecedent conditions, and physical environment are particularly influential on the consumption experience. How, what, and when we consume is largely dependent upon the environment that we are in.

For example, football fans enjoy tailgating and numerous products are essential to convert the occasion into value. Beer, burgers, and brats are standard fare at typical Midwestern tailgates. In Louisiana, jambalaya, gumbo, gator tail, and perhaps even a Cajun band may accompany the beer. The products become artifacts in part of a tailgating ritual. Without these, the experience is less than authentic. **Authenticity** means something (including an experience) is real, genuine, unique, and has a history or tradition.[2] The consumption of authentic things adds value over the consumption of synthetic experiences, particularly when the consumption environment contains high degrees of symbolism or consumers are highly involved in some activity. The very same products, such as fried gator tail, offer less value when they are not contributing to an authentic consumer experience.

authenticity is the degree to which an object, person, or experience seems real, genuine, unique, and part of history or tradition

meaning transference process through which cultural meaning is transferred to a product and onto the consumer

The environment plays a large role in influencing consumption and consumer satisfaction. An American traveler would typically be very upset with a $200 hotel room so small that the door hits the bed when entering the room. However, if the environment is London city center in the U.K., the consumer may be very happy to have such a room at that price. A large hotel room in London would likely damage its authenticity anyway.

14-1d Consumption, Meaning, and Transference

Consumers' lives are very much intertwined with consumption. Value depends on a process called **meaning transference**. From a utilitarian standpoint, the meaning of consumption is straightforward.

A Tattoo Is Taboo??

Big decisions are often filled with anticipation. However, how many things really live up to the anticipation? At times tattoos were considered taboo, and sometimes they still are. A Disney cast member, for instance, cannot have a visible tattoo. Today, young people commonly display tattoos, and perhaps the anticipation of just what the tattoo will mean and will accomplish for the consumer crowds out any negative implications like not being able to be a Disney cast member! The choice to get a tattoo is filled with CB elements. Anticipation comes along with expectations, including the way other consumers will react to the tattoo. If the consumer is satisfied with what the tattoo does, perhaps they'll get another. If the consumer purchases the tattoo to gain acceptance within a group of associates (the sailor effect) and it accomplishes that end, the consumption results in utilitarian value. If the wearing a tattoo produces desirable feelings, then hedonic value results. As most consumers know, a tattoo is a relatively permanent decision. Removing a tattoo is expensive and painful. Thus, a tattoo also sets up a situation ripe for cognitive dissonance. Like many things, when it comes to a tattoo, be sure to know what you are hoping for.

Alfred Wekelo/Shutterstock.com

Consumers buy shoe polish to polish their shoes. That's easy. What is not as straightforward is the hedonic component of consumption. Here, inner meanings, including cultural meaning, must be considered.

Meaning transference begins with culture. Value is affected largely by the meaning of goods, services, and experiences. Marketers work to transfer important cultural ideals or values into products via advertising and the word of mouth that occurs between consumers. If marketers can attach a freedom theme to a product—for example, a motorcycle—then a consumer not only consumes the motorcycle itself, but also the meaning attached to the bike. Ultimately, the meaning of the product becomes an important part of the consumption experience.[3]

14-1e Consumption Outcomes and Emotion

Consumers choose products, services, and experiences that they believe will deliver value by addressing their wants and needs. They anticipate good outcomes from their choices or else they would have made a different choice. Emotions influence CB before, during, and after consumption. Emotions play a role prior to exchange as expectations manifest emotions like anxiety, apprehension, or fear. Imagine the emotions accompanying a student just prior to going off to university for the first time. Fantasies, fun, and feelings all are associated with consumption, and these elements of consumption are closely tied to perceived value.[4] Emotions taking place during a consumption experience affect value directly. Finally, in evaluating a consumption outcome, emotions naturally occur as a result of appraisal. Consumers anticipate what an authentic French restaurant experience will be like based on cognitions that give the concept meaning (i.e., schema), the meaning is either realized or not during a visit to a French restaurant, and the evaluation of that experience in turn creates emotion and adjustments to meaning. Emotions are involved in all phases of consumption and they influence value both directly and indirectly, as illustrated in Exhibit 14.2.

In this portion of the CVF, and in this chapter, we stress how consumer emotions influence consumption outcomes. Consumption, value, and satisfaction are

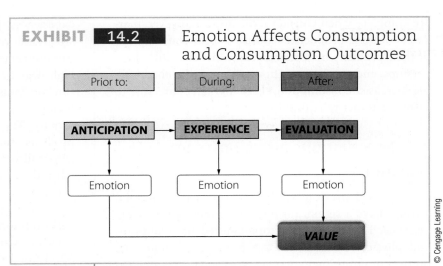

EXHIBIT 14.2 Emotion Affects Consumption and Consumption Outcomes

© Cengage Learning

tied closely together. Not surprisingly, consumers tend to be more satisfied with exchanges they find valuable, as value is at the heart of marketing transactions. Value perceptions, therefore, directly influence consumer satisfaction.[5] However, the link between value and satisfaction is nowhere near perfect, as will be seen later.

> A consumer not only consumes the motorcycle itself, but also the meaning attached to the bike.

14-2 Value and Satisfaction

Many companies try hard to satisfy customers. However, is satisfaction *the* key outcome variable for marketers and consumers? Consider Exhibit 14.3. This chart plots scores for major retailers from the ACSI, which is the American Consumer Satisfaction Index.[6] This index provides satisfaction scores for many major companies across many industries and even some governmental organizations.

Notice that Publix (a large supermarket chain operating in the southeastern United States) has the highest customer satisfaction rating over the entire period, with Nordstrom also scoring higher on the ACSI than practically all other retailers. JCPenney, Dillard's, Target, Dollar General, and Sears

> Is satisfaction the key outcome variable for marketers and consumers?.

EXHIBIT 14.3   The ACSI Scores for U.S. Retailers

top-line performance a business term referring to sales growth (sales being at the top of an earnings statement)

Legend:
- Nordstrom
- Target
- Dollar General
- J.C. Penney
- Kohl's
- Dillard's
- Sears Holdings
- Army and Air Force Exchange Service (AAFES)
- Walmart Stores
- Macy's
- Publix

Source: Based on data from www.theacsi.org, accessed March 29, 2013.

increase customer satisfaction do not always improve **top-line performance**, a business term referring to sales growth.

The importance of value in the consumption experience cannot be overstated. In fact, the reason a firm exists at all is to create value.[8] Value and satisfaction are usually related, but value is the heart of CB and is what consumer seek from consumption experiences.[9] If marketers ever face the decision of providing value or satisfaction, value should be prioritized because, as illustrated by the ACSI, firms can do well even when they do not enjoy the highest industry satisfaction scores, but the firm that does not provide value in some form can't succeed for long.[10]

all have higher satisfaction ratings than Walmart. What does this mean? Has any retailer in recent history enjoyed more success than Walmart? Yet, as the ACSI shows, Walmart is hardly the satisfaction leader. In fact, Walmart's satisfaction ratings are the lowest of all retailers listed, according to the ACSI. What can explain this? The answer lies in value. Even if Walmart does not provide high customer satisfaction, it does provide value leadership, particularly the perception that high utilitarian value results from shopping there. Thus, the track record says Walmart should continue to prioritize value over satisfaction.

Indications are that Walmart executives have learned what drives customers to Walmart. In just the past few years, Walmart has briefly launched campaigns to increase customers satisfaction and overall positive perceptions about the brand. These have included initiatives to make the store atmosphere more comfortable through reduced crowding of aisles and floor space, increased availability of higher quality brands, and an increased emphasis on sustainability. In each case, Walmart found the results unsustainable and quickly shifted back to an emphasis on large assortments at low prices.[7] Managers acknowledge that initiatives that

14-2a What Is Consumer Satisfaction?

Customer satisfaction receives a lot of attention from consumer researchers and marketing managers. However, different people may define satisfaction differently and result in confusion over the exact meaning. As a result, satisfaction is at times confused with numerous closely related concepts like quality,

Courtesy of American Customer Satisfaction Index

Limited-Service Restaurants

	Base-line	95	96	97	98	99	00	01	02	03	04	05	06	07	08	09	10	11	12	Previous Year % Change	First Year % Change
Papa John's	NM	NM	NM	NM	NM	76	77	78	76	NM	78	79	77	76	75	80	79	83		5.1	9.2
All Others	73	74	75	73	74	74	72	73	74	75	NM	78	80	79	80	83	76	81	82	1.2	12.3
Subway	NM	NM	NM	NM	NM	NM	NM	NM	NM	NM	NM	NM	NM	NM	NM	NM	NM	82	N/A	N/A
Little Caesar	72	69	69	73	71	NM	69	70	74	75	NM	74	77	75	75	75	78	80	82	2.5	13.9
Limited-Service Restaurants	69	70	66	68	69	69	70	71	71	74	NM**	76	77	77	78	78	75	79	80	1.3	15.9
Dunkin' Donuts	NM	NM	NM	NM	NM	NM	NM	NM	NM	NM	NM	NM	NM	NM	NM	NM	NM	79	N/A	N/A
Pizza Hut (YUM! Brands)	69	66	63	71	71	68	70	71	70	75	NM	71	76	72	76	74	78	81	78	-3.7	13.0
Wendy's	72	73	71	69	73	71	70	72	74	74	NM	75	76	78	73	76	77	77	78	1.3	8.3
Domino's Pizza	67	70	68	68	70	67	69	73	75	75	NM	71	75	75	77	77	77	77	77	0.0	14.9
Taco Bell (YUM! Brands)	66	66	66	67	64	64	63	66	67	68	NM	72	70	69	70	73	74	76	77	1.3	16.7
Starbucks	NM	NM	NM	NM	NM	NM	NM	NM	NM	NM	NM	NM	77	78	77	76	78	80	76	-5.0	-1.3
KFC (YUM! Brands)	67	68	69	67	64	64	65	63	69	71	NM	69	70	71	70	69	75	75	75	0.0	11.9
Burger King	66	65	67	68	64	66	67	65	68	68	NM	71	70	69	71	69	74	75	75	0.0	13.6
McDonald's	63	63	60	60	61	61	59	62	61	64	NM	62	63	64	69	70	67	72	73	1.4	15.9

The ACSI for famous fast food restaurants. What do you think?

consumer satisfaction
mild, positive emotion resulting from a favorable appraisal of a consumption outcome

consumer dissatisfaction mild, negative affective reaction resulting from an unfavorable appraisal of a consumption outcome

loyalty, and cognitive dissonance. However, satisfaction is distinct from these concepts.

Consumer satisfaction is a mild, positive emotional state resulting from a favorable appraisal of a consumption outcome. Several points distinguish consumer satisfaction from other important consumer behavior concepts:

1. Consumer satisfaction is a *postconsumption* phenomenon because it is a reaction to an outcome.

2. Like other emotions, satisfaction results from a cognitive appraisal. Some refer to this appraisal as the satisfaction judgment; however, the appraisal and the reaction are distinct.

3. Satisfaction as an emotion is relatively mild and does not create strong behavioral motivations.

Other key consumer variables like expectations, quality, or attitude are generally more relevant in explaining preconsumption or even prepurchase phenomena.[11] Nevertheless, managers consider consumer satisfaction to be important because consumers' word of mouth, repeat purchases, and ultimately, consumer loyalty, correlate with reported customer satisfaction. These relationships are discussed in detail in the next chapter.

14-2b What Is Consumer Dissatisfaction?

Recall from the material on consumer information processing (CIP) that consumers react quite differently when responding to losses than when responding to gains. Additionally, some debate exists over whether or not low satisfaction necessarily means a consumer has high dissatisfaction. For reasons like these, consumer behavior theory distinguishes consumer dissatisfaction from consumer satisfaction. Therefore, **consumer dissatisfaction** can be defined as a mild, negative affective reaction resulting from an unfavorable appraisal of a consumption outcome.[12] Even though conceptually dissatisfaction is an opposite concept to satisfaction, the fact that consumers react differently to negative contexts means that dissatisfaction will explain behaviors that satisfaction cannot.

14-3 Other Postconsumption Reactions

Although people often use *satisfaction* as a colloquialism for everything that happens after a consumer buys something, many other things, including other emotions, may also occur post consumption. Among the other important postconsumption reactions

Outcomes Are Cocreated

Consumption is a partnership. Consumer researchers often express that idea by emphasizing the fact that consumers *coproduce* or *cocreate* outcomes.

The consumer's role in cocreating the outcome from a frozen entrée seems very simple. However, nearly 40% of frozen dinner consumers admit to ignoring instructions such as those stating that the food should be stirred halfway through the microwave cooking time. The nonstirred result is a meal scorched on the outside

© iStockphoto.com/Spauln

yet still frozen in the middle. As a result, average customer satisfaction with frozen meals is surprisingly low. Thus, even when the company gets everything right, the consumer is still a partner in creating the value and sometimes the consumer does not make a good partner! Some brands, such as Whole Foods, are turning away from microwave ovens as the recommended way of creating the meals and encouraging partners to use a skillet.

Sources: A. M. Chaker, "Frozen Entrees Give Microwaves a Cold Shower," *The Wall Street Journal*, March 27, 2013, D3. G. Cairins, "Evolutions in Food Marketing, Quantifying the Impact and Policy Implications," *Appetite* 62 (March 2013): 194–97.

that can be overlooked are specific emotions, including delight, disgust, surprise, exhilaration, and even anger. These particular emotions are often much more strongly linked to behavior, because although they are also emotional reactions to appraisals, they are often much stronger.

An angry consumer exhibits much more noticeable and persistent behavior than does a consumer with low satisfaction. The angry consumer likely complains and sometimes shouts and, in extreme cases, begins boycott initiatives against a company that is the target of anger. A consumer with low satisfaction would not likely exhibit any visible signs of irritation. The particular emotion experienced by consumers will do much to determine the behavioral reaction, as we will see in the next chapter, when we discuss complaining in more detail. Any model of what happens after purchase would be remiss not to include possibilities beyond satisfaction.

14-4 Theories of Postconsumption Reactions

Imagine a consumer placing an online order for some perishable food items—say peaches. What does the consumer expect the peaches to be like when they arrive? When will they arrive? How long will they last? Will they taste better than store-bought peaches? The answer to each of these questions involves an expectation before the peaches arrive. Afterwards, the actual outcomes are compared to these expectations. If the event turns out to be less than satisfying, perhaps the expectations were too high or perhaps the performance of the company was too poor. The application of the *disconfirmation model* to this question may help explain consumers' slow adoption of groceries online.[13]

14-4a Expectancy/ Disconfirmation

The most commonly accepted theory of consumer satisfaction is the **expectancy/ disconfirmation theory**. The basic disconfirmation model proposes that consumers enter into a consumption experience with predetermined cognitive expectations of consumption. These expectations provide a benchmark against which actual performance perceptions are judged.

Disconfirmation becomes central in explaining consumer satisfaction. When performance perceptions are more positive than what was expected, **positive disconfirmation** occurs. Positive disconfirmation leads to consumer satisfaction. When performance perceptions do not meet expectations, meaning performance is less than expected, **negative disconfirmation** occurs. Negative disconfirmation leads to dissatisfaction. Finally, if performance perceptions exactly match what was expected, confirmation (sometimes referred to as *neutral disconfirmation*) is said to occur.

The expectancy/disconfirmation approach is shown in Exhibit 14.4. Taken together, disconfirmation represents the cognitive appraisal that produces postconsumption emotions like consumer satisfaction. Using different terminology, disconfirmation is the satisfaction judgment. The blue boxes represent cognitive postconsumption reactions, whereas the green box represents an affective or emotional postconsumption reaction. The relationships between the concepts are explained in the section that follows.

Expectations

Expectations are preconsumption beliefs concerning what will occur during an exchange and/or consumption of a product. Consumer expectations have two components: (1) the probability that something will occur and (2) an

expectancy/disconfirmation theory satisfaction formation theory that proposes that consumers use expectations as a benchmark against which performance perceptions are judged

positive disconfirmation according to the expectancy/disconfirmation approach, a perceived state wherein performance perceptions exceed expectations

negative disconfirmation according to the expectancy/disconfirmation approach, a perceived state wherein performance perceptions fall short of expectations

expectations preconsumption beliefs of what will occur during an exchange and consumption of a product

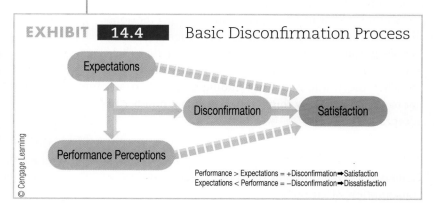

EXHIBIT 14.4   Basic Disconfirmation Process

Performance > Expectations = +Disconfirmation➡Satisfaction
Expectations < Performance = −Disconfirmation➡Dissatisfaction

© Cengage Learning

hope a fundamental emotion evoked by positive, anticipatory appraisals that signal uncertainty about a potentially positive outcome

evaluation of that potential occurrence.[14] Exhibit 14.4 reveals that expectations also can have a direct impact on satisfaction (by the dotted line), independent of their role in the disconfirmation process.[15] This can occur when the consumer has very little involvement. In these cases, little effort is put into either expectation or performance appraisal, and satisfaction formation is largely impacted by consumer expectations alone. In other words, with low involvement, high expectations will be associated directly with increased satisfaction, and low expectations will be associated directly with increased dissatisfaction.

Very high involvement can also create a similar effect. When consumers are very involved with a situation and filled with anticipation, their ability to objectively judge performance can be impaired. Balance theory kicks in and consumers may adjust their reactions automatically as a way of protecting themselves from the realization that they may have made a poor choice. Over the last few years, the anticipation over a new iPhone release nears hysteria. Such high anticipation may cause a consumer to block out negative product performance aspects to adjust to preconsumption expectations. Thus, under conditions of very low or very high involvement, expectations can influence satisfaction directly.

Expectations are the cognitive component of anticipation. Anticipation, though, also involves emotions. **Hope**, for example, is a fundamental emotion evoked by positive, anticipatory appraisals that signal uncertainty about a positive outcome. The consumer anticipates an outcome that could bring about a better situation in some way, and he feels the emotion of hope in return. In this way, hope contrasts with fear, the anticipation of a negative outcome. Consumers that experience anticipatory hope show a greater tendency toward being satisfied relative to consumers who frame expectations based on what ought to happen. Consumers waiting for stores to open before big promotions like Filene's Basement Bridal Event, where wedding dresses go on sale at large discounts, report that their expectations of the event generate emotions from anxiety when they think about not finding a suitable product to hope when they think about finding a number of acceptable choices.[16]

Types of Expectations

Consumers bring different types of expectations into a consumption situation.

Predictive Expectations. Expectations that form about what a consumer thinks will actually occur during an experience.

Normative Expectations. Expectations of what a consumer thinks should happen given past experiences with a product or service.

Ideal Expectations. Expectations about what a consumer really wants to happen during an experience if everything were ideal. In terms of regulatory focus theory, these could be referred to as promotion-based expectations (the expectation being that the experience will improve their overall status and not just maintain the current state)

Equitable Expectations. Expectations that a consumer forms regarding what she thinks should or ought to happen given the level of work that she has put into the experience. From a regulatory focus viewpoint, these can be called prevention-based expectations.

Source of Expectations

How do consumers form expectations? In other words, what are the sources of information that allow consumers to form expectations? In reality, consumers form expectations based on a number of different sources.[17] Word-of-mouth communication from other consumers is an important source of information. When a close friend tells you that a new television show is good, you'll probably hope that this is the case if you plan on watching it. A consumer's experience also influences expectations. If you've gone to a dentist who was caring and respectful of your feelings on the first visit, then you would expect the same kind of treatment during the next visit. Explicit promises such as advertisements and promotions create consumer expectations as well. If a company promises that it will deliver a package within two days, a two-day delivery is what you probably expect! Personal factors also influence expectations. Some people simply expect more out of products and services than do others. Perhaps you know people who expect restaurant meals to be perfect or flights to arrive on time in any conditions. Here, personal factors influence the expectations that they have about the service.

Performance Perceptions

Recall that perception plays a very important role in CB. "Perception *is* reality!" Marketers are well aware of this. Perception directly influences how a consumer interacts with the world.

Perception is also very important for the consumption and postconsumption processes. As is the case with

Consumers expect service providers of most types to be empathetic. If those expectations are not met, quality is diminished.

© iStockphoto.com/sturti

expectations, performance perceptions can also directly influence consumer satisfaction formation independent of the disconfirmation process (dotted line in Exhibit 14.4). This is particularly the case when expectations are low. For example, if a consumer buys a brand of product that he or she knows will be bad, expectations are likely to be low. Even if these low expectations are met by performance perceptions, the consumer may not feel very satisfied. Also, when a consumer has no previous experience or expectation regarding a product (for example, a new product), then perception directly influences satisfaction.[18]

Marketers may think twice about setting expectations too firmly among consumers. Domino's Pizza once emphasized the 30-minute delivery guarantee for their pizzas. Consumers then began to expect this performance so strongly that they became very dissatisfied when the expectation was not met, so much so that the drivers became hazards on the road in an effort to meet the 30-minute deadline. In the end, Domino's had to back off the guarantee to avoid legal liability for accidents incurred by drivers who could easily be accused of driving recklessly in an effort to meet the 30-minute promise.

Confidence in Expectations and the Confirmatory Bias

Another issue that is important in satisfaction theory is the degree to which consumers are confident in their expectations. For example, if a complete stranger tells a consumer that a movie is good, the consumer may not be very confident in his expectations. However, if a family member tells the consumer that a movie is good, then he might feel much more confident in expecting the movie to be good. Research has indicated that when expectations are held with a strong degree of confidence, both disconfirmation and performance perceptions affect satisfaction. However,

when expectations lack a strong degree of confidence, perceived performance more strongly influences satisfaction.[19]

Not only do expectations play a key role in satisfaction formation, they also can affect how consumers see things. That is, expectations can affect performance perceptions.[20] Imagine a student who goes into a class thinking, "This class is going to be really bad!" There is a tendency for an expectation like this to actually alter her perception of the class experience. If the student thinks it's going to be bad, she may very well look for evidence to support this expectation! The term to explain this phenomenon is **confirmatory bias**.

Research shows the confirmatory bias to be particularly present when consumers receive recommendations from the marketer and return policies are lenient. A consumer who has doubts about switching to a different phone is more likely to confirm those doubts and interpret the phone's performance as bad when purchased from a retailer with lenient return policies. In contrast, when a retailer makes no recommendation and has restrictive policies, consumers rely more on actual performance perceptions.[21] The confirmatory bias works in conjunction with self-perception theory. **Self-perception theory** states that consumers are motivated to act in accordance with their attitudes and behaviors. Here, consumers are motivated to perceive their environment through the lens of their expectations. The confirmatory influence of expectations on perceptions is especially strong when consumers are quite confident in what to expect.

Expectations and Service Quality

Service quality can be thought of as the overall goodness or badness of a service provided. Service quality is often discussed as the difference between consumer expectations of different service aspects and the actual service that is delivered. When a gap exists, for example, when a dental hygienist is not as empathetic as a consumer expected, then quality perceptions are diminished. In fact, the **SERVQUAL** scale, a commonly applied approach for measuring service quality, takes this approach. From this perspective, service quality is really a disconfirmation approach.[22] Perhaps it

confirmatory bias tendency for expectations to guide performance perceptions

self-perception theory theory that states that consumers are motivated to act in accordance with their attitudes and behaviors

service quality overall goodness or badness of a service experience, which is often measured by SERVQUAL

SERVQUAL way of measuring service quality that captures consumers' disconfirmation of service expectations

desire level of a particular benefit that will lead to a valued end state

equity theory theory that proposes that people compare their own level of inputs and outcomes to those of another party in an exchange

distributive fairness refers to the way a consumer judges the outcomes of an exchange

interactional fairness captures how fairly a consumer believes he or she was treated when dealing with service personnel in resolving some issue

One of the judgments consumers make about outcomes concerns equity. Does the outcome of their experience seem fair considering all input?

goes without saying, but service quality then becomes a key driver of consumer satisfaction or dissatisfaction.

Desires and Satisfaction

Although expectations play a major role in satisfaction formation, consumer desires are also very important. A **desire** is the level of a particular benefit that will lead to a valued end state. Studies have shown that desires directly impact satisfaction, beyond the influence of disconfirmation alone.[23] What consumers truly desire, rather than expect, from a product, service, or experience is therefore very important.

14-4b Equity Theory and Consumer Satisfaction

Perceptions of fairness can also have an impact on consumer satisfaction. **Equity theory** proposes that consumers cognitively compare their own level of inputs and outcomes to those of another party in an exchange.[24] Equitable exchanges occur when these ratios are equal. In equation form:

$$outcomes_A / inputs_A \approx outcomes_B / inputs_B$$

The equation states that as long as comparisons of outcomes to inputs for consumer A are approximately the same as the same ratio for another party (for example, a company or another consumer), then satisfaction will be positively affected. So an inequitable exchange can occur when a consumer believes that he or she has been taken advantage of by a company or when another customer has been treated more favorably.

When a consumer sets out to buy a computer, she will put quite a bit of effort into finding just the right one. She will take time to visit a store such as Best Buy, talk with friends about what brand to buy, visit websites such as Apple.com, and try to figure out the best way to finance the computer. She considers all these inputs before conducting the transaction. What will the consumer get when she buys the computer? Of course, she will get a computer, but she will also get a warranty, service contract, and maybe even in-home installation. These things represent her outcomes. The term **distributive fairness** refers to the way a consumer judges the outcomes of an exchange. When a consumer asks, "Did I get what I paid for?" she is asking a question of distributive fairness.

The computer salesperson should put time into understanding the consumer's desires and the way she will use the computer and then try to match these with a good arrangement of product features. Perhaps the salesperson will show effort by listening and physically searching store inventory for the most appropriate product. These are inputs for the salesperson. Salesperson outcomes include a salary and any commission tied directly to the sale. When consumers put a lot into an important purchase, they don't like to be shortchanged by an apathetic employee. That wouldn't be fair, and the output-to-input ratios would reflect this. Fairness perceptions affect satisfaction in addition to any influence of disconfirmation. In fact, consumers sometimes feel over rewarded in a service recovery effort. For instance, a passenger whose bags were delayed for an hour was offered $200 from an airline for the inconvenience. This act may come across as more than adequate for what was a relatively small transgression. However, consumers with this impression tend to pay the business back with very high satisfaction.[25] In particular, equity theory plays a role in explaining how consumers react to complaints. The term **interactional fairness** captures how fairly a consumer believes he is treated when dealing with service personnel in resolving some issue.[26]

Inequitable Treatment

Perhaps more often, equity perceptions involve inequitable treatment of customers. A single customer enters a restaurant for lunch and puts in an order. A few minutes later, a couple enters and sits beside the first customer at

Jim Stern/Bloomberg/Getty Images

the next table. They place their order. After ten minutes, the couple receives their food and the original customer is still waiting. To the original customer, this may seem unfair and be a source of dissatisfaction. Thus, service providers need to be keenly aware of how customers are treated in public to maintain perceptions that all customers are treated in much the same way—or at least treated in a fair way.

Inequitable Consumers

Some consumers will try to take advantage of situations. Even though treatment is inequitable, if the inequity is in the consumers' favor, these particular customers may be very satisfied. For example, some consumers may take a minor mishap and complain so fiercely that managers feel compelled to offer something overly generous as a way of calming the consumer down. Other consumers may realize that a cashier has made a significant error and given them significantly too much change and not correct the mistake. These consumers may be satisfied because the equity balance favors them. However, their actions can disadvantage other consumers.

14-4c Attribution Theory and Consumer Satisfaction

Another satisfaction theory focuses on consumer attributions. **Attribution theory** focuses on explaining why a certain event has occurred. When consumers select and consume products, they are motivated to make attributions as to why good or bad things happen. Humans are innately curious. There are three key elements to the attribution theory approach: *locus, control,* and *stability*.[27]

1. **Locus.** Judgments of who is responsible for an event. Consumers can assign the locus to themselves or to an external entity like a service provider. A self-ascribed event occurs when a consumer blames himself for a bad event. For example, a consumer might say to himself, "I have not followed the fitness program, no wonder I haven't lost any weight!" Self-ascribed causes are referred to as internal attributions. If an event is attributed to a product or company, an external attribution is made. For example, a consumer might say, "I exercised just like my personal trainer said and I've still gained weight!! She is clueless!" This type of attribution of blame toward a marketing entity increases consumer dissatisfaction.

2. **Control.** The extent to which an outcome was controllable or not. Here, consumers ask themselves, "Should this company have been able to control this event?" Two consumers are stranded in the Frankfurt airport in Germany overnight because their destination airport, Dallas/Fort Worth, is iced over. One consumer is irate (beyond dissatisfaction) with the airline because he believes the airline should have equipment to clear the ice off the runway—even in the southern part of the country. Another consumer who is booked on the same flight is not happy about the situation but does not blame the airline because she understands that weather events are uncontrollable. Therefore, the situation does not significantly affect her satisfaction process.

attribution theory theory that proposes that consumers look for the cause of particular consumption experiences when arriving at satisfaction judgments

3. **Stability.** The likelihood that an event will occur again in the future. Here, consumers ask themselves, "If I buy this product again, is another bad outcome likely to happen?" Let's briefly return to the Frankfurt airport example. If a customer recently found himself stranded because of weather problems in Dallas due to something other than an ice storm, he naturally comes to believe that this is a stable situation and his satisfaction with the airline is reduced. On the other hand, if the other consumer never found herself stranded due to problems at the Dallas airport, her satisfaction with the airline is not likely to be affected by the current situation. She, unlike the previous consumer, does not have a track record showing a stable problem.

> Effective marketing can target consumers after purchase to take steps to reinforce their customers' decisions to select a brand.

14-4d Cognitive Dissonance

Consumers also can experience what is known as cognitive dissonance following a purchase or a big decision. As was discussed with the balance theory approach, consumers prefer consistency among their beliefs. When faced with the knowledge that a bad decision may have been made, consumers experience dissonance (literally meaning "lack of agreement") between the thought that they are good decision makers and that they made a bad decision.

cognitive dissonance an uncomfortable feeling that occurs when a consumer has lingering doubts about a decision that has occurred

Cognitive dissonance refers to lingering doubts about a decision that has already been made.[28] Dissonance is sometimes known as buyer's regret. For example, a consumer may reach a decision to buy one house and then experience discomfort due to doubt that creeps in when he realizes there were many other attractive houses available in addition to the one purchased.

Cognitive dissonance does not occur for all decisions. For high-ticket items like automobiles or homes, though, dissonance is a real possibility if not a probability. Dissonance has also been responsible for more than a few cold feet in the days before a wedding. These are situations that naturally lend themselves to the experience of dissonance. A consumer is more likely to experience true dissonance following a purchase when the following conditions exist:

1. The consumer is aware that there are many attractive alternatives that may offer comparable value relative to the product/brand purchased.

2. The decision is difficult to reverse.

3. The decision is important and involves risk.

4. The consumer has low self-confidence.

The dissonance among consumers' beliefs following a consumption experience can be very discomforting and be a source of negative postconsumption emotions. Consumers may therefore be motivated to lessen this discomfort. Furthermore, effective marketing can target consumers after purchase to take steps to reinforce their customers' decisions to select a brand. Many universities automatically send graduates university-sponsored magazines in order to maintain relationships and to reinforce the idea that choosing the school was indeed a good idea.

To lessen feelings of discomfort following purchase, consumers may engage in any, or all, of the activities listed in Exhibit 14.5.

Cognitive Dissonance and Satisfaction

Satisfaction and cognitive dissonance are closely related topics. The major difference between the two concepts is that satisfaction is generally felt *after* a consumption experience but dissonance may be experienced even *before* consumption begins. For example, immediately after a decision has been made, a consumer might immediately think, "I should have bought the other one!" The uncertainty of events that might occur provides the basis for dissonance.[29]

EXHIBIT 14.5 Dissonance Reduction Strategies

- Return the product if possible
- Complain about the experience
- Seek positive information about the alternative selected
- Seek negative information about alternatives not selected
- Minimize the perceived importance of the decision

© Cengage Learning

14-5 Consumer Satisfaction/ Dissatisfaction Measurement Issues

There are many ways that marketers can measure consumer satisfaction. Three popular ways are through direct measures, difference scores, and disconfirmation.

- **Direct, Global Measure.** Simply asks consumers to assess their satisfaction on a scale such as:

  How do you rate your overall satisfaction with your stove?

completely dissatisfied	dissatisfied	satisfied	completely satisfied
☐	☐	☐	☐

- **Attribute-Specific.** Assesses a consumer's satisfaction with various components, or attributes, of a product, service, or experience, such as:

  How satisfied are you with the following attribute of your stove?

  Heat of Burners

completely dissatisfied				completely satisfied
1	2	3	4	5

- **Disconfirmation.** Compares the difference between expectations and performance perceptions. This measure can be taken in a direct, subjective fashion, such as:[30]

  Compared to my expectations, this stove performs . . .

much worse than I expected				much better than I expected
1	2	3	4	5

14-5a Improving Satisfaction Measures

Satisfaction is one of the most commonly measured concepts in consumer behavior but also one of the most difficult to measure accurately. For example, the typical four-choice satisfaction approach as shown in the direct global measure example actually proves quite problematic in practice. The problems can be severe and limit the ability to use satisfaction ratings to explain or predict other outcomes, including whether or not the consumer will return.

Consider that marketers measure satisfaction among existing customers most frequently. These customers have already decided to patronize a business. So a pop-up window on Amazon.com may ask a consumer to rate satisfaction with a simple measure of this type. This consumer should already be favorable because she has decided to purposefully visit Amazon.com and shop using this site. Thus, she already feels favorable toward Amazon.com. Therefore, we would expect even without knowing what happened during the visit that the customer would report some degree of satisfaction. In fact, typical consumer responses to this type of measure show that the vast majority of consumers, 80% or more, choose "satisfied" or "completely satisfied." Statistically speaking, these data are **left skewed**, in this instance meaning that the bulk of consumers have indicated that they are satisfied or completely satisfied with the product or service.

Does this reflect reality, or is the scale simply inadequate in truly differentiating consumers experiencing different levels of satisfaction? The truth is that both possibilities are likely true to some extent. From a measurement perspective, giving consumers more choices to respond to may increase the amount of variance displayed in the satisfaction measure and thereby increase its usefulness in trying to use satisfaction to predict and explain other behaviors. An alternative would be to have consumers score their satisfaction on a 0 (no satisfaction) to 100 (complete satisfaction) point scale. The results will still typically show an average satisfaction score above 50 points; however, the statistical properties are much improved,

making for a more useful measure. Even better, a researcher might have respondents rate their satisfaction with multiple scale items.

Exhibit 14.6 displays an improved way of measuring consumer satisfaction using multiple scale items.[31] The scale mitigates problems with skewness and bias by providing scales with more response points and by using different response formats for each response item. The scale also focuses only on satisfaction. Although a marketer may choose to measure only satisfaction, this scale suggests that dissatisfaction should be measured with its own scale. A dissatisfaction scale can be formed by substituting the word *dissatisfaction* for satisfaction in each of the four items. Even if a total of eight items are used (four satisfaction and four dissatisfaction items), a consumer can typically respond to these items in less than one minute.

> **left skewed** distribution of responses consistent with most respondents choosing responses so the distribution is clustered toward the positive end of the scale

---

EXHIBIT 14.6 A Multi-Item Satisfaction Scale

Please rate your satisfaction with your experience in the Delta Airlines Sky Club using the following items. It will take you no longer than 1 minute to complete this survey.

Place an X in the box that best describes the way you feel about your stay in the Delta Airlines Sky Club.

Not satisfied at all	Somewhat satisfied	Satisfied	Very satisfied	Completely satisfied
☐	☐	☐	☐	☐

Indicate the percent to which you feel satisfied with your stay in the Delta Airlines Sky Club using a 100 point scale where 0 = no satisfaction at all and 100 = total satisfaction.

_____ %

Indicate the extent to which you experienced the feeling of satisfaction with your visit to the Delta Airlines Sky Club. Place an X in the box that matches the way you feel.

Did not feel at all	Felt only slightly	Felt a little	Felt somewhat	Felt moderately	Felt very much	Felt Extremely
☐	☐	☐	☐	☐	☐	☐

To what extent do you agree with the following statement:
I feel completely satisfied with my experience with the Delta Airlines Sky Club.

Strongly disagree	Disagree	Slightly disagree	Slightly agree	Agree	Strongly agree
☐	☐	☐	☐	☐	☐

Source: Adapted from Barry J. Babin and Mitch Griffin, "The Nature of Satisfaction: An Updated Examination and Analysis," *Journal of Business Research* 41 (1998): 127–36.

consumer refuse any packaging that is no longer necessary for consumption to take place or, in some cases, the actual good that is no longer providing value to the consumer

The question of whether or not dissatisfaction is more than just low satisfaction can be sorted out statistically. That topic is left for another course.

14-6 Disposing of Refuse

14-6a Disposal Decisions

A final step in consumption is disposal of any consumer refuse. **Consumer refuse** is any packaging that is no longer necessary for consumption to take place or, in some cases, the actual good that is no longer providing value to the consumer. Many consumers have old computers that they no longer use but have not yet disposed of because of various concerns including security issues. At first, this may seem like a straightforward process: consumers simply throw away their trash. However, a number of disposal alternatives are available. These include trashing, recycling, converting to another use, trading, donating, or reselling.[32]

- **Trashing.** One alternative that a consumer has is to simply throw away waste material including unused products, packaging, and by-products. Of course, there are environmental concerns with this alternative. According to the Environmental Protection Agency, approximately 243 million tons of municipal garbage is generated each year, or an average of 4.0 pounds of garbage per person, per day![33] Many

marketers have turned to so-called green marketing initiatives, which aim to use packaging materials that cut down on the environmental impact of waste.

- **Recycling.** Another alternative for consumers is to recycle used products or packaging. Recycling cuts down on garbage while providing raw materials for other new products. Consumers can then buy new products made of recycled materials.

- **Converting.** Consumers can convert products or product packaging into new products in a number of creative ways. For example, consumers often use old t-shirts and socks as car-wash rags.

- **Trading.** Another alternative for consumers is to trade in old products for new products. The automotive industry has encouraged this practice for years. Consumers can often get thousands of dollars off of a new automobile purchase by trading in an old model. Even a car that doesn't run has some value in the form of spare parts.

- **Donating.** Consumers also have the ability to donate used products to various causes. Eyeglasses, clothing, and (surprisingly) automobiles are often donated in order to help other consumers who may not be able to afford new products.

- **Reselling.** One of the most popular methods for permanently disposing of used products is to simply sell them. Garage sales and swap meets are popular

Mr.Reborn55/Shutterstock.com

Satisfaction from the Soul!

The name Emilia-Romagna may not be familiar to a lot of consumers but nonetheless, the name means satisfaction to fashion-conscious women. That's the town in Italy where Louboutin, Ferragama, Prada, Armani, Alexander McQueen, and more produce designer shoes. A recent editorial opined that it was incomprehensible how a woman could find wearing high-heeled shoes satisfying. However, a presumption here is that the women expect the shoes to be comfortable. Also, the view puts forward a presumption that all high-heeled shoes are uncomfortable. In Emilia-Romagna, shoe designers once believed four inches

Richard Peterson/Shutterstock.com

was the limit on a high heel. An innovative designer discovered that by putting a platform under the ball of the foot, the back heel can be raised to just over 5 inches and not over-contort the foot. However, the heel must be made of steel at that point and placed directly under the heel bone. Then, the shoe is not so uncomfortable. Others say the value comes mainly from the way the shoes make women feel—good about themselves, self-confident, and powerful! If so, these things are more important and those consumers don't have high expectations for comfort anyway.

Sources: C. Binkely, "Pushing High Heels to the Limit," *The Wall Street Journal*, April 5, 2012, D1–D2. G. Bowler, "Power Heel' Thesis Fails to Convince," *The Wall Street Journal*, April 20, 2012, A12.

means of disposing of products in this way. Of course, online methods such as eBay and Craigslist are also quite popular with consumers.

14-6b Disposal, Emotions, and Product Symbolism

Consumers often develop emotional bonds with their possessions. As discussed in an earlier chapter, possessions can help express a consumer's self-concept. The decision to part with belongings can therefore be very emotional, especially for older consumers who place much symbolic value on many products.[34] Strong feelings of attachment may be placed on many goods, especially those goods that are considered to be family heirlooms. Selling, giving away, or donating goods can lead some consumers to feel as if they have lost a part of themselves. In other situations, consumers can be quite ready to dispose of products that bring back bad memories, or that lead the consumers to have uneasy feelings about themselves or their past.[35]

The willingness to let go of possessions varies from consumer to consumer. **Packrats** possess a lifestyle trait leading to a strong tendency toward retaining consumption-related possessions.[36] Packrats also are likely to visit garage sales, swap meets, and flea markets to purchase products that serve no immediate need.[37] Even though the term *packrat* is often used loosely, the packrat behavior can be associated with various psychological conditions including obsessive-compulsive disorder. In contrast, most consumers hang onto a relatively manageable number of cherished mementos from the past that bring a great deal of value through nostalgia or personal memories. Things like family photos and love letters are understandably difficult to simply throw away.

One method of disposal is to sell an item. Ebay makes selling unwanted items easy. Also, recent television shows like Cajun Pawn Stars have glamorized pawnshops. A pawnshop provides evidence that there is something to the old cliché that one person's garbage is another's treasure. Even emotional value has a price!

packrats consumers possessing high levels of a lifestyle trait leading to a strong tendency toward retaining consumption-related possessions

Study Tools

Located at the back of the textbook

- ❑ Rip out Chapter in Review Card

Located at www.cengagebrain.com

- ❑ Review Key Terms Flashcards (print or online)
- ❑ Download audio summaries to review on the go
- ❑ Complete practice quizzes to prepare for tests
- ❑ Play "Beat the Clock" to master concepts
- ❑ Watch video on Sephora for a real company example

WHAT DO YOU THINK?
WHAT OTHERS HAVE THOUGHT

①	②	③	④	⑤	⑥	⑦
Strongly disagree	Disagree	Somewhat disagree	Neither agree nor disagree	Somewhat agree	Agree	Strongly agree

When I'm treated unfairly by a business, dissatisfaction describes my feelings well.

Respondents show a tendency toward agreement. About 70 percent selected one of the agree responses. However, 25 percent disagree and perhaps recognize that emotions other than dissatisfaction come into play in these situations. For instance, maybe angry, hurt, or disgusted fits better.

Tim Hall/Cultura/Jupiter Images

Truly loyal customers
are like gold to a company.

WHAT DO YOU THINK?
When I have a good experience with a brand, I reward it by telling my friends how great it is.

STRONGLY DISAGREE   STRONGLY AGREE

VISIT COURSEMATE AT WWW.CENGAGEBRAIN.COM

Consumer Relationships

15

For companies and consumers alike, transactions hopefully represent only a single touchpoint among many that make up the relationships between the two. This chapter focuses on how single interactions between consumers and companies can become long-term relationships.

15-1 Outcomes of Consumption

The story of CB does not end with the transaction. In fact, a transaction can be a starting place. To help bring customers back, many companies offer satisfaction guarantees:

100% Satisfaction or Your Money Back!

Are all companies really interested in complete satisfaction? If consumers could not return to do business again, the pursuit of satisfaction would represent a purely altruistic exercise. Many firms might lose interest in serving customers if the only opportunity to do business with them is in the first transaction. The vast majority of businesses depend on consumers' repeat purchase behavior. Therefore, businesses should be very interested in what happens after the transaction—the outcomes of consumption—and the climax of CB.

This chapter focuses squarely on what happens after the purchase and even after consumption. Exhibit 15.1 illustrates postconsumption CB by expanding the disconfirmation framework traditionally used to represent consumer satisfaction. The green colored boxes represent cognitive reactions experienced by consumers including those that make up the actual disconfirmation process. The disconfirmation process comprising a comparison of what a consumer thought would happen in terms of expectations with the consumer's actual performance perception. A consumer's attributions and equity perceptions also represent cognitive reactions. More specifically, a consumer's equity perceptions are also included among cognitions. Perceptions of justice are included within the equity cognitions.

After studying this chapter, the student should be able to:

15-1 List and define the behavioral outcomes of consumption.

15-2 Know why and how consumers complain and spread word-of-mouth and know the ramifications for the marketing firm.

15-3 Use the concept of switching costs to understand why consumers do or do not repeat purchase behavior.

15-4 Describe each component of true consumer loyalty.

15-5 Understand the role that value plays in shaping loyalty and building consumer relationships.

procedural justice
an equity-based cognition representing the extent that consumers believe the processes involved in processing a transaction, performing a service, or handling any complaint are fair

critical incident exchange between consumers and business that the consumer views as unusually negative with implications for the relationship

complaining behavior
action that occurs when a consumer actively seeks out someone (supervisor, service provider, etc.) to share an opinion with regarding a negative consumption event

Procedural justice, in particular, refers to the extent that consumers believe the processes involved in processing a transaction, performing a service, or handling a complaint is fair. Distributive justice represents how fair the overall outcome is perceived.

Postconsumption cognitions lead to an affective reaction most conventionally represented by consumer satisfaction or dissatisfaction (CS/D). This particular model recognizes that the evaluation process could lead to any number of varying affective outcomes, many of which have stronger behavioral reactions than CS/D. The blue sections in Exhibit 15.1 show the affective variables.

Finally, the exhibit shows behavioral outcomes of the postconsumption process in magenta boxes. Indeed, this is why marketers are interested in pursuing satisfaction. The behaviors that complete this process do much to determine the success or failure of competitive enterprises.

Never has this been truer than in today's relationship marketing era. While the negative behaviors like complaining perhaps receive more attention as reactions to consumption, positive outcomes, including positive word-of-mouth behavior and ultimately the development of a strong relationship, are essential elements to success.

We begin this chapter by looking at some common behaviors that follow consumption. Exhibit 15.1 lists the behaviors; although most seem negative, if properly managed they can be turned by the firm into positive value experiences. The term **critical incident** refers to exchanges between consumers and business that the consumer views as unusually negative.[1] Customers who believe a firm has adequately responded to some negative critical incident are likely to become more loyal, and loyalty is the positive outcome relationship-oriented firms seek.

15-2 Complaining and Spreading WOM

15-2a Complaining Behavior

Complaining behavior occurs when a consumer actively seeks out someone to share an opinion with regarding a negative consumption event. The person may be a service provider, a supervisor, or someone designated by a company to take complaints. Think about this question:

> *How long should a consumer have to wait for service before complaining?*

The answer to this may depend on several factors, including the type of service involved. A 30-minute wait may be unacceptable and evoke negative disconfirmation, a negative affective consequence, and an active complaint if a consumer is waiting to be served for lunch. However, a consumer waiting to see a doctor for 30 minutes may not experience the same reaction because the expectation is that one will wait for 30 minutes or more. Even if one waits longer than expected to see a doctor, the consumer still may not complain for other reasons.

Complainers

Generally, we think of dissatisfied customers as complainers. Not all customers

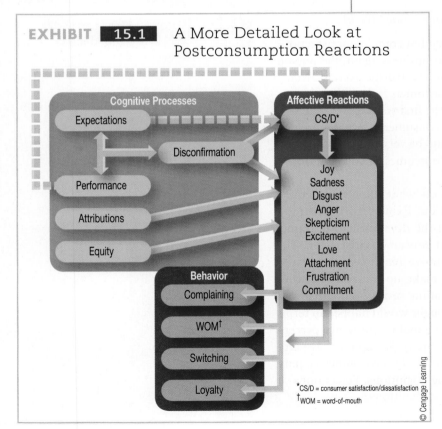

EXHIBIT 15.1 A More Detailed Look at Postconsumption Reactions

*CS/D = consumer satisfaction/dissatisfaction
†WOM = word-of-mouth

© Cengage Learning

Actively listening to the complaints of annoyed customers can lead to greatly improved service.

ALLESALLTAG BILDAGENT/AGE Fotostock

reporting dissatisfaction complain. In fact, far less than half of customers experiencing some dissatisfaction complain to management. This means that for every poor service encounter management hears about from a complaining customer, estimates suggest about 20 other customers had something to complain about but chose not to voice that complaint to management.[2]

What makes a *complainer* different? Consumers who complain experience different emotions than do those who do not complain. In contrast to consumers who are merely dissatisfied, angry consumers are very likely to complain and, at times, the anger becomes very strong and reaches the stage of rage.[3] These consumers complain and more. In addition, consumers high in price sensitivity are more likely to complain than consumers with some indifference about the price paid for a service.[4] In turn, price-sensitive consumers become less loyal following the complaint than do those with less price sensitivity.

A potentially worse outcome for a business occurs when a consumer has a negative experience, realizes this, and then reacts more with disgust than anger. Compared to the angry customer, a disgusted or hopeless consumer is not likely to complain.[5] Consumers' behavioral reactions can be understood by considering whether the emotions they experience evoke approach or avoidance reactions. Negative approach emotions like anger are most likely to precede complaining behavior. Complaining is a relatively mild way of coping with anger.

The consumer who reacts with disgust is unlikely to complain. Disgust evokes an avoidance response, and as a result, a disgusted consumer avoids a potential confrontation and simply goes away.

When the disgusted consumer simply goes away, the information about what caused the problem in the first place also goes away. Complainers, although sometimes unpleasant to deal with, are valuable sources of feedback about potential problems in service quality, product performance, or system malfunction. Unfortunately, the disgusted consumer copes by going away.

When a consumer complains, the marketer has a chance to rectify the negative situation. A consumer who sulks away takes the valuable information with her. A truly consumer-oriented company should encourage customers to complain when things go wrong. If "100% satisfaction" is not just a slogan, the company must encourage its customers to act like whistleblowers when something goes wrong. In this sense, an angry customer is a valuable asset for a business!

> When a customer complains, the marketer has a chance to rectify the negative situation…. An angry customer is a valuable asset.

The Results of Complaining

Exhibit 15.2 provides a summary of what happens when consumers do or do not complain. The fact of the matter is that for consumers as well as marketers, complaining

EXHIBIT 15.2 Complainers versus Noncomplainers

Complainers:
- Tell others when company performs poorly
- Potentially valuable source of information
- More likely to become satisfied with company intervention
- More likely to return following exchange

Noncomplainers:
- May tell others (friends/family) when company performs poorly
- Not as valuable to firm because they don't complain
- Unlikely to return
- Firm must take preemptive action to create satisfaction

Elena Elisseeva/Shutterstock.com

Selecstock/Shutterstock.com

© Cengage Learning

pays off. When consumers complain, more often than not some corrective action is taken that culminates with the consumer feeling satisfied when he reevaluates the situation. A consumer who complains about a noisy hotel room gets moved to another room, perhaps a suite! In such a case, the customer is likely to believe that he was treated fairly after complaining, and these thoughts evoke a more positive outcome. This positive outcome can represent a win-win situation.

The U.S. Better Business Bureau (BBB) reports that over three out of four consumer complaints across all industries are resolved in a way that leaves the customer satisfied.[6] Thus, businesses should actively seek resolutions to consumer complaints. The following list gives service providers advice for handling consumer complaints effectively:[7]

1. Thank the customer for providing the information.
2. Ask questions to clarify the issue.
3. Apologize sincerely.
4. Show empathy for the customer's situation.
5. Explain the corrective action that will take place.
6. Act quickly.
7. Follow up with the customer after the corrective action.

Today it's easier than ever for consumers to complain publicly. Check out websites like these:

- Complaints.com (www.complaints.com)
- Federal Communications Commission (www.fcc.gov/complaints)
- Better Business Bureau (www.bbb.org)

These websites allow consumers to lodge formal complaints, make their complaints public, and get advice on the proper steps to follow should the consumer need to take further official action. Public complaining on such forums also creates a source of negative publicity, as we will see later in the chapter.

The Result of Not Complaining

So, what happens when a consumer does not complain? Let's return to the noisy hotel room. Our customer may simply put up with the inconvenience and end up leaving miserable after a poor night's sleep. Is this the end of the story? Not really! The consumer may well remember this incident and be less likely to do business with this hotel again. He may also complain to others about the episode. Interestingly, though, when marketers can take action to address a negative situation before a consumer complains, a very positive outcome can result. So, imagine that a bell clerk reports the noise in one of the halls of the hotel to management. Management then takes action by calling the adjacent guests to suggest that they move to better rooms. These customers are likely to be very appreciative and become more likely to return again.[8]

Can You Hear Me Now???

Consumers complain to let off steam and to hopefully get a remedy to some critical service incident. If you don't like to deal with complaining customers, then stay away from some industries. The BBB tracks complaints across practically every industry. What industry is number one in receiving complaints? Think about your own experiences and you may not be surprised at the following lists of the five industries where consumers complain the most:

1. Cellular Phone Service and Equipment
2. New Car Dealers

© iStockphoto.com/Don Bayley

3. Television Services (Cable TV, Satellite TV, …)
4. Collection Agencies
5. Banks

What is it about consumers of these products that makes them relatively more likely to complain? The answer may not be obvious, but consumers of these products generally face high switching cost. Thus, consumers who feel entrapped in a relationship may see a complaint to an agency like the BBB as one of their only options when they perceive that the service provided is bad. Can you relate?

Source: "US BBB 2011 Statistics," Better Business Bureau, http://www.bbb.org/us/ (accessed July 4, 2012).

Revenge

On occasion, consumers' verbal complaints to the marketing company do not eliminate the negative emotions they are experiencing. In these instances, consumers may retaliate in the form of revenge-oriented behaviors. These could be as simple as trying to prevent others from using the business by spreading the word about how bad the business is, but the behaviors can become more aggressive. **Rancorous revenge** is when a consumer yells insults and makes a public scene in an effort to harm the business.[9] A vengeful consumer may make derogatory posts on social networks as a way of taking out frustrations. In extreme cases the furious consumer can become violent or try to vandalize the business. **Retaliatory revenge** is a term that captures these extreme types of behavior. Revenge often occurs out of feelings of inequity; in particular, violations of procedural or interactional justice can lead to revenge.[10]

When it comes to rancorous or retaliatory revenge, the customer is definitely not always right! From time to time news stories report extreme consumer behaviors. A Taco Bell customer returned a few minutes after receiving his order and vandalized the restaurant after discovering one taco missing from his bag. Another customer got upset with the service at a Mercedes dealership and drove his car through the glass into the showroom. In the extreme, employees and bystanders are seriously harmed by these behaviors.

15-2b Word-of-Mouth/Publicity

Just because a consumer doesn't complain to the offending company doesn't mean she just keeps the episode inside. **Negative word-of-mouth** (negative WOM) takes place when consumers pass on negative information about a company from one to another. As can be seen from Exhibit 15.2, both the complainer and the noncomplainer may well participate in this kind of potentially destructive behavior. Some estimates suggest that consumers who fail to achieve a valuable consumption experience are likely to tell their story to more than ten other consumers.[11] Recall that as a source of information, WOM is powerful because of relatively high source credibility. The fact that most consumers who participate in WOM speak to multiple consumers makes the matter all the more important.

WOM is not always negative. In fact, **positive WOM** occurs when consumers spread information from one to another about positive consumption experiences with companies. Conventionally, negative WOM is seen as more common than positive WOM. However, in the television industry, consumers appear more likely to spread the word about shows they find valuable rather than those they do not.[12] One study shows that when a shopper has a reversal in orientation from a browser to a buyer within a retail store, he becomes highly likely to tell others about the great experience.[13] Whether positive or negative, WOM exerts very strong influences on other consumers.

rancorous revenge is when a consumer yells insults and makes a public scene in an effort to harm the business in response to an unsatisfactory experience

retaliatory revenge consumer becomes violent with employees and/or tries to vandalize a business in response to an unsatisfactory experience

negative word-of-mouth (negative WOM) action that takes place when consumers pass on negative information about a company from one to another

positive WOM action that occurs when consumers spread information from one to another about positive consumption experiences with companies

negative public publicity action that occurs when negative WOM spreads on a relatively large scale, possibly even involving media coverage

Negative Public Publicity

When negative WOM spreads on a relatively large scale, it can result in **negative public publicity**. Negative public publicity could even involve widespread media coverage. The outcome of such events questions the old cliché that bad publicity is better than no publicity at all. Lululemon, which markets yoga pants that retail for about $100, recently faced an embarrassing episode when customers discovered that their Luon pants, although black, were see-through when stretched. As many companies would do, Lululemon's PR team spread the word that these pants were being promptly recalled.[13a]

Sometimes, negative publicity starts with individual consumer behaviors. Today, consumers have more options than ever when it comes to spreading negative publicity. They can actually talk to one another in person or on the phone about bad company experiences, they can complain to public media like newspapers, or they can complain to websites set up for that purpose, but more and more consumers are turning to social media as a way of spreading negative publicity. YouTube contains many videos with various consumer rants about different companies. One post shows a cable TV service technician asleep on a customer's couch. Facebook contains numerous pages set up as vehicles for consumers to publicly post complaints about companies. These sites can turn a complaint into negative publicity—particularly when the complaint goes viral!

Facebook offers consumers ways of turning negative word-of-mouth into negative public publicity.

Facebook consumer complaints

Companies use software such as Salesforce.com's Radian6 to monitor posts on social media that use the brand's name.[14] At the Gatorade Mission Control Center, employees focus particularly on tweets mentioning Gatorade, sponsored events, or any athletes that endorse the Gatorade brand. Gatorade's own Twitter site has over 125,000 followers. When negative tweets are discovered, the team goes into action. If the tweet constitutes an individual customer complaint, Gatorade tries to reach out to that individual customer. Hopefully, the customer is a follower. When negative tweets begin to show a consistent theme, negative publicity could be the result and Gatorade can respond directly via Twitter to its followers, but they also can release public relations (PR) of their own through Facebook and conventional media outlets to try to quell any damage to the name brand. In the social media world, the key is to respond quickly before negative news goes viral.

Negative publicity can do considerable harm to a brand. British Petroleum, known as BP, suffered serious damage to the brand due to the 2010 oil spill that received worldwide media coverage for months. BP continues to spend millions in community service along the U.S. Gulf Coast and on advertising promoting their social efforts and taking responsibility for the spill. Even though Mother Nature has restored the environment faster than experts expected,[15] BP's image remains lower than before the spill in practically every part of the world.

How should a firm handle negative public publicity? Here are some alternative courses of action:

1. Do nothing; the news will eventually go away.
2. Deny responsibility for any negative event.
3. Take responsibility for any negative events and be visible in the public eye.
4. Release information allowing the public to draw its own conclusion.

What is the best approach?

Doing Nothing

Doing nothing is neither the best nor the worst option. Taking action seems to be a responsible thing to do, but the action might backfire and bring more attention to the issue. For over two decades, June's first days have been known as "Gay Days" at Florida's Walt Disney World theme parks. The event is not sponsored or sanctioned by Disney, but has grown over the years to attract mainstream sponsors such as Bud Light. Tens of thousands of gays and lesbians, often adorned with red t-shirts, visit the Magic Kingdom at the height of the event. The juxtaposition of a brand strongly tied to traditional family values that appeals to children of all ages with the social sensitivities of this event puts Disney in a difficult position. Disney's response is to stay silent.[16] The event attracts thousands of posts to blogs and social media sites, but nothing from Disney. Disney does, however, refund park admissions for any families who are uncomfortable attending the park during these days. Would any open public reaction cause even more problems?

Silence can also be better when a negative claim is ridiculous. For instance, a rumor spread in the mid 2000s that Starbucks refused to provide products to members of the military serving in the Middle East because they were against the war in Iraq. The rumor proved to be false and in fact Starbucks has several programs designed to assist those in military service. Had Starbucks publicly denied this rumor, it only would have given it credibility.

Denying Responsibility

Denials can also be tricky given the potential to bring attention to something that may not even be true. Denials should be made only when the evidence unambiguously supports the actual truth. Even when one is innocent, denials can have lingering effects. Consider the long-term effects on the images of baseball celebrities involved in the steroid scandal. Roger "the Rocket" Clemens, seven-time Cy Young Award winner for the best pitcher in the league, denied taking steroids to the media, to fans, to Congress, and in court. Even though the court found him innocent of lying to Congress, the Clemens brand may be irreparably tarnished.[17] Another famous pitcher, Andy Pettitte, acknowledged taking steroids when confronted with the claim and his image remains positive.

Taking Responsibility

One might easily see that attribution theory plays a role in dealing with negative publicity. If consumers blame the company for the event surrounding the negative publicity, then the potential repercussions appear serious. However, public action to deal with any consequences of a negative event can mollify any negative effects.

One of the most famous negative publicity cases of all time involves Tylenol pain medicine. In the fall of 1982, over half a dozen consumer deaths in the Chicago area were attributed to cyanide traces in Tylenol capsules. Tylenol executives considered their options, including plausible deniability, and decided to take action by immediately having all Tylenol removed from shelves all around the country immediately. In addition, they agreed to take steps to make sure they discovered what had happened and to make sure it could not happen again. The dramatic action helped convince consumers that Tylenol truly cared about the welfare of customers and wanted to make sure this never happened again. Even though they were quite certain they had no culpability in what appears to be senseless murder, they acted in a way that led to a huge short-term loss. However, this action saved Tylenol's reputation. In fact, many younger consumers may wonder how we came to have tamperproof packaging for over-the-counter medications and now practically all food products. While today government mandates require such packaging in many instances, the beginning of tamperproof packaging goes back to Tylenol's response to this potentially damaging negative publicity associated with the murders.

Releasing Information

Sometimes, a company may be able to release some counter-PR to media that allows consumers to make up their own minds about the potential source of any negative PR. If this is done properly, the company does not publicly deny any allegation about the event and instead insists that actions are being taken to get to the bottom of the event.

In the mid 1990s, a consumer made the news by claiming that he was simply drinking a Pepsi when a hypodermic needle began to flow out of the can and stuck his lip. Within two days of this story going public, dozens of consumers from all around the country made the same claim. Pepsi, rather than denying any responsibility, opened the doors of canning operations around North America. Film crews were allowed to come in and videotape cans streaming down an assembly line at high speed. Pepsi released information about the number of canning plants that exist and how they are spread around the country. This action worked to prevent any negative fallout for Pepsi. The media coverage allowed consumers to draw their own conclusions.

Obviously, if a needle would get into some Pepsi cans, the chances that this would happen at multiple canning plants all around the country seemed unlikely. Thus, how could this be happening all over? Also, watching the canning operations made clear the fact that nobody could possibly slip a needle into a can at the speeds the assembly line operates. This entire incident was over in just a couple of weeks. All of the alleged needle victims confessed to making up the stories with the hope of getting some part of any settlement that Pepsi might be forced to pay. Thus, this appears to be a textbook way to deal with negative publicity for an implausible event.

Participating in Negative WOM

One of the factors that helps determine negative word-of-mouth returns to the issue of equity. Consumers who believe they have not been treated with fairness or justice become particularly likely to tell others and, in some cases, report the incident to the media.[18]

Consumers can be angry when they believe they have been wronged in this way, and these actions are a small way of trying to get revenge. Consumers who spread negative WOM without complaining to the company itself are particularly likely to never do business with that company again.[19] This tendency provides all the more reason for companies to make consumers feel comfortable about complaining and creating the impression of genuine concern for the consumer's situation.

Implications of Negative WOM

One reason consumers share negative WOM is as a way of preventing other consumers from falling victim to a company. Thus, negative WOM can hurt sales. However, this is not the only potential negative effect. Negative

The media are a vehicle both for spreading negative publicity and for managing the implications of negative publicity.

third-party endorsement
one form of publicity in which an ostensibly objective outsider (neither the customer nor the business) provides publicly available purchase recommendations or evaluations

WOM also can damage the image of the firm. When a consumer hears the negative WOM from a credible source, that information gets stored and associated with the schema for that brand. Thus, not only is the consumer's attitude toward the brand lowered, but the consumer will also find the firm's advertising harder to believe.[20]

In extreme cases, the negative WOM attached to one company can have effects that spill over to an entire industry. For instance, news attributing accidents at one amusement park to a lack of maintenance will certainly damage the image of that particular amusement park. However, a consumer hearing this news may end up not feeling very comfortable about any similar amusement park. Thus, firms must be wary of negative WOM not just for their own brand, but for the industry as well.[21]

Negative WOM does not affect all consumers and all brands in the same way. Consumers who have very strong, positive feelings about a brand may have a difficult time accepting negative WOM. One reason is due to balance theory, as consumers try to maintain their existing belief systems. If the relationship with the brand is strong, accepting negative information also diminishes the consumer's self-concept. In addition, highly loyal consumers connect the brand with positive emotions such that the emotions help insulate the brand from negative WOM to some degree.[22] Online consumer reviews on product-related and social networking websites influence consumers. A negative review can influence consumers' opinions of products—particularly technologically oriented ones. However, online reviews influence the opinions for relatively unfamiliar brands much more than they do established brands,[23] so new brands need to be particularly wary of "the word of mouse."

Third-Party Endorsements

Not all publicity is negative. Consumers often see publicity as more credible than advertising because the source is someone other than the firm. A **third-party endorsement** represents one form of publicity in which an ostensibly objective outsider (neither the customer nor the business) provides publicly available purchase recommendations. These come in two forms.

The first type makes recommendations based on cumulative consumer ratings. TripAdvisor represents a site that collects consumers' postconsumption evaluations of restaurants, airlines, and hotels, and provides an overall recommendation based on the average ratings.

The web provides a virtually limitless number of opportunities to find third-party endorsements. The consumer is left to find out which are credible.

Consumers tend to trust each other, so these ratings can be influential. However, are all the ratings supplied by actual customers? Web "worksites" like Fiverr.com allow anyone to hire "workers" who will post batches of fake reviews (positive or negative) about any business.[24] Thus, technology provides another mechanism for unethical behavior in the form of manufactured ratings.

The second type involves recommendations from subject experts. Numerous media organizations endorse higher education institutes and programs. Each has its own system for determining the best schools in each category. Universities put considerable effort into finding a place near the top of at least one of these lists. The Academy of Motion Pictures Oscar Award may be the best known third-party product endorsement. Movies that are merely nominated for an Oscar see spikes in sales at the box office and online. Several "authorities" score wines; retailers routinely use these scores as point-of-purchase promotional materials as these endorsements are very influential in a category where most buyers have difficulty discriminating among alternatives. The following are examples of such rating authorities:

1. *Financial Times*: ranks business schools and graduate business programs

2. *U.S. News and World Report*: ranks universities and programs

> The negative WOM attached to one company can affect an entire industry. Accidents due to poor maintenance at an amusement park can damage the image of the entire industry.

3. *Consumer Reports*: rates the latest consumer products from soap to automobiles

4. *Wine Spectator*: rates wines based on blind taste tests by editors on a scale of 50 to 100

5. JD Power: rates autos and many other industries

6. CNET: rates many consumer products, with an emphasis on electronics (reviews.cnet.com)

15-3 Switching Behavior

Exhibit 15.1 suggests that a consumer evaluates a consumption experience, reacts emotionally, and then, perhaps, practices switching behavior. **Switching**, in a consumer behavior context, refers to the times when a consumer chooses a competing choice, rather than the previously purchased choice, on the next purchase occasion. If a consumer visited Waffle House for breakfast last Tuesday, and chooses Panera Bread the next time she goes out for breakfast, the consumer has practiced switching behavior. This could be due to any number of reasons, but perhaps the last experience at Waffle House was less than satisfying.

All things considered, consumers prefer the status quo. Change brings about, well ... change, and this can mean costs that diminish the value of an experience. If the consumer has been a regular Waffle House customer, she now has to learn the new assortment of items available at Panera Bread, may lose any accumulated benefits from being a loyal Waffle House customer, and cannot get all of those free coffee refills at Waffle House.

Thus, the consumer will incur some **switching costs**, or the costs associated with changing from one choice (brand/retailer/service provider) to another. Switching costs are one reason why a consumer may be dissatisfied with a service provider but will continue to do business with them. Switching costs can be divided into three categories:[25]

1. Procedural
2. Financial
3. Relational

15-3a Procedural Switching Costs

Procedural switching costs involve lost time and effort. Although Apple computers have a stellar reputation for being easy to use, many computer users stick with PC models. Why? Even if an Apple MacBook is easy to use, a consumer familiar with a PC-based Windows operating platform would have to forgo this knowledge to learn how to use a MacBook. Thus, the effort that went into learning the PC system is lost and replaced by effort that would be needed to learn how to use an Apple. Thus, when consumers master a technologically complex product, they become very resistant to switching.

15-3b Financial Switching Costs

Financial switching costs consist of the total economic resources that must be spent or invested as a consumer learns how to obtain value from a new product choice. A consumer in Lille, France, plans a summer vacation to the Mexican Riviera. A few weeks later, the consumer hears friends discussing their upcoming vacation in Florida and suffers cognitive dissonance. Even though the vacation to Florida now seems better, he has already purchased airfare for his family and the airlines would impose a €60 penalty on each ticket. This financial cost of switching does much to influence the final decision to go to Mexico. On some occasions, consumers receive services with bundled prices (such as cable, Internet, and phone in one bill). The consumer could potentially perceive, and may actually realize, an increased price if they were to replace only one of the services in the bundle.[26] A financial switching cost would be incurred in this situation.

15-3c Relational Switching Costs

The **relational switching cost** refers to the emotional and psychological consequences of changing from one brand/retailer/service provider to another. Imagine a consumer who has used the same hairstylist for five years. When she goes to college, however, she finds another hair salon that is more convenient. She is greeted by a stylist named Karla just after entering the salon. Although Karla seems nice, the consumer is very uneasy during the entire salon visit. In fact, she even feels a bit guilty for letting Karla do her hair. This uneasiness is an example of a typical relational switching cost.

switching times when a consumer chooses a competing choice, rather than the previously purchased choice, on the next purchase occasion

switching costs costs associated with changing from one choice (brand/retailer/service provider) to another

procedural switching costs lost time and effort

financial switching costs total economic resources that must be spent or invested as a consumer learns how to obtain value from a new product choice

relational switching cost emotional and psychological consequences of changing from one brand/retailer/service provider to another

competitive intensity
number of firms competing for business within a specific category

15-3d Understanding Switching Costs

Exhibit 15.3 demonstrates conventional consumer behavior theory that explains switching costs. Consumers become dissatisfied for any number of reasons, and these reasons and dissatisfaction together determine how likely a consumer is to return on the next purchase occasion.[27] Equity judgments, in particular perceptions of unfair treatment, are particularly prone to lead consumers to switch. Perceptions of unfair prices may make consumers temporarily angry, but they also create lasting memories. When coastal building centers raise plywood prices immediately before a hurricane's landfall, they may enjoy a short-term profit, but consumers will probably remember this and switch to a different retailer the next time they need a building center. Retailers like Home Depot make a point of advertising policies that they maintain prices during weather crises like hurricanes.

Furthermore, even though all types of functional costs can prevent switching, evidence suggests that relational barriers may be the most resistant to influence. Retailers who build up procedural switching costs, particularly through the use of loyalty cards and other similar programs, may gain temporary repeat purchase behavior, but they fail to establish the connection with the customer that wins them true loyalty.[28] Additionally, the inability of web-based retailers to create anything other than procedural loyalty may be responsible for the low levels of loyalty observed for pure-play (Internet-only) retailers.[29]

15-3e Satisfaction and Switching

The intermingling of consumer satisfaction/dissatisfaction and switching costs has received considerable attention. In fact, in addition to the measurement difficulties associated with CS/D, switching costs are another important reason

EXHIBIT 15.3 Factors Contributing to Switching Costs

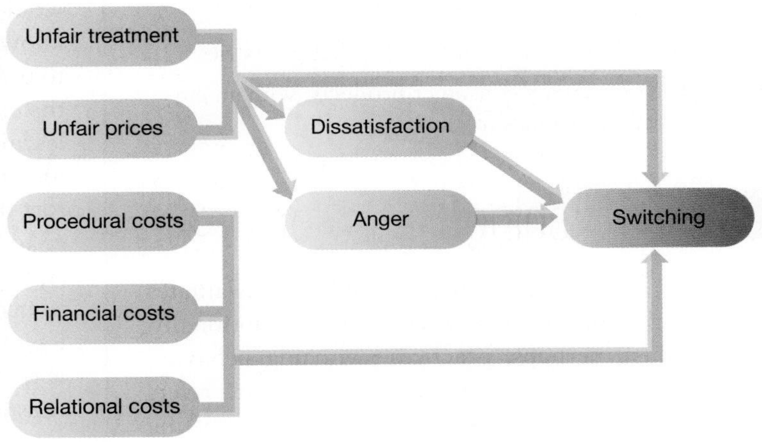

why CS/D results often fail to predict future purchasing behavior. Exhibit 15.4 summarizes how vulnerable a company is to consumer defections based on the interaction between switching costs, competitive intensity, and consumer satisfaction.

As can be seen in Exhibit 15.4, dissatisfaction does not always mean that the consumer is going to switch. Before reaching a conclusion on vulnerability to losing a customer, one also has to take into account at least two other factors. For instance, the amount of competition and the competitive intensity also play a role in determining who switches. **Competitive intensity** refers to the number of firms competing for business within a specific category. Until 1984, American consumers had only one choice for telephone service—"Ma Bell." So competitive intensity was low. Today, consumers have many choices for data services. Consumers can choose among companies such as AT&T, Verizon, or CenturyLink, or Internet calling with a company like Skype. Consumers who are

EXHIBIT 15.4 Vulnerability to Defections Based on CS/D

Customers	High Competitive Intensity		Low Competitive Intensity	
	Switching Costs		Switching Costs	
	Low	High	Low	High
Satisfied	Vulnerable	Low vulnerability	Low vulnerability	No vulnerability
Dissatisfied	Highly vulnerable	Vulnerable	Vulnerable	Low vulnerability

dissatisfied with their phones also tend to stick with them due to the service contract. Service providers, particularly in the U.S.A., subsidize phone prices as long as the consumer's contract is eligible for renewal. If the consumer had to pay full price for a smartphone, few would switch.

When competitive intensity is high and switching costs are low, a company is vulnerable to consumers who will switch providers even when customers are satisfied. The consumer has many companies vying for the business and changing presents little barrier. Today, a consumer has many choices when it comes to getting take-out food, and switching costs are very low. Even if a consumer is satisfied with Chili's take-out, he may try Boston Market next time if a traffic situation makes Boston Market's location slightly more convenient.

In contrast, Exhibit 15.4 suggests that even when consumers are dissatisfied, consumers may not switch. Consider the case when competitive intensity is low, meaning there are few alternatives for the consumer and switching costs are high. In this case, even dissatisfied consumers may return time and time again. In many small- to medium-size markets in the United States, Walmart Supercenters dominate the mass merchandising landscape. Many conventional grocery stores were unable to compete in these markets; as a result, the Walmart Supercenter became practically the only choice for buying groceries on any large scale. Thus, although consumers may experience dissatisfaction, the fact that there are few places to turn to and the costs of switching might involve a long drive to the next larger city in the area makes Walmart only slightly vulnerable to defections due to low consumer satisfaction.

15-4 Consumer Loyalty

15-4a Customer Share

Marketing managers have come to accept the fact that getting business from a customer who has already done business with the company before is easier and less expensive than getting a new customer. This basic belief motivates much of relationship marketing. The rubrics that determine marketing success then switch from pure sales and profit margin toward indicators that take into account marketing efficiencies. One important concept is **customer share**, which is the portion of resources allocated to one brand from among the set of competing brands. Here, *brand* is used loosely to capture any type of consumer alternative including a retailer, service provider, or actual product brand. Some managers use the term **share of wallet** to refer to customer share.

> **customer share** portion of resources allocated to one brand from among the set of competing brands
>
> **share of wallet** customer share

Exhibit 15.5 illustrates customer share. The exhibit shows the choices made by two consumers who each make daily coffee shop visits. On July 1, Bill goes to Starbucks (SB) and spends $5 and Erin does the same thing. On July 2, Bill returns to Starbucks and spends $10. Erin however, goes to CC's (CC) and spends $15. In ten days, Bill chose Starbucks (SB) eight out of ten times and spent $60 out of the $80 total at Starbucks. Erin chose Starbucks only three times out ten visits and spent $20 out of the $70 total at Starbucks. Thus, Starbucks gets considerably greater customer share from Bill than from Erin. The tenet of relationship marketing is that a company's marketing is much more efficient when most of the business comes from repeat customers. In this sense, Bill is a more valuable consumer to Starbucks than Erin is. Starbucks gets a greater share of Bill's coffee business than they do out of Erin.

Customer share represents a behavioral component that is indicative of customer loyalty. Behaviorally, Bill is more loyal than Erin. When customers don't switch, they repeat their purchase behavior over again. At times, they repeat the behavior over and over and over again. We examine the question of whether or not a consumer is truly loyal by examining why a consumer is repeating behavior. This brings us to the concept of consumer inertia.

EXHIBIT 15.5 Customer Share Information for Two Coffee Shop Customers

	Date of Visit										Total Spent
	7-1	7-2	7-3	7-4	7-5	7-6	7-7	7-8	7-9	7-10	
Bill Choice	SB	SB	CC	SB	SB	CC	SB	SB	SB	SB	
$$ Spent	5	10	10	5	15	10	5	5	10	5	$80
Erin Choice	SB	CC	M	M	SB	M	CC	SB	CC	M	
$$ Spent	5	15	5	5	5	5	10	10	5	5	$70

SB = Starbucks
CC = CC's
M = McDonald's

© Cengage Learning

Consumer Inertia

consumer inertia situation in which a consumer tends to continue a pattern of behavior until some stronger force motivates him or her to change

loyalty card/program device that keeps track of the amount of purchasing a consumer has had with a given marketer once some level is reached

In physics, inertia refers to the fact that a mass that is in motion (or at rest) will stay in motion (at rest) unless the mass is acted upon by a greater force. The concept of consumer inertia presents an analogy. **Consumer inertia** means that consumers will tend to continue a pattern of behavior until some stronger force motivates them to change. In fact, resistance to change is one of the biggest reasons why new products fail in the marketplace.[30] Change often means consumers must give something up. For example, many grocers try to take advantage of technology to increase the utilitarian value of getting groceries. The latest approach involves a regular grocery purchase where the customer simply drives up, pays using a credit card, and drives away in a matter of minutes. This seems like a great value-added service. However, it comes at the price of the value that a customer gets by actually entering in the store and getting to see, touch, and smell the products beforehand. Remember that losses loom larger than gains and a potential loss motivates consumers more to continue with their current consumer behavior.

Jean Claude MOSCHETTI/REA/Redux

At this store, you can drive up and collect a regular order of groceries without leaving your car. Will this create loyalty?

Loyalty Programs

Many marketers have experimented with loyalty cards or programs as a way of increasing customer share. Loyalty cards also allow marketers to learn more about customer groups' demographics and shopping patterns. A **loyalty card/program** is a device that keeps track of the amount of purchasing a consumer has had with a given marketer (as well as a list of actual items purchased by the consumer); once some level is reached a reward is offered, usually in terms of future purchase

Spreading the Word!

When do consumers care enough to share their experiences, positive or negative, in an effort to influence other consumers? Well, from the positive perspective, consumers who describe their experience with something more powerful than mere satisfaction, such as delight or excitement, become most likely to post recommendations on social media sites. On the other hand, consumers may be more willing to share negative experiences. In particular, consumers who consider themselves highly involved with technology are quick to post about problems with products like smartphones or tablet computers. Research also suggests that religion may have something to do with spreading negative referrals for brands. Among U.S. Christians, evangelical Protestant consumers are more likely to participate in consumer activism including negative WOM and even brand boycotts.

Monkey Business Images/Shutterstock.com

Sources: K. Swimberghe, L. A. Flurry, and J. M. Parker, "Consumer Religiosity: Consequences for Consumer Activism in the United States," *Journal of Business Ethics* 103 (2011): 453–67. N. N. Bechwati and N. I. Nasr, "Triggers of Offline and Online Consumer Recommendations," *Journal of Consumer Satisfaction, Dissatisfaction and Complaining Behavior* 24 (2011): 56–68.

incentives. Loyalty programs differ somewhat depending on the firms offering them. Today, European firms typically offer the standard reward in terms of a future purchase incentive, but in the United States, loyalty programs more often work by offering on-the-spot discounts on selected items. One result is a two-tiered pricing system where there is one price for customers who comply with the card program, and a higher price for those who do not use the card on those selected items.

However, the results are mixed with respect to the effectiveness of loyalty cards. In fact, they can sometimes even backfire by appealing too strongly to consumers who are bargain shoppers. Consumers with a strong economic orientation display lower customer share with all competitors, instead choosing to shop in the place with the current best offer.[31]

While these programs are referred to as "loyalty" programs, the question occurs as to exactly what constitutes loyalty. Customer share reflects a behavioral component of loyalty by reflecting repeated behavior. Starbucks is noted for having one of the most successful loyalty programs. It periodically rewards consumers with free drinks and other extras based on points earned through purchasing behavior. As recorded in Exhibit 15.5, Bill repeats similar behavior over again and appears to be loyal to Starbucks, but is he really? This question is the focus of the next section.

15-4b Customer Commitment

Bill does appear at least partially loyal to Starbucks. However, repeated behavior alone cannot answer the loyalty question. True consumer loyalty consists of both a pattern of repeated behavior as evidenced by high customer share and a strong feeling of attachment, dedication, and sense of identification with a brand. **Customer commitment** captures this sense of attachment, dedication, and identification. Exhibit 15.6 depicts the components of loyalty. Customer share is behavioral, and commitment is an affective component of loyalty.

Highly committed customers are true assets to a company. They are willing to sacrifice to continue doing business with the brand and serve as a source of promotion by spreading positive WOM. If we look at a consumer with a pattern of consistent behavior like Bill in Exhibit 15.5, the question becomes whether the behavior is simply inertia or motivated by true commitment. Perhaps this particular customer just happens to live next door to a Starbucks and thus getting coffee there is merely the easiest thing to do. If a CC's Coffee Shop were to take over the current Starbucks location, the customer would then buy his coffee there. However, if Bill were truly committed, he would seek out another Starbucks location even if the one next to his place were to close or get leased to a different coffee competitor. This distinguishes inertia from a truly loyal customer. Even if Starbucks is not convenient or the least expensive alternative, the truly loyal consumer will still seek out Starbucks! Indeed, the Starbucks loyalty card is successful not just for the points, but because the visit to Starbucks often brings hedonic value.

The CLV (Customer Lifetime Value equation from Chapter 2) concept demonstrates why high customer commitment is so beneficial to a company. The certainty of a lengthy stream of revenues is much less for a customer acting only on inertia. In addition, the customer acting on inertia alone is likely not contributing on the equity side of the equation as is the truly committed customer. A firm that concentrates on repeated behavior alone, perhaps by always being convenient, can do well but remains more vulnerable to competitors. The reason for the vulnerability is that competitors easily duplicate tangible assets like convenience; but the intangible assets, like the feel associated with a choice or place, or the feelings consumers have for Louis Vuitton or drinking a Coke, are very hard to duplicate.

> **customer commitment** sense of attachment, dedication, and identification
>
> **antiloyal consumers** consumers who will do everything possible to avoid doing business with a particular marketer

EXHIBIT 15.6 True Loyalty Requires Customer Commitment

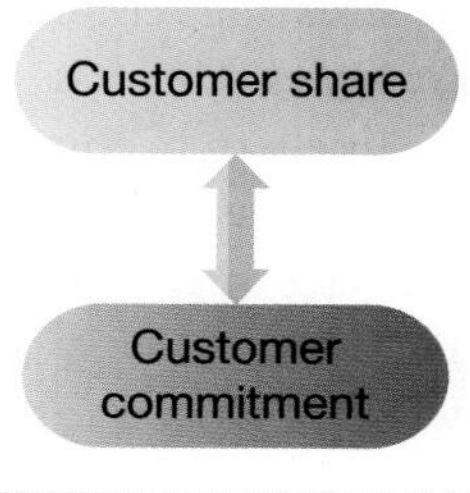

Customer share

⇅

Customer commitment

© Cengage Learning

15-4c Antiloyalty

Loyalty is almost always discussed from a positive perspective. However, at times consumers act in an antiloyal way. **Antiloyal consumers** are those who will do everything possible to avoid doing business with a particular marketer. These consumers generally dislike this particular company severely and the negative emotions that go along with the aversion determine the subsequent reactions. Antiloyalty is often motivated by a bad experience between a consumer and the marketer that the marketer could not redress.

Attributes marketers build into a product to create procedural switching costs are one source of frustration. These attributes include parts that are incompatible with widely available replacements or a mobile phone contract that locks a consumer into a specific service set for a lengthy time period. Consumers may wonder if their mobile phone number is transferable. In fact, many consumers may be frustrated with their mobile phone carrier but feel locked in, particularly if the phone number is not transferable or difficult to transfer.[32]

Antiloyal customers are often consumers who have switched and treat the former marketing partner as a jilted partner. They obviously have no net positive lifetime value for the target firm. Moreover, these antiloyal consumers who are former customers become perhaps the most frequent source for negative word-of-mouth.[33] Thus, antiloyal consumers can be a major force to reckon with.

15-4d Value and Switching

Exhibit 15.7 reproduces the center portion of the Consumer Value Framework (CVF). The exhibit clearly shows that value plays a role in the postconsumption process. During an exchange, the consumer goes through the consumption process, and the result produces some amount and type of value. The value, in turn, shapes what happens next. Thus, the CVF makes up for a shortcoming of the disconfirmation theory approach (as displayed in Exhibit 15.1) by explicitly accounting for value.

For a host of reasons, consumers may end up maintaining a relationship even if they experience dissatisfaction. However, consumers do not maintain relationships in which they find no value. Even if consumers do not enjoy shopping at Walmart, they tend to repeat the behavior because of high utilitarian value. Also, even though a consumer may be able to bank at a more convenient location, he might continue doing business with his original bank because he enjoys the personal relationships he has developed with bank personnel. Thus, both utilitarian and hedonic value can be a key in preventing consumers from switching

EXHIBIT 15.7 Value and Relationship Outcomes

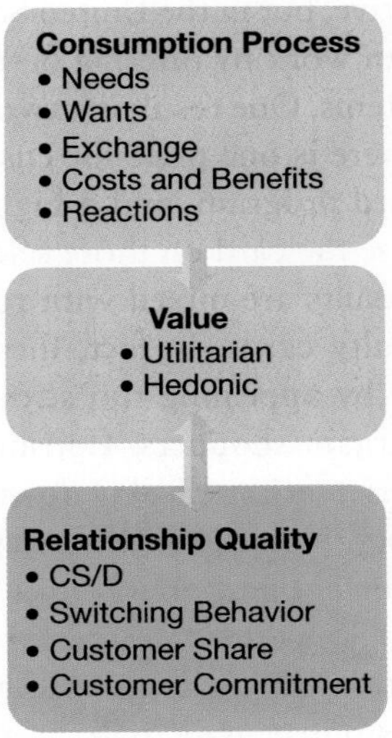

Consumption Process
- Needs
- Wants
- Exchange
- Costs and Benefits
- Reactions

Value
- Utilitarian
- Hedonic

Relationship Quality
- CS/D
- Switching Behavior
- Customer Share
- Customer Commitment

© Cengage Learning

to a competitor and creating true loyalty among consumers.

Is one type of value more important in preventing switching behavior? The answer to this question depends on the nature of the goods or services being consumed. For functional types of services, such as banking, utilitarian value is more strongly related to customer share (and therefore preventing switching) than is hedonic value.[34] However, for more experiential types of services, such as mall shopping, hedonic value is more strongly related to customer share.[35]

Value also is linked to the affective side of loyalty, customer commitment. Again, both value dimensions relate positively to commitment. Hedonic value, however, plays a larger role in creating commitment. In particular, customers who have switched service providers are more likely to become loyal customers when they experience increased hedonic value compared to the previous service provider. Exhibit 15.8 suggests ways that value plays a role in shaping loyalty and preventing switching behavior for different types of businesses.

> Both value dimensions relate positively to commitment. Hedonic value, however, plays a larger role in creating commitment.

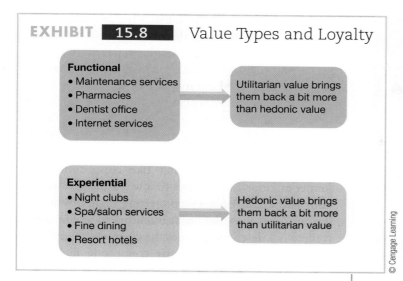

EXHIBIT 15.8 Value Types and Loyalty

Functional
- Maintenance services
- Pharmacies
- Dentist office
- Internet services

→ Utilitarian value brings them back a bit more than hedonic value

Experiential
- Night clubs
- Spa/salon services
- Fine dining
- Resort hotels

→ Hedonic value brings them back a bit more than utilitarian value

© Cengage Learning

15-5 Value, Relationships, and Consumers

15-5a Relationships and the Marketing Firm

Marketers have come to realize that the exchange between a business and a consumer constitutes a relationship. Two factors help make this clear:

1. Customers have a lifetime value to the firm.
2. True loyalty involves both a continuing series of interactions and feelings of attachment between the customer and the firm.

relationship quality
degree of connectedness between a consumer and a retailer

In return, many firms that truly adopt a relationship marketing approach with customers enjoy improved performance.[36] This is particularly the case as the relationship between customer and seller becomes very personal and involves trust.

Taken together, CS/D, complaining behavior, switching, customer share, and commitment all indicate relationship quality. Generally, **relationship quality** represents the degree of connectedness between a consumer and a retailer. When relationship quality is high, the prospects for a continued series of mutually valuable exchanges exist. Relationship quality represents the health of the relationship so that, in all likelihood, healthy relationships continue. When consumers are truly loyal, and this loyalty is returned by the marketer, relationship quality is high.

15-5b Value and Relationship Quality

A healthy relationship between a consumer and a marketer enhances value both for the consumer and the

Loyalty's in the Bag

What does it mean to be in a relationship? A relationship implies sacrifice and a willingness to overlook some inconveniences. Few products say more about a person than her handbag. After all, the bag takes care of your stuff. Like picking a spouse, picking a designer handbag is work. A designer bag should last for decades, so the comparison between choosing bags and husbands isn't so crazy. How many marriages will last two decades? Like husbands, a bag has to be loved even if it's not perfect. A Louis Vuitton Sofia Coppola Duffle goes for nearly $5,000, but it's rugged yet soft. The Yves Saint Laurent Classic 12 Duffle, about $2,500, is sleek and functional—the bag must balance function and style. A Legacy Coach Duffle goes for under $500 and gives a retro look.

The fact that you will be in a long-term relationship means you shouldn't get tired of looking at the object.

© iStockphoto.com/evemilla

Something too trendy is not likely to fit the criteria for a long-term relationship. Therefore, women looking for a long-term relationship in their bags prefer neutral colors, natural fabrics, and a look that will last. The bag may not fit perfectly with every outfit—but it clashes with none. A person can learn a lot from the way a smart consumer buys a handbag!

Sources: Rachel Dodes, "Shopping for a Handbag," *The Wall Street Journal*, February 9–10, 2013, D1–D2. "Bag Style: Set the Tone for Your Look," Harper's Bazaar.com, n.d., http://www.harpersbazaar.com/fashion/fashion-articles/handbag-style-0210#slide-1, accessed March 31, 2013.

A warm relationship with a customer adds value in more ways than one.

marketer.[37] For the consumer, decision making becomes simpler, enhancing utilitarian value, and relational exchanges often involve pleasant relational and experiential elements, enhancing hedonic value. For the marketer, the regular consumer does not have to be resold and thus much of the selling effort required to convert a new customer is not necessary.

In fact, when relationship quality is very strong, the marketer and the customer act as partners. When something bad happens to the marketer, the customer is affected. When something bad happens to the customer, the marketer is affected. Customers and sellers often act very closely as partners in business-to-business contexts. However, relationship quality can be very important in business-to-consumer contexts, too. When a parent sends a child off to college, chances are that a strong relationship exists or will soon exist between the family and the college. The family will don school colors on game day and become a prime target for fundraising campaigns. The strong relationship quality means that the family and the university share many common goals.

Exhibit 15.9 displays some of the characteristics of a marketing relationship that is very healthy. Consider this example. A consumer uses the same travel agent for practically all travel. When the consumer calls the agent, the agent does not have to ask the customer for preferences or personal information, not even a credit card number, because she has all the information about the customer. She knows the customer is a Delta SkyMiles member so she books on Delta whenever possible. She knows the customer doesn't like close connections (under an hour), so she tries to always allow at least an hour and a half between connecting flights. Whenever the customer flies, the agent monitors the flight status. If there is a delay, she phones the customer to exchange information and rebooks any connecting flights, hotel reservations, or car rentals if the delay disrupts the original plans. In this case, we can see that many of the characteristics displayed in Exhibit 15.9 are illustrated. This agent is customer oriented, has a personal relationship with the customer, communicates well, and is competent; the relationship is characterized by trust. Chances are that this customer will be loyal for quite some time.

EXHIBIT 15.9 The Characteristics of Relationship Quality

- **Competence** Consumer views company and service providers as knowledgeable and capable
- **Communication** Consumer and firm understand each other and "speak the same language"
- **Trust** Buyer and seller can depend on each other
- **Equity** Both buyer and seller see equity in exchange and are able to equitably resolve conflicts
- **Personalization** Buyer treats the customer as an individual with unique desires and requirements
- **Customer oriented** Strong relationships are more likely to develop when a firm practices a marketing orientation, and this filters down to service providers and salespeople

© Cengage Learning

WHAT DO YOU THINK?
WHAT OTHERS HAVE THOUGHT

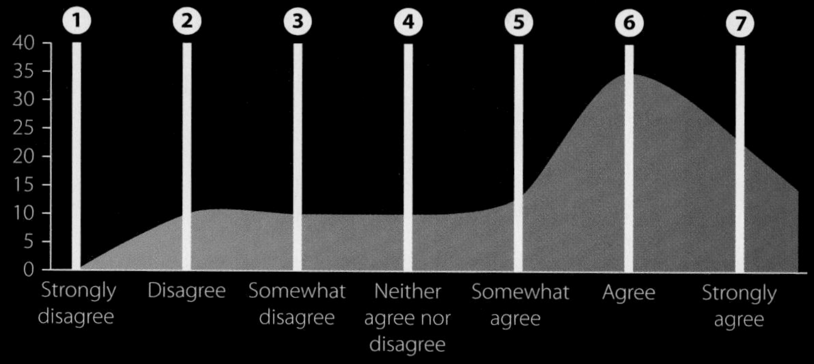

①	②	③	④	⑤	⑥	⑦

40
35
30
25
20
15
10
5
0

Strongly disagree | Disagree | Somewhat disagree | Neither agree nor disagree | Somewhat agree | Agree | Strongly agree

When I have a good experience with a brand, I reward it by telling my friends how great it is.

The response pattern clearly shows how loyal customers can become a powerful marketing tool. Over half of respondents chose either agree or strongly agree and, perhaps even more telling, no respondents expressed strongly disagree as an opinion. Thus, consumers like to spread good news!

Study Tools

Located at the back of the textbook

❑ Rip out Chapter in Review Card

Located at www.cengagebrain.com

❑ Review Key Terms Flashcards (print or online)

❑ Download audio summaries to review on the go

❑ Complete practice quizzes to prepare for tests

❑ Play "Beat the Clock" to master concepts

❑ Watch video on Harley-Davidson for a real company example

study tools

Jason Stitt/Shutterstock.com

Misbehavior violates norms

and also disrupts the flow of consumption activities.

WHAT DO YOU THINK?

Consumers are generally more ethical than the typical businessperson.

STRONGLY DISAGREE   STRONGLY AGREE

VISIT COURSEMATE AT WWW.CENGAGEBRAIN.COM

Consumer and Marketing Misbehavior

16

Most of the time when we think about consumer behavior, we think about behaviors that are generally considered "acceptable" or "normal" by societal standards. A number of important topics, however, fall outside of what would be considered acceptable. In this chapter, we focus on what is referred to as consumer and marketer misbehavior. The term *misbehavior* is used cautiously because opinions regarding what is acceptable or normal depend on our ethical beliefs, ideologies, and even culture. For consumers, examples include shoplifting, downloading music illegally, drinking and driving, engaging in fraud, and bullying one another on the Internet. Marketers sometimes engage in unethical activities as well. They mislead consumers through deceptive advertising, state that regular prices are "sale" prices, and artificially limit the availability of products in order to increase prices. Some marketers will do anything to profit at the cost of consumer satisfaction and value. As we discuss, a fair marketplace depends on ethical behavior by *both* consumers and marketers. When the marketplace is disrupted by misbehavior, both consumers and marketers eventually lose.

16-1 Consumer Misbehavior and Exchange

Consumer misbehavior may be viewed as a subset of the *human deviance* topic. This topic has a long history of research in the fields of sociology and social psychology. We consider misbehavior a subset in part because the term covers only negative or destructive deviance and does not consider positive deviance. Sometimes consumers can deviate from norms with the intention of doing good.

Consumer misbehavior can be defined in numerous ways. We define it as behaviors that are in some way unethical and that

After studying this chapter, the student should be able to:

16-1 Understand the consumer misbehavior phenomenon and how it affects the exchange process.

16-2 Distinguish between consumer misbehavior and consumer problem behavior.

16-3 Discuss marketing ethics and how marketing ethics guide the development of marketing programs.

16-4 Comprehend the role of corporate social responsibility in the field of marketing.

16-5 Understand the various forms of regulation that affect marketing practice.

16-6 Comprehend the major areas of criticism to which marketers are subjected.

consumer misbehavior
behaviors that are in some way unethical and that potentially harm the self or others

moral beliefs beliefs about the perceived ethicality or morality of behaviors

moral equity beliefs regarding an act's fairness or justness

contractualism beliefs about the violation of written (or unwritten) laws

potentially harm the self or others.[1] Misbehavior violates norms and also disrupts the flow of consumption activities. For example, a consumer cursing at employees in a grocery store because she thinks her wait is too long makes other consumers feel uncomfortable. Her actions disrupt others' shopping and may affect their entire afternoon. Chances are the employees who endure the outburst will perform poorly, at least for a while. This single consumer's actions potentially affect all the other customers in the store.

Consumer misbehavior is sometimes called the "dark side" of CB, and words such as *aberrant*, *illicit*, *dysfunctional*, and *deviant* have been used to describe it. Some behaviors are clearly illegal, while others are simply immoral. There's a difference. For example, shoplifting is illegal and almost always considered immoral. Illicitly downloading music, however, is illegal but not always considered immoral. Many students think that if "everyone's doing it," then there's not a problem. Not returning excess change that is mistakenly given at a store is immoral but not illegal.[2] A consumer might purchase a product one day, use it, and then return it for a refund. This may be immoral but not illegal. This practice is called *retail borrowing* and it costs the retail sector billions of dollars annually.

In order for exchanges to occur in an orderly fashion, the expectations of the consumer, the marketer, and even other consumers must coincide with one

Consumers who misbehave harm themselves and others.

Mark Douet/Stone/Getty Images

another.[3] When we see consumers becoming abusive, cutting in line at a movie theatre, or making other people uncomfortable, the exchange process is disrupted. Consumers who make fraudulent insurance claims increase insurance costs. Consumers who engage in retail borrowing increase product costs. Belligerent sports fans turn otherwise joyous occasions into annoying events for everybody. All sorts of misbehaviors affect exchange.

16-1a The Focus of Misbehavior: Value

As we have discussed throughout this text, a central component for understanding consumer behavior is value. It shouldn't be surprising then that the focal motivation for consumer misbehavior is value.[4] However, *how* consumers obtain value is the key issue. Rowdy sports fans think that the best way to obtain value is to be obnoxious. Identity thieves believe that the best way to obtain value is to steal from others. In each instance, consumers seek to maximize the benefits they receive from an action while minimizing, or eliminating, their own costs. Ultimately, others' costs increase. Consumer misbehavior is, quite simply, selfish!

⌐ Moral beliefs and evaluations influence decisions pertaining to marketplace behaviors. ⌐

16-1b Consumer Misbehavior and Ethics

Moral beliefs and evaluations influence decisions pertaining to marketplace behaviors.[5] The effect of moral beliefs on ethical decision making and consumer misbehavior is shown in Exhibit 16.1.

Moral Beliefs

Moral beliefs, or beliefs about the perceived ethicality or morality of behaviors, play a very important role in misbehavior.

Notice that a consumer's moral beliefs are made up of three components: moral equity, contractualism, and relativism.[6]

- **Moral equity** represents beliefs regarding an act's fairness or justness. Do I consider this action to be fair? Is it fair for me to illegally download a video?

- **Contractualism** refers to beliefs about the violation of written (or unwritten) laws. Does this action break

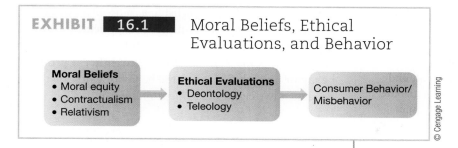

EXHIBIT 16.1 Moral Beliefs, Ethical Evaluations, and Behavior

Moral Beliefs
• Moral equity
• Contractualism
• Relativism

Ethical Evaluations
• Deontology
• Teleology

Consumer Behavior/
Misbehavior

© Cengage Learning

relativism beliefs about the social acceptability of an act in a culture

deontological evaluations evaluations regarding the inherent rightness or wrongness of specific actions

teleological evaluations consumers' assessment of the goodness or badness of the consequences of actions

a law? Does it break an unwritten promise of how I should act? Is pirating videos illegal?

• **Relativism** represents beliefs about the social acceptability of an act. Is this action culturally acceptable? Is pirating acceptable in this culture?

Ethical Evaluations

Consumers bring their moral beliefs into all decision-making settings. Once a consumer enters into a situation that calls for an ethical decision (*Should I download this movie?*), she considers the various alternative courses of action. Here, two sets of ethical evaluations occur: deontological evaluations and teleological evaluations.[7]

Deontological evaluations focus on specific *actions*. Is this action "right"? As such, deontology focuses on *how* people accomplish their goals. The deontological perspective is, in large part, attributed to the work of Immanuel Kant. Kant's *categorical imperative* suggests that one should act in a way that would be considered a universal law for all people facing the same situation.

Teleological evaluations focus on the *consequences* of the behaviors and the individual's assessment of those consequences. How much "good" will result from this decision? With teleological evaluations, consumers consider the perceived consequences of the actions for various stakeholders, the probability that the consequence will occur, the desirability of the consequences for the stakeholders, and the importance of the stakeholder groups to the consumer.[8] Notice from Exhibit 16.1 that moral beliefs influence ethical evaluations, which in turn, influence the decision to engage in misbehavior.

16-1c Motivations of Misbehavior

Moral beliefs and behavioral evaluations indeed play important roles in consumer misbehavior. However, the question remains: why do consumers misbehave? Researchers Ronald Fullerton and Girish Punj offer the following motivations of consumer misbehavior:[9]

• **Unfulfilled Aspirations.** Many consumers have unfulfilled aspirations that influence their misbehavior. An important concept here is *anomie*. Anomie has been conceptualized as both a response to rapid cultural change and an explanation for deviance. To understand anomie as an explanation for deviance, consider the goals that are generally accepted in a culture. The U.S. culture places a great deal of emphasis on attaining material possessions and "getting ahead." However, not all members of the society have the necessary resources to be able to get ahead and enjoy the things that society deems important. As a result, some consumers turn to deviant actions in order to acquire these things. It's when societal goals are out of reach given the accepted means of achieving them that deviance occurs.[10]

• **Thrill Seeking.** The thrill of the action may lead consumers to misbehave. Some consumers get a thrill from defacing the property of companies.

• **Lack of Moral Constraints.** Some consumers simply don't have a set of moral beliefs that are in agreement with society's expectations and see no problem with their behavior. For example, some consumers who sell illegal drugs don't see a problem with the behavior.

• **Differential Association.** Differential association explains why groups of people replace one set of acceptable norms with another set that others view as unacceptable. By acting in opposition to acceptable standards, group members forge their own identities and strengthen group cohesion.[11] For example, prospective gang members may assault innocent bystanders as a way of gaining acceptance into their group.

• **Pathological Socialization.** Consumers may view misbehavior as a way of getting revenge against companies. Stealing from large corporations may seem less severe than stealing from a family-owned retailer, and consumers may believe that big companies somehow deserve what they get. Numerous groups have targeted Walmart over the last few years simply because they believe that the company "deserves it."

consumer problem behavior consumer behavior that is deemed to be unacceptable but that is seemingly beyond the control of the consumer

- **Provocative Situational Factors.** Factors like crowding, wait times, excessive heat, and noise can contribute to consumer misbehavior. A well-mannered, quiet person may become combative if his order is wrong at a busy restaurant.

- **Opportunism.** Misbehavior can also be the outcome of a deliberate decision-making process that weighs the risks and rewards of the behavior. For example, consumers may believe that the rewards associated with stealing outweigh the risks of getting caught.

16-2 Distinguish Consumer Misbehavior from Problem Behavior

Consumer misbehavior can be distinguished from what we refer to as consumer "problem behavior." The misbehavior term is used to describe behavior deliberately harmful to the self or another party during an exchange. **Consumer problem behavior** refers to behaviors that are seemingly outside of a consumer's control. For example, some people compulsively shop. Some people are addicted to drugs or alcohol. In cases like these, consumers may express a desire to stop the behaviors but simply find quitting too difficult.

Although the line between consumer misbehavior and problem behaviors can be blurred, we distinguish between the two areas by considering the issue of self-control. Exhibit 16.2 presents examples of consumer misbehaviors and problem behaviors, but again the line

is blurry. Drug addiction is listed as a problem behavior, but when someone drives under the influence of drugs, the individual risks injuring or killing someone else. Shoplifting could also be considered either a problem behavior or misbehavior, as the behavior can sometimes be clinically diagnosed as *kleptomania*.

16-2a Consumer Misbehavior

Many of the behaviors that are listed in Exhibit 16.2 are discussed frequently in the popular press. For example, you may have heard stories in the news media about the devastating effects of binge drinking or problem gambling. Although there are many different types of consumer misbehavior, we limit our discussion to behaviors that have gathered significant attention.

Shoplifting

Did you know that consumers steal more than $35 million of products every day? That's over $13 billion per year! Shoplifting has become one of the most common U.S. crimes, averaging over 500,000 cases per day! Many shoplifters are repeat offenders, shoplifting on average 1.6 times per week.[12] Consumers' motivations for shoplifting are similar to motivations for other forms of misbehavior. Specifically, consumers shoplift because the temptation can be very strong, they believe that retailers can afford the monetary loss, they believe they probably won't get caught, they seek acceptance into a group, and the act can be exciting.[13]

As we have mentioned, shoplifting can sometimes be diagnosed as kleptomania. Kleptomania is generally triggered by a strong compulsion and the inability of the consumer to fight the urge.

Emotions and Shoplifting. Emotions play a large role in shoplifting. Fear of being caught plays a role in predicting shoplifting intentions, especially among young consumers. Interestingly, the shoplifting intentions of adolescents appear to be more heavily influenced by emotions than by moral beliefs. The opposite occurs in older consumers. Research also shows that consumers who shoplift are

EXHIBIT 16.2	Consumer Misbehavior and Problem Behavior
Consumer Misbehavior	**Consumer Problem Behavior**
• Shoplifting	• Compulsive buying
• Computer-mediated behaviors: illicit sharing of software and music, computer attacks, cyberbullying	• Compulsive shopping
• Fraud	• Eating disorders
• Abusive consumer behavior	• Binge drinking
• Illegitimate complaining	• Problem gambling
• Product misuse: aggressive driving, drunk driving, cell phone use while driving, sexting	• Drug abuse

© Cengage Learning

Some consumers cannot resist the temptation to shoplift.

Chuck Savage/CORBIS/Glow Images

sometimes motivated by repressed feelings of stress and anger.[14]

Age and Shoplifting. Shoplifting behavior appears to peak during the adolescent years. This may be because adolescents are yet to fully mature and often find themselves in the stressful transition from childhood to adulthood. Adolescents also tend to consider shoplifting as being more ethical than do adult shoppers.[15]

Computer-Mediated Behaviors: Illegal Sharing of Software and Music

Due to improvements in technology, consumers often have the ability to illicitly download electronic material from a number of sources. Major problems here include the pirating of computer software, video games, and music.

The software industry continues to lose billions of dollars annually due to piracy. The Business Software Alliance estimated in 2012 that as much as 42% of software loaded on PCs worldwide was obtained illegally and that over $63 billion was lost globally due to illegal use of software products in 2012. What's more, the Alliance estimates that over half of computer users worldwide admit to pirating software.[16] The music industry has also been hit hard by these actions. The U.S. Digital Millennium Copyright Act deems the sharing of copyrighted music as illegal. Although there are numerous legal download services such as iTunes, Zune, and Rhapsody, consumers continue to share music in illegal ways.

Interestingly, research reveals that how consumers view illegal downloading depends on the motivation for the behavior. That is, if the motivation is primarily based on utilitarian value (that is, for personal gain), then the act is viewed as less morally ethical and socially acceptable than if the behavior occurs based on hedonic value (that is, for "fun").[17]

Computer-Mediated Behaviors: Attacks

Computers present other opportunities for misbehavior. Did you know that consumers in the United States send more spam than do consumers in any other nation? Spam clogging up computers and slowing Internet connectivity results in losses of billions of dollars annually in business productivity![18] Computer viruses are another major problem. In fact, it has been estimated that viruses cost U.S. businesses over $55 billion annually.[19] U.S. households suffer losses of nearly $5 billion annually due to viruses.[19a]

Another form of computer misbehavior is *cyberbullying*. Cyberbullying, the attack of innocent people on the Internet, is especially a problem for young consumers. Current research indicates that girls tend to be targeted by, and instigate, cyberattacks more often than boys.[20] However, cyberbullying is a serious issue for both genders. Recent statistics reveal that as many as 32% of online teens have been victims of some type of cyberbullying.[21] Teens can experience lower self-esteem, depression, anxiety, and suicidal thoughts when victimized by cyberbullying.[22]

Consumer Fraud

There are many types of consumer fraud. For instance, consumers fraudulently obtain credit cards, open bank accounts, and turn in insurance claims. Although it is difficult to estimate exactly how much consumer fraud ends up costing consumers, the Coalition Against Insurance Fraud estimates that insurance fraud alone costs Americans at least $80 billion per year.[23]

Identity theft is another major public concern. Statistics reveal that as many as 15 million Americans are victimized by identity theft each year.[24] The Identity

Theft and Assumption Deterrence Act of 1998 and the Identity Theft Penalty Enhancement Act of 2004 were passed in order to curb the crime, but the increased reliance on computers for transactions has contributed to its spread. It is no wonder that information privacy and security concerns are hot topics for consumers.

Abusive Consumer Behavior

As we have discussed, abusive consumers can be a real problem. Consumers who are aggressive or rude to employees and other consumers are considered to be abusive.[25] One early study in the area of problem customers suggested that four categories of customers can be identified: verbally or physically abusive customers, uncooperative customers, drunken customers, and customers who break company policy.[26] Needless to say, employees don't like to deal with customers who act this way, and abusive behaviors can have negative effects on other consumers as well.[27]

One area of abusive behavior that has gained attention is dysfunctional fan behavior. *Dysfunctional fan behavior* is abnormal functioning relating to sporting event consumption. Several college towns have seen riots that have occurred after big losses (or wins) of the home team. Unfortunately, riots can get out of hand quickly. While there are many explanations for such behavior, some think that dysfunctional fan behavior is simply a result of an increasingly violent society.[28]

Another controversial issue today is culture jamming. *Culture jamming* refers to attempts to disrupt marketing campaigns by altering the messages in some meaningful way. For example, billboards are often altered in a way that delivers messages that conflict with those originally intended. Also, websites that attempt to disrupt marketing efforts are often created. Sites like Amexsux.com have popped up in the online world. Of course, calling culture jamming an abusive behavior depends on your own perspective. Proponents believe that their behaviors are a matter of free speech and good for society.

Illegitimate Complaining

Consumers also complain about products and services even when there really isn't a problem. To date, the research on illegitimate complaining remains relatively

Black (and Blue) Friday

"Black Friday" has become a ritual for millions of consumers. For some, it's a fun-filled family tradition. For others, the entire weekend is seen as nothing more than madness.

"Madness" probably is the appropriate term for the event as some people see it. And as retailers continue to move Black Friday back to Thanksgiving Day, the madness only intensifies. Each year there are numerous reports of injuries and assaults that occur during the rush. Sadly, some consumers add to the problem by just going to watch the event, or to cause trouble.

Evidence is beginning to show that some consumers are growing tired of it all. Certain groups have begun to fight back, including the "Occupy Black Friday" movement, which gained momentum during 2012. Local police forces are put on alert each year nationwide on Black Friday, and hospitals know that they will be busier than usual as well.

Although Black Friday is an opportunity for retailers to operate in the "black" by realizing a profit, it seems that some consumers will stop at nothing to get what they

Daniel Acker/Bloomberg/Getty Images

want. For some, Black Friday might as well be called "Black and Blue Friday."

Sources: Philip Caulfield, "As Anxious Black Friday Shoppers Swarm Sale Stores to Nab Post-Thanksgiving Deals, Fights and Hot Tempers Mar Holiday Shopping and Lead to Injuries, Arrests Across the Country," NYDailyNews.com, November 23, 2012, http://www.nydailynews.com/news/national/tensions-black-friday-u-s-article-1.1206877 (accessed March 7, 2013). Eric Lindquist, "Black (and Blue) Friday Adventure," *Leader-Telegram*, November 26, 2011, http://www.leadertelegram.com/blogs/eric_lindquist/article_91152dc0-1875-11e1-8cd3-001cc4c03286.html (accessed May 14, 2012); Aliyah Shahid, "Black Friday Madness Turns Violent," *New York Daily News*, November 25, 2011, http://articles.nydailynews.com/2011-11-25/news/30442767_1_pepper-sprayed-los-angeles-wal-mart-shopper (accessed May 14, 2012).

scarce. However, one study did find that illegitimate complaining is motivated by a desire for monetary gain, a desire to evade personal responsibility for product misuse, a desire to enhance the consumer's ego and look good to others, or a desire to harm a service provider or company.[29]

Product Misuse

Consumers also sometimes use products in ways that were clearly not intended. In some cases, consumers simply misuse products by accident. In others, they knowingly misuse them. For example, some consumers will sniff glue or household cleaners to get high. Marketers therefore work hard to ensure that consumers understand the ways in which products should be used. However, even when warnings and instructions are provided, consumers still misuse products. Injuries that result can be very costly. In fact, statistics from the Consumer Product Safety Commission reveal that deaths and injuries resulting from product consumption cost the United States over $800 billion annually.[30]

Why do consumers use products in unsafe ways? A number of explanations have been offered. Consumers may simply not pay attention to what they are doing, may feel as though they generally get away with risky behaviors, may have a tendency to be error prone, or may focus more on the thrill of misuse rather than the actual risk of the behavior.[31] Although product misuse may apply to any number of products, many issues revolve around automobiles, cell phones, and prescription medication.

Aggressive Driving. Aggressive driving may range from mild displays of anger to seriously violent acts while driving. Although aggressive driving is often thought of as an act by a solitary consumer, aggressive driving problems often involve multiple drivers, as victims often retaliate with their own aggression.[32] Younger, less-educated males have been shown to be more likely to engage in aggressive driving behavior.[33] Situational factors, such as intense traffic congestion and driver stress, as well as personality traits play a part. Traits like instability and competitiveness have been found among aggressive drivers.[34]

Drunk Driving. Statistics reveal that as many as 13,000 people die from alcohol-related traffic accidents in the United States each year and that nearly three out of every ten Americans will be involved in an alcohol-related crash at some point in their lives. Even though drunk driving incidents have decreased in recent years, on average, 30 Americans die from these accidents each day.[35] Sadly, one out of every six fatalities among children aged 14 and younger is due to an alcohol-related accident.[36] Statistics also reveal that men are responsible for four in five episodes of drinking and driving and that young men aged 21–34 are responsible for 32% of all instances of drinking and driving. This is a telling statistic, given that this group only makes up 11% of the total U.S. population.[37] While the cost in terms of human life is high, there is a high monetary cost of drinking and driving. Estimates reveal that drinking and driving costs over $51 billion annually.[38]

Furthermore, one study estimates that nearly 25% of all drivers aged 15–20 who are killed in fatal accidents have blood alcohol levels above 0.08.[39] Of course, this group is under the legal drinking age! Drunk driving and binge drinking are often related. In fact, one study indicated that over 80% of respondents who reported alcohol-impaired driving also reported engaging in binge drinking behaviors.[40]

Cell Phone Use in Cars. There were nearly seven billion cellular subscriptions worldwide as of 2013,[41] and there are currently over 330 million wireless subscriptions in the United States alone.[42] The effective U.S. penetration rate is now over 100% (many consumers have more than one subscription). With such widespread adoption, one area of concern involves the use of cell phones while driving. While not everyone will agree that using a cell phone while driving is misbehavior, the behavior does put others at risk and it is against the law in several U.S. states and in numerous countries worldwide.

© iStockphoto.com/Steve Jacobs

compulsive consumption repetitive, excessive, and purposeful consumer behaviors that are performed as a response to tension, anxiety, or obtrusive thoughts

addictive consumption physiological dependency on the consumption of a consumer product

compulsive buying chronic, repetitive purchasing that is a response to negative events or feelings

compulsive shopping repetitive shopping behaviors that are a response to negative events or feelings

Studies reveal that consumers who use cell phones while driving are four times as likely to get into serious accidents, and the problem is particularly serious for teens. One recent study found that only 43% of teens surveyed, aged 16–17, had *never* texted while driving, which of course suggests that 57% have![43] A 2012 study also revealed that teen girls are twice as likely as teen boys to use cell phones while driving.[44] While the problem appears to be serious among younger drivers, the behavior actually cuts across age groups, and texting is not the only problem. One recent study revealed that 43% of drivers 18–29 surfed the Internet while driving![45]

Currently, ten U.S. states ban talking on a handheld phone while driving, and texting while driving is banned in 39 states and the District of Columbia.[46] Forty-six countries worldwide currently restrict or ban the use of cell phones while driving.[47]

Sexting

One growing form of misbehavior is "sexting." Sexting is taking nude photos of oneself and sending them to another person via cell phone. It seems to occur most frequently among teenaged consumers, and the app Snapchat has been criticized by some as making sexting seem easy and secure.[47a]

Multiple media reports indicate that many teens feel like sexting isn't harmful. Parents and school administrators don't feel the same way. Parents are concerned that the images can be passed from person to person, and even onto the Internet. Sexting also raises moral, ethical, and legal issues.[48] The behavior can result in severe psychological and social problems. The effects of sexting range from minor psychological distress to intense emotional trauma.[49]

16-2b Consumer Problem Behavior

Consumer problem behaviors include other acts that do not necessarily break any specific laws or societal norms. For example, consumers shop too much, rack up large amounts of debt, and sometimes harm their own bodies in desperate attempts to look thin. Psychological problems can cause or influence these behaviors.

Compulsive Consumption

Compulsive consumption refers to repetitive, excessive, and purposeful consumer behaviors that are performed as a response to tension, anxiety, or obtrusive thoughts.[50] The term *compulsive consumption* is often used broadly and consists of a number of specific behaviors related to the purchase and use of consumer products and services.[51] Compulsive consumption should not be confused with *addictive consumption*. **Addictive consumption** refers to a physiological dependency on the consumption of a product. The word *dependency* is important, and in the strictest sense, addictions are characterized by the physical inability to discontinue a behavior, or a physical reliance. A person who is addicted to a product physically needs it. Compulsive consumption often takes two forms: *compulsive buying* and *compulsive shopping*.

Compulsive Buying. **Compulsive buying** may be defined as chronic, repetitive *purchasing* behaviors that are a response to negative events or feelings.[52] The behavior has harmful effects such as the accumulation of debt, domestic problems, and feelings of frustration. Influencers of the behavior include feelings of low self-esteem, obsessive-compulsive tendencies, fantasy-seeking motivations, and materialism,[53] as well as a focus on the short term.[54] Research also reveals that a need for prestige also motivates the behavior, particularly among college students.[55] Among adolescents, the behavior can be a response to family problems.[56] The same negative feelings that influence compulsive buying can also result from the behavior itself. So a consumer who buys compulsively as a reaction to negative feelings often experiences even more negative feelings after going on buying binges.[57] In short, it can be a vicious circle.

Compulsive Shopping. **Compulsive shopping** refers to repetitive *shopping* behaviors. The word *oniomania* is sometimes used to describe this behavior. Compulsive shoppers often feel preoccupied with shopping, exhibit uncontrollable shopping tendencies, and experience guilt from their behaviors.[58] The key difference between compulsive shopping and buying is the buying process itself. Compulsive shoppers tend to focus on the mental highs associated with "the hunt,"[59] whereas compulsive buyers feel the need to buy. Although early research on this issue revealed that compulsive shopping was

EXHIBIT 16.3 Binge Eating Disorder

Binge Eating Disorder Consists of:

- Frequent eating episodes that include large quantities of food in short time periods
- A felt loss of control over eating behavior
- Feelings of shame, guilt, and/or disgust about the amount of food consumed
- The consumption of food when one is not hungry
- The consumption of food in secret

Source: Based on National Eating Disorders Association, www.nationaleatingdisorders.

binge eating consumption of large amounts of food while feeling a general loss of control over food intake

binge drinking consumption of five or more drinks in a single drinking session for men and four or more drinks for women

problem gambling obsession over the thought of gambling and the loss of control over gambling behavior and its consequences

predominately a problem for women, more recent evidence suggests that both women and men engage in compulsive shopping. One study confirmed that equal proportions of men and women are compulsive shoppers (6% of women, 5.5% of men).[60]

Eating Disorders

Binge eating refers to the consumption of large amounts of food while feeling a general loss of control over intake. Binge eating may result in medical complications, including high cholesterol, high blood pressure, and heart disease. Exhibit 16.3 presents a description of the binge eating disorder. The disorder is thought to affect as many as 3.5% of all women and 2% of all men at some point in their lives.[61]

Binge eating has been shown to be associated with compulsive buying and impulsivity, and it is often related to obesity. Consumers who binge-eat and who are also obese are likely to have other psychiatric disorders that require treatment.[62] Unfortunately, many consumers who binge-eat fail to seek treatment. Binge eating is also often associated with *bulimia*, a disorder that includes binge eating episodes followed by self-induced vomiting. *Anorexia*, or the starving of one's body in the pursuit of thinness, is another consumer eating disorder. Eating problems are often associated with other consumer issues. For example, it has been shown that simply paying for food with a credit card leads to unhealthy food choices.[63]

Binge Drinking

Binge drinking is defined as the consumption of five or more drinks in a single drinking session for men and four or more drinks for women,[64] and the behavior is particularly prevalent among full-time college students. A report from 2012 revealed that binge drinking rates among full-time college students are over 39%, compared to 35% for students who are not enrolled full

time.[65] Binge drinking occurs globally. In fact, one study revealed that students in the United Kingdom binge-drink for the sole purpose of getting drunk and feel that getting drunk is a key part of college life.[66]

Binge drinking has been linked to suicide attempts, unsafe sexual practices, legal problems, academic disruptions, and even death.[67] Sadly, over 1,800 college students between the ages of 18 and 24 die each year from alcohol-related unintentional injuries.[68] College students who have higher self-actualization values generally have lower attitudes toward binge drinking, whereas students who value social affiliation tend to have more positive attitudes toward the behavior.[69] Studies also reveal that students who drink excessively often brag about it on social networking sites like Facebook.[70]

Binge drinking behavior actually cuts across demographic groups. One alarming trend is the occurrence of binge drinking among underage consumers, with one study indicating that nearly half of the alcohol consumed on four-year college campuses is consumed by underage consumers.[71] Other statistics reveal that one in five teenagers binge-drink.[72]

Problem Gambling

Problem gambling is another serious issue. This behavior may be described as an obsession with gambling and the loss of control over gambling behavior and its consequences.[73] Consumers who are problem gamblers frequently gamble longer than planned, borrow money to finance their gambling, and feel major depression due to their gambling behaviors. Although casino and online gambling receive much research attention, lottery ticket and scratch ticket purchases can also be considered problem gambling behaviors.[74]

Estimates reveal that as many as two million consumers meet the criteria of pathological gambling and another four to six million could be considered problem gamblers.[75] Problem gamblers exhibit at least some of the criteria for

ethics standards or moral codes of conduct to which a person, group, or organization adheres

marketing ethics societal and professional standards of right and fair practices that are expected of marketing managers as they develop and implement marketing strategies

marketing concept states a firm should focus on consumer needs as a means of achieving long-term success

pathological gambling. Although problem gambling is often thought of as being primarily an issue for middle-aged consumers, approximately 8% of college students gamble problematically.[76] What's more, one study revealed that nearly 70% of seniors older than 65 had gambled at least once in the previous year and nearly 11% were considered at risk for problem gambling.[77] Research indicates that problem gambling is often associated with compulsive buying and drug abuse.[78]

ronstik/Shutterstock.com

Drug Abuse

Both illegal and prescription drugs are problem areas for some consumers. The problem is especially alarming among teens. One study by the Partnership for a Drug-Free America revealed that nearly one in five teenagers report using prescription drugs to get high, and nearly one in ten report abusing cough medicine. A 2012 study revealed that 15% of high school seniors reported using prescription medication to get high.[79]

The abuse of illegal drugs has been a problem for years. Like other behaviors, it is a serious problem that cuts across demographic groups. One estimate reveals that over 40% of high school seniors have tried marijuana.[80] And in 2012, 7% of seniors used it daily.[80a] A 2012 study revealed that fully 31% from 2008 to 2011 and one in ten teens reported using the drug at least 20 times in the last month.[81] The same study revealed that teen abuse of prescription medicines is at 17% and 12% for over-the-counter cough and cold medicines. Of course, it's not only teens who smoke marijuana. Estimates reveal that over 17 million consumers use the drug regularly.[82] A relatively new trend is also the use of "synthetic" marijuana, which many consumers view as being safer than the actual drug. Other drugs, such as cocaine and methamphetamine, are also often abused at alarmingly high rates.

We've discussed only a handful of behaviors that may be considered consumer problem areas here. Space prohibits a complete discussion of several other consumer problem areas.

16-3 Marketing Ethics and Misbehavior

As we have stated, a fair marketplace depends on each party in an exchange acting fairly and with due respect for each other. Whenever anyone acts unethically, inefficiencies result and chances are that somebody will suffer. Marketers, like consumers, can act unethically. Media reports all too often describe company actions that are at best questionable, at times immoral, and at worst illegal. Unscrupulous actions of companies directly impact the marketplace because they upset the value equation associated with a given exchange. When a company misrepresents a product, consumers are led to expect more than is actually delivered.

Not everyone will agree on what behaviors should be considered marketing "misbehaviors." The topic again centers on ethics. The term **ethics** refers to standards or moral codes of conduct to which a person, group, or organization adheres. **Marketing ethics** consist of societal and professional standards of right and fair practices that are expected of marketing managers as they develop and implement marketing strategies.[83] More simply, ethics determines how much tolerance one has for actions that take advantage of others.

Many organizations have explicitly stated rules or codes of conduct for their employees. Exhibit 16.4 presents the Code of Ethics for the American Marketing Association.

Like consumer misbehavior, marketer misbehavior can be viewed as a subset of *deviance*. For marketers to misbehave, they must be aware that an action will be considered unethical and act with deviance to cover intent. Sometimes, marketers don't intend to misbehave but mistakes are made in marketing execution. As in a court of law, proving intent is rarely an easy thing to do.

16-3a Consumerism

The **marketing concept** proposes that all the functions of the organization should work together in satisfying

EXHIBIT 16.4   American Marketing Association Code of Ethics

Preamble The American Marketing Association commits itself to promoting the highest standard of professional ethical norms and values for its members. Norms are established standards of conduct that are expected and maintained by society and/or professional organizations. Values represent the collective conception of what people find desirable, important and morally proper. Values serve as the criteria for evaluating the actions of others. Marketing practitioners must recognize that they not only serve their enterprises but also act as stewards of society in creating, facilitating and executing the efficient and effective transactions that are part of the greater economy. In this role, marketers should embrace the highest ethical norms of practicing professionals and the ethical *values* implied by their responsibility toward stakeholders (e.g., customers, employees, investors, channel members, regulators and the host community).

General Norms:

1. Marketers must do no harm. This means doing work for which they are appropriately trained or experienced so that they can actively add value to their organizations and customers. It also means adhering to all applicable laws and regulations and embodying high ethical standards in the choices they make.

2. Marketers must foster trust in the marketing system. This means that products are appropriate for their intended and promoted uses. It requires that marketing communications about goods and services are not intentionally deceptive or misleading. It suggests building relationships that provide for the equitable adjustment and/or redress of customer grievances. It implies striving for good faith and fair dealing so as to contribute toward the efficacy of the exchange process.

3. Marketers must embrace, communicate and practice the fundamental ethical values that will improve consumer confidence in the integrity of the marketing exchange system. These basic *values* are intentionally aspirational and include honesty, responsibility, fairness, respect, openness and citizenship.

Ethical Values

Honesty—to be truthful and forthright in our dealings with customers and stakeholders. We will tell the truth in all situations and at all times. We will offer products of value that do what we claim in our communications. We will stand behind our products if they fail to deliver their claimed benefits. We will honor our explicit and implicit commitments and promises.

Responsibility—to accept the consequences of our marketing decisions and strategies. We will make strenuous efforts to serve the needs of our customers. We will avoid using coercion with all stakeholders. We will acknowledge the social obligations to stakeholders that come with increased marketing and economic power. We will recognize our special commitments to economically vulnerable segments of the market such as children, the elderly and others who may be substantially disadvantaged.

Fairness—to try to balance justly the needs of the buyer with the interests of the seller. We will represent our products in a clear way in selling, advertising and other forms of communication; this includes the avoidance of false, misleading and deceptive promotion. We will reject manipulations and sales tactics that harm customer trust. We will not engage in price fixing, predatory pricing, price gouging or "bait-and-switch" tactics. We will not knowingly participate in material conflicts of interest.

Respect—to acknowledge the basic human dignity of all stakeholders. We will value individual differences even as we avoid stereotyping customers or depicting demographic groups (e.g., gender, race, sexual orientation) in a negative or dehumanizing way in our promotions. We will listen to the needs of our customers and make all reasonable efforts to monitor and improve their satisfaction on an ongoing basis. We will make a special effort to understand suppliers, intermediaries and distributors from other cultures. We will appropriately acknowledge the contributions of others, such as consultants, employees and coworkers, to our marketing endeavors.

Openness—to create transparency in our marketing operations. We will strive to communicate clearly with all our constituencies. We will accept constructive criticism from our customers and other stakeholders. We will explain significant product or service risks, component substitutions or other foreseeable eventualities that could affect customers or their perception of the purchase decision. We will fully disclose list prices and terms of financing as well as available price deals and adjustments.

Citizenship—to fulfill the economic, legal, philanthropic and societal responsibilities that serve stakeholders in a strategic manner. We will strive to protect the natural environment in the execution of marketing campaigns. We will give back to the community through volunteerism and charitable donations. We will work to contribute to the overall betterment of marketing and its reputation. We will encourage supply chain members to ensure that trade is fair for all participants, including producers in developing countries.

Implementation Finally, we recognize that every industry sector and marketing subdiscipline (e.g., marketing research, e-commerce, direct selling, direct marketing, advertising) has its own specific ethical issues that require policies and commentary. An array of such codes can be accessed through links on the AMA website. We encourage all such groups to develop and/or refine their industry and discipline-specific codes of ethics to supplement these general norms and values.

Source: American Marketing Association Code of Ethics. Copyright 2008 © American Marketing Association. All rights reserved. Reprinted by permission.

consumerism activities of various groups to voice concern for, and to protect, basic consumer rights

Consumer Bill of Rights introduced by President John F. Kennedy in 1962, list of rights that include the right to safety, the right to be informed, the right to redress and to be heard, and the right to choice

its customers' wants and needs. This is important for any business. When businesses begin taking advantage of consumers, consumers lose, businesses lose, and society as a whole eventually loses. In fact, it can be said that the ethical treatment of consumers is a cornerstone of a fair marketplace.[84]

Much of the pressure that has been placed on marketers comes directly from consumer groups. **Consumerism** is used to describe the activities of various groups to protect basic consumer rights. Many years ago, the voice of the consumer simply didn't garner much attention at all. In the early days of mass production, much of the focus was on production efficiencies rather than on the consumer. This changed gradually throughout the 20th century as the marketplace became more competitive. The voice of the consumer grew steadily. The **Consumer Bill of Rights**, which today stands as a foundation of the consumerism movement, was introduced in 1962, and included:

1. The right to safety
2. The right to be informed
3. The right to redress and to be heard
4. The right to choice

16-3b The Marketing Concept and the Consumer

The marketing concept developed greatly in the 1960s. It was early in this time period that Theodore Levitt published the article "Marketing Myopia." Among other things, Levitt's work brought about a new perspective

Being a Champion

Without question, the consequences of drinking too much have severe effects not only on the individual consumer, but on society as a whole. Given all the problems with impaired driving, binge drinking, and alcoholism, it is easy to understand why many consumers view alcoholic beverage marketers with a great deal of contempt.

However, many of these marketers put great effort into promoting a much healthier view of alcohol consumption. One recent effort by Bacardi Limited provides a good illustration of what socially responsible marketing is all about. The company's "Champions Drink Responsibly" campaign is not only a commendable approach to marketing alcohol, but it has also been awarded a "Best International Communication" award by the European Excellence Awards.

In 2011, tennis superstar Rafael Nadal was named the spokesperson for the campaign and was deemed the "Global Social Responsibility Ambassador." This athlete is thought of highly by both his peers and his fans, and this adds to his effectiveness as a public face for the campaign. Bacardi, one of the biggest producers of rum and spirits, is committed to spreading the message that consumers can drink responsibly and still enjoy the time spent with

Olga Besnard/Shutterstock.com

friends. Considering the effects of marketing campaigns on all stakeholders is an important part of the societal marketing concept.

Sources: Kim Brandow, "Rafael Nadal is a Champion Who Drinks Responsibly," Examiner.com, November 27, 2012, http://www.examiner.com/article/rafael-nadal-is-a-champion-who-drinks-responsibly (accessed March 7, 2013); L. Guoyang, "Champions Drink Responsibly (New Launches)," Cosmone.com, February 14, 2013, http://cosmone.com/flavour/new-launches/champions-drink-responsibly (accessed March 7, 2013); Rahim Kanani, "Rafael Nadal: Global Social Responsibility Ambassador for Bacardi Limited," *Huffington Post*, August 24, 2011, http://www.huffingtonpost.com/rahim-kanani/rafael-nadal-global-socia_b_935416.html (accessed March 7, 2013).

that argued that businesses should define themselves in terms of the consumer needs that they satisfy rather than in terms of the products they make. He argued that a firm's long-term health depends on its ability to exist as a consumer-satisfying entity rather than a goods-producing entity. As we have discussed in this text, companies should focus on the *total value concept* and remember that products provide value in multiple ways.

While many companies today adhere to the marketing concept, numerous questions arise regarding actual marketing practice. For example, companies often come under criticism for marketing products that some consider harmful. In particular, the fast-food, cereal, tobacco, and alcohol industries are often under fire from various groups. Even though freedom of choice is a central tenet of the U.S. economic system, these products are among the many that society often considers harmful.

The Marketing Mix and the Consumer

Marketers should use the tools found in the marketing mix carefully as they target consumers. When consumers question the way in which they are treated, they are likely to spread negative information through word of mouth and seek some form of remedy.

One of the most visible elements of the marketing mix is pricing. When consumers believe that a firm's prices are unfair, they are likely to leave the firm and spread negative information about it.[85] Consumers also complain that marketing efforts lead to higher overall prices. Marketers counter by explaining that marketing expenditures allow for increased economies of scale that contribute to lower overall production costs. Pricing issues

are certainly debatable. Exhibit 16.5 presents the four Ps of marketing, as well as their ethical and unethical uses.

The product portion of the marketing mix also commonly comes under fire. Consumers question the extent to which products are actually harmful to them or society in the long run. Many products can lead to short-term satisfaction, but they can also lead to long-term consumer and/or societal problems. Consider the following categories of products, as originally discussed by Philip Kotler:[86]

- **Deficient products** are products that have little to no potential to create value of any type (for example, faulty appliances).

- **Salutary products** are products that are good for both consumers and society in the long run (for example, air bags). These products offer high utilitarian value, but do not provide hedonic value.

- **Pleasing products** are products that provide hedonic value to consumers but may be harmful in the long run (for example, energy drinks).

- **Desirable products** are products that deliver high utilitarian and hedonic value and that benefit both consumers and society in the long run (for example, pleasant-tasting weight-loss products).

© iStockphoto.com/Skip O'Donnell

EXHIBIT 16.5   The Marketing Mix and Business Ethics

Tool	Common Use	Unethical Use
Product	The development of a good, service, or experience that will satisfy consumers' needs.	Failure to disclose that product won't function properly without necessary component parts.
Place	The distribution of a marketing offer through various channels of delivery.	Limiting product availability in certain markets as a means of raising prices.
Price	The marketer's statement of value received from an offering, which may be monetary or nonmonetary.	Stating that a regular price is really a "sales" price. This practice is prohibited by law.
Promotion	Communicating an offering's value through techniques such as advertising, sales promotion, and word of mouth.	Promoting one item as being on sale and then informing the customer that the product is out of stock and that a more expensive item should be bought. This practice, known as "bait and switch," is illegal.

© Cengage Learning

morals personal standards and beliefs used to guide individual action

Marketers clearly want to avoid offering *deficient* products. The difficult issue comes with the marketing of *pleasing* products. Many consumers know that the products they enjoy are harmful, but they buy them anyway! Needless to say, the tobacco industry has been under criticism for years for marketing products that many think are unsafe. Individual responsibility and freedom are important factors in consumer decisions to use these products. Most of the time, these companies deliver both customer satisfaction and value.

The promotion and place elements of the marketing mix can also be questioned. Consumers also question distribution tactics used by marketers. For example, they complain about tickets to major events being made available in only a few select channels. In 2009, Bruce Springsteen fans were enraged when trying to buy tickets to his concerts through Ticketmaster. After logging into the website, they were redirected to the Ticketmaster-owned site TicketsNow.com. Ticket prices were much higher than face value on TicketsNow. Springsteen condemned the practice and Ticketmaster later apologized.[87] A settlement was reached with the FTC in 2010. Ticketmaster was to repay fans the difference between a ticket's face value and the amount paid to a broker through TicketsNow, and brokers on TicketsNow must now disclose when they are listing tickets that they do not actually have.[88] The 2012 Olympic Games were also marred with a ticket scandal.

Consumer Vulnerability and Product Harmfulness

Two important issues to consider when discussing marketing ethics are product harmfulness and consumer vulnerability.[89] A classification of product harmfulness versus consumer vulnerability applied to marketing decision making is presented in Exhibit 16.6. Public criticism of marketing strategies tends to be most intense when a marketer targets vulnerable consumer groups with harmful products. In 2013, a major debate raged throughout the United States on increased regulation of firearms.

Of course, what constitutes a "harmful" product is a question of interpretation, as is the definition of

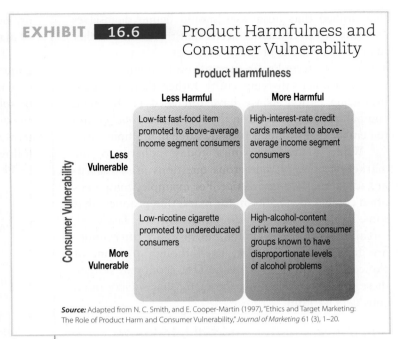

EXHIBIT 16.6 Product Harmfulness and Consumer Vulnerability

Product Harmfulness

	Less Harmful	More Harmful
Less Vulnerable	Low-fat fast-food item promoted to above-average income segment consumers	High-interest-rate credit cards marketed to above-average income segment consumers
More Vulnerable	Low-nicotine cigarette promoted to undereducated consumers	High-alcohol-content drink marketed to consumer groups known to have disproportionate levels of alcohol problems

Consumer Vulnerability

Source: Adapted from N. C. Smith, and E. Cooper-Martin (1997), "Ethics and Target Marketing: The Role of Product Harm and Consumer Vulnerability," *Journal of Marketing* 61 (3), 1–20.

a "vulnerable" consumer. What is a harmful product? What is a vulnerable consumer? Obesity continues to be a major issue in the United States. Public pressure has led fast-food marketers to rethink their menus.

Employee Behavior

Individual employees play an important part in the execution of marketing programs. Although consumers hope that a firm's employees are acting in good faith, this is not always the case. A used car salesperson who sets the odometer back on automobiles should know that the act is unethical and illegal. Some situations, however, are not as straightforward. Consider a salesperson facing the temptation to use bribery as a means of obtaining a sale. In some cultures, this practice is commonplace and acceptable; however, the practice is prohibited in the United States. But what if the salesperson is dealing with a customer who is living in the United States but is from a country where bribes are commonplace?

Individual behavior is guided largely by morals. **Morals** are personal standards and beliefs that are used to guide individual action. Certainly, individuals must answer to their own belief systems.

> Two important issues to consider when discussing marketing ethics are product harmfulness and consumer vulnerability.

16-4 Corporate Social Responsibility

Corporate social responsibility (CSR) may be defined as an organization's activities and status related to its societal obligations.[90] Due to increased pressure from consumer groups, companies are finding that they must be socially responsible. In fact, a popular catchphrase for socially responsible businesses is "doing well by doing good."

There are many ways in which companies can be responsible. Activities such as making donations to causes, supporting minority programs, ensuring responsible manufacturing processes and environmental protectionism, acting quickly when product defects are detected, focusing on employee safety, and encouraging employees to volunteer for local causes are some of the many ways in which companies can exhibit their social responsibility.[91] Basically, the actions described fall into one of three categories:

- *Ethical duties* include acting within expected ethical boundaries.
- *Altruistic duties* include giving back to communities through philanthropic activities.
- *Strategic initiatives* include strategically engaging in socially responsible activities in order to increase the value of the firm.[92]

Socially responsible marketing is associated with favorable consumer evaluations, increased customer satisfaction, and the likelihood of increased sales. This is particularly the case when an individual consumer identifies with the company and the causes to which it contributes. Managers should ensure that their social responsibility efforts guide their marketing programs, as research indicates that brand promotion influences how consumers respond to CSR initiatives.[93]

corporate social responsibility (CSR) organization's activities and status related to its societal obligations

societal marketing concept marketing concept that states that marketers should consider not only the wants and needs of consumers but also the needs of society

16-4a The Societal Marketing Concept

Part of being socially responsible is adopting the **societal marketing concept**. This concept considers the needs of society along with the wants and needs of individual consumers.[94] All firms have many stakeholders, and the effects of marketing actions on all these stakeholder groups should be considered. Some argue that if a product promotion achieves profitability at the expense of the general good, then the effort should not be undertaken. All of the stakeholders of a firm should be considered when marketing programs are initiated. Exhibit 16.7 presents prescriptions for improved marketing ethics.

All Shades of Green

The growth in consumer demand for green products has produced all kinds of opportunities for marketers. Green products continue to gain in popularity and there is much money to be made while helping to save the environment. One emerging problem with green marketing, however, is when products are promoted as being green or environmentally friendly when they really aren't. The practice has become so common that the term *greenwashing* was introduced, and many organizations attempt to fight the practice.

Greenwashing is exactly that: misleading consumers into believing that either a product or the processes used to make the product are green. For example, some products might be promoted as certified green when they really aren't, or they may be promoted as including all natural ingredients when the natural ingredients are actually harmful. Although research in this area is scarce, consumers are turned off by the practice, and it can be considered to be a form of marketer misbehavior.

© iStockphoto.com/Irina Chirkova

Sources: "Greenwashing," SourceWatch.com, http://www.sourcewatch.org/index.php?title=Greenwashing (accessed June 1, 2011); P. Brent, "Greenwashing: It's a Sin," *Marketing* 7, no. 27 (2008): 1.; "Whole Foods Market Imposes One-Year Deadline on Brands to Drop Bogus Organic Label Claims and Calls for Federal Regulation of Personal Care Products," Organic Consumers Association, http://www.organicconsumers.org/bodycare/index.cfm (accessed July 1, 2010).

EXHIBIT 16.7 Prescriptions for Improved Marketing Ethics

- Marketers must put people first and consider the effects of their actions on all stakeholders.
- Actions must be based on standards that go beyond laws and regulations.
- Marketers must be held responsible for the means they use to achieve their desired ends. Focusing on profit motivations is not enough.
- Marketing organizations should focus on training employees in ethical decision making.
- Marketing organizations should embrace and disseminate a core set of ethical principles.
- Decision makers must adopt a stakeholder orientation that leads to an appreciation of how marketing decisions affect all relevant parties.
- Marketing organizations should specify ethical decision-making protocols.

Source: G. R. Laczniak and P. E. Murphy, "Normative Perspectives for Ethical and Socially Responsible Marketing," *Journal of Macromarketing* 26, no. 2 (2006): 154–77.

16-5 Regulation of Marketing Activities

Many federal, state, and local laws were established in order to protect consumers from marketer misbehavior. Federal regulatory bodies such as the Federal Trade Commission (FTC) and the Food and Drug Administration monitor exchanges that take place between consumers and marketers. Other groups, such as the Better Business Bureau and the American Association of Advertising Agencies (AAAA), also play important roles in monitoring marketing activities. Although these groups attempt to bring fairness to the marketplace, it is ultimately up to managers to ensure that the actions of their firms fall within generally accepted business guidelines.

16-5a Marketing and the Law

Exhibit 16.8 presents legislation that has been enacted in an effort to regulate commerce and ensure free trade. Many of these acts are aimed at maintaining or improving the general welfare of consumers in a free marketplace. They also protect the value that consumers receive from exchanges by prohibiting acts such as deceptive advertising and the selling of defective or unreasonably dangerous products.

EXHIBIT 16.8 Major Acts Affecting Commerce and Consumer Safety

Sherman Antitrust Act (1890)	Prohibits restraint of free trade
Federal Food and Drug Act (1906)	Prohibits misleading practices associated with food and drug marketing
Clayton Act (1914)	Restricts price discrimination, exclusive dealing, and tying contracts
Wheeler Lea Act (1938)	Provides FTC with jurisdiction over misleading or false advertising
Fair Packaging and Labeling Act (1966)	Marketers must present proper packaging and content information about products
Child Protection Act (1966)	Prohibits the marketing of dangerous toys
Truth in Lending Act (1968)	Lenders required to disclose complete costs associated with loans
Children's Online Privacy Protection Act (1998)	Establishes rules governing online marketing practices aimed at children
Credit Card Accountability, Responsibility, and Disclosure Act (2009)	Amends Truth in Lending Act to establish fair and transparent practices relating to consumer credit
Helping Families Save Their Homes Act (2009)	Prevents mortgage foreclosures and enhances mortgage availability
Family Smoking Prevention and Tobacco Control Act of 2009	Protects public health by giving the Food and Drug Administration certain authority to regulate the tobacco industry
Wall Street Reform and Consumer Protection Act (2010)	Regulation of financial market practices and consumer protection from various financial and credit practices
Food Safety Modernization Act of 2010	Aims at ensuring the safety of U.S. food supply
Patient Protection and Affordable Care Act of 2010	Aims at decreasing the number of Americans without health insurance

© Cengage Learning 2015

16-6 Public Criticism of Marketing

Unethical marketers intend to do harm in some way, act negligently, and/or manipulate consumers. As we have stated, however, marketers can simply make innocent mistakes. For example, a company may not discover a product defect until it has been released for public consumption. It would then issue a product recall. At issue is the *intent* and *knowledge* of the firm. Consumer perception is also important, as bad events can mean disaster for the firm in terms of lost business, customer boycotts, and bad publicity. We could discuss any number of different issues regarding public criticism of marketing; however, we focus on only a handful of issues here.

16-6a Deceptive Advertising

Deceptive advertising (sometimes called false or misleading advertising) is an important issue for marketers. Deceptive advertising is covered under the Wheeler-Lea Act (1938). This act amended the Federal Trade Commission Act to include false advertising issues. The FTC protects consumers from acts of fraud, deception, and unfair business practices, and the Wheeler-Lea Amendment plays an important role in regulating advertising. The FTC has power to issue cease-and-desist orders and to issue fines against firms that are found guilty of deceptive advertising.

According to the FTC, **deceptive advertising** is advertising that (a) contains or omits information that is important in influencing a consumer's buying behavior and (b) is likely to mislead consumers who are acting reasonably.[95] The extent to which advertisers *intentionally* misrepresent their products is crucial. Although the FTC defines what deceptive advertising is, actual deception can be difficult to prove.

An important distinction in practice is the difference between deceptive advertising and *puffery*. The term **puffery** describes making exaggerated claims about a product's superiority. Puffery differs from deceptive advertising in that there is no overt attempt to deceive a targeted consumer. Consumers often complain that advertisers create unrealistic expectations in their advertisements. For example, marketers of weight-loss products often promote lofty expectations. Advertisers include disclaimers such as "results vary" or "results are not typical" in their advertisements, but consumers rarely notice them. Quite often disclaimers are given very quickly; research indicates that consumers are less likely to purchase products when disclaimers are presented very quickly, especially for unknown or untrusted brands.[96]

In general, objective claims must be substantiated. In fact, the American Advertising Federation (AAF) promotes the idea that advertising claims must be, among other things, truthful and substantiated.[97] The line between puffery and deception can be blurry.

Although regulatory mechanisms are in place to protect consumers from deceptive advertising, most businesses prefer forms of self-regulation over governmental regulation. For this reason, self-regulatory bodies such as the National Advertising Review Council (NARC) work to ensure that advertisements are truthful. The NARC provides guidelines and sets standards for truth and accuracy for national advertisers.[98] National organizations such as the AAAA and the AAF also monitor the advertising practices of their members.

16-6b Marketing to Children

Children typify a vulnerable group because they often lack the knowledge of how to behave as responsible

Marketing to children is a controversial issue.

Jose Luis Pelaez Inc/Blend Images/Jupiter Images

deceptive advertising message that omits information that is important in influencing a consumer's buying behavior and is likely to mislead consumers acting reasonably

puffery practice of making exaggerated claims about a product and its superiority

consumers. Two important issues arise with marketing to children. First, there is the question of whether children can understand that some marketing messages do not offer literal interpretations of the real world. For example, many toys are shown in unrealistic settings. Second, the quantity of marketing messages to which children are exposed can be called into question. It has been estimated that the average American child sees more than 40,000 television commercials per year—or an average of over 100 commercials per day.[99] The Children's Television Act was put into effect to limit the amount of advertising to which children are exposed, with a limit of 10.5 minutes of commercials per hour on weekends and 12 minutes on weekdays. Even with these limitations, approximately $17 billion is spent each year by advertisers targeting the children's market.[100]

The Children's Advertising Review Unit (CARU) of the Better Business Bureau is a self-regulatory body that examines marketing activities that are aimed at children. Among other things, the CARU guidelines state that advertisers should take into account the limited knowledge and comprehension that children have regarding marketing issues. Furthermore, the CARU maintains that advertisers should pay close attention to the educational role that advertising plays in a child's development and that advertising should stress positive behaviors.[101]

Internet marketing is another issue. The Children's Online Privacy Protection Act focuses on the online collection of personal information from children who are 13 years or younger. It specifies what marketers must include in privacy policies, when and how to seek consent from parents, and the responsibilities that marketers have to protect children's privacy and safety online.[102] Yet another issue is how violent advertisements affect children. Research indicates that children who are exposed to these ads may have violent thoughts.[103]

16-6c Pollution

Marketing a product can lead to pollution. Of course, consumption also leads to pollution,[104] and both marketers and consumers play roles in environmental stewardship.

Environmental protection continues to grow in importance, and popular movies and events highlight consumer pressure on businesses and government to increase their role. The Live Earth organization focuses on solving environmental problems, and developed the successful concert of 2007. More recently, the group sponsored the Run for Water in 2010, an event that took place in more than 200 cities around the world.[105] These events are examples of millions of consumers coming together to support the cause. Although experts disagree on the effects of pollution, the issue remains important.

16-6d Planned Obsolescence

Marketers are also criticized for intentionally phasing out products before their usefulness wears out. For example, video game manufacturers are criticized for releasing new and seemingly "improved" gaming consoles even when older models haven't been on the market very long. The practice of managing and intentionally setting discontinue dates for products is known as **planned obsolescence**. Critics charge that it is both wasteful and greedy for marketers to engage in planned obsolescence. Marketers counter by arguing that by continually offering improved products, consumers are able to enjoy improved standards of living and innovation.

16-6e Price Gouging

One area of consumer interest is price gouging. Price gouging is the act of charging a higher than reasonable price for a good, following some kind of natural disaster or event. Price gouging is most often aimed at commodity goods like gasoline. However, it also occurs for other kinds of products and services. Following natural disasters it is common for state officials to warn potential violators to not engage in price gouging. Most laws prohibit sellers from increasing prices more than 25% above average prices over a thirty-day period after a disaster. Retailers were warned to not engage in gouging following the tornado that devastated Tuscaloosa, Alabama, in early 2011 and also in Joplin, Missouri, later the same year. Several businesses were found guilty of gouging after Hurricane Sandy and were forced to pay thousands of dollars in fines. While some argue that the laws amount to price controls, there is no doubt that gouging ultimately harms consumers.[106]

16-6f Manipulative Sales Tactics

High-pressure and manipulative sales pitches are often the cause of consumer dissatisfaction. For example, a realtor might tell a client that several other people have looked at a particular house when they actually haven't. Or a salesperson might tell a customer that a product is in short supply when it really isn't.

Salespeople who adhere to a **sales orientation** are often guilty of these types of high-pressure tactics. To have a sales orientation means that the salesperson is more focused on the immediate sale and short-term results than on long-term customer satisfaction and relationship development. A more appropriate way to approach a sale is to adhere to what is referred to as a customer orientation. When using a **customer orientation**, the salesperson focuses on customer needs. Several studies have shown that having a customer orientation leads to favorable results for salespeople.

Ingratiation tactics are sometimes used by salespeople in order to get a sale. These techniques are often viewed as being manipulative.[107] Techniques such as the foot-in-the-door technique, the door-in-the-face technique, the even-a-penny-will-help technique, and the "I'm working for you!" technique can be called into question. These methods are considered unethical to the extent they are used for manipulation.

- A salesperson using the **foot-in-the-door technique** focuses on simply getting a "foot in the door." When consumers realize that they have opened themselves up to a sales pitch they are more likely to listen to the pitch and they are also more likely to buy a product. The salesperson first makes a small request such as "May I have a few minutes of your time?" and follows with larger request such as "May I show you how this works?" and finally by the largest request of "May I have your order?" The foot-in-the-door technique is based on *self-perception theory*, which proposes that consumers use perceptions of their own actions when forming attitudes. The consumer realizes that he has "let the salesperson in" and has given in to a small request; therefore, he must be the type of person who would give in to larger requests and ultimately buy the product. Of course, salespeople could argue that this is simply good salesmanship.

- With the **door-in-the-face technique**, a salesperson begins by making a really large request such as "Can I get you to buy this car today?" Realizing that very few, if any, customers would say "Yes!" the salesperson prepares for the dreaded "No!" Showing that her feelings are hurt, she guilt-trips the customer with a statement like "Well, can I show you its features?" Many consumers would feel bad about responding negatively to the first request and would allow the salesperson to explain the car's features. This tactic relies on the *reciprocity norm*, which states that individuals are motivated to give back to those who have given them something. By feeling that he just rejected a salesperson, the customer feels that he at least owes the salesperson the courtesy of listening.

- Using the **even-a-penny-will-help technique**, cause-related marketers suggest to potential donors that even the smallest donation will go a long way toward reaching the desired goal, such as ending child abuse, feeding the hungry, or sheltering the homeless.[108] The idea is to make the donor feel ashamed to give such a small amount. Instead of giving the penny, they may give a dollar. This technique is considered unethical to the extent that it relies on feelings of guilt.

- Using the **"I'm working for you!" technique**, salespeople attempt to lead customers into believing that they are working as hard as possible to give them the best deal when in reality they are following a script or routine. A salesperson walks away from his office during a negotiation to "go check with the manager" when he is really going to get coffee. The salesperson returns and says something like "I'm really working for you and here's a good deal!" This technique relies on *equity theory*. Here, the consumer would think that the

sales orientation practice of using sales techniques that are aimed at satisfying the salesperson's own needs and motives for short-term sales success

customer orientation practice of using sales techniques that focus on customer needs

foot-in-the-door technique ingratiation technique used in personal selling in which a salesperson begins with a small request and slowly leads up to one major request

door-in-the-face technique ingratiation technique used in personal selling in which a salesperson begins with a major request and then follows with a series of smaller requests

even-a-penny-will-help technique ingratiation technique in which a marketing message is sent that suggests that even the smallest donation, such as a penny or a dollar, will help a cause

"I'm working for you!" technique technique used by salespeople to create the perception that they are working as hard as possible to close a sale when they really are not doing so

Les and Dave Jacobs/Cultura/Jupiter Images

There are several ways in which sales manipulation may occur.

products liability extent to which businesses are held responsible for product-related injuries

strict liability legal action against a firm whereby a consumer demonstrates in court that an injury occurred and that the product associated with the injury was faulty in some way

negligence situation whereby an injured consumer attempts to show that a firm could foresee a potential injury might occur and then decided not to act on that knowledge

salesperson is working hard, thereby raising the denominator in the equity theory comparison equation and leading to higher levels of satisfaction, and potentially purchase likelihood. Of course, salespeople often do consult with managers and work as hard as possible to give their customers the best deal.

Finding the balance between consumer protection and market freedom is difficult.

16-6g Stealth Marketing

One area of marketing that is currently receiving increased attention is the use of stealth marketing. This type of marketing was discussed in an earlier chapter. Is it ethical for businesses to market products to consumers when the consumers do not realize that they are being targeted by marketing messages? As you may remember from our earlier discussion, with *stealth marketing*, consumers are completely unaware that they are being marketed to (hence, the term stealth). Again, WOMMA (Word of Mouth Marketing Association) is opposed to such tactics and considers their use to be unethical.[109]

16-6h Products Liability

Big business is often criticized for marketing unsafe products. The Consumer Product Safety Commission is the main body that monitors product safety, and the right to be safe is a basic consumer right listed in the Consumer Bill of Rights. Deaths, injuries, and/or property damage from consumer products in the United States cost the nation more than $800 billion annually.[110] Another organization with which consumers are familiar is the Insurance Institute for Highway Safety. This organization focuses on deaths, injuries, and property damage from automobile accidents on the nation's highways.

Product safety is governed in different ways around the world. American consumers are largely protected by regulations resulting from tort law. When a consumer is harmed by a product, he has the right to sue the party believed to be responsible. The issue of **products liability**, which is the extent to which businesses are held responsible for product-related injuries, is determined through this process. At one extreme, the consumer could live by the "buyer beware" principle and face responsibility for all injuries. At the other, firms could be responsible for any consumer injury. In the latter case, the marketplace would be so restricted that few firms could afford to operate.

The primary legal doctrine governing products liability in the United States today is strict liability. With **strict liability**, consumers can win a legal action against a firm if it can be demonstrated in court that an injury occurred and that the product associated with the injury was faulty in some way. This doctrine has become more prominent recently than the former guiding doctrine of negligence. With **negligence**, an injured consumer would have to show that the firm could foresee a potential injury that might occur and then decided not to act on that knowledge. The doctrine of strict liability means that firms face increased exposure to costs associated with product injury lawsuits.

A famous consumer incident involved McDonald's and a customer in the U.S. who spilled coffee onto her legs, burning herself. She obtained counsel and sued McDonald's. Under the negligence doctrine, the plaintiff would have to prove that McDonald's knew such an injury could occur and did nothing to prevent such a mishap, but under strict liability, the consumer needed to demonstrate that an injury occurred and that the product was faulty. In this case, an action under strict liability was pursued on the basis that the consumer was burned and the coffee, being hot, was faulty. The woman ended up winning the lawsuit. A similar action led to Wendy's discontinuing the sale of hot chocolate, because if "being hot" made the chocolate faulty, there was little need in offering the product for sale! Warning labels are now commonplace.

The costs of products liability are high in many industries. Physicians in the United States face huge costs due to the cost of liability insurance they must carry.

Some claim that one of the biggest cost elements to an automobile is the cost of liability exposure, and companies have little choice but to pass these costs on to consumers. So, when a consumer purchases a ladder, a big part of the price covers liability exposure. A potentially bigger cost comes from stifled innovation, as firms fear introducing products that are novel because they could be considered faulty. Companies like Cessna, Piper, and Beechcraft produce piston engine aircraft using the same basic technology that existed in 1950. More innovative aircraft are produced in the "kit plane" industry where consumers have the responsibility of manufacturing the airplane themselves, limiting company liability.

Generally, firms face higher liability costs in the United States than in most other countries. One reason is because liability lawsuits that actually reach a courtroom often involve jury trials. In Europe, most liability actions would be overseen by a magistrate rather than a jury. Juries tend to be more sympathetic and are much more likely to award substantial punitive damages as well as compensatory damages. **Punitive damages** are intended to punish a company for injuries; **compensatory damages** are intended to cover costs incurred by a consumer due to an injury.

The issue of products liability is a good way to illustrate the importance of public policy to consumer behavior. The issue can be complicated and emotional. But while tilting the balance of bearing the burden of product injuries toward firms may, at times, seem reasonable, such tilting actually restricts the market by driving businesses out of certain industries and restricting the choices of consumers. If pharmaceutical firms face costs that are too high and regulations that are too stringent, they may simply stop producing potentially life-saving medications because of product risk. The key to effective public policy is finding the proper balance, offering consumers protection but still providing a high degree of freedom in the marketplace. This, of course, is no easy task.

punitive damages damages that are sought to punish a company for behavior associated with an injury

compensatory damages damages that are intended to cover costs incurred by a consumer due to an injury

Study Tools

Located at the back of the textbook

☐ Rip out Chapter in Review Card

Located at www.cengagebrain.com

☐ Review Key Terms Flashcards (print or online)

☐ Download audio summaries to review on the go

☐ Complete practice quizzes to prepare for tests

☐ Play "Beat the Clock" to master concepts

☐ Watch video on The Putting Lot for a real company example

study tools

WHAT DO YOU THINK?
WHAT OTHERS HAVE THOUGHT

① ② ③ ④ ⑤ ⑥ ⑦

35
30
25
20
15
10
5
0

Strongly disagree | Disagree | Somewhat disagree | Neither agree nor disagree | Somewhat agree | Agree | Strongly agree

Consumers are generally more ethical than the typical businessperson.

Most responses to this question are not very extreme, with a majority of students responding with either *somewhat disagree* or *neutral* responses. Nevertheless, the data do suggest that many students think that consumers can be relatively unethical. How much were these results impacted by introspection? Do students believe that they, themselves, are unethical? This is an interesting question.

PART 5 [CASES]

CASE 5-1

Culture Creates Customer Dissatisfaction?

Written by Mohan Menon, University of South Alabama

It was close to lunch time in Singapore when a long-time customer, Mr. Joe Teng, walked into the offices of Global Voyages and began to raise his voice in anger. He was not in a joyful mood. When employees at the travel agency offered to help, he brushed them aside. He wanted to see the owner to demand his three airline tickets for a flight that night. Mr. Teng had planned to travel to Australia with his family to plan the wedding of his daughter in Sydney. His daughter, who completed her graduate program in environmental sciences at Macquarie University, is working in Sydney. She invited her parents to visit and help her with the wedding in a couple of months.

As Mr. Teng rushed past the row of employee desks, heading toward the back of the office, the owner, Mr. Tarun Yadav, walked out of his office to meet him. "I've been getting my tickets from you for the past four years, and now you make me lose face with my future son-in-law. If I can't leave tonight I would have to postpone the wedding." Mr. Yadav kept his cool in front of his employees and tried to calm the customer down, but in vain. Mr. Teng was in no mood to reason. He wanted his three tickets and nothing else mattered.

The genesis of this service encounter began a few years ago when the customer was referred to Global Voyages by one of Mr. Teng's business acquaintances, who was himself a customer of the travel agency. Global Voyages is a full-service travel agency that primarily serves the corporate market in Singapore and countries in the Asia-Pacific region including China and India. But through referrals Global Voyages developed a significant proportion of business in the retail sector over the years with little or no promotion.

Global Voyages' owner, Mr. Yadav, worked for Thomas Cook, a global full-service travel agency, before establishing his own business. He was with them for about ten years in their Kuala Lumpur, Malaysia, office. He was involved with both corporate and retail clients during that time. At Thomas Cook, Mr. Yadav experienced the peril of retail travel business in the Asian markets and was deliberate in his attempt to target the corporate marketplace with Global Voyages. As with other businesses in the high-context Asian region, retail referrals are sustained if not sought after. Small- and medium-scale businesses welcome referrals, which provide higher marginal revenues with little effort.

Yet many small business owners, like Mr. Yadav, deal with referrals such as Mr. Teng's with trepidation. The reason is cultural, in that consumers develop the bonds of trust with business owners and thus expect to be served without regard for their own "deficient" payment habits. The situation with Mr. Teng's dealings with Global Voyages is illustrative of this phenomenon. Consumers expect prompt and high-quality personal service but seem reluctant to make timely payments. For various reasons, consumers expect unsecured credit for services. Seldom do they skip town without paying, but delayed payments affect a business's cash flow situation.

At the same time, in such high-context cultural societies, repeated pleas or threats for payment are frowned upon and most business owners, such as Mr. Yadav, feel uncomfortable doing so anyway. In the past, he tried having his employees do this "dirty" job with mixed success. Longtime customers sometimes feel slighted by the approach. Travel business is personal in the region, therefore a high level of satisfaction among customers is a prerequisite for building loyalty. Meeting or exceeding customer expectations is the name of the game.

The travel industry has been battered in recent years on several fronts. The economic downturn across the world, including in southeast Asia, a rise in aviation fuel prices, and competition among the major carriers and the low-cost airlines have had a profound negative effect on the travel business. Add to this the pricing pressure from airline websites, third-party consolidator sites, and meta-search sites such as Kayak.com, and it is easy to understand the scope of the problems that contribute to full-service travel agencies being squeezed.

Since travel site switching costs are negligible, younger customers tend to price-shop online and thus are harder for full-service agents to attract. Older travelers, on the other hand, are generally in need of additional help with their travel arrangements and tend to value relationships they've cultivated through the years. They are not very price sensitive and thus patronizing businesses such as Global Voyages provides higher levels of service and satisfaction.

But given his earlier experiences with Thomas Cook, Mr. Yadav also feels that some consumers take advantage of this cultural peculiarity in Asia. Both his corporate accounts and retail clients are generally satisfied with his company, and 80% of them are repeat buyers. His own surveys and audits of travel-related blogs and forums confirm his belief that the company is doing well in the satisfaction ratings. He is fond of adding personal touches to his client interactions. For instance, he and his employees call clients once they reach their destinations to make sure they had pleasant trips and reassure them of help if they need it. At the same time, he uses these personal calls to subtly upsell local attractions or other arrangements they might need. Older clients appreciate this level of attention and often refer their friends and family to the business.

But he has had enough with a few consumers such as Mr. Teng. He feels that their service expectations about Global Voyages are high, yet their reimbursements for services rendered are protracted beyond reason. Customers' vision of what they want from businesses is sometimes colored by their unrealistic expectation of the level of service they feel they deserve within a cultural context. Mr. Teng is not likely to delay payments to service providers in Australia, a country he visits often. Other customers also tend to exhibit such behaviors to varying degrees, and Global Voyages has had to resort to intense coaxing to get paid. Legal maneuvers are rarely utilized, since they might backfire in the high-context culture of Singapore.

This time, he wants to take a stand, yet not in a manner his customers or employees might find hostile. He needs to set the right tone and be the role model that his employees have come to expect. Mr. Yadav also wants his employees to take a stand in similar situations in the future.

Questions

1. What type of expectation does Mr. Joe Teng have about his ticketing situation?

2. Which of the theories of postconsumption reactions might explain Mr. Teng's experience? Why?

3. If the customer is likely to mention his dissatisfaction or negative experience with Global Voyages to his friends and acquaintances, what can Mr. Yadav's business do to combat it?

4. In your opinion, is this a case of customer misbehavior or not? Please justify your answer.

5. Which of the characteristics of relationship quality does Global Voyages exhibit in the case?

6. What would you do if you were the owner of Global Voyages; in other words, how would you deal with the situation?

CASE 5-2

Susan G. Komen for the Cure: Can This Relationship Be Saved?

Written by Mary Anne Doty, Texas A&M University–Commerce

On January 31, 2012, news reports circulated that Susan G. Komen for the Cure had decided to stop funding clinical breast exams through a grant to Planned Parenthood. Initially, Komen cited the congressional investigation of Rep. Cliff Stearns, a conservative legislator who has pushed for abortion restrictions, as the reason for the change in policy barring grants to groups under government investigation. This decision had been made quietly in late November, 2011, with notification to Planned Parenthood in mid-December. As the story broke, Komen found itself in the middle of a controversy. Overnight the organization faced severe criticism (and some praise) as the story mushroomed through television and newspapers, as well as Facebook, Twitter, and other social media.[1]

Susan G. Komen for the Cure has become the largest source of nonprofit funds dedicated to the fight against breast cancer in the world, investing more than $1.9 billion since 1982. In April 2012 their website listed 124 corporate sponsors from varying organizations, including product brands (American Airlines, Ford Motor Company, Mohawk Flooring, and Yoplait Yogurt), retailers (Belk, Lowe's, Old Navy, Walgreens), and sports organizations (Dallas Cowboys, Major League Baseball, Ladies PGA).[2] In thirty years the brand had reached iconic proportions, beloved by people on all parts of the political spectrum. Charity Navigator, a website that rates nonprofit organizations on the percentage of funds used for the organization's mission and on transparency, gave Komen a rating of 4/4 stars, with a score of 62/70.[3] Supporters have a very personal link with the organization because volunteers have given (or walked) in honor of loved ones affected by breast cancer.

As word trickled out about the Komen decision, supporters and critics began sharing opinions through social networking sites. Former Komen supporters responded with anger and disappointment, many expressing feelings of betrayal. While the Komen grants totaled only $680,000 in 2011, an outpouring of donations to Planned Parenthood raised $3 million in three days, including over 10,000 new donors. As the lines were drawn for supporters of both organizations, most chose Planned Parenthood.[4]

The negative publicity also drew attention to many of Komen's practices that had not faced public scrutiny.[5] Among the complaints were: (1) the relatively small percentage of Komen funds that go to medical research for a cure (less than 19%); (2) high salaries of the founder and board members (founder Nancy Brinker is reportedly paid over $400,000 annually); (3) large legal expenses incurred from suing other charities defending the words "for the Cure" in their trademark; and (4) making women's health a political issue.

Susan G. Komen for the Cure did not respond to the social media uproar initially, which angered many of their former supporters.[6] Komen received a strong defense from people who disapproved of Planned Parenthood. Many of these were people who previously did not support Komen's activities because of their grants to Planned Parenthood. In spite of the approval, it was not clear that this segment would replace the funding and other support at risk by the decision.

Corporate sponsors, who generally fear controversial issues, complained that Komen had not informed them of the policy change in advance.[7] While none of the sponsors publicly abandoned Susan G. Komen for the Cure in the short term, they made it clear that better communication was expected if the relationship was to thrive.

After four days of intense negative publicity, Komen announced they were reversing their decision and would consider reinstating the Planned Parenthood grants.[8] Komen founder Nancy Brinker apologized and announced that in the future groups will only be disqualified from receiving grants when they are under investigations that are "criminal and conclusive in nature and not political."

This response was probably a case of "too little, too late" that angered those on both sides of the debate. Planned Parenthood supporters claimed the wording was full of loopholes and not a strong repudiation of the initial decision. Planned Parenthood opponents were angry that the decision was reversed and vowed not to support Komen in the future. The slow response managed to alienate a majority of the public.[9]

When the decision to defund Planned Parenthood's grant became public on February 1, 2012, a number of Komen executives and employees resigned in protest, including a medical advisory board member, a health official, and the directors of several large Komen chapters. After the reversal on February 3, public outcry did not fade away. Karen Handel, Senior Vice President for Public Affairs, received most of the blame for the initial decision and for politicizing Komen policies by focusing on abortion politics rather than detecting and treating breast cancer. Handel, a former political candidate who had campaigned on an anti–Planned Parenthood platform, resigned on February 7.[10]

By February 23, news stories reported Komen hired a consulting firm to assess damage to their brand among supporters.[11] The 20-minute survey tested the wording of various apologies and then measured the credibility of the Komen foundation and its leaders, along with the credibility of other public figures. Komen's problems continued into March when two top executives resigned, the Executive VP and Chief Marketing Officer, as well as the CEO of Komen's New York City affiliate. As the organization struggled to repair its relationship with supporters, some Komen affiliates reported revenues were substantially lower than in previous campaigns, and participation in the Race for the Cure was also down.

It may take years to determine if Komen can repair its relationships and be restored as a premiere charity brand. The damage of these events affects employees in the form of poor morale, former supporters who are angered by Komen's initial decision and are not mollified by the reversal of that decision, corporate sponsors who are leery of future controversy, a public that views Susan G. Komen for the Cure as a tarnished organization, and disappointed anti-abortion groups who remain opposed to Komen. Moving forward, it may be time to reexamine their mission. When the organization was founded in 1982, breast cancer was often a death sentence for women (and a few men) because the prognosis was poor when cancer was detected in later stages. Komen raised awareness of breast cancer and spent millions of

dollars on public education and breast cancer screening. By any measure, those efforts were a resounding success. It may be time for Komen to focus their strategy on research and treatment (as implied by the trademark name, "…for the Cure") and save their education campaigns for less informed segments.

Questions

1. How did social media impact the complaining behaviors of donors and participants for Susan G. Komen for the Cure activities? What types of complaining behaviors were most apparent?

2. What was the response by Susan G. Komen for the Cure to negative public publicity after their decision to stop funding mammograms in partnership with Planned Parenthood? Would you have responded differently had you been in charge?

3. Officials at Susan G. Komen for the Cure seemed unprepared for the intensity of response that they encountered. How would an understanding of the difference between customer loyalty and customer inertia have prepared the Komen officials for the reactions they experienced?

4. Does the Komen organization demonstrate characteristics of relationship loyalty with their donors? Why or why not?

5. Many Komen supporters switched their donations to Planned Parenthood after the negative public publicity. Use the concept of share of wallet to explain why this might have happened.

CASE 5-3

Sports Fans Behaving Badly

Written by Dr. Venessa Funches, Auburn University–Montgomery

It is becoming more and more commonplace to turn on the television, pick up a newspaper, or browse the web and find out about another sports fan behaving badly. You can attend a sporting event from professional to little leagues and you are likely to encounter fans misbehaving. The misbehavior of fans has become legendary. The offenses run the gamut from simple mischief all the way to criminal behavior.

In fact, researchers have identified a subset of fans they term *dysfunctional fans*. "These fans tend to be overly aggressive with opposing teams, fans, and officials oftentimes yelling obscenities or throwing things. These fans are typically disruptive, confrontational, complain a great deal, and abuse alcohol while attending sporting events."[1] In addition, these fans tend to be highly identified with a particular team.[2]

Team identification is defined as the degree to which the fan feels a psychological connection to the team.[3] Fans exhibit high levels of team identification in numerous ways: following the players' careers, being students of team history, attending or watching games, closely watching news coverage, wearing team apparel, just to name a few. There are additional benefits associated with high levels of team identification: an improved state of well-being, a greater sense of community, and strong social connections.[4] In addition, high team identification is also positively correlated to game attendance and merchandise purchasing. Fans who identify highly with their teams consume sports-related products, services, and media such as television, talk radio, and websites at greater levels than their low-identifying counterparts. These high consumption levels are good for business. Unfortunately, there is also a dark side. Some researchers believe that excessive team identification is a determinant factor in fan misbehavior.

Dysfunctional fans are characterized as aggressive males who lack self-control and have positive attitudes toward violent actions.[5] Anecdotal evidence supports the research in this area.

Examples of legendary fan misbehavior include the 2004 NBA brawl between the Pacers and Pistons. A fight broke out between players. After it was brought under control, Ron Artest lay on the scoring table. Suddenly an upset fan threw a drink at him. Artest responded by entering the crowd and throwing punches. The resulting altercation was enormous and included both fans and players. In the end, nine people were injured. Several players were fined and/or suspended from the game as a result of their participation in the fight.[6]

More recently, Harvey Updyke, a 62-year-old avid Alabama fan and retired Texas highway patrolman, called into a popular sports talk show to announce his misbehavior. Updyke told the radio host that he became upset after a disappointing loss to archrival Auburn and decided to retaliate. He allegedly poisoned the famous Toomer's oak trees located on the Auburn campus with a lethal herbicide. The Toomer oak trees represent a coveted symbol for Auburn Tiger fans. The fans traditionally roll these trees with toilet paper after every victory. Updyke is facing criminal charges.[7]

In the latest instance, several Crimson Tide fans poked, prodded, and taunted an incapacitated LSU fan at a burger joint. Eventually one of the fans sexually assaulted the unconscious man in a restaurant after the BCS championship game. Although many people witnessed the incident, no one intervened. The incident was recorded and posted on the web, where it eventually came to the attention of local authorities in New Orleans.[8]

In the heat of the moment sports fans either fail to consider the consequences or believe their inappropriate exploits will remain an unspoken part of the game day experience, repeated only as part of sports folklore. However, this is not the case. Just as in the aforementioned examples, all of these occurrences were heavily scrutinized and reported by the media and gained national attention. Additionally, all of these occurrences were punished and criminally prosecuted. But this inappropriate behavior is not limited to professional sports.

At the conclusion of a teenage baseball tournament, a player from the losing team left the field, making loud and disrespectful comments about the opposing team. A supporter of the winning team consequently punched the player in the head and a fight broke out. By the end of the fight, a spectator had bitten off a man's earlobe and knocked a baby from its mother's arms.[9]

In 2009, sheriff's deputies had to be called out to a little league championship. Apparently, words were exchanged after the game. Then the mother of one player threw a punch at a father of a player from the opposing team. Deputies moved in and quickly gained control of the scene. Both parents were taken into custody.[10]

While this type of fan misbehavior may not be new, it certainly appears to be more frequent and widespread in today's society. Unfortunately, this type of behavior is detrimental to numerous stakeholders, including employees and other consumers. The misbehavior is especially concerning for management of sports organizations because it is their job to deliver positive consumer experiences. Sports fans are expecting to experience an exciting game filled with suspense, drama, and emotional swings. Fan misbehavior like shouting obscenities at officials, throwing items on the field of play, drunken displays, and confrontations can disrupt not only the game but also the positive experience of other fans. Sports fans have many choices when it comes to where to spend their entertainment dollars. Event managers are afraid some fans may decide that sporting events are either unsafe or inappropriate family outings.

As a result, reducing incidents of fan misbehavior is an important concern for managers of sports organizations. Obviously, no one has found the answer yet, but several strategies are presently being used: increasing the number of security personnel present at games, proactively seeking out misbehaving fans through fan tips and increased security surveillance and removing them, and limiting the sale of alcohol. Is this enough? What can be done about fan misbehavior outside of the stadiums? Are the teams responsible in any way? Could teams like Alabama play a role in reducing this type of behavior? If so, what could they do?

Questions

1. Have you ever witnessed fan misbehavior? Describe the experience and how it impacted the value you received from the experience.

2. Is fan misbehavior unethical? Explain your answer.

3. What are the motivations of fan misbehavior?

4. What measures can be taken to prevent or reduce incidents of fan misbehavior?

5. Is fan misbehavior appropriately described as abusive consumer behavior?

ENDNOTES

Chapter 1

1. Dow Jones, "US New Home Sales Fall for Second Month in a Row," March 23, 2012, http://finance.yahoo.com/news/us-home-sales-drop-5-140239145.html, accessed July 24, 2012.
2. J. D. Power, "2012 U.S. Tablet Satisfaction Study Results," September 14, 2012, http://www.jdpower.com/content/study/KjouJRL/2012-u-s-tablet-satisfaction-study-results.htm, accessed May 30, 2013.
3. See C. Glenn Walters and Gordon W. Paul, *Consumer Behavior: An Integrated Approach*, 3rd ed. (Homewood, IL: Irwin, 1970); John L. Howard and Jagdish Sheth, *The Theory of Buyer Behavior* (New York: Wiley, 1969).
4. Deborah J. MacInnis and Valerie S. Folkes, "The Disciplinary Status of Consumer Behavior: A Sociology of Science Perspective on Key Controversies," *Journal of Consumer Research* 36 (April 2010): 899–914.
5. MacInnis and Folkes, "Disciplinary Status."
6. J. Tucker and J. Ryan, *Economics with Emphasis on Free Enterprise System* (Mason, OH: South-Western/Cengage Learning, 2013).
7. "Fast Food for Thought," *The Economist* (July 31, 2011), available at http://www.economist.com/node/21524873.
8. Jennifer Christie, Dan Fisher, John C. Kozup, Scott Smith, Scott Burton, and Elizabeth H. Creyer "The Effects of Bar-Sponsored Alcohol Beverage Promotions Across Binge and Nonbinge Drinkers," *Journal of Public Policy & Marketing* 20 (Fall, 2001): 240–53.
9. Leona E. Tyler, "More Stately Mansions—Psychology Extends Its Boundaries," *Annual Review of Psychology* 32 (1981): 1–20.
10. Carolyn Yoon, Gilles Laurent, Helen H. Fung, Richard Gonzales, Angela H. Gutchess, Trey Hedden, Raphaelle Lambert-Pandraud, Mara Mather, Denise C. Park, Ellen Peters, and Ian Skurnik, "Cognition, Persuasion and Decision Making in Older Consumers," *Marketing Letters* 16, no. 3 (2005): 429–41.
11. W. Pride and O. C. Ferrell, *Foundations of Marketing* (Mason, OH: South-Western/Cengage Learning, 2013).
12. Robert A. Mittelstaedt, "Economics, Psychology, and the Literature of the Subdiscipline of Consumer Behavior," *Journal of the Academy of Marketing Science* 18, no. 4 (1990): 303–11.
13. Interested readers can see MacInnis and Folkes (2010) for more on this debate.
14. M. Bello, "DMVs Hit by Budget Cutbacks: Drivers Face Higher Fees, Longer Waits," *USA Today*, November 23, 2009, 3A.
15. "Editorial: Not Your Father's DMV," *Denver Post*, February 29, 2012, http://www.denverpost.com/opinion/ci_20065131, accessed April 2, 2012. J. P. Meyer, "DMVs Drawn-Out Wait Times Force Denver to Reconsider Furloughs, Budget Cuts," *The Denver Post*, June 1, 2012, http://www.denverpost.com/politics/ci_2012601, accessed February 2, 2013.
16. Monica Yant Kinney, "Speeding Welcome Behind the Counter at License Bureaus," *The Philadelphia Inquirer*, May 17, 2009, B01.
17. J. C. Narver and S. F. Slater, "The Effect of a Market Orientation on Business Profitability," *Journal of Marketing* 54 (October, 1990): 20–35.
18. Seigyoung Auh and B. Menguc, "Diversity at the Executive Suite: A Resource-Based Approach to the Customer Orientation–Organizational Performance Relationship," *Journal of Business Research* 59 (2006): 564–72; N. A. Morgan, "Marketing and Business Performance," *Journal of the Academy of Marketing Science* 40 (January, 2012): 102–119.
19. T. Hult, J. A. Mena, O. C. Ferrell, and L. Ferrell, "Stakeholder Marketing: A Definition and Conceptual Framework," *AMS Review* 1, no. 1 (2011): 44–65.
20. I. Skogland and J. A. Siguaw, "Are Your Satisfied Customers Loyal?" *Cornell Hotel and Restaurant Administration Quarterly* 45 (2004): 221–34; P. D. Berger, N. Eechambadi, G. Morris, D. R. Lehmann, R. Rizley, and R. Venkatesan, "From Customer Lifetime Value to Shareholder Value: Theory, Empirical Evidence and Issues for Future Research," *Journal of Services Research* 9 (2006): 156–67.
21. S. A. Neslin, D. Grewal, R. Leghorn, V. Shankar, M. L. Teerling, J. S. Thomas, and P. C. Verhoef, "Challenges and Opportunities in Multichannel Customer Management," *Journal of Services Research* 9 (2006): 95–112.
22. S. D. Hunt, "Developing Successful Theories in Marketing: Insights from Resource-Advantage Theory," *AMS Review* 1, no. 2 (2011): 72–84.
23. C. M. Christenson, S. Cook, and T. Hall, "Marketing Malpractice: The Cause and the Cure," *Harvard Business Review* 83 (2005): 74–83.
24. A. Arkar, "Six Billion Mobile Phone Subscribers Worldwide: UN Report," 2012, http://www.allvoices.com/contributed-news/13180699-6-billion-mobile-phone-subscribers-worldwide-un-report, accessed February 3, 2013.
25. U.S. Federal Reserve Statistics, http://www.federalreserve.gov, accessed April 1, 2012; CreditCards.com, http://www.creditcards.com, accessed April 2, 2012.
26. Ed Hall, "U.S. National Debt Clock," http://www.usdebtclock.org/, accessed February 4, 2013.
27. W. G. Zikmund and B. J. Babin, *Essentials of Marketing Research* (Mason, OH: South-Western/Cengage Learning, 2013).
28. R. A. Tiwsakul and C. Hackley, "Postmodern Paradoxes in Thai-Asian Consumer Identity," *Journal of Business Research* 65 (April 2012): 490–96.
29. M. Tadajewski, "Remembering Motivation Research: Toward an Alternative Genealogy of Interpretive Consumer Research," *Marketing Theory* 6 (2006): 429–66.
30. Miguel Del Fresno, *Netnografía: Investigación, Análisis e Intervención Social Online* (Barcelona, Spain: Editorial UOC, 2011).
31. Kashmir Hill, "How Target Figured Out a Teen Girl Was Pregnant Before Her Father Did," *Forbes*, February 16, 2012, http://www.forbes.com, accessed February 19, 2012.
32. J. S. Chiou, C. Y. Huang, and H. H. Lee, "The Antecedents of Music Piracy Attitudes and Intentions," *Journal of Business Ethics* 57 (2005): 161–74.
33. "Company Profile," http://www.starbucks.com/about-us/company-information, accessed February 2, 2013.
34. http://www.searsarchives.com/catalogs/history.htm, accessed July 19, 2012.
35. "Quarterly Retail E-Commerce Sales," http://www.census.gov/retail/mrts/www/data/pdf/ec_current.pdf, accessed February 2, 2013.
36. Lenhart, "Teens, Cell Phones and Texting."
37. "Top Sites," http://www.alexa.com/topsites, accessed March 15, 2012.
38. Dennis Jacobe, "Gallup Finds U.S. Unemployment Rate at 10.0% in March," Gallup Economy, March 31, 2011, http://www.gallup.com/poll/146900/gallup-finds-unemployment-rate-march.aspx, accessed April 3, 2012.
39. C. Rohwedder, "U.K. Grocers in Price Fight, and It's Drawing Customers," *The Wall Street Journal*, August 10, 2009, A1. T. Benning, "Slump Strains Church Finances as Need Grows," *The Wall Street Journal*, August 11, 2009, A13.

Chapter 2

1. "My Favorite Things," *SongLyrics.com*, http://www.songlyrics.com/the-sound-of-music/my-favorite-things-maria-lyrics/, accessed July 15, 2012.
2. http://www.harrisinteractive.com/Insights/YouthEquiTrendRankings.aspx, accessed April 4, 2012.
3. Yany Grégoire, T. M. Tripp, and R. Legoux, "When Customer Love Turns into Lasting Hate: The Effects of Relationship Strength and Time on Customer Revenge and Avoidance," *Journal of Marketing* 73 (November 2009): 18–32. Yany Grégoire and Robert Fisher, "The Effects of Relationship Quality on Customer Retaliation," *Marketing Letters* 17, no. 1 (2006): 31–46. Frank Kressmann, M. Joseph Sirgy, Andreas Herrmann, Frank Huber, Stephanie Huber, and Dong-Jin Lee, "Direct and Indirect Effects of Self-image Congruence on Brand Loyalty," *Journal of Business Research* 59 (September 2006): 955–64.
4. G. Jacobson, "CVS aims to personalize retail experience," http://www.chaindrugreview.com/inside-this-issue/news/04-23-2012/cvs-aims-to-personalize-retail-experience, accessed July 30, 2012.
5. L. A. Crosby, W. Marks, and S. L. Johnson, "On Their Behalf," *Marketing Management* 16, no. 2 (2007): 12–13. Michael Treacy and Fred Wiersema, "Customer Intimacy and Other Value Disciplines," *Harvard Business Review* 71 (Jan/Feb 1993): 84–93.
6. B. J. Babin, W. R. Darden and M. Griffin, "Work and/or Fun: Measuring Hedonic

and Utilitarian Shopping Value," *Journal of Consumer Research* 20 (March 1994): 644–56.

7. T. Levitt, "Marketing Myopia," *Harvard Business Review* 38 (July–August 1960): 57–66.

8. T. Wasserman, "Puma Celebrates Darts and Other Hip Pastimes," *Adweek*, August 22, 2010, 26. V. Reklatis, "Analysts See Market-Share Gains for Nike," *Investors' Business Daily*, November 16, 2010, B03.

9. Ferrari information taken from http://www.ferrari.com, accessed April 4, 2012.

10. Jean Halliday, "Total Value Promise a Total Mess for GM Sales," *Advertising Age* 76 (2005): 3.

11. R. Adner, "Match Your Innovation Strategy to Your Innovation Ecosystem," *Harvard Business Review* 84 (April 2006): 98–108.

12. S. L. Vargo and R. F. Lusch, "Service-Dominant Logic: Continuing the Evolution," *Journal of the Academy of Marketing Science* 36 (March 2008): 1–10.

13. P. R. Dickson and J. L. Ginter, "Market Segmentation, Product Differentiation and Marketing Strategy," *Journal of Marketing* 51 (1987): 1–10.

14. More precisely, in economics *price elasticity* represents the proportionate change in demand associated with a proportionate change in price. The slope parameter represents the parameter of the line showing how demand responds to price. Thus, the slope of the line is constant over the range, while the elasticity changes at any point on the line. In addition, to get the actual total quantity demanded, the total size of the population would have to be included in the equation. For simplicity of illustration, they are omitted here.

15. U. R. Orth, M. McDaniel, T. Shellhamer, and K. Lopetcharat, "Promoting Brand Benefits: The Role of Consumer Psychographics and Lifestyle," *Journal of Consumer Marketing* 21 (2004): 97–108.

16. William R. Swinyard and Scott M. Smith, "Why People (Don't) Shop Online: A Lifestyle Study of the Internet Consumer," *Psychology & Marketing* 20 (2003): 567–97. C. Martin, "Consumption Motivation and Perceptions of Malls: A Comparison of Mothers and Daughters," *Journal of Marketing Theory and Practice* 17 (Winter 2009): 49–61.

17. See W. C. Kim and R. Mauborgne, "Blue Ocean Strategy," *Harvard Business Review* (October 2004): 2–10. From a creative thinking view, blue ocean strategies are built around the key words of Reduce, Eliminate, Raise, and Create. Blue ocean strategists often refer to perceptual maps as a strategy canvas.

18. For similar perceptual map illustrations: R. T. Kuo, K. Aksana, and B. Subrota, "Application of Particle Swarm Optimization and Perceptual Map to Tourist Market Segmentation," *Expert Systems with Applications* 39 (August 2012): 5726–8735. L. Xiang, F. Meng, M. Uysal, and B. Milhalik, "Understanding China's Long-Haul Outbound Travel Market: An Overlapped Segmentation Approach," *Journal of Business Research* (in press).

19. L. M. Sciulli and C. Bebko, "Positioning Strategies for Social Cause Organizations: A Multivariate Analysis of Dimensions and Ideals," *Journal of Nonprofit and Public Sector Marketing* 23, no. 2 (2012): 99–133.

20. G. Sunil, D. Hanssens, B. Hardie, W. Kahn, V. Kumar, L. Nathaniel, and N. R. Sriram, "Modeling Customer Lifetime Value," *Journal of Service Research* 9 (November 2006): 139–55.

21. V. Kumar, D. Shah, and R. Venkatesan, "Managing Retailer Profitability—One Customer at a Time!" *Journal of Retailing* 82 (2006): 277–94.

22. Kumar et al., "Managing Retailer Profitability."

Case 1-1

1. IDEO, http://www.ideo.com, accessed April 11, 2012.

2. Cliff Kuang, " IDEO and Steelcase Unveil a School Desk for the Future of Teaching," *Fast Company,* June 16, 2010, http://www.fastcompany.com/1660576/ideo-and-steelcase-unveil-schooldesk-for-the-future-of-teaching, accessed August 1, 2012.

3. Vivek Kemp, "Pediatric Adventures," GE Healthymagination, http://www.healthymagination.com/stories/pediatric-adventures/, accessed August 1, 1012.

Case 1-2

1. T. Shimp and S. Subash, "Consumer Ethnocentrism: Construction and Validation of the CETSCALE," *Journal of Marketing Research* 24, no. 3 (1987): 280–289.

2. "Made in America," *World News with Diane Sawyer*, ABC, 2012, http://abcnews.go.com/WN/fullpage/tour-made-america-house-13001236, accessed October 1, 2012.

3. T. A. Shimp, S. Samiee, and S. Sharma, "The Country-of-Origin Effect and Brand Origin Knowledge: How Little Consumers Know and How Important Knowledge Is," in *European Advances in Consumer Research*, ed. A. Groeppel-Klien and R. E. Frank, 325–26 (Provo, UT: Association for Consumer Research, 2001).

Case 1-3

1. Kashmir Hill, "How Target Figured Out a Teen Girl Was Pregnant Before Her Father Did," *Forbes*, February 16, 2012, www.forbes.com, accessed August 1, 2012.

2. Charles Duhigg, "How Companies Learn Your Secrets," *The New York Times*, February 16, 2012, www.nytimes.com/2012/02/19/magazine/shopping-habits.html, accessed August 1, 2012.

3. Eric Savitz, "IBM Buying DemandTec for $13.20/Share in $440M Deal," *Forbes.com*, December 8, 2011, 21.

4. "The Collaborative Analytics Cloud," *DemandTec, an IBM Company*, 2012, http://www.demandtec.com/mydemandtec/home.

5. Ladka Bauerova, Chris Burritt, and Joao Oliveira, "A Three-Way Food Fight in Brazil," *Business Week*, no. 4172 (April 5, 2010): 70.

6. Ibid.

7. Michael Garry, "GPA Deploys Price Optimization," *SN: Supermarket News* 59, no. 39 (2011): 11.

8. Ibid.

9. Ibid.

10. "SKU (inventory)," Britannica Online Encyclopedia, n.d., http://www.britannica.com/EBchecked/topic/1242199/SKU, accessed August 1, 2012.

11. Garry, "GPA Deploys Price Optimization."

12. Ibid.

13. Ibid.

Case 1-4

1. Laura Petrecca, "Sears, Kmart Parent Company Details 80 Store Closings," *USA Today*, December 29, 2011, http://www.usatoday.com/money/industries/retail/story/2011-12-29/sears-releases-sears-kmart-closings-list/52272742/1, accessed August 2, 2012.

Chapter 3

1. D. L. Levinsky and T. Youm, "The More Food Young Adults Are Served, the More They Overeat," *Journal of Nutrition* 134 (2004): 2546–49; B. J. Rolls, L. S. Roe, and J. S. Meengs, "Reductions in Portion Size and Energy Density of Foods Are Addictive and Lead to Sustained Decreases in Energy Intake," *American Journal of Clinical Nutrition* 83 (2006): 11–17.

2. "Mickelson ExxonMobil Teachers Academy," http://www.exxonmobil.com/Corporate/community_math_academy.aspx, accessed April 24, 2012.

3. G. Antonides, P. C. Verhoef, and M. van Aalst, "Consumer Perception and Evaluation of Waiting Time: A Field Experiment," *Journal of Consumer Psychology* 12, no. 3 (2002): 193–202.

4. J. J. Argo, M. Popa and M. C. Smith, "The Sound of Brands," *Journal of Marketing* 74 (July 2010): 97–109.

5. Rajagopal Raghunathan and Julie R. Irwin, "Walking the Hedonic Product Treadmill: Default Contrast and Mood-Based Assimilation in Judgments of Predicted Happiness with a Target Product," *Journal of Consumer Research* 28 (2010): 355–68.

6. Joan Meyers-Levy and Alice M. Tybout, "Schema Congruity as a Basis for Product Evaluation," *Journal of Consumer Research* 16, no. 1 (1989): 39–54.

7. B. N. Rittichainuwat and G. Chakraborty, "Perceptions of Importance and What Safety Is Enough," *Journal of Business Research* 65 (January 2012): 42–50.

8. P. Aggarwal and A. L. McGill, "Is That Car Smiling at Me? Schema Congruity as a Basis for Evaluating Anthropomorphized Products," *Journal of Consumer Research* 14 (December 2007): 468–79.

9. P. M. Merkile, "Subliminal Perception," *Encyclopedia of Psychology* 7 (2000): 497–99.

10. M. Gable, H. Wilkens, L. Harris, and R. Feinbert, "An Evaluation of Subliminally Embedded Sexual Stimuli in Graphics," *Journal of Advertising* 16 (1987): 26–31.

11. S. J. Broyles, "Misplaced Paranoia over Subliminal Advertising: What's the Big Uproar?" *Journal of Consumer Marketing* 23 (2006): 312–13.

12. T. Verwijerman, J. C. Karremans, W. Stroebe, and D. H. T. Wigboldus, "The Workings and Limits of Subliminal Advertising: The Role of Habits," *Journal of Consumer Psychology* 21 (April 2011), 206–13.

13. S. J. Broyles, "Subliminal Advertising and the Perceptual Popularity of Playing to People's Paranoia," *Journal of Consumer Affairs* 40 (2006): 392–406.

14. G. Lantos, "Ice Cube Sex: The Truth about Subliminal Advertising; Book Review," *Journal of Consumer Marketing* 13 (1996): 62–64.

15. W. B. Key, *Subliminal Seduction: Ad Media's Manipulation of a Not So Innocent America* (New York: Signet, 1974); V. Packard, *The Hidden Persuaders* (New York: D. McKay Co., 1957).

16. W. A. Cook, "Looking Behind Ice Cubes," *Journal of Advertising Research* 33 (March/April 1993): 7–8.

17. "Subliminal Seduction and Other Urban Myths," *Advertising Age* 71 (September 18, 2000): 104–5.

18. J. Vroomen and M. Keetels, "The Spatial Constraint in Intersensory Pairing: No Role in Temporal Ventriloquism," *Journal of Experimental Psychology* 32 (2006): 1063–71.

19. Richard L. Miller, "Dr. Weber and the Consumer," *Journal of Marketing* 26 (1962): 57–67.
20. K. D. Hoffman, L. W. Turley, and S. W. Kelley, "Pricing Retail Services," *Journal of Business Research* 55 (December 2002): 1015–23.
21. K. Kalyanam and T. S. Shively, "Estimating Irregular Pricing Effects: A Stochastic Spline Regression Approach," *Journal of Marketing Research* 35 (1998): 16–29.
22. Miller, "Dr. Weber and the Consumer."
23. C. Y. Yoo, "Unconscious Processing of Web Advertising: Effects on Implicit Memory, Attitude toward the Brand and Consideration Set," *Journal of Interactive Marketing* 22 (Spring 2008): 2–18.
24. Chris Janiszewski, "Preattentive Mere Exposure Effects," *Journal of Consumer Research* 20, no. 3 (1993): 376–92.
25. K. Gustav and Z. Dienes, "Implicit Learning of Nonlocal Musical Rules: Implicitly Learning More Than Chucks," *Journal of Experimental Psychology/Learning, Memory & Cognition* 31 (November 2005): 1417–32; G. Chakraborty, V. Lala, and D. Warran, "What Do Customers Consider Important in B2B Websites?" *Journal of Advertising Research* (March 2003): 50.
26. B. S. Bulik, "Media Morph: People Search," *Advertising Age* 78 (March 28, 2007): 18; J. N. Ballenson, S. Iyengar, N. Yee, and N. A. Collins, "Facial Similarity between Voters and Candidates Causes Influence," *Public Opinion Quarterly* 72, no. 5 (2008): 935–61.
27. C. V. Dimofte and R. F. Yalch, "The Mere Association Effect and Brand Attitudes," *Journal of Consumer Psychology* 21 (2011): 24–37.
28. M. Yang, D. Roskos-Ewoldson, L. Dinu, and L. M. Arpan, "The Effectiveness of 'In-Game' Advertising," *Journal of Advertising* 35 (Winter 2006): 143–52.
29. S. Auty and C. Lewis, "Exploring Children's Choice: The Reminder Effect of Product Placement," *Psychology & Marketing* 21, no. 9 (2004): 697–713.
30. S. H. Ang, S. M. Leong, and W. Yeo, "When Silence Is Golden: Effects of Silence on Consumer Ad Responses," *Advances in Consumer Research* 26 (1999): 295–99.
31. B. David and D. W. Wooten, "From Labeling Possessions to Possessing Labels: Ridicule and Socialization among Adolescents," *Journal of Consumer Research* 33 (2006): 188–98.
32. B. F. Skinner, "The Origins of Cognitive Thought," *American Psychologist* 44, no. 1 (1989): 13–18.
33. Ibid.
34. John C. Malone, Jr., and Natalie M. Cruchon, "Radical Behaviorism and the Rest of the Psychology: A Review/Precis of Skinner's *About Behaviorism*," *Behavior and Philosophy* 29 (2001): 31–57.
35. Saul McLeod, "Behaviorism: Learning Theory," 2007, http://www.simplypsychology.org/behaviorism.html, accessed June 29, 2012.

Chapter 4

1. E. Lepkowska-White and A. Parsons, "Comprehension of Warnings and Resulting Attitudes," *Journal of Consumer Affairs* 35 (2001): 278–94; A. D. Cox, D. Cox, and S. Powell Mantel, "Consumer Response to Drug Risk Information: The Role of Positive Affect," *Journal of Marketing* 74 (July 2010): 31–44.
2. J. J. Argo and K. J. Main, "Meta-Analysis of the Effectiveness of Warning Lavels," *Journal of Public Policy & Marketing* 23 (Fall 2004): 193–208.
3. T. F. Thrasher, M. C. Rousu, D. Hammond, A. Navarro, and J. Corrigan (2011), "Estimating the Impact of Pictorial Health Warnings and 'Plain' Cigarette Packaging: Evidence from Experimental Auctions among Adult Smokers in the U.S.," *Health Policy* 102 (September 2011): 41–48.
4. A. Borges, "Price Matching Guarantees: The Effect of Refund Size and the Moderating Role of Retail Price Strategy," *Recherche et Applications en Marketing* 24, no. 1 (2009): 29–39; M. Kukar-Kinney and R. G. Walters, "Comparison of Consumers to PMGs in Internet and Bricks-and-Mortar Retail Environments," *Journal of the Academy of Marketing Science* 35 (Summer 2007): 197–207.
5. C. Areni and C. Sutton-Brady, "The Universal Color Grid: Color Research Unbiased by Verbal Labels and Protypical Hues," *Journal of Marketing Development and Competitiveness* 5 (2011): 98–102; D. Tsiantar, J. Brau, E. Florian, B. Dumaine, and M. Kimes, "25 Green Myths Debunked," *Fortune*, April 12, 2010, http://money.cnn.com/galleries/2010/technology/1003/gallery.green_myths.fortune/index.html.
6. J. R. Doyle and P. A. Bottemly, "Dressed for the Occasion: Font-Product Congruity in the Perception of Logotype," *Journal of Consumer Psychology* 16, no. 2 (2006): 112–23.
7. H. Noel and B. Vallen, "The Spacing Effect in Marketing: A Review of Extant Findings and Directions for Future Research," *Psychology & Marketing* 26 (November 2009): 951–69.
8. V. Madhubalan and M. Hastak, "The Role of Summary Information in Facilitating Consumers' Comprehension of Nutrition Information," *Journal of Public Policy & Marketing* 21 (2002): 305–18.
9. Y. C. Shen and T. C. Chen, "When East Meets West: The Effect of Cultural Tone Congruity in Ad Music and Message on Consumer Ad Memory and Attitude," *International Journal of Advertising* 25 (2006): 51–70.
10. R. R. Burke and T. K. Srull, "Competitive Interference and Consumer Memory for Advertisements," *Journal of Consumer Research* 15 (June 1988): 55–68.
11. R. R. Dholakia and B. Sternthal, "Highly Credible Sources: Persuasive Facilitator or Persuasive Liabilities?" *Journal of Consumer Research* 3 (1997): 223–32.
12. Renee C. Quinn, "The Power of Branding Through Catchy Advertising, GEICO Commercials," February 24, 2011, http://www.ipwatchdog.com/2011/02/24/the-power-of-branding-through-catchy-advertising-geico-commercials/id=13081/, accessed April 15, 2012. J. Pollack, "Who's Who?" *Advertising Age* 82 (February 21, 2011): 3; J. L. LeBel and N. Cooke, "Branded Food Spokescharacters: Consumers' Contributions to the Narrative of Commerce," *Journal of Product & Brand Management* 17, no. 3 (2008): 143–53.
13. V. A. Taylor and A. B. Bower, "Improving Product Instruction Compliance: If You Tell Me Why, I Might Comply," *Psychology & Marketing* 21 (2004): 229–41.
14. L. Block and T. Kramer, "The Effect of Superstitious Beliefs on Performance Expectations," *Journal of the Academy of Marketing Science* 37 (2009): 161–69.
15. Richard L. Celsi and Jerry C. Olson, "The Role of Involvement in Attention and Comprehension Processes," *Journal of Consumer Research* 15, no. 2 (1988): 210–24.
16. S. Menon and D. Soman "Managing the Power of Curiosity for Effective Web Advertising Strategies," *Journal of Advertising* 31 (2002): 1–14.
17. C. Moorman, "A Quasi-Experiment to Access the Consumer and Informational Determinants of Nutrition Information Processing Activities: The Case of the Nutrition Labeling and Education Act," *Journal of Public Policy & Marketing* 15 (2004): 28–44. See also R. W. Nalor, C. M. Droms, and K. L. Haws, "Eating with a Purpose: Consumer Response to Functional Food Health Claims in Conflicting Versus Complementary Information Environments," *Journal of Public Policy & Marketing* 28 (Fall 2009): 221–33.
18. J. P. Redden, "Reducing Satiation: The Role of Categorization Level," *Journal of Consumer Research* 34 (February 2008): 624–34; C. L. Nordhielm, "The Influence of Levels of Processing on Advertising Repetition Levels," *Journal of Consumer Research* 29 (December 2002): 371–82.
19. M. Griffin, B. J. Babin, and D. Modianos, "Shopping Values of Russian Consumers: The Impact of Habituation in a Developing Economy," *Journal of Retailing* 76 (2000): 33–52.
20. Ralph I. Allison and Kenneth P. Uhl, "Influence of Beer Brand Identification on Taste Perception," *Journal of Marketing Research* 1 (August 1964): 36–39.
21. C. Kaufman-Scarborough, "Seeing Through the Eyes of the Color-Deficient Shopper: Consumer Issues for Public Policy," *Journal of Consumer Policy* 23 (2000): 461–92.
22. K. Vance and S. Virtue, "Metaphoric Advertisement Comprehension: The Role of Cerebral Hemispheres," *Journal of Consumer Behaviour* 10 (2011): 41–50.
23. Ravi Bapna, P. Goes, A. Gupta, and G. Karuga, "Optional Design of the Online Auction Channel: Empirical and Computational Insights," *Decision Sciences* 33 (2002): 557–77.
24. A. D. Cox, D. Cox, and G. Zimet, "Understanding Consumer Responses to Product Risk Information," *Journal of Marketing* 70 (January 2006): 79–91.
25. A. Tversky and D. Kahneman, "The Framing of Decisions and the Psychology of Choice," *Science* 211 (1981): 453–58. J. Cesario, K. S. Corker, and S. Jelinek, "A Self-Regulatory Framework for Message Framing," *Journal of Experimental Social Psychology* 49 (2013): 218–49.
26. S. Rick, "Losses, Gains, and Brains: Neuroeconomics Can Help to Answer Open Questions about Loss Aversion," *Journal of Consumer Psychology* 21 (2011): 453–63.
27. G. M. Fitzsimons, T. L. Chartrand, and G. J. Fitzsimons, "Automatic Effects of Brand Exposure on Motivated Behavior: How Apple Makes You Think Different," *Journal of Consumer Research* 35, no. 1 (2008): 21–35.
28. R. Saini, R. S. Rao, and A. Monga, "Is That Deal Worth My Time? The Interactive Effect of Relative and Referent Thinking on Willingness to Seek a Bargain," *Journal of Marketing* 74 (January 2010): 34–48.
29. C. Spence, "Managing Sensory Expectations Concerning Products and Brands: Capitalizing on the Potential of Sound and Shape Symbolism," *Journal of Consumer Psychology* 22 (2012): 37–54.

30. Keith S. Coulter, Pilsik Choi, and Kent B. Monroe, "Comma N'cents in Pricing: The Effects of Auditory Representation Encoding on Price Magnitude Perception," *Journal of Consumer Psychology* 22 (2012): 395–407; D. Luna and H. M. Kim, "How Much Was Your Shopping Basket? Working Memory Processes in Total Basket Price Estimation," *Journal of Consumer Psychology* 19 (2009): 346–55.

31. M. Vanhuele and X. Drèze, "Measuring the Price Knowledge Consumers Bring to the Store," *Journal of Marketing* 66 (2002): 72–85.

32. A. Krishna, M. Q. Lwin, and M. Morrin, "Product Scent and Memory," *Journal of Consumer Research* 37 (June 2010): 57–67.

33. M. Vanhuele, G. Laurent, and X. Drèze, "Consumers Immediate Memory for Prices," *Journal of Consumer Research* 33 (2006): 153–172.

34. J. C. K. Chan, K. B. McDermott, J. M. Watson, and D. A. Gallo, "The Importance of Material-Processing Interactions in Inducing False Memories," *Memory & Cognition* 33 (2005): 389–95.

35. A. Debenedetti and P. Gomez, "Mental Rumination: How Unwanted and Recurrent Thoughts Can Perturbate the Purchasing Behavior," *Advances in Consumer Research* 37 (2010): 1–6.

36. Celsi and Olson, "The Role of Involvement."

37. J. Saegert, "A Demonstration of Levels of Processing Theory in Memory for Advertisements," *Advances in Consumer Research* 6 (1979): 82–84.

38. Schema taken from top-of-mind associations among a convenience sample of consumers.

39. B. M. Fennis, L. Janssen, K. D. Vohs, "Acts of Benevolence: A Limited-Resource Account of Compliance with Charitable Requests," *Journal of Consumer Research* 35 (April 2009): 906–24.

40. R. S. Moore, "The Sociological Impact of Attitudes Toward Smoking: Secondary Effects of the Demarketing of Smoking," *Journal of Social Psychology* 145 (2005): 703–18.

41. B. McFerran, D. W. Dahl, G. J. Fitzsimons, and A. C. Morales, "Might an Overweight Waitress Make You Eat More? How the Body Type of Others Is Sufficient to Alter Our Food Consumption," *Journal of Consumer Psychology* 20 (2010): 146–51.

42. R. J. Fisher and L. Dubé, "Gender Differences in Responses to Emotional Advertising: A Social Desirability Perspective," *Journal of Consumer Research* 31 (2005): 850–58.

43. L. N. Chaplin and T. M. Lowrey, "The Development of Consumer-Based Consumption Constellations in Children," *Journal of Consumer Research* 36 (February 2009): 757–77.

44. Moore, "The Sociological Impact of Attitudes Toward Smoking."

Chapter 5

1. S. Chatterjee, R. Roy, and A. V. Malshe, "The Role of Regulatory Fit in the Attraction Effect," *Journal of Consumer Psychology* 21 (2011): 473–81; M. Touré-Tillery and A. Fishbach, "The Course of Motivation," *Journal of Consumer Psychology* 21 (2011): 414–23.

2. T. L. Childers, C. L. Carr, J. Peck, and S. Carson, "Hedonic and Utilitarian Motivations for Online Retail Shopping Behavior," *Journal of Retailing* 77 (Winter 2001): 511–35.

3. G. Laurent and J. N. Kapferer, "Measuring Consumer Involvement Profiles," *Journal of Marketing Research* 22 (February 1985): 41–53.

4. D. J. Howard and R. A. Kerin, "Broadening the Scope of Reference Price Advertising Research: A Field Study of Shopping Involvement," *Journal of Marketing* 70 (October 2006): 185–204.

5. H. Kim, K. Park, and N. Schwarz, "Will This Trip Be Exciting? The Role of Incidental Emotions in Product Evaluations," *Journal of Consumer Research* 36 (April 2010): 983–91.

6. R. Plutchik, *Emotions and Life: Perspectives from Psychology, Biology and Evolution* (Washington, DC: American Psychological Association, 2003).

7. E. Fonberg, "Amygdala: Emotions, Motivation, and Depressive States," in *Emotion: Theory, Research, and Experience*, ed. R. Plutchik et al. (New York: Kluwer Press, 1986), 302.

8. B. J. Babin, W. R. Darden, and L. A. Babin, "Negative Emotions in Marketing Research: Affect or Artifact?" *Journal of Business Research* 42 (1998): 271–85; J. A. Russell and J. Snodgrass, "Emotion and the Environment," in *Environment and Psychology*, ed. D. Stokols and I. Altman (New York: John Wiley and Sons, 1987), 245–80.

9. R. Saini and S. C. Thota, "The Psychological Underpinnings of Relative Thinking in Price Comparisons," *Journal of Consumer Psychology* 20 (2010): 185–92.

10. L. Watson and M. Spencer, "Causes and Consequences of Emotions on Consumer Behaviour: A Review and Integrative Cognitive Appraisal Theory," *European Journal of Marketing* 41 (2007): 487–511.

11. J. G. Moulard, M. Kroff, and J. A. G. Folse, "Unraveling Consumer Suspense: The Role of Fear, Hope and Probability Fluctuations," *Journal of Business Research* 65 (March 2012): 340–46; L. Brennan and W. Binney, "Fear, Guilt and Shame Appeals in Social Marketing," *Journal of Business Research* 62 (2010): 140–46.

12. H. Zourrig, J. C. Chebat, and R. Toffoli, "Consumer Revenge Behavior: A Cross-Cultural Perspective," *Journal of Business Research* 62 (2009): 995–1001.

13. B. J. Babin and W. R. Darden, "Good and Bad Shopping Vibes: Spending and Patronage Satisfaction," *Journal of Business Research* 35 (1996): 201–6.

14. N. M. Pucinelli, "Putting Your Best Foot Forward: The Impact of Customer Mood on Salesperson Evaluation," *Journal of Consumer Psychology* 16 (2006): 156–62.

15. R. Raghunathan and J. R. Irwin, "Walking the Hedonic Product Treadmill: Default Contrast and Mood-Based Assimilation in Judgments of Predicted Happiness with a Target Product," *Journal of Consumer Research* 28 (December 2001): 355–68.

16. Y. Jiang, A. Choi, and R. Adaval, "The Unique Consequences of Feeling Lucky: Implications for Consumer Behavior," *Journal of Consumer Psychology* 19 (2009): 171–84.

17. A. S. Koch and J. P. Forgas, "Feeling Good and Feeling Truth: The Interactive Effects of Mood and Processing Fluency on Truth Judgments," *Journal of Experimental Social Psychology* 48 (2012): 481–85.

18. R. B. Cialdini and D. T. Kenrick, "Altruism as Hedonism: A Social Development Perspective on the Relationship of Negative Mood State and Helping," *Journal of Personality and Social Psychology* 34 (1976): 907–14.

19. P. Raghubir, "An Information Processing View of the Subjective Value of Money and Prices," *Journal of Business Research* 59 (2006): 1053–62.

20. See P. Karolein and S. Dewitte, "How to Capture the Heart? Twenty Years of Emotion Measurement in Advertisement," *Journal of Advertising* 46 (2006): 18–37.

21. For an overview, see R. A. Drake and L. R. Myers, "Visual Attention, Emotion, and Action Tendency: Feeling Active or Passive," *Cognition and Emotion* 20 (2006): 608–22.

22. J. A. Russell and G. Pratt, "Affect Space Is Bipolar," *Journal of Personality and Social Psychology* 37 (1979): 1161–78; Babin, Darden, and Babin, "Negative Emotions in Marketing Research."

23. W. J. Havlena and M. B. Holbrook, "The Varieties of Consumption Experience: Comparing Two Typologies of Emotion in Consumer Behavior," *Journal of Consumer Research* 13 (1986): 97–112; R. Kottasz, "Understanding the Influences of Atmospheric Cues on the Emotional Responses and Behaviours of Museum Visitors," *Journal of Nonprofit & Public Sector Marketing* 16 (2006): 95–121.

24. C. White and Y. Yi-Ting, "Satisfaction Emotions and Consumer Behavioral Intentions," *Journal of Services Marketing* 19 (2005): 411–20; J. C. Chebat and W. Sluszrczyk, "How Emotions Mediate the Effects of Perceived Justice on Loyalty in Service Recovery Situation: An Empirical Study," *Journal of Business Research* 56 (2005): 664–73.

25. T. A. Moorradian and J. M. Oliver, "I Can't Get No Satisfaction: The Impact of Personality and Emotion on Postpurchase Processes," *Psychology & Marketing* 14 (1997): 379–93.

26. O. Mascarenhas, R. Kesavan, and M. Bernacchi, "Lasting Customer Loyalty: A Total Customer Experience Approach," *Journal of Consumer Marketing* 23 (2006): 397–405.

27. A. Hiam, "Match Premiums to Marketing Strategies," *Marketing News* 34, no. 20 (2000): 12.

28. D. L. Hoffman and T. P. Novak, "Flow Online: Lessons Learned and Future Prospects," *Journal of Interactive Marketing* 23 (2009): 23–24.

29. T. J. Chou and C. C. Ting, "The Role of *Flow* Experience in Cyber-Game Addiction," *Cyber Psychology & Behavior* 6 (2003): 663–75.

30. Elizabeth Cohen, "Five Clues That You Are Addicted to Facebook," CNNhealth.com, April 23, 2009, http://www.cnn.com/2009/HEALTH/04/23/ep.facebook.addict/index.html, accessed April 18, 2012. L. A. Jelenchick, T. Becker, and M. A. Moreno, "Assessing the Psychometric Properties of the Internet Addiction Test (IAT) in US College Students," *Psychiatry Research*, in press; A. Patterson, "Social Networkers of the World Unite and Take Over: A Meta-Introspective Perspective on the Facebook Brand," *Journal of Business Research* 65 (2012): 527–34.

31. Sylvain Sénécal, J. E. Gharbi, and J. Nantel, "The Influence of Flow on Utilitarian and Hedonic Shopping Values," *Advances in Consumer Research* 29 (2002): 483–84.

32. Donnavieve N. Smith and K. Sivakumar, "Flow and Internet Shopping Behavior," *Journal of Business Research* 57, no. 10 (2004): 1199–1208.

33. L. Dailey, "Navigational Web Atmospherics: Explaining the Influence of Restrictive Navigation Cues," *Journal of Business Research* 57 (2004): 795–803.

34. J. M. Gottman and R. W. Leveson, "Emotional Suppression: Physiology, Self-Report, and Expressive Behavior," *Journal of Personality and Social Psychology* 64 (April 1992): 970–86.

35. J. J. Gross and O. P. John, "Revealing Feelings: Facets of Emotional Expressivity in Self-Reports, Peer Ratings, and Behavior," *Journal of Personality and Social Psychology* 72 (February 1997): 435–48.

36. Particularly when the emotions are consistent with the sex-role expectations of the female social schema. Social schemata were discussed in Chapter 4.

37. H. A. Taute, B. A. Huhmann, and R. Thakur, "Emotional Information Management: Concept Development and Measurement in Public Service Announcements," *Psychology & Marketing* 27 (May 2010): 417–44.

38. E. J. Rozell, C. E. Pettijohn, and R. S. Parker, "Emotional Intelligence and Dispositional Affectivity as Predictors of Performance in Salespeople," *Journal of Marketing Theory and Practice* 14 (2006): 113–24.

39. J. Chang, "Born to Sell?" *Sales & Marketing Management* 155 (2003): 34–39.

40. P. Ferrè, "Effects of Level of Processing on Memory for Affectively Valenced Words," *Cognition and Emotion* 17 (2003): 859.

41. Thomas R. Baird, R. G. Wahlers, and C. K. Cooper, "Non Recognition of Print Advertising: Emotion Arousal and Gender Effects," *Journal of Marketing Communications* 13 (2007): 39–57.

42. K. White and C. McFarland, "When Are Moods Likely to Influence Consumers' Product Preferences? The Role of Mood Focus and Perceived Relevance of Moods," *Journal of Consumer Psychology* 19 (2009): 526–36; A. Merchant, J. B. Ford, and G. Rose, "How Personal Nostalgia Influences Giving to Charity," *Journal of Business Research*, in press, doi.10.1016 /j.busres2010.06.013.

43. J. P. Forgas and J. Ciarrochi, "On Being Happy and Possessive: The Interactive Effects of Mood and Personality on Consumer Judgments, *Psychology & Marketing* 18 (2001): 239–60.

44. J. J. Sierra and S. McQuitty, "Attitudes and Emotions as Determinants of Nostalgic Purchases: An Application of Social Identity Theory," *Journal of Marketing Theory and Practice* 15 (2007): 99–112.

45. R. T. Proyer, T. Platt, and W. Ruch, "Self-Conscious Emotions and Ridicule: Shameful Gelotophobes and Guilt Free Katagelasticists," *Personality and Individual Differences* 49 (2010): 54–58; Brennan and Binney, "Fear, Guilt and Shame Appeals in Social Marketing."

46. S. M. Gountas, T. Ewing, and J. L. Gountas, "Testing Airline Passengers' Responses to Flight Attendants' Expressive Displays: The Effects of Positive Affect," *Journal of Business Research* 60 (2007): 81–83; T. Hennig-Thurau, M. Groth, P. Michael, and D. D. Gremier, "Are All Smiles Created Equal? How Emotional Contagion and Emotional Labor Affect Service Relationships," *Journal of Marketing* 70 (2006): 58–73.

47. J. L. Argo, D. W. Dahl, and A. C. Morales, "Positive Consumer Contagion: Responses to Attractive Others in a Retail Context," *Journal of Marketing Research* 45 (December 2008): 690–701.

Chapter 6

1. For a discussion of individual difference variables in consumer research and marketing practice, see John C. Mowen, *The 3M Model of Motivation and Personality: Theory and Empirical Applications to Consumer Behavior* (Boston: Kluwer Academic Publishers, 2000).

2. This definition is based on a number of different sources in personality psychology literature, including G. W. Allport, *Pattern and Growth in Personality* (New York: Holt, Rinehart, and Winston, 1961); L. A. Pervin and O. P. John, *Personality Theory and Research* (New York: John Wiley & Sons, 1977); Nathan Brody and Howard Ehrlichman, *Personality Psychology: The Science of Individuality* (Upper Saddle River, NJ: Prentice Hall, 1998); and Mowen, *The 3M Model of Motivation and Personality*.

3. Alois Angleitner, "Personality Psychology: Trends and Developments," *European Journal of Personality* 5 (1991): 185–97.

4. A discussion of the debate regarding personality and behavioral consistency across situations may be found in W. Mischel and P. K. Peake, "Some Facets of Consistency: Replies to Epstein, Funder, and Bem," *Psychological Review* 89 (1983): 394–402; S. Epstein, "The Stability of Confusion: A Reply to Mischel and Peake," *Psychological Review* 90 (1983): 179–194; David Buss, "Personality as Traits," *American Psychologist* 44 (1989): 1378–88.

5. For a discussion of psychoanalytical theory and applications to marketing, see Harold H. Kassarjian, "Personality and Consumer Behavior: A Review," *Journal of Marketing Research* 8 (November 1971): 409–18. Also see Harold H. Kassarjian and Mary Jane Sheffet, "Personality and Consumer Behavior: An Update," in *Perspectives in Consumer Behavior*, 4th ed., ed. Harold H. Kassarjian and Thomas S. Robertson, 81–303 (Upper Saddle River, NJ: Prentice Hall, 1991). For a general description of the psychoanalytical approach in psychology, see Brody and Ehrlichman, *Personality Psychology*.

6. Interesting examples of the early use of these motivational techniques can be found in Philip Gustafson, "You Can Gauge Customers' Wants," *Nation's Business* 49 (April 1958): 76–84.

7. Kassarjian, "Personality and Consumer Behavior: A Review."

8. Brody and Ehrlichman, *Personality Psychology*.

9. Stephen J. Gould, "The Emergence of Consumer Introspection Theory (CIT): Introduction to a JBR Special Issue," *Journal of Business Research* 65 (2012): 453–60; Barbara Olsen, "Reflexive Introspection on Sharing Gifts and Shaping Stories," *Journal of Business Research* 65 (2012): 467–74.

10. A. Keinan and R. Kivetz, "Productivity Orientation and the Consumption of Collectible Experiences," *Journal of Consumer Research* 37, no. 6 (2011): 935–50.

11. Buss, "Personality as Traits."

12. G. W. Allport and H. S. Odbert, "Trait Names," *Psychological Monographs* 47, no. 211 (1936): 1–37.

13. Donald R. Lichtenstein, Richard G. Netemeyer, and Scot Burton, "Distinguishing Coupon Proneness from Value Consciousness: An Acquisition-Transaction Utility Theory Perspective," *Journal of Marketing* 54, no. 3 (1990): 54–67.

14. Russell W. Belk, "Materialism: Trait Aspects of Living in the Material World," *Journal of Consumer Research* 12, no. 3 (December 1985): 265–80.

15. Marsha L. Richins, "Special Possessions and the Expression of Material Values," *Journal of Consumer Research* 21, no. 3 (December 1994): 522–33; Belk, "Materialism."

16. Aric Rindfleisch, James E. Burroughs, and Nancy Wong, "The Safety of Objects: Materialism, Existential Insecurity, and Brand Connection," *Journal of Consumer Research* 36 (June 2009): 1–16.

17. Kelly Tian and Russell W. Belk, "Extended Self and Possessions in the Workplace," *Journal of Consumer Research* 32, no. 2 (September 2005): 297–310.

18. Melanie Wallendorf and Eric J. Arnould, "My Favorite Things: A Cross-Cultural Inquiry into Object Attachment, Possessiveness, and Social Linkage," *Journal of Consumer Research* 14, no. 4 (March 1988): 531–47.

19. Belk, "Materialism."

20. Mary Loftus, "Till Debt Do Us Part," *Psychology Today* 37, no. 6 (November/December 2004): 42–50.

21. John L. Lastovicka, Lance A. Bettencourt, Renee Shaw Hughner, and Ronald J. Kuntze, "Lifestyle of the Tight and Frugal: Theory and Measurement," *Journal of Consumer Research* 26, no. 1 (June 1999): 85–98.

22. This definition is based on the works of David F. Midgley and Grahame R. Dowling, "Innovativeness: The Concept and Its Measurement," *Journal of Consumer Research* (1978): 229–42; Everett M. Rogers and Floyd F. Shoemaker, *Communication of Innovations* (New York: The Free Press, 1971); Jonathan B. Hartman, Kenneth C. Gerht, and Kittichai Watchravesringkan, "Re-Examination of the Concept of Innovativeness in the Context of the Adolescent Segment: Development of a Measurement Scale," *Journal of Targeting, Measurement and Analysis for Marketing* 12 (2004): 353–66; Stacy L. Wood and Joffre Swait, "Psychological Indicators of Innovation Adoption: Cross-Classification Based on Need for Cognition and Need for Change," *Journal of Consumer Psychology* 12 (2002): 1–13; Ronald E. Goldsmith and Charles E. Hofacker, "Measuring Consumer Innovativeness," *Journal of the Academy of Marketing Science* 19 (1991): 209–21; Meera A. Venkatraman, "The Impact of Innovativeness and Innovation Type on Product Adoption," *Journal of Retailing* 67 (1991): 51–67.

23. Tanawat Hirunyawipada and Audhesh K. Paswan, "Consumer Innovativeness and Perceived Risk: Implications for High Technology Product Adoption," *Journal of Consumer Marketing* 23/24 (2006): 182–98; Elizabeth C. Hirschman, "Innovativeness, Novelty Seeking, and Consumer Creativity," *Journal of Consumer Research* 7 (1980): 283–95; Kenneth C. Manning, William O. Bearden, and Thomas J. Madden, "Consumer Innovativeness and the Adoption Process," *Journal of Consumer Psychology* 4 (1995): 329–45; A. V. Citrin, D. E. Sprott, S. N. Silverman, and D. E. Stem, "Adoption of Internet Shopping: The Role of Consumer Innovativeness," *Industrial Management & Data Systems* 100 (2000): 294–300.

24. John Cacioppo and Richard Petty, "The Need for Cognition," *Journal of Personality and Social Psychology* 42 (January 1982): 116–31.

25. Curt Haugtvedt, Richard Petty, John Cacioppo, and Theresa Steidley, "Personality and Ad Effectiveness: Exploring the Utility of Need for Cognition," in *Advances in Consumer Research*, Vol. 15, ed. Michael Houston (Provo, UT: Association for Consumer Research, 1988): 209–12.

26. These assertions based on Yong Zhang, "Responses to Humorous Advertising: The Moderating Effect of Need for Cognition," *Journal of Advertising* 25, no. 1 (1996): 15–31; Sanjay Putrevu, "Consumer Responses toward Sexual and Nonsexual Appeals: The Influence of Involvement, Need for Cognition, and Gender," *Journal of Advertising* 37, no. 2 (2008): 57–70.

27. John C. Mowen, "Exploring the Trait of Competitiveness and Its Consumer Behavior Consequences," *Journal of Consumer Psychology* 14 (2004): 52–63.

28. Robert B. Cialdini, Richard J. Borden, Avril Thorne, Marcus R. Walker, Stephen Freeman, and Lloyd R. Sloan, "Basking in Reflected Glory: Three (Football) Field Studies," *Journal of Personality and Social Psychology* 34, no. 3 (1976): 366–75.

29. M. Snyder, *Public Appearances, Private Realities: The Psychology of Self-Monitoring* (New York: W. H. Freeman, 1987).

30. Aron O'Cass, "A Psychometric Evaluation of a Revised Version of the Lennox and Wolfe Revised Self-Monitoring Scale, *Psychology & Marketing* 17, no. 5 (2000): 397–418; Timothy Graeff, "Image Congruence Effects on Product Evaluations: The Role of Self-Monitoring and Public/Private Consumption," *Psychology & Marketing* 13, no. 5 (1996): 481–99.

31. Researchers who have contributed to the development of the Five-Factor Model and associated consumer research include: P. T. Costa and R. R. McCrae, *The NEO Personality Inventory Manual* (Odessa, FL: Psychological Assessment Resources, 1985); L. R. Goldberg, "The Development of Matters for the Big-Five Factor Structure," *Psychological Assessment* 4 (1992): 26–42; J. Wiggins, *The Five-Factor Model of Personality* (New York: Guilford Press, 1996); Eric G. Harris and John C. Mowen, "The Influence of Cardinal, Central-, and Surface-Level Personality Traits on Consumers' Bargaining and Complaining Behaviors," *Psychology & Marketing* 18, no. 11 (November 2001): 1150–85; Eric G. Harris and David E. Fleming, "Assessing the Human Element in Service Personality Formation: Personality Congruency and the Five Factor Model," *Journal of Services Marketing* 19, no. 4 (2005): 187–98; John C. Mowen and Nancy Spears, "Understanding Compulsive Buying among College Students," *Journal of Consumer Psychology* 8, no. 4 (1999): 407–30; Seth Finn, "Origins of Media Exposure: Linking Personality Traits to TV, Radio, Print, and Film Use," *Communication Research* 24, no. 5 (October 1997): 507–30; Elena Fraj and Eva Martinez, "Influence of Personality on Ecological Consumer Behaviour," *Journal of Consumer Behaviour* 5 (2006): 167–81.

32. Notable works in this area include H. J. Eysenck, *Dimensions of Personality* (London: Routledge & Kegan Paul, 1947); Allport, *Pattern and Growth in Personality*; S. V. Paunonen, "Hierarchical Organization of Personality and Prediction of Behavior," *Journal of Personality and Social Psychology* 74 (1998): 538–56; Mowen, *The 3M Model of Motivation and Personality*.

33. This section is based on a number of sources that have discussed problems with the trait approach in CB, including Kassarjian, "Personality and Consumer Behavior: A Review"; Kassarjian and Sheffet "Personality and Consumer Behavior: An Update"; John L. Lastovicka and Eric A. Joachimsthaler, "Improving the Detection of Personality-Behavior Relationships," *Journal of Consumer Research* 14, no. 4 (March 1988): 583–87; Mowen, *The 3M Model of Motivation and Personality*.

34. Hans Baumgartner, "Toward a Personology of the Consumer," *Journal of Consumer Research* 29, no. 2 (September 2002): 286–92; also Dan P. McAdams, "Personality, Modernity, and the Storied Self: A Contemporary Framework for Studying Persons," *Psychological Inquiry* 7, no. 4 (1996): 295–321.

35. Jennifer Aaker, "Dimensions of Brand Personality," *Journal of Marketing Research* 34, no. 3 (August 1997): 347–56.

36. K. P. Gwinner and J. Eaton, "Building Brand Image through Event Sponsorship: The Role of Image Transfer," *Journal of Advertising* 38 (1999): 47–57.

37. Vanitha Swaminathan, Karen M. Stilley, and Rohini Ahluwalia, "When Brand Personality Matters: The Moderating Role of Attachment Styles," *Journal of Consumer Research* 35 (April 2009): 985–1002.

37a. R. Tsiotsou, "Developing a Scale for Measuring the Personality of Sports Teams," *Journal of Services Marketing* 26, no. 4/5 (2012): 238–52.

38. David A. Aaker, *Building Strong Brands* (New York: Free Press, 1996); also Bill Snyder, "Highly Trusted Brands Run More Risk of Offending Customers," March 1, 2003, http://www.gsb.stanford.edu/news /research/mktg_goodbrands .shtml, accessed May 24, 2010.

38a. L. Malar, B. Nyffenegger, H. Krohmer, and W. Hoyer, "Implementing an Intended Brand Personality: A Dyadic Perspective," *Journal of the Academy of Marketing Science* 40, no. 5 (2012): 728–44.

39. Traci H. Freling, Jody L. Crosno, and David H. Henard, "Brand Personality Appeal: Conceptualization and Empirical Validation," *Journal of the Academy of Marketing Science* 39 (2011): 392–406.

40. Susan Fournier, "Consumers and Their Brands: Developing Relationship Theory in Consumer Research," *Journal of Consumer Research* (March 1998): 343–73; Jennifer Aaker, Susan Fournier, and S. Adam Brasel, "When Good Brands Do Bad," *Journal of Consumer Research* (June 2004): 1–16.

40a. S. J. Long-Tolbert and B. S. Gammoh, "In Good and Bad Times: The Interpersonal Nature of Brand Love in Service Relationships," *Journal of Services Marketing* 26, no. 6/7 (2012): 391–402.

41. Harris and Fleming, "Assessing the Human Element in Service Personality Formation."

42. Aaker, Fournier, and Brasel, "When Good Brands Do Bad."

43. W. Lazer, "Lifestyle Concepts and Marketing," in *Towards Scientific Marketing*, ed. S. Greyer (Chicago: American Marketing Association, 1963).

44. Rob Lawson and Sarah Todd, "Consumer Lifestyles: A Social Stratification Perspective," *Marketing Theory* 2 (2002): 295–307.

45. Ana M. Gonzalez and Laurentino Bello, "The Construct 'Lifestyle' in Market Segmentation: The Behaviour of Tourist Consumers," *European Journal of Marketing* 36 (2002): 51–85.

46. These assertions come from the works of Karen Benezra, "The Fragging of the American Mind," *Brandweek*, June 1998, S12–S19; Trent Johnson and Johan Bruwer, "An Empirical Confirmation of Wine-Related Lifestyle Segments in the Australian Wine Market," *International Journal of Wine Marketing* 15 (2003): 5–33; A. Taylor, "Porsche Slices Up Its Buyers," *Fortune,* January 16, 1995, 24; Natural Marketing Institute website, www.nmisolutions .com/lohasd_segment.html, accessed May 24, 2010.

47. This section is based on information obtained on the SBI International website, http://www.strategicbusinessinsights.com /vals/presurvey.shtml, accessed May 25, 2010.

48. This information is based on materials found at http://enus.nielsen.com/tab /product_families/nielsen_claritas/prizm, accessed May 25, 2010.

49. Cecilia L. Ridgeway and Henry A. Walker, "Status Structures," in *Sociological Perspectives on Social Psychology,* ed. Karen S. Cook, Gary A. Fine, and James S. House, 281–310 (Boston: Allyn and Bacon, 1995).

50. George H. Mead, *Mind, Self, and Society* (Chicago: University of Chicago Press, 1934); David Glen Mick, "Consumer Research and Semiotics: Exploring the Morphology of Signs, Symbols, and Significance," *Journal of Consumer Research* 13, no. 2 (September 1986): 196–213; Morris B. Holbrook, "The Millennial Consumer in the Texts of Our Times: Exhibitionism," *Journal of Macromarketing* 21 (2001): 81–95; Himadri Roy Chaudhuri and Sitanath Majumdar, "Of Diamonds and Desires: Understanding Conspicuous Consumption from a Contemporary Marketing Perspective," *Academy of Marketing Science Review* (2006): 1.

51. See also Hope Jensen Schau and Mary Gilly, "We Are What We Post? Self-Presentation in Personal Web Space," *Journal of Consumer Research* 30, no. 3 (December 2003): 385–404; Kaye D. Trammell and Ana Keshelashvili, "Examining the New Influencers: A Self-Presentation Study of A-List Blogs," *Journalism and Mass Communication Quarterly* 82, no. 4 (Winter 2005): 968–83.

52. Jennifer Aaker, "The Malleable Self: The Role of Self-Expression in Persuasion," *Journal of Marketing Research* 36, no. 1 (February 1999): 45–57.

53. These concepts are based on M. Joseph Sirgy, "Self-Concept in Consumer Behavior: A Critical Review," *Journal of Consumer Research* 9, no. 3 (December 1982): 287–300; Russell Belk, "Possessions and the Extended Self," *Journal of Consumer Research* 15, no. 2 (September 1988): 139–68.

54. Aaron C. Ahuvia, "Beyond the Extended Self: Loved Objects and Consumers' Identity Narratives," *Journal of Consumer Research* 32, no. 1 (June 2005): 171–84; Jennifer Escalas and James R. Bettman, "Self-Construal, Reference Groups, and Brand Meaning," *Journal of Consumer Research* 32, no. 3 (December 2005): 378–89.

55. Lon Nguyen Chaplin and Debrah Roeder John, "The Development of Self-Brand Connections in Children and Adolescents," *Journal of Consumer Research* 32, no. 1 (June 2005): 119–30.

56. Debra Trampe, Diederik A. Stapel, and Frans W. Siero, "The Self-Activation Effect in Advertisements: Ads Can Affect Whether and How Consumers Think About the Self," *Journal of Consumer Research* 37, no. 6 (2011): 1030–45.

57. Dirk Smeesters and Naomi Mandel, "Positive and Negative Media Image Effects on the Self," *Journal of Consumer Research* 32, no. 4 (March 2006): 576–82; Marsha Richins, "Social Comparison and the Idealized Images of Advertising," *Journal of Consumer Research* 18, no. 1 (June 1991): 71–83; Sarah Grogan, *Understanding Body Dissatisfaction in Men, Women, and Children* (London: Routledge, 1999).

58. Darren W. Dahl, Jennifer J. Argo, and Andrea C. Morales, "Social Information in the Retail Environment: The Importance of Consumption Alignment, Referent Identity, and Self-Esteem," *Journal of Consumer Research* 38 (February 2011): 860–71.

59. Cheryl Lu-Lien Tan, "Fashion Group Sets Guides to Rein in Ultra-Thin Models," *The Wall Street Journal,* January 8, 2007, B4.

60. Brandon Keim, "Media Messes with Mens' Minds Too," *Psychology Today* 39, no. 5 (September/October 2006): 26.

61. Michael Hafner,, "How Dissimilar Others May Still Resemble the Self: Assimilation and Contrast after Social Comparison," *Journal of Consumer Psychology* 14 (2004): 187–96.

62. "Celebrating 15 Years of Trustworthy Plastic Surgery Statistics," The American Society for Aesthetic Plastic Surgery, March 20, 2012, http://www.surgery.org/media/news-releases/celebrating-15-years-of-trustworthy-plastic-surgery-statistics, accessed April 11, 2012.

63. Eric Bui, Rachel Rodgers, Lionel Cailhol, Phillippe Birmes, Henri Chabrol, and Laurent Schmitt, "Body Piercing and Psychopathology: A Review of the Literature," *Psychotherapy and Psychosomatics* 79 (2010): 125–29.

64. Joan Jacobs Brumberg, "Are We Facing an Epidemic of Self-Injury?" *Chronicle of Higher Education* 53 (2006): B6–B8.

65. R. Braithwaite, A. Robillard, T. Woodring, T. Stephens, and K. J. Arriola, "Tattooing and Body Piercing among Adolescent Detainees: Relationship to Alcohol and Other Drug Use," *Journal of Substance Abuse* 13 (2001): 5–16; J. Grief and W. Hewitt, "The Living Canvas: Health Issues in Tattooing, Body Piercing, and Branding," *Advances for Nurse Practitioners* 12 (1998): 26–31; Jonathan W. Roberti and Eric A. Storch, "Psychosocial Adjustment of College Students with Tattoos and Piercings," *Journal of College Counseling* 8, no. 1 (Spring 2005): 14–19.

66. Jeff W. Totten, Thomas J. Lipscomb, and Michael A. Jones, "Attitudes toward and Stereotypes of Persons with Body Art: Implications for Marketing Management," *Academy of Marketing Studies Journal* 13, no. 2 (2009): 77–96.

67. M. Joseph Sirgy, Dhruv Grewal, Tamara Mangleburg, and Jae-ok Park, "Assessing the Predictive Validity of Two Methods of Measuring Self-Image Congruence," *Journal of the Academy of Marketing Science* 25, no. 3 (Summer 1997): 229–41.

68. M. Joseph Sirgy and A. Coskun Samli, "A Path Analytic Model of Store Loyalty Involving Self-Concept, Store Image, Geographic Loyalty, and Socioeconomic Status," *Journal of the Academy of Marketing Science* 13, no. 3 (Summer 1985): 265–91.

68a. S. Hosany and D. Martin, "Self-Image Congruence in Consumer Behavior," *Journal of Business Research* 65 no. 5 (2012): 685–91.

69. Aaker, "The Malleable Self."

70. Alexander Chernev, Ryan Hamilton, and David Gal, "Competing for Consumer Identity: Limits to Self-Expression and the Perils of Lifestyle Branding," *Journal of Marketing* 75 (May 2011): 66–82.

71. Melea Press and Eric J. Arnould, "How Does Organizational Identification Form? A Consumer Behavior Perspective," *Journal of Consumer Research*, 38 (December 2011): 650–66; Grahame R. Dowling and Tayo Otubanjo, "Corporate and Organizational Identity: Two Sides of the Same Coin," *AMS Review* 1, no. 3/4 (2011): 171–82.

71a. P. W. Fombelle, C. B. Jarvis, J. Ward, and L. Ostrom, "Leveraging Customers' Multiple Identities: Identity Synergy as a Driver of Organizational Identification," *Journal of the Academy of Marketing Science* 40, no. 4 (2012): 587–604.

Chapter 7

1. This definition is based on a summary of several works in the social psychology and consumer behavior literature, including Alice Eagly and Shelly Chaiken, *The Psychology of Attitudes* (New York: Harcourt Brace, 1993); John Cacioppo, Stephen Harkins, and Richard Petty, "The Nature of Attitudes and Cognitive Responses and Their Relations to Behavior," in *Cognitive Responses in Persuasion*, ed. Richard Petty, Thomas Ostrom, and Timothy C. Brock (Hillsdale, NJ: Lawrence Erlbaum, 1981); L. L. Thurstone, "The Measurement of Social Attitudes," in *Readings in Attitude Theory and Measurement*, ed. M. Fishbein (New York: Wiley, 1931).

2. The information in this section is based on Daniel Katz, "The Functional Approach to the Study of Attitudes," *Public Opinion Quarterly* 24, no. 2 (1960): 163–204.

3. Heather Gibson, Cynthia Willming, and Andrew Holdnak, "We're Gators . . . Not Just Gator Fans: Serious Leisure and University of Florida Football," *Journal of Leisure Research* 34, no. 4 (2003): 397–425.

4. Michael Ray, "Marketing Communications and the Hierarchy-of-Effects," in *New Models for Mass Communications*, ed. P. Clarke, 147–76 (Beverly Hills, CA: Sage, 1973).

5. Herbert Krugman, "The Impact of Television Advertising: Learning without Involvement," *Public Opinion Quarterly* 29 (Fall, 1965): 349–56.

6. A recent example of the experiential nature of consumption may be found in Russell Belk, Guliz Ger, and Soren Askegaard, "The Fire of Desire: A Multisited Inquiry into Consumer Passion," *Journal of Consumer Research* 30, no. 3 (2003): 326–51.

7. Martin Fishbein and Icek Ajzen, *Belief, Attitude, Intention, and Behavior: An Introduction to Theory and Research* (Reading, MA: Addison-Wesley, 1975).

8. A number of researchers have addressed this issue, including Linda F. Alwitt and Ida E. Berger, "Understanding the Link Between Environmental Attitudes and Consumer Product Usage: Measuring the Moderating Role of Attitude Strength," in *Advances in Consumer Research,* vol. 20, ed. Leigh McAlister and Michael Rothschild, 189–94 (Provo, UT: Association for Consumer Research, 1992); Allan Wicker, "Attitudes Versus Actions: The Relationship of Verbal and Overt Behavioral Responses to Attitude Objects," *Journal of Social Issues* 25 (Autumn 1969): 41–78.

9. Icek Ajzen and Martin Fishbein, "Attitude-Behavior Relations: A Theoretical Analysis and Review of Empirical Research," *Psychological Bulletin* 84, no. 5 (September 1977): 888–918.

10. Michael J. Ryan and E. H. Bonfield, "Fishbein's Intentions Model: A Test of External and Pragmatic Validity," *Journal of Marketing* 44, no. 2 (1980): 82–95.

11. More on this model may be found in Art Sahni Notani, "Moderators of Perceived Behavioral Control's Predictiveness in the Theory of Reasoned Action," *Journal of Consumer Psychology* 7, no. 3 (1998): 247–71. Also, an interesting presentation of the planned behavior model applied to food choice may be found in Mark T. Conner, "Understanding Determinants of Food Choice: Contributions from Attitude Research," *British Food Journal* 95, no. 9 (1993): 27–32.

12. Andrew A. Mitchell and Jerry Olson, "Are Product Attribute Beliefs the Only Mediator of Advertising Effects on Brand Attitude?" *Journal of Marketing Research* 18 (1981): 318–32.

13. Several studies have approached this issue, including Scott MacKenzie and Richard Lutz, "An Empirical Examination of the Structural Antecedents of Attitude towards the Ad in an Advertising Pretesting Context," *Journal of Marketing* 53 (April 1989): 48–65; Scot Burton and Donald Lichtenstein, "The Effect of Ad Claims and Ad Context on Attitude towards the Advertisement," *Journal of Advertising* 17, no. 1 (1988): 3–11.

14. Tom J. Brown and Peter A. Dacin, "The Company and the Product: Corporate Associations and Consumer Product Responses," *Journal of Marketing* 61 (January 1997): 68–84.

15. Sankar Sen and C. B. Bhattacharya, "Does Doing Good Always Lead to Doing Better? Consumer Reactions to Corporate Social Responsibility," *Journal of Marketing Research* 38 (May 2001): 225–43.

16. Edward Group, "The Benefits of Apple Cider Vinegar," Global Healing Center, August 4, 2008, http://www.globalhealingcenter.com/natural-health/the-benefits-of-apple-cider-vinegar/, accessed April 18, 2012.

17. Richard E. Petty, John T. Cacioppo, and David Schuman, "Central and Peripheral Routes to Advertising Effectiveness: The Moderating Role of Involvement," *Journal of Consumer Research* 10, no. 2 (1983): 135–46.

18. Richard L. Celsi and Jerry C. Olson, "The Role of Involvement in Attention and Comprehension Processes," *Journal of Consumer Research* 15, no. 2 (September 1988): 210–24; Deborah J. MacInnis and C. Whan Park, "The Differential Role of Characteristics of Music on High- and Low-Involvement Consumers' Processing of Ads," *Journal of Consumer Research* 18, no. 2 (September 1991): 161–73.

19. Fritz Heider, *The Psychology of Interpersonal Relations* (New York: John Wiley, 1958).

20. Steve DiMeglio, "Tiger Woods Gets New Endorsement with Nutrition Company," *USA Today*, November 21, 2011, http://content.usatoday.com/communities/gameon/post/2011/11/tiger-woods-new-endorsement-fuse-science-/1, accessed April 18, 2012.

21. A number of studies have addressed these issues, including Cristel Russell and Barbara B. Stern, "Consumers, Characters, and Products: A Balance Model of Sitcom Product Placement Effects," *Journal of Advertising* 35, no. 1 (2006): 7–21; Arch Woodside, "Advancing Means-End Chains by Incorporating Heider's Balance Theory and Fournier's Consumer-Brand Relationship Typology," *Psychology & Marketing* 21, no. 4 (2004): 279–94; Jennifer Edson Escalas and James R. Bettman, "Self-Construal, Reference Groups, and Brand Meaning," *Journal of Consumer Research* 32, no. 3 (2005): 378–89, Janet S. Fink, Heidi Parker, Brett Martin, and Julie Higgins, "Off-Field Behavior of Athletes and Team Identification: Using Social Identity and Balance Theory to Explain Fan Reactions," *Journal of Sport Management* 23, no. 2 (2009): 142–57.

22. Muzafer Sherif and Carl Hovland, *Social Judgment: Assimilation and Contrast Effects in Communication and Attitude Change* (New Haven, CT: Yale University Press, 1961).

22a. D. Allan, "Radio Advertising: Blip Commercials," *Journal of Business Research* 65, no. 6 (2013): 880–81.

23. Donna L. Hoffman and Thomas P. Novak, "Marketing in Hypermedia Computer-Mediated Environments: Conceptual Foundations," *Journal of Marketing* 60, no. 3 (1996): 50–68.

24. This estimate based on data from http://www.internetworldstats.com/stats.htm, accessed February 4, 2013.

25. Hoffman and Novak, "Marketing in Hypermedia Computer-Mediated Environments."

25a. A. O'Cass and J. Carlson, "An Empirical Assessment of Consumers' Evaluations of Web Site Service Quality: Conceptualizing and Testing a Formative Model," *Journal of Services Marketing* 26, no. 6 (2012): 419–34.

26. Sid C. Dudley, "Consumer Attitudes toward Nudity in Advertising," *Journal of Marketing Theory and Practice* 7, no. 4 (1999): 89–96.

27. Michael S. LaTour, "Female Nudity in Print Advertising: An Analysis of Gender Differences in Arousal and Ad Response," *Psychology & Marketing* 7, no. 1 (1990): 65–81.

28. Penny M. Simpson, Steve Horton, and Gene Brown, "Male Nudity in Advertisements: A Modified Replication and Extension of Gender and Product Effects," *Journal of the Academy of Marketing Science* 24, no. 3 (1996): 257–62.

29. Ming-Hui Huang, "Romantic Love and Sex: Their Relationship and Impacts on Ad Attitudes," *Psychology & Marketing* 21, no. 1 (2004): 53–73.

30. Martin Eisend, "A Meta-Analysis of Humor in Advertising," *Journal of the Academy of Marketing Science* 37 (Summer 2009): 191–203.

31. H. S. Krishnan and D. Chakravarti, "A Process Analysis of the Effects of Humorous Advertising Executions on Brand Claims Memory," *Journal of Consumer Psychology* 13, no. 3 (2003): 230–45.

32. Yong Zhang, "The Effect of Humor in Advertising: An Individual-Difference Perspective," *Psychology & Marketing* 13, no. 6 (1996): 531–45.

33. Thomas W. Cline, Moses B. Altsech, and James J. Kellaris, "When Does Humor Enhance or Inhibit Ad Responses?" *Journal of Advertising* 32, no. 3 (2003): 31–46.

34. Amitava Chattopadhyay, "Humor in Advertising: The Moderating Role of Prior Brand Evaluations," *Journal of Marketing Research* 29 (November 1990): 466–76.

35. Stephen M. Smith, "Does Humor in Advertising Enhance Systematic Processing?" in *Advances in Consumer Research*, vol. 20, ed. L. McAlister and M. Rothschild, 155–58 (Provo, UT: Association of Consumer Research, 1993).

36. Michael S. LaTour and Herbert J. Rotfeld, "There Are Threats and (Maybe) Fear-Caused Arousal: Theory and Confusions of Appeals to Fear and Fear Arousal Itself," *Journal of Advertising* 3 (Fall 1997): 45–59.

37. Punam Anand Keller and Lauren Goldberg Block, "Increasing the Persuasiveness of Fear Appeals: The Effect of Arousal and Elaboration," *Journal of Consumer Research* 22, no. 4 (1996): 448–59.

38. Ron Lennon, Randall Renfro, and Bay O'Leary, "Social Marketing and Distracted Driving Behaviors among Young Adults: The Effectiveness of Fear Appeals," *Academy of Marketing Studies Journal*, 14, no. 2 (2010): 95–113.

39. John C. Mowen, Eric G. Harris, and Sterling A. Bone, "Personality Traits and Fear Response to Print Advertisements: Theory and an Empirical Study," *Psychology & Marketing* 21, no. 11 (2004): 927–43.

40. Robert F. Potter, Michael S. LaTour, Kathryn A. Braun-LaTour, and Tom Reichert, "The Impact of Program Context on Motivational System Activation and Subsequent Effects on Processing a Fear Appeal," *Journal of Advertising* 35, no. 3 (2006): 67–80.

41. John F. Tanner, James B. Hunt, and David R. Eppright, "The Protection Motivation Model: A Normative Model of Fear Appeals," *Journal of Marketing* 55, no. 3 (1991): 36–45.

42. Charles R. Duke, Gregory M. Pickett, Les Carlson, and Stephen J. Grove, "A Method for Evaluating the Ethics of Fear Appeals," *Journal of Public Policy & Marketing* 1 (Spring 1993): 120–30.

43. E. Deanne Brocato, Douglas A. Gentile, Russell N. Laczniak, Julia A. Maier, and Mindy Ji-Song, "Television Commercial Violence: Potential Effects on Children," *Journal of Advertising*, 39, no. 4 (2010): 95–107.

44. Michael L. Capella, Ronald Paul Hill, Justine M. Rapp, and Jeremy Kees, "The Impact of Violence Against Women in Advertisements," *Journal of Advertising*, 39, no. 4 (2010): 37–51.

45. Benjamin J. Blackford, James Gentry, Robert L. Harrison, and Les Carlson, "The Prevalence and Influence of the Combination of Humor and Violence in Super Bowl Commercials," *Journal of Advertising*, 49, no. 4 (2011): 123–33.

46. Alan G. Sawyer, and Daniel J. Howard, "Effects of Omitting Conclusions in Advertisements to Involved and Uninvolved Audiences," *Journal of Marketing Research* 28 (November 1991): 467–74.

47. William L. Wilkie and Paul W. Ferris, "Comparison Advertising: Problems and Potential," *Journal of Marketing* 39 (October 1973): 7–15.

48. Paul W. Miniard, Michael J. Barone, Randall L. Rose, and Kenneth C. Manning, "A Further Assessment of Indirect Advertising Claims of Superiority over All Competitors," *Journal of Advertising* 35, no. 4 (2006): 53–64.

49. Dennis D. Stewart, Cheryl B. Stewart, Clare Tyson, Vinci Gail, and Tom Fioti, "Serial Position Effects and the Picture-Superiority Effect in the Group Recall of Unshared Information," *Group Dynamics: Theory, Research, and Practice* 8, no. 3 (2004): 166–81.

50. Curtis P. Haugtvedt and Duance T. Wegener, "Message Order Effects in Persuasion: An Attitude Strength Perspective," *Journal of Consumer Research* 21 (June 1994): 205–18.

51. H. Rao Unnava, Robert E. Burnkrant, and Sunil Erevelles, "Effects of Presentation Order and Communication Modality on Recall and Attitude," *Journal of Consumer Research* 21 (December 1994): 481–90.

52. Cong Li, "Primacy Effect or Recency Effect? A Long-Term Memory Test of Super Bowl Commercials," *Journal of Consumer Behaviour* 9 (October 2009): 32–44.

53. S. P. Jain and S. S. Posavac, "Prepurchase Attribute Verifiability, Source Credibility, and Persuasion," *Journal of Consumer Psychology* 11, no. 3 (2001): 169–80.

54. Pamela M. Homer and Lynn R. Kahle, "Source Expertise, Time of Source Identification, and Involvement in Persuasion," *Journal of Advertising* 19, no. 1 (1990): 30–39.

55. Xiaoli Nan, "The Influence of Source Credibility on Attitude Certainty: Exploring the Moderating Effects of Time of Source Identification and Individual Need for Cognition," *Psychology & Marketing* 26, no. 4 (2009): 321–32.

56. Elizabeth Wilson and Daniel L. Sherrell, "Source Effects in Communication and Persuasion Research: A Meta-Analysis of Effect Size," *Journal of the Academy of Marketing Science* 21, no. 2 (1993): 101–112.

57. Josh Wiener and John C. Mowen, "The Impact of Product Recalls on Consumer Perceptions," *The Journal of the Society of Consumer Affairs Professionals in Business* (Spring 1985): 18–21.

58. Barbara A. Lafferty, Ronald E. Goldsmith, and Stephen J. Newell, "The Dual Credibility Model: The Influence of Corporate and Endorser Credibility on Attitudes and Purchase Intention," *Journal of Marketing Theory & Practice* 10, no. 3 (2002): 1–12.

59. Brian D. Till and Michael Busler, "The Match-Up Hypothesis: Physical Attractiveness, Expertise, and the Role of Fit on Brand Attitude, Purchase Intent, and Brand Beliefs," *Journal of Advertising* 3 (Fall 2000): 1–13; Shelly Chaiken, "Communicator Physical Attractiveness and Persuasion," *Journal of Personality and Social Psychology* 37 (August 1979): 1387–97.

60. Michael Baker and Gilbert Churchill, "The Impact of Physically Attractive Models on Advertising Effectiveness," *Journal of Marketing Research* 14 (November 1977): 538–55.

61. Yoon-Soon Kang and Paul M. Herr, "Beauty and the Beholder: Toward an Integrative Model of Communication Source Effects," *Journal of Consumer Research* 33, no. 1 (2006): 123–30; also Debra Trampe, Diederik A. Stapel, Frans W. Siero, and Henriette Mulder, "Beauty as a Tool: The Effect of Model Attractiveness, Product Relevance and Elaboration Likelihood on Advertising Effectiveness," *Psychology & Marketing* 27 (December 2010): 1101–1121.

62. Marketing Evaluations, Inc., http://www .qscores.com, accessed May 28, 2010.

63. Marc-Andre Reinhard and Matthias Messner, "The Effects of Source Likeability and Need for Cognition on Advertising Effectiveness under Explicit Persuasion," *Journal of Consumer Behaviour* 8, no. 4 (2009): 179–91.

64. James Lynch and Drue Schuler, "The Matchup Effect of Spokesperson and Product Congruency: A Schema Theory Interpretation," *Psychology & Marketing* 11 (September–October 1994): 417–45; Michael A. Kamins, "An Investigation into the 'Match-Up' Hypothesis in Celebrity Advertising: When Beauty May Be Only Skin Deep," *Journal of Advertising* 19, no. 1 (1990): 4–13.

Case 2-1

1. "Indoor Rock Climbing," Find Sports Now, http://www.findsportsnow.com/learn /indoor-rock-climbing.

2. Jessika Toothman, "What Is the History of Rock Climbing?" How Stuff Works, http: //adventure.howstuffworks.com/outdoor -activities/climbing/history-of-rock -climbing1.htm.

3. "Climbing Gyms," Centrahealth, http://www .centrahealth.com/health-library/c/609 -climbing-gyms.

Case 2-2

1. David Katzmaier and Matthew Moskov-ciak, "The Basics of TV Power," *CNET,* April 21, 2010, http://reviews.cnet.com /green-tech/tv-power-efficiency/.

2. Gary Merson, "HDTV Viewing Distance Chart," HD Guru, 2006, http://hdguru .com/wp-content/uploads/2006/11/hdtv _distance_chart.pdf.

Case 2-3

1. A. Troianovski, S. E. Ante, and J. E. Vascel-laro, "Mom, Please Feed My Apps!" *The Wall Street Journal*, June 11, 2012, C1.

2. Steven Russolillo, "Zynga Shares Plunge Below $5; Circuit Breaker Triggered," *The Wall Street Journal*, June 12, 2012, C1.

3. Daisuke Wakabayashi and Spencer E. Ante, "Mobile Game Fight Goes Global," *The Wall Street Journal*, June 14, 2012, B1.

4. Troianovski, Ante, and Vascellaro.

5. Daisuke and Spencer.

Chapter 8

1. C. Whan Park and V. Parker Lessig, "Students and Housewives: Differences in Susceptibility to Reference Group Influence," *Journal of Consumer Research* 4 (September 1977): 102–10.

2. H. Andrew Michener and Michelle P. Wasserman, "Group Decision Making," in *Sociological Perspectives on Social Psychology*, ed. Karen S. Cook, Gary Alan Fine, and James S. House (Boston: Allyn and Bacon, 1995), 336–61.

3. Paul Webley and Ellen K. Nyhus, "Parents' Influence on Children's Future Orientation and Saving," *Journal of Economic Psychology* 27, no. 1 (2006): 140–49.

4. Albert M. Muniz, Jr., and Thomas C. O'Guinn, "Brand Community," *Journal of Consumer Research* 27, no. 4 (2001): 412–32.

4a. Z. Zhou, Q. Zhang, S. Chenting, and N. Zhou, "How Do Brand Communities Generate Brand Relationships? Intermediate Mechanisms," *Journal of Business Research* 65 (2012): 890–95.

5. James H. Alexander, John W. Schouten, and Harold F. Koening, "Building Brand Community," *Journal of Marketing* 66, no. 1 (2002): 38–54.

6. Dana-Nicoleta Lascu and George Zinkhan, "Consumer Conformity: Review and Applications for Marketing Theory and Practice," *Journal of Marketing Theory and Practice* 7, no. 3 (1999): 1–12.

7. Jill Ross and Ross Harradine, "I'm Not Wearing That! Branding and Young Children," *Journal of Fashion Marketing and Management* 8, no. 1 (2004): 11–26.

8. Juan Ramos, "Tobacco Company Undermines Global Treaty on Facebook," Suite101 website, May 28, 2010, http: //www.suite101.com/article/tobacco -company-undermines-global-treaty-on -facebook-a242242, accessed June 17, 2010.

9. Karen H. Smith and Mary Ann Stutts, "The Influence of Individual Factors on the Effectiveness of Message Content in Antismoking Advertisements Aimed at Adolescents," *Journal of Consumer Affairs* 40, no. 2 (2006): 261–93; Merri Rosenberg, "Anti-Smoking Ads Aimed at Peers," *New York Times*, February 17, 2002, http: //query.nytimes.com/gst/fullpage.html? sec=health&res=9D06E5D8163FF934A25 751C0A9649C8B63.

10. Nancy Albers-Miller, "Consumer Misbehavior: Why People Buy Illicit Goods," *The Journal of Consumer Marketing* 16, no. 3 (1999): 273–87.

11. Kenneth J. Gergen and Mary Gergen, *Social Psychology* (New York: Harcourt Brace Jovanovich, 1981).

12. J. R. P. French and B. Raven, "The Bases of Social Power," in *Studies in Social Power*, ed. D. Cartwright (Ann Arbor, MI: Institute for Social Research, 1959).

13. Park and Lessig, "Students and Housewives."

14. William O. Bearden and Michael J. Etzel, "Reference Group Influence on Product and Brand Purchase Decisions," *Journal of Consumer Research* 9, no. 2 (1982): 183–94.

15. Park and Lessig, "Students and Housewives."

16. Bearden and Etzel, "Reference Group Influence."

17. Aaron Smith, "Neighbors Online," Pew Research Center, June 9, 2010, http:// pewresearch.org/pubs/1620/neighbors -online-using-digital-tools-to-communicate -monitor-community-developments, accessed July 17, 2012.

18. Sarah Perez, "Social Networking Now More Popular on Mobile than Desktop," ReadWriteWeb, February 18, 2010, www .readwriteweb.com/archives/social _networking_now_more_popular_on _mobile_than_desktop.php, accessed July 17, 2012.

19. "Top Sites," Alexa, http://www.alexa.com /topsites, accessed September 12, 2012.

20. "Key Facts," Facebook, http://newsroom .fb.com/Key-Facts, accessed May 31, 2013.

21. "Twitter 101," Twitter, https://business .twitter.com/audiences-twitter/, accessed February 12, 2013.

22. Alexa.com, http://www.alexa.com/topsites, accessed February 12, 2013.

23. "Facebook to Acquire Instagram," Facebook, April 9, 2012, http://newsroom .fb.com/News/Facebook-to-Acquire -Instagram-141.aspx, accessed September 12, 2012.

24. SocialVibe, http://www.socialvibe.com/info /faq.html, accessed June 10, 2010.

25. Stylehive.com blog, http://blog.stylehive .com/index.php/about/, accessed July 17, 2012; also Foursquare, www.foursquare .com, accessed June 10, 2010.

26. Jessica Guynn, "Pinterest Pierces the Ranks of the Social-Networking Elite," *Los Angeles Times*, April 13, 2012, http://latimes.com/business/la-fi-pinterest-20120413,0,6102779.story, accessed April 12, 2012.

27. William O. Bearden, Richard G. Netemeyer, and Jesse E. Teel, "Measurement of Consumer Susceptibility to Interpersonal Influence," *Journal of Consumer Research* 15, no. 4 (1989): 473–81.

28. Rajeev Batra, Pamela M. Homer, and Lynn R. Kahle, "Values, Susceptibility to Normative Influence, and Attribute Importance Weights: A Nomological Perspective," *Journal of Consumer Research* 11, no. 2 (2001): 115–28.

29. David B. Wooten and Americus Reed II, "Playing It Safe: Susceptibility to Normative Influence and Protective Self-Presentation," *Journal of Consumer Research* 31, no. 3 (2004): 551–56.

30. David B. Wooten and Randall L. Rose, "Attention to Social Comparison Information: An Individual Difference Variable Affecting Consumer Conformity," *Journal of Consumer Research* 16, no. 4 (1990): 461–71.

31. Ronald A. Clark and Ronald E. Goldsmith, "Global Innovativeness and Consumer Susceptibility to Interpersonal Influence," *Journal of Marketing Theory and Practice* 14, no. 4 (2006): 275–85.

32. Cheng Lu Wang and Allan K. K. Chan, "A Content Analysis of Connectedness vs. Separateness Themes Used in U.S. and P.R.C. Print Advertisements," *International Marketing Review* 18, no. 2 (2001): 145–57; Cheng Lu Wang and John C. Mowen, "The Separateness-Connectedness Self-Schema: Scale Development and Application to Message Construction," *Psychology & Marketing* 14 (March 1997): 185–207.

33. Wang and Mowen, "The Separateness-Connectedness Self-Schema."

34. Jiang Lan, Joandrea Hoegg, Darren W. Dahl, and Amitava Chattopadhyay, "The Persuasive Role of Incidental Similarity on Attitudes and Purchase Intentions in a Sales Context," *Journal of Consumer Research* 36, no. 5 (2010): 778–91.

35. Wang and Chan, "A Content Analysis of Connectedness vs. Separateness Themes."

36. Jennifer J. Argo, Darren W. Dahl, and Rajesh V. Manchanda, "The Influence of a Mere Social Presence in a Retail Context," *Journal of Consumer Research* 32, no. 2 (2005): 207–12.

37. Darren W. Dahl, Rajesh V. Manchanda, and Jennifer J. Argo, "Embarrassment in Consumer Purchase: The Roles of Social Presence and Purchase Familiarity," *Journal of Consumer Research* 28, no. 3 (2001): 473–81.

38. He Yi, Qimei Chen, and Dana L. Alden, "Consumption in the Public Eye: The Influence of Social Presence on Service Experience," *Journal of Business Research* 65 (2012): 302–10.

39. "WOM 101: Organic vs. Amplified Word of Mouth," Word of Mouth Marketing Association (WOMMA), http://www .womma.org/wom101/04/, accessed July 18, 2012.

40. Tom J. Brown, Thomas E. Berry, Peter A. Dacin, and Richard F. Gunst, "Spreading the Word: Investigating Antecedents of Consumers' Positive Word-of-Mouth Intentions and Behaviors in a Retailing

Context," *Journal of the Academy of Marketing Science* 33, no. 2 (2005): 123–38.

41. Cindy M. Y. Chung, "The Consumer as Advocate: Self-Relevance, Culture, and Word-of-Mouth," *Marketing Letters* 17, no. 4 (2006): 269–84; Florian von Wangenheim, "Postswitching Negative Word-of-Mouth," *Journal of Service Research* 8, no. 1 (2005): 67–78.

42. Paula Bone, "Word-of-Mouth Effects on Short-Term and Long-Term Product Judgments," *Journal of Business Research* 32, no. 3 (1995): 213–23.

43. Barry J. Babin, Yong-Ki Lee, Eun-Ju Kim, and Mitch Griffin, "Modeling Consumer Satisfaction and Word-of-Mouth: Restaurant Patronage in Korea," *Journal of Services Marketing* 19, no. 3 (2005): 133–39.

44. "Health," Pew Internet & American Life Project, http://www.pewinternet.org/topics /Health.aspx, accessed June 11, 2010.

45. "Teens and Mobile Phones," Pew Research Center, http://www.pewinternet.org /Reports/2010/Teens-and-Mobile-Phones .aspx?r=1, accessed June 12, 2010.

46. See www.bzzagent.com, yelp.com/faq, and www.digg.com.

47. "How Ford Got Social Marketing Right," *Bloomberg BusinessWeek*, January 8, 2010, http://www.businessweek.com/managing /content/jan2010/ca2010018_445530.htm, accessed June 12, 2010.

48. Andrew M. Kaikati and Jack G. Kaikati, "Stealth Marketing: How to Reach Consumers Surreptitiously," *California Management Review* 46, no. 4 (2004): 6–22.

49. "Days of Our Lives Botches Product Placements," Fox News, November 16, 2010, http://www.foxnews.com /entertainment/2010/11/16/days-lives-product-placements-cheerios-chex/, accessed April 14, 2012.

50. Federico de Gregorio and Yongjun Sung, "Understanding Attitudes Toward and Behaviors in Response to Product Placement: A Consumer Socialization Framework," *Journal of Advertising* 39, no. 1 (2010): 83–96.

51. "Unethical Word-of-Mouth Marketing Strategies," Word of Mouth Marketing Association (WOMMA), http://www.womma .org/ wom101/06/.

52. "Ford Gets Women Involved in 'What Women Want' for Instant Buzz," Market Autopsy Blog, http://www.marketing -autopsyblog.com/customer-facing/ford -bloggers-involved-women-instant-buzz/, accessed April 14, 2012.

53. Michael Solomon, "The Missing Link: Surrogate Consumers in the Marketing Chain," *Journal of Marketing* 50 (October 1986): 208–18.

54. Everett M. Rogers, *Diffusion of Innovations*, 4th ed. (New York: The Free Press, 1995).

55. Ayalla Ruvio, "Consumer's Doppelganger: A Role Model Perspective on Intentional Consumer Mimicry," *Journal of Consumer Behaviour*, forthcoming.

56. AARP Public Policy Institute (2012), "Multigenerational Households Are Increasing," online content retrieved at: http://assets .aarp.org/rgcenter/ppi/econ-sec/fs221 -housing.pdf, accessed September 12, 2012.

57. U.S. Census Bureau, www.factfinder .census.gov, accessed June 12, 2010.

57a. O. Winslow, "Census: Nonfamily Households Surge," *News Day*, April 25, 2012, http: //www.newsday.com/news/nation /census -nonfamily-households-surge-1.3682787, accessed February 11, 2013.

58. DivorceRate, http://www.divorcerate.org/, accessed April 12, 2012.

59. Shankar Vidantam, "Marriage Economy: I Couldn't Afford to Get Divorced," NPR, December 20, 2011, http://www.npr.org /2011/12/20/144021297/marriage -economy-i-couldnt-afford-to-get-divorced, accessed April 12, 2012.

60. R. Jaslow, "U.S. Birth Rate Lowest Since 1920: Blame the Economy?" *CBS News*, November 30, 2012, http://www.cbsnews .com/8301-204_162-57556442/u.s-birth -rate-lowest-since-1920-blame-the-economy/, accessed February 12, 2013.

61. D'Vera Cohn, "Marriage Rate Declines and Marriage Age Rises," Pew Research Center, December 14, 2011, http://www.pewsocial -trends.org/2011/12/14/marriage-rate -declines-and-marriage-age-rises/, accessed April 12, 2012.

62. "51% of American Women Living Without a Spouse," Women Lifestyle website, April 8, 2012, http://womenlifestyle.com /entry/51-american-women-living -spouse/, accessed April 12, 2012.

63. U.S. Census Bureau, http://www.census .gov/hhes/families/data/cps2012.html, accessed February 12, 2013.

64. "The New Demography of American Motherhood," Pew Research Center, http: //pewsocialtrends.org/pubs/754/new -demography-of-american-motherhood, accessed June 11, 2010.

65. Gretchen Livingston and D'Vera Cohn, "More Women Without Children," Pew Research Center Publications, 2010, http: //pewresearch.org/pubs/1642/more-women -without-children/, accessed April 22, 2011.

66. Wendy Koch, "Number of Single Men Adopting Foster Kids Doubles; Historic Shift From When Kids Went Only to Married Couples," *USA Today*, June 15, 2007, 5A.

67. Robert E. Wilkes, "Household Life-Cycle Stages, Transitions, and Product Expenditures," *Journal of Consumer Research* 22, no. 1 (1995): 27–41.

68. Jessica Dickler, "Boomerang Kids: 85% of College Grads Moving Home," CNN Money, http://money.cnn.com/2010/10/14 /pf/boomerang_kids_move_home/index.htm, accessed April 25, 2011.

69. Kim Parker, "The Boomerang Generation," Pew Social and Demographic Trends, Pew Research Center, March 15, 2012, http: //pewsocialtrends.org/2012/03/15/the -boomerang-generation/, accessed April 12, 2012.

69a. K. Parker, "The Boomerang Generation," Pewsocialtrends.org, March 15, 2012, http://www.pewsocialtrends .org /2012/03/15/the-boomerang-generation/, accessed February 11, 2013.

70. John Chatzky, "Your Adult Kids Are Back. Now What?" *Money* 36, no. 1 (2007): 32–35.

71. "A Generation Caught Between Two Others," MSNBC, February 13, 2007, http: //www.msnbc.msn.com/id/17134636/, accessed April 3, 2009.

72. Ari Houser and Mary Jo Gibson, "Valuing the Invaluable: The Economic Value of Family Caregiving, 2008 Update," AARP Public Policy Institute, November 2008, http://assets.aarp.org/rgcenter/il/i13 _caregiving.pdf, accessed April 3, 2009.

73. Houser and Gibson, "Valuing the Invaluable."

74. James W. Gentry, Suraj Commuri, and Sunkyu Jun, "Review of Literature on Gender in the Family," *Academy of Marketing Science Review* 1 (2003): 1–18.

75. Christina K. C. Lee and Sharon E. Beatty, "Family Structure and Influence in Family Decision Making," *Journal of Consumer Marketing* 19, no. 1 (2002): 24–41.

76. Michael A. Belch and Laura A. Willis, "Family Decisions at the Turn of the Century: Has the Changing Structure of Households Impacted the Family Decision-Making Process?" *Journal of Consumer Behaviour* 2, no. 2 (2002): 111–25; Richard Fry and D'Vera Cohn, "New Economics of Marriage: The Rise of Wives," Pew Research Center, January 19, 2010, http://pewresearch.org/pubs/1466 /economics-marriage-rise-of-wives?src=prc -latest&proj=peoplepress, accessed June 11, 2010.

77. Statistics in this section are based on the following: "Kid Power," *Chain Store Age* 83, no. 3 (2007): 20; "Spending on Kids Seems Recession-Resistant," MSNBC, http://www .msnbc.msn.com/id/27312338/ns/business -eye_on_the_economy/, accessed April 25, 2011; Michelle Koetters, "Tweeners' Money Talks," *Knight Ridder Tribune Business News*, May 14, 2007, 1; Steve Maich, "The Little Kings and Queens of the Mall," *Maclean's* 119, no. 25 (2006): 37.

78. This definition is based on Scott Ward, "Consumer Socialization," in *Perspectives in Consumer Behavior*, ed. Harold H. Kassarjian and Thomas S. Robertson, 380 (Glenview, IL: Scott, Foresman, 1980).

Chapter 9

1. D. Nelson, "It Costs How Much to Get Married These Days?" ConsumerAffairs.com, March 11, 2013, http://www.consumeraffairs .com/news/it-costs-how-much-to-get-married -these-days-you-might-be-surprised-031113 .html, accessed March 12, 2013.

2. Linda Presley, "The Cost of Weddings Spirals in China," BBC News, July 22, 2011, http: //www.bbc.co.uk/news /business-14208448, accessed May 5, 2012.

3. R. Ahmed, "Dunkin Donuts and Starbucks to Duke It Out in India," *The Wall Street Journal*, February 22, 2012, B8.

4. David Greenwald, "Katy Perry Heads to Boot Camp in 'Part of Me' Video," Bill-board.com, March 21, 2012, http://www .billboard.com/news/katy-perry-heads-to -boot-camp-in-part-of-1006536952.story# /news/katy-perry-heads-to-boot-camp -in-part-of-1006536952.story, accessed May 6, 2012.

5. G. McCracken, "Culture and Consumption: A Theoretical Account of the Structure and Movement of the Cultural Meaning of Consumer Goods," *Journal of Consumer Research* 13 (1986): 71–84.

6. T. Lenartowicz and K. Roth, "A Framework for Culture Assessment," *Journal of International Business Studies* 30 (1999): 781–98; T. Lenartowicz and K. Roth, "Culture Assessment Revisited: The Selection of Key Informants in IB Cross-Cultural Studies," Annual Meeting of the Academy of International Business, Sydney, Australia, November 16–19, 2001.

7. J. W. Overby, R. B. Woodruff, and S. F. Gardial, "The Influence of Culture on Consumers' Desired Value Perceptions: A Research Agenda," *Marketing Theory* 5 (June 2005): 139–63.

8. See Geert Hofstede, http://www.geert -hofstede.com/geert_hofstede_resources .shtml, for an overview, accessed August 3, 2010.

9. For a concise review of Hofstede's value dimensions, see A. M. Soares, M. Farhangmehr, and A. Shoham, "Hofstede's Dimensions of Culture in International Marketing Studies," *Journal of Business Research* 60 (2007): 277–84.

10. E. C. Hirschman, "Men, Dogs, Guns and Cars," *Journal of Advertising* 32 (Spring 2003): 9–22.

11. P. K. Petrova, R. B. Cialdini, and S. J. Sills, "Consistency-Based Compliance Across Cultures," *Journal of Experimental and Social Psychology* 43 (2007): 104–11.

12. Hofstede (2010).

13. J. M. Jung and J. J. Kellaris, "Responsiveness to Authority Appeals Among Young French and American Consumers," *Journal of Business Research* 59 (June 2006): 735–44.

14. J. M. Jung and J. J. Kellaris, "Cross-National Difference in Proneness to Scarcity Effects: The Moderating Roles of Familiarity, Uncertainty Avoidance and Need for Cognitive Closure," *Psychology & Marketing* 21 (September 2004): 739–53.

15. S. Erevelles, R. Abhik, and L. Yip, "The Universality of the Signal Theory for Products and Services," *Journal of Business Research* 52 (May 2001): 175–87.

16. D. Martin, "Uncovering Unconscious Memories and Myths for Understanding International Tourism Behavior," *Journal of Business Research* 63 (2010): 372–83; J. C. Mowen, X. Fang, and K. Scott, "A Hierarchical Model Approach for Identifying the Trait Antecedents of General Gambling Propensity and of Four Gambling-Related Genres," *Journal of Business Research* 62 (2009): 1262–68.

17. J. K. M. Marta, A. Singhapakdi, D. Lee, M. J. Sirgy, K. Koonmee, and B. Virakul, "Perceptions about Ethics Institutionalization and Quality of Work Life: Thai versus American Marketing Managers," *Journal of Business Research* (2012), doi:10.1016/j.jbusres.2011.08.013.

18. G. Hofstede, *Culture's Consequences* (Thousand Oaks, CA: Sage Publications, 2001).

19. K. Keysuk and C. Oh, "On Distributor Commitment in Marketing Channels for Industrial Products: Contrast Between the United States and Japan," *Journal of International Marketing* 10 (2002): 72–107; S. Ryu, S. Kabadavi, and C. Chung, "The Relationship Between Unilateral and Bilateral Control Mechanisms: The Contextual Effect of Long-Term Orientation," *Journal of Business Research* 60 (July 2007): 681–89.

20. Hofstede, *Culture's Consequences*.

21. C. L. Wang, "Guanxi vs. Relationship Marketing: Exploring Underlying Differences," *Industrial Marketing Management* 36 (2007): 81–86.

22. S. Worthington, "Entering the Market for Financial Services in Transitional Economies," *International Journal of Bank Marketing* 23 (2005): 381–96.

23. X. Ren, S. Oh, and J. Noh, "Managing Supplier-Retailer Relationships: From Institutional and Task Environment Perspectives," *Industrial Marketing Management* 39 (2010): 593–604.

24. P. M. Byrne, "Thinking Beyond BRIC," *Logistics Management* 46 (2007): 24–26.

25. For example, see T. E. Muller, "Targeting the CANZUS Baby-Boomer Explorer and Adventurer Market," *Journal of Vacation Marketing* 6 (2000): 154–69.

26. M. Laroche, Z. Yang, C. Kim, and M. O. Richard, "How Culture Matters in Children's Purchase Influence: A Multi-Level Investigation," *Journal of the Academy of Marketing Science* 35 (Winter 2007): 113–26.

27. J. Bokale, "Supermarkets Bolster Focus on Children's Ranges," *Marketing* 6 (February 2008): 1.

28. K. Chankon, M. Laroche, and M. Tomiuk, "The Chinese in Canada: A Study of Ethnic Change with Emphasis on Gender Roles," *Journal of Social Psychology* 144 (February 2004): 5–27.

29. M. Laroche, K. Chankon, M. Tomiuk, and D. Belisle, "Similarities in Italian and Greek Multidimensional Ethnic Identity: Some Implications for Food Consumption," *Canadian Journal of Administrative Science* 22 (2005): 143–67.

30. T. Bristol and T. F. Mangleburg, "Not Telling the Whole Story: Teen Deception in Purchasing," *Journal of the Academy of Marketing Science* 33 (Winter 2005): 79–95.

31. H. L. Adams and L. R. Williams, "Advice from Teens about Dating: Implications for Healthy Relationships," *Children and Youth Services Review* 33 (2011): 254–64; R. A. Tiwsakul and Ch. Hackley, "Postmodern Paradoxes in Thai-Asian Consumer Identity," *Journal of Business Research* 65 (2012): 490–96.

32. A. Bakir, G. M. Rose, and A. Shoham, "Consumption Communication and Parental Control of Children's Viewing: A Multi-Rater Approach," *Journal of Marketing Theory and Practice* 13 (Spring 2005): 47–58; L. Carlson and S. Grossbart, "Parental Style and Consumer Socialization in Children," *Journal of Consumer Research* 15 (June 1988): 77–94.

33. C. Miller, F. Bram, J. Reardon, and I. Vida, "Teenagers' Response to Self- and Other-Directed Anti-Smoking Messages," *International Journal of Market Research* 49 (2006): 515–33.

34. A. E. Clark and Y. Loheac, "It Wasn't Me, It Was Them! Social Influence in Risky Behavior by Adolescents," *Journal of Health Economics* 26 (2007): 763–84; K. J. Kelly, M. D. Slater, and D. Karan, "Image Advertisements' Influence on Adolescents' Perceptions of the Desirability of Beer and Cigarettes," *Journal of Public Policy & Marketing* 21 (Fall 2002): 295–304.

35. M. Mourali, M. Laroche, and F. Pons, "Individual Orientation and Consumer Susceptibility to Interpersonal Influence," *Journal of Services Marketing* 19 (2005): 164–73.

36. A. S. Matilla and P. G. Patterson, "The Impact of Culture on Consumers' Perceptions of Service Recovery Efforts," *Journal of Retailing* 80 (2004): 196–207.

37. Mei Fong, "Tired of Laughter, Beijing Gets Rid of Bad Translations," *The Wall Street Journal*, February 5, 2007, A1.

38. See M. Griffin, B. J. Babin, and D. Modianas, "Shopping Values of Russian Consumers: The Impact of Habituation in a Developing Economy," *Journal of Retailing* 76 (2000): 33–52.

39. N. Spielmann and M. Delvert, "To Adopt or Standardize: A New Standard for Copywriting," presented at 2011 AMS World Marketing Congress, Reims, France, July 20, 2011, www.globish.com, accessed May 7, 2012.

40. K. S. Dallimore, B. A. Sparks, and K. Butcher, "The Influence of Angry Customer Outbursts on Service Providers' Facial Displays and Affective States," *Journal of Services Marketing* 10 (August 2007): 78–92.

41. L. A. Wang, J. Baker, J. A. Wagner, and K. Wakefield, "Can a Retail Web Site Be Social?" *Journal of Marketing* 71 (July 2007): 143–57; L. Qiu and I. Bernbasat, "Online Consumer Trust and Live Help Interfaces: The Effects of Text-to-Speech Voice and Three-Dimensional Avatars," *Journal of Human-Computer Interaction* 19 (2005): 75–94.

42. T. Kramer, S. Spolter-Weisfeld, and M. Thakker, "The Effect of Cultural Orientation on Consumer Responses to Personalization," *Marketing Science* 26 (March/April 2007): 246–58.

43. G. C. Pigliasco, "Lost in Translation: From Omiyage to Souvenir: Beyond Aesthetics of the Japanese Ladies' Gaze in Hawaii," *Journal of Material Culture* 10 (July 2005): 177–96.

44. J. N. Sheth, "Rise of Chindia and Its Impact on World Marketing," presented at the 2007 Academy of Marketing Science World Marketing Congress, Verona, Italy, July 13, 2007.

44a. L. Burkitt and E. Glazer, "Web Redraws China's Beauty Market," *The Wall Street Journal*, February 11, 2013, B6.

45. Y. Strizhakova, R. A. Coulter, and L. Price, "Branded Products as a Passport to Global Citizenship: Perspectives from Developed and Developing Countries," *Journal of International Marketing* 16, no. 4 (2008): 57–85.

46. Sheth, "Rise of Chindia."

47. See www.transparency.org for an overview of culture and corruption around the world.

Chapter 10

1. M. B. Beverland, F. Farrelly, and P. G. Quester, "Authentic Subcultural Membership: Antecedents and Consequences of Authenticating Acts and Authoritative Performances," *Psychology & Marketing* 27 (July 2010): 608–716.

2. J. Berger and C. Heath, "Who Drives Divergence? Identity Signaling, Outgroup Similarity, and the Abandonment of Cultural Tastes," *Journal of Personality and Social Psychology* 95 (2008): 593–607.

3. Benjamin Zimmer, "Life in These, Uh, This United States," Language Log, November 24, 2005, http://itre.cis.upenn.edu/~myl/languagelog/archives/002663.html, accessed August 6, 2010.

4. Joel Garreau, *The Nine Nations of North America* (New York: Avon, 1981).

5. L. R. Kahle, "The Nine Nations of North America and the Value Basis of Geographic Segmentation," *Journal of Marketing* 50 (April 1986): 37–47.

6. Blayne Cutler, "Welcome to the Borderlands," *American Demographics* (February 1991): 44–49, 57.

7. S. Guimond, S. Brunot, A. Chatard, D. M. Garcia, D. Martinot, N. R. Branscombe, M. Desert, S. Haque, and V. Yzerbyt, "Culture, Gender, and the Self: Variations and Impact of Social Comparison Processes," *Journal of Personality and Social Psychology* 92 (June 2007): 1118–34.

8. Y. Sung and S. F. Tinkham, "Brand Personality Structures in the United States and Korea: Common and Culture-Specific Factors," *Journal of Consumer Psychology* 15, no. 4 (2005): 334–50.

9. D. Ball, "Women in Italy Like to Clean but Shun the Quick and Easy," *The Wall Street Journal*, April 25, 2006, A1.

10. M. Bustillo and M. E. Lloyd, "Best Buy Seeks Female Shoppers," *The Wall Street Journal,* June 16, 2010, B5.

11. R. A. Smith, "Wanted: Guy Shoppes for Fashion Sites," *The Wall Street Journal,* July 22, 2010, B1.

12. B. T. Yoram and M. Jarymowicz, "The Effect of Gender on Cognitive Structuring: Who Are More Biased, Men or Women?" *Psychology* 1 (2010): 80–87.

13. Statistics in this chapter are taken from the U.S. Census Bureau (www.census.gov) or the CIA Factbook (www.cia.gov).

14. J. E. Lueg and R. Z. Finney, "Interpersonal Communication in the Consumer Socialization Process: Scale Development and Validation," *Journal of Marketing Theory and Practice* 15 (Winter 2007): 25–39.

15. "International Survey Shows that Coca-Cola and McDonald's Are Teenagers' Favorite Brands," Business Wire, February 8, 1999, http://findarticles.com/p/articles/mi_m0EIN/is_1999_Feb_8/ai_53724844/, accessed July 19, 2012.

17. A. Muk and B. J. Babin, "U.S. Consumers' Adoption–Non-Adoption of Mobile SMS Advertising," *Journal of Mobile Marketing* 1 (June 2006): 21–29.

18. "Global Teen Culture—Does It Exist?" *Brand Strategy* 167 (January 2003): 37–38.

19. R. S. Parker, A. D. Schaefer, and C. M. Hermans, "An Investigation Into Teens' Attitudes Towards Fast-Food Brands in General: A Cross-Culture Analysis," *Journal of Foodservice Business Research* 9, no. 4 (2006): 25–40.

20. Demographic categories in this section are based on Paul Taylor and Scott Keeter, eds., "Millennials: A Portrait of Generation Next," Pew Research Center online report, 2011, http://pewresearch.org/millennials, accessed April 28, 2011.

21. Catherine Siskos, "Generation X Socks It Away," *Kiplinger's Personal Finance Magazine* 52, no. 5 (1998): 20.

22. This information based on Nancy Gibbs, "Generation Next," *Time,* March 11, 2010, http://www.time.com/time/magazine/article/0,9171,1971433-2,00.html, accessed August 10, 2010.

23. Paul Taylor and Scott Keeter, eds., "Millennials: A Portrait of Generation Next," Pew Research Center, February 2010, http://pewsocialtrends.org/assets/pdf/millennials-confident-connected-open-to-change.pdf, accessed August 10, 2010.

24. B. Steinberg, "Study: Young Consumers Switch Media 27 Times in an Hour," *Advertising Age,* April 9, 2012, http://adage.com/article/news/study-young-consumers-switch-media-27-times-hour/234008/, accessed June 6, 2012.

25. "Young, Underemployed and Optimistic," Pew Research Center, February 9, 2012, http://www.pewsocialtrends.org/files/2012/02/young-underemployed-and-optimistic.pdf, accessed June 12, 2012; Hadley Malcolm, "Millennials Use Alternative Financial Services," *USA Today,* May 17, 2012, B1.

26. The Center for Generational Diversity Studies, www.generationaldiversity.com/index.php?/fap.html, accessed June 14, 2012.

27. Angela Cross-Bystrom, "What You Need to Know about Generation Z," IMediaConnection, www.imediaconnection.com/content/27425.asp, accessed June 18, 2012.

28. P. Boski, "Humanism–Materialism: Centuries-Long Polish Cultural Origins and 20 Years of Research," in *Indigenous and Cultural Psychology: Understanding People in Context,* ed. U. Kim, K. S. Yang, and K.-K. Hwang, 373–402 (New York: Springer, 2006).

29. T. Benning, "Slump Strains Church Finances as Need Grows," *The Wall Street Journal,* August 11, 2009, A13.

30. Valerie A. Taylor, Diane Halstead, and Paula J. Haynes, "Consumer Responses to Christian Religious Symbols in Advertising," *Journal of Advertising* 39, no. 2 (2010): 79–92.

31. O. Sandikci and G. Ger, "Veiling in Style: How Does a Stigmatized Practice Become Fashionable?" *Journal of Consumer Research* 37 (June 2010): 15–36.

32. "French MPs Vote to Ban Islamic Full Veil in Public," BBC News, July 13, 2010, http://www.bbc.co.uk/news/10611398, accessed August 9, 2010.

33. M. A. Zolfagharian and Q. Sun, "Country of Origin, Ethnocentrism and Bicultural Consumers: The Case of Mexican Americans," *The Journal of Consumer Marketing* 27 (2010): 345.

34. "Marketing to Asian Americans," *AdWeek Media,* May 26, 2008, http://www.adweekmedia.com/aw/content_display/custom-reports/mtaa/e3i70fa56666e6c5bccfb3fe3b2dc4c015b, accessed August 8, 2010.

35. This definition based on George Ritzer, *Sociological Theory,* 4th ed. (New York: McGraw-Hill, 1996).

36. Charles M. Schaninger, "Social Class Versus Income Revisited: An Empirical Investigation," *Journal of Marketing Research* (May 1981): 192–208.

37. Lloyd W. Warner and Paul S. Hunt, eds., *The Social Life of a Modern Community* (New Haven, CT: Yale University Press, 1941).

38. C. R. Schwartz and R. D. Mare, "Trends in Educational Assortative Marriage from 1940 to 2003," *Demography* 42, no. 4 (2005): 621–46; E. C. Snyder, "Attitudes: A Study of Homogamy and Marital Selectivity," *Journal of Marriage and Family* 26, no. 3 (1964): 332–36.

39. This definition based on Jack Eller, *Cultural Anthropology: Global Forces, Local Lives* (New York: Routledge, 2009), and Jonathan H. Turner, *Sociology: Studying the Human System* (Santa Monica, CA: Goodyear Publishing, 1981).

40. Lisa Ling and Katie Hinman, "Under Las Vegas: Tunnels Stretch for Miles," ABC News, September 23, 2009, http://abcnews.go.com/Nightline/las-vegas-strip-home-homeless/story?id=8652139, accessed August 11, 2010; also Ashley Powers, "A Life Saved from the Shadows," *Los Angeles Times,* December 22, 2009, http://articles.latimes.com/2009/dec/22/nation/la-na-tunnel22-2009dec22, accessed August 11, 2010.

41. An Hodgson, "China's Middle Class Reaches 80 Million," Euromonitor International, July 25, 2007, http://www.euromonitor.com/Chinas_middle_class_reaches_80_million, accessed August 11, 2010.

42. This section based on Vincent Fernando, "Faber: India's Middle Class Will Soon Be Larger than America's," *Business Insider,* February 15, 2010, http://www.businessinsider.com/faber-dont-ignore-india-2010-2, accessed August 11, 2010; also Eric Beinhocker, Diana Ferrell, and Adil Zainulbhai, "Tracking the Growth of India's Middle Class," *McKinsey Quarterly,* August 2007, http://www.mckinseyquarterly.comTracking_the_growth_of_Indias_middle_class_2032, accessed August 11, 2010.

43. C. Goulding and M. Saren, "Performing Identity: An Analysis of Gender Expressions at the Whitby Goth Festival," *Consumption Markets & Culture* 12 (March 2009): 27–46.

44. Bob Martin, "Wife Shortage Looms in China," *Culture Briefings,* Geotravel Research Center, http://www.culturebriefings.com/articles/chwifesh.html, accessed August 12, 2010; also "Study: China Faces 24M Bride Shortage by 2020," CNN, January 11, 2010, http://www.cnn.com/2010/WORLD/asiapcf/01/11/china.bride.shortage/index.html, accessed August 12, 2010.

45. "Asian Youth Trends," *American Demographics* 26, no. 8 (2004): 14.

Case 3-2

1. Focus groups conducted at New Mexico State University, 2011.

2. Focus groups conducted at New Mexico State University, 2011.

3. Laura Deaton Morarity, "Whisper to a Scream," *Marketing Health Services* (Summer 2009): 9–13.

4. http://www.flashmobamerica.com/, accessed April 1, 2012.

Case 3-3

1. Solomon, Michael R. *Consumer Behavior,* 9th ed. Upper Saddle River, New Jersey: Prentice Hall, 2011.

2. Neuborne, Ellen and Kerwin, Kathleen. "Generation Y," *Business Week* Online. February 15, 1999, accessed March 23, 2012.

3. Smith, J. Walker. "10 Truths about Millennials," Warc, July 8, 2011, http://popsurvey.blogspot.com/2011/07/10-truths-about-millennials.html, accessed March 30, 2012.

4. Chau, Joanna. "Millennials Are More 'Generation Me' Than 'Generation We'," *The Chronicle of Higher Education.* March 15, 2012, http://chronicle.com/article/Millennials-Are-More/131175/, accessed April 13, 2012.

5. Babin, Barry and Harris, Eric. *CB4.* Mason, Ohio: South-Western/Cengage Learning, 2012.

6. Kane, Sally. "Generation Y," Legalcareers.about.com, accessed March 23, 2012.

7. Babin, Barry and Harris, Eric. *CB4.* Mason, Ohio: South-Western/Cengage Learning, 2012.

8. Chau, Joanna. "Millennials Are More 'Generation Me' Than 'Generation We'," *The Chronicle of Higher Education.* March 15, 2012, http://chronicle.com/article/Millennials-Are-More/131175/, accessed April 13, 2012.

9. Babin, Barry and Harris, Eric. *CB4.* Mason, Ohio: South-Western/Cengage Learning, 2012.

10. Smith, J. Walker. "10 Truths about Millennials," Warc, July 8, 2011, http://popsurvey.blogspot.com/2011/07/10-truths-about-millennials.html, accessed March 30, 2012.

Chapter 11

1. R. Dhar and S. M. Nowlis, "The Effect of Time Pressure on Consumer Choice Deferral," *Journal of Consumer Research* 25 (March 1999): 369–84.

2. M. G. Bublitz, L. A. Peracchio, and L. G. Block, "Why Did I Eat That? Perspectives on Food Decision Making and Dietary Restraint," *Journal of Consumer Psychology* 20 (July 2010): 239–58.

3. C. M. Henderson, J. T. Beck, and R.W. Palmatier, "Review of the Theoretical Underpinnings of Loyalty Programs," *Journal of Consumer Psychology* 21 (2011): 256–76.

4. Junsang Lim and Sharon E. Beatty, "Factors Affecting Couples' Decisions to Jointly Shop," *Journal of Business Research* 64, no. 7 (2011): 774–81.

5. S. M. Nowlis, "The Effect of Time Pressure on the Choice Between Brands that Differ in Quality, Price and Product Features," *Marketing Letters* 6 (October 1995): 287–96.

6. R. Suri and K. B. Monroe, "The Effects of Time Constraints on Consumers' Judgments of Prices and Products," *Journal of Consumer Research* 30 (June 2003): 92–104.

7. J. Wagner and M. Mokhtari, "The Moderating Effect on Household Apparel Expenditure," *Journal of Consumer Affairs* 34, no. 2 (2000): 22–78.

8. S. Roslow, T. Li, and J. A. F. Nicholls, "Impact of Situational Variables and Demographic Attributes in Two Seasons on Purchase Behavior," *European Journal of Marketing* 34, no. 9 (2000): 1167–80.

9. C. Yoon, C. Cole, and M. P. Lee, "Consumer Decision Making and Aging: Current Knowledge and Future Decisions," *Journal of Consumer Psychology* 19 (2009): 2–16. Bublitz et al., "Why Did I Eat That?"

10. H. Okamura, A. Tsuda, J. Yajima, H. Mark, S. Horiuchi, N. Troyoshima, and T. Matsuishi, "Short Sleeping Time and Psychological Responses to Acute Stress," *International Journal of Psychophysiology*, 2010, doi 10.1016/j.ijpsycho.2010.0/.010.

11. G. Saad and E. Stenstrom, "Calories, Beauty and Ovulation: The Effects of the Menstrual Cycle on Food and Appearance-Related Consumption," *Journal of Consumer Psychology* 22 (2012): 102–113.

12. G. Zhuang, A. S. Tsang, N. Zhou, F. Li, and J. A. Nicholls, "Impacts of Situational Factors on Buying Decisions in Shopping Malls," *European Journal of Marketing* 40 (2006): 17–43.

13. D. M. Koo and Y. Y. Choi, "Knowledge Search and People with High Epistemic Curiosity," *Competence in Human Behavior* 26 (2010): 12–22.

14. T. J. L. Van Rompay, J. Krooshoop, J. W. M. Verhoeven, and A. T. H. Pruyn, "With or Without You: Interactive Effects of Retail Density and Need for Affilliation on Shopping Pleasure and Spending," *Journal of Business Research* 65 (2012): 1126–31.

15. B. J. Babin, W. R. Darden, and M. Griffin, "Work and/or Fun: Measuring Hedonic and Utilitarian Shopping Value," *Journal of Consumer Research* 20, no. 4 (1994), 644–56.

16. A. G. Close and M. Kukar-Kineey, "Beyond Buying: Motivations Behind Consumers' Online Shopping Cart Use," *Journal of Business Research* 63 (September 2010), 986–92.

17. W. R. Darden and B. J. Babin, "Exploring the Concept of Affective Quality: Expanding the Concept of Retail Personality," *Journal of Business Research* 29 (February 1994): 101–109.

18. S. Ramanathan and P. Williams, "Immediate and Delayed Emotional Consequences of Indulgence: The Moderating Influence of Personality Type on Mixed Emotions," *Journal of Consumer Research* 34 (2007): 212–23.

19. T. L. Childers, C. L. Carr, J. Peck, and S. Carson, "Hedonic and Utilitarian Motivations for Online Shopping Behavior," *Journal of Retailing* 77 (2001): 511–35.

20. A. Mukhopadhyay and G. V. Johar, "Indulgence as Self-Reward for Prior Shopping-Restraint: A Justification Based Mechanism," *Journal of Consumer Psychology* 19 (July 2009): 334–45.

21. I. H. A. Franken and P. Muris, "Gray's Impulsivity Dimension: A Distinction Between Reward Sensitivity and Rash Impulsiveness," *Personality & Individual Differences* 40 (July 2006): 1337–47; Ramanathan and Williams, "Immediate and Delayed Emotional Consequences of Indulgence."

22. U. M. Dholakia, "Temptation and Resistance: An Integrated Model of Consumption Impulse Formation and Enactment," *Psychology & Marketing* 17 (November 2000): 955–82.

23. C. Kaufman-Scarborough and J. Cohen, "Unfolding Consumer Impulsivity: An Existential-Phenomenological Study of Consumers with Attention Deficit Disorder," *Psychology & Marketing* 21 (August 2004): 637–69.

24. S. E. Beatty and E. M. Ferrell, "Impulse Buying: Modeling Its Precursors," *Journal of Retailing*, 74 (1998): 161–91.

25. X. Zhang, V. R. Prybutok, and D. Strutton, "Modeling Influences on Impulse Purchasing Behaviors During Online Marketing Transactions," *Journal of Marketing Theory and Practice* 15 (Winter 2007): 79–89.

26. B. J. Babin and W. R. Darden, "Consumer Self-Regulation in a Retail Environment," *Journal of Retailing* 71 (Spring 1995): 47–70.

27. M. Herzenstein, S. S. Posavac, and J. J. Brakus, "Adoption of New and Really New Products: The Effects of Self-Regulation Systems and Risk Salience," *Journal of Marketing Research* 44 (May 2007): 251–260.

28. Darden and Babin, "Exploring the Concept of Affective Quality"; J. A. Russell and G. Pratt, "A Description of the Affective Quality Attributable to Environments," *Journal of Personality and Social Psychology* 38 (1980): 311–22.

29. M. J. Bitner, "Servicescapes: The Impact of the Physical Environment on Customers and Employees," *Journal of Marketing* 56 (April 1992): 57–71.

30. S. K. Koernig, "E-Scapes: The Electronic Physical Environment and Service Tangibility," *Psychology & Marketing* 20 (2003): 151–67; Yong-Ki Lee, Choong-Ki Lee, Seung-Kon Lee, and Barry J. Babin, "Festivalscapes and Patrons' Emotions, Satisfaction, and Loyalty," *Journal of Business Research* 61, no. 1 (2008): 56–64.

31. M. K. Brady, C. M. Voorhees, J. J. Cronin, and B. L. Boudreau, "The Good Guys Don't Always Win: The Effect of Valence on Service Perceptions and Consequences," *Journal of Services Marketing* 20 (2006): 83–91.

32. G. Williams, "It's a Style Thing," *Entrepreneur* 32 (March 2004): 34; Dawn Iacobucci and Amy Ostrom, "Gender Differences in the Impact of Core and Relational Aspects of Services on the Evaluation of Service Encounters," *Journal of Consumer Psychology* 2, no. 3 (1993): 257–86.

33. D. L. Haytko and J. Baker, "It's All at the Mall: Exploring Adolescent Girls' Experiences," *Journal of Retailing* 80 (Spring 2004): 67–83.

34. Barry J. Babin, Jean-Charles Chebat, and Richard Michon, "Perceived Appropriateness and Its Effect on Quality, Affect and Behavior," *Journal of Retailing and Consumer Services* 11 (September 2004): 287–98; R. Michon, J. C. Chebat, and L.W. Turley, "Mall Atmospherics: The Interaction Effects of the Mall Environment on Shopping Behavior," *Journal of Business Research* 58 (May 2005): 576–83.

35. O. R. Orth and A. Bourrain, "Ambient Scent and Consumer Exploratory Behavior: A Causal Analysis," *Journal of Wine Research* 16 (2005): 137–50.

36. Michon et al., "Mall Atmospherics."

37. L. W. Turley and J. C. Chebat, "Linking Retail Strategy, Atmospheric Design and Shopping Behavior," *Journal of Marketing Management* 18 (2002): 125–44; R. E. Milliman, "The Influence of Background Music on the Behavior of Restaurant Patrons," *Journal of Consumer Research* 13 (September 1986): 286–89; Babin, Chebat, and Michon "Perceived Appropriateness" (see note 34).

38. A. E. Crowley, "The Two-Dimensional Impact of Color on Shopping," *Marketing Letters* 4 (1993): 59–69; J. Bellizi and R. E. Hite, "Environmental Color, Consumer Feelings and Purchase Likelihood," *Psychology & Marketing* 59 (Spring 1992): 347–63; B. J. Babin, D. M. Hardesty, and T. A. Suter, "Color and Shopping Intentions: The Intervening Effect of Price Fairness and Affect," *Journal of Business Research* 56 (2003): 541–51.

39. Babin, Hardesty, and Suter, "Color and Shopping Intentions."

40. C. Dennis, A. Newman, R. Michon, J. J. Brakus, and L. T. Wright, "The Mediating Effects of Perception and Emotion: Digital Signage in Mall Atmospherics," *Journal of Consumer and Retail Services* 17 (2010): 205–15.

41. P. Cotlet, M. C. Lichtlé, and V. Plichon, "The Role of Value in a Services: A Study in a Retail Environment," *Journal of Consumer Marketing* 23 (2006): 219–27; S. A. Eroglu, K. Machleit, and T. F. Barr, "Perceived Retail Crowding and Shopper Satisfaction: The Role of Shopping Values," *Journal of Business Research* 58 (August 2005): 1146–53.

42. B. Price and D. Murray, "Match-Up Revisited: The Effect of Staff Attractiveness on Purchase Intentions in Younger Adult Females: Social Comparative and Produce Relevance Effects," *Journal of International Business and Economics* 9 (2010): 55–76; S. K. Koering and A. L. Page, "What If Your Dentist Looked Like Tom Cruise? Applying the Match-up Hypothesis to a Service Encounter," *Psychology & Marketing* 19 (January 2002): 91–110; D. Grace, "An Examination of Consumer Embarrassment and Repatronage Intentions in the Context of Emotional Service Encounters," *Journal of Retailing and Consumer Services* 16 (January 2009): 1–9.

43. A. Borges, J. C. Chebat, and B. J. Babin, "Does a Companion Always Enhance the Shopping Experience?" *Journal of Retailing and Consumer Services* 17 (July 2010): 294–99; Lim Beatty, "Factors Affecting Couples' Decisions to Jointly Shop."

44. N. Mande and E. J. Johnson, "When Web Pages Influence Choice: Effects of Visual Primes on Experts and Novices," *Journal of*

Consumer Research 20 (September 2002): 235–45.

45. Y. J. Wang, M. S. Minor, and J. Wei, "Aesthetics and the Online Shopping Environment: Understanding Consumer Responses," *Journal of Retailing* 87 (2011): 46–58.

46. L. C. Wang, J. Baker, J. Wagner, and K. Wakefield, "Can a Web Site Be Social?" *Journal of Marketing* 71 (July 2007): 143–57.

47. Art Markman, "Spending and Credit Cards," *Psychology Today* blog, January 26, 2010, http://www.psychologytoday .com/blog/ulterior-motives/201001 /spending-and-credit-cards, accessed June 2, 2012.

48. B. O'Connell, "MasterCard: 'Contactless' Consumers Spend More Cash," Main Street, http://www.mainstreet.com/article /moneyinvesting/credit/debt/mastercard -contactless-consumers-spend-more-cash, accessed June 2, 2012.

49. C. Heath and J. B. Soll, "Mental Budgeting and Consumer Decisions," *Journal of Consumer Research* 23 (June 1996): 40–52.

50. First Data, *Consumer Insights into the U.S. Gift Card Market: 2011* (Atlanta: First Data Market Strategies International, 2011).

51. Steve Stolz, "What Happens to Unused Gift Cards?" Her Geek Life, January 26, 2012, http://hergeeklife.com/2012/01/26/what -happens-to-unused-gift-cards/, accessed June 3, 2012.

52. Y. J. Wang, M. D. Hernandez, and M. S. Minor, "Web Aesthetics Effects on Perceived Online Service Quality and Satisfaction in an E-Tail Environment: The Moderating Role of Purchase Task," *Journal of Business Research* 53 (2010): 935–42.

53. R. Michon, H. Yu, D. Smith, and J. C. Chebat, "The Shopping Experience of Female Fashion Leaders," *International Journal of Retail and Distribution Management* 35, no. 6 (2007), 488–501; W. R. Swinyard, "The Effects of Mood, Involvement, and Quality of Store Experience on Shopping Intentions," *Journal of Consumer Research* 20 (September 1992): 271–80.

54. Luiza Oleszczuk, "Worst Black Friday Casualties: Is Walmart the Most Dangerous Place to Shop?" November 26, 2011, http: //www.christianpost.com/news/worst -black-friday-casualties-is-walmart-the -most-dangerous-place-to-shop-video -63055/, accessed June 3, 2012.

Chapter 12

1. Alison Jing Xu and Robert W. Wyer, Jr., "The Effect of Mind-Sets on Consumer Decision Strategies," *Journal of Consumer Research* 34, no. 4 (2007): 556–66.

2. Richard P. Bagozzi and Utpal Dholakia, "Goal Setting and Goal Striving in Consumer Behavior," special issue, *Journal of Marketing* 63 (1999): 19–32.

3. Robert Lawson, "Consumer Decision Making within a Goal-Driven Framework," *Psychology & Marketing* 14, no. 5 (1997): 427–49.

4. Mary Frances Luce James R. Bettman, and John W. Payne, "Trade-off Difficulty: Determinants and Consequences for Consumer Decisions," *Monographs of the Journal of Consumer Research Series* 1 (Spring 2001); Kalyani Menon and Laurette Dube, "Ensuring Satisfaction by Engineering Salesperson Response to Customer Emotions," *Journal of Retailing* 76, no. 3 (2000): 285–307.

5. John C. Mowen, "Beyond Consumer Decision Making," *Journal of Consumer Marketing* 5, no. 1 (1988): 15–25.

6. "POP Sharpens Its Focus," *Brandweek* 44, no. 24 (2003): 31–36.

7. V. Kanti Prasad, "Socioeconomic Product Risk and Patronage Preferences of Retail Shoppers," *Journal of Marketing* 39 (July 1975): 42–47; Grahame R. Dowling and Richard Staelin, "A Model of Perceived Risk and Intended Risk-Handling Activity," *Journal of Consumer Research* 21, no. 1 (1994): 119–34.

8. This definition is based on Richard Oliver, *Satisfaction: A Behavioral Perspective on the Consumer* (New York: McGraw-Hill, 1997).

9. Louise O'Brien and Charles Jones, "Do Rewards Really Create Loyalty?" *Harvard Business Review* 73 (May/June 1995): 75–82.

10. Kevin Lane Keller, *Strategic Brand Management: Building, Measuring, and Managing Brand Equity* (Upper Saddle River, NJ: Prentice Hall, 1998).

11. David A. Aaker, *Building Strong Brands* (New York: The Free Press, 1997), 21.

12. Richard W. Olshavsky and Donald H. Granbois, "Consumer Decision Making—Fact or Fiction?" *Journal of Consumer Research* 6, no. 2 (1979): 93–100.

13. Don Moyer, "Satisficing," *Harvard Business Review* 85, no. 4 (2007): 144; Barry Schwartz, Andrew Ward, John Monterosso, Sonja Lyubomirsky, Katherine White, and Darrin R. Lehman, "Maximizing versus Satisficing: Happiness Is a Matter of Choice," *Journal of Personality and Social Psychology* 83, no. 5 (2002): 1178–97.

14. Itamar Simonson and Aner Sela, "On the Heritability of Consumer Decision Making: An Exploratory Approach for Studying Genetic Effects on Judgment and Choice," *Journal of Consumer Research* 37, no. 6 (2011): 951–66.

15. Gordon C. Bruner III and Richard J. Pomazal, "Problem Recognition: The Crucial First Stage of the Consumer Decision Process," *Journal of Consumer Marketing* 5, no. 1 (1988): 51–63.

16. M. Joseph Sirgy, *Social Cognition and Consumer Behavior* (New York: Praeger, 1983).

17. Sharon Beatty and Scott M. Smith (1987), "External Search Effort: An Investigation across Several Product Categories," *Journal of Consumer Research* 14 (1): 83–95.

18. Peter H. Bloch, Daniel L. Sherrell, and Nancy M. Ridgway, "Consumer Search: An Extended Framework," *Journal of Consumer Research* 13, no. 1 (1986): 119–26.

19. Benjamin Scheibehenne, Rainer Greifeneder, and Peter M. Todd, "Can There Ever Be Too Many Options? A Meta-Analytic Review of Choice," *Journal of Consumer Research* 37, no. 3 (2011): 409–25; Nicholas H. Lurie, "Decision Making in Information-Rich Environments: The Role of Information Structure," *Journal of Consumer Research* 30, no. 4 (2004): 473–87.

20. Girish Punj and Richard Brookes, "Decision Constraints and Consideration Set Formation in Consumer Durables," *Psychology & Marketing* 18, no. 8 (2004): 843–64; Allan D. Shocker, Moshe Ben-Akiva, Bruno Boccara, and Prakash Nedungadi, "Consideration Set Influences on Consumer Decision Making and Choice: Issues, Models, and Suggestions," *Marketing Letters* 2, no. 3 (1991): 181–97.

21. Bas Donkers, "Modeling Consideration Sets across Time: The Relevance of Past Consideration," in *American Marketing Association Conference Proceedings*, vol. 13 (Chicago: American Marketing Association, 2002), 322.

22. John R. Hauser and Birger Wernerfelt, "An Evaluation Cost Model of Consideration Sets," *Journal of Consumer Research* 16, no. 4 (1990): 393–408.

23. Nobuhiko Terui, Masataka Ban, and Greg M. Allenby, "The Effect of Media Advertising on Brand Consideration and Choice," *Marketing Science* 30 (2011): 74–91.

24. Cheryl Burke Jarvis, "An Exploratory Investigation of Consumers' Evaluations of External Information Sources in Prepurchase Search," in *Advances in Consumer Research*, vol. 25, ed. Joseph W. Alba and J. Wesley Hutchinson (Provo, UT: Association for Consumer Research, 1998).

25. Melissa Bishop and Nelson Barber, "A Market Segmentation Approach to Esteem and Efficacy in Information Search," *Journal of Consumer Marketing* 29, no. 1 (2012): 13–21.

26. D. R. Lichtenstein, N. M. Ridgway, and R. P. Netemeyer, "Price Perceptions and Consumer Shopping Behavior," *Journal of Marketing Research* 30 (1993): 234–45.

27. Jane J. Lee, "Scienceshot: Radiohead Was Right," ScienceMag.org, April 23, 2012, http://news.sciencemag.org/sciencenow /2012/04/scienceshot-radiohead-was-right .html?ref=hp, accessed April 25, 2012.

28. Torsten Bornemann and Christian Homberg, "Psychological Distance and the Dual Role of Price," *Journal of Consumer Research* 38 (October 2011): 490–504.

29. Barbara Bickart and Robert M. Schindler, "Internet Forums as Influential Sources of Consumer Information," *Journal of Interactive Marketing* 15, no. 3 (2001): 31–40.

30. Brian T. Ratchford, Myung-Soo Lee, and Debabrata Talukdar, "The Impact of the Internet on Information Search for Automobiles," *Journal of Marketing Research* 40, no. 2 (2003): 193–209.

31. Moutusy Maity, Maxwell K. Hsu, and Lou E. Pelton, "Consumers' Online Information Search: Gen Yers Finding Needles in the Internet Haystack," *Journal of Marketing Channels* 19, no. 1 (2012): 49–76; Charla Mathwick and Edward Rigdon, "Play, Flow, and the Online Search Experience," *Journal of Consumer Research* 31, no. 2 (2004): 324–32.

32. Dan Ariely, "Controlling the Information Flow: Effects on Consumers' Decision Making and Preferences," *Journal of Consumer Research* 27, no. 2 (2000): 233–48.

33. David Mazursky and Gideon Vinitzky, "Modifying Consumer Search Processes in Enhanced On-Line Interfaces," *Journal of Business Research* 58, no. 10 (2005): 1299–1309.

34. Information in this section based in part on Anonymous (2012), "February/March 2012 Trend Briefing: Point-Know-Buy: Why Infolusty, Spontaneity-Loving Consumers Will Embrace Instant Visual Information

Gratification," online content retrieved at Trendwatching.com, http://trendwatching.com/trends/pointknowbuy/, accessed October 1, 2012.

35. Beatty and Smith, "External Search Effort."

36. Narasimhan Srinivasan and Brian T. Ratchford, "An Empirical Test of a Model of External Search for Automobiles," *Journal of Consumer Research* 18 (1991): 233–42; Eric J. Johnson and Edward J. Russo, "Product Familiarity and Learning New Information," *Journal of Consumer Research* 11 (1984): 542–50; William L. Moore and Donald R. Lehmann, "Individual Differences in Search Behavior for a Nondurable," *Journal of Consumer Research* 7 (1980): 296–307.

37. Sridhar Moorthy, Brian T. Ratchford, and Debabrata Talukdar, "Consumer Information Search Revisited: Theory and Empirical Analysis," *Journal of Consumer Research* 23, no. 4 (1997): 263–77; also see Joseph W. Alba and J. Wesley Hutchinson, "Dimensions of Consumer Expertise," *Journal of Consumer Research* 13, no. 4 (1987): 411–54.

38. Beatty and Smith, "External Search Effort."

39. G. R. Dowling and R. Staelin, "A Model of Perceived Risk and Intended Risk-Handling Activity," *Journal of Consumer Research* 21, no. 1 (1994): 119–34; Konrad Dedler, I. Gottschalk, and K. G. Grunert, "Perceived Risk as a Hint for Better Information and Better Products," in *Advances in Consumer Research*, vol. 8, ed. Kent Monroe (Ann Arbor, MI: Association for Consumer Research, 1981), 391–97.

40. Nitin Mehta, Surendra Rajiv, and Kannan Srinivasan, "Price Uncertainty and Consumer Search: A Structural Model of Consideration Set Formation," *Marketing Science* 22, no. 1 (2003): 58–84.

41. Charles F. Hofacker and Jamie Murphy, "Consumer Web Page Search, Clicking Behavior, and Reaction Time," *Direct Marketing: An International Journal* 3, no. 2 (2009): 88–96.

42. Beatty and Smith, "External Search Effort."

43. Ibid.

44. Noel Capon and Mariane Burke, "Individual, Product Class, and Task-Related Factors in Consumer Information Processing," *Journal of Consumer Research* 7, no. 3 (1980): 314–26; Joseph Newman and Richard Staelin, "Prepurchase Information Seeking for New Cars and Major Household Appliances," *Journal of Marketing Research* 7 (August 1972): 249–57.

45. Cathy J. Cobb and Wayne D. Hoyer, "Direct Observation of Search Behavior in the Purchase of Two Nondurable Products," *Psychology & Marketing* 2, no. 3 (1988): 161–79; Newman and Staelin, "Prepurchase Information Seeking."

46. Girish Punj, "Presearch Decision Making in Consumer Durable Purchases," *Journal of Consumer Marketing* 4, no. 1 (1987), 71–83.

47. Kristy E. Reynolds, Judith Anne Garretson Folse, and Michael A. Jones, "Search Regret: Antecedents and Consequences," *Journal of Retailing* 82, no. 4 (2006): 339–48.

Chapter 13

1. Charles M. Futrell, *ABCs of Relationship Selling*, 7th ed. (Boston: McGraw-Hill, 2003).

2. James H. Myers and Mark Alpert, "Determinant Buying Attitudes: Meaning and Measurement," *Journal of Marketing* (October 1968): 13–20.

3. Terrell G. Williams, "Social Class Influences on Purchase Evaluation Criteria," *Journal of Consumer Marketing* 19, no. 2/3 (2002): 249–76; Ravi Dhar and Klaus Wertenbroch, "Consumer Choice between Hedonic and Utilitarian Goods," *Journal of Marketing Research* 37 (February 2000): 60–71; Elizabeth C. Hirschman and S. Krishnan, "Subjective and Objective Criteria in Consumer Choice: An Examination of Retail Store Choice," *Journal of Consumer Affairs* 15, no. 1 (1981): 115–27.

4. Barry Schwartz, "The Tyranny of Choice," *Scientific American* 290, no. 4 (2001): 70–75.

5. Michel T. Pham, Joel B. Cohen, John W. Pracejus, and G. David Hughes, "Affect Monitoring and the Primacy of Feelings in Judgment," *Journal of Consumer Research* 28, no. 2 (2001): 167–88.

6. Gerald J. Gorn, Marvin E. Goldberg, and Kunal Basu, "Mood, Awareness, and Product Evaluation," *Journal of Consumer Psychology* 2, no. 3 (1993): 237–56.

7. Georgios A. Bakamitsos, "A Cue Alone or a Probe to Think? The Dual Role of Affect in Product Evaluations," *Journal of Consumer Research* 33 (December 2006): 403–12.

8. C. Page Moreau, Arthur B. Markman, and Donald R. Lehmann, "What Is It? Categorization Flexibility and Consumers' Responses to Really New Products," *Journal of Consumer Research* 27, no. 4 (2001): 489–98.

9. This discussion is based on Joseph W. Alba and J. Wesley Hutchinson, "Dimensions of Consumer Expertise," *Journal of Consumer Research* 13, no. 4 (1987): 411–54.

10. Michael D. Johnson and Claes Fornell, "The Nature and Methodological Implications of the Cognitive Representation of Products," *Journal of Consumer Research* 14, no. 2 (1987): 214–28.

11. Madhubalan Viswanathan and Terry L. Childers, "Understanding How Product Attributes Influence Product Categorization: Development and Validation of Fuzzy Set-Based Measures of Gradeness in Product Categories," *Journal of Marketing Research* 36, no. 1 (1999): 75–94.

12. Mita Sujan and Christine Dekleva, "Product Categorization and Inference Making: Some Implications for Comparative Advertising," *Journal of Consumer Research* 14, no. 3 (1987): 372–78.

13. Niraj Dawar and Philip Parker, "Marketing Universals: Consumers' Use of Brand Name, Price, Physical Appearance, and Retailer Reputation as Signals of Product Quality," *Journal of Marketing* 58, no. 2 (1994): 81–95.

14. Deborah Roedder John and Mita Sujan, "Age Differences in Product Categorization," *Journal of Consumer Research* 16, no. 4 (1990): 452–60.

15. Alba and Hutchinson, "Dimensions of Consumer Expertise."

16. Williams, "Social Class Influences on Purchase Evaluation Criteria."

17. Mark Bergen, Shantanu Dutta, and Steven M. Shugan, "Branded Variants: A Retail Perspective," *Journal of Marketing Research* 33, no. 1 (1996): 9–19.

18. Barbara Fasolo, Gary H. McClelland, and Peter M. Todd, "Escaping the Tyranny of Choice: When Fewer Attributes Make Choice Easier," *Marketing Theory* 7, no. 1 (2007): 13–26.

19. Michael D. Giebelhausen and Stacey G. Robinson, "Worth Waiting For: Increasing Satisfaction by Making Consumers Wait," *Journal of the Academy of Marketing Science* 39 (2011): 889–905.

20. Debanjan Mitra and Peter N. Golder, "How Does Objective Quality Affect Perceived Quality?" *Marketing Science* 25, no. 3 (2006): 230–47.

21. Ford Motor Company, "Ford's Swap Your Ride Campaign Proves a Real Eye-Opener for Consumers," http://media.ford.com/article_display.cfm?article_id=34341, accessed May 11, 2011.

22. Dawar and Parker, "Marketing Universals."

23. Elizabeth G. Miller and Barbara E. Kahn, "Shades of Meaning: The Effect of Color and Flavor Names on Consumer Choice," *Journal of Consumer Research* 32, no. 1 (2006): 86–92.

24. J. Jacoby, D. E. Speller, and C. A. Kohn, "Brand Choice Behavior as a Function of Information Load: Replication and Extension," *Journal of Consumer Research* 1 (1974): 33–41; Naresh K. Malhotra, "Information Load and Consumer Decision Making," *Journal of Consumer Research* 8 (1982): 419–30.

25. Fasolo et al., "Escaping the Tyranny of Choice."

26. Ran Kivetz and Itamar Simonson, "The Effects of Incomplete Information on Consumer Choice," *Journal of Marketing Research* 37, no. 4 (2000): 427–48.

27. Joseph F. Hair, Jr., Rolph Anderson, Ronald L. Tatham, and William C. Black, *Multivariate Data Analysis*, 5th ed. (Upper Saddle River, NJ: Prentice Hall, 1998).

28. Peter Wright, "Consumer Choice Strategies: Simplifying vs. Optimizing," *Journal of Marketing Research* 12 (February 1975): 60–67.

29. Hirschman and Krishnan, "Subjective and Objective Criteria in Consumer Choice"; Julie Baker, A. Parasuraman, Dhruv Grewal, and Glenn B. Voss, "The Influence of Multiple Store Environmental Cues on Perceived Merchandise Value and Purchase Intentions," *Journal of Retailing* 66, no. 2 (2002): 120–42.

30. Yoo-Kyoung Seock and Jessie H. Chen-Yu, "Website Evaluation Criteria Among U.S. College Student Consumers with Different Shopping Orientations and Internet Channel Usage," *International Journal of Consumer Studies* 31, no. 3 (2007): 204–12; Soyoung Kim, Reginald Williams, and Yulee Lee, "Attitude toward Online Shopping and Retail Website Quality: A Comparison of U.S. and Korean Consumers," *Journal of International Consumer Marketing* 16, no. 1 (2003): 89–111.

Case 4-1

1. Bertolucci, Jeff, "Smartphone Sales Boom—Who Needs a Laptop?" *PCWorld.com*, February 4, 2012, http://www.pcworld.com/article/249313/smartphone_sales_boom_who_needs_a_laptop.html, accessed June 5, 2012.

2. Kain, Erik, "Smartphone Shipments Top PCs for First Time Ever," *Forbes*, February 4, 2012, http://www.forbes.com/sites/erikkain/2012/02/04/smartphone-shipments-top-pcs-for-the-first-time-ever/, accessed June 5, 2012

3. Thomas, Knowlton, "Smartphones Outsell PCs for First Time Ever, Tablets Lead Growth by a Long Shot," Techvibes.com, February 3, 2012, http://www.techvibes.com/blog/smartphones-outsell-pcs-for-the-first-time-ever-tablets-lead-growth

-by-a-long-shot-report-2012-02-03, accessed June 5, 2012.

4. Kyrnin, Mark, "Tablet PCs vs. Laptops," About.com, (2012), http://compreviews .about.com/od/buyers/a/Tablets-vs-Laptops .htm, accessed June 5, 2012.

5. Ibid.

6. Wingfield, Nick, "Time to Leave the Laptop Behind," *The Wall Street Journal*, February 23, 2009, http://online.wsj.com/article /SB122477763884262815.html, accessed June 5, 2012.

7. Chan, Eric, "Size Matters: Tablets vs. Smartphones," *Businessweek*, March 16, 2011, http://www.businessweek.com /technology/content/mar2011/tc20110316 _121017.htm, accessed June 5, 2012.

Case 4-2

1. Datamonitor, 2012. New Balance Athletic Shoe Company.

2. Tiffany Yannetta, "The Flatiron New Balance Concept Store Is No Joke," August 12, 2011. http://ny.racked.com/ archives/2011/08/12/the_flatiron_new_bal -ance_concept_store_is_no_joke.php, accessed March 28, 2012.

3. "New Balance Sees 15 Percent Growth This Year." SGB, September 2011. Available at http://www.alacrastore.com/storecontent /Business-and-Industry/275234714.

4. Bergeron, Natalie (2012). New Balance interview via email. March 17, 2012.

5. Mary Johnson, "New Balance Opens Its First North American 'Experience' Store in the Flatiron," August 12, 2011. Retrieved March 28, 2012, http://www.dnainfo .com/20110812/murray-hill-gramercy/new -balance-opens-its-first-north-american -experience-store-flatiron.

6. Piktelis, Judy (2012). New Balance interview.

7. Dedham Quick facts (2012), http: //quickfacts.census.gov/qfd/states/25 /2516530.html.

8. Dedham Demographics, http://dedham .areaconnect.com/statistics.htm.

9. Legacy Place, http://www.legacyplace.com/.

10. Piktelis.

11. Kings Events (2012). http://www .kingsdedham.com/kings/events.php.

12. Piktelis.

13. "New Balance, Red Sox Strike Sponsor-ship Deal," *Team Business*, 3(2) (April 4, 2011): 12.

Chapter 14

1. Robert B. Woodruff, "Customer Value: The Next Source for Competitive Advantage," *Journal of the Academy of Marketing Science* 25, no. 2 (1997): 139–53.

2. M. B. Beverland and F. Farrelly, "The Quest for Authenticity in Consumption: Consumers' Purposive Choice of Authentic Cues to Shape Experienced Outcomes," *Journal of Consumer Research* 36 (February 2010): 838–56.

3. Grant McCracken, "Culture and Consumption: A Theoretical Account of the Structure and Movement of the Cultural Meaning of Consumer Goods," *Journal of Consumer Research* 13, no. 1 (1986): 71–84.

4. Morris B. Holbrook, "Consumption Experience, Customer Value, and Subjective Personal Introspection: An Illustrative Photographic Essay," *Journal of Business Research* 59 (2006): 714–25; Elizabeth C. Hirschman, and Morris B. Holbrook, "Hedonic Consumption: Emerging Concepts, Methods, and Propositions," *Journal of Marketing*, 46 (1983): 92–101.

5. Paul G. Patterson and Richard G. Spreng, "Modeling the Relationship Between Perceived Value, Satisfaction, and Repurchase Intentions in a Business-to-Business, Services Context: An Empirical Investigation," *International Journal of Industry Management* 8, no. 5 (1997): 414–34.

6. The American Consumer Satisfaction Index, www.theacsi.org, accessed July 5, 2012.

7. Jack Neff, "What Scandal? Walmart Rides Low Prices to Regain Mojo," *Advertising Age*, June 4, 2012, 1–19.

8. Stanley Slater, "Developing a Customer Value-Based Theory of the Firm," *Journal of the Academy of Marketing Science* 25, no. 2 (1997): 162–67.

9. Morris B. Holbrook, "Emotion in the Consumption Experience: Toward a Model of the Human Consumer," in *The Role of Affect in Consumer Behavior: Emerging Theories and Applications*, ed. Robert A. Peterson et al. (Lexington, MA: Heath, 1986), 17–52.

10. Barry J. Babin and Kevin William James, "A Brief Retrospective and Introspective on Value," *European Business Review* 22 (2010): 471–78.

11. This definition is based in part on Robert A. Westbrook and Richard L. Oliver, "The Dimensionality of Consumption Emotion Patterns and Consumer Satisfaction," *Journal of Consumer Research* 18, no. 1 (1991): 84–91.

12. Barry J. Babin and Mitch Griffin, "The Nature of Satisfaction: An Updated Examination and Analysis," *Journal of Business Research* 41 (1998): 127–36.

13. Y. C. Cho, "Analyzing Online Customer Dissatisfaction toward Perishable Goods," *Journal of Business Research* 64 (2011): 1245–50.

14. Richard L. Oliver, "Measurement and Evaluation of Satisfaction Processes in Retail Settings," *Journal of Retailing* 57 (Fall 1983): 25–48.

15. Gilbert A. Churchill, Jr., and Carol Surprenant, "An Investigation into the Determinants of Consumer Satisfaction," *Journal of Marketing Research* 19, no. 4 (1982): 491–504.

16. S. Dobsha and E. Foxman, "Mythic Agency and Retail Conquest," *Journal of Retailing* 88 (2012): 291–307; R. Trudel, K. Murray, and J. Cotte, "Beyond Expectations: The Effect of Regulatory Focus on Consumer Satisfaction," *International Journal of Marketing Research* 29 (2012): 93–97.

17. Valarie A. Zeithaml, Leonard L. Berry, and A. Parasuraman, "The Nature and Determinants of Customer Expectations of Service," *Journal of the Academy of Marketing Science* 21, no. 1 (1993): 1–12.

18. David K. Tse and Peter C. Wilton, "Models of Consumer Satisfaction Formation: An Extension," *Journal of Marketing Research* 24, no. 2 (1988): 204–12; Stephen A. LaTour and Nancy C. Peat, "Conceptual and Methodological Issues in Consumer Satisfaction Research," in *Advances in Consumer Research*, vol. 6, ed. William L. Wilkie (Ann Arbor, MI: Association of Consumer Research, 1979).

19. Richard A. Spreng and Thomas J. Page, Jr., "The Impact of Confidence in Expectations on Consumer Satisfaction," *Psychology & Marketing* 18, no. 11 (2001): 1187–1204.

20. Stephen J. Hoch and John Deighton, "Managing What Consumers Learn from Experience," *Journal of Marketing* 53, no. 2 (1989): 1–20.

21. Y. Kim and B. Wansink, "How Retailers' Recommendations and Return Policies Alter Product Evaluations," *Journal of Retailing*, (2012), 88:4, 528–541.

22. For a discussion of this topic, see F. A. Carrilat, J. Fernando, and J. P. Mulki, "The Validity of the SERVQUAL and SERVPREF Scales," *International Journal of Service Industry Management* 18 (May 2007): 472–90. Also see C. Bebko, L. M. Sciulli, and R. K. Garg, "Consumers' Level of Expectations for Services and the Role of Implicit Service Promises," *Services Marketing Quarterly* 28 (2006): 1–23.

23. Richard A. Spreng, Scott B. MacKenzie, and Richard W. Olshavsky, "A Reexamination of the Determinants of Consumer Satisfaction," *Journal of Marketing* 60, no. 3 (1996): 15–32.

24. J. Stacey Adams, "Inequity in Social Exchange," in *Advances in Experimental Social Psychology*, vol. 2, ed. Richard Berkowitz (New York: Academic Press, 1965), 267–99.

25. D. C. Barnes, M. B. Beauchamp, and C. Webster, "To Delight, or Not to Delight? This Is the Question Service Firms Must Address," *Journal of Marketing, Theory and Practice* 18 (Summer 2010): 275–83.

26. P. Aggarwal and R. P. Larrick, "When Consumers Care About Being Treated Fairly: The Interaction of Relationship Norms and Fairness Norms," *Journal of Consumer Psychology* 22 (2012): 114–27.

27. Bernard Wiener, "Attributional Thoughts about Consumer Behavior," *Journal of Consumer Research* 27, no. 3 (2000): 382–87.

28. L. Festinger, *A Theory of Cognitive Dissonance* (Stanford, CA: Stanford University Press, 1957).

29. Jillian C. Sweeney, Douglas Hausknecht, and Geoffrey N. Soutar, "Cognitive Dissonance after Purchase: A Multidimensional Scale," *Psychology & Marketing* 17, no. 5 (2000): 369–87.

30. J. Paul Peter, Gilbert A. Churchill, Jr., and Tom J. Brown, "Caution in the Use of Difference Scores in Consumer Research," *Journal of Consumer Research* 19, no. 4 (1993): 655–62.

31. Babin and Griffin, "The Nature of Satisfaction."

32. Jacob Jacoby, Carol K. Berning, and Thomas F. Dietvorst, "What About Disposition?" *Journal of Marketing* 41, no. 2 (1977): 22–28.

33. "Municipal Solid Waste Generation, Recycling, and Disposal in the United States: Facts and Figures for 2009," Environmental Protection Agency, http: //www.epa.gov/wastes/nonhaz/municipal /pubs/msw2009-fs.pdf, accessed July 2, 2013.

34. Linda L. Price, Eric J. Arnould, and Carolyn Folkman Curasi, "Older Consumers' Disposition of Special Possessions," *Journal of Consumer Research* 27, no. 2 (2000): 179–82.

35. John L. Lastovicka and Karen V. Fernandez, "Three Paths to Disposition: The Movement of Meaningful Possessions to Strangers," *Journal of Consumer Research* 31, no. 4 (2005): 813–23.

36. K. L. Haws, R. W. Naylor, R. A. Coulter, and W. O. Bearden, "Keeping It All without Being Buried Alive: Understanding Product Retention Tendency," *Journal of Consumer Psychology* 22 (2012): 224–36.

37. Robin A. Coulter and Mark Ligas, "To Retain or to Relinquish: Exploring the Disposition Practices of Packrats and Purgers," *Advances in Consumer Research* 30 (2003): 38–43.

Chapter 15

1. J. Van Doorn and P. C. Verhoef, "Critical Incidents and the Impact of Satisfaction on Customer Share," *Journal of Marketing* 72 (July 2008): 123–42.
2. Tom Costello, "Meet Your Complaining Customers, What Causes Them to Complain, and How Complaints Affect Your Business," July 2, 2012, http://www .hospitalitynet.org/news/4056742.html, accessed March 31, 2013.
3. M. Kalamas, M. Laroche, and L. Makdessian, "Reaching the Boiling Point: Consumers' Negative Affective Reactions to Firm-Attributed Service Failures," *Journal of Business Research* 61 (2008): 813–24.
4. P. Williams, M. Sajid Khan, N. Ul Ashil, and E. Naumann, "Customer Attitudes of Stayers and Defectors in B2B Services: Are They Really Different?" *Industrial Marketing Management* 40 (July 2011): 805–15.
5. C. M. Voorhees, M. K. Brady, and D. M. Horowitz, "A Voice from the Silent Masses: An Exploratory and Comparative Analysis of Non-Complaining," *Journal of the Academy of Marketing Science* 34 (September 2006): 513–27.
6. Better Business Bureau, http://www .bbb.org/us/, accessed July 4, 2012.
7. Simos, "Seven Steps to Handle Complaints."
8. L. S. Alvarez, R. V. Casielles, and A. M. D. Martin, "Analysis of the Role of Complaint Management in the Context of Relationship Marketing," *Journal of Marketing Management* 27 (February 2011): 143–64.
9. J. R. McColl-Kennedy, P. G. Patterson, A. K. Smith, and M. K. Brady, "Customer Rage Episodes: Emotions, Expressions and Behaviors," *Journal of Retailing* 85 (2009): 222–37.
10. H. Zourrig, J.C. Chebat, and R. Tofoli, "Consumer Revenge Behavior: A Cross-Cultural Perspective," *Journal of Business Research*, 62 (2009): 995–1001; Kalamas et al., "Reaching the Boiling Point."
11. C. A. Hart, J. L. Heskett, and E. W. Sasser, "The Profitable Art of Service Recovery," *Harvard Business Review* 68, no. 4 (1990): 148–56.
12. J. Romaniuk, "Word of Mouth and the Viewing of Television Programs," *Journal of Advertising Research* 47 (December 2007), 462–70.
13. K. E. Reynolds, M. A. Jones, C. F. Musgrove, and S. T. Gillison, "An Investigation of Retail Outcomes Comparing Two Types of Browsers," *Journal of Business Research* 65 (2012): 1090–95.
13a. "Lululemon Recalls See-Through Pants," *Advertising Age* 84, no. 12 (2013): 5.
14. L. Klie, "Hearing 140 Million Voices," *Customer Relationship Management* (June 2012): 21–26.
15. "BP Oil Spill, Two Years Later: Natural Recovery Far Greater Than Expected," *Science Daily*, http://www.sciencedaily.com /releases/2012/04/120417152648 .htm, accessed July 4, 2012.
16. J. Cloud, "Gay Days in the Magic Kingdom," *Time*, June 21, 2010, 69–70.
17. T. Schoenberg, "Clemens Lied to Protect Brand, U.S. Says as Trial Ends," *Business-Week*, June 12, 2012, http://www.business -week.com/news/2012-06-12/clemens-lied -to-protect-brand-u-dot-s-dot-says-as-trial -ends, accessed July 4, 2012.

18. J. G. Blodgett, D. H. Granbois, and R. G. Walters, "The Effects of Perceived Justice on Complainants' Negative Word-of-Mouth Behavior and Repatronage Intentions," *Journal of Retailing* 69 (Winter 1993): 399–428.
19. P. M. Nyer and M. Gopinath, "Effects of Complaining Versus Negative WOM on Subsequent Changes in Satisfaction: The Role of Public Commitment," *Psychology & Marketing* 22 (December 2005): 937–53.
20. F. Lange and M. Dahlen, "Too Much Bad PR Can Make Ads Ineffective," *Journal of Advertising Research* 46 (December 2006): 528–42; J. Aaker, S. Fournier, and B. S. Adam, "When Good Brands Go Bad," *Journal of Consumer Research* 31 (June 2004): 1–16.
21. Lange and Dahlen, "Too Much Bad PR Can Make Ads Ineffective."
22. C. Pullig, R. C. Netemeyer, and A. Biswas, "Attitude Basis Certainty and Challenge Alignment: A Case of Negative Publicity," *Journal of the Academy of Marketing Science* 34 (Fall 2006): 528–42.
23. Z. Feng and X. Zhang, "Impact of Online Consumer Reviews on Sales: The Moderating Role of Product and Consumer Characteristics," *Journal of Marketing* 74 (March 2010): 133–48.
24. S. McCartney, "The Big Flaws in Hotel Rankings," *The Wall Street Journal*, April 5, 2012, D1–D3.
25. T. A. Burnham, J. K. Frels, and V. Mahajan, "Consumer Switching Costs: A Typology, Antecedents and Consequences," *Journal of the Academy of Marketing Science* 31 (Spring 2003): 109–26.
26. M. L. Andrews, R. L. Benedicktus, and M. K. Brady, "The Effect of Incentives on Customer Evaluations of Service Bundles," *Journal of Business Research* 63 (2010): 71–76.
27. C. Antón, C. Camarero, and M. Carrero, "The Mediating Effect of Satisfaction on Consumers' Switching Intention," *Psychology & Marketing* 24 (June 2007): 511–538.
28. M. A. Jones, K. E. Reynolds, D. L. Mothersbaugh, and S. E. Beatty, "The Positive and Negative Effects of Switching Costs on Relational Outcomes," *Journal of Services Research* 9 (May 2007): 335–55.
29. G. Balabanis, N. Reynolds, and A. Simintiras, "Base of E-Store Loyalty: Perceived Switching Barriers and Satisfaction," *Journal of Business Research* 59 (February 2006): 214–24.
30. J. T. Gourville, "Eager Sellers and Stony Buyers: Understanding the Psychology of New-Product Adoption," *Harvard Business Review* 84 (June 2006): 99–106.
31. A. W. Magi, "Share of Wallet in Retailing: The Effects of Consumer Satisfaction, Loyalty Cards and Shopper Characteristics," *Journal of Retailing* 79 (Summer 2003): 97–106.
32. Dong H. Shin and Won Y. Kim, "Mobile Number Portability on Customer Switching Behavior: In the Case of the Korean Mobile Market." *Info* 9 (2007): 38–54.
33. F. V. Wangenheim, "Postswitching Negative Word of Mouth," *Journal of Services Research* 8 (2005): 67–78.
34. H. C. Chiu, Y. C. Hsieh, Y. C. Li, and L. Monle, "Relationship Marketing and Consumer Switching Behavior," *Journal of Business Research* 58 (December 2005): 1681–89.

35. B. J. Babin and J. P. Attaway, "Atmospheric Affect as a Tool for Creating Value and Gaining Share of Customer," *Journal of Business Research* 49 (August 2000): 91–99.
36. R. W. Palmatier, R. P. Dant, D. Grewal, and K. R. Evans), "Factors Influencing the Effectiveness of Relationship Marketing: A Meta-Analysis," *Journal of Marketing* 70 (October 2006): 136–53.
37. R. W. Palmatier, L. K. Scheer, M. B. Houston, K. R. Evans, and S. Gopalakrishna, "Use of Relationship Marketing Programs in Building Customer-Salesperson and Customer-Firm Relationships: Differential Influences on Financial Outcomes," *International Journal of Research in Marketing* 24 (2007): 210–23.

Chapter 16

1. R. A. Fullerton and G. Punj, "Repercussions of Promoting an Ideology of Consumption: Consumer Misbehavior," *Journal of Business Research* 57 (2004): 1239–49.
2. Aubry R. Fowler III, Barry J. Babin, and Amy K. Este, "Burning for Fun or Money: Illicit Consumer Behavior in a Contemporary Context," paper presented at the Academy of Marketing Science Annual Conference, May 27, 2005, Tampa, FL.
3. Fullerton and Punj, "Repercussions of Promoting an Ideology of Consumption."
4. Fowler et al., "Burning for Fun or Money."
5. Scott J. Vitell, "Consumer Ethics Research: Review, Synthesis and Suggestions for the Future," *Journal of Business Ethics* 43, no. 1/2 (March 2003): 33–47.
6. Barry J. Babin and Laurie A. Babin, "Effects of Moral Cognitions and Consumer Emotions on Shoplifting Intentions," *Psychology & Marketing* 13 (December 1996): 785–802.
7. Vitell, "Consumer Ethics Research."
8. Shelby Hunt and Scott Vitell, "A General Theory of Marketing Ethics," *Journal of Macromarketing* 6, no. 1 (Spring 1986): 5–16.
9. This section is based on Fullerton and Punj, "Repercussions of Promoting an Ideology of Consumption."
10. Robert Merton, *Social Theory and Social Structure* (New York: Free Press, 1968).
11. V. Lee Hamilton and David Rauma, "Social Psychology of Deviance and Law," in *Sociological Perspectives on Social Psychology*, ed. Karen S. Cook, Gary A. Fine, and James S. House, 524–47 (Boston: Allyn and Bacon, 1995).
12. Information and statistics provided by the National Association for Shoplifting Prevention (NASP), a nonprofit organization (www.shopliftingprevention.org), accessed May 27, 2011.
13. Dena Cox, Anthony D. Cox, and George P. Moschis, "When Consumer Behavior Goes Bad: An Investigation of Adolescent Shoplifting," *Journal of Consumer Research* 17, no. 2 (September 1990): 149–59.
14. Babin and Babin, "Effects of Moral Cognitions"; Cynthia Webster, "Exploring the Psychodynamics of Consumer Shoplifting Behavior," *American Marketing Association Conference Proceedings* 11 (2000): 360–65.
15. Barry J. Babin and Mitch Griffin, "A Closer Look at the Influence of Age on Consumer Ethics," *Advances in Consumer Research* 22 (1995): 668–73.
16. "Shadow Market: 2011 BSA Global Software Piracy Study," Business Software Alliance, May 2012, http://portal.bsa.org

/globalpiracy2011/downloads/study_pdf/2011_BSA_Piracy_Study-Standard.pdf, accessed May 15, 2012.

17. Fowler et al., "Burning for Fun or Money."

18. Corilyn Shropshire, "Spam Floods In-boxes," *Knight Ridder Tribune Business News*, January 23, 2007, 1; "U.S. Branded 'Biggest Spam and Virus Host,'" *Precision Marketing*, January 26, 2007, 9.

19. Mark Smail, "Are We Risking Our Digital Lives?" Technewsworld.com, January 20, 2010, http://www.technewsworld.com/story/69145.html, accessed June 30, 2010.

19a. Statisticbrain.com, July 11, 2012, http://www.statisticbrain.com/computer-virus-statistics/, accessed March 4, 2013.

20. Beth Herskovits, "APA Shows Public How Psychology Fits into Their Lives," *PR Week,* January 2, 2006, 19.

21. Amanda Lenhart, "Cyberbullying: What the Research Is Telling Us . . . ," Pew Internet & American Life Project, http://www.pewinternet.org/Presentations/2010/May/Cyberbullying-2010.aspx, accessed May 27, 2011.

22. R. S. Tokunaga, "Following You Home from School: A Critical Review and Synthesis of Research on Cyberbullying Victimization," *Computers in Human Behavior* 26 (2010): 277–87.

23. Coalition Against Insurance Fraud, http://www.insurancefraud.org, accessed May 14, 2012.

24. Identifytheft.com, http://www.identitytheft.info/victims.aspx, accessed May 11, 2012.

25. Kathryne Dupre, Tim Jones, and Shirley Taylor, "Dealing with the Difficult: Understanding Difficult Behaviors in a Service Encounter," *American Marketing Association Proceedings*, 2001, 173–80.

26. Mary J. Bitner, Bernard H. Booms, and Lois Mohr, "Critical Service Encounters: The Employee's Viewpoint," *Journal of Marketing* 58, no. 4 (1994): 95–106.

27. Lloyd Harris and Kate L. Reynolds, "The Consequences of Dysfunctional Customer Behavior," *Journal of Service Research* 6, no. 2 (November 2003): 144–61.

28. Scott Thorne, "An Exploratory Investigation of the Characteristics of Consumer Fanaticism," *Qualitative Market Research* 9, no. 1 (2006), 51–72; Robert W. Pimentel and Kristy E. Reynolds, "A Model for Consumer Devotion: Affective Commitment with Proactive Sustaining Behaviors," *Academy of Marketing Science Review*, Volume 8, no. 7 (2004): 1–45; Kirk L. Wakefield and Daniel L. Wann, "An Examination of Dysfunctional Sports Fans: Method of Classification and Relationships with Problem Behaviors," *Journal of Leisure Research* 38 (2006): 168–86; Kenneth A. Hunt, Terry Bristol, and R. Edward Bashaw, "A Conceptual Approach to Classifying Sports Fans," *Journal of Services Marketing* 13 (1999): 439–49; Bill Saporito, "Why Fans and Players Are Playing So Rough," *Time,* December 6, 2004, 30–35.

29. Kate L. Reynolds and Lloyd C. Harris, "When Service Failure Is Not Service Failure: An Exploration of the Forms and Motives of 'Illegitimate' Customer Complaining," *Journal of Services Marketing* 19 (2005): 321–35.

30. Consumer Products Safety Commission, http://www.cpsc.gov, accessed March 17, 2008.

31. Jeffrey Stoltman and Fred Morgan, "Psychological Dimensions of Unsafe Product

Usage," in *Marketing Theory and Applications*, 4th ed., ed. Rajan Varadarajan and Bernard Jaworski (Chicago: American Marketing Association, 1993).

32. "Road Rage Leads to More Road Rage," National Safety Commission, December 6, 2006, http://www.nationalsafetycommission.com, accessed March 17, 2008.

33. Jim Crimmins and Chris Callahan, "Reducing Road Rage: The Role of Target Insight in Advertising for Social Change," *Journal of Advertising Research* (December 2003): 381–90.

34. Sterling A. Bone and John C. Mowen, "Identifying the Traits of Aggressive and Distracted Drivers: A Hierarchical Trait Model Approach," *Journal of Consumer Behaviour* 5, no. 5, (2006): 454–65; also D. A. Hennessy and D. L. Wiesenthal, "The Relationship Between Traffic Congestion, Driver Stress, and Direct Versus Indirect Coping Behaviors," *Ergonomics* 40 (1997): 348–61.

35. "Impaired Driving," Centers for Disease Control and Prevention, http://www.cdc.gov/Motorvehiclesafety/Impaired_Driving/index.html, accessed May 8, 2012.

36. "Impaired Driving: Get the Facts," Centers for Disease Control and Prevention, http://www.cdc.gov/MotorVehicleSafety/Impaired_Driving/impaired-drv_factsheet.html, accessed June 17, 2009.

37. "Drinking and Driving: A Threat to Everyone," Centers for Disease Control and Prevention, October 4, 2011, http://www.cdc.gov/vitalsigns/drinkinganddriving/?s_cid=vitalsigns-092-bb#LatestFindings, accessed May 8, 2012.

38. L. Blincoe, A. Seay, E. Zaloshnja, T. Miller, E. Romano, S. Luchter et al., *The Economic Impact of Motor Vehicle Crashes, 2000* (Washington, DC: U.S. Dept. of Transportation), National Highway Traffic Safety Administration, 2002).

39. "Underage Drinking," Under *Your Influence* website (National Highway Traffic Safety Administration), http://underyourinfluence.org/underage-drinking, accessed March 4, 2013.

40. Kyran P. Quinlan, Robert D. Brewer, Paul Siegel, David A. Sleet, Ali H. Mokdad, Ruth A. Shults, and Nicole Flowers, "Alcohol Impaired Driving among U.S. Adults 1993–2003," *American Journal of Preventive Medicine* (May 2005): 346–50.

41. International Telecommunication Union, http://www.itu.int/ITU-D/ict/facts/material/ICTFactsFigures2013.pdf, accessed March 4, 2013.

42. CTIA-The Wireless Association, http://www.ctia.org/advocacy/research/, accessed May 8, 2012.

43. "Cell Phones and Driving," Insurance Information Institute, http://www.iii.org/issues_updates/cellphones-and-driving.html, accessed May 8, 2012.

44. Carol Ronis, "Teen Driver Safety," AAA Foundation, 2012, http://www.aaafoundation.org/pdf/DistractedDrivingAmongNewlyLicensedTeenDriversPR.pdf, accessed May 8, 2012.

45. "Cell Phones and Driving," Insurance Information Institute.

46. Governors Highway Safety Association, http://www.ghsa.org/html/stateinfo/laws/cellphone_laws.html, accessed March 7, 2013.

47. "Countries That Ban Cell Phone Use While Driving," June 6, 2009, http://www.cellular-news.com/car_bans/, accessed May 8, 2012.

47a. Erik Pineda, "It Turns Out 'Safe Sexting' Tool Snapchat Is Not 100% Secured," *International Business Times*, January 13, 2013, http://au.ibtimes.com/articles/420882/20130105/turns-out-safe-sexting-tool-snapchat-100.htm, accessed March 7, 2013.

48. D. Searcy, "Currents: A Lawyer, Some Teens and a Fight over Sexting," *The Wall Street Journal*, April 21, 2009, A17; A. Kingston, "The Sexting Scare," *Maclean's*, March 16, 2009, 52; W. Koch, "Teens Caught 'Sexting' Face Porn Charges," *USA Today*, March 11, 2009, http://www.usatoday.com/tech/wireless/2009-03-11-sexting_N.htm, accessed June 18, 2009.

49. Renee St. Pierre, "Sexting Behaviours among Teens: Dating and Romance in the Digital Age?" *International Centre for Youth Gambling Problems and High-Risk Behaviors* 11, no. 3 (2011), available at www.youthgambling.com, accessed May 9, 2012.

50. This definition is based on Thomas C. O'Guinn and Ronald J. Faber, "Compulsive Buying: A Phenomenological Exploration," *Journal of Consumer Research* 16, no. 2 (1989): 147–57.

51. Rajan Nataraajan and Brent G. Goff, "Manifestations of Compulsiveness in the Consumer-Marketplace Domain," *Psychology & Marketing* 9 (1992): 31–44.

52. This definition is based on Ronald Faber and Thomas O'Guinn, "A Clinical Screener for Compulsive Buying," *Journal of Consumer Research* 19, no. 3 (1992): 459–69.

53. Elizabeth C. Hirschman, "The Consciousness of Addiction: Toward a General Theory of Compulsive Consumption," *Journal of Consumer Research* (September 1992): 155–79; O'Guinn and Faber, "Compulsive Buying"; Helga Dittmar, "A New Look at Compulsive Buying: Self-Discrepancies and Materialistic Values as Predictors of Compulsive Buying Tendencies," *Journal of Social and Clinical Psychology* (September 2005): 832–59.

54. Jeff Joireman, Jeremy Kees, and David Sprott, "Concern with Immediate Consequences Magnifies the Impact of Compulsive Buying Tendencies on College Students' Credit Card Debt," *Journal of Consumer Affairs* 44, no. 1 (2010): 155–78.

55. Kay M. Palan Paula C. Morrow, Allan Trapp II, and Virginia Blackburn, "Compulsive Buying Behavior in College Students: The Mediating Role of Credit Card Abuse," *Journal of Marketing Theory and Practice* 19, no. 1 (2011): 81–96.

56. James A. Roberts, Chris Manolis, and John F. Tanner, Jr., "Adolescent Autonomy and the Impact of Family Structure on Materialism and Compulsive Buying," *Journal of Marketing Theory and Practice* 14, no. 4 (2006): 301–14.

57. James A. Roberts, "Compulsive Buying among College Students: An Investigation of Its Antecedents, Consequences, and Implications for Public Policy," *Journal of Consumer Affairs* 32, no. 2 (1998): 295–319; O'Guinn and Faber, "Compulsive Buying."

58. D. W. Black, "Assessment of Compulsive Buying," in *I Shop, Therefore I Am: Compulsive Buying and the Search for Self*, ed. A. L. Benson, 191–216 (Northvale, NJ: Jason Aronson, 2000).

59. Jessica Parker-Pope, "This Is Your Brand at the Mall: Why Shopping Makes You Feel So Good," *The Wall Street Journal*, December 6, 2005, D1.

60. Lorrin M. Koran, Ronald J. Faber, Elias Aboujauode, Michael D. Large, and Richard T. Serpe, "Estimated Prevalence of Compulsive Buying Behavior in the United States," *The American Journal of Psychiatry* (October 2006): 1806–12.

61. Binge-eating.com, http://www.binge-eating.com/, accessed May 9, 2012.

62. Susan Yanovski and Billinda K. Dubbert, "Association of Binge Eating Disorder and Psychiatric Comorbidity in Obese Subjects," *The American Journal of Psychiatry* (October 1993): 1472–79.

63. Manoj Thomas, Kalpesh Kaushik Desai, and Satheeshkumar Seenivasan, "How Credit Card Payments Increase Unhealthy Food Purchases: Visceral Regulation of Vices," *Journal of Consumer Research* 38 (June 2011): 126–39.

64. National Institute for Alcohol Abuse and Alcoholism, http://www.niaaa.nih.gov, accessed March 17, 2008.

65. Substance Abuse and Mental Health Services Administration, http://www.samhsa.gov/data/NSDUH/2k11Results/NSDUHresults2011.htm#3.1.6, accessed March 7, 2013.

66. Maira G. Piacentini and Emma N. Banister, "Getting Hammered? . . . Students Coping with Alcohol," *Journal of Consumer Behaviour* 5, no. 2 (2006): 145–56.

67. H. Wechsler, J. E. Lee, M. Kuo, M. Seibring, T. F. Nelson, and H. P. Lee, "Trends in College Binge Drinking During a Period of Increased Prevention Efforts: Findings from Four Harvard School of Public Health Study Surveys," *Journal of American College Health* 50 (2002): 203–17; C. A. Presley, M. A. Leichliter, and P. W. Meilman, *Alcohol and Drugs on American College Campuses: A Report to College Presidents: Third in a Series* (Carbondale, IL: Core Institute, Southern Illinois University, 1998).

68. "A Snapshot of Annual High-Risk College Drinking Consequences," College Drinking—Changing the Culture, July 1, 2010, www.collegedrinkingprevention.gov/StatsSummaries/snapshot.aspx, accessed June 1, 2011.

69. Soyeon Shim and Jennifer Maggs, "A Cognitive and Behavioral Hierarchical Decision-Making Model of College Students' Alcohol Consumption," *Psychology & Marketing* 22, no. 8 (2005): 649–68.

70. Megan A. Moreno, Dimitri A. Christakis, Katie G. Egan, Libby N. Brockman, and Tara Becker, "Associations Between Displayed Alcohol References on Facebook and Problem Drinking among College Students," *Archives of Pediatric Adolescent Medicine* 166, no. 2 (2012): 157–63.

71. National Institute on Alcohol Abuse and Alcoholism (2002). *A Call to Action: Changing the Culture of Drinking at U.S. Colleges,* National Institutes of Health, US Department of Health and Human Services.

72. Institute of Medicine National Research Council of the National Academies. (2003). Bonnie, Richard J. and Mary Ellen O'Connell, eds. "Reducing Underage Drinking: A Collective Responsibility." (Washington, DC: The National Academies Press).

73. This definition is based on Richard G. Netemeyer, Scot Burton, Leslie K. Cole, Donald A. Williamson, Nancy Zucker, Lisa Bertman,

and Gretchen Diefenbach, "Characteristics and Beliefs Associated with Probable Pathological Gambling: A Pilot Study with Implications for the National Gambling Impact and Policy Commission," *Journal of Public Policy & Marketing* 17, no. 2 (1998): 147–60.

74. George Balabanis, "The Relationship Between Lottery-Ticket and Scratch-Card Buying Behaviour, Personality and Other Compulsive Behaviors," *Journal of Consumer Behaviour* 2, no. 1 (2002): 7–22.

75. Statistics based on information found at National Council on Problem Gambling, www.ncpgambling.org/i4a/pages/Index.cfm?pageID=3315#widespread, accessed May 9, 2012.

76. J. L. McComb and W. E. Hanson, "Problem Gambling on College Campuses," *NASPA Journal* 46, no. 1 (2009): 1–29.

77. Suzi Levens, Anne-Marie Dyer, Cynthia Zubritsky, Kathryn Knott, and David W. Oslin, "Gambling Among Older, Primary Care Patients," *American Journal of Geriatric Psychiatry* 13 (2005): 69–76; Peggy Sue Loroz, "Golden-Age Gambling: Psychological Benefits and Self-Concept Dynamics in Aging Consumers' Consumption Experiences," *Psychology & Marketing* 25, no. 1 (2004): 323–50.

78. Hyokjin Kwak, George M. Zinkhan, and Elizabeth P. Lester Roushanzamir, "Compulsive Comorbidity and Its Psychological Antecedents: A Cross-Cultural Comparison Between the U.S. and South Korea," *The Journal of Consumer Marketing* 21 (2004): 418–34; Netemeyer et al., "Characteristics and Beliefs Associated with Probable Pathological Gambling."

79. Drugabuse.gov website, http://www.druga-buse.gov/publications/drugfacts/high-school-youth-trends, accessed March 4, 2013.

80. "Marijuana: Facts Parents Need to Know," March 2011, http://www.drugabuse.gov/publications/marijuana-facts-parents-need-to-know, accessed August 3, 2012.

80a. National Institute on Drug Abuse, http://www.drugabuse.gov/news-events/news-releases/2012/12/regular-marijuana-use-by-teens-continues-to-be-concern, accessed March 4, 2013.

81. Cassie Goldberg, "National Study: Teen 'Heavy' Marijuana Use Up 80% Since 2008; One in Ten Teens Report Using Marijuana at Least 20 Times a Month," The Partnership for a Drug-Free America, May 2, 2012, http://www.drugfree.org/newsroom/pats-2011, accessed May 11, 2012.

82. "Results from the 2010 National Survey on Drug Use and Health: Summary of National Findings," NSDUH Series H-41, HHS Publication No. (SMA) 11-4658 (Rockville, MD: Substance Abuse and Mental Health Services Administration, 2011), http://oas.samhsa.gov/SDUH/2k10NSDUH/2k10Results.pdf, accessed May 11, 2012.

83. This definition is based on Gene R. Laczniak and Patrick E. Murphy, "Normative Perspectives for Ethical and Socially Responsible Marketing," *Journal of Macromarketing* 26, no. 2 (2006): 154–77.

84. Rhoda H. Karpatkin, (1999), "Toward a Fair and Just Marketplace for All Consumers: The Responsibilities of Marketing Professionals," *Journal of Public Policy & Marketing* 18 (1), 118–22.

85. Lan Xia, Kent B. Monroe, and Jennifer L. Cox, "The Price Is Unfair! A Conceptual Framework of Price Fairness Perceptions," *Journal of Marketing* 68 (October 2004): 1–15; Margaret C. Campbell, "Perceptions of Price Fairness: Antecedents and Consequences," *Journal of Marketing Research* 36 (May 1999): 187–99.

86. Philip Kotler, "What Consumerism Means for Marketers," *Harvard Business Review* 50 (May–June 1972): 48–57.

87. Larry McShan, "Bruce Springsteen Slams Ticketmaster over Working on a Dream Ticket Sales," *New York Daily News*, February 4, 2009, www.nydailynews.com/gossip/2009/02/04/2009-02-04_bruce_springsteen_slams_ticketmaster_ove.html, accessed June 19, 2009.

88. Ben Sisario, "Ticketmaster Reaches Settlement on Complaints of Deceptive Sales," *The New York Times*, February 19, 2010, http://www.nytimes.com/2010/02/19/arts/music/19ticket.html, accessed May 14, 2012.

89. N. Craig Smith and Elizabeth Cooper-Martin, "Ethics and Target Marketing: The Role of Product Harm and Consumer Vulnerability," *Journal of Marketing* 61, no. 3 (1997): 1–20.

90. This definition is based on Tom J. Brown and Peter A. Dacin, "The Company and the Product: Corporate Associations and Consumer Product Responses," *Journal of Marketing* 61, no. 1 (1997): 68–84.

91. Sankar Sen and C. B. Bhattacharya, "Does Doing Good Always Lead to Doing Better? Consumer Reactions to Corporate Social Responsibility," *Journal of Marketing Research* 38, no. 2 (2001): 225–43.

92. Geoffrey P. Lantos, "The Boundaries of Strategic Corporate Social Responsibility," *Journal of Consumer Marketing* 18, no. 7 (2001): 595–630. These assertions based on several works including Xueming Luo and C. B. Bhattacharya, "Corporate Social Responsibility, Customer Satisfaction, and Market Value," *Journal of Marketing* 70, no. 4 (2006): 1–18; Donald R. Lichenstein, Minette E. Drumwright, and Bridgette M. Braig, "The Effect of Corporate Social Responsibility on Customer Donations to Corporate-Supported Nonprofits," *Journal of Marketing* 68, no. 4 (2004): 16–32; Sen and Bhattacharya, "Does Doing Good Always Lead to Doing Better?"; Brown and Dacin, "The Company and the Product."

93. Carlos J. Torelli, Alokparna Basu Monga, and Andrew M. Kaikati, "Doing Poorly by Doing Good: Corporate Social Responsibility and Brand Concepts," *Journal of Consumer Research* 38 (February 2011): 948–63.

94. Kotler, "What Consumerism Means for Marketers."

95. Federal Trade Commission, www.ftc.gov/bcp/conline/pubs/buspubs/ad-faqs.shtm, accessed March 17, 2008.

96. Kenneth C. Herbst, Eli J. Finkel, David Allan, and Grainne M. Fitzsimons, "On the Dangers of Pulling a Fast One: Advertisement Disclaimer Speed, Brand Trust, and Purchase Intention," *Journal of Consumer Research* 38 (February 2011): 909–18.

97. American Advertising Federation, www.aaf.org, accessed May 14, 2012.

98. National Advertising Review Council, www.narcpartners.org/, accessed March 17, 2008.

99. "Television Advertising Leads to Unhealthy Habits in Children, Says APA Task Force," American Psychological Association, February 23, 2004, www.apa.org/releases/childrenads.html, accessed August 2007.

100. Anup Shah, "Children as Consumers," Global Issues, November 21, 2010, www.globalissues.org/article/237/children-as-consumers#Advertisingtochildrenisbig business, accessed May 14, 2012.

101. Children's Advertising Review Unit, Better Business Bureau, www.caru.org/guidelines/index.aspx, accessed July 2, 2010.

102. Online content retrieved at Federal Trade Commission website, http://www.ftc.gov/ogc/coppa1.htm, accessed October 29, 2012.

103. E. Deanne Brocato, Douglas A. Gentile, Russell N. Laczniak, Julia A. Maier, and Mindy Ji-Song, "Television Commercial Violence: Potential Effects on Children," *Journal of Advertising* 39, no. 4 (2011): 95–107.

104. Marie-Louis Fry and Michael Jay Polonsky, "Examining the Unintended Consequences of Marketing," *Journal of Business Research* 57 (2004): 1303–6.

105. Live Earth, http://liveearth.org/en/liveearth, accessed June 1, 2011.

106. M. J. Ellington, "Price Gouging Law Takes Effect with State of Disaster Declaration," TimesDaily.com, April 29, 2011, www.timesdaily.com/article/20110429/news/110429779?Title=Price-gouging-law-takes-effect-with-state-disaster-declaration, accessed June 1, 2011; Brent Martin, "Attorney General Worries about Price-Gouging in Wake of Joplin Tornado," Missouri.net, May 23, 2011, www.missourinet.com/2011/05/23/attorney-general-worries-about-price-gouging-in-wake-of-joplin-tornado-audio/, accessed June 1, 2011; "Kentucky Gas Stations Fined for Price Gouging after Katrina," Wlky.com, August 1, 2006, www.wlky.com/r/9608663/detail.html, accessed June 1, 2011.

107. Alice M. Tybout, Brian Sternthal, and Bobby J. Calder, "Information Availability as a Determinant of Multiple-Request Effectiveness," *Journal of Marketing Research* 20 (August 1988): 280–90; John C. Mowen and Robert Cialdini, "On Implementing the Door-in-the-Face Compliance Strategy in a Marketing Context," *Journal of Marketing Research* 17 (May 1980): 253–58; Jonathan L. Freedman and Scott C. Fraher, "Compliance without Pressure: The Foot-in-the-Door Technique," *Journal of Personality and Social Psychology* 4 (August 1966): 195–202.

108. Robert Cialdini and David Schroeder, "Increasing Compliance by Legitimizing Paltry Contributions: When Even a Penny Helps," *Journal of Personality and Social Psychology* 34 (October 1976): 599–604.

109. "Unethical Word-of-Mouth Marketing Strategies," WOMMA, www.womma.org/wom101/06/, accessed March 17, 2008.

110. Consumer Product Safety Commission, www.cpsc.gov/about/about.html, accessed March 17, 2008.

Case 5-2

1. Associated Press, "Bloom Is Off the Pink for Some," *Dallas Morning News,* February 5, 2012, 7A.

2. "About Us," Susan G. Komen for the Cure, http://www.komen.org/AboutUs/AboutUs.html, accessed March 18, 2012.

3. Charity Navigator–America's Largest Charity Evaluator, http://www.charitynavigator.org/.

4. Park, Alice, "Public Backlash Spurs Komen to Renew Ties with Planned Parenthood," *Time,* February 3, 2012, http://healthland.time.com/2012/02/03/planned-parenthood-credits-social-media-for-publicizing-its-position-against-komen-foundation/, accessed August 3, 2012.

5. Begley, Sharon and Janet Roberts, "Insight: Komen charity under microscope for funding, science," Reuters.com, February 8, 2012, http://www.reuters.com/article/2012/02/08/us-usa-healthcare-komen-research-idUS-TRE8171KW20120208.

6. Ramizer, Marc, "Swift Outcry on Social Media Played Key Role," *Dallas Morning News,* February 4, 2012, 1A.

7. Robinson-Jacobs, Karen and Melissa Repko, "Komen's Sponsors Rattled," *Dallas Morning News,* February 5, 2012, 1D.

8. Bassett, Laura, "Susan G. Komen Executives Resign amid Reports of Internal Troubles," *Huffington Post,* March 20, 2012, http://www.huffingtonpost.com/2012/03/20/susan-g-komen-executives-resign_n_1368213.html, accessed August 3, 2012; Laura Bassett and Lisa Belkin, "Susan G. Komen Officials Resign as Backlash Gains Steam," *Huffington Post,* February 2, 2012, http://www.huffingtonpost.com/2012/02/02/susan-g-komen_n_1250651.html, accessed August 3, 2012.

9. Ramizer, Marc, "Swift Outcry on Social Media Played Key Role," *Dallas Morning News,* February 4, 2012, 1A.

10. Preston, Jennifer, "After Outcry, a Senior Official Resigns at Komen," *The New York Times,* February 7, 2012, http://www.nytimes.com/2012/02/08/us/after-outcry-a-top-official-resigns-at-komen-cancer-charity.html?_r=1.

11. Basset, Laura, "Susan G. Komen Hires Consulting Firm to Assess Damage to Reputation," *Huffington Post,* February 23, 2012, http://www.huffingtonpost.com/2012/02/23/susan-g-komen-planned-parenthood_n_1297483.html.

Case 5-3

1. Courtney, Jesse J., and Daniel L. Wann, "The Relationship between Sport Fan Dysfunction and Bullying Behaviors," *North American Journal of Psychology* 12, no. 1 (2010): 191–98.

2. Smith, J., and Wann, D. L. (2006). Relationship of dysfunctional sport fandom with dislike for rivals in a sample of college students, *Perceptual and Motor Skills,* 102, 719–720.

3. Trail, G.T., J. S. Fink, and D. F. Anderson, (2003). Sport spectator consumption behavior, *Sport Marketing Quarterly,* 12 (1), 8–17.

4. Wakefield, Kirk L., and Daniel L. Wann (2006). "An Examination of Dysfunctional Sport Fans: Method of Classification and Relationships with Problem Behaviors," *Journal of Leisure Research,* Vol. 38 (2), 168–186.

5. Smith and Wann, "Relationship of dysfunctional sport fandom with dislike for rivals."

6. Burleson, Duane, "NBA Suspends Artest for Rest of Season," http://nbcsports.msnbc.com/id/6549074/, accessed April 10, 2012.

7. Austen, Ben, "Aubs Eat Boogers," *GQ,* September 2011, www.gq.com/sports/profiles/201109/college-football-alabama-auburn-rivalry, accessed April 10, 2012.

8. McCarthy, Brendan, "Fan Misbehavior: Revelry Gone Awry in the Sports World," *The Times-Picayune,* www.nola.com/crime/index.ssf/2012/01/fan_misbehavior_revelry_gone_a.html, accessed April 10, 2012.

9. "Parents Brawl at Little League Game," www.cbsnews.com/2100-201_162-527602.html, accessed April 10, 2012.

10. "Fight at Little League Game Brings Deputies to Stonehouse Park," www.ranchomurieta.com/node/10962, accessed April 10, 2012.

GLOSSARY

A

ABC approach to attitudes approach that suggests that attitudes encompass one's affect, behavior, and cognitions (or beliefs) toward an object

absolute threshold minimum strength of a stimulus that can be perceived

accommodation state that results when a stimulus shares some but not all of the characteristics that would lead it to fit neatly in an existing category, and consumers must process exceptions to rules about the category

acculturation process by which consumers come to learn a culture other than their natural, native culture

acquisitional shopping activities oriented toward a specific, intended purchase or purchases

action-oriented consumers with a high capacity to self-regulate their behavior

actual state consumer's perceived current state

adaptation level level of a stimulus to which a consumer has become accustomed

addictive consumption physiological dependency on the consumption of a consumer product

advertiming ad buys that include a schedule that runs the advertisement primarily at times when customers will be most receptive to the message

aesthetic labor effort put forth by employees in carefully managing their appearance as a requisite for performing their job well

affect feelings associated with objects or experienced during events

affect-based evaluation evaluative process wherein consumers evaluate products based on the overall feeling that is evoked by the alternative

affective quality retail positioning that emphasizes a unique environment, exciting décor, friendly employees, and, in general, the feelings experienced in a retail place

age-based microculture term that describes the finding that people of the same age end up sharing many of the same values and develop similar consumer preferences

aggregation approach approach to studying personality in which behavior is assessed at a number of points in time

AIO statements activity, interest, and opinion statements that are used in lifestyle studies

antecedent conditions situational characteristics that a consumer brings to information processing

anthropology study in which researchers interpret relationships between consumers and the things they purchase, the products they own, and the activities in which they participate

anthropomorphism giving humanlike characteristics to inanimate objects

antiloyal consumers consumers who will do everything possible to avoid doing business with a particular marketer

aspirational group group in which a consumer desires to become a member

assimilation state that results when a stimulus has characteristics such that consumers readily recognize it as belonging to some specific category

associative network network of mental pathways linking all knowledge within memory; sometimes referred to as a semantic network

atmospherics emotional nature of an environment or the feelings created by the total aura of physical attributes that comprise a physical environment

attention purposeful allocation of information-processing capacity toward developing an understanding of some stimulus

attention to social comparison information (ATSCI) individual difference variable that assesses the extent to which consumers are concerned about how other people react to their behavior

attitude-behavior consistency extent to which a strong relationship exists between attitudes and actual behavior

attitude-toward-the-object (ATO) model attitude model that considers three key elements including beliefs consumers have about salient attributes, the strength of the belief that an object possesses the attribute, and evaluation of the particular attribute

attitude tracking effort of a marketer or researcher to track changes in consumer attitudes over time

attitudes relatively enduring overall evaluations of objects, products, services, issues, or people

attribute a product feature that delivers a desired consumer benefit

attribute-based evaluation evaluative process wherein alternatives are evaluated across a set of attributes that are considered relevant to the purchase situation

attribute correlation perceived relationship between product features

attribution theory theory that proposes that consumers look for the cause of particular consumption experiences when arriving at satisfaction judgments

augmented product actual physical product purchased plus any services such as installation and warranties necessary to use the product and obtain its benefits

authenticity the degree to which an object, person, or experience seems real, genuine, unique, and part of history or tradition

autobiographical memories cognitive representation of meaningful events in one's life

autonomic measures means of recording responses based on either automatic visceral reactions or neurological brain activity

awareness set set of alternatives of which a consumer is aware

B

background music music played below the audible threshold that would make it the center of attention

balance theory theory that states that consumers are motivated to maintain perceived consistency in the relations found in a system

behavioral influence decision-making perspective assumes many consumer decisions are actually learned responses to environmental influences

behavioral intentions model model developed to improve on the ATO model, focusing on behavioral intentions, subjective norms, and attitude toward a particular behavior

behaviorist approach to learning theory of learning that focuses on changes in behavior due to association, without great concern for the cognitive mechanics of the learning process

benefit perceived favorable result derived from a particular feature

benefits positive results of consumption

bicultural used to describe immigrants as they face decisions and form preferences based on their old or new cultures

binge drinking consumption of five or more drinks in a single drinking session for men and four or more drinks for women

binge eating consumption of large amounts of food while feeling a general loss of control over food intake

bipolar situation wherein if one feels joy he or she cannot also experience sadness

blue ocean strategy positioning a firm far away from competitors' positions so that it creates an industry of its own and, at least for a time, isolates itself from competitors

body esteem positivity with which people hold their body image

body language nonverbal communication cues signaled by somatic responses

boomerang kids young adults, between the ages of 18 and 34, who move back home with their parents after they graduate from college

bounded rationality idea that consumers attempt to act rationally within their information processing constraints

brain dominance refers to the phenomenona of hemispheric lateralization. Some people tend to be either right-brain or left-brain dominant

brand community group of consumers who develop relationships based on shared interests or product usage

brand inertia what occurs when a consumer simply buys a product repeatedly without any real attachment

brand loyalty deeply held commitment to rebuy a product or service regardless of situational influences that could lead to switching behavior

brand personality collection of human characteristics that can be associated with a brand

brand personality appeal a product's ability to appeal to consumers based on the human characteristics associated with it

BRIC acronym that refers to the collective economies of Brazil, Russia, India, and China

buzz marketing marketing efforts that focus on generating excitement among consumers and that are spread from consumer to consumer

C

CANZUS acronym that refers to the close similarity in values between Canada, Australia, New Zealand, and the United States

central cues information presented in a message about the product itself, its attributes, or the consequences of its use

central route to persuasion path to persuasion found in ELM where the consumer has high involvement, motivation, and/or ability to process a message

Chindia combined market and business potential of China and India

chunk single memory unit

chunking process of grouping stimuli by meaning so that multiple stimuli can become one memory unit

circadian cycle rhythm (level of energy) of the human body that varies with the time of day

classical conditioning change in behavior that occurs simply through associating some stimulus with another stimulus that naturally causes some reaction; a type of unintentional learning

cognition thinking or mental processes that go on as we process and store things that can become knowledge

cognitive appraisal theory school of thought proposing that specific types of appraisal thoughts can be linked to specific types of emotions

cognitive dissonance an uncomfortable feeling that occurs when a consumer has lingering doubts about a decision that has occurred

cognitive interference notion that everything else that the consumer is exposed to while trying to remember something is also vying for processing capacity and thus interfering with memory and comprehension

cognitive organization process by which the human brain assembles sensory evidence into something recognizable

cognitive psychology study of the intricacies of mental reactions involved in information processing

cognitive structuring term that refers to the reliance on schema-based heuristics in making decisions

cohort a group of people who have lived the same major experiences in their lives

collectivism extent to which an individual's life is intertwined with a large cohesive group

compensatory damages damages that are intended to cover costs incurred by a consumer due to an injury

compensatory model attitudinal model wherein low ratings for one attribute are compensated for by higher ratings on another

compensatory rule decision rule that allows consumers to select products that may perform poorly on one criterion by compensating for the poor performance on one attribute by good performance on another

competitive intensity number of firms competing for business within a specific category

competitiveness enduring tendency to strive to be better than others

complaining behavior action that occurs when a consumer actively seeks out someone (supervisor, service provider, etc.) to share an opinion with regarding a negative consumption event

comprehension the way people cognitively assign meaning to (i.e., understand) things they encounter

compulsive buying chronic, repetitive purchasing that is a response to negative events or feelings

compulsive consumption repetitive, excessive, and purposeful consumer behaviors that are performed as a response to tension, anxiety, or obtrusive thoughts

compulsive shopping repetitive shopping behaviors that are a response to negative events or feelings

conditioned response response that results from exposure to a conditioned stimulus that was originally associated with the unconditioned stimulus

conditioned stimulus object or event that does not cause the desired response naturally but that can be conditioned to do so by pairing with an unconditioned stimulus

confirmatory bias tendency for expectations to guide performance perceptions

conformity result of group influence in which an individual yields to the attitudes and behaviors of others

congruity how consistent the elements of an environment are with one another

conjoint analysis technique used to develop an understanding of the attributes that guide consumer preferences by having consumers compare product preferences across varying levels of evaluative criteria and expected utility

conjunctive rule noncompensatory decision rule where the option selected must surpass a minimum cutoff across all relevant attributes

connected self-schema self-conceptualization of the extent to which a consumer perceives himself or herself as being an integral part of a group

consideration set alternatives that are considered acceptable for further consideration in decision making

consistency principle principle that states that human beings prefer consistency among their beliefs, attitudes, and behaviors

consumer affect feelings a consumer has about a particular product or activity

consumer behavior set of value-seeking activities that take place as people go about addressing realized needs

consumer behavior as a field of study study of consumers as they go about the consumption process; the science of studying how consumers seek value in an effort to address real needs

Consumer Bill of Rights introduced by President John F. Kennedy in 1962, list of rights that includes the right to safety, the right to be informed, the right to redress and to be heard, and the right to choice

consumer culture commonly held societal beliefs that define what is socially gratifying

consumer (customer) orientation way of doing business in which the actions and decision making of the institution prioritize consumer value and satisfaction above all other concerns

consumer dissatisfaction mild, negative affective reaction resulting from an unfavorable appraisal of a consumption outcome

consumer ethnocentrism belief among consumers that their ethnic group is superior to others and that the products that come from their native land are superior to other products

consumer inertia situation in which a consumer tends to continue a pattern of behavior until some stronger force motivates him or her to change

consumer involvement degree of personal relevance a consumer finds in pursuing value from a particular category of consumption

consumer misbehavior behaviors that are in some way unethical and that potentially harm the self or others

consumer problem behavior consumer behavior that is deemed to be unacceptable but that is seemingly beyond the control of the consumer

consumer refuse any packaging that is no longer necessary for consumption to take place or, in some cases, the actual good that is no longer providing value to the consumer

consumer satisfaction mild, positive emotion resulting from a favorable appraisal of a consumption outcome

consumer search behavior behaviors that consumers engage in as they seek information that can be used to satisfy needs

consumer self-regulation tendency for consumers to inhibit outside, or situational, influences from interfering with shopping intentions

consumer socialization the process through which young consumers develop attitudes and learn skills that help them function in the marketplace

Consumer Value Framework (CVF) consumer behavior theory that illustrates factors that shape consumption-related behaviors and ultimately determine the value associated with consumption

consumerism activities of various groups to voice concern for, and to protect, basic consumer rights

consumption process by which goods, services, or ideas are used and transformed into value

consumption frequency number of times a product or service is consumed in a given period of time

contractualism beliefs about the violation of written (or unwritten) laws

contrast state that results when a stimulus does not share enough in common with existing categories to allow categorization

core societal values (CSV) commonly agreed-upon consensus about the most preferable ways of living within a society

corporate social responsibility (CSR) organization's activities and status related to its societal obligations

corporate strategy way a firm is defined and its general goals

costs negative results of consumption

counterarguments thoughts that contradict a message

credibility extent to which a source is considered to be both an expert in a given area and trustworthy

critical incident exchange between consumers and business that the consumer views as unusually negative

crowding density of people and objects within a given space

cultural distance representation of how disparate one nation is from another in terms of their CSV

cultural norm rule that specifies the appropriate consumer behavior in a given situation within a specific culture

cultural sanction penalty associated with performing a nongratifying or culturally inconsistent behavior

customer commitment sense of attachment, dedication, and identification

Customer Lifetime Value (CLV) approximate worth of a customer to a company in economic terms; overall profitability of an individual consumer

customer orientation practice of using sales techniques that focus on customer needs

Customer Relationship Management (CRM) systematic information management system that collects, maintains, and reports detailed information about customers to enable a more customer-oriented managerial approach

customer share portion of resources allocated to one brand from among the set of competing brands

D

deceptive advertising message that omits information that is important in influencing a consumer's buying behavior and is likely to mislead consumers acting "reasonably"

declarative knowledge cognitive components that represent facts

demographic analysis a profile of a consumer group based on their demographics

demographics observable, statistical aspects of populations such as age, gender, or income

deontological evaluations evaluations regarding the inherent rightness or wrongness of specific actions

desired state perceived state for which a consumer strives

desire level of a particular benefit that will lead to a valued end state

determinant criteria criteria that are most carefully considered and directly related to the actual choice that is made

dialects variations of a common language

differentiated marketers firms that serve multiple market segments each with a unique product offering

diffusion process way in which new products are adopted and spread throughout a marketplace

discriminative stimuli stimuli that occur solely in the presence of a reinforcer

disjunctive rule noncompensatory decision rule where the option selected surpasses a relatively high cutoff point on any attribute

dissociative group group to which a consumer does not want to belong

distributive fairness refers to the way a consumer judges the outcomes of an exchange

divergence situation in which consumers choose membership in microcultures in an effort to stand out or define themselves from the crowd

door-in-the-face technique ingratiation technique used in personal selling in which a salesperson begins with a major request and then follows with a series of smaller requests

dostats Russian word that can be roughly translated as "acquiring things with great difficulty"

dual coding coding that occurs when two different sensory traces are available to remember something

durable goods goods that are usually consumed over a long period of time

E

echoic storage storage of auditory information in sensory memory

ecological factors physical characteristics that describe the physical environment and habitat of a particular place

economics study of production and consumption

ego component in psychoanalytic theory that attempts to balance the struggle between the superego and the id

ego-defensive function of attitudes function of attitudes whereby attitudes work as defense mechanisms for consumers

elaboration extent to which a consumer continues processing a message even after an initial understanding is achieved

elaboration likelihood model attitudinal change model that shows attitudes are changed based on differing levels of consumer involvement through either central or peripheral processing

elasticity reflects how sensitive a consumer is to changes in some product characteristic

elimination-by-aspects rule (EBA) noncompensatory decision rule where the consumer begins evaluating options by first looking at the most important attribute and eliminating any option that does not meet a minimum cutoff point for that attribute and where subsequent evaluations proceed in order of importance until only one option remains

emotion a specific psychobiological reaction to a human appraisal

emotional contagion extent to which an emotional display by one person influences the emotional state of a bystander

emotional effect on memory relatively superior recall for information presented with mild affective content compared to similar information presented in an affectively neutral way

emotional expressiveness extent to which a consumer shows outward behavioral signs and otherwise reacts obviously to emotional experiences

emotional intelligence awareness of the emotions experienced in a given situation and the ability to control reactions to these emotions

emotional involvement type of deep personal interest that evokes strongly felt feelings simply from the thoughts or behavior associated with some object or activity

emotional labor effort put forth by service workers who have to overtly manage their own emotional displays as part of the requirements of the job

encoding process by which information is transferred from workbench memory to long-term memory for permanent storage

enculturation way people learn their native culture

enduring involvement ongoing interest in some product or opportunity

episodic memory memory for past events in one's life

epistemic shopping activities oriented toward acquiring knowledge about products

equity theory theory that proposes that people compare their own level of inputs and outcomes to those of another party in an exchange

ethics standards or moral codes of conduct to which a person, group, or organization adheres

ethnic identification degree to which consumers feel a sense of belonging to the culture of their ethnic origins

ethnography qualitative approach to studying consumers that relies on interpretation of artifacts to draw conclusions about consumption

etiquette customary mannerisms consumers use in common social situations

evaluative criteria attributes that consumers consider when reviewing alternative solutions to a problem

even-a-penny-will-help technique ingratiation technique in which a marketing message is sent that suggests that even the smallest donation, such as a penny or a dollar, will help a cause

exchange acting out of the decision to give something up in return for something of greater value

exemplar concept within a schema that is the single best representative of some category; schema for something that really exists

expectancy/disconfirmation theory proposes that consumers use expectations as a benchmark against which performance perceptions are judged and this comparison is a primary basis for satisfaction/dissatisfaction

expectations beliefs of what will happen in some future situation

experiential decision-making perspective assumes consumers often make purchases and reach decisions based on the affect, or feeling, attached to the product or behavior under consideration

experiential shopping recreationally oriented activities designed to provide interest, excitement, relaxation, fun, social interaction, or some other desired feeling

expertise amount of knowledge that a source is perceived to have about a subject

explicit memory memory that develops when a person is exposed to, attends, and tries to remember information

exposure process of bringing some stimulus within proximity of a consumer so that the consumer can sense it with one of the five human senses

extended decision making consumers move diligently through various problem-solving activities in search of the best information that will help them reach a decision

extended family three or more generations of family members

external influences social and cultural aspects of life as a consumer

external search gathering of information from sources external to the consumer such as friends, family, salespeople, advertising, independent research reports, and the Internet

extinction process through which behaviors cease due to lack of reinforcement

F

family household at least two people who are related by blood or marriage who occupy a housing unit

feature performance characteristic of an object

femininity sex role distinction within a group that emphasizes the prioritization of relational variables such as caring, conciliation, and community; CSV opposite of masculinity

figure object that is intended to capture a person's attention; the focal part of any message

figure–ground distinction notion that each message can be separated into the focal point (figure) and the background (ground)

financial switching costs total economic resources that must be spent or invested as a consumer learns how to obtain value from a new product choice

fit how appropriate the elements of a given environment are

five-factor model multiple-trait perspective that proposes that the human personality consists of five traits: agreeableness, extroversion, openness to experience (or creativity), conscientiousness, and neuroticism (or stability)

flow extremely high emotional involvement in which a consumer is engrossed in an activity

foot-in-the-door technique ingratiation technique used in personal selling in which a salesperson begins with a small request and slowly leads up to one major request

foreground music music that becomes the focal point of attention and can have strong effects on a consumer's willingness to approach or avoid an environment

formal group group in which a consumer formally becomes a member

framing a phenomenon in which the meaning of something is influenced (perceived differently) by the information environment

functional quality retail positioning that emphasizes tangible things like a wide selection of goods, low prices, guarantees, and knowledgeable employees

functional theory of attitudes theory of attitudes that suggests that attitudes perform four basic functions

G

geodemographic techniques techniques that combine data on consumer expenditures and socioeconomic variables with geographic information in order to identify commonalities in consumption patterns of households in various regions

Globish a simplified form of English that reduces the vocabulary to around 1500 words and eliminates grammatical complications

glocalization idea that marketing strategy may be global but the implementation of that strategy at the marketing tactics level should be local

golden section the preferred ratio of objects, equal to 1.62 to 1.00

ground background in a message

group influence ways in which group members influence attitudes, behaviors, and opinions of others within the group

guanxi (pronounced "gawn-zeye") Chinese term for a way of doing business in which parties must first invest time and resources in getting to know one another and becoming comfortable with one another before consummating any important deal

guerrilla marketing marketing of a product using unconventional means

H

habitual decision making consumers generally do not seek information at all when a problem is recognized and select a product based on habit

habituation process by which continuous exposure to a stimulus affects the comprehension of, and response to, the stimulus

habitus mental and cognitive structures through which individuals perceive the world based largely on their standing in a social class

haptic perception interpretations created by the way some object feels

hedonic motivation drive to experience something emotionally gratifying

hedonic shopping value worth of an activity because the time spent doing the activity itself is personally gratifying

hedonic value value derived from the immediate gratification that comes from some activity

hierarchical approaches to personality approaches to personality inquiry that assume that personality traits exist at varying levels of abstraction

hierarchy of effects attitude approach that suggests that affect, behavior, and cognitions form in a sequential order

homeostasis state of equilibrium wherein the body naturally reacts in a way so as to maintain a constant, normal bloodstream

homogamy the finding that most marriages comprise people from similar classes

hope a fundamental emotion evoked by positive, anticipatory appraisals that signal uncertainty about a potentially positive outcome

household decision making process by which decisions are made in household units

household life cycle (HLC) segmentation technique that acknowledges that changes in family composition and income alter household demand for products and services

I

iconic storage storage of visual information in sensory memory and the idea that things are stored with a one-to-one representation with reality

id the personality component in psychoanalytic theory that focuses on pleasure-seeking motives and immediate gratification

ideal point combination of product characteristics that provide the most value to an individual consumer or market segment

idiographic perspective approach to personality that focuses on understanding the complexity of each individual consumer

implicit memory memory for things that a person did not try to remember

impulsive consumption consumption acts characterized by spontaneity, a diminished regard for consequences, and a need for self-fulfillment

impulsive shopping spontaneous activities characterized by a diminished regard for consequences, spontaneity, and a desire for immediate self-fulfillment

impulsivity personality trait that represents how sensitive a consumer is to immediate rewards

"I'm working for you!" technique technique used by salespeople to create the perception that they are working as hard as possible to close a sale when they really are not doing so

individual difference variables descriptions of how individual consumers differ according to specific trait patterns of behavior

individual differences characteristic traits of individuals, including personality and lifestyle

individualism extent to which people are expected to take care of themselves and their immediate families

inept set alternatives in the awareness set that are deemed to be unacceptable for further consideration

inert set alternatives in the awareness set about which consumers are indifferent or do not hold strong feelings

informal group group that has no membership or application requirements and that may have no code of conduct

information intensity amount of information available for a consumer to process within a given environment

information overload situation in which consumers are presented with so much information that they cannot assimilate the variety of information presented

information processing perspective learning perspective that focuses on the cognitive processes associated with comprehension and how these precipitate behavioral changes

informational influence ways in which a consumer uses the behaviors and attitudes of reference groups as information for making his or her own decisions

innovativeness degree to which an individual is open to new ideas and tends to be relatively early in adopting new products, services, or experiences

instrumental conditioning type of learning in which a behavioral response can be conditioned through reinforcement—either punishment or rewards associated with undesirable or desirable behavior

intentional learning process by which consumers set out to specifically learn information devoted to a certain subject

interactional fairness captures how fairly a consumer believes he or she was treated when dealing with service personnel in resolving some issue

internal influences things that go on inside of the mind and heart of the consumer

internal search retrieval of knowledge stored in memory about products, services, and experiences

interpretive research approach that seeks to explain the inner meanings and motivations associated with specific consumption experiences

involuntary attention attention that is beyond the conscious control of a consumer

involvement the personal relevance toward, or interest in, a particular product

J

JMD just meaningful difference; smallest amount of change in a stimulus that would influence consumer consumption and choice

JND just noticeable difference; condition in which one stimulus is sufficiently stronger than another so that someone can actually notice that the two are not the same

judgments mental assessments of the presence of attributes and the consequences associated with those attributes

K

knowledge function of attitudes function of attitudes whereby attitudes allow consumers to simplify decision-making processes

L

learning change in behavior resulting from some interaction between a person and a stimulus

left skewed distribution of responses consistent with most respondents choosing responses so the distribution is clustered toward the positive end of the scale

lexicographic rule noncompensatory decision rule where the option selected is thought to perform best on the most important attribute

lifestyles distinctive modes of living, including how people spend their time and money

limited decision making consumers search very little for information and often reach decisions based largely on prior beliefs about products and their attributes

long-term memory repository for all information that a person has encountered

long-term orientation values consistent with Confucian philosophy and a prioritization of future rewards over short-term benefits

loyalty card/program device that keeps track of the amount of purchasing a consumer has had with a given marketer

M

market maven consumer who spreads information about all types of products and services that are available in the marketplace

market orientation organizational culture that embodies the importance of creating value for customers among all employees

market segmentation separation of a market into groups based on the different demand curves associated with each group

marketing multitude of value-producing seller activities that facilitate exchanges between buyers and sellers

marketing concept states a firm should focus on consumer needs as a means of achieving long-term success

marketing ethics societal and professional standards of right and fair practices that are expected of marketing managers as they develop and implement marketing strategies

marketing mix combination of product, pricing, promotion, and distribution strategies used to implement a marketing strategy

marketing myopia a common condition in which a company views itself in a product business rather than in a value, or benefits producing, business. In this way, it is shortsighted.

marketing strategy way a company goes about creating value for customers

marketing tactics ways marketing management is implemented; involves price, promotion, product, and distribution decisions

masculinity role distinction within a group that values assertiveness and control; CSV opposite of femininity

Maslow's hierarchy of needs a theory of human motivation which describes consumers as addressing a finite set of prioritized needs

matchup hypothesis hypothesis that states that a source feature is most effective when it is matched with relevant products

materialism extent to which material goods have importance in a consumer's life

meaning transference process through which cultural meaning is transferred to a product and onto the consumer

meaningful encoding coding that occurs when information from long-term memory is placed on the workbench and attached to the information on the workbench in a way that the information can be recalled and used later

memory psychological process by which knowledge is recorded

memory trace mental path by which some thought becomes active

mental budgeting memory accounting for recent spending

mere association effect the transfer of meaning between objects that are similar only by accidental association

mere exposure effect that which leads consumers to prefer a stimulus to which they've previously been exposed

message congruity extent to which a message is internally consistent and fits surrounding information

message effects how the appeal of a message and its construction affect persuasiveness

metaphor in a consumer context, an ad claim that is not literally true but figuratively communicates a message

metric equivalence statistical tests used to validate the way people use numbers to represent quantities across cultures

microculture a group of people who share similar values and tastes that are subsumed within a larger culture

modeling process of imitating others' behavior; a form of observational learning

moderating variable variable that changes the nature of the relationship between two other variables

mood transient and general affective state

mood-congruent judgments evaluations in which the value of a target is influenced in a consistent way by one's mood

mood-congruent recall consumers will remember information better when the mood they are currently in matches the mood they were in when originally exposed to the information

moral beliefs beliefs about the perceived ethicality or morality of behaviors

moral equity beliefs regarding an act's fairness or justness

morals personal standards and beliefs used to guide individual action

motivational research era era in consumer research that focused heavily on psychoanalytic approaches

motivations inner reasons or driving forces behind human actions that drive consumers to address real needs

multiattribute attitude model a model that combines a number of pieces of information about belief and evaluations of attributes of an object

multiple store theory of memory theory that explains memory as utilizing three different storage areas within the human brain: sensory, workbench, and long-term

multiple-trait approach approach in trait research wherein the focus remains on combinations of traits

N

need for cognition refers to the degree to which consumers enjoy engaging in effortful cognitive information processing

negative disconfirmation according to the expectancy/disconfirmation approach, a perceived state wherein performance perceptions fall short of expectations

negative public publicity action that occurs when negative WOM spreads on a relatively large scale, possibly even involving media coverage

negative reinforcement removal of harmful stimuli as a way of encouraging behavior

negative word-of-mouth (negative WOM) action that takes place when consumers pass on negative information about a company from one to another

negligence situation whereby an injured consumer attempts to show that a firm could foresee a potential injury might occur and then decided not to act on that knowledge

netnography a branch of ethnography that studies the behavior of online cultures and communities

neuroscience the study of the central nervous system including the brain

niche marketing plan wherein a firm specializes in serving one market segment with particularly unique demand characteristics

nodes concepts found in an associative network

nomothetic perspective variable-centered approach to personality that focuses on particular traits that exist across a number of people

noncompensatory rule decision rule in which strict guidelines are set prior to selection and any option that does not meet the guidelines is eliminated from consideration

nondurable goods goods that are usually consumed quickly

nonlinear effect a plot of an effect that does not make a straight line

nonverbal communication information passed through some nonverbal act

nostalgia a yearning to relive the past that can produce lingering emotions

nuclear family a mother, a father, and a set of siblings

O

olfactory refers to humans' physical and psychological processing of smells

one-to-one marketing plan wherein a different product is offered for each individual customer so that each customer is treated as a segment of one

ongoing search search effort that is not necessarily focused on an upcoming purchase or decision but rather on staying up to date on the topic

opinion leader consumer who has a great deal of influence on the behavior of others relating to product adoption and purchase

orientation reflex natural reflex that occurs as a response to something threatening

outshopping shopping in a city or town to which consumers must travel rather than in their own hometowns

P

PAD pleasure–arousal–dominance; a self-report measure that asks respondents to rate feelings using semantic differential items

packrats consumers possessing high levels of a lifestyle trait leading to a strong tendency toward retaining consumption-related possessions

paths representations of the association between nodes in an associative network

peer pressure extent to which group members feel pressure to behave in accordance with group expectations

perceived risk perception of the negative consequences that are likely to result from a course of action and the uncertainty of which course of action is best to take

perception consumer's awareness and interpretation of reality

perceptual attributes attributes that are visually apparent and easily recognizable

perceptual map tool used to depict graphically the positioning of competing products

peripheral cues nonproduct-related information presented in a message

peripheral route to persuasion path to persuasion found in ELM where the consumer has low involvement, motivation, and/or ability to process a message

personal elaboration process by which people imagine themselves somehow associating with a stimulus that is being processed

personal shopping value (PSV) overall subjective worth of a shopping activity considering all associated costs and benefits

personality totality of thoughts, emotions, intentions, and behaviors that a person exhibits consistently as he or she adapts to the environment

persuasion attempt to change attitudes

phenomenology qualitative approach to studying consumers that relies on interpretation of the lived experience associated with some aspect of consumption

physical characteristics tangible elements or the parts of a message that can be sensed

planned obsolescence act of planning the premature discontinuance of product models that perform adequately

pleasure principle principle found in psychoanalytic theory that describes the factor that motivates pleasure-seeking behavior within the id

positive disconfirmation according to the expectancy/disconfirmation approach, a perceived state wherein performance perceptions exceed expectations

positive reinforcers reinforcers that take the form of a reward

positive WOM action that occurs when consumers spread information from one to another about positive consumption experiences with companies

power distance extent to which authority and privileges are divided among different groups within society and the extent to which these facts of life are accepted by the people within the society

preattentive effects learning that occurs without attention

prepurchase search search effort aimed at finding information to solve an immediate problem

price information that signals the amount of potential value contained in a product

primacy effect occurs when the information placed early in a message has the most impact

primary group group that includes members who have frequent, direct contact with one another

priming cognitive process in which context or environment activates concepts and frames thoughts and therefore both value and meaning

PRIZM popular geodemographic technique that stands for Potential Ratings Index by ZIP Market

problem gambling obsession over the thought of gambling and the loss of control over gambling behavior and its consequences

procedural justice an equity-based cognition representing the extent that consumers believe the processes involved in processing a transaction, performing a service, or handling any complaints are fair

procedural switching costs lost time and extended effort spent in learning ways of using some product offering

product potentially valuable bundle of benefits

product categories mental representations of stored knowledge about groups of products

product contamination refers to the diminished positive feelings someone has about a product because another consumer has handled the product

product differentiation marketplace condition in which consumers do not view all competing products as identical to one another

product enthusiasts consumers with very high involvement in some product category

product involvement the personal relevance of a particular product category

product placements products that have been placed conspicuously in movies, television shows, music, or video games

product positioning way a product is perceived by a consumer

production orientation approach where innovation is geared primarily toward making the production process as efficient and economic as possible

products liability extent to which businesses are held responsible for product-related injuries

prospect theory theory that suggests that a decision, or argument, can be framed in different ways and that the framing affects risk assessments consumers make

prototype schema that is the best representative of some category but that is not represented by an existing entity; conglomeration of the most associated characteristics of a category

psychoanalytic approach to personality approach to personality research, advocated by Sigmund Freud, that suggests personality results from a struggle between inner motives and societal pressures to follow rules and expectations

psychobiological a response involving both psychological and physical human responses

psychographics quantitative investigation of consumer lifestyles

psychology study of human reactions to their environment, including behavior and mental processes

puffery practice of making exaggerated claims about a product and its superiority

punishers stimuli that decrease the likelihood that a behavior will persist

punitive damages damages that are sought to punish a company for behavior associated with an injury

purchasing power parity (PPP) total size of the consumer market in each country in terms of total buying power

Q

qualitative research tools means for gathering data in a relatively unstructured way, including case analysis, clinical interviews, and focus group interviews

quality perceived overall goodness or badness of some product

quantitative research approach that addresses questions about consumer behavior using numerical measurement and analysis tools

quartet of institutions four groups responsible for communicating the CSVs through both formal and informal processes from one generation to another: family, school, church, and media

R

rancorous revenge is when a consumer yells, insults, and makes a public scene in an effort to harm the business in response to an unsatisfactory experience

rational decision-making perspective assumes consumers diligently gather information about purchases, carefully compare various brands of products on salient attributes, and make informed decisions regarding what brand to buy

reality principle the principle in psychoanalytic theory under which the ego attempts to satisfy the id within societal constraints

recency effect occurs when the information placed late in a message has the most impact

reference group individuals who have significant relevance for a consumer and who have an impact on the consumer's evaluations, aspirations, and behavior

regulatory focus theory puts forward the notion that consumers orient their behavior either through a prevention or promotion focus.

relational switching cost emotional and psychological consequences of changing from one brand/retailer/service provider to another

relationship marketing activities based on the belief that the firm's performance is enhanced through repeat business

relationship quality degree of connectedness between a consumer and a retailer, brand, or service provider

relativism beliefs about the social acceptability of an act in a culture

renquing the idea that favors given to another are reciprocal and must be returned

repetition simple mechanism in which a thought is kept alive in short-term memory by mentally repeating the thought

researcher dependent subjective data that requires a researcher to interpret the meaning

resource-advantage theory theory that explains why companies succeed or fail; the firm goes about obtaining resources from consumers in return for the value the resources create

response generation reconstruction of memory traces into a formed recollection of information

retail personality way a retail store is defined in the mind of a shopper based on the combination of functional and affective qualities

retaliatory revenge consumer becomes violent with employees and/or tries to vandalize a business in response to an unsatisfactory experience

retrieval process by which information is transferred back into workbench memory for additional processing when needed

reversal theory tries to explain how environmental elements can lead to near 180-degree changes in shopping orientation

role conflict a situation involving conflicting expectations based on cultural role expectations

role expectations the specific expectations that are associated with each type of person within a culture or society

rumination unintentional but recurrent memories of long-ago events that are spontaneously (not evoked by the environment) triggered

S

sales orientation practice of using sales techniques that are aimed at satisfying the salesperson's own needs and motives for short-term sales success

sandwich generation consumers who must take care of both their own children and their aging parents

satisficing practice of using decision-making shortcuts to arrive at satisfactory, rather than optimal, decisions

schema cognitive representation of a phenomenon that provides meaning to that entity

schema-based affect emotions that become stored as part of the meaning for a category (a schema)

script schema representing an event

search regret negative emotions that come from failed search processes

seasonality regularly occurring conditions that vary with the time of year

secondary group group to which a consumer belongs whose contact is less frequent than that found in a primary group

selective attention process of paying attention to only certain stimuli

selective distortion process by which consumers interpret information in ways that are biased by their previously held beliefs

selective exposure process of screening out certain stimuli and purposely exposing oneself to other stimuli

self-concept totality of thoughts and feelings that an individual has about himself or herself

self-congruency theory theory that proposes that much of consumer behavior can be explained by the congruence of a consumer's self-concept with the image of typical users of a focal product

self-conscious emotions specific emotions that result from some evaluation or reflection of one's own behavior, including pride, shame, guilt, and embarrassment

self-esteem positivity of the self-concept that one holds

self-improvement motivation motivation aimed at changing the current state to a level that is more ideal, not at simply maintaining the current state

self-monitoring tendency for consumers to observe and control behavior in ways that agree with social cues and influence

self-perception theory theory that states that consumers are motivated to act in accordance with their attitudes and behaviors

semantic coding type of coding wherein stimuli are converted to meaning that can be expressed verbally

semiotics study of symbols and their meanings

sensation consumer's immediate response to a stimulus

sensory memory area in memory where a consumer stores things exposed to one of the five senses

separated self-schema self-conceptualization of the extent to which a consumer perceives himself or herself as distinct and separate from others

serial position effect occurs when the placement of information in a message impacts recall of the information

service quality overall goodness or badness of a service experience, which is often measured by SERVQUAL

servicescape physical environment in which consumer services are performed

SERVQUAL way of measuring service quality that captures consumers' disconfirmation of service expectations

sex role orientation (SRO) family's set of beliefs regarding the ways in which household decisions are reached

sex roles societal expectations for men and women among members of a cultural group

shaping process through which a desired behavior is altered over time, in small increments

share of wallet customer share

shopping involvement personal relevance of shopping activities

shopping set of value-producing consumer activities that directly increase the likelihood that something will be purchased

signal attribute that consumer uses to infer something about another attribute

signal theory explains ways in which communications convey meaning beyond the explicit or obvious interpretation

single-trait approach approach in trait research wherein the focus is on one particular trait

situational influences things unique to a time or place that can affect consumer decision making and the value received from consumption

situational involvement temporary interest in some imminent purchase situation

social buying consumer buying behavior that takes place on social networking sites

social class a culturally defined group to which a consumer belongs based on resources like prestige, income, occupation, and education

social comparison a naturally occurring mental personal comparison of the self with a target individual within the environment

social couponing type of buying where consumers receive a coupon, or deal, by joining a special social networking website

social environment elements that specifically deal with the way other people influence consumer decision making and value

social judgment theory theory that proposes that consumers compare incoming information to their existing attitudes about a particular object or issue and that attitude change depends upon how consistent the information is with the initial attitude

social media media through which communication occurs

social networking website website that facilitates online social networking

social networks consumers connecting with one another based on common interests, associations, or goals

social power ability of an individual or a group to alter the actions of others

social psychology study that focuses on the thoughts, feelings, and behaviors that people have as they interact with other people

social schema cognitive representation that gives a specific type of person meaning

social stereotype another word for social schema

social stratification the division of society into classes that have unequal access to scarce and valuable resources

socialization learning through observation of and the active processing of information about lived, everyday experience

societal marketing concept marketing concept that states that marketers should consider not only the wants and needs of consumers but also the needs of society

sociology the study of groups of people within a society, with relevance for consumer behavior because a great deal of consumption takes place within group settings or is affected by group behavior

source attractiveness the degree to which a source's physical appearance matches a prototype for beauty and elicits a favorable or desirous response

source effects characteristics of a source that influence the persuasiveness of a message

spreading activation way cognitive activation spreads from one concept (or node) to another

stakeholder marketing an orientation in which firms recognize that more than just the buyer and seller are involved in the marketing process and a host of primary and secondary entities affect and are affected by the value creation process

state-oriented consumers with a low capacity to self-regulate their behavior

status symbols products or objects that are used to signal one's place in society

stealth marketing guerrilla marketing tactic in which consumers do not realize that they are being targeted for a marketing message

stigmatization a situation in which consumers are marked in some way that indicates their place in society

strategy a planned way of doing something to accomplish some goal

strict liability legal action against a firm whereby a consumer demonstrates in court that an injury occurred and that the product associated with the injury was faulty in some way

subliminal persuasion behavior change induced by subliminal processing

subliminal processing way that the human brain deals with very low-strength stimuli, so low that the person has no conscious awareness

superego component in psychoanalytic theory that works against the id by motivating behavior that matches the expectations and norms of society

support arguments thoughts that further support a message

surrogate consumer consumer who is hired by another to provide input into a purchase decision

susceptibility to interpersonal influence individual difference variable that assesses a consumer's need to enhance the image others hold of him or her by acquiring and using products, conforming to the expectations of others, and learning about products by observing others

switching times when a consumer chooses a competing choice, rather than the previously purchased choice, on the next purchase occasion

switching costs costs associated with changing from one choice (brand/retailer/service provider) to another

symbolic interactionism perspective that proposes that consumers live in a symbolic environment and interpret the myriad of symbols around them, and that members of a society agree on the meanings of symbols

T

tag small piece of coded information that helps with the retrieval of knowledge

target market identified segment or segments of a market that a company serves

teleological evaluations consumers' assessment of the goodness or badness of the consequences of actions

temporal factors situational characteristics related to time

theory of planned action attitudinal measurement approach that expands upon the behavioral intentions model by including a perceived control component

third-party endorsement one form of publicity in which an ostensibly objective outsider (neither the customer nor the business) provides publicly available purchase recommendations or evaluations

time pressure urgency to act based on some real or self-imposed deadline

top-line performance a business term referring to sales growth (sales being at the top of an earnings statement)

total value concept business practice wherein companies operate with the understanding that products provide value in multiple ways

touchpoints direct contacts between the firm and a customer

tradition customs and accepted ways of everyday behavior in a given culture

trait distinguishable characteristic that describes one's tendency to act in a relatively consistent manner

trait approach to personality approaches in personality research that focus on specific consumer traits as motivators of various consumer behaviors

translational equivalence two phrases share the same precise meaning in two different cultures

trustworthiness how honest and unbiased the source is perceived to be

U

uncertainty avoidance extent to which a culture is uncomfortable with things that are ambiguous or unknown

unconditioned response response that occurs naturally as a result of exposure to an unconditioned stimulus

unconditioned stimulus stimulus with which a behavioral response is already associated

underlying attributes attributes that are not readily apparent and can be learned only through experience or contact with the product

undifferentiated marketing plan wherein the same basic product is offered to all customers

unintentional learning learning that occurs when behavior is modified through a consumer-stimulus interaction without any effortful allocation of cognitive processing capacity toward that stimulus

universal set total collection of all possible solutions to a consumer problem

unplanned shopping shopping activity that shares some, but not all, characteristics of truly impulsive consumer behavior; being characterized by situational memory, a utilitarian orientation, and feelings of spontaneity

utilitarian function of attitudes function of attitudes in which consumers use attitudes as ways to maximize rewards and minimize punishment

utilitarian influence ways in which a consumer conforms to group expectations in order to receive a reward or avoid punishment

utilitarian motivation drive to acquire products that can be used to accomplish something

utilitarian shopping value worth obtained because some shopping task or job is completed successfully

utilitarian value value derived from a product that helps the consumer with some task

V

VALS popular psychographic method in consumer research that divides consumers into groups based on resources and CB motivations

value a personal assessment of the net worth obtained from an activity

value co-creation the realization that a consumer is necessary and must play a part in order to produce value

value consciousness the extent to which consumers tend to maximize what they receive from a transaction as compared to what they give

value-expressive function of attitudes function of attitudes whereby attitudes allow consumers to express their core values, self-concept, and beliefs to others

value-expressive influence ways in which a consumer internalizes a group's values or the extent to which consumers join groups in order to express their own closely held values and beliefs

verbal communication transfer of information through either the literal spoken or written word

viral marketing marketing method that uses online technologies to facilitate WOM by having consumers spread messages through their online conversations

visceral responses certain feeling states that are tied to physical reactions/behavior in a very direct way

W

want way a consumer goes about addressing a recognized need

Weber's Law law that states that a consumer's ability to detect differences between two levels of a stimulus decreases as the intensity of the initial stimulus increases

word-of-mouth (WOM) information about products, services, and experiences that is transmitted from consumer to consumer

workbench memory storage area in the memory system where information is stored while it is being processed and encoded for later recall

world teen culture speculation that teenagers around the world are more similar to each other than to people from other generations in the same culture

Chinglish, 182, 184
Choice, 240–241
Christianity, 199–200
Chunk, 77
Chunking, 76, 77–78
Circadian cycle, 220
Cirque de Soleil, 36
Class. *See* **Social class**
Classical conditioning, 61
Clayton Act, 10, 322
Clemens, Roger, 294
Clowns, 54
Clutter, 52
CNET, 297
Coca-Cola, 112, 196
Code of ethics, American Marketing Association, 317
Coercive power, 151
Cognition
defined, 26
emotion and, 97–101
need for, 108
Cognitive appraisal theory, 90–91
Cognitive dissonance, 283–284
Cognitive interference, 77
Cognitive organization, 50–51
Cognitive perspective. *See* **Information processing perspective**
Cognitive psychology, 7
Cognitive structuring, 195
Cohort, 196
Cohort effect, 115
Collaborative analytics, 43–44
Collectivism, 174
Collegiate sports, 212–213
Color, 67, 230–232
Columbia Records, 160
Commodities, 35
Communication
basic model, 136
changes in, 20, 182
computer-mediated environment, 136–137
culture and, 171, 181, 182–187
elements of, 182–187
interactive, 136–137
nonverbal, 184–187
verbal, 182–183
Companhia Brasileira de Distribuicao Grupo Pao de Acucar (GPA), 43
Companions, shopping, 221, 233
Company response to negative publicity, 294–295, 329–330
Compensatory damages, 327
Compensatory model, 127
Compensatory rules, 264
Competition, consumer orientation and, 9–10
Competitive intensity, 298
Competitiveness, 108–109
Competitive shopping, 312
Complainers, 290–291
Complaining behavior, 290–293
addressing, 292
consequences, 291–292
defined, 290

emotion and, 291
illegitimate, 312–313
incidence of, 290, 292
industries commonly subject to, 292
Comprehension
cognitive and affective aspects, 66
defined, 49, 65
environmental characteristics, 73–74
influences on, 65–74
internal factors, 66
marketing role, 60
message characteristics, 67–70
message receiver characteristics, 70–73
signal theory, 66
Compulsive buying, 314
Compulsive consumer behavior, 100, 228
Compulsive consumption, 314–315
Compulsive shopping, 314–315
Computer viruses, 311
Conditioned response, 61
Conditioned stimulus, 61
Confirmatory bias, 281
Conformity, 149–150
Congruity, 229
Conjoint analysis, 264
Conjunctive rule, 265
Connected self-schema, 156–157
Consideration set, 248–249
Consistency principle, 134
Conspicuous consumption, 109
Consumer (customer) orientation, 9–10
See also **Consumer relationships; Customer orientation**
Consumer affect, 92
Consumer affluence, 206
Consumer behavior
abusive, 312
changing nature of, 18–21
children's role in, 166
complaining behavior, 290–293
decision making and, 14–16
defined, 5
demographic effects, 206–208
effects of, 3–4
as field of study, 6–8, 16–18
as human behavior, 5–6
marketing strategy and, 11–14, 37–38
perceptual process, 52–54
personality and, 103–106
personality traits in, 106–111
process of, 5, 240
relationship marketing and, 10–11
self-concept and, 116–118
significance of, 11–16
society and, 14
See also **Consumer misbehavior**

Consumer behavior as a field of study, 6–8, 16–18
Consumer Bill of Rights, 318, 326
Consumer budgeting, 234–235
Consumer culture
defined, 170
popular culture, 171–172
role expectations, 172
See also **Culture**
Consumer dissatisfaction, 278
Consumer doppelganger effect, 162
Consumer ethnocentrism, 41–42, 179
Consumer fraud, 311–312
Consumer identity, 118–119
Consumer inertia, 300
Consumer Introspection Theory, 106
Consumer involvement, 87–89
Consumerism, 316, 318
Consumer loyalty, 299–303
Consumer misbehavior, 307–316
abusive behavior, 312
computer-mediated, 311–312
consequences, 308
defined, 307
driving misbehavior, 313–314
ethics and, 308–309
fraud, 311–312
identity theft, 311–312
illegitimate complaining, 312–313
motivations of, 309–310
problem behavior vs., 310, 314–316
product misuse, 313–314
shoplifting, 310–311
value and, 308
Consumer problem behavior, 310, 314–316
binge drinking, 315
compulsive consumption, 314–315
drug abuse, 316
eating disorders, 315
problem gambling, 315–316
Consumer Product Safety Commission, 326
Consumer refuse, 286–287
Consumer relationships, 289–304
company responses, 294–295
complaining behavior, 290–293
consumer orientation, 9–10
loyalty, 299–303
outcomes of consumption, 289–290
relationship quality, 24–25, 303–304
switching behavior, 297–299
value and, 302–303
word-of-mouth, 293–297
Consumer Reports, 297

Consumers
attitudes, 121–145
treatment of, 8–11
Consumer satisfaction, 276–278
attribution theory, 283
cognitive dissonance, 283–284
consumer's role in, 278
defining, 277–278
desires and, 282
equity theory, 282–283
expectancy theory, 279–282
measurement issues, 284–285
switching and, 298–299
Consumer search behavior, 247–248
See also **External search**
Consumer self-regulation, 226–228
Consumer socialization, 166
Consumer Value Framework (CVF)
components, 24–28
defined, 24
postconsumption process, 302
Consumer vulnerability, 320
Consumption
cocreation of, 278
defined, 6
external influences, 26–27
internal influences, 26
process of, 5–6, 274
situational influences, 27
Consumption frequency, 274
Contractualism, 308
Contrast, 52, 59
Contrast effects, 135
Control, 283
Conversion, of products, 286
Core societal values (CSV), 173–177
Corporate associations, 130
Corporate social responsibility, 321
Corporate strategy, 31
Cosmetic surgery, 117–118
Costs, 5
Council of Fashion Designers of America (CFDA), 117
Counterarguments, 70
Country music, 198
Country of origin, 41–42
Credibility, 70, 139–140, 152
Credit Card Accountability, Responsibility, and Disclosure Act, 322
Credit cards, 234–235, 274
Creeps, the, 54
Critical incident, 290
CRM. *See* **Customer Relationship Management (CRM)**
Crowding, 232–233
CSV scoreboard, 176–177
See also **Core societal values (CSV)**
Cultural distance, 177–178
Cultural norms, 171
Cultural sanctions, 171
Cultural values. *See* **Core societal values (CSV)**

consumer search, 250
decision-making aids, 261
disclosure of information, 116
gaming, 144–145
marketing to children, 324
reference groups, 147
shopping, 20, 225, 233–234
social media, 154–157
viral marketing, 160
word-of-mouth and, 158–159, 296
Interpretive research, 16–18, 19
Introspections, 106
Involuntary attention, 59
Involvement
attention and, 59–60
consumer, 87–89
decision making and, 252
emotional, 89, 95–96
enduring, 89
expectations affected by, 280
memory and, 76
message reception, 71
motivation and, 87–89
product, 88
shopping, 89
situational, 89
types, 88–89
iPads, 246
iPhones, 246
Islam, 200, 207

J

Japan, 174, 203, 204
JMD (just meaningful difference), 56
JND (just noticeable difference), 55, 262
Joneses, The (film), 160
Judaism, 200
Judgments, 261–262

K

Kant, Immanuel, 309
Kardashian sisters, 45
Kelley, David, 40
Kennedy, John F., 318
KFC, 79
KGOY (Kids Growing Older, Younger), 166, 198
KISS Army, 148
Kit plane industry, 327
Kleptomania, 310
Knauer, Tracy, 269
Knowledge
associative networks, 80
declarative, 80
prior, 70–71
Knowledge function of attitudes, 123
Kosher diet, 200
Kotler, Philip, 319
Kuang, Cliff, 40

L

Labeling. *See* Food labeling
Ladik, Daniel, 108
Laptops, 268–269
Las Vegas, 225–226
Latitudes of acceptance, 135
Latitudes of rejection, 135
Laughter, 97
See also Humor
Learning
behaviorist approach, 60
defined, 47
information processing approach, 60–61
intentional, 60
unintentional, 53, 56, 60–63
Left skewed, 285
Legacy Recordings, 160
Legislation, on commerce and consumer safety, 322
Legitimate power, 150
Legoux, Renaud, 108
Levitt, Theodore, 12, 318
Lexicographic rule, 265, 266
Libido, 104
Life expectancy, 207
Lifestyles, 113–114
Likeability, of sources, 140
Limited decision making, 244
Live Earth, 324
Livingsocial, 156
Locus, 283
Logos, 74
Long-term memory, 78–79
Long-term orientation, 176
Looking-glass self, 117
L'Oreal, 69
Loss leaders, 43
Low-involvement hierarchy, 124–125
Low-involvement processing, 134
Loyalty cards/programs, 300–301
Lucky Brand, 68
Lululemon, 293
Luxuries, group influence on, 154

M

Male identity, 83
Manipulative sales tactics, 324–326
Mannerisms, 185
Manners, 186–187
Marketing
changing nature of, 18
to children, 323–324
consumer behavior and, 7–8
consumer relationships, 10–11, 303
decision making and, 261
defined, 7
generational influence, 198
Internet, 160
public criticism of, 323–327

regulation of, 322
subliminal, 53–54
word-of-mouth, 160–161
Marketing concept, 316, 318–320
Marketing ethics, 316–320
consumerism, 316, 318
consumer vulnerability, 320
defined, 316
employee behavior, 320
marketing concept, 318–320
prescriptions for, 322
product harmfulness, 320
public criticism and, 323–327
societal marketing concept, 321
Marketing mix, 33, 319–320
Marketing myopia, 30
Marketing strategy
consumer behavior, 11–14, 37–38
defined, 30
value, 30–33
Marketing tactics, 31
Market mavens, 161
Market orientation, 10
Markets
perceptual maps, 35–37
segmentation, 33–35
Market segmentation, 33–35, 194–195
Marriage
cultural factors, 169, 186
same-sex, 163
social class and, 203
Masculinity, 174
Maslow's hierarchy of needs, 86–87
Matchup hypothesis, 140
Materialism, 107
Maximizing, 108
McDonald's, 11, 170, 198, 326
Meaningful encoding, 76, 77
Meaningfulness, of sources, 140
Meaning transference, 275–276
Media
cultural influence of, 180–181
gender segmentation, 194–195
negative publicity, 295
Memory
aids to, 76–79
capacity, 76
defined, 74
duration, 75, 76
episodic, 82
implicit vs. explicit, 56–59
involvement, 76
long-term, 78–79
multiple store theory, 74–75
retrieval, 78
sensory, 74
workbench, 75–76
Memory trace, 78
Mental budgeting, 235
Merchandising, 232
Mere association effect, 58
Mere exposure effect, 56–58

Message appeal, 137–138
Message congruity, 69
Message construction, 138–139
Message effects, 136–139
Message reception, 70–73
brain dominance, 72–73
expectations, 72
familiarity/habituation, 71–72
intelligence/ability, 71
involvement, 71
physical limits, 72
prior knowledge, 70–71
Messages
appeals of, 137–138
congruity, 69
construction of, 138–139
environmental characteristics, 73–74
figure and ground, 69
framing, 73–74
information intensity, 73
physical characteristics, 67–68
reception of, 70–73
simplicity-complexity, 68–69
sources of, 69–70, 139–140
timing, 74
Metaphor, 73
Metric equivalence, 183
Microcultures, 191–215
age-based, 195–196
cultural hierarchy, 191–192
defined, 191
demographic analysis, 204–205
ethnic, 200–202
generational, 196–198
income and social class, 202–203
international, 203–204
regional, 193–194
religious, 198–200
role expectations, 192
sex roles, 194–195
street, 203, 204
trends affecting consumer behavior, 206–208
U.S., 193–203
values, 193
Microsoft, 11
Millennials, 197–198, 214–215
Mobile devices, 14, 15, 154, 268–269
See also Cell phones; Smartphones
Mobile gaming, 144–145
Modeling, 181
Moderating variables, 88
Mood, 91, 236, 258
Mood-congruent judgments, 91
Mood-congruent recall, 97–98
Moral beliefs, 308–309
Moral equity, 308
Morals, 320
Motivation, and decision making, 241
Motivational research era, 105
Motivations
classifications of, 86–87

Tailgating, 275
Target, 18, 43
Target market, 33
Tattoos, 118, 275
Team names, 264
Technology
  communication devices,
    268–269
  consumer behavior, 19–20
  consumer search aids,
    250–251
  televisions, 143–144
Teen culture, 196
Teleological evaluations, 309
Telephone service, 298–299
Televisions, 143–144
Temporal factors, 219
Tesco, 11
Text messaging, 158, 314
  See also Sexting
Theory of planned action, 129
Theory of reasoned action.
    See **Behavioral intentions
    model**
Third-party endorsements,
    296–297
Thrill-seeking, 309
Ticket distribution, 320
Ticketmaster, 320
Time
  advertising and, 220
  cultural factors, 184–185
  for decision making, 252
  situational influences,
    219–220
Time of day, 220
Time of year, 219
Time pressure, 219
Timing, 74
TinyCo, 144–145
Top-line performance, 277
Total value concept,
    32–33, 319
Touchpoints, 10, 11
Toyota, 11, 13
Trading, 286
Tradition, 173
Trait approach to personality,
    105–106, 110
Trait impulsivity, 109
Traits
  consumer research on,
    106–111
  defined, 105
  five-factor model, 109–110
  nomothetic vs. idiographic
    approaches, 105–106
  personality research based
    on, 105–106, 110
  single- vs. multiple-trait
    approaches, 106

Trait superstition, 109
Trait vanity, 109
Translation, 182–183
Translational equivalence,
    182–183
Trashing, 286
Travel industry, 328–329
TripAdvisor, 296
Trustworthiness, 70, 140
Truth in Lending Act, 322
Tutone, Tommie, 77
Twitter, 20, 155, 161, 199, 294
Tylenol, 295

U

Unanticipated needs, 247
Uncertainty avoidance,
    175–176, 179
Unconditioned response, 61
Unconditioned stimulus, 61
Underlying attributes, 260
Undifferentiated marketing, 13
Unilever, 117
Unintentional learning
  classical conditioning, 61
  defined, 60
  instrumental conditioning,
    61–62
United Kingdom, 208
United States. *See* **CANZUS**
  demographic analysis, 205
  ethnic/racial groups,
    200–202
  microcultures, 193–203
  religion, 199–200
  social class, 195, 202–203
Unit relations, 134
Universal set, 248
University sports, 212–213
Unplanned shopping, 225–226
Unrealistic expectations, 323
Updyke, Harvey, 331
U.S. Census Bureau, 162, 205
U.S. Digital Millennium Copy-
    right Act, 311
U.S. Food and Drug Adminis-
    tration (FDA), 68–69, 71,
    244, 259, 322
*U.S. News and World
    Report*, 296
**Utilitarian function of at-
    titudes**, 122–123
Utilitarian influence, 152
Utilitarian motivation, 87,
    88, 241
Utilitarian shopping value, 223
Utilitarian value, 29, 240–241,
    257, 302

V

VALS, 114–115
Value, 23–39
  alternative evaluation,
    257–258
  co-creation of, 33
  consumer behavior and, 3–5
  consumer misbehavior, 308
  consumer relationships,
    302–303
  consumer satisfaction and,
    276–278
  Consumer Value Frame-
    work, 24–28
  consumption and, 273
  culture and, 170–178
  decision making and,
    240–241
  defined, 28
  equation for, 28–29
  hedonic, 29–30
  lifetime, 38–39
  marketing and, 7
  meaning transference,
    275–276
  microcultures and, 193
  online shopping, 20
  reference groups and,
    152–153
  of search effort, 252
  shopping activities
    and, 223
  situations and, 217–218
  social media and social
    networking, 155
  types, 29–30
  utilitarian, 29
  word-of-mouth and, 158
Value co-creation, 33
Value consciousness, 106–107
**Value-expressive function of
    attitudes**, 123
Value-expressive influence,
    152–153
Vegetables, 261
Veils, 200
Verbal communication,
    182–183
Verizon, 30
Vespa, 195
Vicary experiment, 53–54
Violence, in advertising, 138
Viral marketing, 160
Virtual products, 12
Viruses, computer, 311
Visceral responses, 90
Visual search, 251
Von Furstenberg, Diane, 117

W

Wade, Dwayne, 140
Wall Street Reform and Con-
    sumer Protection Act, 322
Walmart, 13, 28, 277,
    299, 309
Wants, 5, 247, 321
Weber's Law, 55
Website construction, 250
Weddings, 186
Wendy's, 326
Wheeler Lea Act, 322, 323
Window shopping, 223
Wine Spectator, 297
Word-of-mouth (WOM),
    157–162
  buzz marketing, 160
  consumer characteristics,
    300
  defined, 157
  diffusion process, 161–162
  digital age, 158–159,
    293–294
  effects of, 295–296
  informational influence,
    152
  negative, 158–159,
    293–297
  opinion leaders, 161
  organic vs. amplified, 158
  positive vs. negative,
    158–159, 293
  stealth marketing, 160
  and value, 158
Word of Mouth Marketing
    Association (WOMMA),
    158, 160–161, 326
Workbench memory, 75–76
World teen culture, 196

Y

Yelp.com, 158
Yipit, 156
YouTube, 155, 293

Z

Zeitgeist, 71
Zynga, 12, 144–145

CHAPTER 1 **PREP** *CARD*
WHAT IS CB, AND WHY SHOULD I CARE?

Learning Outcomes

With the growth in eReader usage among students, this edition of *CB* features a numbering system for major headings that we recommend you use instead of page numbers when creating assignments.

1-1   Understand the meaning of *consumption* and *consumer behavior*.

1-2   Describe how competitive marketing environments lead to better outcomes for consumers.

1-3   Explain the role of consumer behavior in business and society.

1-4   Be familiar with basic approaches to studying consumer behavior.

1-5   Appreciate how dynamic the field of consumer behavior continues to be.

Chapter 1 Outline

Multimedia

PPT—THE HIGHLIGHTS

- Slide 6 Exhibit 1.1 The Basic Consumption Process
- Slide 12 Some Terminology
- Slide 15 Why Study CB?
- Slide 20 Exhibit 1.4 Different Ways of Doing Business
- Slide 23 CB and Personal Growth

VIDEOS ON DVD AND COURSEMATE

CB Scenario Video

Run time: 0:38 minutes

 At an auction, goods are offered up for sale and sold to the buyer offering the highest bid. The auctioneer calls out the item and the latest bid. The bidders must decide whether or not they want to bid on a particular object. The amount buyers bid for an object depends on how much value they perceive is associated with the object. Often goods offered up for auction have no intrinsic worth but may hold special meaning or value for the buyer.

CHAPTER VIDEO SUMMARY

Travelocity

Run time: 16:09 minutes

 Faced with the challenges of plunging sales, Travelocity, the pioneer in Internet travel business, decided to spruce up its marketing strategies. It introduced the concept of "Travelocity Guarantee," which ensured that promises made to customers would be fulfilled at all costs. The interest of the customer was strategically put before short-term organizational inconveniences. This, coupled with Travelocity's emphasis on relevance marketing and an intelligent exploitation of the media, revived its sales once again. Apart from successfully designing user experience through extensive usability analysis, a big part of Travelocity's success lies in humanizing the brand and winning the trust of its customers.

Ask your students:

1. What impact did "Travelocity Guarantee" have on the purchasing decisions of consumers?

2. How did Travelocity seek to improve the traveling experiences of tourists opting for its services?

3. Why is partnering important in online businesses?

Discussion Questions

1. What does the term "chain reaction" refer to in discussing the role of consumer behavior in greater society?

2. How does a stakeholder orientation compare with a marketing orientation?

3. How can consumer behavior contribute to public policy?

Key Terms

Lecture Example

New York Mayor Michael Bloomberg's proposed ban on the sale of sodas and other such beverages larger than 16 ounces at restaurants, movie theatres, and street carts elicited mixed reactions from the public. The proposed ban was the consequence of research studies that indicated that the consumption of beverages had increased among children and adults, and this was a contributing factor to the increasing levels of obesity among Americans.

While the beverage industry has made efforts to reduce calories in products, their best sellers have always been the high-calorie drinks. This indicates that consumers prefer these beverages even though they are aware of their high-calorie content. The proposed ban is an attempt to modify consumer behavior and preferences through legislation, but soda companies are fighting back.

Source: Leon Stafford, "Soda Makers in a New Kind of Cola War," *Atlanta Business News*, June 3, 2012, http://www.ajc.com/business/soda-makers-in-a-1451241.html

Group Activity

As a group, visit a residential construction site and interview someone considering the purchase of a new home. Prepare a brief report that tries to tell from the qualitative interview with the consumer what motivations are driven by the desire for a new home. In particular, try to estimate the types of things a consumer will add to the new home to make the "house" a "home." Also, try to estimate the number of people (a chain of people) who benefit economically from the purchase of a new home. Start by trying to guess how many workers are directly involved in planning, designing, and constructing the new home, then consider how many people in the distribution channel are touched, such as the workers for suppliers of flooring, lumber, appliances, etc.

Assignments

Review the following situations, and discuss the relevance of consumer behavior to explain each scenario:
- A student selling a textbook back to the college bookstore
- A student purchasing a value meal from an on-campus fast-food stand
- A family purchasing a new home
- A corporate CEO taking a prospective customer to lunch
- A consumer injured during a pick-up football match who is given a tetanus shot at a first aid clinic
- A consumer in a third-world nation who is considering the purchase of a battery-operated television from a government-owned store

Beyond the Class

A selection of materials is in the Instructor's Manual.

CHAPTER 1—UPDATES TO CB THIS YEAR

Page 4—Updated number of apps available for iPad to 250,000 from 200,000

Page 5—Edits in "The Basic CB Process" to better reflect the hedonic value aspects of tablets that have become more obvious over time

Page 5—New Tiny Zoo example under Benefits

Page 9—Revised number of Denver DMV employees

Page 14—Updated worldwide cell phone statistics and used China to illustrate 1 billion quantity instead of Europe and NorthAmerica. Also, updated total number of phones worldwide to 6 billion.

Page 15—*Hold the Phone! Consumers and Their Phones* box feature updated with statistics on children with cell phones

Page 16—Updated statistics on U.S. national debt to $16.5 trillion

Page 17—New box feature *Facing Myopia* replaces *A CB Life: The Modern Way* box feature

Page 20—Updated Internet retailing statistics and updated unemployment data

WHAT'S INSIDE Key topics in this chapter: the consumer value framework, consumer value (utilitarian and hedonic value), how firms and consumers create value, the psychology of the consumer, perceptual maps, and consumer's lifetime value for a long-term orientation.

CHAPTER 2 **PREP** *CARD*
VALUE AND THE CONSUMER BEHAVIOR VALUE FRAMEWORK

Learning Outcomes

With the growth in eReader usage among students, this edition of *CB* features a numbering system for major headings that we recommend you use instead of page numbers when creating assignments.

2-1 Describe the consumer value framework, including its basic components.

2-2 Define consumer value and compare and contrast two key types of value.

2-3 Apply the concepts of marketing strategy and marketing tactics to describe the way firms go about creating value for consumers.

2-4 Explain the way market characteristics like market segmentation and product differentiation affect marketing strategy.

2-5 Analyze consumer markets using elementary perceptual maps.

2-6 Justify consumers' lifetime value as an effective focus for long-term business success.

Chapter 2 Outline

Multimedia

PPT—THE HIGHLIGHTS

- Slide 6 Exhibit 2.2: The Consumer Value Framework (CVF)
- Slide 13 External Influences
- Slide 18 Types of Value
- Slide 21 Exhibit 2.4: Consumption Activities Can Fall into Any of These Categories
- Slide 38 Customer Lifetime Value (CLV)

VIDEOS ON DVD AND COURSEMATE

CHAPTER VIDEO SUMMARY

E-Business at Evo

Run time: 7:49 minutes

When ski enthusiast Bryce Phillips launched Evo from his garage in 2001, the sports-equipment company consisted of an Internet connection, used ski gear, and a single employee. Today the Seattle-based ski-and-snowboard retailer is the premier online destination for closeout-model equipment and apparel. Consumers of ski and water sport products choose Evo for its online shopping experience, discounted brand name merchandise, and no-haggle customer service. The retailer's website also delivers value through detailed product reviews and Evo-hosted travel opportunities.

Ask your students:

1. According to Bryce, what is the heart and soul of Evo?

2. How does Evo offer value to its customers?

3. Name a significant competitive advantage of Evo.

Key Terms

affect 26

augmented product 32

blue ocean strategy 36

cognition 26

Consumer Value Framework (CVF) 24

corporate strategy 31

Customer Lifetime Value (CLV) 38

Customer Relationship Management (CRM) 24

elasticity 34

external influences 26

hedonic value 29

ideal points 36

individual differences 26

internal influences 26

market segmentation 33

marketing mix 33

marketing myopia 30

marketing strategy 30

marketing tactics 31

perceptual map 36

product differentiation 35

product positioning 35

relationship quality 25

situational influences 27

social environment 27

strategy 30

target market 33

total value concept 32

utilitarian value 29

value 28

value co-creation 33

Lecture Example

Walmart, considered the world's largest retailer, is facing stiff competition from Amazon these days. Shoppers, who are primarily focused on value, are now turning to the world's largest online retailer, Amazon, for many common purchases. Walmart's target consumers were those who were primarily interested in low prices and not the overall shopping experience. This is where Walmart is losing out to competitor Amazon, which scores by providing more value to the shopper with competitive prices and free shipping for many products.

Source: Brad Tuttle, "Today's Value Shopper Heads to Amazon, Not Walmart," *Time Moneyland*, April 10, 2012, http://moneyland.time.com/2012/04/10/todays-value-shopper-heads-to-amazon-not-walmart/

Discussion Questions

1. What is the difference between an internal influence and an external influence?
2. In what ways can using Twitter to tweet to others provide value? What type of value does tweeting provide?
3. How do marketing firms assess the value of a given customer?

Group Activity

Assign each team member to closely examine a different component of the CVF (internal influences, external influences, etc.). Develop and act out a short skit in which each person explains to a store clerk why they are selecting a specific type of smartphone to purchase, in terms only of the concepts that go along with the particular component of the CVF. In other words, is there a certain type of device that would be more likely to be selected based on external influences rather than internal? In the skit, each person must use the following words: value, hedonic value, utilitarian value, motivation, benefits, cost, and time. Have some fun with this activity!

Assignments

List ten fast-food restaurants. Consider what a typical lunch would be like at each place. Use their websites if you need to review the menu. Rank them from least to most expensive. Then, using the same ten restaurants, rank them from the least to the most healthy. Form "dimensions" with these rankings and then create a perceptual map illustrating the fast-food market formed by these ten restaurants.

Beyond the Class

A selection of materials is in the Instructor's Manual.

CHAPTER 2—UPDATES TO CB THIS YEAR

Page 26—Replaced athletic shoe price example with one introducing the idea of feature creep

Page 27—New box feature *Fill'er Up!* replaces *Starving for a Vacation?* box feature

Page 28—New example about convenience stores

Page 29—New example of utilitarian value

Pages 31–32—New example about Best Buy repositioning themselves as a services company

Page 35—Updated the price of an ounce of Chanel No. 5 perfume

Page 37—New information about BlackBerry's BB10 Smartphone in the *Assume Crash Position?* box feature

WHAT'S INSIDE Key topics in this chapter: preliminary stages of consumer perception, phases in the consumer perception process, concept of just noticeable difference (JND), implicit and explicit memory, enhancing a consumer's attention, and differences in unintentional and intentional learning.

CHAPTER 3 **PREP** *CARD*

CONSUMER LEARNING STARTS HERE: PERCEPTION

Learning Outcomes

With the growth in eReader usage among students, this edition of *CB* features a numbering system for major headings that we recommend you use instead of page numbers when creating assignments.

3-1 Define learning and perception and how the two are connected.

3-2 List and define phases of the consumer perception process.

3-3 Apply the concept of the JND.

3-4 Contrast the concepts of implicit and explicit memory.

3-5 Know ways to help get a consumer's attention.

3-6 Understand key differences between intentional and unintentional learning.

Chapter 3 Outline

Multimedia

PPT—THE HIGHLIGHTS

- Slide 7 Elements of Consumer Perception
- Slide 10 Exhibit 3.3 Sensing, Organizing, and Reacting
- Slide 22 JND: Marketing Implications
- Slide 26 Mere Exposure Effect
- Slide 31 Factors that Get Attention

VIDEOS ON DVD AND COURSEMATE

CB Scenario Video

Run time: 3:02 minutes

 Consumers at a store are surprised to discover that the delicious aromas of fruit and chocolate aren't all from the products on the shelves. The store uses "scent air machines" to make customers hungry and encourage them to buy more. The aromas trigger the associations hardwired into our brains and stimulate consumer wants. The staff in the store noted that sales in the produce department at the store increased after the introduction of the machines.

CHAPTER VIDEO SUMMARY

Culver's Restaurants

Run time: 9:07 minutes

 Specializing in quick service in a fast-paced environment, Culver's is not the average American fast-food restaurant. What differentiates Culver's from other sandwich-and-hamburger-serving restaurants is its strong focus on the customer. That each customer leaves happy is the creed of Culver's. As much as in 1984 when Culver's was started, this unwavering focus on customers is still closely tied to its current marketing strategy. Culver's treats its customers with great respect and personal care, and they, in turn, come back for the good food and great experience they have had.

Ask your students:

1. What distinguishes Culver's from the average American fast-food restaurants?

2. What factors have contributed to Culver's phenomenal growth since 1984?

3. What advertising strategy did Culver's adopt in its early days? Was it successful?

VISIT LOGIN.CENGAGE.COM FOR ADDITIONAL MATERIALS TO ENHANCE YOUR LECTURES!

CHAPTER 3 CONSUMER LEARNING STARTS HERE: PERCEPTION

Key Terms

Lecture Example

Food safety remains a primary area of concern for consumers who have become increasingly conscious of the food they eat at home or in restaurants. Topping the list of consumer concern is the level of mercury found in fish and other seafood. Import alerts generated by the FDA for mercury in fish are enough to make consumers anxious about the safety of what they consume. Consumers are believed to have a better understanding of the food safety issue facing them, and their perception often becomes the reality. Retailers and restaurateurs must therefore act proactively, to help regain consumer confidence that is already on a steep decline.

Source: "Today's Consumers—Perception is Reality," *Huff Post*, September 9, 2010, http://www.huffingtonpost.com/malcolm-wittenberg/todays-consumers-percepti_b_706712.html

Discussion Questions

1. What does consumer perception mean?
2. What are the three possible results from the cognitive organization process? Give examples of each.
3. Define attention. What are ways that consumer attention can be enhanced?

Group Activity

Write a 100-word short story about your professor's Saturday morning (as you imagine it—you do not need to actually interview him or her about Saturday). What do you imagine that your professor does on Saturday morning? Make sure you include at least three brand names in the story. Write the story down; then, in class or with some other group of at least 20 people, have one person in the group first read the story and then quietly tell the story to the next person (the person behind him or her) without referring to the written version. Have the story passed only verbally from one to another until it finally reaches the last person in the class. Then, have that person tell the story to the entire class. How did the class do and what makes remembering such a short story so difficult?

Assignments

Ask a friend who has never studied marketing or consumer behavior to flip through a popular magazine, such as *Sports Illustrated* or *People*. Ask them to find examples of attempted subliminal persuasion. Have them discuss the ads and explain their choices. What do you think of their opinions?

Beyond the Class

A selection of materials is in the Instructor's Manual.

CHAPTER 3—UPDATES TO CB THIS YEAR

Page 50—New example about cosmopolitan restaurants dining in the dark to highlight your senses

Page 50—New box feature *Sensing is Believing* replaces *Oversensitive or Overperceptive* box feature

Page 51—New pull quote

Page 54—Revised box feature *Uncanny!* replaces *Gives Me the Creeps!* box feature

Page 55—Revised Quantity example about computer paper

Page 55—Revised Add-on Purchases example about a coat and scarf

Page 60—New pull quote

Page 62—Revised example of career day at a university under Shaping section

Pages 62–63—New example of extinction

WHAT'S INSIDE Key topics in this chapter: theory and evidence addressing how consumers learn when they are trying to learn something, factors that affect what gets comprehended in a marketing message, how consumers form memory and how that memory is represented, how knowledge is stored, and how it relies upon categories captured with concepts like schema, social schema, and exemplar.

CHAPTER 4 **PREP** *CARD*
COMPREHENSION, MEMORY, AND COGNITIVE LEARNING

Learning Outcomes

With the growth in eReader usage among students, this edition of *CB* features a numbering system for major headings that we recommend you use instead of page numbers when creating assignments.

4-1 Identify factors that influence consumer comprehension.

4-2 Explain how knowledge, meaning, and value are inseparable using the multiple stores memory theory.

4-3 Understand how the mental associations that consumers develop are a key to learning.

4-4 Use the concept of associative networks to map relevant consumer knowledge.

4-5 Apply the cognitive schema concept in understanding how consumers react to products, brands, and marketing agents.

Chapter 4 Outline

Multimedia

PPT—THE HIGHLIGHTS

- Slide 3 Exhibit 4.1: The Components of Consumer Information Processing
- Slide 24 Exhibit 4.6: The Multiple Store Approach to Memory
- Slide 27 Mental Processes Assisting Learning
- Slide 35 Associative Network
- Slide 41 Exhibit 4.10 Category Exemplars

VIDEOS ON DVD AND COURSEMATE

CB Scenario Video

A menu is displayed for customers at a restaurant. The menu provides a list of the available dishes and their prices. A group of consumers places an order. The chef prepares lobsters in the kitchen. Restaurant customers are served meals in an outdoor setting.

CHAPTER VIDEO SUMMARY

Cold Stone Creamery

Run time: 6:35 minutes

Cold Stone Creamery has a mission to create the ultimate ice cream experience. Success at Cold Stone begins with the official goal to "make people happy," and employees deliver pure bliss to customers in the form of delectable ice cream treats and toppings. But careful planning and goal setting are critical to achieving any corporate mission, and Cold Stone's Pyramid of Success 2010 campaign communicates important messages that are memorable and comprehensible to workers and consumers alike.

Ask your students:

1. During one's experience at Cold Stone Creamery, what type of memory is drawn on?

2. How does Cold Stone Creamery cater to different ethnic groups?

Key Terms

adaptation level 72
associative network 79
brain dominance 72
chunk 77
chunking 76
cognitive interference 77
comprehension 65
counterarguments 70
credibility 70
declarative knowledge 80
dostats 72
dual coding 76
echoic storage 75
elaboration 79
encoding 75
episodic memory 82
exemplar 81
expectations 72
expertise 70
figure 69
figure–ground distinction 69
framing 73
golden section 68
ground 69
habituation 72
haptic perception 75
iconic storage 75
information intensity 73
long-term memory 78
meaningful encoding 76
memory 74
memory trace 78
message congruity 69
metaphor 73
multiple store theory of memory 74
nodes 80
nostalgia 79
paths 80
personal elaboration 79
physical characteristics 67
priming 73
prospect theory 73
prototype 81
repetition 76
response generation 78
retrieval 75
rumination 79
schema 80
script 81
semantic coding 78
sensory memory 74
signal theory 66
social schema 82
social stereotype 82
spreading activation 78
support arguments 70
tag 79
trustworthiness 70
workbench memory 75

Lecture Example

Putting the real Harley rider in the spotlight, the latest evolution of Harley-Davidson's "No Cages" campaign poses a veritable challenge to stereotypes. The focal point of the new campaign, titled "E Pluribus Unum," or "out of many, one," is a series of digital videos of real Harley-Davidson riders and a corresponding stereotype. The ads are engineered to initiate conversations through social platforms and Harley-Davidson's website.

The E Pluribus Unum campaign cashes in on the element of surprise to inspire people to think about riding Harleys.

Source: "Harley-Davidson Tackles Stereotypes in New Advertising Campaign," *The New York Times*, March 1, 2012, http://markets.on.nytimes.com/research/stocks/news/press_release.asp?docTag=201203011410PR_NEWS_USPRX_AQ63091&feedID=600&press_symbol=145197

Discussion Questions

1. Are traditional product warning labels effective? What are some reasons why they are not effective? Do you believe adding pictures to cigarette warning labels will make them more effective?

2. Consider the atmosphere created by a specialty fashion merchandiser like Lucky stores (or similar, like Anthropologie, Ralph Lauren, Polo, etc.). Define figure and ground and describe its effects in the context of a shopping environment.

3. Of the four types of mental processes to help remember things discussed in the chapter, which is most effective? Does this have implications for the way you study?

Group Activity

This activity is aimed at researching the schema for a brand. Choose one of these brands: Facebook, Motorola, or Red Bull. Have each member of your team go and interview a different consumer using free association techniques. Ask the consumer:

"Name the first five things that come into your mind when you hear the name _____."

After all the interviews are complete, discuss the results using terminology from the chapter. Based on the results, show the schema by drawing it on a poster board. Give the class a brief presentation that analyzes the meaning of the brand and the implications of this meaning for its growth.

Assignments

Prepare a short position statement that describes your agreement or disagreement with the following statement: "All product safety labels should be presented in multiple languages (at least the three most common languages in the area) and without the use of colors."

Beyond the Class

A selection of materials is in the Instructor's Manual.

CHAPTER 4—UPDATES TO CB THIS YEAR

Page 68—New example about alphanumeric names when creating new products, brands, or models

Page 78—New example of Easter to describe memory trace

Page 81—New example of exemplar

Page 81—New example of cobranding

Page 82—New box feature *Bike, Trike or Hike?* replaces *May I Read Your Table?* box feature

Page 83—New example of social schemas

WHAT'S INSIDE Key topics in this chapter: human behavior and what drives it, basic consumer motivations and a general hierarchy of motivations, consumer emotions, and the schema-based affect.

CHAPTER 5 **PREP** *CARD*
MOTIVATIONS AND EMOTION: DRIVING CONSUMER BEHAVIOR

Learning Outcomes

With the growth in eReader usage among students, this edition of *CB* features a numbering system for major headings that we recommend you use instead of page numbers when creating assignments.

5-1 Understand what initiates human behavior.

5-2 Classify basic consumer motivations.

5-3 Describe consumer emotions and demonstrate how they help shape value.

5-4 Apply different approaches to measuring consumer emotions.

5-5 Understand how different consumers express emotions in different ways.

5-6 Define and apply the concepts of schema-based affect and emotional contagion.

Chapter 5 Outline

Multimedia

PPT—THE HIGHLIGHTS

- Slide 5 Motivations
- Slide 11 Exhibit 5.2: Utilitarian and Hedonic Motivations Lead to Consumer Behaviors
- Slide 17 Cognitive Appraisal Theory
- Slide 23 PANAS and PAD
- Slide 28 Exhibit5.7: Emotional Intelligence Consists of Multiple Elements

VIDEOS ON DVD AND COURSEMATE

CB Scenario Video
Run time: 0:07 minutes

 A consumer in a supermarket pushes her shopping trolley along the aisles, quickly filling it with groceries and staples from the many products available on the shelves.

CHAPTER VIDEO SUMMARY

Jordan's Furniture
Run time: 9:24 minutes

 Business is about understanding people, their needs, emotions, and motivations. Jordan's Furniture is a good example of a successful business that derives much of its success from influencing consumer behavior to its advantage. The two brothers, Eliot and Barry, who run Jordan's, have devised a unique marketing strategy that couples entertainment with furniture shopping. Jordan's advertising line is interesting and robust at the same time: from radio to funny ads for the TV, Jordan's Furniture has a face of its own, a furniture shop to which people return not only for the high-quality products, but also for the unique experience it offers.

Ask your students:

1. What is unique about the marketing strategy adopted by Jordan's Furniture?

2. Why did Jordan's Furniture decide to couple entertainment with shopping? How successful is the strategy?

3. What advantages did Jordan's Furniture secure by studying consumer behavior?

Key Terms

Lecture Example

Pairing products with rich emotional experiences is one of the most effective ways of building brand loyalty. The Disney experience is a case in point, where the Walt Disney Company has been successful in creating an iconic brand by designing great experiences for consumers. Every visit to the Disney theme parks is a memorable experience. Disney achieved unparalleled brand loyalty by engineering this emotion of happiness and wonder that consumers effortlessly associate with the brand.

Source: "Testing the User Experience: Consumer Emotions and Brand Success," UX Matters, October 19, 2009, http://www.uxmatters.com/mt/archives/2009/10/testing-the-user-experience-consumer-emotions-and-brand-success.php

Discussion Questions

1. Define the concept of consumer motivation. What two orientations are driven by consumer motivations?
2. What is consumer involvement and what different types of involvement play a role in CB?
3. What is emotional contagion? Do you think it could affect the schema-based affect for some type of service provider? Explain.

Group Activity

Prepare a short video that depicts the concept of aesthetic labor in the marketplace and the emotions that accompany such attempts. Pay particular attention to depicting the visceral reactions that show emotion. Either take the video in an actual services environment (ask permission before doing so, as many service establishments frown on having photos or videos taken) or act out the roles played by service providers and customers. Be prepared to explain your video in class and demonstrate how it illustrates at least five concepts from the chapter.

Assignments

Interview four friends concerning the feelings they have toward Facebook activities. Ask them about how they would feel if they were deprived of using Facebook for a week, ten days, or two months. Do you believe any of the friends may be addicted to Facebook?

Beyond the Class

A selection of materials is in the Instructor's Manual.

CHAPTER 5—UPDATES TO CB THIS YEAR

Page 87—Revised Exhibit 5.1, An Illustration of Consumer Motivations According to Maslow's Hierarchy

Page 88—Revised Exhibit 5.2, Utilitarian and Hedonic Motivations Lead to Consumer Behaviors

Page 88—Revised Exhibit 5.3, Typical High and Low Product Involvement

Page 89—In situational involvement section, changed "air conditioner" to "water heater" example

Page 90—New pull quote

Page 91—New DQ example within Affect section

Page 94—New box feature *Feeling Guilty* replaces *Naturally Wired* box feature

Page 95—New examples in the Emotional Involvement section

Page 97—New example of the Superbowl 2013 ads in the What's Funny section

Page 99—Revised Exhibit 5.9 Examples of Schema-Based Affect

WHAT'S INSIDE Key topics in this chapter: personality and consumer behavior, major traits in consumer research, lifestyle and demographics, self-concept as it relates to consumer behavior, and issue of self-congruency.

CHAPTER 6 **PREP** *CARD*

PERSONALITY, LIFESTYLES, AND THE SELF-CONCEPT

Learning Outcomes

With the growth in eReader usage among students, this edition of *CB* features a numbering system for major headings that we recommend you use instead of page numbers when creating assignments.

6-1 Define personality and know how various approaches to studying personality can be applied to consumer behavior.

6-2 Discuss major traits that have been examined in consumer research.

6-3 Understand why lifestyles, psychographics, and demographics are important to the study of consumer behavior.

6-4 Comprehend the role of the self-concept in consumer behavior.

6-5 Understand the concept of self-congruency and how it applies to consumer behavior issues.

Chapter 6 Outline

Multimedia

PPT—THE HIGHLIGHTS

- Slide 16 Important Traits Studied
- Slide 21 Personology Approach
- Slide 25 VALS
- Slide 33 Self-Concept
- Slide 38 Self-Congruency Theory

VIDEOS ON DVD AND COURSEMATE

CB Scenario Video

Run time: 0:27 minutes

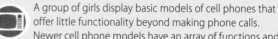

A group of girls display basic models of cell phones that offer little functionality beyond making phone calls. Newer cell phone models have an array of functions and capabilities. Touchscreen phones and smartphones allow users to perform a variety of tasks in addition to phone calls—scheduling appointments, online shopping, and entertainment.

CHAPTER VIDEO SUMMARY

Wheelworks

Run time: 9:30 minutes

Since 1977, Wheelworks has been a hub of the East Coast cycling community. The Boston-based bicycle shop has earned both national and consumer's choice awards for its selection and service. Because cycling is a lifestyle pursuit that generates excitement among recreational enthusiasts and professional competitors alike, sales personnel at Wheelworks bypass hard selling and focus instead on educating consumers, promoting bicycle clubs, and sharing their passion for riding.

Ask your students:

1. What is the key to Wheelworks' success?

2. How does Wheelworks motivate the sales force to provide excellent customer service?

VISIT LOGIN.CENGAGE.COM FOR ADDITIONAL MATERIALS TO ENHANCE YOUR LECTURES!

CHAPTER 6 PERSONALITY, LIFESTYLES, AND THE SELF-CONCEPT

Key Terms

Lecture Example

In a crowded market, it is difficult to sell without any real product differentiation. So, when Nestlé launched a new luxury chocolate in an already saturated market, it was just expected that the food giant's latest offering would be a class apart. So it was. Nestlé launched Maison Cailler, which allowed customers to discover their "chocolate personality"; it emphasized building "stronger relationships." Although tasting chocolate is an innovative idea, taste is a tricky thing to personify. However, since consumers have relationships with brands, personality traits are considered important in the context of these relationships.

Source: "Maison Cailler, Nestle's New Luxury Chocolate Brand, Markets 'Stronger Relationships Through Chocolate,'" *Huff Post*, January 25, 2012, http://www.huffingtonpost.com/2012/01/25/maison-cailler_n_1231093.html

Discussion Questions

1. Describe the trait approach to studying consumer personality. What is meant by nomothetic and idiographic approaches?

2. What are the distinctions between lifestyles, psychographics, and demographics? How can consumer researchers use information based on these concepts?

3. What is meant by the terms *symbolic interactionism* and *semiotics*? How do these concepts apply in the daily life of a consumer?

Group Activity

Have team members collect various lifestyle magazines that they subscribe to, or read regularly. Examples would be cooking magazines, paintball magazines, athletic magazines such as *ESPN* or *Sports Illustrated*. Bring the magazines back to the group but do not reveal who brought in each magazine. Have team members try to guess who brought in each magazine. Are they correct? How do magazines like these reflect our lifestyles?

Assignments

Browse various websites of popular products such as Coca-Cola, Honda Motor Company, Dell, or any other website that comes to mind. Take note of websites that include messages that suggest that a consumer's identity is expressed through using the products. Do you use products to express your identity? Which ones? In what ways?

Beyond the Class

A selection of materials is in the Instructor's Manual.

CHAPTER 6—UPDATES TO CB THIS YEAR

Page 103—Demographics are now mentioned in opening paragraph and a new example of the band Kings of Leon

Page 104—New pull quote

Page 105—New LARP example in the Psychoanalytic Approach and Motivation Research section

Page 105—New example about Nick to illustrate nomothetic approach

Page 108—New box feature *A Sisyphean Effort* replaces *Buy It Now* box feature

Pages 108–109—New example of competitions that are growing in popularity

Page 109—Revised Exhibit 6.1 Examples of Other Traits in Consumer Research

Page 111—New research findings about brand personality concept

Page 111—New information in the Formation of Brand Personality section

Page 112—New information about service employees playing a part in formation of brand love

Page 113—New pull quote

Page 118—New example of self-congruency theory

Page 119—New information about identifying with an organization

WHAT'S INSIDE Key topics in this chapter: attitude and attitude components, functions of attitudes, hierarchy of effects, consumer attitude models, attitude change theories, message, and source effects to influence persuasion.

CHAPTER 7 **PREP** *CARD*
ATTITUDES AND ATTITUDE CHANGE

Learning Outcomes

With the growth in eReader usage among students, this edition of *CB* features a numbering system for major headings that we recommend you use instead of page numbers when creating assignments.

7-1 Define attitudes and describe attitude components.

7-2 Describe the functions of attitudes.

7-3 Understand how the hierarchy of effects concept applies to attitude theory.

7-4 Comprehend the major consumer attitude models.

7-5 Describe attitude change theories and their role in persuasion.

7-6 Understand how message and source effects influence persuasion.

Chapter 7 Outline

Multimedia

PPT—THE HIGHLIGHTS

- Slide 8 Functions of Attitudes
- Slide 14 Exhibit 7.2 Hierarchy of Effects
- Slide 17 Attitude-Toward-the-Object (ATO) Model
- Slide 27 Persuasion
- Slide 38 Message Appeal

VIDEOS ON DVD AND COURSEMATE

CB Scenario Video

Run time: 1:02 minutes

 An advertisement for Coca-Cola has a group of polar bears slipping and sliding on the ice in pursuit of a bottle of Coke.

CHAPTER VIDEO SUMMARY

Southwest Airlines

Run time: 6:57 minutes

 For over forty years, Southwest Airlines has remained true to its goal of being a low-cost carrier that provides excellent customer service. A large part of the Southwest culture is its fun-loving employees, who enjoy working at Southwest, and encourage customers to enjoy their flying experiences as well. The airline ensures that every aspect of the customer's flying experience is the best it can be by gathering in-depth qualitative and quantitative research about its services and working to improve based on customer feedback.

Ask your students:

1. Explain how Southwest's marketing message performs each of the four functions of consumer attitude.

2. Explain Southwest's strategy and positioning in the context of social judgment theory.

VISIT LOGIN.CENGAGE.COM FOR ADDITIONAL MATERIALS TO ENHANCE YOUR LECTURES!

CHAPTER 7 ATTITUDES AND ATTITUDE CHANGE

Key Terms

Lecture Example

Increasing gas prices have had a significant impact on consumer behavior. Consumers have realized that the only way to counter the rise in gas prices is to drive less and opt for fuel-efficient cars. They have also started making less frequent trips to retail stores to save on gas. This demonstrates the knowledge aspect of consumer attitude, which allows consumers to simplify their decision-making processes.

Source: Brad Tuttle, "With High Gas Prices, Americans Are Already Driving Less, Buying Better MPG Cars," *Time Moneyland*, March 1, 2012, http://moneyland.time.com/2012/03/01/with-high-gas-prices-americans-are-already-driving-less-buying-better-mpg-cars/

Discussion Questions

1. Describe the ABC approach to consumer attitudes. How do the various components apply to your daily life as a consumer?

2. What is meant by the hierarchy of effects? Differentiate between the high-involvement, low-involvement, experiential, and behavioral influence hierarchies. In what situations are you most likely to observe each hierarchy at work?

3. How can marketers attempt to change beliefs or evaluations directly? How effective do you think these attempts can be?

Group Activity

Have students break up into teams and visit a local shopping mall and a number of popular retail stores. Have them take note of the music that is played in each retail store. Popular clothing retailers like American Apparel, PacSun, and Hollister are great for this exercise. Have each group assess how well the music in the store matches its image. Have the students focus specifically on any music that is played from their favorite bands. Does this music influence their attitudes toward the stores? Have them visit stores that they do not like. What do they find? Do they like the music that is played in stores that they don't like? Have the groups present their results to the class. This exercise can encourage some great class discussions.

Assignments

Visit the popular website Pinterest. How does, or how could, this site influence your attitudes towards the products or hobbies that are being suggested? Do you think sites like Pinterest can be effective in changing your attitude about a product?

Beyond the Class

A selection of materials is in the Instructor's Manual.

CHAPTER 7—UPDATES TO CB THIS YEAR

Page 122—Revised Exhibit 7.1, Functions of Consumer Attitudes

Page 123—New example of high school boys wanting to fit in by wearing the right clothes

Page 130—New box feature *Make the Switch* replaces *Don't Forget the Mail!* box feature

Page 134—Revised Exhibit 7.6 and surrounding text

Page 136—New introduction to Message and Source Effects and Persuasion section

Page 136—Revised Internet statistics

Page 136—New research findings that social media influences consumer loyalty and WOM

WHAT'S INSIDE Key topics in this chapter: different types of reference groups that influence consumers and value perceptions; social power that reference groups have on perceptions; differences between utilitarian, informational, and value-expressive group influence; the importance of word-of-mouth communications; household influence on consumer behavior; and the role of social media and networking in influencing groups.

CHAPTER 8 **PREP** *CARD*

GROUP AND INTERPERSONAL INFLUENCE

Learning Outcomes

With the growth in eReader usage among students, this edition of *CB* features a numbering system for major headings that we recommend you use instead of page numbers when creating assignments.

8-1 Understand the different types of reference groups that influence consumers and how reference groups influence value perceptions.

8-2 Describe the various types of social power that reference groups exert on members.

8-3 Comprehend the difference between informational, utilitarian, and value-expressive reference group influence.

8-4 Understand social media's role in consumer behavior.

8-5 Understand the importance of word-of-mouth communications in consumer behavior.

8-6 Comprehend the role of household influence in consumer behavior.

Chapter 8 Outline

Multimedia

PPT—THE HIGHLIGHTS

- Slide 7 Types of Groups
- Slide 15 Exhibit 8.1: Types of Social Power
- Slide 18 Categories of Influence
- Slide 33 Buzz Marketing
- Slide 40 Household Purchase Roles

VIDEOS ON DVD AND COURSEMATE

CB Scenario Video

Run time: 0:24 minutes

 A woman prepares street food on a busy street while another woman eats it quickly, standing in the street. In a restaurant, a customer is able to order a meal at leisure, referring to a menu and having the chef prepare the meal while he waits.

CHAPTER VIDEO SUMMARY

Teen Research Unlimited

Run time: 8:10 minutes

 Gathering information is key to marketing success. For businesses interested in selling products to teens, Teenage Research Unlimited (TRU) is an invaluable research partner. The marketing research firm has been studying teen habits since the 1980s, and data gleaned from TRU's focus groups and surveys reveals the ways in which teens are influenced by reference groups and each other. According to analysts, the teenage consumer segment will continue to grow in importance, especially in the age of cell phones, iPods, and social networking.

Ask your students:

1. Why is gathering information important for marketers?

2. How do companies benefit from the information obtained by TRU?

3. Why is the teenage group important to marketers?

VISIT LOGIN.CENGAGE.COM FOR ADDITIONAL MATERIALS TO ENHANCE YOUR LECTURES!

CHAPTER 8 GROUP AND INTERPERSONAL INFLUENCE

Key Terms

Lecture Example

Put simply, word-of-mouth (WOM) communication is friendly banter. Its power to shape public opinion can hardly be overstated. In WOM communication, it is the customers who do the marketing, i.e., talk about products and services on behalf of the marketers. These customers are mostly loyalists and enthusiasts who help provide compelling reasons to other potential buyers to buy a particular product or avail themselves of a specific service. If a customer is happy with a product or service, positive WOM is more likely. However, marketers must be wary of negative WOM as it can prove to be substantially damaging to both reputation and future prospects.

Source: "Word of Mouth Marketing—Powerful Messaging via an Affordable Medium," *Huff Post*, August 18, 2010, http://www.huffingtonpost.com/april-rudin/marketing-via-word-of-mou_b_641002.html

Group Activity

Have students break up into teams. Have each team begin a group page on Facebook for their particular team, restricting membership to only team members. Have students use the group as a discussion board for this project. Have each team member post a question on their own walls about a particular product or brand. For example, a question might be: "Does anyone know where I can get a good deal on a used car?" or "I'm looking for a new hair stylist, does anyone have any ideas?" Each member is to take notes of the responses they get and then report it back to the team on Facebook. Let this continue over the course of several weeks, including several different questions. At the end of the exercise, have students report on the types of responses they got from Facebook for the various questions, the usefulness of the information they obtained, and also how useful their new group was for discussion purposes. Have them summarize their findings to class. Make sure they focus on the usefulness of the Facebook group as compared to meeting face-to-face. How useful was the experience? Did they learn anything new regarding the questions that they asked?

CHAPTER 8—UPDATES TO CB THIS YEAR

Page 147—New reference to Snapchat

Page 149—New pull quote

Page 149—New discussion about recent research on brand communities and consumer commitment

Page 151—Revised Exhibit 8.1, Types of Social Power

Page 153—New box feature *Student Groups Bring Value* replaces *Valuable Alumni Groups* box feature

Page 154—A brief reference to the popularity of smartphone apps

Page 155—New statistics for Facebook, Twitter, and MySpace

Page 155—Snapchat is used as an example of the popularity of sending photos and videos between consumers. The "Ourtime.com" website has been referenced.

Page 155—Game apps, including Words with Friends, Ruzzle, and What's the Word, have been included to illustrate how consumers can connect while playing games.

Page 158—New pull quote

Page 160—Concepts "branded content" and "advertisement" have been added to the section on stealth marketing

Page 163—New statistics have been added for: the growth in nonfamily households, the declining U.S. birth rates, the number of children in the USA who live with only one parent. Exhibit 8.5, U.S. Children Younger Than Age 18 by Household Type 2012 statistics have been updated

Page 165—A new statistic for the percentage of boomerang kids who feel like they don't make enough money to live on their own

Page 166—New statistics have been added to the *Pets Are Family Too!* box feature

WHAT'S INSIDE Key topics in this chapter: culture and the meaning of objects and activities, key dimensions of core societal values, acculturation and enculturation, elements of verbal and nonverbal communication, and current emerging markets and opportunities.

CHAPTER 9 **PREP** *CARD*

CONSUMER CULTURE

Learning Outcomes

With the growth in eReader usage among students, this edition of *CB* features a numbering system for major headings that we recommend you use instead of page numbers when creating assignments

9-1 Understand how culture provides the true meaning of objects and activities.

9-2 Use the key dimensions of core societal values to apply the concept of cultural distance.

9-3 Define acculturation and enculturation.

9-4 List fundamental elements of verbal and nonverbal communication.

9-5 Discuss current emerging consumer markets and scan for opportunities.

Chapter 9 Outline

Multimedia

PPT—THE HIGHLIGHTS

- Slide 5 Exhibit 9.1 Culture, Meaning, and Value
- Slide 13 Exhibit 9.5 CSV Differences Scores Relative to American Consumers
- Slide 17 Exhibit 9.6: Characteristics of Fast and Slow Acculturation
- Slide 26 Exhibit 9.10 Nonverbal Communication Affects the Message Comprehended
- Slide 31 Glocalization

VIDEOS ON DVD AND COURSEMATE

CB Scenario Video

Run time: 4:57 minutes

 As the first wave of Baby Boomers reach 65, marketers are preparing for the changing needs of the Me generation. Stores are modifying their designs to make it easier for aging consumers to access products despite their physical limitations. Companies are developing technologies that can be used to help older people live safer and fuller lives. In the next few years, the buying power of the Baby Boomer cohort will ensure that marketers take good care of this market segment.

CHAPTER VIDEO SUMMARY

Lonely Planet

Run time: 7:54 minutes

 The challenges of working in an international marketing environment are both varied and numerous. Businesses with a global presence must be both brave and distinctive in order to prosper. Lonely Planet aims to provide travelers with consistent information leading to memorable personal experiences. It emphasizes marketing as a means of communicating effectively with customers, and attributes much of the success of global businesses to a robust branding strategy.

Ask your students:

1. What are the factors that can be attributed to the global success of Lonely Planet?

2. How does Lonely Planet seek to distinguish itself from its peers?

3. Discuss Lonely Planet's position on branding.

VISIT LOGIN.CENGAGE.COM FOR ADDITIONAL MATERIALS TO ENHANCE YOUR LECTURES!

CHAPTER 9 CONSUMER CULTURE

Key Terms

Lecture Example

The use of pop culture in selling products is hardly a novel concept. Pepsi's latest campaign featuring the hip-hop artist Nicki Minaj is in line with the trend that rolled out ads such as the "the choice of a new generation" in the 1980s and "had the right one, baby" in the 1990s. Minaj will feature in Pepsi's "Live for Now" campaign. The campaign indicates a renewed focus on marketing, a drive probably initiated by Wall Street, and focuses on improving beverage sales in North America. Brad Jakeman, president of the company's Global Enjoyment Brands and chief creative officer of PepsiCo Global Beverages Group, wants the brand to win back its position as a true pop culture icon. Consequently, the campaign in the coming years will feature entertainers and artists.

Source: "Using Pop Culture to Sell Cola," *Sowetan Live*, May 2, 2012, http://www.sowetanlive.co.za/news/business/2012/05/02/using-pop-culture-to-sell-cola

Discussion Questions

1. Why are culture and meaning inseparable?
2. What is meant when one says that "culture gives meaning to objects and activities"?
3. Describe the concepts of translational equivalence and metric equivalence and how they relate to communication differences across cultures

Group Activity

Ask someone from the international department at a nearby university to visit your classroom, or have an international student pay a visit so that students can experience consumer culture. Have the student or representative discuss Exhibit 9.1 on culture, meaning, and value. This activity allows students to understand the impact of marketing in cultures around the world. This activity could end up as a panel discussion if two or more students hail from other countries.

Assignments

Design an advertisement that intends to communicate the benefits of a facial cream to family skin care for each of the following consumer markets. Consider the relative role of verbal and nonverbal communication in doing so.

- Germany
- Egypt
- Japan
- Israel
- New Zealand

CHAPTER 9—UPDATES TO CB THIS YEAR

Page 169—Updated average spending on weddings.

Page 172—Replaced Katy Perry example with one for Miley Cyrus as a female pop icon.

Page 172—Revised Exhibit 9.2, Societal Role Expectations Vary

Page 173—New pull quote

Page 174—New example about Korean consumers

Page 175—New pull quote

Page 176—New example of high uncertainty avoidance with German consumers and new example of consumer credit in China

Page 177—New examples of businesses in the cultural distance section.

Page 181—Revised Exhibit 9.8, Modeling and the Quartet

Page 182—New box feature *Horse of a Different Color* replaces *Culture of Its Own* box feature

Page 188—New example of how Chindian consumers are spending their money on luxuries

CHAPTER 10 PREP *CARD*

MICROCULTURES

Learning Outcomes

With the growth in eReader usage among students, this edition of *CB* features a numbering system for major headings that we recommend you use instead of page numbers when creating assignments.

10-1 Apply the concept of microculture as it influences consumer behavior.

10-2 Know the major U.S. microcultural groups.

10-3 Realize that microculture is not a uniquely American phenomenon.

10-4 Perform a demographic analysis.

10-5 Identify major cultural and demographic trends.

Chapter 10 Outline

Multimedia

PPT—THE HIGHLIGHTS

- Slide 5 Exhibit 10.1 The Hierarchical Nature of Culture and Microculture
- Slide 15 Religious Microculture
- Slide 22 Microcultures Exist Globally
- Slide 24 Demographics
- Slide 27 Cultural and Demographic Trends Affecting CB

VIDEOS ON DVD AND COURSEMATE

CB Scenario Video

Run time: 0:29 minutes

 An advertisement for Discovercard contrasts two types of family vacations. The father of a family lists the activities they've undertaken during "learning" family vacations: watching a cow give birth, cleaning up after an accident at a nuclear plant, improving the family dynamics through role play. The kids in the family are not impressed by any of these. However, families who want a fun vacation, the ad says, use Discovercard to visit Universal Orlando Resort.

CHAPTER VIDEO SUMMARY

Vans

Run time: 7:23 minutes

 At Vans, the focus is on building strong and enduring relationships thorough strategic PR. The expenditure on advertising at Vans is huge, and involves print, online, TV, and outdoor ads. Vans is also engaged in sponsoring events in order to promote bonding and spread its culture. It also deals in cause marketing and athlete endorsements—activities that are perceived to strengthen the brand. Besides conventional marketing, Vans also focuses on interactive marketing and collaborations as part of its product-oriented marketing strategy. With the expansion of its product line, the focus on brand promotion has now shifted to mixing branding ads with product-driven ads. With the changing face of technology, Vans plans to do more interactive marketing in the future.

Ask your students:

1. Explain how Vans' target audience influences the company's advertising and marketing strategies. Why, in your opinion, are these strategies necessary for the company to target its audience?

2. Describe the primary demographic characteristics of Vans' target audience. How do you think these will change in the next twenty years?

VISIT LOGIN.CENGAGE.COM FOR ADDITIONAL MATERIALS TO ENHANCE YOUR LECTURES!

CHAPTER 10 MICROCULTURES

Key Terms

Lecture Example

Struggling to find its way out of the recession, the hotel industry has set its eyes on a new patron. This group, popularly known as the Millennials, are those in their 20s and mid 30s. Obsessed with social media and technology, Generation Y, as they are sometimes called, are avid travelers. Besides comfort, they look for innovative service and are likely to spend more on designer hotels. Hoteliers have been prompt in seizing this new trend as a valuable opportunity. Wi-Fi access, power consoles, and airportlike check-in kiosks are fast becoming regular features of the modern hotel. As some industry experts claim, this trend is no passing fad, but an enduring change.

Source: "The Millennials Check In," *The New York Times,* March 12, 2012, http://www.nytimes.com/2012/03/13/business/young-travelers -drive-changes-in-hotel-industry.html?_r=1&pagewanted=all

Discussion Questions

1. How do microcultures affect value?
2. What are some of the distinguishing characteristics of the Millennial microculture in the USA?
3. What is the major factor that is influencing the increase in cultural diversity worldwide?

Group Activity

Divide students into groups comprising different microcultures. Of course, this will vary depending on the enrollment of your university or college. An easy choice would be different ethnic microcultures, but religious, income, or generation might apply as well.

Have them discuss the differences in value that they receive from various products. Examples would include things like mp3 players, laptop computers, various kinds of music, different fashions, activities they enjoy in their spare time, etc. They could even discuss how they view things like sex roles. Ask the students to attempt to come to a better appreciation of how their peers in different microcultures view the value of these things. You could even have them report their findings and opinions to the class.

This is a great way to emphasize a key point of Chapter 10—that the value we receive from things is largely influenced by the microcultures that we belong to. A word of caution would be to try to keep the discussions away from politics and/or religion. Of course, this is at your discretion as the professor. Discussions may become quite lively.

Assignments

Using a popular geodemographic tool such as PRIZM, find information about your local college town. What social classes are present in your town according to this tool? Are all of the social classes presented in the textbook present in your town?

Beyond the Class

A selection of materials is in the Instructor's Manual.

CHAPTER 10—UPDATES TO CB THIS YEAR

Page 194—Revised Exhibit 10.3, Regional Differences and Preferences among U.S. Consumers

Page 195—New box feature *Changing Class?* replaces *Going Metro or Retro?* box feature

Page 196—New Coca-Cola example

Page 200—New pull quote

Page 201—Revised Exhibit 10.6, Ethnic/Racial Groups in the United States Based on U.S. Census Projections

Page 206—Revised Exhibit 10.8, Demographic Profile for the State of Missouri

Page 208—Revised Exhibit 10.9, Projected Birthrates per Couple and Life Expectancies for Countries around the World (2014)

WHAT'S INSIDE   Key topics in this chapter: how values vary in situations; how time affects consumer behavior; shopping as a consumer activity; types of purchases: unplanned, impulsive, and compulsive shopping; atmospherics; and antecedent conditions.

CHAPTER 11 **PREP** *CARD*

CONSUMERS IN SITUATIONS

Learning Outcomes

With the growth in eReader usage among students, this edition of *CB* features a numbering system for major headings that we recommend you use instead of page numbers when creating assignments.

11-1 Understand how value varies with situations.

11-2 Know the different ways that time affects consumer behavior.

11-3 Analyze shopping as a consumer activity using the different categories of shopping activities.

11-4 Distinguish the concepts of unplanned, impulse, and compulsive consumer behavior.

11-5 Use the concept of atmospherics to create consumer value.

11-6 Understand what is meant by antecedent conditions.

Chapter 11 Outline

Multimedia

PPT—THE HIGHLIGHTS

- Slide 9 Advertiming
- Slide 11 Shopping Activities
- Slide 16 Personality Traits
- Slide 20 Atmosphere Elements
- Slide 23 Antecedent Conditions

VIDEOS ON DVD AND COURSEMATE

CB Scenario Video

Run time: 2:37 minutes

Customers at an electronics store are looking at the latest phones on display. They check out the features on the touchscreen phone, asking about the different kinds of apps that come with it. A saleswoman explains the features of a particular phone to a customer. Various phones are on display—the Apple iPhone, Samsung Nexus, and Nokia N8—and this gives consumers the chance to compare their features before buying.

CHAPTER VIDEO SUMMARY

Murray Cheese

Run time: 6:02 minutes

At Murray Cheese, atmosphere is everything. The company prides itself on its distinctive environment, one in which customers' needs are placed at the forefront of the retail effort. Though employees are well-informed about the various products on the shelves, the primary focus is on helping customers pick out cheeses that are the best for them. The staff is friendly and approachable and make it easier for customers to be open about their requirements. A large part of the sales in the store are initiated by customers trying out the cheeses for themselves. This helps the employees open conversations about products customers may not be familiar with, and boosts sales. With an advertising budget of $0, it's techniques like these that create buzz, and keep customers coming in to the stores.

Ask your students:

1. How would you describe the shopping experience that Murray Cheese tries to create for customers? Is it experiential, impulsive, acquisitional, or epistemic? Give reasons for your answer.

2. Does the retail personality at Murray Cheese emphasize its affective or utilitarian quality? Explain why this is necessary for the company.

Beyond the Class

A selection of materials is in the Instructor's Manual.

Key Terms

Lecture Example

Faced with customers stealthily scanning the prices of items in order to purchase them for less online, Target worked this trend to its advantage, encouraging customers to use the free Shopkick app on their phones to scan items in the stores. This allows the customer to accumulate points that can be traded for gift cards. This option was introduced at Target stores with the intention of getting customers to visit Target more often and look at a lot of items that they otherwise wouldn't notice. This could lead to impulse buying. The app also displays all the in-store deals and promotions, and thus gives consumers an affordable and exciting shopping experience at the store.

Source: Brad Tuttle, "Scan This! Target Encourages Shoppers to Scan Items with Smartphones Nationwide," *Time Moneyland*, May 25, 2012, http://moneyland.time.com/2012/05/25/scan-this-target-encourages-shoppers-to-scan-items-with-smartphones-nationwide/

Group Activity

Assign each member of your team to visit a local hypermart at different times of the day. Make sure at least one member is assigned to each of these hours: 8 AM, 11 AM, 2 PM, 6 PM, 11 PM, and 3 AM. Observe the following:

a. Approximately how full is the parking lot?

b. On average, how full are the shopping carts of customers?

c. On average, how friendly do the other shoppers seem?

d. How many cash registers are open for transactions?

Try to apply the circadian cycle in explaining differences in behavior. Prepare a brief presentation for the class.

Assignments

Take a field trip to a lifestyle shopping center or shopping mall and use the observations made there to come up with answers. Observe the behavior of the shoppers going to and from stores. In general, how would you characterize their movements and appearance:

• Hurried or relaxed?
• Distracted or focused?
• Continuing the shopping trip or heading to the exits?
• Alone or with others?
• Empty-handed or with hands full of purchases?

Note the time of day, week, and month. How do you believe temporal situational influences are playing a role in consumers' behaviors as you described using points above?

CHAPTER 11—UPDATES TO CB THIS YEAR

Page 218—New pull quote
Page 221—New shopping example
Page 222—Revised Exhibit 11.2, Types of Shopping Activities
Page 222—New example of acquisitional shopping
Page 225—New example of unplanned shopping
Page 227—Revised Exhibit 11.5, Retail Approaches to Encouraging Impulse Purchases
Page 231—New box feature *Fascinating* replaces *Don't Lose Control* box feature
Page 232—New example about Victoria's Secret and Burberry
Page 234—New statement about cash payments emphasizing the sacrifice required for purchase

WHAT'S INSIDE   Key topics in this chapter: activities involved in the consumer decision-making process, three major decision research perspectives, consideration set in the decision-making process, and factors that influence the amount of consumer search.

CHAPTER 12 **PREP** *CARD*

DECISION MAKING I: NEED RECOGNITION AND SEARCH

Learning Outcomes

With the growth in eReader usage among students, this edition of *CB* features a numbering system for major headings that we recommend you use instead of page numbers when creating assignments.

12-1   Understand the activities involved in the consumer decision-making process.

12-2   Describe the three major decision-making research perspectives.

12-3   Explain the three major types of decision-making approaches.

12-4   Understand the importance of the consideration set in the decision-making process.

12-5   Understand the factors that influence the amount of search performed by consumers.

Chapter 12 Outline

Multimedia

PPT—THE HIGHLIGHTS

- Slide 4 Exhibit 12.1: Basic Consumption Process and Decision Making
- Slide 8 Exhibit 12.3: Perspectives on Consumer Decision Making
- Slide 12 Exhibit 12.4: Decision-Making Approaches
- Slide 17 Exhibit 12.5: Consideration Set
- Slide 23 Factors Influencing Amount of Search

VIDEOS ON DVD AND COURSEMATE

CB Scenario Video

Run time: 0:18 minutes

 A woman is shopping online using her personal laptop to access the Internet. She chooses the option of free shipping for her items. She surfs the Internet and uses her tablet simultaneously to search for more options and shopping offers.

CHAPTER VIDEO SUMMARY

Consumer Behavior at Scholfield Honda

Run time: 5:49 minutes

 Buying an automobile is a lengthy process, and the sales associates at Scholfield Honda are experts at identifying how different shoppers arrive at different purchase decisions. Though some drivers are habitual Honda buyers, most consumers research brands and models before driving a vehicle off the lot. Whether an individual is shopping for a sports car, SUV, hybrid, or convertible, the issues of fuel efficiency, size, quality, and price are important considerations in the decision-making process.

Ask your students:

1. What do customers feel about the alternative fuel vehicles?

2. According to the sales consultant of Scholfield Honda, what are the steps that customers generally follow to reach a buying decision?

3. Why does the management of Scholfield Honda encourage customers who are keen on comparing Honda vehicles with other cars?

Key Terms

actual state 246

awareness set 248

behavioral influence decision-making perspective 242

brand inertia 245

brand loyalty 245

consideration set 248

consumer search behavior 247

desired state 246

experiential decision-making perspective 242

extended decision making 243

external search 249

habitual decision making 245

inept set 249

inert set 249

information overload 248

internal search 248

limited decision making 244

ongoing search 247

perceived risk 243

prepurchase search 247

price 249

quality 250

rational decision-making perspective 242

satisficing 245

search regret 253

universal set 248

Lecture Example

A primary job for marketers is to understand the decision-making process that operates behind consumer purchases. With ever-increasing amounts of information about products as well as viable alternatives available to customers, sometimes what a company offers is different from what the consumer wants. This discrepancy can negatively affect the sales of a company. For example, according to a study conducted by Polk, an auto industry data company, 35% or less of hybrid buyers will purchase another one. This decision has been facilitated by the cost factor of hybrids and includes concerns over fuel economy problems, with many owners trading in their hybrids for electric cars. Growing strength of fuel economy among compact and midsize competitors has also contributed to hybrid owners' decision not to become repeat buyers.

Source: Bob Holt, "Hybrid Car Buyers May Go Electric," *New Jersey News Room*, April 11, 2012, http://www.newjerseynewsroom.com/science -updates/consumer-reports-survey-says-hybrid-buyers-will-not-buy-hybrid-again

Discussion Questions

1. Describe each of the activities that are present in the consumer decision-making process.
2. How do the various types of risks influence consumer decision-making approaches?
3. What types of technologies are affecting consumer search behavior?

Group Activity

Have students divide into teams. The size can vary depending on class size. Tell the class that the assignment will be to find information about buying a new product. (The purpose is to use a product category with which they probably have little direct experience. An example might be "buying new bedroom furniture.") Have each team focus on one specific type of information source and tell the group that they are to collect information from only their specified source. For example, assign one group "friends," one group "Internet," one group "apps," one group "salespeople," one group "advertisements," etc. Have the groups gather information that is relevant to purchasing the new product. Have the groups report on the information that they gather and how useful they thought the search process was. Have them also comment on how much they enjoyed gathering the information and how easy the process was. What observations do they make? This is a good exercise for sparking conversation on what types of information sources students prefer. (It is likely that the Internet and smartphone apps will be most popular and useful for the students.)

Assignments

Describe a recent situation that you faced in which you think the decision-making model discussed in the chapter applies well. What type of decision approach did you take? Why?

Beyond the Class

A selection of materials is in the Instructor's Manual.

CHAPTER 12—UPDATES TO CB THIS YEAR

Page 240—New example using visual search applications when searching for a business suit

Page 240—Revised Exhibit 12.2, Consumer Decision-Making Process

Page 241—New pull quote

Page 243—New example about risks associated with mp3 players.

Page 244—New box feature *Safety Risks* replaces *Now Hear This* box feature.

Page 245—"Maximizers" is discussed directly after the discussion of "Satisficing" consumers

Page 247—Box feature *Give Me Shelter* now includes references to the Mobile, Alabama, and Hattiesburg, Mississippi, tornadoes of 2012 and 2013

Page 249—New pull quote

Page 251—New apps included: SnapShot Showroom app and iWant as an illustration of GPS-based technologies

WHAT'S INSIDE Key topics in this chapter: difference between evaluative criteria and determinant criteria, how values affect the evaluation of alternatives, importance of product categorization in the evaluation of alternatives process, and compensatory and noncompensatory rules that guide consumer choice.

CHAPTER 13 **PREP** *CARD*

DECISION MAKING II: ALTERNATIVE EVALUATION AND CHOICE

Learning Outcomes

With the growth in eReader usage among students, this edition of *CB* features a numbering system for major headings that we recommend you use instead of page numbers when creating assignments.

13-1 Understand the difference between evaluative criteria and determinant criteria.

13-2 Comprehend how value affects the evaluation of alternatives.

13-3 Explain the importance of product categorization in the evaluation of alternatives process.

13-4 Distinguish between compensatory and noncompensatory rules that guide consumer choice.

Chapter 13 Outline

Multimedia

PPT—THE HIGHLIGHTS

- Slide 5 Evaluative and Determinant Criteria
- Slide 8 Value and Alternative Evaluation
- Slide 12 Exhibit 13.4: Superordinate and Subordinate Categorization
- Slide 15 Factors Determining Evaluative Criteria Used
- Slide 20: Consumer Choice: Decision Rules

VIDEOS ON DVD AND COURSEMATE

CB Scenario Video

Run time: 3:15 minutes

Several experts on choice discuss the counterintuitive effects large numbers of options have on consumers. Rather than increasing the likelihood of consumers finding the best options for them, a variety of choices distresses, confuses, or overwhelms consumers—and may even prevent them from making a purchase.

CHAPTER VIDEO SUMMARY

Ford Motor Company

Run time: 8:00 minutes

Shopping for a fuel-efficient SUV was easy in 2005 when Ford introduced the Escape, the first and only hybrid on the market. But today there are dozens of alternative energy models on the road, and consumers looking for the most environmentally friendly SUV have many options from which to choose. The Ford brand continues to benefit from its association with historic firsts in auto manufacturing, but some consumers ignore brand history and simply choose the vehicle that performs best on a single important feature, such as fuel economy.

Ask your students:

1. Why would Ford create a hybrid SUV? What makes the Escape attractive to consumers?

2. How did Ford approach the pricing of the Escape? What effect does this have on consumers' decisions?

Key Terms

Lecture Example

Ethical and green consumerism may be increasingly shaping consumer behavior and marketing practices, but when it comes to actual purchases, a key focus on environmental sustainability may be overshadowed by the consumer's evaluation of a product's perceptual attributes. Most participants in a survey by the Carbon Trust in London said they would buy products labeled with carbon footprints only if they cost the same as conventional products. In 2009, William Young and his colleagues at the University of Leeds found that 30% of people in the U.K. said they were very concerned about the environment, but ethically sourced foods only account for 5% of the market. According to Young, most consumers choose products based on the price, along with other factors like brand name and appearance.

Source: Tom DeLay, "Green Consumer Attitudes Questioned," UPI.com, April 12, 2012, http://www.upi.com/Science_News/2012/04/12/Green-consumer-attitudes-questioned/UPI-77281334263043/

Discussion Questions

1. What is the relationship between utilitarian and hedonic value and the evaluation of alternatives?

2. At what level do product comparisons across features or attributes take place according to the product categorization approach? What examples can you think of for product comparisons at this level?

3. In what ways does the conjunctive rule differ from the elimination-by-aspects rule?

Group Activity

Form groups of five to six (depending on class size) and assign each group a specific product category. There assignment will be to visit a local retailer and evaluate three different options of the category using the four noncompensatory rules and the ATO approach that was discussed in Chapter 7. The following list of products provides examples: TVs, car stereos, washing machines, laptops, refrigerators, automobiles, motorcycles, cell phones, video game consoles, watches, and apartment complexes. Ask students how realistic the various noncompensatory approaches were in their opinion. Also, ask them to compare the noncompensatory approaches with the ATO approach. Which did they think was most appropriate? Have them report their findings to class.

Assignments

Compare the websites of three major retailers like Sears, Target, and Walmart to their in-store atmosphere. How well does the website represent the physical stores? Which combination of website and brick-and-mortar store do you think is best? Why?

Beyond the Class

A selection of materials is in the Instructor's Manual.

CHAPTER 13—UPDATES TO CB THIS YEAR

Page 256—Addition of "hyperchoice" concept in first paragraph of the Evaluation of Alternatives: Criteria section

Page 256—Revised Exhibit 13.2, Product, Feature, and Benefit

Page 258—New example of fast-food marketers combating boredom

Page 258—New pull quote

Page 259—New box feature *Tastes Like…Water!* replaces *Go Team* box feature

Page 260—New example for product knowledge has been changed to a college basketball player understanding what to look for in an athletic shoe.

Page 261—New example for marketing communications has been changed to the example of Hallmark Cards.

Page 261—New box feature *This Looks Good!* replaces *It's My Big Day!* box feature.

Page 263—New pull quote

Page 264—New box feature *Birds of Prey* replaces the *Seeing Green* box

WHAT'S INSIDE Key topics in this chapter: the link from consumption value to satisfaction; importance of satisfaction in consumer behavior; emotions that can affect postconsumption behavior; expectancy disconfirmation, equity, and attribution theory approaches; problems with commonly applied satisfaction measures; and how consumers dispose of products.

CHAPTER 14 **PREP** *CARD*

CONSUMPTION TO SATISFACTION

Learning Outcomes

With the growth in eReader usage among students, this edition of *CB* features a numbering system for major headings that we recommend you use instead of page numbers when creating assignments.

14-1 Gain an appreciation of the link from consumption to value to satisfaction.

14-2 Discuss the relative importance of satisfaction and value in consumer behavior.

14-3 Know that emotions other than satisfaction can affect postconsumption behavior.

14-4 Use expectancy disconfirmation, equity, and attribution theory approaches to explain consumers' postconsumption reactions.

14-5 Understand problems with commonly applied satisfaction measures.

14-6 Describe some ways that consumers dispose of products.

Chapter 14 Outline

Multimedia

PPT—THE HIGHLIGHTS

- Slide 5 Exhibit 14.1: Basic Consumption Process
- Slide 13 Consumer Satisfaction
- Slide 15 Other Postconsumption Reactions
- Slide 17 Theories of Postconsumption Reactions
- Slide 29 Disposing of Refuse

VIDEOS ON DVD AND COURSEMATE

CB Scenario Video

Run time: 0:15 minutes

A batch of shrimps is sizzling over a flame. Two customers look over the menu of a restaurant, Mezzaluna. The menu is displayed on a board with a list of the dishes and their prices. Inside the restaurant, customers chat and drink as they wait for their orders to be served.

CHAPTER VIDEO SUMMARY

Sephora Retailing for Success

Run time: 8:00 minutes

At Sephora, shopping is all about experiencing products. When the French cosmetics retailer came to America in the late 1990s, it immediately opened its counters to free trials of makeup, fragrances, and skin care items. The try-before-you-buy concept is a hit with female customers, and sales associates at Sephora are always on hand to facilitate and educate. The company's loyalty program ensures that satisfied customers keep coming back for more.

Ask your students:

1. Visit the Sephora website and browse the online store. How does Sephora use the online environment to promote its products without the advantage of letting customers try before they buy?

2. Sephora is working out the details of a new loyalty program and they have asked you to give your input and advice. What do you tell them? How should they integrate this new program with the retailing mix they have already adopted?

VISIT LOGIN.CENGAGE.COM FOR ADDITIONAL MATERIALS TO ENHANCE YOUR LECTURES!

CHAPTER 14 CONSUMPTION TO SATISFACTION

Key Terms

Lecture Example

A new study by McKinsey links satisfaction with consistency and highlighted that companies with a consistent value proposition and a clear way of offering it do much better. According to the study, the companies that have the most satisfied consumers also report the tightest distribution of responses. It revealed that among U.S. consumers, multi-category retailers have the highest customer satisfaction ratings while subscription-based industries are struggling with issues of customer satisfaction. Cost-driven cuts made to service in the downturn due to decreasing revenue may be the reason attributed to the dismal state of customer satisfaction in transaction-based services.

Source: "Retailers Top Service Charts," Warc, April 16, 2012, http://www.warc.com/Content/News/_Retailers_top_service_charts .content?CID=&ID=82dd7566-a92b-4ae6-9f2c-58632958ad5b&q=Retailers+top+service+charts&qr=

Discussion Questions

1. Distinguish durable and nondurable goods. Provide an example of each. How do you think the postconsumption processes may vary based on this distinction?

2. Explain the way confirmatory bias may work in postpurchase processes.

3. What are the problems associated with measuring consumer satisfaction?

Group Activity

Get together in groups of four. Individually visit Facebook, Twitter, or Pinterest to look for comments from consumers that you believe illustrate some of the concepts in this chapter. Make notes of and/or print some of the evidence. Discuss the findings with your group to find the best illustrations and present those in class.

Assignments

What is a "packrat"? Ask three friends permission to take a photo of their rooms. Which do think is the biggest packrat? Prepare a brief report explaining your conclusion.

Beyond the Class

A selection of materials is in the Instructor's Manual.

CHAPTER 14—UPDATES TO CB THIS YEAR

Page 274—New example about Google Checkout payments

Page 276—New pull quote

Page 277—Revised Exhibit 14.3, The ACSI Scores for U.S. Retailers

Page 277—New ACSI scores for fast-food restaurants

Page 278—New box feature *Outcomes are Co-Created* replaces *On Your Mark, Get Set, Shop!* box feature

Page 280—New example of preconsumption expectations

Page 283—New pull quote

Page 286—Revised statistics about trashing

CHAPTER 15 **PREP** *CARD*
CONSUMER RELATIONSHIPS

Learning Outcomes

With the growth in eReader usage among students, this edition of *CB* features a numbering system for major headings that we recommend you use instead of page numbers when creating assignments.

15-1 List and define the behavioral outcomes of consumption.

15-2 Know why consumers complain and the ramifications of complaining behavior for a marketing firm.

15-3 Use the concept of switching costs to understand why consumers do or do not repeat purchase behavior.

15-4 Describe each component of true consumer loyalty.

15-5 Understand the role that value plays in shaping loyalty and building consumer relationships.

Chapter 15 Outline

Multimedia

PPT—THE HIGHLIGHTS

- Slide 5 Exhibit 15.1: A More Detailed Look at Postconsumption Reactions
- Slide 10 Handling Service Complaints Effectively
- Slide 22 Exhibit 15.4: Vulnerability to Defections Based on CS/D
- Slide 27 Exhibit 15.6: True Loyalty Requires Customer Commitment
- Slide 35 Exhibit 15.9: Characteristics of Relationship Quality

VIDEOS ON DVD AND COURSEMATE

CB Scenario Video

Run time: 1:04 minutes

A woman stands in her kitchen, using a smartphone to place an order online. She later shops online, from the privacy of her home, using her laptop. The products she ordered online are then delivered to her doorstep.

CHAPTER VIDEO SUMMARY

Harley-Davidson

Run time: 7:58 minutes

Come August, Sturgis, a small town in South Dakota, is set abuzz with motorcycle riders who gather there for the biggest motorcycle rally in the world. That the event is dominated by Harley-Davidson motorcycles is hardly a surprise. Participating in events helps Harley not only to pursue new customers, but also to interact with current owners of its motorcycles. Harley emphasizes providing a unique experience to its riders and fostering a sense of community. Besides facilitating the customization of its motorcycles, it also offers shipping service and programs such as the Harley Owners' Group. By building strong relations, the company has been successful in turning its customers into its best salespeople.

Ask your students:

1. How does Harley-Davidson benefit from frequent face-to-face interactions with customers?

2. How did Harley-Davidson build the phenomenal brand loyalty it currently enjoys?

3. Discuss the marketing strategies of Harley-Davidson.

VISIT LOGIN.CENGAGE.COM FOR ADDITIONAL MATERIALS TO ENHANCE YOUR LECTURES!

CHAPTER 15 CONSUMER RELATIONSHIPS

Key Terms

antiloyal consumers 301
competitive intensity 298
complaining behavior 290
consumer inertia 300
critical incident 290
customer commitment 301
customer share 299
financial switching costs 297
loyalty card/program 300
negative public publicity 293
negative word-of-mouth 293
positive WOM 293
procedural justice 290
procedural switching costs 297
rancorous revenge 293
relational switching cost 297
relationship quality 303
retaliatory revenge 293
share of wallet 299
switching costs 297
switching 297
third-party endorsement 296

Lecture Example

Switching costs vary with products. While switching cell phones is fraught with barriers, replacing a car is not. High switching costs may often lead to the abuse of brand loyalty by companies. Conversely, the removal of switching costs may lead to a drop in price. The prevailing view on switching costs affirms that a reduction in such costs would lead companies to lower prices in order to gain new customers. In an environment where the competitive intensity is high and switching costs low, dissatisfied customers are more likely to opt for a switch.

Source: "The High Cost of Loving Your Phone," *The New York Times*, June 11, 2010, http://www.nytimes.com/2010/06/13/technology/13every.html

Discussion Questions

1. What are the cognitive and affective components that help shape postconsumption behavior?
2. What are the different ways in which a firm can react to negative public publicity? Which way is *almost* always a bad response?
3. Explain which types of firms are most vulnerable and least vulnerable to customer defections.

Group Activity

For each of the following product areas, list your favorite brand and estimate the customer share you allocate to that brand:

- Gasoline
- Supermarkets
- Phone service
- Hair stylists
- Consumer electronics
- Soft drinks

Then, in groups of three or four, discuss results and try to determine which group member is the most likely to be a "loyal" consumer.

Assignments

Describe complaining behavior and discuss places where a marketer should be on the watch for evidence of problems with their service or value propositions based on complaining.

Beyond the Class

A selection of materials is in the Instructor's Manual.

CHAPTER 15—UPDATES TO CB THIS YEAR

Page 291—New complainers example
Page 291—New pull quote
Page 293—New example of an irate customer experience
Page 293—New example about negative public policy
Page 294—Revised number of Gatorade followers on Twitter
Page 296—New pull quote

Page 297—New third-party endorsers
Page 297—New Switching Behavior example
Page 299—New competitive intensity example
Page 302—New pull quote
Page 302—New box feature *Loyalty's in the Bag* replaces *The Price of Loyalty* box feature

CHAPTER 16 **PREP** *CARD*
CONSUMER AND MARKETING MISBEHAVIOR

Learning Outcomes

With the growth in eReader usage among students, this edition of *CB* features a numbering system for major headings that we recommend you use instead of page numbers when creating assignments

16-1 Understand the consumer misbehavior phenomenon and how it affects the exchange process.

16-2 Distinguish between consumer misbehavior and consumer problem behavior.

16-3 Discuss marketing ethics and how marketing ethics guide the development of marketing programs.

16-4 Comprehend the role of corporate social responsibility in the field of marketing.

16-5 Understand the various forms of regulation that affect marketing practice.

16-6 Comprehend the major areas of criticism to which marketers are subjected.

Chapter 16 Outline

Multimedia

PPT—THE HIGHLIGHTS

- Slide 10 Motivations of Misbehavior
- Slide 12 Consumer Misbehavior and Problem Behavior
- Slide 28 Consumer Bill of Rights
- Slide 38 Exhibit 16.7: Prescriptions for Improved Marketing Ethics
- Slide 40 Exhibit 16.8: Major Acts Affecting Commerce and Consumer Safety

VIDEOS ON DVD AND COURSEMATE

CB Scenario Video
Run time: 3:38 minutes

A "textiquette" expert talks about the increasing acceptance of texting in almost any social situation, whether it's on a date, at a wedding, or even in bed. A survey revealed a definite difference in texting behavior among people from different generations, with people under 35 significantly more likely to find texting acceptable in most situations, as compared to people over 35. The rise of texting as a mode of communication may even hamper face-to-face interactions, and it is recommended that people draw boundaries for their own texting behavior.

CHAPTER VIDEO SUMMARY

The Putting Lot
Run time: 6:36 minutes

Lack of recreational space and activity in an industrial neighborhood drove the co-organizers of the Putting Hole to convert a vacant lot into an urban mini-golf course. Initiated through friendly discussions, the project saw the participation of many neighborhood volunteers who wanted to engage in a community project that focused on neighborhood sustainability. BUSHWICKBK.com, a local blog, was the first to report an article on the Putting Hole. It was not long before different blogs picked up from the article and the Putting hole was featured on NYT and various radio shows. It is a perfect story of how a "hyper local" idea made it big.

Ask your students:

1. Explain the ethos of the Putting Lot in terms of the societal marketing concept.

2. Would you describe the Putting Lot's corporate social responsibility strategy as ethical or altruistic? Justify your answer.

Key Terms

Lecture Example

Many legal provisions are instituted to protect consumers from marketing misbehavior. Such legislation is aimed at maintaining or improving the general welfare of consumers in a free marketplace and also mutually benefitting marketers. For example, in Connecticut, consumers as well as farmers are pushing for a legislation that will make labeling of genetically modified food compulsory. Organic farmers say they stand to benefit from better informed consumers who may reject genetically modified products and instead choose organic food. Preliminary findings in an academic study found that consumers would pay more for food labeled as free of genetically modified ingredients. The farmers feel that Connecticut's legislation is specifically intended to help organic food producers while at the same time being a wonderful way to raise the consciousness of consumers.

Source: Stephen Singer, "Organic Farmers Hope for Boost with Rivals' Labels," *Bloomberg BusinessWeek*, April 15, 2012, http://www.businessweek.com

Group Activity

Have students break up into teams (sizes based on class size). Assign each group the responsibility of interviewing a local business leader about one of the consumer misbehaviors listed in the text and how often they think it occurs in your community. In what ways do they attempt to combat the problem? For example, a group could interview a local retail manager about the occurrence of shoplifting in their store. A group could interview a computer store manager about the prevalence of computer viruses in the community, and a group could interview a facilities manager about the frequency of dysfunctional sports behavior at your school's facilities. Another group could get information about local police efforts to combat texting and driving, or drinking and driving. Have the groups report back to the class about the responses they get. This is a good exercise for both expanding on the content of the book and highlighting the extent to which the misbehaviors occur in your immediate area. It is likely that students will be surprised by the extent to which these misbehaviors occur locally.

Assignments

Survey fellow students at about how much they tend to trust marketers. What companies do they trust? What companies do they distrust? For those that state that they distrust marketers, ask them why. What would it take to gain the confidence of these students?

CHAPTER 16—UPDATES TO CB THIS YEAR

Page 308—New pull quote

Page 310—New statistic about shoplifting incidents in the United States

Page 311—New statistic about U.S. households losing $5 billion annually due to computer viruses

Page 312—Revised Black and Blue Friday box feature

Page 313—New statistic for the percentage of 15- to 20-year-old drivers who are killed in accidents

Page 313—New estimate of the total number of cellular subscriptions in the world

page 314—Reference to the widespread criticism of the Snapchat app as a sexting tool

Page 315—A reference to a 2012 study that compares binge drinking across full-time and part-time students has been added.

Page 316—A 2012 study that reveals that 15% of U.S. high school seniors report using prescription medications to get high has been added.

Page 316—A new estimate of 6.5% of U.S. high school seniors using marijuana daily has been added.

Page 318—New box feature *Being a Champion* replaces *Pay for Pain* box feature

Page 320—The ticket scandal of the 2012 Olympic games is discussed.

Page 320—A new reference to the 2012 gun control debate has been added.

Page 320—New pull quote

Page 322—Revised Exhibit 16.8, Major Acts Affecting Commerce and Consumer Safety